# LAW AND LEGACY IN MEDICAL JURISPRUDENCE

AF167700

Graeme Laurie stepped down from the Chair of Medical Jurisprudence at the University of Edinburgh in 2019. This edited collection pays tribute to his extraordinary contributions to the field. Graeme often spoke about the importance of 'legacy' in academic work and forged a remarkable intellectual legacy of his own, notably through his work on genetic privacy, human tissue and information governance, and the regulatory salience of the concept of liminality. The essays in this volume animate the concept of legacy to analyse the study and practice of medical jurisprudence. In this light, legacy reveals characteristics of both benefit and burden, as both an encumbrance to and a facilitator of the development of law, policy and regulation. The contributions reconcile the ideas of legacy and responsiveness and show that both dimensions are critical to achieving and sustaining the health of medical jurisprudence itself as a dynamic, interdisciplinary and policy-engaged field of thinking.

EDWARD S. DOVE is Lecturer in Health Law and Regulation at the University of Edinburgh. His research examines confidentiality and data protection law as well as the regulatory work of research ethics committees and other bodies involved in health research. He is the author of *Regulatory Stewardship of Health Research: Navigating Participant Protection and Research Promotion* (2020).

NIAMH NIC SHUIBHNE is Professor of European Union Law at the University of Edinburgh, and a joint editor of the *Common Market Law Review*. Her research examines questions of substantive EU law from a constitutional perspective. She recently completed a project on equal treatment for EU citizens, funded by a Leverhulme Trust Major Research Fellowship (2016–19).

# LAW AND LEGACY IN MEDICAL JURISPRUDENCE

Essays in Honour of Graeme Laurie

Edited by

## EDWARD S. DOVE
*University of Edinburgh*

## NIAMH NIC SHUIBHNE
*University of Edinburgh*

CAMBRIDGE
UNIVERSITY PRESS

Shaftesbury Road, Cambridge CB2 8EA, United Kingdom

One Liberty Plaza, 20th Floor, New York, NY 10006, USA

477 Williamstown Road, Port Melbourne, VIC 3207, Australia

314–321, 3rd Floor, Plot 3, Splendor Forum, Jasola District Centre, New Delhi – 110025, India

103 Penang Road, #05–06/07, Visioncrest Commercial, Singapore 238467

Cambridge University Press is part of Cambridge University Press & Assessment, a department of the University of Cambridge.

We share the University's mission to contribute to society through the pursuit of education, learning and research at the highest international levels of excellence.

www.cambridge.org
Information on this title: www.cambridge.org/9781108828895

DOI: 10.1017/9781108903295

First published 2022
First paperback edition 2023

*A catalogue record for this publication is available from the British Library*

*Library of Congress Cataloging-in-Publication data*
Names: Laurie, G. T. (Graeme T.), honouree. | Dove, E. S. (Edward S.), editor. | Nic Shuibhne, Niamh, editor.
Title: Law and legacy in medical jurisprudence : essays in honour of Graeme Laurie / edited by Edward S Dove, University of Edinburgh; Niamh Nic Shuibhne, University of Edinburgh.
Description: 1. | Cambridge [UK] ; New York, NY : Cambridge University Press, 2022. | Includes index.
Identifiers: LCCN 2021031092 (print) | LCCN 2021031093 (ebook) | ISBN 9781108842433 (hardback) | ISBN 9781108828895 (paperback) | ISBN 9781108903295 (ebook)
Subjects: LCSH: Medical laws and legislation. | Medical genetics – Law and legislation. | Medical ethics. | Human chromosome abnormalities – Diagnosis – Moral and ethical aspects. | Laurie, G. T. (Graeme T.)
Classification: LCC K3601 .L387 2022 (print) | LCC K3601 (ebook) | DDC 344.04/1–dc23
LC record available at https://lccn.loc.gov/2021031092
LC ebook record available at https://lccn.loc.gov/2021031093

ISBN    978-1-108-84243-3    Hardback
ISBN    978-1-108-82889-5    Paperback

# CONTENTS

# CONTRIBUTORS

FABIANA ARZUAGA, Professor of Regulation of Biotechnology and Patent Law; Chair of the Advisory Commission in Cellular Therapies and Regenerative Medicine at the Ministry of Science, Technology and Productive Innovation of Argentina

RICHARD ASHCROFT, Professor of Bioethics and Deputy Dean, City Law School, City, University of London

MICHAEL J. S. BEAUVAIS, Academic Associate, Centre of Genomics and Policy, McGill University

MARGARET BRAZIER, Professor of Law, University of Manchester

ROGER BROWNSWORD, Professor of Law, King's College London

RUTH CHADWICK, Professor Emerita, Cardiff University; Honorary Visiting Professor, University of Leeds

SHARON COWAN, Professor of Feminist and Queer Legal Studies, University of Edinburgh

EDWARD S. DOVE, Lecturer in Health Law and Regulation, University of Edinburgh

LAURA DOWNEY, Research Fellow, University of Birmingham

MURRAY EARLE, Lecturer in Medical Law, University of Edinburgh

AGOMONI GANGULI-MITRA, Lecturer and Chancellor's Fellow in Bioethics and Global Health Ethics, University of Edinburgh

LAWRENCE O. GOSTIN, Professor of Global Health Law, Georgetown University

SHAWN H. E. HARMON, Research Associate, IWK Health Centre; Part-Time Faculty, Dalhousie University; Attorney, C3 Legal; Honorary Fellow, University of Edinburgh (2018–2021)

CALVIN WAI-LOON HO, Associate Professor of Law and Co-Director of the Centre for Medical Ethics and Law, University of Hong Kong

NILS HOPPE, Professor of Ethics and Law in the Life Sciences, Leibniz University Hannover

EMILY JACKSON, Professor of Law, London School of Economics and Political Science

BARTHA MARIA KNOPPERS, Canada Research Chair in Law and Medicine, McGill University

SHEILA MCLEAN, Professor Emerita of Law and Ethics in Medicine, University of Glasgow

JEAN V. MCHALE, Professor of Health Care Law, University of Birmingham

AISLING MCMAHON, Associate Professor in Law, Maynooth University

CATRIONA MCMILLAN, British Academy Postdoctoral Fellow, University of Edinburgh

ERIC M. MESLIN, President and CEO, Council of Canadian Academies

JOSÉ MIOLA, Chair in Law and Social Justice, University of Leeds

ALEXANDRA MULLOCK, Senior Lecturer in Medical Law, University of Manchester

NIAMH NIC SHUIBHNE, Professor of European Union Law, University of Edinburgh

EMILY POSTAN, Chancellor's Fellow in Bioethics, University of Edinburgh

MUIREANN QUIGLEY, Professor of Law, Medicine, and Technology, University of Birmingham

NAYHA SETHI, Chancellor's Fellow in Data Driven Innovation, University of Edinburgh

ANNIE SORBIE, Lecturer in Medical Law and Ethics, University of Edinburgh

MARK J. TAYLOR, Associate Professor in Health Law and Regulation, University of Melbourne

DAVID M. R. TOWNEND, Professor of Law and Legal Philosophy in Health, Medicine and Life Sciences, Maastricht University

JUSTIN YUK CHEONG WONG, Student, Harvard College

# FOREWORD

It is a pleasure to have been invited to write the foreword for this excellent collection of essays to celebrate the enormous contribution that Graeme Laurie has made, both to the academic discipline of medical law and to the wider community.

I have known Graeme for many years, having taught him as an undergraduate specialising in medical law at the University of Glasgow. I also supervised his PhD and was able to give him his first research position at the same university. I would like to be able to say that I spotted Graeme's potential from the beginning – and I did! He was an excellent student, bright and enquiring, and his PhD (subsequently turned into an excellent book) was a masterpiece of originality and thoughtfulness. Graeme was not just an outstanding student/colleague – he was also a charismatic and generous friend, as I am sure everyone with whom he has collaborated since then will agree.

Graeme joined the University of Edinburgh in 1995. For many academics, the 'ivory tower' is sufficiently challenging. While Graeme continued to teach, research, publish and present at conferences around the world, and lead on the School of Law's research strategy, he also demonstrated a genuine commitment to contributing his expertise to the wider world beyond academia. His creation and leadership of the J. Kenyon Mason Institute for Medicine, Life Sciences and the Law not only is an homage to his mentor, the late Professor Ken Mason, but has generated significant research projects and student enthusiasm over the years, enhancing the University of Edinburgh's profile in this important area. Graeme's elevation to the Chair of Medical Jurisprudence in 2005 would have come as no surprise to anyone familiar with the man and with his work – indeed, I am sure it was welcomed by all. His contribution to academia has also been recognised by his election as a Fellow of the Royal Society of Edinburgh, Scotland's most prestigious award, as well as Fellowships of the Academy of Medial Sciences and the Royal College of Physicians of Edinburgh.

Graeme's external roles are too many to mention here, but amongst them are his Chairmanship of the UK Biobank Ethics and Governance Council, his Chairmanship of the Privacy Advisory Committee in Scotland and his membership of important bodies such as the Nuffield Council on Bioethics, the British Medical Association's Medical Ethics Committee and the Council of Canadian Academies' Expert Panel on Timely Access to Health and Social Data for Health Research and Health System Innovation. In addition, Graeme has generated (or collaborated to generate) millions in research funding – an astonishing success in these days when grants are incredibly difficult to come by and increasingly competitive – resulting not just in excellent research outputs but also, as is typical of Graeme, in work that is valuable in practical as well as theoretical terms.

It is this awareness of the potential relevance of academic enterprise to the community as a whole that, in my view, serves to enhance his contribution and reputation even further than his academic output would already have done. No isolationist, he has always acknowledged and fulfilled the promise that 'town and gown' can not only live together but learn from each other.

There will, no doubt, be considerable sadness that Graeme has chosen to step down early from his Chair. He has contributed so much, and doubtless had much more that he could have contributed, and I am sure he will be sorely missed by his students and colleagues. However, I am also sure that there will be many – myself included – who applaud his courage and vision to explore new horizons. On behalf of all of his friends and colleagues, I wish him and Ian every happiness in their future ventures and a long and happy retirement. It has been a pleasure to have played a small part in Graeme's career, but even more to have been able to call this outstanding young man a friend.

*Sheila McLean*

# PREFACE

In September 2019, Graeme Laurie stepped down from the Chair of Medical Jurisprudence at the University of Edinburgh, to which he had been appointed in August 2005. Graeme has been a teacher, mentor, supervisor and colleague to countless students and fellow academics over the years at two institutions with which he is fondly associated: his alma mater and first employer the University of Glasgow and, latterly, the University of Edinburgh. It was with deep appreciation and affection – though certainly a touch of sadness as well – that we at Edinburgh Law School received Graeme's news that he would be transitioning from the full-time Chair position to a part-time Professorial Fellow role (thereby maintaining his cherished focus on research mentorship and PhD supervision). With this volume, we are endeavouring to honour Graeme's contributions to the university and to the field in as fitting a way as we can. Additionally, as Graeme views himself as both a Scot and a European and is also an intrepid global traveller and a keen student of cultures and languages, perhaps it is apt that a North American medical lawyer and an Irish EU lawyer are editing this volume!

We are deeply grateful to each contributor for their persistence, hard work and patience in putting together this volume: everyone deserves special thanks for writing, reading and editing these pieces in the midst of a once-in-a-century (we hope) pandemic of infectious disease that challenged us, both personally and professionally, in significantly disruptive ways for much of 2020 and 2021. No doubt, the SARS-CoV-2/Covid-19 pandemic will leave a tragic legacy; certainly, it will leave an instructive one for medical jurisprudence regarding both painful failures (foremost, many governments' lack of adequate preparation and inability to curtail rates of infection and death) and uplifting successes (foremost, the incredibly fast timeline and global sharing of the virus's original genomic sequence and the subsequent discovery, regulatory approval and distribution of multiple safe and effective vaccines).

We also thank Finola O'Sullivan and Marianne Nield at Cambridge University Press for supporting this project from the outset and through to publication, and Ella Keating and Ruby Reed-Berendt for their careful and invaluable research assistance in the final stages.

It has been our privilege to work with Graeme over the years. We owe him more than we could write (and certainly more than he would be comfortable reading) and we can only hope that this volume does some justice to his work – to his legacy – and stimulates further thinking on where law and legacy in medical jurisprudence might and ought to go. To paraphrase Lawrence Gostin's astute words from the Afterword, legacy notwithstanding, there is so much more thinking and giving to do; and as Shawn Harmon reminds us in his chapter, 'we are all stewards' in some way in helping to shape this field and continuing to build on Graeme's legacy, within and well beyond the academy. Many collections of this kind are convened when someone might be 'gone, but not forgotten'. We consciously decided to offer this tribute while Graeme is neither forgotten nor gone; in his role as Professorial Fellow, the making of his legacy continues; indeed, we can already hear him briskly declaring, 'Next!'

*ESD and NSS*
*Edinburgh, April 2021*

# TABLE OF CASES

## UK

# ECHR

# EPO

# EU

# USA

# Canada

# TABLE OF LEGISLATION

## UK Statutes

Abortion Act 1967
Anatomy Act 1832
Anatomy Act 1984
Care Act 2014
Corneal Grafting Act 1952
Corneal Tissue Act 1986
Coroners and Justice Act 2009
European Communities Act 1972
Human Fertilisation and Embryology Act 1990
Human Fertilisation and Embryology Act 2008
Human Organ Transplants Act 1989
Human Rights Act 1998
Human Tissue (Scotland) Act 2006
Human Tissue Act 1961
Human Tissue Act 2004
Human Transplantation (Wales) Act 2013
Local Government Act 1986
Local Government Act 1988
Mental Capacity Act 2005
Organ Donation (Deemed Consent) Act 2019
Suicide Act 1961
Surrogacy Arrangements Act 1985

## Statutory Instruments

Anatomy Regulations 1988 (SI 1988/44)
Health Research Authority (Establishment and Constitution) Order 2011 (SI 2011/
    2323)
Health Research Authority Regulations 2011 (SI 2011/2341)
Health Research Regulations 2018 (SI 2018/314) (Ireland)
Human Fertilisation and Embryology Authority (Disclosure of Donor Information)
    Regulations 2004

Human Tissue (Quality and Safety for Human Application) Regulations 2007
Medical Device (Amendment etc.) (EU Exit) Regulations 2019 (SI 2019/791)
Medical Device Regulations 2002 (SI 2002/618)
Medicines for Human Use (Clinical Trials Regulations) 2004

## Human Tissue Act Code of Practices

Code of Practice F: Deceased Organ and Tissue Donation
Code of Practice F: Donation of Solid Organs and Tissue for Transplantation

## European Union Regulations

Council Regulation (EU) 2017/746 on in vitro diagnostics medical devices [2017] OJ
    L117/176
Regulation (EU) 2017/745 on medical devices, amending Directive 2001/83/EC,
    Regulation (EC) No 178/2002 and Regulation (EC) No 1223/2009 and repealing
    Council Directives 90/385/EEC and 93/42/EEC [2017] OJ L117/1
Council Regulation 679/2016 on the protection of natural persons with regard to the
    processing of personal data and on the free movement of such data, and repealing
    Directive 95/46/EC (General Data Protection Regulation) [2016] OJ L119
Regulation (EU) No 536/2014 on clinical trials on medicinal products for human use,
    and repealing Directive 2001/20/EC [2014] OJ L158/1
Regulation (EC) No 178/2002 laying down the general principles and requirements of
    food law, establishing the European Food Safety Authority and laying down pro-
    cedures in matters of food safety [2002] OJ L31

## European Union Directives

Directive (EC) 23/2004 on setting standards of quality and safety for the donation,
    procurement, testing, processing, preservation, storage and distribution of human
    tissues and cells [2004] OJ L102/48
Directive 2001/83/EC on the Community code relating to medicinal products for
    human use [2001] OJ L311/67
Directive 2001/20/EC on the approximation of the laws, regulations and administrative
    provisions of the Member States relating to the implementation of good clinical
    practice in the conduct of clinical trials on medicinal products for human use, [2001]
    L121/34
Council Directive 98/79/EEC concerning in vitro diagnostic medical devices [1998] OJ
    L331/1
Council Directive 98/44EC on the legal protection of biotechnological inventions
    [1998] OJ L213/13
Council Directive 93/42/EEC concerning medical devices [1993] OJ L169/1
Directive 90/385/EEC concerning active implanted medical devices [1990] OJ L189/17

## Council of Europe Conventions

Council of Europe, European Convention for the Protection of Human Rights and
Fundamental Freedoms, as amended by Protocols Nos 11 and 14, 4 November 1950
Convention for the protection of Human Rights and Dignity of the Human Being with
regard to the Application of Biology and Medicine: Convention on Human Rights
and Biomedicine, ETS No 164, 4 April 1997 entered into force 1 December 1999
(otherwise known as the Oviedo Convention)

## International Conventions

Vienna Convention on the Law of Treaties (UN Treaty Series 1155 adopted
23 May 1969, in force 27 January 1980)

## United Nations

United Nations General Assembly, 'Convention on the Rights of Persons with
Disabilities' (United Nations Doc A/RES/61/106, 24 January 2007)
United Nations General Assembly, 'Convention on the Rights of the Child' (UN Treaty
Series vol. 1577, 20 November 1989)
United Nations General Assembly, 'International Covenant on Economic, Social and
Cultural Rights' (UNGA Resolution A/RES/2200A(XXI) adopted
16 December 1966, in force 3 January 1976)

## Foreign Statutes

Canadian Charter of Rights and Freedoms
Constitution Act 1982 (Canada)
Data Protection 2018 (Ireland)
Patent and Trademark Law Amendments Act 1980 (USA)

# ABBREVIATIONS

| | |
|---|---|
| AAAS | American Association for the Advancement of Science |
| ADR | administrative data research |
| ADRN | Administrative Data Research Network (UK) |
| AEMPS | Spanish Agency of Medicines and Medical Products |
| AHRC SCRIPT | Arts and Humanities Research Council Research Centre for Studies in Intellectual Property and Technology Law |
| AI | artificial intelligence |
| AIDS | acquired immune deficiency syndrome |
| AIP | access and intellectual property policy |
| ALS | amyotrophic lateral sclerosis |
| ANMAT | National Administration of Drugs, Foods and Medical Devices (Argentina) |
| API | application programming interface |
| APTA | Argentine Network of Patients for Advanced Therapies |
| ARC | average relative citations |
| ART | assisted reproductive technology |
| ASC | Access Sub-Committee (UK Biobank) |
| ATMP | advanced therapy medicinal product |
| AWT | artificial womb technology |
| BDF | big data in health and research |
| BRCA | breast cancer gene |
| CEO | chief executive officer |
| CESCR | United Nations Committee on Economic, Social and Cultural Rights |
| CIOMS | Council for International Organizations of Medical Sciences |
| Covid-19 | Coronavirus disease 2019 |
| CRISPR | clustered regularly interspaced short palindromic repeats |
| DNA | deoxyribonucleic acid |
| DPP | Director of Public Prosecutions (England and Wales) |
| EAC | Ethics Advisory Committee (UK Biobank) |
| EBM | evidence-based medicine |
| ECA | European Communities Act 1972 |
| ECHR | European Convention on Human Rights |

| | |
|---|---|
| ECtHR | European Court of Human Rights |
| EGC | Ethics and Governance Council (UK Biobank) |
| EGF | Ethics and Governance Framework (UK Biobank) |
| ELSI | ethical, legal and social implications |
| EMA | European Medicines Agency |
| EPC | European Patent Convention 1973 |
| EPO | European Patent Office |
| EPOrg | European Patent Organisation |
| ESRC | Economic and Social Research Council (UK) |
| FDA | Food and Drug Administration (USA) |
| GA4GH | Global Alliance for Genomics and Health |
| GDPR | Regulation (EU) 2016/679 of the European Parliament and of the Council on the protection of natural persons with regard to the processing of personal data and on the free movement of such data [2016] OJ L119/1 (General Data Protection Regulation) |
| GGF | Good Governance Framework |
| HCT/Ps | human, cellular and tissue products |
| HFEA | Human Fertilisation and Embryology Authority (UK) |
| HHGE | heritable human genome editing |
| HL | House of Lords (UK) |
| HRCDC | Health Research Consent Declaration Committee (Ireland) |
| HRR | health research regulation |
| HTA | Human Tissue Authority (UK) |
| HUGO | Human Genome Organization |
| ICD | internal cardiac defibrillators |
| ICESCR | International Covenant on Economic, Social and Cultural Rights |
| ICMJE | International Committee of Medical Journal Editors |
| ICU | intensive care unit |
| IEAG | Interim Ethics and Governance Group (UK Biobank) |
| INCUCAI | El Instituto Nacional Central Único Coordinador de Ablación e Implante (Argentina) |
| IP | intellectual property |
| IPR | intellectual property rights |
| IRB | institutional review board |
| IT | information technology |
| IVDR | Council Regulation (EU) 2017/746 on in vitro diagnostics medical devices [2017] OJ L117/176 |
| IVF | in vitro fertilisation |
| LCJ | Lord Chief Justice |
| LJ | Lord Justice |
| LLM | Master of Laws |
| MB | megabyte |

| MDR | Regulation (EU) 2017/45 of the European Parliament and Council on medical devices [2017] OJ L117/1 |
| MHRA | Medicines and Healthcare Products Regulatory Agency (UK) |
| MISST | mobile imaging, pervasive sensing, social media and location tracking |
| MMDB | Medicines and Medical Devices Bill 2019–20 |
| MOH | Ministry of Health |
| MOST | Ministry of Science, Technology and Productive Innovation (Argentina) |
| MP | Member of Parliament |
| MRC | Medical Research Council (UK) |
| MSP | Member of Scottish Parliament |
| NHS | National Health Service |
| NICE | National Institute for Health and Care Excellence (UK) |
| ORCID | open researcher and contributor ID |
| OSTP | Office of Science and Technology Policy (USA) |
| PDF | portable document format |
| PI | principal investigator |
| PSC | Patient Safety Commissioner |
| QB | Queen's Bench |
| QC | Queen's Counsel |
| REC | research ethics committee |
| REF | Research Excellence Framework (UK) |
| SHIP | Scottish Health Informatics Programme |
| STEM | science, technology, engineering and mathematics |
| TRIPS | Agreement on Trade-Related Aspects of Intellectual Property Rights |
| UDHR | Universal Declaration of Human Rights |
| ULTRA | Unrelated Live Transplant Regulatory Authority |
| UN | United Nations |
| UNESCO | United Nations Educational, Scientific and Cultural Organization |
| WHO | World Health Organization |
| WMA | World Medical Association |

~

# Introduction

EDWARD S. DOVE AND NIAMH NIC SHUIBHNE

How might an individual scholar generate and maintain a legacy in their field of study? We present this collection of chapters in tribute to Graeme Laurie's extraordinary contribution to the field of medical jurisprudence, as well as to legal and interdisciplinary scholarship more generally and to the development of policy and practice in the UK and beyond. The aim of the volume is to animate and interrogate a concept that Graeme so often talks about – *legacy* – as a dimension of the study and practice of 'medical jurisprudence'.

Graeme has often spoken about the importance of legacy in our individual and collective academic work[1] and has forged a remarkable intellectual legacy of his own, notably through his work on genetic privacy,[2] human tissue,[3] information governance[4] and the regulatory salience of the anthropological concept of liminality.[5] These contributions can be traced

---

[1] See, for example, Nayha Sethi, Graeme Laurie and Shawn Harmon, 'International Academic Conferences: Significance and Legacy of the 13th World Congress of the International Association of Bioethics' (2016) 16 *Medical Law International* 105, 106, in which the authors reflect on the 13th World Congress of the International Association of Bioethics (IAB 2016, which was hosted in Edinburgh) and write: 'how do we generate and maintain legacy and help to keep communities consistently engaged over time?'. See also Graeme Laurie, 'Pause for Reflection . . . and Respect' (2015) 12 *SCRIPTed: A Journal of Law, Technology and Society* 82, 84, an editorial in which Graeme reflects on the Edinburgh Law School postgraduate student-run journal *SCRIPTed*, which he helped to found in 2004, and writes: '[i]t had not struck me until now, however, how much *SCRIPTed* is a legacy platform – with postgraduates passing the torch of responsibility and quality from one team to the next, and always in precarious circumstances of funding and the vagaries of the multiple demands of modern academic life'.

[2] See, for example, Graeme Laurie, *Genetic Privacy: A Challenge to Medico-legal Norms* (Cambridge University Press 2002).

[3] See, for example, Kenyon Mason and Graeme Laurie, 'Consent or Property? Dealing with the Body and Its Parts in the Shadow of Bristol and Alder Hey' (2001) 64 *Modern Law Review* 710.

[4] See, for example, his influential work with the Scottish Government, *Joined-Up Data for Better Decisions: Guiding Principles for Data Linkage* (Scottish Government 2012).

[5] See, for example, Graeme Laurie, 'Liminality and the Limits of Law in Health Research Regulation: What Are We Missing in the Spaces in-Between?' (2017) 25 *Medical Law Review* 47.

1

through more personal legacies, too. When Graeme moved from the University of Glasgow to the University of Edinburgh in 1995 as a lecturer in law, having been supervised and mentored by the pioneering medical lawyer Professor Sheila McLean,[6] he was immediately taken under the wing of Professor J Kenyon (Ken) Mason, Regius Professor of Forensic Medicine at Edinburgh 1973–85 and thereafter a valued Honorary Fellow in the School of Law. Ken Mason was figuratively and literally a towering figure in forensic medicine and medical jurisprudence, and he inspired in Graeme a strong sense of intellectual rigour, teaching excellence and legacy-formation. We see the legacy of Ken Mason throughout Edinburgh Law School, foremost through the research institute established and named in his honour in 2012,[7] as well as in several of the courses he was instrumental in creating (such as 'Fundamental Issues in Medical Jurisprudence') and co-creating with Graeme (such as 'Contemporary Issues in Medical Jurisprudence', which enables groups of students to design and lead seminars on topical medical law and ethics issues[8]) and through the next generation of scholars he influenced, including Graeme and many of the contributors to this volume.

What does legacy *mean*, though? – to ask a type of question that would remind many of Ken Mason. We may start with a look at the dictionary. According to the Cambridge Dictionary, legacy is 'something that is a part of your history or that remains from an earlier time',[9] and one example provided is that '[t]he Greeks have a rich legacy of literature'.[10] This provides a useful starting point. In one sense, it seems that legacy speaks to what it means to be human and a member of society by way of *leaving a lasting mark*. Second, while it elucidates what we contribute individually, it also elucidates what we contribute as *connected members in a community*.

---

[6] For an appreciation of Sheila McLean's work, see Pamela Ferguson and Graeme Laurie (eds), *Inspiring a Medico-legal Revolution: Essays in Honour of Sheila McLean* (Routledge 2015).

[7] J Kenyon Mason Institute for Medicine, Life Sciences and the Law (more commonly known as the Mason Institute). See Mason Institute, available at www.law.ed.ac.uk /research/research-centres-and-networks/mason-institute/about-the-mason-institute (accessed 29 March 2021). See also Sheila McLean (ed), *First Do No Harm: Law, Ethics and Healthcare* (Routledge 2006).

[8] Graeme himself has referred to Contemporary Issues in Medical Jurisprudence as a 'legacy' of his teaching: a course largely of his design that empowers students to flourish as independent researchers and seminar leaders.

[9] Cambridge Dictionary, available at https://dictionary.cambridge.org/ (accessed 29 March 2021).

[10] Ibid.

These ideas resonate with our collective efforts as academics to leave something behind (intellectually and otherwise) for others to take up. We aspire, as Eric Meslin writes, to have 'informed new ways of knowing . . . [and to have] disrupted (positively) the ways of knowing that had been used before';[11] in so doing, we might reveal – and shape, even in some small way – what kind of world we want to live in and leave to future generations. In this understanding, legacy, as 'the central arc that connects the past, present and future',[12] is the linked chain of experiences shared, decisions made and actions taken that marks our collective bond, connecting us to that which has come before us and what may, through our efforts exerted in the past and present, come after us. In other words, legacy enables us, for Mark Taylor and David Townend, 'to reach for [ideas] better suited to our shared future'.[13]

However, as Jean McHale underlines, it is not just that we *can* map the future but that we *need* to do so,[14] charting, through that endeavour, some known pathways but also, notes Fabiana Arzuaga, 'pathways into the unknown', be it in our personal or professional capacity.[15] Moreover, thinking in particular of the role of legacy in law, policy and regulation, 'part of that creation [of pathways] may mean (or demand) a fundamental re-visioning of the legal setting itself, its instruments, institutions, and regulatory or governance mechanisms'; which means, in turn, that '[w]e must be prepared to ask whether existing systems (and their assumptions and values) are capable of responding to the demands being made of them and of delivering the future that we want'.[16]

Richard Ashcroft underlines the non-linear relationship among past, present and future in thinking about legacy because 'the scope of a legacy can change: the present looks back to the past and downplays an issue that might have been important to the previous generation, and introduces elements of the past that had previously been neglected as important after all'.[17] Fundamentally, though, as scholars, we reap what others have sown. Our ideas and our outputs are a reflection, in part, of those

---

[11] Chapter 6.
[12] Chapter 8.
[13] Chapter 17.
[14] Chapter 14.
[15] Chapter 15.
[16] Ibid., referring to Graeme Laurie, Shawn Harmon and Fabiana Arzuaga, 'Foresighting Futures: Law, New Technologies, and the Challenges of Regulating for Uncertainty' (2012) 4 *Law, Innovation and Technology* 1.
[17] Chapter 2.

contributions made by academics of times present and past. Likewise, we might find that law, more generally, is a reflection of societal norms and events – be they enduring or recently formed – that shape our conduct as citizens in a polity.

How can these dimensions of legacy catalyse transformative change in medical jurisprudence? More specifically, what fruits can we reap from the intellectual efforts of Graeme Laurie? What can we learn from his scholarship and wider contributions as a public intellectual who sought at times to break new ground and depart from the burdens of legacy while appreciating, at the same time, lessons of value produced by both scholars and events of the past?

## Graeme Laurie: Dimensions of a Legacy

In this volume, many of Graeme's dearest colleagues and academic friends reflect on these ideas in a range of fields, and from a variety of perspectives and disciplines, yet connected in some way to the study and practice of 'medical jurisprudence' (the meaning of which we return to a little further on). Through synthesis of and further reflection on their findings, we seek as editors in this chapter to construct the profile of the concept of legacy as a lens through which the evolution of medical jurisprudence can be analysed and assessed. As we indicated earlier, the role of legacy in medical jurisprudence may be seen in various lights, both positive and negative. Yet all of its dimensions are necessary fully to round out the nature and trajectory of the field – in terms of what it was, what it is and where it is going – and to appreciate how Graeme's own contributions have given shape to it and charted a path for others to follow.

We consider that Graeme's legacy to law and medical jurisprudence takes three forms. First, it takes the form of the *intellectual legacy* that his scholarship contributes to the advancement of the field. We return to his specific contributions in more detail later in this introduction, but, in a general sense, we were struck by how many contributors to this volume emphasised Graeme's affinity for and advancement of *ideas*; captured by Annie Sorbie as 'his almost superhuman ability to detect and tease out the kernel of an idea'.[18] For Sharon Cowan, Emily Postan and Nayha Sethi, this is evidenced most strongly through Graeme's deployment of 'evocative and often highly visual concepts that provide centres of critical and

---

[18] Chapter 4.

interpretive gravity in his own work and, subsequently, in that of others'[19] – concepts such as privacy as a state of separateness; legal foresighting for new and emerging technologies; liminality and the experience of transition; and reflexive governance in biobanking.

The sheer range of conceptual contributions that Graeme has produced to date – an 'immense' personal intellectual legacy that has never 'sacrificed depth for breadth', as Margot Brazier and Alexandra Mullock put it[20] – demonstrates his openness not just to ideas but to *new* ideas; it demonstrates, in other words, his innate intellectual curiosity. But Cowan, Postan and Sethi also identify another reason why this work appeals to Graeme: '[d]espite the law's association with rules and bright lines, the interpretation of open-ended and pliable concepts is a crucial part of permitting the law to be responsive and to evolve – a facility that is particularly important where its objects are rapidly developing medical practices or biotechnologies'.[21]

Importantly, as Roger Brownsword emphasises, 'Graeme has invited readers to think outside the black-letter box of medical law.'[22] We understand this dimension of his legacy beyond law in two senses. At one level, Graeme's pursuit of 'concept-driven inquiries' is progressed through '*interdisciplinary thinking* . . . [exemplifying] the value of looking to other disciplines for theoretical tools and framing devices'.[23] For Bartha Knoppers, Ruth Chadwick and Michael Beauvais, Graeme's interdisciplinary approach is characterised by his 'sustained efforts to bring ethical considerations to the fore of biomedical research and to ensure the development of agile, fit-for-purpose governance', reflecting a 'reciprocal relationship [across disciplines]. Indeed, the silence of law at the forefront of biomedical science is an invitation for creative policy-making that is embedded within the scientific endeavour itself.'[24]

In another sense, however, Graeme's work journeys to 'areas where the law does not reach'; for example, 'thinking about how ethical and other normative frameworks can inform the governance and practices of medicine and the biosciences'.[25] Graeme's Wellcome-funded Liminal Spaces project ('Confronting the liminal spaces of health research

---

[19] Chapter 1.
[20] Chapter 10.
[21] Chapter 1.
[22] Chapter 3.
[23] Chapter 1 (emphasis added).
[24] Chapter 8.
[25] Chapter 1.

regulation'), which ran from 2014 to 2021 and which he considers one of his milestone career accomplishments, exemplifies his calling into question the conventional categories of law, especially to underline what then gets lost 'in-between'. This evidences, for Shawn Harmon, that while Graeme 'has been and remains concerned with what can and ought to guide actors in the health-care setting, and how law might be deployed to assist in this regard', he also creates 'action spaces that are encouraging, sensible and comprehensible, all within environments where the law might be quite limited in what it can accomplish'.[26] As Graeme himself expressed in his monograph *Genetic Privacy*, '[l]aw has its limits, and an examination of these is as much a part of the search for an answer as is a thorough examination of any statute or body of case-law . . . ultimately it is in the exploration of the limits of legal intervention that the symbiosis of privacy and law will be found'.[27]

Those who have worked with or been supervised or taught by Graeme will recall his familiar expression of 'recognising the limits of law'. This is not at all a statement of lack of interest in the law or a diminishment of law's power. Rather, it stems from a deep appreciation of the awesomeness of law. Calvin Wai-Loon Ho and Justin Yuk Cheong Wong point to this vital qualifier in their observation that Graeme's openness to the world beyond law does not suggest his

> . . . lack of confidence in the law[;] such a proposition could not be further from the truth. Rather than draw on the analytic of alterity to critique the 'other', Graeme has instead turned the critical lens inward and demonstrated to us all what the law could and should be, particularly for those whose life and work are deeply enmeshed with it. Far from denigrating the relevance of law to health-related research, this deeply introspective approach reveals to us how the zest of law must itself be sustained.[28]

Crucially, then, as this chapter and those that follow will demonstrate, legacy can be both an advantage and a potential burden – and sometimes it can be both simultaneously: it can generate a platform from which innovative thinking and policy can develop, and it can also generate a stasis that constrains or encumbers progress (or seeds the beginnings of dangerous or unjust practices). In that light, another defining characteristic of Graeme's intellectual legacy is his ability to navigate and negotiate the obstacles that legacy can produce.

---

[26] Chapter 18.
[27] Laurie (n 2) 27.
[28] Chapter 7.

A second form that Graeme's legacy to law and medical jurisprudence takes is his *impact legacy*, particularly through his work in knowledge exchange and co-creation at the highest levels of policy and practice. If you ask Graeme what professors should do, he typically answers: 'they should profess'. Nevertheless, Graeme's own work is not confined to the ivory tower; it has been coloured by his consistent engagement 'with the messiness of the real world'. As Sorbie writes, '[i]f legacy is understood not only as something that connects us to what has gone before and enables us to move forward with the benefit of that wisdom but also as a means of community building and facilitating future progress and innovation, then this is indeed what Graeme has accomplished'.[29] In that light, Graeme's work can be

> ... unified by a number of interrelated objectives, which, stated very broadly, are to improve the behaviour of life science innovators, the performance of health system regulators, and the outcomes of life science and health research and medical interventions. And, finally, it can be said to have at its centre the empowerment of people and communities, particularly those who have traditionally been silenced or pushed to the peripheries of decision-making.[30]

Finally, third, Graeme has produced an extraordinary *personal legacy* – as mentor, project leader, supervisor and teacher, and exemplified by his belief in and commitment to creating space for others to conceive and generate their own legacies. All who know him would attest that Graeme is studiously devoid of affectation, pretence or haughty seniority. From undergraduates to postdoctoral researchers, from new hires to old(er) hands: Graeme treats all equally and with respect, as a peer and as a person-in-full, with views that deserve to be recognised and valorised, trusting the experience and wisdom of others to have a role in decision-making within the multidisciplinary field that is 'medical jurisprudence'. Connecting personal legacy back to intellectual legacy, Eric Meslin observes astutely that

> ... whereas the first few years of Graeme's publication record are filled primarily with single-authored papers, the later years include more jointly authored works, as befits a senior scholar with an interest in and commitment to mentoring, but also one who has recognised that one of the most energising (and fruitful) ways of exploring complex topics at the intersection of law, medicine and science is to have co-authors from these fields.[31]

---

[29] Chapter 4.
[30] Chapter 18.
[31] Chapter 6.

In light of this, it is not surprising to see that his long-standing and focused attention in his own research has been on 'understanding and vindicating the interests of those actors who have habitually been left out of governance and policymaking: participants and publics'.[32] Graeme's alertness to providing space extends also, as another dimension of his impact legacy, to a 'persistent concern for understanding and vindicating the interests of those actors who have habitually been left out of governance and policy-making: participants and publics'.[33] In his extended work with UK Biobank, the Scottish Health Informatics Programme and the Scottish Government, among other bodies, Graeme has consistently advocated for furthering the voices of publics – engaging (with) and respecting them – and feeding those voices coherently into policy-making and governance processes to make health policy not only more informed but also more legitimate and more accountable to society. That is a profound part of *his* legacy because it is a profound part of Graeme himself.

### 'Medical Jurisprudence'

As Richard Ashcroft notes, '[t]he field of law and medical ethics is now flourishing all around the (academic) world. But it is salutary to recall that this is a recent development, and that even now it is a vexed question to define its scope and principles.'[34] In that spirit, and before looking in more depth at the concept of legacy, we should also briefly dissect the meaning of 'medical jurisprudence' and consider the legacy of this term as compared to its close semantic siblings such as 'medical law', 'health law' and 'health-care law'.

Ashcroft further argues that '[n]omenclature matters; naming tells us what is to be studied and what is of interest. It can also imply what is to be left out.'[35] In that light, he asks the following critical questions and explains why it is important that we ask them:

> Are we looking at 'law and medical ethics' or 'medical law and ethics' or 'medical law' or 'health-care law' or 'health law' or 'medical jurisprudence'? While to a great extent these pick out significant areas of overlap, the differences matter. For are we primarily concerned with what medical practitioners do, and how this is supervised and regulated by the law? Or

---

[32] Ibid.
[33] Chapter 18.
[34] Chapter 2.
[35] Ibid.

are we mainly concerned with the legal framework within which professional self-governance through 'professional ethics' operates? Perhaps we
are most concerned with how the law is used to protect and promote
health, or with the legal framework of the public delivery of health
services.[36]

The University of Edinburgh has long embraced the term 'medical
jurisprudence', stemming from the Chair of Medical Jurisprudence,
which has existed at the University since 1807 – initially in the Faculty
of Law and then the Faculty of Medicine, before returning to the Law
School in 2005 when Graeme accepted it. The 'Medical' dimension of the
Chair thus has an institutional as well as a clinical legacy at Edinburgh,
itself an institution long associated with esteemed medical education. But
we might also note Ashcroft's caution that 'the relative dominance of the
medical forms of names of the field (medical law, medical ethics, medical
jurisprudence, medical regulation . . .) is broadly borne out by the relative
dominance of the concerns of the medical profession in what is
discussed'.[37]

'Jurisprudence' is, according to the Cambridge Dictionary, 'the study
of law *and the principles on which law is based*'.[38] This suggests a wider
term than 'law' per se, which is itself notoriously difficult to pin down but,
depending on one's philosophical persuasion, might be somewhat safely
defined as a system of rules of a particular country, group or area of
activity. 'Jurisprudence' suggests something more scholarly, austere and
quasi-theological. Even if so, we do not think that the term is innately or
significantly divergent from its semantic siblings. True, it may be that
'health law' is more encompassing than 'medical law' or 'medical jurisprudence', if only because health is a broader term that takes us beyond
the clinical context, but this should not be treated as an impermeable
division. After all, Graeme, as Chair of Medical Jurisprudence, regularly
progressed the law and law's underlying principles in areas well beyond
the doctor–patient relationship, the hospital, or what we might otherwise
associate with law and the treatment of illness and injuries. His work also
reflects Ashcroft's observation that there are 'two ways for "medical law"
to be "medical": it can be "medical law" because it focuses on medical
practice (however broadly drawn); but it can also be "medical law"
because it focuses on the health impacts of law'.[39]

---

[36] Ibid.
[37] Ibid.
[38] See n 9 (emphasis added).
[39] Chapter 2.

Beyond our claim that medical jurisprudence can be seen as closely related to – and in harmony with – other terms used to demarcate this field of 'law and health' (as the chapters in this volume evidence rather convincingly), it is particularly important to underline that medical jurisprudence has never been a purely legal domain; it 'should be more than a manual of time-honoured precedents and principles'.[40] For example, work from José Miola,[41] among others, has shown that while medical jurisprudence is a field (and practice) that has not always engaged well with other domains, foremost ethics,[42] it necessarily must (and must do so faithfully) if it is to be seen as coherent and regulating well – that is, robustly and legitimately – the practices of health care and health research. In other words, 'lawyers will accept that it makes no sense to study medical law without also taking seriously the application of medical ethics, and that medical jurisprudence needs to set medical law in its social, political and economic context'.[43] Perhaps more than other cognate areas, medical jurisprudence *needs* this engagement with ethics (and, we would add, human rights) for the very reason that those caring for and interacting with others – health professionals, researchers and so on – predominate in this field and do so in ways that are often more intimate and more pronounced than in many other areas of law.

This engagement with and connection to other areas is not limited to ethics, though that is, perhaps unsurprisingly, the most significant other field to which medical jurisprudence is bonded.[44] Graeme's work demonstrates how a core 'legacy' component of medical jurisprudence is its disciplinary and methodological openness to fields *beyond* (applied) ethics, too, such as life science and medicine, as well as to the social sciences, including sociology, politics and anthropology. Of course, medical jurisprudence's 'bread-and-butter' will always be astute commentary on developments in case law and statutes. But in recent years, we have also seen scholars – foremost Graeme, we submit – who harness concepts and research findings from non-legal disciplines and apply them to make better sense of developments in science, medicine and health

---

[40] Chapter 3.
[41] José Miola, *Medical Ethics and Medical Law: A Symbiotic Relationship* (Hart 2007).
[42] And, to be fair, few other areas of law have successfully achieved this either.
[43] Chapter 3.
[44] We note that the subject area in Edinburgh Law School is called 'Medical Law and Ethics', which is also the name of the associated LLM programme. It would be hard (even if interesting) to imagine other cognate legal fields taking the same approach, be it 'EU Law and Ethics' or otherwise.

technologies; to advocate for smarter ways to get the regulatory environment right; and to chart better, more innovative ways to engage publics to contribute to debates about effective and acceptable uses of technologies for regulatory purposes. The legacy of Graeme's disciplinary and methodo- logical openness in medical jurisprudence is reflected in many of the chapters in this volume, such as Catriona McMillan and Agomoni Ganguli- Mitra's assessment of the ethics and governance of reproduction,[45] wherein they harness the concept of liminality and insights from bioethics critically to assess two contemporary examples of human reproduction, namely surro- gacy and ectogenesis, as a means to consider how both ought to be regulated, and regulated better.

This pivot away from rule-bound scripture and 'black-letter' attitude, as Ho and Wong call it,[46] enables those in the field (whatever they choose to call it) to cope with an innately complex set of challenges, characterised by 'uncertain risks, uncertain futures and uncertain outcomes'.[47] Phrased another way, the problems and issues addressed by medical jurispru- dence require analysis and responses influenced by scholarship that reaches well beyond the juridical field. It is for this reason that Lawrence Gostin concludes that:

> The field of 'medical jurisprudence', to use the University of Edinburgh parlance, has come a long way. It is not just about medicine and what happens in the clinic; it also explores health systems, including public health services. It is not just about health systems but also upstream social and commercial determinants of health. And it is not just all-of- government but also all-of-society.[48]

At the same time, though, Ashcroft offers a tempering caution in sug- gesting that '[i]nasmuch as we can have, or want, a normative theory of (medical) law, ... we will get more at this stage from a jurisprudential study of medical law *as law* (both in doctrine and in action) than from a philosophical study of medical law as concretised medical ethics'.[49]

As the chapters in this volume taken together demonstrate, the legacy of medical jurisprudence is characterised by its gradual expansion from the clinic to health systems; its interdisciplinary foray into elements of good governance in the area of health; and its deeper connection among

---

[45] Chapter 5.
[46] Chapter 7.
[47] Ibid.
[48] Afterword.
[49] Chapter 2.

law, ethics and other fields (realised through establishing relationships with scholars in moral philosophy, science and medicine, and the social sciences). Academics working in the field of medical jurisprudence pursue 'a set of different epistemic trajectories, most often grounding the work in legal and jurisprudential thinking, but not uncommonly taking on topics using applied ethics, human rights or social science frames'; moreover, '[t]his diversity is consistent with the trajectories of like-minded scholars working at the intersection of law, medicine and ethics, just as it would be for those of us in the humanities and social sciences working at other "intersections" in the disciplinary landscape, including applied ethics, science and technology studies, or global health'.[50]

In many ways, this is part of the legacy contributed by Graeme himself. To that end, we now turn to the concept of legacy more substantively.

## Delineating Dimensions of Law and Legacy in Medical Jurisprudence

It is not only medical jurisprudence itself that is imbued with legacy. Individuals, too, both receive and produce legacy, and here we pick up on several of the chapters' themes to highlight how individual contributions within the field – such as Graeme Laurie's ground-breaking work on liminality in law, the right not to know and genetic privacy, and principles-based governance – have secured lasting legacy across jurisdictions and across sectors.

More specifically, through this collection of chapters, we illustrate Graeme's contributions by unpacking both the burdens and the benefits of legacy. We seek to demonstrate, first, that legacy is a concept of relevance for the medical jurisprudence field. By this, we suggest that legacy is a useful and significant analytical lens for the field of medical jurisprudence, through which a range of substantive examples can be presented and evaluated, and through different disciplinary approaches. Second, reflecting across the chapters in this volume, we uncover the surface persona of legacy by identifying its Janus-faced 'encumbering' and 'facilitating' functions. In other words, legacy reveals characteristics of both benefit and burden – as both an encumbrance to and a facilitator of the development of law, policy and regulation.

---

[50] Chapter 6.

However, third, we also acknowledge the clotted quality of the 'encumbrance' and 'facilitator' functions of legacy. When we first conceived the project, we sketched an essentially binary understanding of legacy: surely it *either* encumbers *or* facilitates progress – whether that progress concerns legal concepts, their reflection in policy or their application in practice – and the former surely must be conceived as negative and discouraged while the latter is positive and welcomed. But then we were confronted with, for example, Mark Taylor and David Townend's analysis of 'beneficial encumbrance',[51] and Knoppers, Chadwick and Beauvais's framing of the 'CRISPR' baby story in China in 2018 as 'a controversy, potentially even a scandal, [and yet] this watershed moment left a legacy that may actually be understood in positive terms'.[52]

Through the generosity of all of the contributors and their willingness to reflect on the implications of legacy across a range of contexts and case studies, the concept that has emerged is therefore far less binary and more complex than we originally imagined it might be. Overall, the chapters manage to reconcile the ideas of legacy and 'responsiveness' and, importantly, to show that both dimensions are critical to achieving and sustaining the health of medical jurisprudence as a dynamic, interdisciplinary and policy-engaged field of thinking.

We were also challenged to reflect on what we are 'doing' with legacy: managing it? Negotiating it? Navigating it? Channelling it? Overcoming it? Transcending it? Harnessing it? For different contexts and to achieve different objectives, it turns out that we are sometimes doing all of those things – and that Graeme's work offers us the tools that might be needed to do them successfully. In what follows, we first outline the 'encumbrance' and 'facilitative' qualities of legacy in more detail before considering the complicated relationship between these dimensions.

### Medical Jurisprudence: Encumbered by Legacy

Controversial or sensitive events in society, science and medicine – but, crucially, also responses to them – may create a jurisprudential legacy that can take different forms. Sometimes, an event-specific legal or regulatory form that has little application outside a specific context can produce problematic responsiveness – law becomes *encumbered* by its

---

[51] Chapter 17, in which the authors observe that '[a]n encumbrance, colloquially and in law, is a restriction, a block on something, a limitation. But the notion of a barrier to an activity, especially in the area of law, is not necessarily one-sided or wholly negative'.

[52] Chapter 8.

history – resulting in blunt, inappropriate regulatory tools. Moreover, whereas individuals traditionally have a reverence for their legacy and therefore, not uncommonly, seek actively to shape their lives in a way that leaves a net benefit for posterity (foremost, we could say, one's family), in the jurisprudential context it may be that events (or scandals) can emerge out of a confluence of actions and are not attributable to one or even several identifiable individuals. In that light, those ascribed with agency – the judge, the regulator, the Secretary of State – may not have much, if any, concern about the 'legacy' implications because they may be only indirectly implicated in the event and perceive a limited ability to shape the law in any profound manner. Phrased another way, legacy's burden in medical jurisprudence can result as much from decisions executed incrementally, over a number of years, as it can from either 'grand' actions or complete inaction.

In these respects, legacy inflicts a burden on or presents a challenge to medical jurisprudence. This comes through particularly in Chapters 7, 9, 10 and 11. Jackson's Chapter 11 forensically examines the legacy of the Warnock Report concerning the ethics of human assisted reproduction techniques, which ultimately led to the Human Fertilisation and Embryology Act 1990. Jackson argues that as well-regarded an impact as the Warnock Report has been in regulating assisted reproduction, changes in societal values *and* technology have taken us far beyond some of the Report's language, particularly in relation to gene editing technologies, egg freezing, same-sex parenthood, trans parenthood and surrogacy. Here, legacy can hold us back, so 'it should not be surprising that a statute based on recommendations made so long ago is "inevitably showing its age" . . . At some point, it may be sensible to embark upon a law reform process that does not just tweak and update the current statute but goes back to first principles and starts again'.[53]

Hoppe and Miola's Chapter 9 examines the burden of legacy through the genesis of the Human Tissue Act 2004 in the wake of the Alder Hey organ retention scandal and, more recently, the public response to the introduction of the *care.data* programme in England. As they observe from their analysis of the 'regulatory corset' produced through responding to these troubling events, it is not uncommonly the case that scandals drive regulatory reform in societies, but not always in proportionate response or with due legislative skill:

---

[53] Chapter 11.

... the more scandalous a trigger event is, the more energy the subsequent regulation deploys. While stakeholders may accept this as proportionate in the immediate aftermath of the scandal itself, the resulting regulation very rarely applies only to that scandal; rather, it unfolds prospective power in all cases which cannot be adequately distinguished. The regulation is the scandal's legacy, impacting future actions that were not even contemplated when the regulatory need was identified.[54]

Hoppe and Miola are not entirely enthusiastic about the Human Tissue Act 2004, which emerged in the aftermath of the Alder Hey scandal. As for the *care.data* programme, which led to serious concerns about the misuse of confidential NHS patient data in England, they warn us that the result may not be poorly drafted legislation but, rather, a regulatory stasis where legacy, from both this specific scandal and those in times past, prevents much, if any, change at all – in this case, appropriate information governance mechanisms to harness the research potential of NHS patient data. This was a story of 'an initiative that seeks to [. . .] learn the lessons of the past on the basis of the treasure trove of NHS data that is already available – but it does so in a way which squanders public trust in the shortest conceivable amount of time':

> The story of *care.data* is that this snapshot is not just relevant to legal rules, and that legacy can prevent as well as erode. . . . What we can see here, then, is the opposite of the story in relation to the law governing tissue donation. In the case of data and privacy, the government was prevented from changing rules by the legacy of previous (mis)behaviours and mistrust. Legacy, it would appear, operates both as a positive catalyst for change and as a conservative force that prevents it. These might be considered micro-interactions, but they do have one thing in common: in both cases, the interests of patients are protected at the expense of what might be seen as the greater good. This can be explained by looking at the wider picture and considering the general trajectory of medical law as a whole, where the impact of legacy is also evident.[55]

Brazier and Mullock trace similar themes in their Chapter 10, cautioning against legacy constructed through *perceptions* and exploring, for example, how different perceptions of the significance of bodies endure to haunt us – including through simple *avoidance* of tough problems.[56]

---

[54] Chapter 9.
[55] Ibid. Also underlining the critical importance of public trust for securing legacy, see Chapter 7.
[56] Chapter 10.

One crucial way in which Graeme's work provides a route through precisely this kind of legacy encumbrance is, as Cowan, Postan and Sethi note in Chapter 1, by:

> ... problematis[ing] the law's tendency to create silos through categorisation of regulatory activities, subjects and objects. These categorisations are themselves legacies left over from previous regulatory regimes, which may at their time of inception have been fit for purpose but no longer remain so and which, paradoxically, may frustrate the original goals of legislation or regulation.[57]

In particular, Graeme's deployment of liminality 'encourages us to break free from these constraints and to reimagine regulatory landscapes as constantly evolving, influenced by and impacting upon diverse disciplines, regulatory objects and actors'.[58] He challenges us to overcome, as Muireann Quigley and Laura Downey write, 'an encumbrance which keeps boundaries and binaries in place' and thus contributes to the freezing of regulation, such that regulation itself becomes stuck.[59]

Aspects of Graeme's work provide tools, in other words, for making lemonade out of lemons, and for actively shifting the narrative from encumbrance to facilitation. To quote Harmon, for example:

> ... contrary to many contemporary deployments of public interest arguments, [Graeme and colleagues argue that] the public interest could and should be understood as an 'encourager' and an 'enabler' rather than as a 'red light' barrier. In other words, rather than functioning to highlight and help avoid socially harmful outcomes, the public interest could also – and more helpfully – underscore the desirable, providing it was sufficiently explored and unpacked.[60]

Otherwise, legacy becomes, as Taylor and Townend put it, 'a secure foundation only for future failure'.[61] Avoiding that fate calls for regulatory courage and indeed a boldness of regulatory vision and ambition, another quality of legacy to which we now turn.

### *Medical Jurisprudence: Facilitated by Legacy*

Graeme's rallying call for a process of regulatory reimagination bridges to the idea that legacy can also be *facilitative*. By this, we mean that legacy

---

[57] Chapter 1.
[58] Ibid.
[59] Chapter 13.
[60] Chapter 18.
[61] Chapter 17.

can play a crucial role in *shifting* the law towards (among other things) protecting, promoting and regulating health research in the public interest. Hoppe and Miola recognise, too, in this understanding, 'the rationality of a legislature that is bounded by, among other things, prior experiences'.[62] While McMillan and Ganguli-Mitra are alert to the fact that the 'role [of legacy] within law and regulation should be treated with caution [and l]aw's legacy can indeed be a burden', they harness Graeme's appeal to liminality, which, 'as a lens, allows us to speak of and examine our present and, moreover, prepare ourselves for the future in liminal periods triggered by emerging technology and evolving social and political landscapes'.[63]

Supporting the work of preparation, legacy in its best sense manifests, for Knoppers, Chadwick and Beauvais, an ethical lineage – a repository of tried and tested ideas and innovations, leaving the best of these in place. In other words, '[t]he legacy of past events and subsequent developments shape our understanding of those events, give shape to our present moment and direct our future course ... The initial principles are never replaced; rather, there is a gradual accretion of experience and of wisdom that translates to new social and scientific contexts.'[64] Moreover, Ashcroft reminds us that 'disruptive or disturbing knowledge that redraws boundaries and resets expectations' – dynamics that we construe in a wholly positive sense for present purposes – 'can often be appreciated properly only in hindsight'.[65] In this sense, building the future requires a foundation, one which is provided by a legacy informed by learning.

Knoppers, Chadwick and Beauvais further highlight the interesting dynamics of legacy in fields of rapid change. While acknowledging that '[e]ffective, robust policy, as a creature of ethics and law, requires some (but not total) cohesion with scientifically relevant categories' – and that '[w]here scientific advances blur the boundaries of certain concepts with either ethical or legal relevance, policy-makers must carefully interpret the implications of such advances' – they suggest, at the same time, that '[a]ttention to lessons learnt and their legacy helps prudence to become wisdom'.[66] The virtue of legal certainty further animates this facilitative conception of legacy, realised through tools that are very familiar to lawyers: precedent, predictability and proportionality.

---

[62] Chapter 9.
[63] Chapter 5.
[64] Chapter 8
[65] Chapter 2.
[66] Chapter 8.

Importantly, though, the idea of legacy as facilitative does not have to imply that legacy is a static good; we should, indeed, 'be cautious of irreflexively miming legal norms of the past'.[67] Broad legal or regulatory forms that are rooted in the experience of best practice yet can apply reflexively across a variety of situations, including those unforeseen, can be produced. Harmon's Chapter 18 exemplifies this dynamic understanding of legacy, tracing the positive legacy dimensions of the human right to share in scientific advancement and its benefits.

## Medical Jurisprudence and Legacy's Complexities

However, the contributors to this volume perhaps demonstrate, above all, that legacy in law and medical jurisprudence may well – and perhaps most commonly – fall somewhere 'in-between' encumbrance and facilitator: that is, legacy, as a Janus-faced concept, can both (and sometimes simultaneously) *restrain society from progress* (be it legislative-based or values-based), on the one hand, yet also *empower society to forge change* (or maintain what is seen as good) for public benefit, on the other hand.[68] In this way, as Hoppe and Miola suggest, legacy is a kind of 'pendulum' that swings back and forth over time, with the law responding to events that conspire to show the limitations and/or benefits of prioritising the individual interests over the collective good: '[l]egacy, it would appear, operates both as a positive catalyst for change and as a conservative force that prevents it'.[69]

We see this dual-faced nature of legacy in Jean McHale's Chapter 14 on the UK Biobank's Ethics and Governance Council.[70] The Council produced a number of outputs – widely viewed as world-leading for biobank governance – that reflected its own development of 'reflexive governance', inspired and shaped by Graeme's work. And yet, the Council was, at the same time, encumbered by the absence of a clear, legally enforceable framework, which ultimately led to its quiet dissolution. We also see it in Aisling McMahon's Chapter 16 on institutional legacy vis-à-vis the imprint of legacy within particular decision-making frameworks, including normative predispositions that may develop. This conception of legacy focuses on shared institutional understandings and historical legacies around a particular concept or provision within that decision-making

---

[67] Chapter 5.
[68] See, for example, Chapter 14.
[69] Chapter 9.
[70] Chapter 14.

framework. Using the morality provisions as interpreted by the European Patent Office since the adoption of Directive 98/44/EC (the 'Biotechnology Directive') as a case study, McMahon demonstrates how 'the potential for encumbrance created by these types of [institutional] legacy is not necessarily negative in nature'.[71] In other words, there may be important reasons why a decision-making body will have specific legacies, which may relate to the legal competences of that body or to ensuring that the body does not act ultra vires its own powers. And yet:

> ... at times, legacy within decision-making can act to perpetuate past ways of doing things where discretion applies in favour of the decision-making body. This can be problematic as it limits scope for adaptation within legal decision-making and potentially limits law's responsiveness. Legacy as encumbrance can be particularly problematic within the medico-legal space, given that science and medicine are advancing at pace, and related social norms are also constantly evolving. This in turn may lead to a heightened need for decision-makers to interpret existing laws for evolving situations within the medico-legal context and require the exercise of discretion to facilitate legal adaptation or responsiveness.[72]

Murray Earle develops similar themes in the context of medically assisted suicide, where he examines the legacy of regulatory failure that results when institutional balance falls out of kilter, with one set of institutions in a polity having to deal with the inaction(s) of another and raising the unwelcome spectre of permanent liminality.[73] In Earle's view, unless and until both the courts and the legislature act to overcome a status (stasis?) quo with which many in society are becoming increasingly uncomfortable, 'the UK runs the risk of a legacy of failure, which is out of kilter with the current medico-legal trend towards personal autonomy'.[74]

Finally, the chapters in this volume suggest that even if we can identify the positive and negative dimensions of legacy – at times both operating simultaneously – it also remains the case that legacy, like so many concepts deployed in medical jurisprudence, is difficult to pin down (much less 'measure'). But we suggest that its uncertainty in both form and function ought to be better recognised and valued. As far as uncertainty goes, Knoppers, Chadwick, and Beauvais observe in their chapter on biomedical research policy that uncertainty is 'inevitable' in law, even

---

[71] Chapter 16.
[72] Ibid.
[73] Chapter 12.
[74] Ibid.

when we look to the law for examples of legacy that create a thread of jurisprudential development over time:

> We can see the inevitability of uncertainty in the legal sphere even in relation to legacies which one might believe to be certain or watertight. In the context of the law of succession, legacies can and frequently do turn out in ways that are very different from those intended. . . . More generally, there are at least two ways in which intentions can be frustrated. The first is through interpretation; the second is a result of events . . ..[75]

In consequence, they advise that 'in mapping our ethical future, we need to have regard to the ways in which ethical legacies will continue to be challenged by interpretation, events, and by a combination of the two'.[76] Phrased another way, legacy is not linear, and we would be foolhardy to assume otherwise.

We can perhaps measure *aspects* of legacy, as Brownsword does in his chapter in terms of 'the leadership, encouragement and inspiration that Graeme has provided to the many young researchers who have worked with him at Edinburgh and who have now gone on to become leading scholars in their own right'.[77] Maybe it is possible, similarly, to attempt to measure the legacy of, say, one's published work or the measure of one's practical impact outside the academy.

But Meslin reminds us that 'not everything that can be measured matters, and not everything that matters can be measured'.[78] Even by the ostensibly robust metrics of academic legacy – leadership, encouragement, inspiration; quantity and quality of published work; demonstrable impact beyond the academy by way of, for example, advancing policy and practice – such 'measures' can go only so far, and do only so much, to reveal the person's (or the concept's) complete value and significance.

And so, even in a volume dedicated to analysing legacy through one person's work and through specific developments in one field, the field of medical jurisprudence, we must recognise these contributions as apertures; they provide us a clearer view as to a person's character and indelible influence, and a clearer view of the shaping of a field, but 'they are not hinged doors opening straight upon life'.[79]

---

[75] Chapter 8.
[76] Ibid.
[77] Chapter 3.
[78] Chapter 6.
[79] Henry James, Preface, *The Portrait of a Lady* (Norton 1975 [1908]) 7.

# 'Doing' Medical Law *and* Ethics

## Putting Interdisciplinarity to Work

SHARON COWAN, EMILY POSTAN AND NAYHA SETHI

## 1.1 Introduction

Interdisciplinary work is hard work, as anyone who has done it knows. In the current research funding environment, it more often than not means working in teams, collaborating across countries, cultures and languages, as well as disciplines. It can be challenging to bring together a group of people – and a range of discourses – from different disciplines, not only because of the ever-increasing time constraints under which academics operate but also because truly interdisciplinary work means negotiating different approaches to research methods, terminology, normative import, ethical boundaries, writing and publishing conventions, and so on. Interdisciplinarity can also mean working as a solo researcher, using the methods and perspectives of disciplines other than one's own to inform, shape and enrich a line of enquiry or a set of specific research questions. Working alone avoids many of the challenges inherent in large interdisciplinary projects, allowing the writer to frame and realise their own research goals. The lone interdisciplinary scholar faces other challenges, including the onerous task of familiarising themselves with the conventions and epistemological parameters of other disciplines. However, as we will explore, interdisciplinarity brings benefits as well as challenges, including the opportunity to paint a more complex picture, create a unified or multi-stranded voice, and construct an intellectual contribution that is more than the sum of its parts.

In this chapter, we explore more specifically the benefits – and challenges – of taking an interdisciplinary approach to the field of medical law *and* ethics, where the '*and*' operates both as a descriptive conjunctive term and as a way of positioning the two in relation to each other. Their conjunction questions the compartmentalisation of medical law (and medical jurisprudence, traditionally perhaps a narrower, doctrinally oriented field of study) as the concern of academic (and practising) lawyers, and the study of ethics as the concern of philosophers. It does so not by bolting on ethics as an afterthought or treating medical law and ethics as if they were separable 'parts of pop-bead necklaces'.[1] Rather, different perspectives have to be brought together at a fundamental level to challenge the assumption that each field of study is truly independent from the other. The composite field of 'medical law and ethics', itself already explicitly interdisciplinary in name, can also then be opened up to critical engagement with other disciplines such as sociology, philosophy, political theory, policy studies, health sciences and anthropology, as well as critical perspectives such as feminism[2] and critical race theory.[3] Indeed, it is an inherently porous and evolving field of study. In our view, this broader understanding of 'medical law and ethics' moves us towards more socially and ethically grounded contextual studies of medical and health-care practice.

The interdisciplinarity of medical law and ethics is reflected in its research focus: the objective is no longer simply to excavate the development of the law or to interrogate legal decision-making. Nor is the aim limited to examining the social and human impacts of the practices of medical law and regulation (though these remain substantial and critical aspects). Rather, medical law and ethics extends also to thinking about how ethical and other normative frameworks can inform the governance and practices of medicine and the biosciences in areas where the law does not, or cannot, reach (for example, because it is normatively ill-equipped to do so, or because it is ill-suited to keep pace with developments in medical knowledge and technology). As we will explore, 'doing' medical law and ethics necessitates an interdisciplinary approach of the sort that has been embraced by our friend and colleague Graeme Laurie, in teaching and in research.

---

[1] Elizabeth Spelman, *Inessential Woman: Problems of Exclusion in Feminist Thought* (Beacon Press 1988) 15.

[2] See, for example, the work of Julie McCandless, Sally Sheldon and Marie Fox.

[3] Chandra Ford and Collins Airhihenbuwa, 'Critical Race Theory, Race Equity, and Public Health: Toward Antiracism Praxis' (2010) 100 (Suppl 1) *American Journal of Public Health* S30; 'Commentary: Just What Is Critical Race Theory and What's It Doing in a Progressive Field like Public Health?' (2018) 28 (Suppl 1) *Ethnicity & Disease* 223. See also Khiara Bridges, Terence Keel and Osagie Obasogie (eds), 'Critical Race Theory & the Health Sciences' (2017) 43 *American Journal of Law and Medicine*.

In this chapter, in keeping with this book's overarching theme, we suggest that it is timely and important to consider what is the legacy of interdisciplinarity for scholars today, and whether – and if so, how – we might choose to continue or disrupt it. This includes asking what might be risked by engaging in interdisciplinarity. We begin by setting out what we mean by interdisciplinarity in our context, before moving on to showcase three ways that Graeme's research and teaching exemplify the openness of spirit and the intellectual curiosity that are required to engage meaningfully in interdisciplinarity. In doing so, we explore the enriching and enabling features of interdisciplinary approaches, and the dividends that can come from working in interdisciplinary ways. However, interdisciplinarity should not be employed just for its own sake, or as an end in itself[4] – rather, it is a means of understanding multi-faceted problems, and its success depends upon how we define the term, and why and how it is utilised.

## 1.2   Implementing Interdisciplinarity

In essence, interdisciplinarity integrates insights from a range of disciplines into a novel framing or understanding of an issue. As noted, the aim of presenting a new, interdisciplinary approach can be achieved either through collaboration with scholars from a range of disciplines or as a lone scholar using insights and methods from cognate – or indeed entirely unrelated – disciplines. As becomes evident in our case studies, Graeme has engaged in both.

### 1.2.1   *How Is Interdisciplinarity Defined?*

It appears that there is no unitary or unified definition of interdisciplinarity; Callard and Fitzgerald have described it as 'a term that everyone invokes and none understands'.[5] At its broadest, interdisciplinary studies have been described by Barthes as 'creating a new object, which belongs to no one'.[6]

---

[4] William Twining, 'Law and Anthropology: A Case Study of Inter-disciplinary Collaboration' (1973) 7 *Law and Society Review* 561.

[5] Felicity Callard and Des Fitzgerald, *Rethinking Interdisciplinarity across the Social Sciences and Neurosciences* (Palgrave Macmillan 2015) 4.

[6] Roland Barthes, *The Rustle of Language* (University of California Press 1989), cited in Erin McClellan and Amanda Johnson, '"Deep Interdisciplinarity" as Critical Pedagogy:

According to Krishnan,[7] one difficulty lies in properly distinguishing between crossdisciplinarity, multidisciplinarity and transdisciplinarity. For Krishnan, crossdisciplinarity refers to the borrowing of methods or conclusions from another discipline – essentially, how do other disciplines answer this question (or, how would one discipline answer a question raised in another discipline)? – while multidisciplinarity frequently involves a team of researchers from different disciplines, often led by a principal investigator, working together to solve a common problem. Transdisciplinarity, on the other hand, says Krishnan, can mean working with people outside of the academic context: for example, 'stakeholders', civic society and so on (though, of course, it might also imply practices that transcend the boundaries of individual disciplines to create a new approach or knowledge base altogether). Notwithstanding these apparent distinctions, we agree with Krishnan that all of these (and potentially others) are types of interdisciplinary work, and we will say more later about how Graeme's work has embraced these approaches to varying degrees.

### 1.2.2   Why Turn to Interdisciplinarity?

An interdisciplinary approach is necessitated, says Newell, 'by complexity, specifically by the structure and behaviour of complex systems'.[8] Of course, we need not accept Newell's view that interdisciplinarity is merited in the study only of complex systems (where complex appears to have a particularly scientific connotation). We might argue that interdisciplinarity is merely a useful way of better understanding a particular issue from overlapping yet distinct perspectives, regardless of whether or not the 'system' or issue in question is 'complex'. In fact, many issues and systems – such as the practice of medicine, or legal decision-making – may appear to some as straightforward, until we subject them to an interdisciplinary perspective.

---

Teaching at the Intersections of Urban Communication and Public Place and Space' (2014) 5 *International Journal of Critical Pedagogy* 5, 9.

[7]  Armin Krishnan, 'Five Strategies for Practicing Interdisciplinarity' (*ESRC National Centre for Research Methods NCRM Working Paper Series*, 2009) http://eprints.ncrm.ac.uk/782/1/ strategies_for_practising_interdisciplinarity.pdf (accessed 19 January 2021). See also Simon Penny, 'Rigorous Interdisciplinary Pedagogy: Five Years of ACE' (2009) 15 *International Journal of Research into New Media Technologies* 31 for a discussion of 'deep' versus 'shallow' interdisciplinarity.

[8]  William Newell, 'A Theory of Interdisciplinary Studies' (2001) 19 *Issues in Integrative Studies* 1.

Newell lists seven diverse motivations for interdisciplinary study – the three most relevant to our discussion here are social, political and epistemological critique; social, economic and technological problem solving; and production of new knowledge. Similarly, Turner suggests that interdisciplinarity is the result of an increasing focus on 'problem solving' in the context of complicated social issues that cannot be resolved on a 'monodisciplinary' basis; interdisciplinarity is therefore inherently critical of existing disciplinary boundaries.[9] He argues that there is some consensus that the study of health and illness is particularly well-suited to interdisciplinary approaches because of the complexity of disease and illness, as well as the 'multicausality of social, individual, biological and cultural phenomena'.[10]

The field of medical law and ethics covers a wide range of disparate and complicated issues – not only the intricacies of legal rules, which by themselves can be technical and complex, but also ethical values and discretion in clinical decision-making, as well as government policy on public health and on the appropriate boundaries of medical research, and so on. Navigating this terrain is clearly both a legal and an ethical project, but it also has social and political impacts, and relies on technology and fast-paced knowledge development. In short, 'doing' medical law and ethics requires attention to a diverse array of complex issues. It is not difficult to see, then, how it might be thought that doing medical law and ethics requires an interdisciplinary approach.

How do these motivations to work interdisciplinarily translate into practice? How might we use interdisciplinarity to best effects? Or, as Callard and Fitzgerald have put it, '[w]hat, we ask, would a delicate, difficult, transgressive, risky, playful, and genuinely *experimental* interdisciplinarity . . . look like?'.[11]

### 1.2.3   How Is Interdisciplinarity Best Utilised?

We can see the answer to this question in Graeme's research and teaching over the last twenty-five years, much of which is interdisciplinary, as our case studies below will highlight (though, as is evidenced by other chapters in this collection, his powerful contributions to legal scholarship in his own 'voice' are also abundantly clear). Graeme's interdisciplinary

---

[9] Bryan Turner, 'The Interdisciplinary Curriculum: From Social Medicine to Postmodernism' (1990) 12 *Sociology of Health and Illness* 1, 2–3.
[10] Ibid., 4.
[11] Callard and Fitzgerald (n 5) 4 (emphasis in original).

approach to his work reminds us that what look like neat compartments of study, within the university at least, have more porous parameters than we might think.[12] His work displays many of the features that Klein has identified as characteristic of interdisciplinarity,[13] notably, defining problems that need to be solved. In Graeme's research, these include the right not to know, the regulation of personal data and tissue, governance of health research, and intellectual property concerns. Doing interdisciplinary work also requires identifying the knowledge systems and disciplines (that is, theories, literatures and methods) needed to address those problems; such as, in Graeme's case, sociology, anthropology, bioethics and philosophy. It involves constructing an integrated framework and deploying common or shared concepts and vocabulary to understand those problems (such as liminality, or spatial privacy, as explored further in our case studies). These are, as Newell says,[14] epistemological issues, but, in Graeme's case, they are also practical issues of team management and motivation, skills that are as rare as they are essential but that Graeme, as anyone who has worked with him knows, has down to a fine art.

Can interdisciplinary work have beneficial impacts on the real world? Recent experience of the Covid pandemic has shown how crucial social science and humanities perspectives are to forming inclusive and evidence-based public health and health-care responses.[15] However, Turner is sceptical that disciplines such as sociology can make much impact on the day-to-day practice of medicine,[16] since they are always to some degree 'subordinate' to medicine.[17] He suggests instead that it is usually a crisis of confidence or legitimacy that prompts change within medical practice. Medicine is clearly a powerful discipline within contemporary society. Law, however, is another. One of the reasons why it is interesting and important to research and teach medical ethics and law together, as Graeme has done, is that there are often epistemological as well as ethical

---

[12] Turner (n 9) 2. See also Raphael Foshay (ed), *Valences of Interdisciplinarity: Theory, Practice, Pedagogy* (AU Press 2011) who argues that universities are inherently interdisciplinary.

[13] Julie Thompson Klein, *Interdisciplinarity: History, Theory, and Practice* (Wayne State University Press 1990) 188–9.

[14] Newell (n 8) 14.

[15] Cecilia Vindrola-Padros, Georgia Chisnall, Silvie Cooper et al, 'Carrying Out Rapid Qualitative Research During a Pandemic: Emerging Lessons from COVID-19' (2020) 30 *Qualitative Health Research* 2192.

[16] Turner (n 9) 12.

[17] Ibid., 19.

conflicts between the two, and these must be resolved in a very practical sense for the sake not only of health-care practitioners and patients but also of governments, researchers and others. Two of our case studies point specifically to these challenges.

As noted already, interdisciplinary engagement can entail the practical and intellectual challenges of navigating the methods, literatures and languages of disciplines in which one has not been trained – and doing so in a way that is respectful of their provenance but also robust enough to challenge territoriality. It also invites a new class of concerns about how to situate and where to publish one's research.

Some of these concerns are noted by Callard and Fitzgerald. In outlining their worries about interdisciplinarity in its current form,[18] they question whether an interdisciplinary approach is inherently constructive or progressive, and whether it can be a distraction or an exercise conducted as a result of institutional or other pressures. On the last point, Callard and Fitzgerald note Barry and Born's critique that '[i]nterdisciplinarity has come to be at once a governmental demand, a reflexive orientation within the academy and an object of knowledge'.[19] This is perhaps most apparent in research council funding priorities and university 'vision' statements and goals.

Interdisciplinarity's 'reflexive orientation' is evident in the recent growth in interdisciplinary courses and relatedly in the formation of 'hybrid' scholars trained in multiple disciplines, who are equipped with a diverse set of skills belonging to multiple and distinct disciplinary homes. Yet, while there can be many merits to such career profiles, there are also distinct downsides. A lack of deep training in any one discipline can carry encumbrances. For example, a researcher can experience the disorientation of having many, potentially competing, sites of intellectual enquiry without the comfort of the disciplinary foundations and boundaries of a single home discipline.

Even where scholars are trained in one discipline, they may be employed in departments or schools that are predominantly the terrain of another discipline (such as a social scientist in a medical school or a philosopher or criminologist in a law school). This can result in the researcher experiencing a continual need to justify themselves as 'belonging' in another discipline's 'home', and to demonstrate their value in

---

[18] Callard and Fitzgerald (n 5) 4.

[19] Andrew Barry and Georgia Born, *Interdisciplinarity: Reconfigurations of the Social and Natural Sciences* (Routledge 2013) 4. The book examines the current 'preoccupation' with interdisciplinarity.

a way that other colleagues perhaps may not. There might also be unrealistic expectations that a researcher has to encounter, such as those relating to their breadth of expertise in their home discipline: 'you trained in law, you must know about all contract/criminal/negligence/intellectual property law'. This can produce a sense of 'disciplinary homelessness' and, in turn, increased exposure to precarity of employment.

Despite these potential challenges, we agree with Callard and Fitzgerald that just as interdisciplinarity is not inherently progressive, neither is it inherently risky.[20] Rather, its success lies in the way that it is utilised. We move now to show, through our three cases studies, that Graeme's approach has been particularly instructive and constructive in this regard, both through his own contributions to interdisciplinarity and in how this has influenced our individual and team working.

### 1.3   Case Study 1: Interdisciplinarity and Pedagogy: A Legacy of Openness (Sharon Cowan)

My professional connection with Graeme Laurie began before I took up my post as a lecturer at Edinburgh Law School in 2004 because he was on my interview panel. The interview was for a lectureship in criminal law and medical jurisprudence, and I was nervous because my knowledge of medical jurisprudence (or medical law as it was named at my previous institution) was limited to reproductive rights and the legal regulation of transgender identity and health care. Somehow, I persuaded the panel that I was appointable. When I took up the post, I became even more nervous because the kind and intellectually curious Dr Laurie who interviewed me was going on sabbatical for a year. Since, by the time I joined the School, the medical jurisprudence team comprised only Graeme and the esteemed emeritus professor J Kenyon Mason, and every class was co-taught by two teachers, this left me in my first year of a new post teaching with the very eminent and – at the time – rather intimidating Professor Mason. Before being appointed as an Honorary Fellow in Law in 1985, Ken Mason, as he was known, was the Regius Professor of Forensic Medicine at the University of Edinburgh. As such, he brought medical experience and expertise directly into our classroom, a rare thing for a law school. Graeme became an integral part of the medical jurisprudence team (which originally included Professor

---

[20] Callard and Fitzgerald (n 5) 12.

Alexander McCall Smith) in 1995 and it became clear when I arrived almost a decade later that my new colleagues had forged a formidable and unique partnership, and that I was being welcomed into a rather unusual unit. From 2004 onwards, the three of us became co-teachers, colleagues and then friends.

Ken passed away in January 2017. I have missed him dearly, and in ways that are difficult to document. His many legacies have been memorialised in the work of the Mason Institute, named after him, as well the Festschrift in his honour, *First Do No Harm*.[21] Graeme has consciously taken forward many of Ken's intellectual legacies. Here, though, I would like to speak about one of the great joys that, for me, is an important legacy of having worked with Graeme – my time spent with him co-teaching medical jurisprudence.

As well as teaching with Ken, I taught side-by-side with Graeme for thirteen years, where I had some of the best teaching moments of my career. The co-taught classroom creates particular opportunities for interdisciplinary teaching and learning. Without being overly reductive, with Ken as a medic, Graeme a private lawyer and me a queer, feminist criminal lawyer, we each brought very different perspectives that led us to different reasoning, and often different outcomes (though, perhaps surprisingly, also sometimes similar outcomes!), when presented with a thorny medico-legal ethical problem. Modelling 'compassionate debate' in the classroom in this way supports critical inquiry as students see simultaneously a variety of views – that here were informed by different disciplinary epistemologies – and participate in the process of knowledge as relative and situated.[22]

In fostering the open-spirited classroom that he and Ken created, Graeme's classrooms were exciting places to be. When we taught together, I never saw Graeme with a single note in his hand, though I observed many intrigued and engaged faces, and every session was fresh and inspiring. I was a newcomer to the discipline, yet it was obvious to me that his knowledge of medical law was deep and all-encompassing, but he was also keen to try new ways of teaching and learning, designing new curricula and courses that kept us in tune with the fast-developing discipline of medical law and ethics, and reaching out to other disciplines that could inform our teaching. Part of this journey, and building on the foundations of a single course at Edinburgh Law School, was the creation of a world-leading LLM programme in 'Medical Law and Ethics' (designed and developed in partnership with a colleague appointed to

[21] Sheila McLean (ed), *First Do No Harm: Law, Ethics and Healthcare* (Routledge 2006).
[22] McClellan and Johnson (n 6) 8, 11.

initiate the programme, Shawn Harmon). One of the core undergraduate and postgraduate courses is still called 'Fundamental Issues in Medical Jurisprudence', recognising the roots of the subject area (and reflecting the title of the established Chair in Medical Jurisprudence) as grounded within the theoretical analysis of legal decision-making on medical matters. Yet, naming the LLM programme 'Medical Law and Ethics' – as well as further appointments of colleagues including Agomoni Ganguli-Mitra and Emily Postan, who specialise in researching and teaching bioethics – allows for ethics to have a more conspicuous role in the study of the intersection of law and medicine within Edinburgh Law School, and also reflects the title of the well-established Mason and McCall Smith's *Law and Medical Ethics* textbook, originally co-authored by Ken and Alexander McCall Smith, with later editions edited by Ken and Graeme and then by Graeme and others. Embracing a law and medical ethics framework reflects a further shift to engage with a more international and interdisciplinary student body; today, LLM students enrolled in the Medical Law and Ethics programme come from a wide range of backgrounds, including medical practice, dental practice, nursing, health-care administration and the humanities, as well as law.

An open engagement with interdisciplinarity and the internationalisation of health as 'global' is apparent across Graeme's research career to date, but it is also discernible in his approach to teaching. During my time as his co-teacher, Graeme spearheaded the development of an innovative 'flipped' course, named 'Contemporary Issues in Medical Jurisprudence'. Students in this course were put into groups, and each group picked a seminar topic which they researched and for which they produced the class handout. Groups were encouraged to choose topics that demonstrated the cutting-edge and interdisciplinary nature of contemporary medico-legal ethical dilemmas. The students then became the teachers of the two-hour discursive class, and each group's skills as researchers and seminar leaders were assessed. This was an original approach that the students invariably found terrifying at first but ultimately empowering and rewarding.

Group work, and specifically co-operative learning and interactive engagement, has been shown to be particularly useful for law students, improving student experiences of learning as well as outcomes.[23] Moreover, learning through the method of inquiring into current social

---

[23]  Mary Keyes and Kylie Burns, 'Group Learning in Law' (2008) 17 *Griffith Law Review* 357; Alex Steel, Julian Laurens and Anna Huggins, 'Class Participation as a Learning and Assessment Strategy in Law: Facilitating Students' Engagement, Skills Development and Deep Learning' (2013) 36 *University of New South Wales Law Journal* 30.

'culture-embedded' problems can lead to what Goredetsky and colleagues have called 'contextual learning', which is informed by interdisciplinary bodies of knowledge.[24] Using such methods to teach law – a subject that is often carved into neat, divisible and separable parts and sub-parts – can be risky and challenging; students, who might be exposed to this approach in only one or two elective subjects and not as part of the core curriculum, may resist the critical epistemological challenges that come with more interdisciplinary learning. But such learning is enhanced and dynamic because it is initiated by the students themselves, and 'reflects the present or developing epistemologies that dominate or will dominate [their] lives'.[25]

The independence and confidence that these teaching methods instil surpass the skills produced through the 'banking' method of learning,[26] where the 'expert' teacher 'deposits' knowledge in the 'novice' student, that often characterises the teaching of law. For Friere, the teacher is a 'catalyst, or animator' creating space for students to 'become creative subjects of the learning process rather than passive objects'.[27] Graeme has always taken on this role of animator in his teaching. His willingness to introduce such non-traditional methods of interdisciplinary teaching, learning and assessment, which fundamentally transformed an already well-established and popular syllabus, speaks to his own openness to continual learning, and his capacity persistently to challenge himself and others around him. I am fortunate enough to have witnessed and learned from this first-hand for more than a decade.

The openness of spirit that marks Graeme's teaching is, of course, also manifest in his *research*.

## 1.4   Case Study 2: Two Mantras for Interdisciplinary Research (Nayha Sethi)

### 1.4.1   The 'So What?' Question

Graeme's colleagues and students will be familiar with the 'So what?' question, a critical tool, akin to a mantra, persistently invoked by him to encourage us to reflect upon the implications of our own research. It is

---

[24] Malka Gorodetsky et al, 'Contextual Pedagogy: Teachers' Journey Beyond Interdisciplinarity' (2003) 9 *Teachers and Teaching* 21.

[25] Ibid., 31.

[26] Paulo Friere, *The Pedagogy of the Oppressed* (Herder and Herder 1970).

[27] Gillian Calder, 'Performance, Pedagogy and Law: Theatre of the Oppressed in the Law School Classroom' in Zenon Bańkowski and Maksymilian Del Mar (eds), *The Moral Imagination and the Legal Life: Beyond Text in Legal Education* (Routledge 2012) 223.

interconnected with related questions: 'What will have changed as a result of this work?', 'What does this mean for others working on this topic?', 'What are the real-world implications?', 'How can these be translated into practice?' and 'What value and impact will this new knowledge generate?'. 'So what?' and associated inquiries speak to Graeme's commitment, apparent throughout his expansive body of work, towards ensuring that our scholarship within and beyond medical law and ethics remains connected to, and contributes towards, the world beyond academia (what Krishan has termed 'transdisciplinarity', as noted in Section 1.2.1). For some, the significance of our research within the academy or out in the 'real world' is easily discernible. Others, though, may have experienced episodic existential crises, approaching the 'So what?' question with some trepidation. Graeme's contributions remind us that looking to other disciplines and to actors within and outwith academia offers invaluable opportunities for identifying how, and ensuring that, our academic work can satisfactorily meet the considerations laid out under the umbrella of the 'So what?' question.

This is evidenced, for example, in Graeme's sustained engagement with social sciences to generate empirically grounded governance solutions across a variety of health research contexts, including DNA databases[28] and electronic health records. My first academic post working with Graeme was at the University of Edinburgh on the Scottish Health Informatics Programme (SHIP). This initiative aimed to establish a research platform for electronic health records held by NHS Scotland, and we were responsible for shaping and delivering the legal workstream. Graeme stressed at the outset that building a governance framework solely based on ethical and legal issues was not an option. Rather, it would necessitate close collaboration with social science colleagues on the Public Engagement workstream of the project.

Having a background in law, including the completion in 2009 of the 'Fundamental Issues in Medical Jurisprudence' LLM course at Edinburgh, I was relatively familiar with key ethico-legal issues of data use and health research. Collaboration with social scientists, however, presented an entirely new explorative lens. As a young legal scholar, the idea that social scientists were concerned with telling a story, devoid of

---

[28] Gillian Haddow et al, 'Tackling Community Concerns about Commercialisation and Genetic Research: A Modest Interdisciplinary Proposal' (2007) 64 *Social Science & Medicine* 272.

the doctrinal inflexibility which lawyers can tend so confidently to impose, often without critical reflexivity or acknowledgement upfront, was certainly novel. Rather than merely asking what the law prescribed, or what the ethical implications of various data access permeations were, our colleagues, led by medical sociologist Professor Sarah Cunningham-Burley, were guided by a distinct set of concerns: 'What do publics think?', 'What are different stakeholders concerned about?', 'Are the governance approaches under proposal acceptable?', 'Why or why not?'. We explored such questions through a variety of sociologically informed methods, including workshops, focus groups, consultations, systematic reviews and questionnaires. Throughout, our social scientist colleagues reminded us of their consternation over the 'tokenistic' ways in which public engagement is often annexed to grant proposals and subsequently funded projects; it is frequently about paying lip service, but stops short of meaningful deliberation. It was clear that Graeme was committed to ensuring that we would not reinforce this pattern but, rather, challenge it.

We incorporated the findings from this research directly into our Principled Proportionate Governance Framework,[29] which was reflective of and informed by stakeholder and – crucially – public concerns. Indeed, advocating for the inclusion of public and stakeholder perspectives has remained a key theme in much of Graeme's work.[30] As I have noted elsewhere, alongside colleagues from other disciplines, the importance of meaningful engagement is particularly pertinent today given the recent growth in data-driven initiatives and associated data controversies.[31] Graeme's scholarship reminds us that in appealing to other disciplines, wondering what they might have to offer us, it is equally important to consider what we in our own disciplines may be able to offer in return and that this responsibility extends beyond the walls of academia into 'the real world'.

---

[29] Graeme Laurie and Nayha Sethi, 'Towards Principles-Based Approaches to Governance of Health-Related Research Using Personal Data' (2013) 4 *European Journal of Risk Regulation* 43.

[30] See, for example, Pam Carter, Graeme Laurie and Mary Dixon-Woods, 'The Social Licence for Research: Why care.data Ran into Trouble' (2015) 41 *Journal of Medical Ethics* 404.

[31] See, for example, Mhairi Aitken et al, 'Why the Public Need a Say in How Patient Data Are Used for Covid-19 Responses' (2020) 5 *International Journal of Population Data Science* Letters to the Editor; and James Shaw, Nayha Sethi and Christine Cassel, 'Social License for the Use of Big Data in the COVID-19 Era' (2020) 3 *npj Digital Medicine* 128.

Participating in a larger interdisciplinary team for the Liminal Spaces project more recently[32] has provided additional learning opportunities, including lively discussions, masterfully stewarded by Graeme, focusing on methodological approaches (or lamented lack thereof!); theoretical frameworks; epistemology; and on one particular occasion the somewhat amusing but crucial realisation that we were appealing to the same terminologies – including 'normativity', 'case study', 'embodiment', even 'liminal' – in very different ways. These interactions provided cautionary tales against assuming shared understanding of key terms. No matter how trite our own interpretations of 'basic' terminology may seem to us, clarification of key terms, communication and exploration of areas of divergence as well as complementarity are imperative from the outset. But beyond this, interdisciplinary working challenges us to question the ways in which we frame research problems, the critical lenses we choose to employ and the need to be alert to, declare and justify them. The enriched insights to be gained from adjusting these lenses make interdisciplinarity well worth the effort. In turn, it is these enriched insights that can tend to reveal to us multiple and diverse responses to the enduring 'So what?' question. These are often responses that we simply would not be able to discover without actively engaging with other disciplines beyond the law and with other actors beyond the academic setting to reveal to us the varied real and potential impacts of our scholarship.

### 1.4.2   Originality, Significance and Rigour

Anyone participating in a UK university Research Excellence Framework (REF) assessment will be familiar with the holy trinity of 'originality, significance and rigour'. For Graeme, this was another key mantra (and one for which he was often playfully teased!). His work demonstrates that engaging with other disciplines can provide fruitful dividends for fulfilling these criteria. For example, a recurring theme through his work is his plea to legal scholars to avoid the temptation of dismissing offhand caricatures of law/regulation as an encumbrance to those wishing to 'get on with their research'. Rather, he suggests that it is our responsibility as medico-legal scholars to understand, demonstrate and effectively communicate the ways in which law can act as a facilitator.

---

[32] www.liminalspaces.ed.ac.uk/ (accessed 20 January 2021).

But equally, if regulatory challenges are to be overcome, we must acknowledge the limits of the law.[33] Graeme's work is exemplary in showing us how robust engagement (rigour) with other disciplines such as social sciences, philosophy and anthropology can provide legal scholars with the novel (original) insights that are necessary to enable us to do this in ways that are impactful (significant). This approach has influenced my scholarship, much of which focuses on supporting context-sensitive decision-making in health research.[34] For example, I have considered the diverse functions that rules and principles can perform, and the repercussions of adopting rules-based and principles-based approaches for those charged with navigating complicated regulatory landscapes within health research. My doctoral thesis considered how best practice instantiations can provide context-sensitive and practically grounded support to decision-makers in determining what to do.[35] Subsequently, I have explored this further in the context of conducting research and innovation during global health emergencies.[36]

Most recently, I was inspired by Graeme's revival of the anthropological concept of liminality and its novel application to health research regulation. Graeme problematises the law's tendency to create silos through categorisation of regulatory activities, subjects and objects.[37] These categorisations are themselves legacies left over from previous regulatory regimes, which may at their time of inception have been fit for purpose but no longer remain so and which, paradoxically, may frustrate the original goals of legislation or regulation. Graeme argues that liminality encourages us to break free from these constraints and to reimagine regulatory landscapes as constantly evolving, influenced by and impacting upon diverse disciplines, regulatory objects and actors. Through embracing a liminal approach, he suggests recasting boundaries

---

[33] Graeme Laurie, 'Liminality and the Limits of Law in Health Research Regulation: What Are We Missing in the Spaces in-Between?' (2017) 25 *Medical Law Review* 47.

[34] Nayha Sethi, 'Reimagining Regulatory Approaches: On the Essential Role of Principles in Health Research Regulation' (2015) 12 *SCRIPTed Journal of Law, Technology and Society* 91.

[35] Nayha Sethi, 'Remaining Rooted Whilst Branching Out: An Investigation of Rules and Principles in Decision-Making' (PhD thesis, University of Edinburgh 2016).

[36] Nayha Sethi, 'Research During Global Health Emergencies: On the Essential Role of Best Practice' (2018) 11 *Public Health Ethics* 237.

[37] Graeme Laurie and Shawn Harmon, 'Through the Thicket and Across the Divide: Successfully Navigating the Regulatory Landscape in Life Sciences Research' in Emilie Cloatre and Martyn Pickersgill (eds), *Knowledge, Technology and Law* (Routledge 2014) 121.

laid down in law – such as those around data and tissue use in health research – to reveal what may be missing from the spaces in between.[38]

I have applied liminality to my own scholarship, including in exploring the relationships between treatment, research and innovation.[39] I argue that predominant regulatory categorisations of these activities, and the bases for differentiating between them, are in many instances obsolete and problematic from practical and regulatory perspectives. They are ignorant of the experiences of key regulatory actors and subjects (publics, patients, researchers, doctors, regulators) and objects (treatments, surgeries, devices, data, tissue). I suggest that liminality offers more holistic understandings of medical innovation that reflect existing processes and relationships. Such recasting provides a novel conceptualisation of medical innovation as a shared space where both practice/treatment and research coexist.

The value of appealing to liminality is clear to me and, I hope, convincing to those who have engaged with the work of the Liminal Spaces team. But, as discussed further in Case Study 3, employing an abstract concept from another discipline can be challenging. Concepts and methodologies carry their own legacies within the disciplines from which they have originated, and choosing to engage with these as a relative 'novice' necessitates a considered approach and explicit acknowledgement of, but not deterrence by, these legacies.

Graeme's application of liminality has been instructive and inspiring in this regard. It demonstrates that we must be up to the task of familiarising ourselves with, and embedding ourselves within, entirely unfamiliar domains while simultaneously guiding our audiences (expert and non-expert) through them. For example, engaging robustly with anthropological literature on liminality and communicating it to non-anthropologist audiences was intimidating for me, as was dealing with the scepticism and disciplinary territoriality that can come with treading outside our own disciplinary, theoretical and methodological homes. But, somewhat paradoxically, Graeme has demonstrated that it is precisely through engaging with other disciplines that we can in turn learn how to harness these very skills. This necessitates a generous amount of openness of spirit in all directions, which is one of the most important legacies Graeme has gifted us, and one that also

---

[38] Laurie (n 33).

[39] Nayha Sethi, 'Regulating for Uncertainty: Bridging Blurred Boundaries in Medical Innovation, Research and Treatment' (2019) 11 *Law, Innovation and Technology* 112.

permeates his work that brings to life the interdisciplinarity of the *conceptual* foundations of medical law and ethics.

## 1.5   Case Study 3: Interdisciplinarity in Conceptual Work (Emily Postan)

As noted in Section 1.2.2, Newell suggests that one possible motivation for interdisciplinary work is epistemological critique.[40] One aspect of this may be the pursuit of conceptual clarity, relevance and utility. In what ways can interdisciplinary approaches contribute to these qualities in the concepts we use in our medical law and ethics scholarship? This is a question that I have confronted in my own bioethics research, and one for which Graeme's work provides an object lesson. My own experiences recounted here are offered as an illustration of a way in which interdisciplinarity may play out in the work of a solo researcher.

As scholars, we often pride ourselves on the appositeness and impact of the concepts we generate and use in our work. This is perhaps particularly so for those with backgrounds in philosophy. Achieving conceptual precision and transparency is the very business of philosophy. Where some might see captivating neologisms or welcome interpretive looseness, the antennae of a philosopher are primed to twitch at the risk of obfuscation or elision.[41] For example, when an anthropologist colleague expressed scepticism about the value of research in which I sought to characterise the impacts of biological information on our identities – objecting that identity was too contested an idea to make this a cogent line of inquiry – my instinct was to double-down, to demarcate precisely the sense of identity where I judged critical interests might be most at stake. Noting such differences of approach, to what extent can and should interdisciplinary thinking, and specifically engagement with the ways that those in other fields use language and identify objects of concern, contribute to the conceptual work we do in medical law and ethics? And what might it teach us about the extent to which we police the boundaries of these concepts?

Graeme's research exemplifies the value of looking to other disciplines for theoretical tools and framing devices. His scholarship is way-marked by the evocative and often highly visual concepts that provide centres of

---

[40] Newell (n 8).
[41] See, for example, Adam Henschke, 'Did You Just Say What I Think You Said? Talking About Genes, Identity and Information' (2010) 3 *Identity in the Information Society* 435.

critical and interpretive gravity in his own work and, subsequently, in that of others. Perhaps most prominent among these are his interrogation of genetic privacy[42] and his recent work on liminality in the practices and regulation of health research,[43] each of which is discussed in depth in other chapters in this volume.

Graeme's application of the concept of liminality invites a fresh perspective on the ways in which the objects and practices of health research may cross or fall between traditional regulatory boundaries, and on the shifting identities and responsibilities of all actors.[44] Meanwhile, with his influential work on privacy, Graeme introduces to the lexicon of medical law and ethics the compelling idea of 'spatial privacy', characterised as a state of 'physical or psychological separateness' that 'should not be invaded without due cause'.[45] In doing so, he has provided an invaluable tool for approaching long-standing ethical and legal puzzles, including the so-called 'right not to know' genetic information about ourselves.

The concepts of liminality and spatial privacy, as developed by Graeme, are inescapably interdisciplinary in both their genesis and their impact. As noted in Case Study 2 (Section 1.4), liminality has its origins in anthropological literature and the team Graeme built to work on this project comprised lawyers, anthropologists, sociologists and bioethicists. Meanwhile, his interpretation of privacy draws not only on legal but also on philosophical, psychological, sociological and historical scholarship.[46] The gaps addressed by each of these concept-driven inquiries reflect not only Graeme's appreciation of inadequacies in the law but also his sensitivity to the human dilemmas and experiences confronted by clinical geneticists, patients, health researchers, participants and regulators, and the ways these disrupt, or are overlooked by, existing legal and ethical frameworks. The enduring impact and

---

[42] Graeme Laurie, *Genetic Privacy: A Challenge to Medico-legal Norms* (Cambridge University Press 2002).

[43] Laurie (n 33).

[44] Graeme Laurie et al, 'Charting Regulatory Stewardship in Health Research: Making the Invisible Visible' (2018) 27 *Cambridge Quarterly of Healthcare Ethics* 333; Catriona McMillan et al, 'Beyond Categorisation: Refining the Relationship Between Subjects and Objects in Health Research Regulation' (2021) 13 *Law Innovation and Technology* (volume 13, 194–222).

[45] Laurie (n 42) 64.

[46] Graeme's monograph opens by recognising the many disciplines in which, and the actors for who, questions of privacy arise – 'Privacy is a problem. Or[,] rather, privacy causes problems. It causes problems for sociologists, psychologists, anthropologists, philosophers, politicians, doctors, lawyers, governments, states, communities, groups and individuals' (n 42) 1.

relevance of Graeme's analyses to policy-makers and practitioners is evidenced by his many expert advisory roles. These include his work with the Nuffield Council on Bioethics and the Ethics and Governance Council of UK Biobank. The practical legacy of his work is undoubtedly attributable to its interdisciplinary roots and ambitions, and Graeme's intentions to speak to audiences beyond law and beyond the academy.

My own work – examining the ways in which our encounters with information about our bodies and biology may impact on our capacities to develop and inhabit our own identities – owes much to Graeme's work on privacy.[47] This is not least because my research also seeks to characterise a critical interest engaged by access to information about ourselves, and Graeme (alongside one of my co-authors here) provided immeasurably supportive supervision of my doctoral research.[48] But it is also because interdisciplinary research was key to my development of a conception of identity as embodied self-narrative and in which biological information can play ethically significant roles. Reflecting my own disciplinary training, I embarked on this inquiry by drawing upon philosophical theories of narrative self-constitution. I then moved into less-familiar territories, to develop and refine the core philosophical conception in light of social scientific analyses and empirical accounts of the nature and experiences of identity construction and the socio-cultural and epistemic contexts in which this takes place.

As a bioethicist working within a law school, my aim is that my research will transcend abstract ethical debate, to convey the real-world importance of understanding and attending to the concepts, interests and values I seek to characterise. This is one of the key strengths of the field of medical law and ethics – that it permits those of us working within the field to draw on the complementary normative, critical and conceptual tools of each 'parent' discipline, while focusing our gaze on practical challenges posed by health, medicine and the biosciences. My hope is that, through drawing upon diverse framings and materials offered by a range of disciplines, the robustness and practical utility of my resultant conceptual analysis, normative frameworks and recommendations will be enhanced. Nevertheless, my approach still betrays marked discipline-specific prejudices about the locus of authority for conceptual matters and, indeed, in the assumption that it makes sense to look for a source of

---

[47] Emily Postan, 'Defining Ourselves: Personal Bioinformation as a Tool of Narrative Self-Conception' (2016) 13 *Journal of Bioethical Inquiry* 133.

[48] Emily Postan, 'Defining Ourselves: Narrative Identity and Access to Personal Biological Information' (PhD thesis, University of Edinburgh 2017).

authority at all. For example, rather than premising my project in identity and bio-information on the ways that the law or publics have construed the value of this information to identity, I instead sought first to characterise how these interests *ought* to be understood.

This approach felt so natural that I was wrong-footed when Graeme asked why embodied narrative self-constitution (rather than some alternative account) was an appropriate foundation. My answer – 'because it rings true, is carefully and consistently characterised, and has been robustly defended against critiques and counterarguments' – felt naïve when held up to the twin mirrors of practical policy application and findings from inductive empirical studies. That something rings true and is consistent and defensible is no guarantee of truth or relevance. And our assessment of these characteristics is inescapably the product of our particular preoccupations and perspectives. The imperative to remain alert to the biases and limitations of our own perspectives, and to adjust for them as far as we can, is ever-present and particularly acute when the outputs are intended (optimistically) to have application in the real world. Interdisciplinary thinking and working offer possible routes out of our myopia and ways to widen our vision. The growth of the discipline of empirical bioethics is one example of a recent interdisciplinary development that seeks to enrich, and enhance the practical applicability of, bioethics scholarship and, by association, that of medical law and ethics.[49]

Learning how to work with materials and ideas from multiple disciplines – particularly where this brings the empirical and the jurisprudential together with the conceptual and the theoretical – is valuable, even necessary. But, as noted at the start of this chapter, it is not always a comfortable experience. It forces us to confront limitations in our own critical tools and understandings. It can make our premises seem question-begging and our conclusions overdetermined. In projects in which the central aim is precisely to draw attention to and characterise particular concepts, it may highlight the instability, contested nature or implicit normativity of these concepts in ways that resist easy resolution. For example, in my own research, when the courts invoke a 'right to identity' in ways that are both promiscuous and ambiguous about what 'identity' means, should I take this as a welcome indication that the law protects identity interests, or that the jurisprudence is dispiritingly

---

[49] See, for example, Jonathan Ives, Michael Dunn and Alan Cribb (eds), *Empirical Bioethics: Theoretical and Practical Perspectives* (Cambridge University Press 2016).

inchoate and inadequate? Similarly, how should I incorporate the views of study participants who report that genetic information is critical to their identities, but justify this on problematically essentialist grounds?

Part of reconciling abstracted ideals and complex realities may be to hold the conceptual and linguistic reigns a little less tightly, to explore and find productive spaces in the ambiguity and differences of interpretation that we encounter through interdisciplinary work. This still does not always come easily to me. Here, my (re)training in medical law has been instructive. Despite the law's association with rules and bright lines, the interpretation of open-ended and pliable concepts is a crucial part of permitting the law to be responsive and to evolve – a facility that is particularly important where its objects are rapidly developing medical practices or biotechnologies.

Conceptual plasticity and ambiguity are not, however, unalloyed virtues. Much of the value of interdisciplinary conceptual work lies in equipping diverse parties, who bring different formations, interests and goals, with a shared lexicon with which to conduct analyses and debates. This means that even if (and when) they disagree, they do not do so because they are talking past each other, using apparently similar words in wildly different ways or resorting to exclusionary jargon. Achieving this requires that the ideas and terms proffered for shared usage are themselves compelling and comprehensible – perhaps not always simple, but not mired in the specialist language or arcane debates of isolated scholarly traditions. The ideas developed in Graeme's work offer precisely these qualities. For example, the idea of spatial privacy exemplifies this kind of accessibility, enabled by the evocative metaphor that – among other things – privacy involves protection of a secluded space, free from unwanted intrusion. This is a perfect example of a concept that is not only a product of interdisciplinary work; it is also itself capable of transcending disciplinary boundaries, of making itself understood and useful wherever it lands.

This case study has focused on the way that interdisciplinarity is experienced and exercised in the context of conceptual work as part of solo academic projects, but of course much of Graeme's work, including his work on genetic privacy, has never been entirely solo, and has often been undertaken in applied contexts and in teaching, as we have discussed. As all three case studies have shown, Graeme's work in 'doing' medical law and ethics – as a collaborative scholar, project leader and co-teacher – exemplifies the many rewards, and sometimes challenges, of rigorous and committed interdisciplinarity.

## 1.6  Conclusion

As Amir Krishnan has suggested:

> Although all researchers are certainly well advised to look beyond their own discipline, it is also clear that little could be gained by choosing an interdisciplinary research strategy just for the sake of it. In the end, it very much depends on the problem that the researcher aims to solve whether a disciplinary or an interdisciplinary approach would be more successful.[50]

Across our three case studies, we have shown the crucial role of interdisciplinary perspectives in 'doing' medical law and ethics, highlighting the hard work, intellectual challenges, practical constraints and compromises that are often involved in interdisciplinary work. However, we have also demonstrated why it is essential to make these efforts, and the rewards that may be reaped in terms of the quality, practical utility and uptake of the products of the work, whether working in teams or individually, and whether the work is conceptual, applied or pedagogical.

Built on his long interdisciplinary partnership with Ken Mason, Graeme's academic agility and intellectual curiosity reflect a willingness to take risks in order to maximise the benefits that an interdisciplinary perspective can bring to 'doing' medical law and ethics. His research and teaching have left their legacy: a culture of collaboration and disciplinary – and personal – openness of spirit, all of which are essential to address the legal, regulatory and ethical challenges posed by medicine, health care and the biosciences.

Collaborating on this chapter has provided the three of us with the opportunity, from different perspectives, and with different approaches, to celebrate together our experiences of the joy and stimulation of teaching and researching with Graeme. And through this celebration we have shown the importance of developing accessible and relevant concepts and methods for 'doing' medical law and ethics that can offer a common currency across and among disciplines, for those within and outwith the academy.

---

[50]  Krishnan (n 7) 2.

# A Philosopher Looks at 'Law and Medical Ethics'

RICHARD ASHCROFT

## 2.1 Introduction

I am honoured to be part of this volume celebrating Graeme Laurie's contribution to law and medical ethics.[1] For more than twenty-five years, Graeme has been one of the most important scholars in this field, setting consistently high standards of clarity, rigour, insight and imagination. Not only is he distinguished and brilliant in his research, he is kind and thoughtful as a teacher, supervisor, mentor and friend. I have benefited intellectually from his writing and conversation in so many ways over the years. I want to pay particular tribute to Graeme as my fellow co-editor of the Cambridge University book series in Bioethics and Law (formerly, Cambridge Medicine, Law and Bioethics). Anyone who has published in this series, or submitted a proposal, will agree with me when I say that Graeme's judgement, generosity and patience in assessing proposals and manuscripts are second to none.

---

[1] I need to make a disclaimer here about the kind of writing this is. All academic work this year has been disrupted by the Covid-19 pandemic: working from home as well as changing jobs and moving into a new office building has made accessing my research books, which are in storage, triply impossible. As I am forced by circumstances to write in a far less 'scholarly' way than I would prefer, I have decided to make a virtue of it; thus, what I present here is neither a research article nor a scholarly contribution but an essay reflecting what I have come to think about the nature of 'law and medical ethics'. I apologise for any errors of fact or emphasis which may arise and ask that you treat it as a 'conversation piece', or even an attempt at what Edward Said called 'late style': a style which, knowing that time is short, is determined to get to the point without prevarication, hesitation or piety, including the pieties of scholarship. As Bob Dylan sang: 'Let us not talk falsely now, the hour is getting late.' Edward Said, *On Late Style: Music and Literature Against the Grain* (Bloomsbury 2006); Bob Dylan, 'All Along the Watchtower' (1967).

One of Graeme's many contributions to academic law is his steward-ship and development of a celebrated textbook now known as *Mason and McCall Smith's Law and Medical Ethics*. In this chapter, I will discuss the importance of textbooks generally in academic work and, in particular, the critical role they play in defining academic fields. I will venture the very strong claim that without 'medical law textbooks' there would have been no 'medical law'. Textbooks assemble and organise diverse mater-ials into *legacy*, which is being handed on to readers and students; and in the case of the most successful textbooks, they are themselves handed on as a legacy down a lineage of authors. They have a powerful shaping influence over what counts as valuable in that field, in terms of the scope of its subject matter, methods, materials, disciplinary frameworks and, indeed, heroes and villains. I will discuss the way the *naming* of the field matters, too, and how textbooks add something central to that.

Finally, I will discuss the ways in which textbooks influence how far a field is 'open' to new problems or methods or 'closed', inasmuch as there is a strong norm of what counts as a contribution to the field (and, importantly, what does not). This touches on the question of the rela-tionship between textbooks and theory, and more widely on the relation-ships among law, ethics and philosophy. In particular, in 'law and medical ethics', there is a profound issue concerning whether we think of the relationship between law and medical ethics as one in which these are two adjacent systems of norms; or whether law should be seen as somehow the practical realisation of a set of ethical principles, to be judged on how far and how well it succeeds in that; or whether there is a (medical) jurisprudence which provides a 'rational reconstruction' of legal doctrine as it applies to the field of practice it regulates (here, medicine).[2]

## 2.2   Research, Scholarship and Textbooks

In UK higher education, a distinction has been drawn between 'research' and 'scholarship'. An intensional definition is a definition which tries to specify a thing or a concept by giving its essential characteristics.[3]

---

[2] The term 'rational reconstruction' is borrowed from the philosophy of science, and specifically from Imre Lakatos, 'History of Science and Its Rational Reconstructions' in Imre Lakatos (eds John Worrall and Gregory Currie), *The Methodology of Scientific Research Programmes: Philosophical Papers Volume 1* (Cambridge University Press 1978).

[3] On intensional and extensional definitions, see Roy Cook, 'Intensional Definition' in Roy Cook, *A Dictionary of Philosophical Logic* (Edinburgh University Press 2009).

'Research' can be defined intensionally as organised academic work which contributes new knowledge; scholarship, likewise, can be defined intensionally as the organisation of that knowledge into a form in which it can be taught and applied. So far, that is a useful distinction and relatively harmless. But the moment we reflect on this research/scholarship distinction, we notice something troubling. In the humanities, at least, new knowledge can arise precisely out of the collation and organisation of existing knowledge. Indeed, the novelty of new knowledge can be established only by showing how it relates to existing knowledge (the recognised *legacy* of the field, perhaps). There is an interdependence between research and scholarship which causes the apparent clarity of the distinction marked in these intensional definitions to crumble.

The other way to make a definition is to give the extension of the terms – to give a (representative, if not complete) list of things which share the feature being defined. Increasingly in UK universities, research is defined extensively as 'those academic activities producing outputs which can be submitted for and rated by the Research Excellence Framework'.[4] Researchers are then defined as 'academic staff who conduct activities whose outputs are submissible for the Research Excellence Framework'. Scholarship is defined extensionally as 'academic outputs which are not submissible for the Research Excellence Framework'. It is the practice in many UK universities to consider as submissible only such work as would score at least 3* in the Research Excellence Framework; this means that a large body of 'research' slides from being 'good though not outstanding' to 'not very good' to 'not research at all', and thus falls under the extensional definition of scholarship. Scholarship then attracts a value judgement as being 'unimportant', 'poor quality' or even 'unnecessary'.

There are other bad ways to define research extensionally, many of which are alive and well in higher education today (in the UK and beyond), such as: research is that which attracts research funding. Or: research is that which gets cited. Or: research is that which is peer reviewed and published in 'top ranked journals'. And so on. Now consider what falls outside these definitions, one way or another: interdisciplinary research; public engagement; creative and performance arts; analytical literature reviews; policy papers. The best of all of these make distinctive contributions to knowledge – but often disruptive or

---

[4] Research Excellence Framework, www.ref.ac.uk (accessed 17 March 2021); for a trenchant critique, see Derek Sayer, *Rank Hypocrisies: The Insult of the REF* (SAGE 2015).

disturbing knowledge that redraws boundaries and resets expectations and which can often be appreciated properly only in hindsight. Consider also the ways in which the restless pressure to find novelty within the tight constraints of metrics and peer review can lead to hasty and unscholarly 'research'. Consider the field of 'AI ethics', much of which proceeds on the basis that because the technology itself is new, the ethical debates around it must also be new, and thus ignores, by and large, decades of work in philosophy and the social sciences about ethics and social interests in science, technology and medicine. Here, we might say that it is sometimes important strategically to ignore or even erase the legacy of prior work in order to establish one's status as an authority.[5]

This reflection on research and scholarship leads me to consider the importance of textbooks. The writing of textbooks is somewhat frowned upon in the current research environment of UK higher education. On the one hand, they are seen as 'merely' scholarship. It is very hard, or so it is thought, to write a textbook which produces 'new knowledge'. As such, textbooks are not research outputs. On the other hand, writing a textbook is hard work. To write in an accessible way, while remaining accurate and avoiding oversimplification, is difficult. Publishers expect the authors of textbooks to revise and update their books regularly, partly because the field changes (obviously so, in law, as new cases are reported, and new statutes and guidelines promulgated), but also because textbooks are literally the stock in trade for academic publishers: they subsidise the publication of monographs and other 'research' publications. There is a commercial pressure to ensure that textbooks maintain steady sales, often in a niche in which there are other competing texts. Maintaining and updating textbooks is time-consuming, and thus can be seen as a diversion from 'research'. And while the income from textbooks is often a useful supplement to an academic salary, it is the rare textbook which makes its author or authors rich. So, given these pressures, we have to conclude that the main reason textbook authors do it is love of the field and their students.

Graeme Laurie has been involved in the writing and renewal of the landmark *Mason and McCall Smith's Law and Medical Ethics* since its sixth edition (2002, the last for which Alexander McCall Smith was a co-author). Since its tenth edition (2016), he took over from J. K. (Ken) Mason as senior co-author on Ken's retirement from the team. Ken sadly

---

[5] I am reminded, inevitably, of Harold Bloom's provocative work on influence in poetry: Harold Bloom, *The Anxiety of Influence* (Oxford University Press 1973).

died in 2017. With Shawn Harmon and Edward Dove, Graeme published its current, eleventh, edition in 2019.[6] As such, he is better placed than most to understand the demands of textbook writing, and generations of students will attest to his love for his field, be they readers and users of the book or, even more fortunately, taught personally by him. We should also recall here his other major textbook, *Contemporary Intellectual Property*.[7] But, important as this is, to see a textbook as 'only' a teaching aid for students is to misunderstand its overall significance. In a nutshell: if we want to understand what 'law and medical ethics' is, we have to understand its textbooks.

## 2.3     What Is 'Law and Medical Ethics'?

The field of law and medical ethics is now flourishing all around the (academic) world.[8] But it is salutary to recall that this is a recent development, and that even now it is a vexed question to define its scope and principles. For one thing, the relationship between law and ethics is controversial. The epigraph to *Mason and McCall Smith's Law and Medical Ethics* is from Coleridge LCJ in *R v. Instan*:

> It would not be correct to say that every moral obligation involves a legal duty; but every legal duty is founded on a moral obligation.[9]

And yet, every law student is sternly taught US Supreme Court Justice Oliver Wendell Holmes's dictum that 'this is a court of law, not a court of justice', or, as Ward LJ rephrased it in his judgment in *Re A (Conjoined Twins)*, 'the court is a court of law, not a court of morals'.[10] Students fortunate enough to study jurisprudence in the course of their legal studies are made aware of the tensions and problems in legal reasoning and doctrine arising from navigating between these dicta. Within 'law

---

[6] The first edition was published by Butterworths; from its seventh edition (2005) it has been published by Oxford University Press. The latest edition is Graeme Laurie, Shawn Harmon and Edward Dove, *Mason and McCall Smith's Law and Medical Ethics* (11th edn, Oxford University Press 2019).

[7] Hector MacQueen, Charlotte Waelde and Graeme Laurie, *Contemporary Intellectual Property: Law and Policy* (Oxford University Press 2007) (and two subsequent editions – the book is now in its fourth edition, but Graeme has handed on his role).

[8] Out of respect for Graeme's own work, I am going to refer to the field as 'law and medical ethics' throughout, both with reference to that work and to designate all the overlapping fields (medical law and ethics, health law and so on) I discuss in this section. It is a shorthand only, for my purposes here.

[9] [1893] 1 QB at 453.

[10] [2000] EWCA Civ 254 (22 September 2000); [2000] 4 All ER 961.

and medical ethics' (the field), numerous scholars have ventured theoretical accounts of the ethical foundations of the law, and of the ethical principles which should guide its developments, both through judicial reasoning and through the adoption of statutes. Such commentators necessarily articulate (even if sometimes only in fragmentary and partial ways) ideas of what the law is, what it is for and what its limits may be. We will return to this debate in Section 2.5.

A second debate turns on a question of nomenclature. Are we looking at 'law and medical ethics' or 'medical law and ethics' or 'medical law' or 'health-care law' or 'health law' or 'medical jurisprudence'? While to a great extent these pick out significant areas of overlap, the differences matter. For are we primarily concerned with what medical practitioners do, and how this is supervised and regulated by the law? Or are we mainly concerned with the legal framework within which professional self-governance through 'professional ethics' operates? Perhaps we are most concerned with how the law is used to protect and promote health, or with the legal framework of the public delivery of health services. We might be concerned only with doctors, or we might focus on nurses, midwives, dentists, physiotherapists or any or all of the varied kinds of personnel and organisations involved in health-related work.

There is considerable openness here. I recall vividly the first time I heard the philosopher Susan Sherwin's argument that bioethics should include gun control as one of its central topics; my initial reaction was one of disbelief. Important as it is, surely gun control was not a topic in bioethics.[11] But, as time has passed, I have changed my mind. It is important, and bioethicists can and should discuss it. This highlights an interesting feature of 'legacy' in that, to some extent, the scope of a legacy can change: the present looks back to the past and downplays an issue that might have been important to the previous generation, and introduces elements of the past that had previously been neglected as important after all.[12] The turn to 'public health ethics' over the past fifteen years has underscored the point. We have seen how focusing on the health impacts of law and public policy can transform the terms of debate and public

---

[11] Susan Sherwin, 'Whither Bioethics? How Feminism Can Help Reorient Bioethics' (2008) 1 *International Journal of Feminist Approaches to Bioethics* 7.

[12] To some extent, legacy is a question of genealogy. See Michel Foucault, 'Nietzsche, Genealogy, History' in Paul Rabinow (ed), *The Foucault Reader* (Penguin 1984); and Friedrich Nietzsche, *On the Genealogy of Morals* (various edns, originally published 1889) and 'On the Use and Abuse of History for Life' in his *Untimely Meditations* (various edns, first published 1874).

attitudes in several areas. Partly this is because of the value that the public places on health, and partly this is because the authority of scientific knowledge in warranting claims about health and health-care policy and practice can – sometimes – be stronger than other kinds of evidence introduced in support of particular policy positions. There are limits to this process, however. Evidence can be missing or controversial; authorities can disagree; different values (health and liberty, for example) can conflict; and, within health, different goals may also conflict. In the midst of the current Covid-19 pandemic, one framing of debates about constraints on social activities is trading off the physical health benefits (of reducing exposure to infection risks) against the mental health costs (of reducing access to educational settings and other communal activities).

This last example reminds us further of the tendency for 'mental health law' – not to speak of social care law and disability law – to develop independently or even separately from 'medical law'. A second conclusion here is that we can distinguish two ways for 'medical law' to be 'medical': it can be 'medical law' because it focuses on medical practice (however broadly drawn); but it can also be 'medical law' because it focuses on the health impacts of law. The controversy around medical aid in dying is a case in point: on the one hand, it is a debate about the legal control of what doctors are allowed to do to or for patients who wish to die; on the other hand, it is a debate about the health impacts of the law of homicide.

Nomenclature matters; naming tells us what is to be studied and what is of interest. It can also imply what is to be left out. The relative dominance of the medical forms of names of the field (medical law, medical ethics, medical jurisprudence, medical regulation . . .) is broadly borne out by the relative dominance of the concerns of the medical profession in what is discussed. There is no especially good reason why issues relating to nursing or social care should be given so little attention in curricula or textbooks or research funding other than the sociological and historical fact of the power and dominance of the medical profession. The feminist critique of medicine (and of medical law) that far more attention is devoted to specifying what may be done to women than to women's agency remains valid. It is arguable that the relative invisibility of nursing and other kinds of care perceived as 'gendered female' reproduces this logic.

## 2.4 Law and Medical Ethics in Theory and Practice

The wide variety and the indeterminate scope of labels for 'law and medical ethics' have, from one point of view, an easy explanation: it is that, from the perspective of the legal system itself, 'medical law' has no distinct existence. There is no medical court: cases involving medical decisions and conduct can appear before judges sitting in most of the different kinds of court in the system, depending on what offence has been charged or cause of action laid or authorisation sought. There is no distinct medical cause of action. There are degrees of professional specialisation, in clinical negligence or professional misconduct or judicial review. But few, if any, professionals would define themselves as 'medical lawyers'.[13] This is a point made with particular force by Ian Kennedy in his writings in the late 1970s and early 1980s, in his 1980 Reith Lectures on *The Unmasking of Medicine* and in establishing the teaching of medical law and ethics (in England at least) at King's College, London as a distinct area of study.[14] Compare, for example, Glanville Williams's important monograph on *The Sanctity of Life and the Criminal Law* (1957).[15] Reading back from the maturely established field of law and medical ethics from the 1990s onward, one might expect to pick this up as an important precursor to Kennedy's work. It is, of course. But Williams did not seek to contribute to 'law and medical ethics' – he had no such conception. Instead, he was seeking to understand the underlying structure of the law of homicide. Similarly, when Patrick Atiyah published *Accidents, Compensation and the Law* in 1970, he did refer from time to time to cases relating to medically induced injuries, but took no special interest in them as such.[16] Medical negligence generated leading cases in the law of torts from time to time, but Atiyah had no particular interest in the law of torts as a tool of medical regulation. So not only is it now a trite observation of legal history that until recently the law took no particular interest in medicine (often explained as a kind of professional deference), neither did the academic commentators on the law.

When Kennedy, Sheila McLean and others began to constitute a field of law and medical ethics, they had to argue that one could discern a distinct legal approach to the law and to assemble materials in support of that view out of a heterogeneous array of sources. This is obvious in *The Unmasking of Medicine* (1981), where Kennedy draws extensively from sources in medical sociology, politics and philosophy, as well as legal materials. But, in his more academic writing, he *constructs*, rather than *finds*, medical law out of cases in the law of torts as well as contract

---

[13] Coroners are an arguable exception.
[14] Ian Kennedy, *The Unmasking of Medicine* (Allen and Unwin 1981).
[15] Glanville Williams, *The Sanctity of Life and the Criminal Law* (Alfred A. Knopf 1957).
[16] Patrick Atiyah, *Accidents, Compensation and the Law* (Weidenfeld and Nicholson 1970).

law, criminal law and equity law. For instance, in his collection of previously published papers *Treat Me Right: Essays in Medical Law and Ethics* (1988), his method of approach is clearly visible.[17] He typically takes a problem in medical practice or regulatory policy, and then develops a legal argument around it, making use of standard techniques of common law case-based reasoning. When, as is often the case, he finds that the law 'on the books' is wanting, he is unafraid of introducing extralegal materials in support of principled arguments for law reform, be that directly through statute or through suggesting ways in which future cases on point should be decided. I remember, on first reading this volume right at the start of my career in bioethics, just how often Kennedy pointed out that decisions were reached on the basis of 'policy', which did not mean explicit government policy or a specific kind of ethical principle but, rather, a judge's (or the court's) particular sense of the shape of the law and how it ought to work. I remember thinking, with the kind of unfairness that perhaps is the privilege of the non-lawyer, that this was a bit of a fudge. I had the impression that Kennedy probably thought so too, which is perhaps why he felt empowered effectively to invent a whole new field, teach it and prescribe how it ought to go.

I cannot stress enough the importance for 'law and medical ethics', at least in its first phases, of common law reasoning, applied to cases arising as they may. Occasional, though before 1980 very rare, specific statutory innovations might arise (such as the Abortion Act (1967)). But rather than looking for a philosophical structure grounded in *medical ethics*, one had to look for philosophical principles (if any) in the nature of the common law – and look for them, as a common lawyer must, in the *rationes decidendi* of particular cases. An analogous case may be found in the development of the European Convention on Human Rights (ECHR) out of common law principles, only to be returned in the form of statute in the Human Rights Act.[18]

Out of these materials, Kennedy, with Andrew Grubb, assembled *Medical Law: Text and Materials* (first edition 1989), which is a far more diverse and wide-ranging collection than most similar texts in

---

[17] Ian Kennedy, *Treat Me Right: Essays in Medical Law and Ethics* (Oxford University Press 1988).

[18] See Brian Simpson, *Human Rights and the End of Empire: Britain and the Genesis of the European Convention* (Oxford University Press 2001). Some of my own thoughts on the relationship between human rights, common law and bioethics may be found in Richard Ashcroft, 'Could Human Rights Supersede Bioethics?' (2010) 10 *Human Rights Law Review* 639.

established areas of legal practice and scholarship tended to be.[19] And it is arguable that, from that point on, it became possible to speak of 'law and medical ethics' as a field, with other academic writers beginning to reshape and restructure it, to find overarching principles in it that are 'principles of medical law' and to articulate theories of what 'law and medical ethics' is and should be. One such theory was Kennedy's own, essentially that medicine, while important, was arrogant and over-mighty in its attitude to patients and to the law, and that the law relating to medicine should be restructured around patient autonomy and individual rights. To the extent that the law reflected these principles, it was good law, and to the extent that it did not, it needed to change. This, to some degree, oversimplifies Kennedy's position, both inasmuch as he was wary of the 'consumer society' and insofar as he always recognised the importance of social systems for understanding patients' and professionals' interests and behaviour. Echoes of this approach persist to the present day, whereby academic medical lawyers – and even judges – look for traces of 'respect for autonomy' in the legal record.

I have emphasised Kennedy and his approach to 'law and medical ethics' because it is impossible to overlook his influence, through the quality of his scholarship, his force of personality and his contributions to public life. But it would be remiss of me to ignore other streams contributing to the early formation of 'law and medical ethics'. We need only recall the roots of medical law in forensic medicine (J. K. Mason), feminist legal scholarship and civil rights (Sheila McLean), public law and human rights (Genevra Richardson and Larry Gostin) and, of course, philosophical, theological and medical writing about medical ethics (Alasdair Campbell, Raanan Gillon, Len Doyal, Mary Warnock, to name but a few). And I have neglected any discussion of the important centre of academic work on law and medical ethics at Manchester. Margaret (Margot) Brazier complicates my story somewhat, owing to the depth and brilliance of her scholarship, her extended engagement in dialogue with philosophical bioethics and her hugely influential role in training many of the leading academic medical lawyers active in the UK today.[20] I had the privilege of joining the Cambridge Bioethics and Law

---

[19] Ian Kennedy and Andrew Grubb, *Medical Law* (Butterworths 1989). One might add that if one wanted to establish that a new field was real and had 'really' been there all along, a 1,200-page textbook has a powerful rhetorical, as well as gravitational, force.

[20] Something worth pointing out about Margaret's contribution to medical law is that her own textbook, while rigorous and detailed, was at the same time addressed to the general reader, as part of the Penguin Law series. This is now in its sixth edition, the second to be

series as junior co-editor to Margot and Graeme, before her retirement from that role. I have not had the opportunity to discuss the ideas of this chapter with her, alas. But my impression, formed from conversations with her over the years, is that while she, like Kennedy, is a brilliant practitioner of common law reasoning, with a profound respect for legal history, unlike Kennedy, she is sceptical of what I have called elsewhere 'philosophical grafts', and more willing to respect the complexity and subtlety of law rather than see it as something to be rationalised.[21] That is for her to say, but this is my impression.

The Kennedy construction of 'law and medical ethics' must therefore be seen as a strategic intervention, both creating a field where none existed and implying that it has always been there. One might speak here of the 'invention of a tradition', or indeed a legacy.[22] I have argued that Kennedy's method of construction, bringing medical practice and common law materials into dialogue, suggests that practice is prior to theory, and moreover that the kind of theory we should expect is the kind of theory which common law reasoning can sustain.[23] Well, you may ask, what is the contrast I am drawing?

One answer to this is that I am suggesting that one cannot theorise 'law and medical ethics' before medical law exists. Secondly, good (legal) theory should grasp the nature of what it is trying to explain. It should work 'with the grain' of its materials rather than against it. However, there is an obvious problem here. It is that once 'law and medical ethics' does exist, it does not leave the world as it was. The (intellectual) world has changed. Although its construction solves certain problems, it creates others. Moreover, some of the drivers behind its construction – such as changes in social attitudes towards health and the professions and technological changes – continue to become ever more salient and some of the problems which arise prove not to be easily solved within the case law framework which supplies the basic architecture of 'medical

---

co-authored with Emma Cave and the first to be published by Manchester University Press. Margaret Brazier and Emma Cave, *Medicine, Patients and the Law* (Manchester University Press 2016).

[21] Richard Ashcroft, 'Law and the Perils of Philosophical Grafts' (2018) 44 *Journal of Medical Ethics* 72.

[22] Eric Hobsbawm and Terence Ranger (eds), *The Invention of Tradition* (Cambridge University Press 1983); Benedict Anderson, *Imagined Communities: Reflections on the Origin and Spread of Nationalism* (Verso 1983).

[23] This is a topic I would like to develop at length; the starting point would be the work of Michael Lobban, in particular *The Common Law and English Jurisprudence, 1760–1850* (Oxford University Press 2001).

law and ethics'. Thus, although we may retain our view of what a theory *of* medical law should be like, there is an increasing need for theory *within* medical law which can assist in guiding changes. For many practical purposes this was – and is – supplied by medical ethics.

I am not saying that 'medical law' is somehow concretised medical ethics. The entire gist of my argument so far is a denial of that proposition. That is not how 'law and medical ethics' came about. 'Medical ethics' does not explain its shape, structure or genesis. (Indeed, the history of 'medics' ethics' is not well explained by and does not well explain 'medical ethics' either.)[24] Instead, I am saying that 'medical law' came to draw on 'medical ethics' as a set of tools for crafting solutions to new problems arising out of social and technological change. The case of *Re A (Conjoined Twins)* is exemplary in this regard,[25] as we can see the judges wrestle both with the limits of the existing common law and with how far they might draw on and apply extra-legal materials from medical ethics in order to cope with those limits. If, in the minds of the judges, those ethical principles were 'always already' there, as philosopher Martin Heidegger might have said, they would have had much less difficulty.[26] Once again, we see the common law making a legacy by finding, indeed I would say consciously constructing, one. And so, we see the conflict between 'common law theory' and 'medical ethics theory' brought to life. But in the end a decision was reached, the primacy of the common law reasserted itself, and the law had subtly changed, with the result that 'theory in the law' became a little more reconciled with 'theory of the law', and 'law and medical ethics' came a little closer to being a unified entity than it had been before. Or so, at any rate, those who believe the case was rightly decided might believe.

## 2.5  Law, Medical Ethics and 'Underlying Principles'

I think there are a number of reasons why so many commentators seek to find underlying ethical principles in 'law and medical ethics', even though the history of the field should dissuade them. Three I propose are: (1) a fixation on legislation, and a tradition of English jurisprudence from Bentham to Hart; (2) a kind of philosophical rationalism, which sees social phenomena, like the law, as surface phenomena overlaying

---

[24] My debt to Duncan Wilson's *The Making of British Bioethics* (Manchester University Press 2014) is deep.

[25] See n 10.

[26] Martin Heidegger, *Being and Time* (various edns, first published 1927).

a deeper progress of reason (be that reason divine or dialectical, as with Finnis or Gewirth); and (3) a reliance on American jurisprudential traditions, which focus on constitutional interpretation. This search for principle reflects one way of thinking about legacy in law: as the coming to concreteness of deeper principles through what Hegel called 'the cunning of reason'.[27] My own search for principle is more pragmatist in orientation, more empirical and inductive, focusing on the legacy of cases as decided and intertwined with the legislative acts of Parliament.

First, it certainly makes sense to look for the principle animating legislation when interpreting and applying it – this is a standard rule of interpretation. It also makes sense when legislating to be clear about the purpose one is pursuing in doing so, and to seek to achieve that through drafting. And in the field of health-care practice and public health and health technologies, it is generally the case that proposals for legislation start from trying to address some moral principle or moral trouble. So, to look for moral principles underlying statute law is not a quixotic thing to do. But the principle may come under considerable strain and adaptation, given the process of passage of bills through parliament. And as no statute stands free and clear of the rest of the law, or the society implementing it, the moral consequence of legislation can be rather different from the moral principle animating the proposal leading to its adoption. We ought to be cautious, therefore, about the idea that there is anything simple and straightforward about reading off 'underlying principles' from legislation and assuming that these are 'underlying principles' in the network of law into which that legislation is introduced.[28]

Although it may be a tricky business to find 'underlying ethical principles' in statute law, it is certainly harder to do so in case law, other than following the careful process of tracing *ratio* to *ratio*. But a different approach is to seek ethical principles underpinning the legal system as a whole. The aim then is to read those foundational principles into particular legal rules (or, in failing, use these principles as a critique of defective rules). Elegant versions of this strategy can be found in the

---

[27] Friedrich Hegel, *The Phenomenology of Spirit* (various edns, first published 1807).

[28] A fascinating case study of the mess and compromise of making law is Michael Mulkay's study of the passage of the first Human Fertilisation and Embryology Act, *The Embryo Research Debate: Science and the Politics of Reproduction* (Cambridge University Press 1997). The argument here is a sort of recapitulation of the Hart-Devlin debate. Although my philosophical and political instincts lie more with Hart, Devlin was the better lawyer. See HLA Hart, *Law, Liberty and Morality* (Stanford University Press 1963); and Patrick Devlin, *The Enforcement of Morals* (Oxford University Press 1965).

natural law theories advanced by John Finnis (drawing on the Catholic natural law tradition stretching back to the Middle Ages) and Deryck Beyleveld and Roger Brownsword (drawing on Alan Gewirth's theory of 'the dialectical nature of morality').[29] To discuss this strategy in detail would require far more space than I have here, but one difficulty is that these supposed 'underlying principles' are essentially extra-legal in nature. It is difficult to see how they can be derived simply from patient study of the law itself without invoking some exterior philosophical theory and stipulating that this theory is the best explanation of the form and content of the law as we find it.

This is open to the standard legal realist critique that the law is what lawyers and judges, empirically, do.[30] To the extent that lawyers and judges draw on such 'underlying principles' explicitly, they have legal force, but for the most part as rhetorical resources in argument, rather than as metaphysical constraints on what law is, may or should be. We can achieve some moderate agreement on certain kinds of underlying principle which are demonstrably invoked or taken for granted, such as the principles of 'the rule of law'. But we are, for the realist, on a fool's errand if we go looking for anything deeper than this, such as 'respect for autonomy'. Glanville Williams's exploration of the *Sanctity of Life and the Criminal Law* is an exemplary, patient exploration of just how far one can get in trying to trace a moral principle through a body of law, and how quickly one finds complexity and contradiction.[31] A less controversial way of putting it is to say that *even if* we could invoke such moral principles, applying them in practice requires immense care and judgement and, in fact, rather than *explaining* law, one finds that one is simply *doing* it – case by case.[32]

A third approach which seeks 'underlying principles' holds that there are indeed such principles but they are contained *within* the body of the law. This approach draws on jurisprudential writing in the American tradition which focuses on constitutional interpretation. Exemplary here is the work of Ronald Dworkin.[33] Of course, within a tradition which has

---

[29] John Finnis, *Natural Law and Natural Rights* (Oxford University Press 1979); Deryck Beyleveld and Roger Brownsword, *Law as a Moral Judgement* (Sweet & Maxwell 1986); Alan Gewirth, *Reason and Morality* (University of Chicago Press 1980).

[30] Karl Llewellyn, *The Bramble Bush: The Classic Lectures on Law and the Law School* (Oxford University Press 2008, first published 1930).

[31] Williams (n 15).

[32] I would like here to pay tribute to Richard Huxtable, with whom I first debated these ideas more than twenty years ago. I am sure Richard still disagrees with me.

[33] For example, Ronald Dworkin, *A Matter of Principle* (Harvard University Press 1985).

a foundation in a written constitution, where it is a practical matter of legal interpretation to read legal rules in light of that constitution (or to show how they are 'unconstitutional' and thus not legal rules at all), it is natural to focus on 'the practice of principle'.[34] It may be that this approach is particularly attractive to legal academics because it confers on them a certain importance in the courts themselves, as experts on abstract reasoning and authors of amicus briefs.[35] A similar approach can be taken in jurisdictions which adopt codifications of bodies of law, in whole or in part. But the legal systems of the United Kingdom are not structured around a constitution or 'basic law'. Certain statutes have been adopted which seek to take on a similar structural role (notably, the Human Rights Act 1998 and the European Communities Act 1972). But they do not have the same status as 'final word' in legal reasoning that a written constitution has.

It is also important to consider how cases are decided in light of the Human Rights Act 1998. Section 3 subsection 1 of the Act instructs us that 'so far as it is possible to do so, primary legislation and subsidiary legislation must be read and given effect in a way which is compatible with Convention rights', which subsection 2 and section 4 qualify by allowing that under some circumstances it is not possible to read such legislation as compatible with Convention rights. And while the courts may issue a 'Declaration of Incompatibility', such a Declaration does not override or cancel such incompatible legislation. Thus, in effect, the principles in the Human Rights Act 1998 (the principles of the European Convention on Human Rights, that is to say) are *not* underlying principles. They are not prior to and do not govern the interpretation and application of legal rules; they must be read alongside such rules and, in the end, if there is an inconsistency, this is a political and not a legal matter.[36]

---

[34] Jules Coleman, *The Practice of Principle: In Defence of a Pragmatist Approach to Legal Theory* (Oxford University Press 2003).

[35] Dworkin (n 33). But see also Raoul van Caeneghem, *Judges, Legislators and Professors: Chapters in European Legal History* (Cambridge University Press 1987).

[36] I have written elsewhere about the relationship among law, human rights and bioethics, a relationship I have described as 'troubled'. My view is that human rights discourse provides a common language for law and bioethics to communicate in a principled way. But what I propose is not that human rights is a foundational discourse underpinning law and bioethics. Rather, I think it provides a way for different parties to move forward and find consensus, particularly in international contexts as a sort of tool of construction. It brings things together, rather than showing how they were together all along (when, manifestly, they weren't). Richard Ashcroft, 'The Troubled Relationship between

## 2.6   The Importance of Textbooks

I began by noting the low status that textbooks have in the current
climate of 'research excellence'. I then noted the continuing instability
of the naming and scope of the field of 'law and medical ethics'. I argued
that this has an institutional and historical explanation, relating to the
way in which in the UK 'law and medical ethics' was not found but rather
constructed by a generation of scholars, centrally, but certainly not
exclusively, by Ian Kennedy. A critical intervention was the publication
of a textbook which both defined and demonstrated the existence of
a field of 'law and medical ethics'. I argued that this first textbook took
a distinctively 'common law' approach to its subject matter, and that in
this case theory followed textbook, rather than theory defining and
unifying the material then gathered into a textbook. Whereas a reader
concerned with 'medical ethics' might expect medical law to reflect
medical ethics, and perhaps move to reflect ever more perfectly the
'principles of medical ethics', I argue that this does not explain the genesis
of medical law or how it evolves in the common law tradition. But the
continuing dialogue between law and medical ethics can be fruitful in
showing ways in which medical law can change: while medical ethics
does not ground a 'theory of medical law', it can still play the role of
a 'theory in medical law'.

Allowing that medical ethics can play a role as theory within medical
law, the question then arises of whether there can be some (other) theory
*of* medical law, what some have called a medical jurisprudence. One
natural response, in line with my historically oriented account of the
development of medical law out of common law methods and materials,
would be to say that there is no theory of medical law which is not
a theory of the law as such. That is, medical law is distinctive in its subject
matter but not in its methods or functions. One could go further and say
that there can be no theory of medical law because there can be no theory
of law. This kind of theoretical nihilism can be given a positive justification along similar lines to nihilism about the idea of a social science or
about the idea of a theory (or philosophy) of history. In brief: law is what
law does, and that's all there is to say about its nature.[37] I would not go so
far. I think that the methods of interpretative, empirical social science

Bioethics and Human Rights' in Michael Freeman (ed), *Current Legal Issues Volume 11:
Law and Bioethics* (Oxford University Press 2008) 3.

[37] This leads one into a vast literature, but one can do worse than look at Peter Winch, *The
Idea of a Social Science and Its Relation to Philosophy* (Routledge 1958), even today.

have a lot to tell us about the shape and development of the law, and indeed of medical law, particularly in the realist tradition of jurisprudence, and related work in feminist, intersectional and critical legal studies. Inasmuch as we can have, or want, a normative theory of (medical) law, I think we will get more at this stage from a jurisprudential study of medical law *as law* (both in doctrine and in action) than from a philosophical study of medical law as concretised medical ethics.[38]

In closing, I am picking up the theme of textbooks once more. The argument that textbooks are not mere afterthoughts in the development of a discipline but can in fact be crucial in discipline formation – in setting out the scope of the discipline, the methodological canons, the chief problems requiring engagement and solution, and exemplars of what count as good solutions to such problems – is not new. It can be traced back to American physicist and philosopher of science Thomas Kuhn, in his *The Structure of Scientific Revolutions* (1962).[39] As my teacher John Forrester wrote:

> One of the many suggestions in Kuhn's book that has aroused great interest but insufficient subsequent research was his pointing to textbooks as the way in which to understand how modern scientific knowledge works. And it is not just the compendious organisation of the textbook that accomplishes this task; the only way to become a scientist is to plough through all those dreary textbook 'problems'. The general principles and arguments enunciated in the general section of each chapter of a textbook are the window-dressing on the real acculturation process: the problems show the neophyte how to do science, provide model ways of asking questions as much as model answers.[40]

The textbook is thus, for Kuhn, not just a compendium of knowledge; it is a tool of practical learning, a resource for research and a common ground on which a community forms – a community of teachers, students, researchers and practitioners. To a degree, the legal professions and the

---

[38] For instance, by bringing together Patricia Collins and Sirma Bilge, *Intersectionality* (Polity Press 2016).

[39] Thomas Kuhn, *The Structure of Scientific Revolutions: Fiftieth Anniversary Edition* (University of Chicago Press 2012).

[40] John Forrester, *Thinking in Cases* (Polity Press 2017) 8. The chapter I am quoting from, 'If p Then What? Thinking in Cases', was first published under that title in (1996) 9 *History of the Human Sciences* 1. It is a tour de force considering the different ways in which case-based reasoning works in law, medicine, psychoanalysis, theology and the sciences. See also Stephen Toulmin and Albert Jonsen, *The Abuse of Casuistry: A History of Moral Reasoning* (University of California Press 1988).

legal academy acknowledge this through naming practices – every criminal lawyer has her 'Archbold', and every medical lawyer has her 'Mason and McCall Smith' (or so I should hope!). The original author of a leading textbook is honoured even unto the eleventh edition and beyond.

I referred above to the commercial pressures on publishers and authors to maintain and update textbooks in a competitive market. Textbooks have different aspirations: some aim to be definitive doctrinal restatements of a body of law with suggestions for reform.[41] Some aim to reshape how we think about the law and its practice from a socio-legal standpoint or with a particular explicit political point of view.[42] Some aim, modestly but importantly, to help students new to a subject to find their way in, without ambitions of being the last word on the subject. And so on. But in the case of new and emerging fields like 'law and medical ethics', textbooks often embody a theoretical argument about the relationship between law and medical ethics, and how one illuminates our understanding of the other. Sometimes this argument is explicit – for example, in Shaun Pattinson's *Medical Law and Ethics* (now in its sixth edition, 2020), which develops an ethically informed account of medical law based on the Sheffield Natural Law school; or in Jonathan Montgomery's *Health Care Law* (which sadly went into only two editions, the last in 2002), which takes a programmatic stance on the need to see medical law in the context of the law of the National Health Service as a health system.[43]

Some of the texts taking this explicit approach are relatively 'closed' in that the author's theoretical approach guides the reader fairly briskly through the material; others are more 'open' in laying out materials for the reader's inspection and inviting them to take up a stance of their own construction.[44] But I would argue that even 'open' texts are not completely open, in that they stipulate a certain scope for the field, what materials are relevant to it, and how to understand the various strands of legal reasoning. And below the level of theorising about 'law and medical ethics' in terms of general principle, we find that most textbook authors

---

[41] For instance, Rachael Mulheron, *Principles of Tort Law* (Cambridge University Press 2016).

[42] For instance, Alison Diduck and Felicity Kaganas, *Family Law, Gender and the State: Text, Cases and Materials* (Hart 2016), which seeks expressly to be a feminist restatement of family law.

[43] Shaun Pattinson, *Medical Law and Ethics* (6th edn, Thomson Reuters 2020). Jonathan Montgomery, *Health Care Law* (2nd edn, Oxford University Press 2002).

[44] I see Emily Jackson, *Medical Law: Text, Cases and Materials* (5th edn, Oxford University Press 2019) as being open in this sense.

have their own perspectives on at least some topics covered, which again can be taken as exemplary models for stating and solving problems, as Kuhn suggests, quite as much as they are to be taken at face value as being 'the right way' to think about abortion or genetic information, say.

In sum, a textbook is not a monograph; it is not a book-length theoretical statement built out of evidence and argument to lead to a conclusion which is the author's (interim) final word on the subject. I hope I have persuaded you that textbooks are *much* more interesting than that. You just have to know how to read them; and good textbooks teach you how they are to be read. In that regard, *Mason and McCall Smith's Law and Medical Ethics* is a *very* good textbook. It is thorough and wide-ranging, written on the basis of decades of scholarship and research by its various authors, carefully updated, open for the reader, but rich in argument and analysis which teach the reader how to 'do' law and medical ethics by example.[45] Long live the textbook, long live *Mason and McCall Smith's Law and Medical Ethics*, long live its legacy. Long live Graeme Laurie.

---

[45] Consider chapter 7 of *Mason and McCall Smith's Law and Medical Ethics* on 'Genetic Information and the Law', which is a masterly summary of the scientific, medical, legal, regulatory and ethical issues and materials. It is reliable as an introduction to the field. But read it alongside Graeme's journal articles and his monograph *Genetic Privacy: A Challenge to Medico-Legal Norms* (Cambridge University Press 2002), and you will clearly see the themes and preoccupations of the latter in the former. *Ars est celare artem.*

# Thinking Outside the Box

## Graeme Laurie's Legacy to Medical Jurisprudence

ROGER BROWNSWORD

### 3.1 Introduction

It is a great pleasure to contribute to this Festschrift for Graeme Laurie, whose legacy to 'medical jurisprudence' – conceived of as the discipline of 'medical law and bioethics'[1] – can be measured in several dimensions. Not least, it is a legacy that can be measured in terms of the leadership, encouragement and inspiration that Graeme has provided to the many young researchers who have worked with him at Edinburgh and who have now gone on to become leading scholars in their own right. It can also be measured in relation to Graeme's practical impact outside the academy – for example, in his important shaping of the relationship of 'critical friendship' between the Ethics and Governance Council and UK Biobank.[2] In this contribution, however, my focus will be on the legacy of Graeme's published work, from his seminal monograph on genetic privacy to his most recent exploration of 'liminality' and the regulation of health-care research.[3]

---

[1] Graeme Laurie, Shawn Harmon and Edward Dove, *Mason and McCall Smith's Law and Medical Ethics* (11th edn, Oxford University Press 2019) 2, para 1.03.

[2] Graeme Laurie, 'Reflexive Governance in Biobanking: On the Value of Policy Led Approaches and the Need to Recognise the Limits of Law' (2011) 130 *Human Genetics* 347; 'The Ethics and Governance Council (EGC) as a "critical friend"' in UK Biobank Ethics and Governance Council, 'Past, Present, Future: The Ethics and Governance of Big Biobanks Conference' (*Wellcome Trust*, 3–5 November 2014) 5; and 'What Does It Mean to Take an Ethics+ Approach to Global Biobank Governance?' (2017) 9 *Asian Bioethics Review* 285.

[3] See Graeme Laurie, *Genetic Privacy* (Cambridge University Press 2002); Samuel Taylor-Alexander et al, 'Beyond Regulatory Compression: Confronting the Liminal Spaces of Health Research Regulation' (2016) 8 *Law, Innovation and Technology* 149; and

Distinctively, in his writing – and conspicuously so in his most recent work on liminality, where the conceptual starting points are in anthropology and specifically in the ethnographic research of Arnold van Gennep[4] – Graeme has invited readers to think outside the black-letter box of medical law. Or, as I will put it, to think outside the box of doctrinal 'Law 1.0'.[5]

Precisely how this invitation is accepted will vary from one person to another. Once we start thinking outside the box, we open our minds to extended fields of inquiry, to new questions and to new focal points for our research. Already, lawyers will accept that it makes no sense to study medical law without also taking seriously the application of medical ethics,[6] and that medical jurisprudence needs to set medical law in its social, political and economic context.[7] In my case, the invitation to think outside the box takes us straight to the many developments in genetics, robotics, nano- and neuro-technologies, additive manufacturing, big data and artificial intelligence (AI) that promise to transform medical practice.

With the benefit of Graeme's legacy, we should be able to ask the right questions about the governance of medical practices that are undergoing a rapid technological transformation. While some of these questions will invite Law 1.0 inquiries about the application of historic principles and values to new technologies, many will be of a quite different 'Law 2.0' regulatory nature.[8] Here, the challenge is to articulate a regulatory environment that is ethically acceptable, effective and fit for our time. However, Law 2.0 is itself a box outside of which we might need to

---

Graeme Laurie, 'Liminality and the Limits of Law in Health Research Regulation: What Are We Missing in the Spaces in-Between?' (2017) 25 *Medical Law Review* 47.

[4] Arnold van Gennep, *The Rites of Passage* (University of Chicago Press 2011).

[5] See Roger Brownsword, *Law, Technology and Society: Re-imagining the Regulatory Environment* (Routledge 2019) and *Law 3.0: Rules, Regulation and Technology* (Routledge 2020).

[6] Famously, as Hoffmann LJ put it at the Court of Appeal stage of the proceedings in *Airedale NHS Trust* v. *Bland* [1993] 1 All ER 821 at 850: 'This is not an area in which any difference can be allowed to exist between what is legal and what is morally right. The decision of the court should be able to carry conviction with the ordinary person as being based not merely on legal precedent but also upon acceptable ethical values.' See, for example, the approach adopted in Shaun Pattinson, *Medical Law and Ethics* (5th edn, Sweet & Maxwell 2017) and, of course, in Laurie et al (n 1).

[7] See, for example, the Preface to Jonathan Herring, *Medical Law and Ethics* (7th edn, Oxford University Press 2018), in which the author says that the book 'is designed to provide readers with coverage not only of medical law, but also of the context, philosophical, social, and political within which the law operates'.

[8] Brownsword (n 5).

think, and with this regulatory challenge in mind, a further thought occurs. Recalling Lawrence Lessig's seminal work on the regulatory significance of the coding of hardware and software,[9] might it now be the time to think in a more general way about the use of emerging technologies as regulatory tools? In other words, should we open a conversation, a 'Law 3.0' conversation, about the effective and acceptable use of technologies for regulatory purposes?[10]

My contribution to this Festschrift is in four main parts. First, I introduce the idea of a field of legal inquiry in which we find three coexisting and interacting mindsets and conversations: the doctrinal conversation of Law 1.0, the regulatory conversation of Law 2.0, and an embryonic conversation about governance by technologies, Law 3.0. Second, assuming a Law 2.0 approach, I outline the key challenges associated with getting the regulatory environment right for new technologies, whether these technologies are applied for medical or other purposes. Third, I discuss how medical jurisprudence should engage with a stream of new health-related technologies that entrust medical functions to smart machines and take humans out of the loop. While much of the engagement here will be in Law 2.0 mode, there might also be some Law 3.0 thinking as regulatory functions are entrusted to the machines. Finally, doubling up on thinking out of the box, by juxtaposing the idea of liminality – which, in Graeme's hands, becomes a lens for viewing afresh the regulatory processes associated with health-care research – with the field of legal inquiry proposed in this chapter, I consider some applications of the former to the latter.

## 3.2   The Field of Law and the Frames of Law

In my introductory remarks, I have flagged up my proposal that we should think outside the doctrinal box by conceiving of our field of inquiry as one comprising three coexisting and interacting conversations (Laws 1.0, 2.0 and 3.0). Before speaking to each of these conversations, and for the avoidance of misunderstanding, some short methodological comments are in order.

---

[9] Lawrence Lessig, *Code and Other Laws of Cyberspace* (Basic Books 1999).
[10] See Roger Brownsword, 'Law 3.0: A Conversation for the New Decade' (21 July 2020) *Georgetown Journal of International Affairs*, https://gjia.georgetown.edu/2020/07/21/law-3-0-a-conversation-for-the-new-decade/ (accessed 16 August 2020).

### 3.2.1   A Methodological Note

Two aspects of what I am proposing as the field of legal inquiry, with its three coexisting mindsets and conversations, merit some short remarks. One aspect is the specification of the field; the other concerns the framing of inquiry within the field.[11]

First, legal scholars have a variety of cognitive interests. However, the specification of the field of legal inquiry defines the limits of scholarship that is appropriately designated as legal; and, in practice, this can constrain the pursuit of particular interests that lie beyond the boundaries of the field. Where the field of law is coextensive with Law 1.0, then legal inquiry will be limited to doctrinal scholarship. Scholars who wish to examine, say, the impact of law in practice or its relationship to informal governance, or to evaluate legal doctrine for its economic efficiency or its alignment with ethical values, will find themselves operating beyond the generally recognised boundaries of legal scholarship. Not only that; questions might be asked about whether the products of such scholarship really belong in the law section of the library.[12]

In response, there is likely to be pressure to extend the boundaries of the field – for example, by proposing that 'contextual' studies of law should be recognised as lying within, or even as constituting, the field.[13] Like many legal scholars, I have a cognitive interest in the context in which law is made, applied and adjudicated but, specifically, in the technological features of that context. My sense is that these features become increasingly important to an understanding of law as societies become more technologically reliant and sophisticated. Accordingly, I want to specify the field of law in a way that enables technology-focused lines of inquiry to be pursued as articulations of legal scholarship and which, at the same time, does not disable other lines of inquiry. Hence, my proposal.

Second, within the field so specified, the overall framing of inquiry is given by three ideal-typical mindsets that reflect a particular way that lawyers will engage with new technologies. In Law 1.0, the mode of

---

[11] See generally Roger Brownsword, 'Framers and Problematisers: Getting to Grips with Global Governance' (2010) 1 *Transnational Legal Theory* 287 and 'Field, Frame and Focus: Methodological Issues in the New Legal World' in Rob van Gestel, Hans Micklitz and Ed Rubin (eds), *Rethinking Legal Scholarship* (Cambridge University Press 2016) 112.

[12] We might note, for example, that Stewart Macaulay's seminal article 'Non-contractual Relations in Business: A Preliminary Study' (1963) 28 *American Sociological Review* 55 was published in a sociology, not law, journal.

[13] See the findings in Fiona Cownie, *Legal Academics* (Hart 2004).

engagement is to ask how traditional legal principles apply to new technological phenomena (for example, to ask how the principles of contract law apply to so-called smart contracts); in Law 2.0, it is to ask how new technologies are best regulated; and in Law 3.0, it is to ask how new technologies might be employed as regulatory tools. The field so constructed prompts a narrative that features a double technological disruption of law. In the first disruption, the traditional doctrinal coherentist mindset of Law 1.0 is destabilised by the emergence of a Law 2.0 mindset, the logic of which is more purposive and regulatory-instrumentalist. This is followed by a second disruption when regulatory instrumentalism is taken in the more technocratic direction of Law 3.0 (at which point technology comes to be seen as a possible solution to regulatory problems). With each mindset, there are different questions that are focal and different conversations that ensue.[14]

Because the three mindsets are ideal-types, they and their accompanying narratives should not be misunderstood either as essays in legal history or as accounts of disruption as necessarily a force for the good. With regard to the former, I will leave it to legal historians to judge just how important, say, the development of the railways actually was for the shaping of nineteenth-century contract law and tort law;[15] and how important the technologies of industrialisation were in encouraging a regulatory approach that ushered in a catalogue of strict liability crimes.[16] With regard to the latter, while I do think that the disruption of Law 1.0 was necessary as societies were transformed by technological developments, a regulatory mindset that is wholly instrumentalist is a very dangerous one: as Robert Merton put it so eloquently, we need to beware civilisations and technocrats that are 'committed to the quest for continually improved means to carelessly examined ends'.[17]

Finally, an obvious question is how my ideal-types relate to other similar sounding framings. While I cannot here attempt to answer this question in relation to all the examples that might be given, let me at least indicate how I view the relationship between Laws 1.0, 2.0 and 3.0 and

---

[14] In addition to the references in n 5, see Roger Brownsword, 'Law and Technology: Two Modes of Disruption, Three Legal Mindsets, and the Big Picture of Regulatory Responsibilities' (2018) 14 *Indian Journal of Law and Technology* 1 and 'Law Disrupted, Law Re-imagined, Law Re-invented' (2019) 1 *Technology and Regulation* 10.

[15] See, for example, Miquel Martin-Casals (ed), *The Development of Liability in Relation to Technological Change* (Cambridge University Press 2010); and Morton Horwitz, *The Transformation of American Law 1780–1860* (Harvard University Press 1977).

[16] Seminally, see F Sayre, 'Public Welfare Offences' (1933) 33 *Columbia Law Review* 55.

[17] In his Foreword to Jacques Ellul, *The Technological Society* (Vintage Books 1964) vi.

Max Tegmark's Life 1.0, 2.0 and 3.0.[18] According to Tegmark, we can conceive of life developing through three stages. In Life 1.0, the 'biological' stage, life forms (such as bacteria) simply evolve; in Life 2.0, the 'cultural' stage, which is where we humans find ourselves, biology still develops through evolution but humans are able to learn new skills and develop new tools and technologies; and in Life 3.0, the 'technological' stage, biology is freed from its evolutionary shackles, life forms now being able, as Tegmark puts it, to design both their hardware and their software. In this developmental story, humans instantiate Life 2.0 and the three conversations of Laws 1.0, 2.0 and 3.0 all fall within this cultural stage. That said, both narratives highlight the increasing significance of technological development and the overall direction of travel, whether it is to making a life form the master of its own destiny or to increasing the effective control exercised by regulators.

### 3.2.2   The Lens of Law 1.0

The lens of Law 1.0 is doctrinal and essentially 'coherentist'. For present purposes, we can treat coherentist thinking as being defined by the following five characteristics.

First, for coherentists, what matters above all is the integrity and internal consistency of legal doctrine. This is viewed as desirable in and of itself. Second, coherentists are not concerned with the fitness of the law for its regulatory purpose. Third, coherentists approach new technologies by asking how they fit within existing legal categories (and then try hard to fit them in) – for example, developments in both biotechnology and information technology have raised questions about the way in which fundamental concepts and distinctions in property law map onto a range of 'things', such as detached human tissue, gametes and personal data.[19] Fourth, coherentists believe that legal reasoning should be anchored to guiding general principles of law. Fifth, coherentists assume that the function of private law, together with its guiding principles, is largely concerned with *ex post* correction and compensation. To be sure, there might be limited preventive measures available to litigants, but, for the most part, private law is geared to specifying which acts or omissions

---

[18]  Max Tegmark, *Life 3.0* (Allen Lane 2017).
[19]  For discussion of the property paradigm and its application to stored sperm samples, see Shawn Harmon and Graeme Laurie, '*Yearworth v North Bristol NHS Trust*: Property, Principles, Precedents and Paradigms' (2010) 69 *Cambridge Law Journal* 476.

constitute wrongs and to remedying such wrongs as and when they occur.

It is worth lingering over the coherentist tendency to ask not whether the prevailing (and disrupted) rules are fit for purpose but how new phenomena can be fitted into traditional classification schemes or how they comport with general principles of law. For coherentists, the focus is on the recognised legal concepts, categories and classifications; and this is accompanied by a certain reluctance to abandon these concepts, categories and classifications with a view to contemplating a bespoke response. For example, rather than recognise new types of intellectual property, coherentists will prefer to tweak existing laws of patents and copyright.[20] As Graeme and his team have put it in the context of the regulation of health-care research, our thinking gets trapped (and, in turn, traps researchers) in historic categories and silos; and the distinctions that organise the jurisprudence do not allow for phenomena that are, so to speak, in an intermediate or transitional state of 'in-betweenness'.[21]

Coherentism is, thus, the natural language of litigators and judges, who seek to apply the law in a principled way. It is also the default mode of thinking for many lawyers who take it that being trained 'to think like a lawyer' is synonymous with being trained to apply general principles of law to situations and phenomena both familiar and novel.

### 3.2.3   The Lens of Law 2.0

Law 2.0 prompts a quite different, regulatory-instrumentalist conversation. It can be characterised by the following six features.

First, regulatory instrumentalism is not concerned with the internal consistency of legal doctrine. When regulatory instrumentalists raise questions about consistency, they are typically making sure that particular regulatory interventions will complement others in serving specified regulatory objectives. Second, the conversation is entirely focused on whether the law is instrumentally effective in serving specified regulatory purposes. Regulatory instrumentalists ask not whether the law is 'coherent' – other than in the sense of asking whether a group of related interventions pushes in the required regulatory direction – but whether

---

[20] Compare Julie Cohen, *Between Truth and Power* (Oxford University Press 2019) 24.

[21] See, in particular, Taylor-Alexander et al (n 3); Laurie (n 3); and Catriona McMillan et al, 'Beyond Categorisation: Refining the Relationship between Subjects and Objects in Health Research Regulation' (2021) 13 *Law Innovation and Technology* 194.

it works.[22] Third, regulatory instrumentalism has no reservation about enacting new bespoke laws if this is an effective and efficient response to a question raised by new technologies. Fourth, the anchoring points for regulatory instrumentalists are not the general principles that are established in the jurisprudence but, rather, current policy purposes and objectives. Fifth, alongside its policy focus, regulatory instrumentalism in relation to new technologies tends to be orientated towards striking an acceptable balance between benefits and risks. Sixth, the tilt of the risk-management mindset that goes with regulatory instrumentalism is towards *ex ante* prevention rather than *ex post* correction.

Regulatory instrumentalism is, thus, the (democratically) mandated language of legislators, policy-makers and regulatory agencies who talk the talk of Law 2.0. Conversely, while judges might have some responsibility for applying the spirit of policy-driven legislation, it is precisely the initiation and setting of regulatory policy or making regulatory 'corrections' that we think falls beyond the mandate of unaccountable judges.[23]

Law 2.0 is relentlessly instrumentally rational. The question is: what works, and what will serve certain specified purposes? When a regulatory intervention does not work, it is not enough to restore the status quo; rather, further regulatory measures should be taken, learning from previous experience, with a view to realising the regulatory purposes more effectively. Hence, the purpose of the criminal law is not simply to respond to wrongdoing (as corrective justice demands) but to reduce crime by adopting whatever measures of deterrence promise to work. Similarly, in a safety-conscious community, the purpose of tort law is not simply to respond to wrongdoing but to deter practices and acts where agents could easily avoid creating risks of injury and damage. For regulatory instrumentalists, the path of the law should be progressive: we should be getting better at regulating crime and improving levels of

---

[22] Compare Edward Rubin, 'From Coherence to Effectiveness' in Rob van Gestel, Hans Micklitz and Edward Rubin (eds), *Rethinking Legal Scholarship* (Cambridge University Press 2017) 328: in the modern administrative state, the 'standard for judging the value of law is not whether it is coherent but rather whether it is effective, that is, effective in establishing and implementing the policy goals of the modern state'.

[23] That said, there are occasions when coherentist-minded judges will respond in a more regulatory way to pressing policy concerns. See, for example, Cristie Ford, *Innovation and the State* (Cambridge University Press 2017) 174: noting that, in the absence of railroad legislation, '[c]ourts were the primary public players, and it was courts that solved the railways' short-term cash flow problem(s). In view of the perceived public interest in keeping the railroads running, judges modified existing security contracts and the law of liens, *often to the bewilderment of the business community*' (emphasis added).

safety; and, similarly, as Graeme has argued, whether the policy focus is on supporting beneficial innovation or protecting the interests of patients and research participants, we should be getting better at regulating health-care treatment and research.

### 3.2.4   The Lens of Law 3.0

If the seeds of Law 2.0 are sown as soon as we start thinking that legal rules and principles might not be 'fit for (regulatory) purpose', the seminal, and radical, thought in Law 3.0 is that 'technology might be the solution to our regulatory problems'. Instead of conceiving of law in Fullerian terms as an enterprise of subjecting human conduct to the governance of *rules*,[24] made, administered and enforced by *humans*, Law 3.0 invites us to contemplate law as an enterprise of subjecting human conduct to the governance of *technology*,[25] operationalised to some extent by smart machines. While 'smart' regulation in both Law 2.0 and Law 3.0 is essentially about employing the optimal mix of regulatory instruments,[26] the range of instruments in Law 3.0 is far more extensive. Moreover, the employment of technological measures changes the complexion of the regulatory environment in ways that threaten to compromise the context for both individual autonomy and human dignity.[27]

The regulatory problems to which technology might be seen as a solution can span the entire range of regulatory functions. It might be that the rules simply do not work (non-compliance is the problem), or that non-compliance is under-detected, or that the administration of the rules is inaccurate or inconsistent, and so on. As a response to these problems, the technological solution might be to preclude the practical option of non-compliance (for example, as where products are designed to preclude infringement of IPRs), to nudge regulatees towards compliance, to reinforce the signals given by the rules (particularly, for example, by employing surveillance and identification technologies) and to support and guide human decision-makers in their application of the rules

---

[24] Lon Fuller, *The Morality of Law* (Yale University Press 1969).

[25] Compare Alain Supiot, *Governance by Numbers* (Hart 2017).

[26] Seminally (in a Law 2.0 paradigm), see Neil Gunningham and Peter Grabosky, *Smart Regulation* (Clarendon Press 1998).

[27] See Roger Brownsword, 'Lost in Translation: Legality, Regulatory Margins, and Technological Management' (2011) 26 *Berkeley Technology Law Journal* 1321, and 'Law, Liberty and Technology' in Roger Brownsword, Eloise Scotford and Karen Yeung (eds), *The Oxford Handbook of Law, Regulation and Technology* (Oxford University Press 2017) 41. See further Section 3.4 of this chapter.

(for example, as in cricket and soccer where decisions made by umpires and referees are subject to review by off-field humans aided by various technologies).

As will be apparent from the foregoing, in a Law 3.0 conversation, the idea of what is a 'technical' or 'technological' solution is very broad. The solutions might be 'architectural' so that buildings and spaces are designed to reduce the opportunities for crime, or accident and injury, or the unnecessary use of energy, and the like; and they might be old-fashioned and visible (like locks on doors and border walls) or high tech and futuristic (like biometric entry systems or smart invisible borders). Technological solutions might be incorporated in the design of products or processes (simply by automating a process, humans might be removed from potentially dangerous situations); and, in principle, the technical measures might be incorporated in wearables or even in humans themselves. Accordingly, in a Law 3.0 conversation where the purpose is, let us suppose, to improve the safety of both patients and health-care workers in hospitals, the questions might include whether the environment would be improved by locking more doors, by introducing surveillance technologies, by replacing humans with robots, by making more use of AI, and so on.[28]

If we can say that, ideal-typically, it is in the courts that we have the forum for Law 1.0 conversations, and in the executive branch and the legislature that we have the forum for Law 2.0 conversations, what should we say about the forum for Law 3.0 conversations? Arguably, Law 3.0 conversations should start in the executive and the legislature, where the ground rules for the use of technological solutions are established, and where particular delegations of responsibility for the development of such solutions can be agreed.[29] However, the actuality is that, in practice, technological measures are employed for regulatory purposes by both public and private actors (for example, by the police, revenue commissioners and financial regulators as much as by bigtech corporations, banks and insurance companies) without there being any prior public

---

[28] Compare, for example, Roger Brownsword, 'Regulating Patient Safety: Is It Time for a Technological Response?' (2014) 6 *Law, Innovation and Technology*, 1; and Will Brown, 'Rwanda Deploys Robots to Fight Covid-19' (*The Telegraph*, 20 May 2020) www.telegraph.co.uk/global-health/science-and-disease/rwanda-deploys-robots-fight-covid-19/ (accessed 28 August 2020).

[29] Compare Laurence Diver, 'Digisprudence: The Design of Legitimate Code' *Law, Innovation and Technology* (forthcoming). The DOI is 10.1080/17579961.2021.1977217.

authorisation or debate.[30] In this sense, Law 3.0 is a conversation that is everywhere and yet, publicly, transparently, and officially, nowhere.

### 3.2.5    Which Lens?

The choice between Law 1.0, Law 2.0 and Law 3.0 is not just a matter of which lens a researcher of medical law (or, indeed, any other area of law) might productively use. For practical purposes, it can make a big difference whether a particular question is put to a court (where the conversation and the lens are Law 1.0) or to a body that has a more regulatory Law 2.0 or even Law 3.0 approach.

For example, in his book *Birth Rights and Wrongs*,[31] Dov Fox discusses US medical jurisprudence as it bears on compensatory claims made by parties whose reproductive plans have been frustrated by negligent acts, negligent advice, negligent omissions, and so on, of those medical professionals who deal with new reproductive techniques and tests. Fox sketches the landscape in the following way:

> Different kinds of reproductive wrongs call for different kinds of rights. In some cases, procreation is *deprived* – as when a lab technician drops the tray of embryos that are an infertile couple's last chance to have biological children, or when a doctor leads an eagerly expecting pregnant woman to abort by misinforming her that her healthy fetus would be born with a fatal disease. In other cases, procreation is *imposed* – as when a pharmacist fills a woman's birth control prescription with prenatal vitamins, or when a surgeon botches the sterilization that parents of five had sought because they were already struggling to make ends meet. Procreation is *confounded* when an IVF clinic fertilizes a patient's eggs with sperm from a stranger instead of her spouse, or when a sperm bank neglects to inform prospective parents that the anonymous donor it called 'perfect' had actually dropped out of college, been convicted of burglary, and diagnosed with schizophrenia.[32]

---

[30] On the use of new technologies in the criminal justice system, see, for example, Benjamin Bowling, Amber Marks and Cian Murphy, 'Crime Control Technologies: Towards an Analytical Framework and Research Agenda' in Roger Brownsword and Karen Yeung (eds), *Regulating Technologies* (Hart 2008) 51; Amber Marks, Benjamin Bowling and Colman Keenan, 'Automatic Justice? Technology, Crime, and Social Control' in Roger Brownsword, Eloise Scotford and Karen Yeung (eds), *The Oxford Handbook of Law, Regulation and Technology* (Oxford University Press 2017) 705; and Roger Brownsword and Alon Harel, 'Law, Liberty and Technology; Criminal Justice in the Context of Smart Machines' (2019) 15 *International Journal of Law in Context* 107. On bigtech companies, see in particular Shoshana Zuboff, *The Age of Surveillance Capitalism* (Profile Books 2019).

[31] Dov Fox, *Birth Rights and Wrongs* (Oxford University Press 2019).

[32] Ibid., 165–6.

Although some courts have responded positively and imaginatively to such cases, Fox is critical of the widespread failure of US courts to do so. Where the negligence at issue involves the loss or destruction or mis-transfer of embryos, courts tend to decline to compensate because the resulting 'harm' or 'loss' does not fit with the usual (Law 1.0) understanding of physical damage or damage to 'property'; and where the negligence involves failing to prevent a pregnancy or the birth of a child with a particular inherited condition, the courts tend to hold that the birth of a child (even an unplanned child) is a cause for celebration rather than compensation.

Where the courts cannot, or do not, use their imagination to rework tort principles or traditional ideas of what can count as property, or to invoke notions of privacy or human dignity,[33] to apply to such cases, we have reached the limits of Law 1.0. Instead, there will be a Law 2.0 conversation about what needs to be done to current rules or which new rules are required in order to protect the reasonable expectations and legitimate interests of consumers of reproductive services. Further, if there seem to be technological solutions that are available, there might also be a Law 3.0 conversation. As Joshua Fairfield remarked, when writing in a related context, 'if courts [or, we might say, the rules of contract law] will not protect consumers, robots will'.[34]

In the next part of the chapter, where our focus is on the regulatory thinking of Law 2.0, it will become apparent that even though, by virtue of thinking out of the box, we might be asking the right questions, it does not follow that those questions are easily answered.

### 3.3   Getting the Regulatory Environment Right

For regulators who aspire to get the regulatory environment right, a Law 2.0 mindset might pose the right questions but, with rapidly developing and contested technologies, the answers can be elusive. Technology, in short, is a problematic target for regulators.[35]

---

[33] Compare Roger Brownsword, 'Human Dignity as the Basis for Genomic Torts' (2003) 42 *Washburn Law Journal* 413.

[34] Joshua Fairfield, 'Smart Contracts, Bitcoin Bots, and Consumer Protection' (2014) 71 *Washington and Lee Law Review Online* 36, 39.

[35] For a thoughtful discussion, see Martin Ebers, 'Regulating AI and Robotics' in Martin Ebers and Susana Navas (eds), *Algorithms and the Law* (Cambridge University Press 2020) 37.

Everyone wants 'better' regulation. Everyone wants regulation that is effective and 'fit for purpose'. Everyone wants regulation that is targeted, sustainable and connected. No one wants over-regulation; and no one wants under-regulation. However, the starting point has to be the legitimacy and acceptability of the purposes and policies that drive the regulatory enterprise and the acceptability of the positions taken up by regulators. In other words, it is with regulatory legitimacy that we must start, and then we can think about the challenges of regulatory connection and regulatory effectiveness.[36]

### 3.3.1  Regulatory Legitimacy and the Triple Licence for New Technologies

Elsewhere, I have argued that regulatory legitimacy hinges on the measures in question – whether employed by public or by private regulators – and the applications and uses of particular technologies satisfying the terms of a triple licence.[37]

The first and most important element of the triple licence is that the measures or applications in question must be compatible with respect for the preconditions of human social existence (with the preconditions that constitute the global commons).[38] The second strand of the triple licence, the community licence, demands that, within a particular community, the measures or applications should be compatible with the fundamental values of that community – with the values that give the community its

---

[36] For these generic challenges of regulation, see Roger Brownsword, *Rights, Regulation and the Technological Revolution* (Oxford University Press 2008); and Roger Brownsword and Morag Goodwin, *Law and the Technologies of the Twenty-First Century* (Cambridge University Press 2012).

[37] Roger Brownsword (n 5) and 'Law, Technology, and Society: In a State of Delicate Tension' (2020) 36 *Politeia* 26.

[38] To avoid any misunderstanding, it should be emphasised that, in my usage, 'the global commons' is not to be limited to, or equated with, 'the international spaces situated beyond the limits of national jurisdiction, open to use by the international community and closed to appropriation by treaty or custom'. Compare Scott Shackelford, *Governing New Frontiers in the Information Age* (Cambridge University Press 2020) xxii–xxiii. Rather, compare Karen Yeung, 'Why Worry about Decision-Making by Machine?' in Karen Yeung and Martin Lodge (eds), *Algorithmic Regulation* (Oxford University Press 2019) 42, cautioning that we should not ignore the possible systemic risks arising from algorithmic decision-making and saying that 'if we fail to ensure that adequate safeguards are put in place, [this] may erode our moral, cultural, and political foundations (the "commons") which could fatally undermine our democratic political system and with it our individual freedom, autonomy, and capacity for self-determination which our socio-cultural infrastructure ultimately seeks to nurture and protect'.

distinctive identity, that make it the particular community that it is (in the way, for example, that the EU has articulated its distinctive values in the Charter of Fundamental Rights).[39] Finally, the third element of the triple licence is the social licence, a licence that hinges on regulators reaching a reasonable accommodation of whatever plurality of views (for example, views about the importance of innovation and the balance of benefits and risks) there might be in their community (and which they identify through their consultative and deliberative processes).

While the criteria relating to the first-tier commons licence are cosmopolitan and non-negotiable, the criteria relating to the community and the social licences are contingent, depending on the fundamental values and interests recognised in each particular community. Conflicts among commons-related interests, community values, and individual or group interests are to be resolved by reference to the lexical ordering of the tiers: interests in a higher tier always outrank those in a lower tier (first-tier commons interests outranking all other interests, and second-tier community values outranking the mere interests of individuals or groups). Granted, this does not resolve all issues about trade-offs and compromises because we still have to handle horizontal conflicts *within* a particular tier; but, by identifying the tiers of the triple licence, we take an important step towards giving some structure to the bigger picture of regulatory legitimacy.

Now, it is sometimes said that we need to have a new social contract or compact for the application of modern technologies;[40] the triple licence might be presented as just such a contract or compact. However, it needs to be understood that the first element of the licence is fundamental to each and every community's contract; this is a non-negotiable standard term. Once we get to the second and third elements of the licence, each community has some freedom to take its own distinctive position. It is, of course, essential that the fundamental values to which a particular community commits itself, or its accommodations of plurality, are consistent

---

[39] 2012 OJ C-326/391 https://eur-lex.europa.eu/legal-content/EN/TXT/?uri=CELEX%3A12012P%2FTXT (accessed 22 August 2021). For the relationship between community values, expressed in a constitutional form, and the commons conditions, see Roger Brownsword, 'Migrants, State Responsibilities, and Human Dignity' (2021) 34 *Ratio Juris* 6.

[40] See, for example, Anneke Lucassen, Jonathan Montgomery and Michael Parker, 'Ethics and the Social Contract for Genomics in the NHS' (*Annual Report of the Chief Medical Officer 2016: Generation Genome*) https://assets.publishing.service.gov.uk/government/uploads/system/uploads/attachment_data/file/631043/CMO_annual_report_generation_genome.pdf (accessed 19 January 2021).

with (or cohere with) the commons conditions. Provided that this is the case, then regulatory legitimacy turns on maintaining fidelity with the community's constitutive values and taking up positions that are somewhere in the range of reasonableness. No doubt, there will be many interpretive questions here, but the exercise is internal to the commitments of the particular community and its practice in accommodating competing and conflicting interests. Accordingly, in principle, the fundamental values of Community A might be quite different from those of Community B and again from those of Community C; and the practical accommodations in Community A might also be different from those reached in Community B and again in Community C. At this level, there can be a plurality of communities each with their own distinctive community and social licences.

To elaborate on this picture of plurality, while the regulatory environment will reflect a mix of local politics, preferences and priorities, we can identify three generic desiderata – or, at any rate, these are desiderata for communities in which citizens expect to enjoy the benefits of innovation but also expect technologies to be safe and applied in ways that respect fundamental values. Here, regulators will face a triple demand:

- to support rather than stifle beneficial innovation;
- to provide for acceptable management of risks to human health and safety and the environment; and
- to respect fundamental community values (such as privacy and confidentiality, freedom of expression, liberty, justice, human rights and human dignity).

The challenges of these three demands reside both in the tensions *among* them and in the tensions hidden *within* them.[41]

Regulators will find that while the innovation lobby will argue for light-touch regulation (for strong intellectual property rights, for tax breaks, for subsidies, and so on), other parties will argue that (a) there need to be proper *ex ante* risk assessments and precautions in place and (b) adequate regulatory oversight might be needed to protect fundamental values. This, it will be said, demands a 'proportionate' response by regulators, weighing the burden on innovators (and, possibly, the delayed public enjoyment of benefits) against community concerns for safety and

---

[41] See Roger Brownsword, 'Law, Regulation, and Technology: Supporting Innovation, Managing Risk and Respecting Values' in Todd Pittinsky (ed), *Handbook of Science, Technology and Society* (Cambridge University Press 2019) 109.

respect for values. However, 'proportionality' is itself contestable and, by framing the question in these terms, we restate rather than resolve the challenge.

Tensions *among* the demands aside, each of the demands hinges on a deeply contested concept. In the case of the first demand, we should ask: what kind of innovation is 'beneficial'? Beneficial to whom, beneficial in meeting whose needs, beneficial relative to which human interests? Beneficial when – at once, within the next five years, or at some unspecified time in the future?

With regard to the second demand, we should ask: what is an 'acceptable' risk, and to whom is the burden of risk 'acceptable'? Notoriously, the view of professional risk-assessors differs from the lay view in characterising a technology as 'low risk' (inviting a leap to 'safe') as long as the likelihood of the harm is low, even though anyone would see the harm in question as extremely serious (for example, a commercial air crash is very rare but typically deadly). Moreover, how is the risk distributed? Who benefits, and who bears the risk?[42]

Last, but not least, which values are to be treated as guiding? Which value system do we support – one based on rights, one based on duties, or one geared towards maximising utility? If we base ourselves on rights, then which rights; if on duties, then which duties; and if on utility, then which variant do we adopt? If, instead, we are guided directly by values such as privacy or human dignity, liberty or justice, equality or solidarity, then which of the many conceptions of these values are to be taken as the reference standard?

It follows that there might be many triple licences, displaying different cultural preferences and different community-defining aspirations, but it bears repetition that, in all places, there should be no green light for technological measures and applications unless they meet the requirements of the non-negotiable commons licence.

### 3.3.2 Regulatory Connection

One of the distinctive challenges presented to regulators by rapidly developing modern technologies is, quite simply, the pace of their development. How do regulators get connected to these technologies, and how

---

[42] Compare Maria Lee, 'Beyond Safety? The Broadening Scope of Risk Regulation' (2009) 62 *Current Legal Problems* 242; and Jonathan Wolff, 'Five Types of Risky Situation' (2010) 2 *Law, Innovation and Technology* 151.

do they stay connected to their further articulation and application? As John Perry Barlow famously remarked: 'Law adapts by continuous increments and at a pace second only to geology in its stateliness. Technology advances in . . . lunging jerks, like the punctuation of biological evolution grotesquely accelerated. Real world conditions will continue to change at a blinding pace, and the law will get further behind, more profoundly confused. This mismatch is permanent.'[43] Whether one looks at the regulation of information technology or the regulation of biotechnology – or, for that matter, at the regulation of nanotechnology or the technologies associated with the new brain sciences, let alone blockchain, AI and machine learning – there seems to be ample support for Barlow's thesis. Indeed, it is arguable that the pace of technological development, already too fast for the law, is accelerating. While this is not an easy matter to measure, there are at least two respects in which modern information technology, in addition to being significant in its own right, plays a key enabling role relative to other technologies: facilitating basic research in biotechnology (spectacularly so in the case of sequencing the human genome) as well as the commercial exploitation of the products of other technologies.

Technology is capable of leaving the law behind at any phase of the regulatory cycle: namely, before regulators have anything resembling an agreed position, before the terms of the regulation are finalised, and once the regulatory scheme is in place. For example, a new technology might emerge very quickly, catching regulators (at any rate, national legislators) cold; or it might be that a controversial new technology develops and circulates long before regulators are able to agree upon the terms of their regulatory intervention. While regulators are getting up to speed, or pondering their options and settling their differences, the technology moves ahead, operating in what for the time being at least amounts to, if not a regulatory void, a space in need of regulatory attention. As Michèle Finck (thinking about the Internet and, potentially, distributed blockchain technologies) rightly remarks, '[w]hen systems with regulation-defiant features are adopted on a large scale, social norms will shift to reject regulatory intervention. In such a setting regulation not only becomes hard from a technical perspective; it also becomes politically unattainable.'[44]

---

[43] John Perry Barlow, 'The Economy of Ideas: Selling Wine Without Bottles on the Global Net' (*Wired*, 3 January 1994) www.wired.com/1994/03/economy-ideas/ (accessed 19 January 2021).

[44] Michèle Finck, *Blockchain Regulation and Governance in Europe* (Cambridge University Press 2019) 64.

Moreover, even (or especially) when regulatory frameworks have been put in place, they enjoy no immunity against technological change. For example, and as Emily Jackson explores in Chapter 11 in this volume, the UK Human Fertilisation and Embryology Act 1990 was overtaken by developments in embryology as well as by the unanticipated use of new embryo-screening procedures to identify embryos that would be tissue compatible with a born child needing a bone marrow transplant (the 'saviour sibling' cases).[45] For this reason, it is arguable that informal, bottom-up governance of spaces in which dynamic technological developments are anticipated is a better option – one that is likely to be more agile, more flexible, more adaptive, more responsive, more reflexive and better connected to both the technology and stakeholders – than hard-wired legislative frameworks.[46]

### 3.3.3 Regulatory Effectiveness

A good deal of research effort has been expended in tracking the impact of particular legal interventions. Some interventions work reasonably well, but many do not – many are relatively ineffective or have unintended negative effects.[47] For example, if well-intended *ex ante* regulation of health-care innovation is too complex or onerous, or the *ex post* liability regime too burdensome, this might discourage investment in what might be highly beneficial research and development. Moreover, we also know that the cross-boundary effects of the online provision of goods and services have compounded the challenges faced by regulators. If we synthesise this body of knowledge, what do we understand about the conditions for regulatory effectiveness?

First, we appreciate that the problems might lie with the regulators themselves. For example, where regulators are incompetent or corrupt (whether in the way that they set the standards or in their monitoring of compliance or in their responses to non-compliance), where they are 'captured' by regulatees or where they are operating with inadequate resources, the effectiveness of the intervention will be compromised.[48]

---

[45] For discussion, see Roger Brownsword, *Rights, Regulation and the Technological Revolution* (Oxford University Press 2008) ch. 6.

[46] Compare Laurie (2014) (n 2).

[47] See, for example, Stuart Biegel, *Beyond Our Control? Confronting the Limits of Our Legal System in the Age of Cyberspace* (MIT Press 2001); and Tom Gash, *Criminal: The Truth About Why People Do Bad Things* (Allen Lane 2016).

[48] The resourcing issue is a point made recurrently in Cristie Ford (n 23).

Second, it might be regulatees who are the problem. Generally, it seems that regulators do better when they act with the backing of regulatees (with a consensus rather than without it). The lesson of the well-known Chicago study, for example, is that compliance or non-compliance hinges not only on self-interested instrumental calculation but also (and significantly) on the normative judgements that regulatees make about the morality of the regulatory standard, about the legitimacy of the authority claimed by regulators and about the fairness of regulatory processes.[49] However, regulatee resistance can be traced to more than one kind of perspective. Business people (from producers and retailers through to banking and financial service providers) may respond to regulation as rational economic actors, viewing legal sanctions as a tax on certain kinds of conduct; professional people (such as lawyers, accountants and doctors) tend to favour and follow their own codes of conduct; the police are stubbornly guided by their own 'cop culture'; consumers can resist by declining to buy; and, occasionally, resistance to the law is required as a matter of conscience – witness, for example, the peace tax protesters, physicians who ignore what they see as unconscionable legal restrictions, members of religious groups who defy a legally supported dress code, and the like.

In all these cases, the critical point is that regulation does not act on an inert body of regulatees: in practice, regulatees will respond to regulation – sometimes by complying with it, sometimes by ignoring it, sometimes by resisting or repositioning themselves, sometimes by relocating, and so on. Sometimes, those who oppose the regulation will seek to overturn it by lawful means; at other times, by unlawful means. Sometimes, the response will be strategic and organised; at other times, it will be chaotic and spontaneous. But regulatees have minds and interests of their own; they will respond in their own way, and the nature of the response will be an important determinant of the effectiveness of the regulation.

Third, the problem might be various kinds of external distortion or interference with the regulatory signals. Some kinds of third-party interference are well-known: for example, regulatory arbitrage (which is a feature of company law and tax law) is nothing new. However, even where regulatory arbitrage is not being actively pursued, the effectiveness of local regulatory interventions can be reduced as regulatees take up more attractive options that are available elsewhere.

---

[49] Tom Tyler, *Why People Obey the Law* (Princeton University Press 2006).

Although externalities of this kind continue to play their part in determining the fate of a regulatory intervention, it is the emergence of the Internet that has most dramatically highlighted the possibility of interference from third parties. As long ago as the closing years of the last century, David Johnson and David Post predicted that national regulators would have little success in controlling extraterritorial online activities, even though those activities have a local impact.[50] While national regulators are not entirely powerless,[51] the development of the Internet has dramatically changed the regulatory environment, creating new vulnerabilities to cybercrime and cyberthreats, as well as new online suppliers and community cultures. As a result, local regulators are left wondering how they can control access to drugs, alcohol, gambling or direct-to-consumer genetic testing services when Internet pharmacies or online drinks suppliers or casinos or the like, all of which are hosted on servers that are located beyond the national borders, direct their goods and services at local regulatees.

### 3.3.4   Taking Stock

At the best of times, getting the regulatory environment right is a complex challenge. Law 2.0 is not plain sailing. When new technologies disrupt social and economic life, the particular challenges of regulatory legitimacy, regulatory connection and regulatory effectiveness (the focal conversation points in Law 2.0) are amplified. Clearly, there is a great deal more to be said about these challenges, and especially about the triple licence benchmarking of regulatory legitimacy. For present purposes, however, we have enough to set the context for the kind of conversations that we will introduce in the next part of the chapter.

## 3.4   Medical Jurisprudence and Health-Related Technologies

In this part of the chapter, we can anticipate the prospect of widespread automation of health care, with smart machines undertaking a broad spectrum of functions – making decisions about triage and treatment;

---

[50]   David Johnson and David Post, 'Law and Borders – The Rise of Law in Cyberspace' (1996) 48 *Stanford Law Review* 1367.
[51]   Compare, for example, Jack Goldsmith and Tim Wu, *Who Controls the Internet? Illusions of a Borderless World* (Oxford University Press 2006). For the important regulatory role that online intermediaries can play – in lieu of national regulatory enforcement – see Natasha Tusikov, *Chokepoints* (University of California Press 2016).

dispensing medicines; directing, informing and communicating with patients; diagnosing conditions; interpreting genetic data, brain and body images; maintaining and controlling patient records (and the data therein); undertaking surgical procedures; and so on – as a result of which humans are largely taken out of the loop.

In the first instance, these technological developments will prompt a Law 2.0 conversation where there will be much discussion about the acceptability of health-care services being delivered in this way. However, to the extent that these technological changes take on regulatory functions – for example, supplementing or replacing various health and safety rules, or making decisions about which patients should be prioritised for scarce intensive care unit (ICU) resources – it is a Law 3.0 conversation that we need to have. In both cases, Law 2.0 or Law 3.0, the fundamental question is whether any and all of these applications will qualify for the triple technological licence.

Accordingly, we begin these conversations by asking whether the technological measures or applications in question would satisfy the conditions for, respectively, a commons, a community and a social licence.

### 3.4.1   Are the Conditions for a Commons Licence Met?

The first question for regulators is whether new technologies for health care and research present any threat to the existence conditions for humans, to the generic conditions for self-development and to the context for moral development. It is only once this question has been answered that we get to the question of compatibility with the community's particular constitutive values and then, after that, to a balancing judgement. For example, if governance is to be 'human-centric', it is not enough that no individual human is exposed to an unacceptable risk or actually harmed; to be fully human-centric, technologies must be designed to respect both the commons and the constitutive values of particular human communities.

#### 3.4.1.1   The Existence Conditions

Famously, Stephen Hawking remarked that 'the advent of super-intelligent AI would be either the best or the worst thing ever to happen to humanity'.[52] As the best thing, AI would contribute to '[the

---

[52] Stephen Hawking, *Brief Answers to the Big Questions* (John Murray 2018) 188.

eradication of] disease and poverty[53] as well as '[helping to] reverse paralysis in people with spinal-cord injuries'.[54] However, on the downside, some might fear that, in our quest for greater safety and well-being, we will develop and embed ever more intelligent devices to the point that there is a risk of the extinction of humans – or, if not that, then a risk of humanity surviving 'in some highly suboptimal state or in which a large portion of our potential for desirable development is irreversibly squandered'.[55] If this concern is well-founded, then communities will need to be extremely careful about how far and how fast they go with intelligent devices.

Of course, this is not specifically a concern about the use of smart machines in hospitals: the concern about the existential threat posed to humans by smart machines arises across the board, and, indeed, concerns about existential threats are provoked by a range of emerging technologies.[56] In such circumstances, a regulatory policy of precaution and zero risk is indicated; while stewardship might mean that the development and application of some technologies that we value have to be restricted, this is better than finding that they have compromised the very conditions on which the enjoyment of such technologies is predicated.[57]

### 3.4.1.2   The Conditions for Self-Development and Agency

The developers of smart devices are hungry for data – data from patients, data from research participants, data from consumers and data from the general public. This raises concerns about privacy and data protection. A characteristic Law 3.0 response would be to check that data protection rules are fit for purpose in their protection of the interests of data subjects and, at the same time, to explore the possibility

---

[53] Ibid., 189.

[54] Ibid., 194.

[55] See Nick Bostrom, *Superintelligence* (Oxford University Press 2014) 281n. 1; and Martin Ford, *The Rise of the Robots* (Basic Books 2015) ch. 9.

[56] For an indication of the range and breadth of this concern, see, for example, 'Resources on Existential Risk', *Technologies and Policies Berkman Center for Internet and Society Harvard University* (2015) https://futureoflife.org/data/documents/Existential%20Risk%20Resources%20(2015–08–24).pdf (accessed 19 January 2021).

[57] Compare, for example, Deryck Beyleveld and Roger Brownsword, 'Complex Technology, Complex Calculations: Uses and Abuses of Precautionary Reasoning in Law' in Marcus Duwell and Paul Sollie (eds), *Evaluating New Technologies: Methodological Problems for the Ethical Assessment of Technological Developments* (Springer 2009) 175; and 'Emerging Technologies, Extreme Uncertainty, and the Principle of Rational Precautionary Reasoning' (2012) 4 *Law Innovation and Technology* 35.

of developing privacy-protecting designs.[58] However, even where there is a commitment (as in the EU) to a high level of protection for data subjects, this will be satisfactory only if regulators have a clear understanding of privacy and associated informational interests as well as a correct reading of the level of interests that are engaged.[59]

In the memorable opening pages of his monograph *Genetic Privacy*,[60] Graeme highlighted how protean a concept privacy is, with applications to both spaces and information. While it is widely accepted that our privacy interests (in a broad sense) are 'contextual',[61] it is important to understand not just that 'there are contexts and contexts' but that there is a Context in which we all have a common interest. What most urgently needs to be clarified is whether any interests that we have in privacy and data protection touch and concern the essential conditions (the Context).

If, on analysis, we judge that privacy reaches through to the interests that agents necessarily have in the commons conditions, particularly in the conditions for self-development and agency, it is neither rational nor reasonable for agents, individually or collectively, to authorise acts that compromise these conditions (unless they do so in order to protect some more important condition of the commons). As Bert-Jaap Koops has so clearly expressed it, privacy has an 'infrastructural character'; 'having privacy spaces is an important presupposition for autonomy [and] self-development';[62] without such spaces, there is no opportunity to be

---

[58] Compare Lee Bygrave, 'Hardwiring Privacy' in Brownsword, Scotford and Yeung (n 27) 755. For a recent review of the use, development and limits of a range of privacy enhancing technologies (PETs), see The Royal Society, 'Protecting Privacy in Practice' (2019) https://royalsociety.org/-/media/policy/projects/privacy-enhancing-technologies /privacy-enhancing-technologies-report.pdf (accessed 19 January 2021). One of the recommendations made in this report is that government and regulators should 'support organisations to become intelligent users of PETs'. So, for example, 'the Information Commissioner's Office (ICO) should provide guidance about the use of suitably mature PETs to help organisations minimise risks to data protection, and this should be part of the ICO's Data Protection Impact Assessment guidelines. Such guidance would need to cover how PETs fit within an organisation's overall data governance infrastructure, since the use of PETs in isolation is unlikely to be sufficient.'

[59] See Roger Brownsword, 'Infosoc 2018: Informational Rights, Informational Wrongs, and Regulatory Responsibilities' (Bournemouth University Working Papers in Law, 2018) https://microsites.bournemouth.ac.uk/law-review/files/2018/03/Infosoc-2018-wps.pdf (accessed 20 August 2020), and 'In Our Connected Societies: Respecting and Protecting Consumers and Data Subjects' (2020, on file with author).

[60] See n 3.

[61] See, for example, Daniel J. Solove, *Understanding Privacy* (Harvard University Press 2008); and Helen Nissenbaum, *Privacy in Context* (Stanford University Press 2010).

[62] Bert-Jaap Koops, 'Privacy Spaces' (2018) 121 *West Virginia Law Review* 611, 621.

oneself.[63] On this reading, privacy is not so much a matter of protecting goods (informational or spatial) in which one has a personal interest as it is about protecting infrastructural goods in which there is either a common interest (engaging first-tier responsibilities) or a distinctive community interest (engaging second-tier responsibilities).[64]

By contrast, if privacy (and, likewise, data protection) is simply a legitimate informational interest that has to be weighed in an 'all things considered' balance of interests, then we should recognise that what each community will identify as a privacy interest and as an acceptable balance of interests might well change over time. To this extent, our reasonable expectations of privacy might be both 'contextual' and contingent on social practices.

### 3.4.1.3   The Conditions for Moral Development and Moral Agency

I take it that the fundamental aspiration of *any* moral community is that regulators and regulatees alike should act on their own moral judgement, trying to do the right thing and freely doing it for the right reason. Where we are technologically assisted, it is important, as Shannon Vallor insists, that our conduct remains 'our *own conscious activity and achievement* rather than passive, unthinking submission'[65] – or, as I have argued on many occasions elsewhere, we should be concerned if technological management leaves agents with no practical option other than to do what those who manage the technology judge to be the right thing.[66] Accordingly, if automated health-care technologies relieve researchers and clinicians from their moral responsibilities, even though well-intended, this might result in

---

[63] Compare, too, Maria Brincker, 'Privacy in Public and the Contextual Conditions of Agency' in Tjerk Timan, Bryce Clayton Newell and Bert-Jaap Koops (eds), *Privacy in Public Space* (Edward Elgar 2017) 64; and, similarly, Margaret Hu, 'Orwell's *1984* and a Fourth Amendment Cybersurveillance Nonintrustion Test' (2017) 92 *Washington Law Review* 1819, 1903–4.

[64] Compare the discussion of 'mass surveillance' in European Commission, 'White Paper: On Artificial Intelligence – A European Approach to Excellence and Trust' (COM Brussels, 19 February 2020) 11 https://ec.europa.eu/info/sites/info/files/commission-white-paper-artificial-intelligence-feb2020_en.pdf (accessed 19 January 2021).

[65] Shannon Vallor, *Technology and the Virtues* (Oxford University Press 2016) 203 (emphasis in original).

[66] See, for example, Roger Brownsword, 'Code, Control, and Choice: Why East Is East and West Is West' (2005) 25 *Legal Studies* 1; 'So What Does the World Need Now? Reflections on Regulating Technologies' in Roger Brownsword and Karen Yeung (eds), *Regulating Technologies* (Hart 2008) 23; and 'Lost in Translation: Legality, Regulatory Margins, and Technological Management' (2011) 26 *Berkeley Technology Law Journal* 1321.

a significant compromising of their dignity, qua the conditions for moral agency.[67]

### 3.4.2    Are the Conditions for a Community Licence Met?

Although many think that 'personalised' medicine is the future, we should ask whether the technologies that enable personalised medicine are compatible with the distinctive values of our particular community. As Karen Yeung asks, is the use of automated personalisation techniques 'compatible with, or antagonistic to, the basic right of all human beings to be treated with equal concern and respect'?[68] Possibly, as Yeung suggests, the answer to this question will vary from one social and political context to another. This difficulty notwithstanding, it is a question that must be asked before a community licence can be granted.

In line with this, in its White Paper on AI, the European Commission recurrently insists that AI should be 'based on European values',[69] implicitly inviting consultees to respond by reference to their understanding of European values. According to the Commission, 'it is vital that European AI is grounded in our values and fundamental rights such as human dignity and privacy protection'.[70] Elaborating on this, it continues:

> The use of AI can affect the values on which the EU is founded and lead to breaches of fundamental rights, including the rights to freedom of expression, freedom of assembly, human dignity, non-discrimination based on sex, racial or ethnic origin, religion or belief, disability, age or sexual orientation, as applicable in certain domains, protection of personal data and private life, or the right to an effective judicial remedy and a fair trial, as well as consumer protection.[71]

Relative to such community values, then, we might wonder whether automated health care comports with respect for human dignity. For example, what should we make of the views of one of Sherry Turkle's interviewees, 'Richard', who seems to prefer less adequate human carers to more caring robots?[72] As Turkle reads Richard's views:

---

[67] Compare Karen Yeung and Mary Dixon-Woods, 'Design-Based Regulation and Patient Safety: A Regulatory Studies Perspective' (2010) 71 *Social Science and Medicine* 502.

[68] See n 38 at 37.

[69] European Commission (n 64) 1. Notably, the constitutional commitments in Article 2 TEU, and in the Charter of Fundamental Rights (n 39).

[70] Ibid., 2.

[71] Ibid., 11.

[72] Sherry Turkle, *Alone Together* (Basic Books 2011).

> For Richard, being with a person, even an unpleasant, sadistic person, makes him feel that he is still alive. It signifies that his way of being in the world has a certain dignity, even if his activities are radically curtailed. For him, dignity requires a feeling of authenticity, a sense of being connected to the human narrative. It helps sustain him. Although he would not want his life endangered, he prefers the sadist to the robot.[73]

The problem is that robots and smart machines might provide excellent care for patients, but the fact of the matter is that humans know that machines, even intelligent machines, 'do not really care'.[74] As with the case of personalised care, it is not entirely clear whether the use of caring robots engages only matters of personal preference or whether it goes deeper to community-defining values such as human dignity; and if the latter, then it remains to determine how such a contested concept is to be interpreted and applied in particular cases. Again, though, none of these difficulties exempt regulators from asking the questions.

### 3.4.3   Are the Conditions for a Social Licence Met?

Within each community, there will be many debates about questions that do not implicate either the commons conditions or the community's particular fundamental values. Judgements about benefits and risks, and about the distribution of benefits and risks, might be varied and conflictual. In many communities, these questions will be managed by a process of inclusive consultation and democratic deliberation structured by a concern that the governing regulatory framework should not 'over-regulate' and risk stifling potentially beneficial innovation; but nor should it 'under-regulate' and expose citizens to unacceptable risks.[75]

It is imperative, of course, that the interests brought into the balance are not higher-tier values or conditions. For example, in its report on *Ethics Guidelines for Trustworthy AI*,[76] the European Commission's independent high-level expert group on AI takes it as axiomatic that the development and use of AI should be 'human-centric'. To this end,

---

[73] Ibid., 281–2.

[74] Compare Roger Brownsword (n 28).

[75] As Mario Martini puts it in 'Regulating Algorithms' in Ebers and Navas (n 35) 135: 'What is needed ... is a healthy balance between the risk of suffocating innovation and the foundations of a digital humanism. In the tradition of the Enlightenment era, the categorical imperative should point the way ahead for the digital world. Technology should always serve the people – not the other way around.'

[76] European Commission (Brussels, 8 April 2019) https://ec.europa.eu/digital-single-market/en/news/ethics-guidelines-trustworthy-ai (accessed 19 January 2021).

the group highlights four key principles for the governance of AI, namely: respect for human autonomy; prevention of harm; fairness; and explicability. Where tensions arise among these principles, they should be dealt with by 'methods of accountable deliberation' involving 'reasoned, evidence-based reflection rather than intuition or random discretion'.[77] Nevertheless, it is emphasised that there might be cases where 'no ethically acceptable trade-offs can be identified. Certain fundamental rights and correlated principles are absolute and *cannot be subject to a balancing exercise* (e.g. human dignity).'[78] Accordingly, regulators need to be sensitive to 'red lines' or 'third rails' in their communities where fundamental values are engaged.

In its White Paper on AI, which builds on the expert group's report, the Commission proposes a risk-based approach such that 'the new regulatory framework for AI should be effective to achieve its objectives while not being excessively prescriptive [and disproportionately burdensome]'.[79] It follows that regulators should focus on high-risk uses of AI. Paradigmatically, such uses will involve some high-risk activity in a high-risk sector. Thus, while health care is a high-risk sector, some uses of AI are less risky than others. As the Commission notes, 'a flaw in the appointment scheduling system in a hospital will not normally pose risks of such significance as to justify legislative intervention'.[80] Presumably, this would contrast with, say, the use of AI in surgical procedures where a patient's life might be at stake if 'something goes wrong'. In these paradigmatically high-risk cases, human oversight is required. In the Commission's own words: '[t]he objective of trustworthy, ethical and human-centric AI can only be achieved by ensuring an appropriate involvement by human beings in relation to high-risk applications'.[81]

That said, if the accommodation of interests is to be adequate, it might not be enough that there is human involvement in relation to health-care outcomes (or products) – to be acceptable, human involvement in the process might also be very important.[82] Consider, for example, the case of Ernest Quintana. At the particular Californian hospital where Ernest was

---

[77] Ibid., 13.
[78] Ibid. (emphasis added).
[79] European Commission (n 64) 17.
[80] Ibid.
[81] Ibid., 21.
[82] Indeed, this is a key point that emerges from the liminality research; see McMillan et al (n 21); and compare Yeung (n 38).

a patient, his family were shocked to learn that a 'robot' displaying a doctor on a screen was used to tell Ernest that the medical team could do no more for him and that he would soon die.[83] What should we make of this? Should we read the family's shock as simply expressing a preference for the human touch – for a particular kind of process or mode of communication – or as going deeper to the community's constitutive values or even to the commons conditions? Depending on how this question is answered, regulators will know whether a simple balance of interests is appropriate. They will know which element of the triple licence is at issue.

### 3.4.4 Taking Stock

In our illustrative conversation, we have more questions than answers. Decentring humans, entrusting health-care and regulatory functions to smart machines, is no small matter. Regulators need to be sure that their communities are ready for such changes to the delivery of health care and the governance of health-related matters. Even if regulators are satisfied that, having consulted with their communities, they can sign off on the terms of a social licence for automation, they still need to be sure that a proposed application is consistent with the community's constitutive values and compatible with respect for the global commons. While much more could be said about the triple licence – for example, about the way in which the scheme helps us to understand which aspects of the regulatory enterprise are cosmopolitan and which are local; what is really 'exceptional' about pandemics; how we should now interpret appeals to the public interest; and so on[84] – perhaps the most important point is that the scheme is an antidote to a tendency to resort to a 'flattening' and 'balancing' of interests. While we can be quite good at recognising the range of competing and conflicting interests at stake, we are not so good at recognising the different levels, weights and significances of these interests. This is already a problem in Law 2.0, but it becomes even more important in Law 3.0, where technological tools are being used

---

[83] See Michael Cook, 'Bedside Manner 101: How to Deliver Very Bad News' (*Bioedge*, 17 March 2019) www.bioedge.org/bioethics/bedside-manner-101-how-to-deliver-very-bad-news/12998 (accessed 7 April 2020).

[84] For further consideration of some of these questions, see Roger Brownsword (n 39); and Roger Brownsword and Jeffrey Wale, 'In Ordinary Times, in Extraordinary Times: Consent, Newborn Screening, Genetics, and Pandemics' (2021) *BioDiritto* 129.

for regulatory purposes, to retrieve a sense of the depth of particular interests.

## 3.5   Liminality and Law

With both liminality and my proposed (technology-sensitive) field of legal inquiry, we have examples of thinking out of the box, of seeing a familiar picture in a different light. However, what if we use the lens of liminality to view the field comprising Laws 1.0, 2.0, and 3.0? Bearing in mind the familiar caution that once we have a hammer, everything starts to look like a nail, I suggest that liminality provokes questions about at least three significant features of the field. These features relate to transitional processes, to phenomena that fall in between organising conceptual frameworks or categories, and to parties who can facilitate transition.

One of the standard examples of liminality is the transition of humans from childhood to adulthood with whatever rites of passage are customary in a particular community. In my proposed field of legal inquiry, there are two difficult transitions: from Law 1.0 to Law 2.0, and from Law 2.0 to Law 3.0. In both cases, we can say that what has been 'the centre' of law is no longer so. In Law 1.0, it is the courts, judges, cases, precedents and principles that are central; but, in the transition to Law 2.0, none of these remains central. Instead, it is the legislature, the politicians and government policy that are at the centre. This is not to say that the mindset of Law 1.0 is no longer important. Far from it; during the transition, judges will regard legislation as an exception to the common law, to be treated with suspicion, to be interpreted restrictively, and so on. However, adjusting to a world of shared legal competences is no easy transition. That said, the transition to Law 3.0, where it is humans and rules that are being decentred, is even more difficult. No wonder, as we have seen in the previous part of the chapter, that we cling to the idea that smart machines should operate in a human-centric way. We are in a liminal space, and on the other side of the space, even if the machines do not kill us, not only are we humans no longer at the centre of the legal action but it is also moot whether we will still be 'in control'.[85]

Liminality is sensitive to persons or phenomena that fall between categories. In the standard example of a teenager who might not yet be

---

[85]   See the fine analysis in Hin-Yan Liu, 'The Power Structure of Artificial Intelligence' (2018) 10 *Law, Innovation and Technology* 197, 222; and the reservations expressed in Rebecca Crootof '"Cyborg Justice" and the Risk of Technological-Legal Lock-In' (2019) 119 *Columbia Law Review* 1.

an adult but who is also no longer a child,[86] the context is a linear process in which one stage (and category) follows another. However, we can also find cases of 'in-between' phenomena in contexts that are not linear in this way – for example, we might say that AI-enabled devices are more than mere tools but without assuming that they are on the way to becoming human beings.[87] Similarly, in health care, we can face classificatory problems with an innovation that is neither a drug nor a device, or a procedure which is neither established clinical practice nor research, and so on.

Problems of this kind can arise in relation to any conceptual scheme, whether it derives from the principles of Law 1.0 or from the bespoke regulatory frameworks of Law 2.0. Taking this a step further, it would be interesting to take a harder look at the possibilities that we now have for multiple framings of issues. Some of these framings are invited within a particular regulatory framework (as with data protection, where issues can be framed in a transactionalist way with consent being central or in a regulatory way with reasonable practice and legitimate interest being central), or they can arise between different regulatory frameworks (as with devices and drugs), or it might be a choice between a Law 1.0 framing and a Law 2.0 approach,[88] or, again, it might be the coexistence of different logics in Law 1.0 and Law 3.0 that provides the options.[89] As if this were not enough, the triple licence scheme, which is integral to my understanding of regulatory legitimacy, invites contestation around what

---

[86] A puzzle famously addressed in *Gillick* v. *West Norfolk and Wisbech Area Health Authority* [1986] AC 112.

[87] See, for example, Mireille Hildebrandt, *Smart Technologies and the End(s) of Law* (Edward Elgar 2015).

[88] For a fine example of principled contractual Law 1.0 thinking coming into tension with Law 2.0 regulatory reasoning, see Catharine MacMillan, 'The Mystery of Privity: *Grand Trunk Railway Company of Canada v Robinson* (1915)' (2015) 65 *University of Toronto Law Journal* 1.

[89] See, for example, Roger Brownsword, 'Smart Contracts: Coding the Transaction, Decoding the Legal Debates' in Philipp Hacker et al (eds), *Regulating Blockchain: Technosocial and Legal Challenges* (Oxford University Press 2019) 311; and 'Smart Transactional Technologies, Legal Disruption, and the Case of Network Contracts' in Larry di Matteo, Michel Cannarsa and Cristina Poncibò (eds), *The Cambridge Handbook of Smart Contracts, Blockchain Technology and Digital Platforms* (Cambridge University Press 2019) 313. While I cannot here say more about the 'legacy' effects of earlier ideal-typical mindsets on later ideal-typical mindsets, this is clearly a feature of the coexistence of these different mindsets and their respective articulations. In a Law 3.0 conversation, whether or not these legacy effects are judged to be positive or negative (an encumbrance) will depend on a number of considerations, but the crucial question should be whether or not they assist compliance with the conditions of the triple licence.

is a condition of the commons, what is a community value and what is a mere interest. Moreover, as we have seen, there are values that might be plausibly argued to engage more than one tier of this scheme. Liminality, it might be said, is ubiquitous in the field of law so conceived.

Finally, how are we to negotiate all of this? In the case of Law, it is not simply a matter of facilitating the transition towards Law 3.0. Unlike textbook liminal processes, there is no inevitability about making this transition. We need to be sure that the use of technological solutions is compatible with the maintenance of the global commons, and each community should address the question of the kind of society that it distinctively wants to be – doing all that, moreover, in a context of rapid social and technological change. As Wendell Wallach rightly insists:

> Bowing to political and economic imperatives is not sufficient. Nor is it acceptable to defer to the mechanistic unfolding of technological possibil-ities. In a democratic society, we – the public – should give approval to the futures being created. At this critical juncture in history, an informed conversation must take place before we can properly give our assent or dissent.[90]

Yet, with no established forum for an informed Law 3.0 conversation, who will facilitate more general participation in the debates that need to be had? So long as law schools see their principal mission as being to train prospective legal practitioners to think in a Law 1.0 way, they will not be the facilitators. However, this seems to me to be a missed opportunity. Many law schools already view their mission in terms of putting law 'in context' and it is a short, but vital step to including technology within that context. If law schools were to reimagine their mission, they could become – and, of course, I would argue that they *should* become – key facilitators of a properly informed and inclusive Law 3.0 conversation.[91]

### 3.6   Conclusion

In this chapter, I have spoken to the many welcome legacies of Graeme Laurie's scholarship. Although Graeme has made more than his fair share of contributions to commentary on and analysis of those high-profile

---

[90] See Wendell Wallach, *A Dangerous Master* (Basic Books 2015) 10.
[91] For elaboration, see Roger Brownsword, 'Teaching the Law of Contract in a World of New Transactional Technologies' in Warren Swain and David Campbell (eds), *Reimagining Contract Law Pedagogy: A New Agenda for Teaching (Legal Pedagogy)* (Routledge 2019) 112.

cases that are the landmarks of medical law, his work reflects the view that medical jurisprudence should be more than a manual of time-honoured precedents and principles.

For my own part, I have argued that medical jurisprudence also needs to speak to the challenge of getting the regulatory environment right and especially so when new technologies, carrying both potential health-care benefits and potential risks, are coming on stream so rapidly. It is not just clinicians and researchers who should try to avoid harming their patients and participants while trying to benefit them or others; regulators, too, have responsibilities for supporting beneficial innovation while also ensuring that new technologies (whether employed in health-care practice or as regulatory tools) meet the conditions of what I have termed the triple licence.

Above all, this chapter is a tribute to Graeme's willingness to think out of the box that is Law 1.0. Once we think outside that box, there is an opportunity to maintain the relevance and critical power of medical jurisprudence as the conversation moves on: first becoming more regulatory, as in Law 2.0, and then turning to technology as a regulatory tool in Law 3.0. We need to reimagine what is involved in 'thinking like a lawyer' and it is in boldly going beyond doctrinal commentary that I see the enduring legacy of Graeme Laurie's scholarship.

# 4

## The Public Interest in Health Research

### From Concept to Context

ANNIE SORBIE

## 4.1 Introduction

I had never met Graeme Laurie until I came to work with him. There is some circularity here, as this is how Laurie describes his introduction to the late and great Professor Ken Mason in 1995, almost twenty years previously.[1] We had spoken, though – a telephone call while I was visiting family – to discuss an opportunity to join his Wellcome-funded Liminal Spaces project to pursue a PhD on the concept of 'the public interest'. As I stood in a cramped hallway, surrounded by holiday detritus, Graeme and Gill Haddow conducted what I later realised was, in all but name, an interview. For my part, I was struck immediately by two things about the man. First was his enthusiasm for medical law and ethics and, in particular, how this could usefully be brought to bear on health research regulation (HRR). This intellectual curiosity was evident in his openness to different perspectives, both within and beyond the academy; in my case, insights from a related area of legal practice. Despite coming from different starting points, Graeme and I both approached 'medical jurisprudence' as a broad church. The cases I dealt with in practice reached across areas of law and were not confined to the traditional doctor-patient relationship. Nor was the advice I provided exclusively on 'the law'; ethical, social and political considerations and contexts were often as, if not more, important. As elaborated in this chapter, this would prove to be an excellent fit with Graeme's commitment to interdisciplinary research, and his appreciation of both the role and the limitations of the

---

[1] Graeme Laurie, 'The Autonomy of Others: Reflections on the Rise and Rise of Patient Choice in Contemporary Medical Law' in Sheila McLean (ed), *First Do No Harm: Law, Ethics and Healthcare* (Routledge 2006) 131.

law. Second was his almost superhuman ability to detect and tease out the kernel of an idea. And a great deal of teasing was required as I struggled to translate my practical experiences of the law and regulation into the language of academic discourse.

It was the thorny issue of the public interest that led to our paths crossing. In the abstract, this enigmatic concept presents very real challenges: it is uncertain and changeable, hard to define and deeply contextual. Indeed, the public interest is more likely to elicit exasperation from colleagues – as those from different disciplines talk across one another – than enthusiasm. However, despite this (or perhaps because of this), the public interest also speaks to one of the central challenges of medical jurisprudence – the relationship between individual and collective interests. This is a consideration that runs through myriad areas of study and practice in health, where our focus shifts from the traditional doctor-patient encounter to matters that engage wider community interests. Consider, for example, the allocation of health resources or, rather topically at the moment, public health interventions to control the spread of contagious disease. Graeme has been at the forefront of these considerations in HRR, where the turn towards large-scale projects, combining data and/or tissue from many thousands of participants, often across national borders, has created an environment where the individual consent encounter (between a researcher and a participant) may no longer be practical or meaningful. In looking beyond the 'consent or anonymise' binary,[2] he has underlined the need to identify new governance mechanisms that can engage with the multiple interests engaged; one candidate that emerges is the public interest.

One aspect of the legacy of Graeme's work on the role of the public interest has been to reinvigorate this previously neglected concept in HRR. His research has delivered new and innovative governance frameworks that are able to meet the challenges of health research in the twenty-first century. However, his legacy can also be seen in his commitment to capacity building through his intellectual and practical support for colleagues. Through the Liminal Spaces project, Graeme has created a space for others to engage in further work on this topic, both locally and internationally, thus inspiring a wider community of scholars. In this chapter, I reflect on Graeme's work on the public interest, with a specific focus on his commitment to the shift from the law on the page to the law

---

[2] Graeme Laurie, 'Liminality and the Limits of Law in Health Research Regulation: What Are We Missing in the Spaces in-Between?' (2017) 25 *Medical Law Review* 47, 52.

in action. Here I could draw on any number of texts from his corpus of research, but I restrict myself to first considering his framing of the public interest in his 2002 monograph *Genetic Privacy and the Law: A Challenge to Medico-legal Norms*.[3] Graeme has developed his ideas from this book in various ways but, given my focus on his commitment to the operationalisation of the public interest, I consider in particular his work with the Scottish Informatics Programme (SHIP)[4] and the Administrative Data Research Network (ADRN) Scotland.[5]

## 4.2   The Public Interest: A Concept Within and Beyond the Law

Graeme's willingness to tackle contested concepts that are hard to pin down can be seen in his treatment of privacy in *Genetic Privacy*. Here, he scrutinises privacy not only as a concept in its own right but also as one that is deeply contextual and has implications for established principles (and key areas) in medical jurisprudence, such as patient autonomy and confidentiality.

   Within the first few pages of *Genetic Privacy*, Graeme deftly characterises the problems caused by privacy and points in particular to the exacerbation of these, given the 'group nature'[6] of claims in relation to familial genetic information. The unique definition of privacy that he proposes there is explored elsewhere in this present volume, as are the ways that his analysis underpins subsequent developments in the area of familial genetic information. However, there is much here too for the public interest scholar. From the outset, Graeme directly engages with the tensions created at the public/private interface:

> [W]hile individual interests are given more importance in democratic communities, public interests are, at the same time, afforded greater weight. This increases tension at the interface between the public and private areas of life and requires that we define as clearly as possible where the boundaries of the two spheres lie. It is a function of privacy to provide a mechanism to ensure that such boundaries are well constituted.[7]

---

[3] Graeme Laurie, *Genetic Privacy: A Challenge to Medico-legal Norms* (Cambridge University Press 2002), referred to hereafter as 'Genetic Privacy'.
[4] (2009–13) www.scot-ship.ac.uk/index.html (accessed 21 January 2021).
[5] (2015–18) http://masoninstitute.org/our-research/administrative-data-research-centre-scotland-adrc-s/ (accessed 21 January 2021).
[6] Laurie (n 3) 4.
[7] Ibid., 10.

Given the significant contribution made by Graeme's thesis to the advancement of the concept of privacy, one might not expect also to find such careful attention to the public interest. However, his reader finds development of this concept here, both within and beyond the law, as well as consideration of how this may be operationalised in order to deliver real-world benefits. These three features of Graeme's work are addressed in this chapter. In particular, I highlight how his work on the public interest has stood the test of time, both legally (in view of subsequent case law) and contextually (with reference to his broader conceptualisation of the public interest in the context of HRR).

I turn first to the case law on which Graeme relies in order to develop his approach to the public interest at the start of *Genetic Privacy*. In particular, he refers to *X* v. *Y*,[8] in which the High Court granted the application of a health authority for an injunction to prevent a newspaper publishing the names of two doctors in general practice who were receiving treatment for AIDS. The Court acknowledged that it had to balance 'various competing public interests',[9] both in the freedom of the press and in public debate but also in the preservation of individuals' confidentiality so that medical attention could be sought without fear of this being revealed. This multifaceted conception of the public interest, as further developed by Graeme in his work, remains good law. Indeed, this approach has been reflected in case law that followed the publication of his book. The House of Lords' consideration of *Campbell* v. *MGN Ltd*[10] concerned the publication by a newspaper of pictures of the supermodel Naomi Campbell emerging from a Narcotics Anonymous meeting. Unlike *X* v. *Y*, *Campbell* was litigated after the enactment of the Human Rights Act 1998, engaging both Article 8 (right to respect for private and family life) and Article 10 (freedom of expression) of the European Convention on Human Rights (ECHR).[11] While the absorption of these rights into the common law action for breach of confidence gave this 'new strength and breadth',[12] we still observe the Court undertaking a balancing exercise, albeit now with reference to ECHR rights, of

---

[8] [1988] 2 ALL ER 648.
[9] Ibid., [25].
[10] [2004] UKHL 22.
[11] In *Genetic Privacy* (n 3), Laurie does consider the earlier case of *Douglas and Others* v. *Hello! Ltd* [2001] 2 All ER 289, which was also considered after the enactment of the Human Rights Act 1998. He comments (at 249) that '[i]t remains to be seen what the UK courts will make of this right'.
[12] [2004] UKHL 22 [32] citing *A* v. *B plc* [2002] EWCA Civ 337; [2003] QB 195, 202, para 4.

the multiple interests at stake. By a slim majority of three to two, the House of Lords reversed the decision of the appeal court and found that that publication by the *Mirror* newspaper was an infringement of Campbell's Article 8 right, for which she was entitled to damages.

The more recent case of *Lewis* v. *Secretary of State for Health* also echoes this pluralistic approach to the public interest in a slightly different context.[13] Here, the High Court had to decide whether it should authorise the disclosure of deceased patients' medical records to the Redfern Inquiry (a UK inquiry into the removal of tissue for analysis from individuals who had worked in the nuclear industry). Again, the judge recognised the multiple public interests at play, though ultimately found that he had 'not the slightest doubt that this is an appropriate case in which to hold that the public interest in disclosure of the material sought outweighs the other public interest, namely, that of maintaining the confidentiality of medical records and information, provided, of course, proper safeguards are put in place to ensure that no inappropriate information becomes public'.[14] Together, this run of case law, both before and following the publication of Graeme's monograph, emphasises the inherent flexibility of the public interest in law, as it is deployed in different contexts.

However, Graeme's work also offers a broader conceptualisation of the public interest in the context of health, and its ability to account for, rather than necessarily polarise, public and private interests. This second feature of his work is illustrated as he steps outside of the courtroom in order to consider the public interest in its broader socio-political setting. He acknowledges that the relationship between public and private interests may, at first blush, appear an uneasy one, noting that '[p]aradoxically ... it is the development of a public interest in the welfare of individuals that has proved to be one of the greatest threats to individual privacy in the last century'.[15] Those who know Graeme may permit themselves a wry smile at the reviewer who described his views as 'rather worryingly Thatcherite'[16] when he remarked that 'Western societies are typified by a glut of legislation stemming from paternalistic attitudes of the state towards its citizens. Thus, we find legislation prohibiting or severely restricting sales of alcohol and other drugs, limiting

---

[13] [2008] EWHC 2196 (QB).

[14] Ibid., [58].

[15] Laurie (n 3) 9.

[16] Donna Dickenson, 'Book Review: Genetic Privacy: A Challenge to Medico-legal Norms' (2003) 29 *Journal of Medical Ethics* 373.

the purchase of lottery tickets, and requiring the wearing of seat belts or safety helmets when using motor vehicles.'[17] Nonetheless, he goes on to stake his claim that 'just as there are public and private reasons to protect privacy, the effective protection of privacy can serve both public and private ends'.[18] In *Genetic Privacy*, Graeme further develops this claim in the context of health with specific reference to the use of familial genetic information. However, with the benefit of hindsight, we can also see how embedded this thinking has become in the realm of HRR more broadly. For example, the main statutory objective of the Health Research Authority, as set out in the Care Act 2014, now encompasses the dual aims of protecting participants and the public, and promoting these interests in the conduct of safe and ethical research.[19]

A third feature of Graeme's work is his commitment to tackling the difficulties inherent in operationalising the public interest. His engagement with the messiness of the real world is evident when he notes: '[t]he classic tension is that between the public interest in protecting private interests such as privacy and confidentiality, and the promotion of other public interests that protect the community from harm and further its collective interests. However, the devil is in the detail of determining what is meant by public interest in each case.'[20] In considering this question, Graeme analyses, amongst other initiatives, the operation of the Icelandic Health Sector Database.[21] He also nods to a new 'Population Biomedical Collection in the United Kingdom involving up to 500,000 participants',[22] which would go on to become the UK Biobank.[23] This shift from the law on the page to the law in action is a recurrent theme that can be seen throughout Graeme's work and is typified by his collaborative work, as described further in Section 4.3. In this way, he challenges us not only to engage in rigorous conceptual work but also to take the next step to ascertain how this can be operationalised to deliver good governance. As he notes, in doing so we must both acknowledge the role of the law and recognise that this is only 'one piece in the puzzle':[24] 'Law has its limits, and an examination of these is as much a part of the search for an answer as is

---

[17] Laurie (n 3) 9.
[18] Ibid., 10.
[19] Care Act 2014, s 110.
[20] Laurie (n 3) 279.
[21] Ibid., ch. 5.
[22] Ibid., 297.
[23] Laurie went on to chair the UK Biobank Ethics and Governance Council from 2006 to 2010. See further Chapter 14 in this volume.
[24] Laurie (n 3) preface.

a thorough examination of any statute or bod of case-law . . . ultimately it is in the exploration of the limits of legal intervention that the symbiosis of privacy and law will be found.'[25]

In Section 4.3, I consider two examples of Graeme's work – SHIP and the ADRN – where the public interest has been leveraged within broader governance frameworks in HRR, with reference to both the role and the limits of the law.

## 4.3   The Public Interest in Action: Towards Good Governance in HRR

SHIP was an interdisciplinary collaboration that involved researchers around Scotland in partnership with NHS Scotland.[26] Graeme and Nayha Sethi led the information governance research stream of this project, which aimed to build better systems for the safe, efficient and productive use of health data for research purposes. In presenting their research, they delivered a comprehensive survey of the legal and policy data sharing landscape in their first working paper, noting the complexity that this has generated: '[t]he many different actors, vague and sometimes conflicting rules/guidance and difficulty reconciling privacy and public interest considerations all add to the labyrinthine structure of the law and considerable confusion in practice'.[27]

Now set in a profoundly practical context, Graeme's conceptual work from *Genetic Privacy* is evident in the unpacking of (among other issues) the concept of the public interest and its potential to encompass both public and private interests. In particular, he and Sethi posit that '[t]here is a public interest both in advancing medical research and in ensuring adequate protection of individual privacy and these should be balanced against each other'.[28] Further, they conclude their first working paper thus: '[r]espect for patient privacy and the public interest are both core guiding principles[;] whilst they are often competing considerations, a balance between the two should be sought'.[29]

---

[25]  Ibid., 26–7.
[26]  www.isdscotland.org/Products-and-Services/eDRIS/SHIP/ (accessed 21 January 2021).
[27]  Graeme Laurie and Nayha Sethi, 'Information Governance of Use of Health-Related Data in Medical Research in Scotland: Current Practices and Future Scenarios' (*SHIP Core Programme 2 Working Paper No. 1 Wellcome Trust*, 2011) 9 www.scot-ship.ac.uk/publica tions.html (accessed 21 January 2021).
[28]  Ibid., 21.
[29]  Ibid., 88.

Building on this work, their second working paper further develops the public interest in two key ways: first, as a threshold concept 'which – if not met – will automatically result in rejection of a research proposal'.[30] Second, the paper underlines the need for good governance frameworks 'to promote a defensible view of public interest and to require applicants to demonstrate sufficiently that their research promotes public interests, or at least has a reasonable likelihood of doing so'.[31] Here, the work is not only conceptually robust but also determinedly normative. The Governance Impact Assessment that resulted from the earlier work on SHIP proposes ten core questions that challenge stakeholders to test potential governance models and whether they are fit for purpose.[32] It pushes back against the 'law first' approach: in identifying six overarching features of a robust governance system, the need for governance to be, among other matters, 'transparent and accessible' and 'understandable and navigable' comes before the final requirement that it should be 'legal and ethical'.[33] This realignment of the law as 'a piece of the puzzle' exposes the tendency discussed elsewhere in Graeme's work for concerns (whether well founded or not) around complex legal frameworks to manifest themselves in a culture of caution where 'doing nothing *is* an option'.[34]

A second key output from this research was the Good Governance Framework (GGF),[35] which consists of four components: '(1) Guiding Principles and Best Practice; (2) Safe, Effective and Proportionate Governance; (3) Roles and Responsibilities of Data Controllers and (4) Researcher Training'. The GGF was launched in 2012 and not only facilitated 'faster, more transparent and consistent access to researchers, within and beyond the NHS'[36] but also directly informed Scottish

---

[30] Graeme Laurie and Nayha Sethi, 'Information Governance of Use of Health-Related Data in Medical Research in Scotland: Towards a Good Governance Framework' (*SHIP Core Programme 2 Working Paper No. 2 Wellcome Trust*, 2012) 19 www.scot-ship.ac.uk/publications.html (accessed 21 January 2021).

[31] Ibid., 19.

[32] Laurie and Sethi (n 27) including, for example: '[h]ow does the model reflect public expectations and impact on public confidence?' (89).

[33] Ibid.

[34] Annie Sorbie et al, 'Examining the Power of the Social Imaginary through Competing Narratives of Data Ownership in Health Research' (2021) *Journal of Law & the Biosciences*, https://doi.org/10.1093/jlb/lsaa068 (emphasis in original).

[35] Laurie and Sethi (n 30).

[36] Andrew Morris, 'Case Study 6: Delivering the Good Governance Framework of the Scottish Health Informatics Programme (SHIP)' (*Research Excellence Framework*) 3 https://impact.ref.ac.uk/casestudies/CaseStudy.aspx?Id=23972 (accessed 21 January 2021).

government policy on data access and linkage. The work on data linkage has subsequently been endorsed internationally, by the Council of Canadian Academies[37] and by Ireland's Health Research Board.[38] These reports also acknowledge the contribution of the work of Administrative Data Research Network (ADRN) Scotland, where Graeme led the legal work package.[39] Here, too, the public interest was operationalised to deliver good governance, this time in the context of administrative data.

ADRN Scotland was one of four Administrative Data Research Centres established in each of the countries of the UK in order to 'facilitate linkage of routinely collected administrative data, thereby stimulating opportunities for innovative research and policymaking'.[40] At the time, little attention had been given to the governance of the broader category of administrative data, as compared to health data specifically. The first SHIP working paper referenced this lacuna, noting that, while SHIP was delivered in the specific context of health data for research, 'the lessons that can be learned from our work – and the model that we proffer – are applicable to a much broader range of governance settings, such as local authority and other public/private instances of data sharing'.[41]

If the challenges of governing health data are significant, those relating to the broader category of administrative data (with health data being a subset of this) are manifold. In particular, Graeme and Leslie Stevens highlight that 'the public sector operates within a widely documented "culture of caution" surrounding the retention and use of administrative data, where concerns are fuelled not by the law or actual procedures of data sharing but rather ... the perceptions of risk by all parties that will come from actually attempting to do so'.[42] One might wonder, then, whether two lawyers are best placed to propose solutions where

---

[37]  Council of Canadian Academies, 'Accessing Health and Health-Related Data in Canada: The Expert Panel on Timely Access to Health and Social Data for Health Research and Health System Innovation' (Ottawa, 2015) www.research.ed.ac.uk/portal/files/21835672/ HealthDataFullReportEn.pdf (accessed 21 January 2021).
[38]  Rosalyn Moran, 'Proposals for an Enabling Data Environment for Health and Related Research in Ireland: A Discussion Document' (Health Research Board Ireland 2016) www .hrb.ie/fileadmin/publications_files/Proposals_for_an_Enabling_Data_Environment _for_Health_and_Related_Research_in_Ireland.pdf (accessed 21 January 2021).
[39]  Graeme Laurie and Leslie Stevens, 'Developing a Public Interest Mandate for the Governance and Use of Administrative Data in the United Kingdom' (2016) 43 *Journal of Law and Society* 372.
[40]  Ibid., 362.
[41]  Laurie and Sethi (n 27) 1.
[42]  Laurie and Stevens (n 39) 362.

ostensibly the law is not the problem? Perhaps unsurprisingly (and also as a lawyer!), I would suggest that, to the contrary, it is in situations such as this that Graeme's approach – which recognises the symbiotic relationship among law, ethics and data sharing cultures – is most needed. In this case, and as a first step towards transforming cultures around administrative data sharing, they propose a decision-making template 'that consolidates the complex legal and ethical considerations at stake when data custodians must decide whether to permit use of administrative data for research purposes'.[43] At the heart of this is a commitment to a 'public interest mandate' to shift the focus away from 'partial legal solutions' and towards meaningful changes to organisational cultures.[44] Here, the public interest is deployed not as an additional regulatory regime and/or burden but, rather, as a device that can refocus stakeholders' attention to the multiple (public) interests that are at stake.[45] Echoing earlier literature, it is made clear that 'the public interest lies in both the robust protection of individual privacy and uses of data that stand to result in wider public benefit'.[46]

Some examples of the types of research use that this may include are offered, though the temptation to offer an overly prescriptive definition of the public interest is resisted. Instead, it is made clear that this will need to be determined on a case-by-case basis by organisations in line with their own values and the contexts in which they operate. Again, the shift from the theoretical to the practical is evident in the normative claims that those who hold data should publicly and transparently commit themselves to the safe and ethical use of data in the public interest, and those who seek data must clearly articulate the public interest benefits of their work. This, it is argued, can cultivate a shared vision for data use both internally, within organisations, and externally, with publics and other stakeholders.[47]

## 4.4  Implications for Medical Law: Liminal Spaces and Beyond

The preceding discussion has focused on just a small subsection of Graeme's corpus of research in HRR since the publication of *Genetic Privacy* in 2002. However, even this brief consideration has demonstrated his contribution to the development of the concept of the public interest, both within and beyond the law, and his commitment to

---

[43] Ibid., 364.
[44] Ibid., 365.
[45] Ibid., 387.
[46] Ibid.
[47] Ibid., 388.

operationalising this to deliver good governance. In doing this, I have illustrated the continuing relevance of Graeme's research and how, through his work with SHIP and then ADRN Scotland, he has reinvigorated a previously neglected concept and positioned it as a worthy candidate for further scrutiny in HRR. Graeme's work has delivered and informed new and innovative governance frameworks, such as the GGF, that are able to meet the challenges of sharing and linking health and administrative data for research in the twenty-first century, both nationally and internationally.

In this final section, I will further consider the legacy of Graeme's work on the role of the public interest with a focus on how he has inspired and continues to inspire a community of scholars through his leadership of the Wellcome-funded Liminal Spaces project,[48] which launched in 2014. First, I will consider the international reach of his work, with a focus on his curatorship of the World Congress of Bioethics that convened in Edinburgh in 2016, before ending with some more personal reflections on Graeme's legacy in my own work.

Liminal Spaces was a culmination of Graeme's work in HRR: an ambitious project to deliver the first-ever integrated, interdisciplinary and cross-cutting analysis of HRR as it impacts on the realisation of extraordinary improvements in human health. Graeme leveraged his previous experience of interrogating the gaps between documented law and research practice in order to promote a holistic approach, which had been absent in HRR. Using the metaphor of 'regulatory liminal spaces', he identified four kinds of regulatory gap that exist between documented law and everyday health research practice: clogged spaces, empty spaces, transitional spaces and dangerous spaces. The Liminal Spaces project was motivated by a concern that HRR has thus far failed to capture core individual and collective values, and the public interest explicitly features in the fourth strand – dangerous spaces – where he asked: how can public interest and public benefit be more effectively reflected in HRR?

Shortly after I joined the project, Edinburgh hosted the 13th World Congress of the International Association of Bioethics in Edinburgh in June 2016, with Graeme and Nayha Sethi at the helm.[49] This international meeting of more than 700 delegates was shaped around the theme

---

[48] www.law.ed.ac.uk/research/research-projects/liminal-spaces/ (accessed 4 September 2021).

[49] Edward Dove et al, 'Conference Report: 13th World Congress of the International Association of Bioethics, Edinburgh 14–17 June 2016 (IAB2016)' (2016) 13 *SCRIPTed* 202.

'Individuals, Public Interests and Public Goods', drawing on the interplay between autonomy and the rights of the individual, on one hand, and wider public interests and/or public benefits, on the other. The Wellcome-funded Liminal Spaces symposium 'What Does It Mean to Regulate in the Public Interest?' brought together an international and interdisciplinary group of scholars who each responded to this question by reflecting on diverse areas of HRR.[50] With characteristic intellectual generosity, Graeme asked me to chair this event, and a number of the symposium's contributors feature elsewhere in this volume. The preceding discussion of Graeme's work makes it plain how his influence can be seen in the two key themes that emerged from the symposium discussions:

> This first is that the public interest need not be balanced against private or personal interests. Using the anthropological concept of liminality to probe this further, we would suggest that if the health research regulatory landscape is reimagined as a coherent whole, with multiple interests in play, we can continue to deepen our understand of the public interest as a concept. This leads us to the second theme that emerged, namely a commitment on the part of the speakers to reintegrate the concept of the public interest to real world practice, and to consider how this concept could deliver tangible benefits, whether this be in the context of data sharing, health research participation, proportionate governance or organ donation.[51]

The symposium also framed a statement of intent for future work in the Liminal Spaces project, which has since been delivered in a number of ways, both within and beyond the team.[52] In the remainder of this chapter, I focus first on the collective work of the Liminal Spaces team on a Delphi study, and then on Graeme's influence on my own collaborative and individual work.

Our Delphi study was conceived to leverage the skills of the different disciplinary backgrounds of researchers within the Liminal Spaces team. As such, we aimed to deliver the first interdisciplinary and cross-cutting analysis of HRR as it is experienced by stakeholders in the UK context.[53] In relation to the public interest, among other contested concepts and

---

[50] Annie Sorbie, 'Conference Report: Liminal Spaces Symposium at the IAB 2016: What Does It Mean to Regulate in the Public Interest?' (2016) 13 *SCRIPTed* 374.

[51] Ibid., 380.

[52] Laurie has also worked extensively with colleagues at the National University of Singapore – see, for example, Owen Schaefer et al, 'Clarifying How to Deploy the Public Interest Criterion in Consent Waivers for Health Data and Tissue Research' (2020) 21 *BMC Medical Ethics* 1.

[53] Isabel Fletcher et al, 'Co-production and Managing Uncertainty in Health Research Regulation: A Delphi Study' (2020) 28 *Health Care Analysis* 99.

practices, we sought to better understand and unpack how this was enacted in HRR in order to animate this concept. In our findings, we identified that our participants reached strong agreement or consensus on seven statements, including that '[v]alues such as the public interest and public benefit as used in health regulation need further elaboration in practice (73.9%)'.[54] Interestingly, we also found marked disagreement or divergence among our participants, in that at least a quarter agreed and the same number disagreed on points such as that '[r]egulatory frameworks help researchers to focus on delivering public benefits and interests'.[55]

In considering the overarching theme of regulatory uncertainty, we identified that conceptualisations of the public interest were often considered by participants alongside practices of involvement, while identifying the need for greater clarity around both of these in HRR. This underlines the interconnectedness of different approaches in this context, and how these may bear upon and inform one another, thus directing us to look at governance holistically. This scrutiny of the ways that concepts are used and constructed, both within and across disciplines, has proven to be a recurring theme in my collaborative and individual work. This is best illustrated by two recent publications on the topic of health data sharing: first, on how notions of ownership can impact upon stakeholders' willingness to share health data; and second, on the role of the public interest.

The first collaborative example of our research on how concepts in HRR are understood and operationalised is provided by the Wellcome-funded *DataTerms* project. Here, Graeme and I worked with David Townend, who led the project (and who also co-contributes Chapter 17 in this volume), and Wifak Gueddana, a social scientist. This research responded to the funder's experience that, in discussions around the use, reuse and sharing of health data in research, terminology was frequently used in relation to the 'ownership' of data sets, and more specifically (though anecdotally) as a barrier to sharing. In our co-authored article, we reported on original empirical research that responded to the question: in health research, in what ways, if at all, do notions of ownership (broadly conceived) of health-related data impact on sharing practices?[56] By exploring stakeholders' hopes, promises and expectations through the

---

[54] Ibid., 104.
[55] Ibid., 105.
[56] Sorbie et al (n 34) 1.

paradigm of 'competing narratives', we found that formal legal property-type appeals to ownership appear to have far less power in the narratives about data than the ethical and social concerns that underpin responsible biomedical research. Graeme and David, with their characteristic generosity, invited me, at the time relatively new to the academy, to use my own research to shape the direction of the project and later to take the lead on our co-authored article. However, this research bears a number of Graeme's hallmarks: international collaboration, willingness to look beyond the law and openness to using a range of disciplinary approaches to tackle a 'real-world' problem.

This invaluable experience links to my second example, a sole-authored article that stemmed from my experiences of working in multidisciplinary teams and observing different approaches to shared concepts, such as the public interest, both from my time in practice and also in the academic sphere.[57] In particular, I became interested in the apparent disconnect between legal notions of what purports to be in the public interest and the empirical views of actual publics. While a narrow 'inward-looking' legal conception of the public interest may be criticised for lacking social legitimacy, it was clear, too, that it was problematic simply to extrapolate outputs from public engagement work into policy or law. Given the limitations of each of these accounts of the public interest, I reframed the discussion through the application of a processual approach, drawing attention to the ways in which multiple actors, processes and interests interact, change and evolve over time in the health research endeavour. This shed light on how legal notions of the public interest, and attitudes of actual publics towards data sharing, might in fact be reconciled. Through this analysis, I argued that understanding the ways in which the public interest can be crafted both within and beyond the law helps to better inform the development of health research regulation. In many ways, this article was where I found my own voice on the role of the public interest in HRR. Within the supportive academic research environment engendered by Graeme's leadership, I was able to reach beyond disciplinary boundaries to articulate my early intuitions around the public interest. This was an extension of my previous research on novel data sharing initiatives,[58] and

---

[57] Annie Sorbie, 'Sharing Confidential Health Data for Research Purposes in the UK: Where Are "Publics" in the Public Interest?' (2019) 16 *Evidence and Policy* 249.

[58] Annie Sorbie 'Medical Data Donation, Consent and the Public Interest After Death: A Gateway to Posthumous Data Use' in Jenny Krutzinna and Luciano Floridi (eds), *The Ethics of Medical Data Donation* (Springer Philosophical Studies Series 2019) 115, www.ncbi.nlm.nih.gov/books/NBK554077/.

a gateway to subsequent work on the development of the public interest as a core concept in HRR.[59]

## 4.5   Final Thoughts

The preceding discussion, first of Graeme's individual work and then of his collaborative work, makes plain the influence that he has had on my own research in HRR. It was the Liminal Spaces project that provided me with the intellectual (and economic) breathing space to do this work. But Graeme's influence also stretches far beyond the topic of the public interest, and even HRR: there are even more fundamental elements of his approach that have influenced, and will continue to bear upon, my own. In particular, there are two phrases that I am sure will be familiar to those of us who have had the benefit of working with Graeme. As I type, I can hear them both in my head in his accent, which is emblematic of the west coast of Scotland.[60]

'So what?' At first blush, this line of enquiry may sound a little abrupt, but our discussions on these important points – *what is the problem that requires attention? why now? why does it matter?* – are always softened by good coffee (and/or good wine!) and good humour. As can be seen from his own track record, Graeme has led by example here, consistently seeking to operationalise concepts that may otherwise remain dormant and fail to realise their transformational potential. He has pushed me to carve out my own contribution to the development of the concept of the public interest, and how it can be animated in order to ensure that governance structures are able to keep apace of the health research landscape.

'Be bold!' This is perhaps a particularly important reminder for law-yers, as we may be tempted to remain within the familiar territory of carefully parsed legislation and case law. However, Graeme demonstrates that law is a piece of the puzzle, the importance of which should be neither overlooked nor overblown. His work has illustrated how the law may be characterised (or indeed caricatured) as being variously 'the problem' or 'the solution', when in reality it is almost always part of a bigger picture. This openness – to consideration of both the strengths

---

[59] Annie Sorbie, 'The Public Interest' in Graeme Laurie et al, *The Cambridge Handbook of Health Research Regulation* (Cambridge University Press 2021).

[60] By coincidence, both my father and Graeme are from Prestwick, a seaside town on the west coast of Scotland, though I should make it clear that Graeme is, of course, *by far* the younger of the two.

and the limitations of the law – has translated to my work in two key ways.

The first is one of approach and the need to bring to bear the full range of methodological tools at our disposal in order to unpick complex real-world problems. Graeme's commitment to interdisciplinary research can be seen in his large-scale collaborations, such as SHIP and ADRN, as well as in his stewardship of the Liminal Spaces team, comprising lawyers, ethicists, philosophers and social scientists. In my own work, I have learned that ambitious and truly interdisciplinary collaborations take trust, patience and a willingness from all involved to step outside of our comfort zones. However, the return on this commitment is the production of truly innovative work, where the sum is greater than the parts. The second is a reflection of Graeme's own determinedly normative approach blended with a commitment to delivering outputs with practical significance. In this way, he has also challenged me not only to engage in rigorous theoretical work around the public interest but also to consider how, in concrete ways, this concept can facilitate the conduct of responsible health research.

Looking back to that telephone call in a hallway, it has a certain 'sliding doors' quality to it, in that, in some ways, it was unremarkable – a discussion about an exciting but abstract opportunity – yet, in other ways, it changed everything: a new country, a new career. It was apparent to me immediately that Graeme would be an excellent principal investigator and colleague, but I did not know that he would also become my mentor and friend. I recall one conversation in particular, during which we talked about the type of academic we wanted to be. I am not sure that before that point I had even realised that this was a choice to be made. We considered the relative merits of, among other things, publishing in 'the best' journals, carrying out meaningful and impactful research, and making a difference in policy and law. By any measure, Graeme has excelled in all of these areas. However, what transcends these individual achievements is his desire not only to contribute himself but to contribute collectively and collaboratively in order to pave the way for others to do so, too. Graeme has undertaken this role for me, and also for countless others, both intellectually, in terms of his ideas and outputs, and practically, in terms of the support he has offered as we have forged our own careers. If legacy is understood not only as something that connects us to what has gone before and enables us to move forward with the benefit of that wisdom but also as a means of community building and facilitating future progress and innovation, then this is indeed what Graeme has accomplished.

# Taking the Legacy Forward

### Reflections on Graeme Laurie's Approach to Liminality and Its Relevance for the Ethics and Governance of Reproductive Technologies

CATRIONA MCMILLAN AND AGOMONI GANGULI-MITRA

## 5.1 Introduction

In February 2014, Graeme Laurie was awarded a Wellcome Senior Investigator Award in Medical Humanities, entitled *Confronting the Liminal Spaces of Health Research Regulation*. The Liminal Spaces project,[1] which began in October 2014, set out to provide the first-ever interdisciplinary, cross-cutting analysis of health research regulation (HRR) by confronting the 'gaps' between law and research in practice. As principal investigator (PI), Graeme managed a team of eight PhD students and research fellows, including both of us. It is with a sense of great fondness that we write this chapter, for not only has Graeme's project shaped our own work, but he himself has acted as our 'academic steward' at the start of our careers. It is indeed befitting that we write this chapter at this stage, having both recently been led out of our own liminal identities as researchers. Throughout our challenging, rewarding and occasionally uncertain career pathways, Graeme has acted not only as an outstanding PI and manager but also as a dedicated and caring mentor and friend. In this chapter, we reflect on Graeme's work on liminality and the wider contributions that it has made to the field of HRR and beyond, by drawing on its relevance for our own shared research interest: the ethics and governance of human reproduction.

Liminality is a concept developed by French anthropologist Arnold van Gennep in his seminal work *The Rites of Passage*,[2] an ethnographic work

---

[1] WT103360MA (2014–21) www.liminalspaces.ed.ac.uk/ (accessed 19 February 2021).

[2] Arnold van Gennep, *The Rites of Passage* (University of Chicago Press 1960 [1909]).

published in the early twentieth century exploring ritual practices in tribal communities across the globe. Van Gennep posited that when human beings transition from one social status to another, such as from childhood to adulthood, the following three-stage pattern always occurs: 'the [i] rites of separation from a previous world, *preliminal rites*, those executed during the [ii] transitional stage *liminal* (or *threshold*) rites, and the [iii] cere-monies of incorporation into the new world *post-liminal rites*'.[3] For van Gennep, the second stage signified the crossing of a threshold,[4] a change of status, and a moment of *becoming* 'which disturbs the life of society and the individual'.[5] He noted that the function of these rites of passage was to reduce the harmful effects of that disruption. The presence of an inde-pendent actor to guide those experiencing transition is a central feature of liminality literature, the actor sometimes referred to as the 'Master of Ceremonies'.[6] Building on this, in the mid-twentieth century, the anthro-pologist Victor Turner developed liminality in the context of non-ritual societies.[7] He suggested that the liminal space is one where existing constraints and norms cease to apply.[8] Liminality is therefore accompan-ied by the dissolution of established hierarchies and social order, and the time-space in which it occurs can be viewed as a nexus for transformation and reflection.[9] Where liminality is triggered by chaos or crisis, or where a clear end point (third phase, see above) is not clear, liminality literature has taught us that three features might emerge: (i) 'permanent liminality'; (ii) the rise of a 'trickster'; and (iii) 'mimesis', a tendency towards an imitative pattern of behaviour in the absence of a clear path to take out of liminality.[10] Liminality does not explain social phenomena;[11] rather, it

---

[3] Ibid., 21.

[4] The term 'liminality' derives from the Latin for threshold: 'limen'.

[5] van Gennep (n 2) 13.

[6] Arapd Szakolczai, 'Liminality and Experience: Structuring Transitory Situations and Transformative Events' in Agnes Hovarth, Bjørn Thomassen and Harald Wydra (eds), *Breaking Boundaries: Varieties of Liminality* (Berghahn Books 2015) 18.

[7] Victor Turner, *The Ritual Process: Structure and Anti-structure* (Aldine Transaction 1969).

[8] Ibid., 95.

[9] Samuel Taylor-Alexander et al, 'Beyond Regulatory Compression: Confronting the Liminal Spaces of Health Research Regulation' (2016) 8 *Law, Innovation and Technology* 149.

[10] Graeme Laurie, 'How Do We Make Sense of Chaos? Navigating Health Research Regulation through the Liminality of the Brexit Process' (2018) 18 *Medical Law International* 110.

[11] See Bjørn Thomassen, *Liminality and the Modern: Living Through the in-Between* (Ashgate 2014) 7.

allows us to examine them. In other words, liminality just *is*. The lasting relevance of this concept to transformations within society is evidenced by its development by scholars such as Turner[12] and, much later, Thomassen,[13] Rabinow,[14] Szakolczai[15] and Squier,[16] among others.[17] Through his distinctive interdisciplinary approach to legal scholarship (discussed in Chapter 1 of this volume), Graeme drew on these scholars, and many others, across a multiplicity of disciplines to build on liminality even further in the context of HRR.

In the following sections, we explore the legacy of Graeme's work, both individual and collaborative, on the Liminal Spaces project through three examples. First, we briefly highlight some of the key themes that arose out of this project and their legacy for HRR. This is followed by two examples on the ethics and regulation of human reproduction. First, in the context of surrogacy, we consider the various liminal identities brought on by the practice of surrogacy, and the different ways in which such liminality is mediated by the presence of various actors, interests and regulatory spaces. We then highlight the resonance of liminality for the regulation of ectogenesis, whereby the process of gestation occurs *ex utero* in an artificial womb. Although this technology is not yet possible, recent advances call us to examine how it might be regulated if and when it becomes a reality. A liminal lens, as applied to technology (which has the potential to disrupt the gestational process as we know it), challenges us to ask critical questions surrounding existing legal paradigms for the threshold for personhood and legal rights. Each example draws on some of the key themes arising from the project including the processual, the marginal, uncertainty, thresholds, the experiential and the quality of 'in-between-ness', all of which may be found in the daily practice of health research. In this way, we aim to illustrate not only the importance of the legacy of certain concepts in ongoing academic research but also the legacy left by a scholar's engagement with such concepts in ways that inspire and shape future academics.

---

[12] Turner (n 7).

[13] Thomassen (n 11).

[14] Paul Rabinow, *French DNA: Trouble in Purgatory* (University of Chicago Press 1999).

[15] See Szakolczai (n 6).

[16] Susan Squier, *Liminal Lives: Imagining the Human at the Frontiers of Biomedicine* (Duke University Press 2004).

[17] See, for example, Paul Stenner and Eduard Moreno-Gabriel, 'Liminality and Affectivity: The Case of Deceased Organ Donation' (2013) 6 *Subjectivity* 229.

## 5.2 Liminality: A Legacy for Health Research Regulation

Health research is subject to a plethora of legal and quasi-legal instruments worldwide, at both national and international levels. In the UK, there is an array of structures and actors implementing these instruments, including the Medicines and Healthcare Products Regulatory Agency,[18] the Human Fertilisation and Embryology Authority[19] and the Human Tissue Authority.[20] It is to these complex regulatory *spaces* – it would be a misnomer to call this vast network of enterprises *the* regulatory space[21] – that Graeme has devoted much of his writings over the years. Some of these spaces have emerged in response (some would say in knee-jerk fashion) to scandals (for example, Alder Hey) or otherwise from a diverse research agenda. In sum, this has resulted in a collection of piecemeal, somewhat disconnected legislation and regulatory frameworks. For Graeme, the research 'problem' for the Liminal Spaces project was law's tendency to fix artificially constructed 'objects' of health research within a series of 'largely disconnected ecosystems', where each silo (for example, 'tissue', 'embryo', 'data') is separately regulated. Indeed, '[a] multiplicity of regulators attach to these legislative structures creating not only a highly complex and tightly regulated landscape, but also an associated taxonomy of regulated "objects" such as "data", "tissue", "embryos", "devices", "ATMPs", and "clinical trials", each bounded by its own legal definition and bespoke sets of regulatory rules of production, storage, use, and market approval'.[22] While each of these spaces is engaged in the same endeavour, there are few means to learn lessons among them.[23] Additionally, creating silos where regulatory categories themselves create the bounded objects that are the focus of governance results in largely overlooking a key aspect of health research – human beings – who as both participants and researchers undergo 'potentially transformative' processes by engaging in research.[24] The regulatory taxonomy described above makes the research 'object' (for

---

[18] Charged with implementing the EU Medical Device Regulation, for example (Regulation 2017/745/EU on medical devices, 2017 OJ L117/1).

[19] Given its powers under the Human Fertilisation and Embryology Act 1990 (as amended).

[20] Instituted by the Human Tissue Act 2004, which followed the Bristol and Alder Hey organ scandals. See further Chapter 9 in this volume.

[21] Graeme Laurie, 'Liminality and the Limits of Law in Health Research Regulation: What Are We Missing in the Spaces in-Between?' (2016) 25 *Medical Law Review* 47, 50.

[22] Laurie (n 21) 48–9.

[23] Ibid.

[24] Ibid., 70.

example, embryo, tissue, personal data) rather than the 'subject' (the embodied person) the focus of regulatory attention.[25] As such, the Liminal Spaces project set out to examine, and to understand more deeply, the spaces in between the regulatory 'silos' that have been created in health research. It was Graeme's belief, and one that team members embraced, that the concept of liminality captured an important, previously neglected feature of the *experiential* nature of research. Treating human research as a liminal process and experience is crucial not only in order fully to appreciate the human dimensions of research but also as a key to understanding why certain aspects of research and research governance either fail or continue to operate sub-optimally.

Since HRR is an inherently human and experiential process, value and guidance may be found in looking across regulatory landscapes, as well as in viewing these regulatory space(s) as a holistic enterprise bound up with human experiences. It allows us to make the invisible *visible*, such as when we cast a light on the underappreciated role of 'regulatory stewards'[26] in HRR (be they Research Ethics Committee chairs or managers, or managers in the Medical Research Council's Regulatory Support Centre). The concept of liminality also proved to be a useful lens through which to examine another aspect of HRR governance: the ethics of research and, more specifically, both ethics approval of research and the social value of health research. Viewing ethics approval of health research as a form of 'rite of passage', we come to see it as a process that transforms patients or healthy volunteers into the role of research participants.[27] This speaks to the experiential nature of health research. Additionally, liminality allows us to shed a new light on the concept of social value, a key component to the justification of health research as an endeavour, as well as for specific studies and protocols. What justifies research is its social value, the prospect of research resulting in generalisable knowledge that will benefit future patients. The path to knowledge generation can be fraught with unexpected turns, including serendipitous findings and unexpected outcomes, and once research has been

---

[25] See also Catriona McMillan et al, 'Beyond Categorisation: Refining the Relationship between Subjects and Objects in Health Research Regulation' (2021) 13(1) *Law, Innovation and Technology* 194.

[26] See Graeme Laurie et al, 'Charting Regulatory Stewardship in Health Research Regulation: Making the Invisible Visible' (2018) 27(2) *Cambridge Quarterly Healthcare Ethics* 333; Edward Dove, *Regulatory Stewardship of Health Research: Navigating Participant Protection and Research Promotion* (Edward Elgar 2020).

[27] Agomoni Ganguli-Mitra et al, 'Reconfiguring Social Value in Health Research through the Lens of Liminality' (2017) 31 *Bioethics* 87.

approved and has begun, it enters a liminal phase (with an unknown outcome). The nature and scope of social value therefore evolve and should be revisited and reviewed, with the concepts of both 'social' and 'value' dynamic to a certain degree, and constantly in the making.[28]

For some scholars, liminality is not always positive. As mentioned earlier, 'mimesis', 'permanent liminality' or the 'trickster' may emerge where there is no clear path out of liminality. For Szakolczai, where there is no possibility for a 'leading out' of liminality, 'permanent liminality' may occur, that is, a state of permanent crisis or chaos.[29] In this state, a 'schism' may occur, where groups 'split off'.[30] These analogies were particularly pertinent to Graeme's work on the liminality of Brexit, which for him was 'quintessentially a liminal moment in (European) human history'.[31] HRR is of course a central feature of the contributions of EU law to the UK; the standards in EU regulatory frameworks, such as the General Data Protection Regulation[32] and the Clinical Trials Regulation,[33] represent the 'gold standard' of robust and ethical scientific research worldwide since the end of World War II. Yet the longevity of these contributions to UK regulatory frameworks was thrown into a state of uncertainty when, on 23 June 2016, 52 per cent of the British electorate voted to leave the EU. In the following years, the UK government's public dialogue failed to capture concerns surrounding how the complexities of HRR, which will be profoundly impacted by the Brexit process, would be tackled. It is this key problem that Graeme addressed.[34] Whether at a 'macro level' – the status of the UK in Europe and the world – or on the 'micro level' of particular regulatory frameworks, a clear *telos* or end point for the liminal process of Brexit must be identified.[35] As he concluded:

> For citizens facing the liminality of the Brexit process, this suggests that the need for a representative of order has never been greater. Moreover, liminal processes predict the emergence of tricksters who seek to take

---

[28] Ibid., 90.
[29] Arpad Szakolczai, *Reflexive Historical Sociology* (Routledge 2000) 220.
[30] Victor Turner, *From Ritual to Theatre: The Human Seriousness of Play* (PAJ Books 1982) 104.
[31] Laurie (n 10) 118.
[32] Regulation 2016/679/EU on the protection of natural persons with regard to the processing of personal data and on the free movement of such data, 2016 OJ L119/1.
[33] Regulation 536/2014/EU on clinical trials on medicinal products for human use, 2014 OJ L158/1.
[34] Laurie (n 10) 110.
[35] Ibid., 133.

advantage of uncertainty and emerging chaos. In the health research context, this means that it is all the more incumbent on local agents and actors – such as current regulators – to assume the role of representatives of order.[36]

A key point that Graeme makes here, and throughout his work, is that a reversion to law for comfort in times of uncertainty such as this can be a 'misguided step'.[37] A liminal lens, as applied to HRR, invites a 'radical rethinking about how health research is experienced. This ... demands that law and legal architectures accommodate liminal regulatory spaces, even when these appear antithetical to the commonly accepted social roles of law itself.'[38] As the Liminal Spaces project's Delphi exercise showed, embracing uncertainty – and moving away from strict rule-based regimes and 'compliance culture' – may represent a brighter future for health research.[39]

A liminal lens, for Graeme, highlights the tendency of law and regulation to 'fix' regulatory objects and, moreover, divorce them from their source, the research subject. For him, 'both of these points suggest a need to approach the management of regulation in processual and potentially transformative terms'.[40] The notion of 'processual regulation' was developed in various ways throughout the project, by individual and team works.[41] Its key contribution in each iteration is a way of thinking about law in more reflexive terms, in a way that places the human experience centrally in the governance of health research. This culminated in the project's final major output, *The Cambridge Handbook of Health Research Regulation*,[42] which offers a collection of writings from contributors across the globe that analyse key concepts, and stubborn and emergent issues in HRR, with a view to exploring what a 'Learning Health Research Regulation System'[43] could look like.

---

[36] Ibid.

[37] Ibid.

[38] Laurie (n 21) 71.

[39] Isabel Fletcher et al, 'Co-production and Managing Uncertainty in Health Research Regulation: A Delphi Study' (2020) 28 *Health Care Analysis* 99.

[40] Laurie (n 21) 68.

[41] See Taylor-Alexander et al (n 9); Catriona McMillan, *The Human Embryo in vitro: Breaking the Legal Stalemate* (Cambridge University Press 2021); Annie Sorbie, 'Sharing Confidential Health Data for Research Purposes in the UK: Where Are "Publics" in the Public Interest?' (2020) 16 *Evidence and Policy* 249.

[42] Graeme Laurie et al (eds), *The Cambridge Handbook of Health Research Regulation* (Cambridge University Press, 2021).

[43] See Graeme Laurie, 'Introduction', ibid.

At the time of this volume's publication, the Liminal Spaces project will have drawn to a close after a successful six-plus years. The concept and the legacy of liminality in the context of health continue, however, to resonate with our own work. The broad applicability of liminality and the lessons from the project's collective research beyond the realms of HRR speak to Graeme's scholarly intuition in identifying and developing concepts and ideas that meaningfully engage with a wide range of scholarship. They also testify to the legacy of his skilled mentorship. It is with great pleasure that, in the rest of this chapter, we progress the resonance of liminality for our own research.

## 5.3   Exploring the Many Liminalities of Surrogacy

The regulation of women's bodies and reproductive labour is fraught not only with ethical and legal concerns but also with considerable political interests, exposing the governance of new reproductive technologies and intervention to myriad ethical and legal tensions. The interests of those most closely involved and affected are sometimes in danger of falling through the gaps created by this potentially chaotic ecosystem. Surrogacy – especially international, contract-based surrogacy – is subject to a variety of regulatory instruments which, much like the silos created by HRR, give rise to spaces that are often devoid of systematic governance structures. The details of a surrogacy agreement, parental rights, the rights and interests of surrogates, and the citizenship of children born of surrogacy, among other aspects, are often left to national regulation, which is subject to strong political and economic interests and which can, at times, conflict with other regulatory regimes across the world. In the absence of harmonised global instruments, the practice has proliferated within the private health sector and in specific regions of the world, often moving away from regulations that are considered restrictive,[44] or countries where the costs of surrogacy are considered prohibitive,[45] to regions where both regulation and costs are perceived as more welcoming. These newly formed spaces, though mediated by national and international structures, engage the interests of a variety of actors, including surrogates, commissioning parents, physicians, surrogacy brokers and lawmakers. Such spaces are also populated by various

---

[44]  Emily Jackson, 'UK Law and International Commercial Surrogacy: "The Very Antithesis of Sensible"' (2016) 4 *Journal of Medical Law and Ethics* 199.

[45]  Vida Panitch, 'Global Surrogacy: Exploitation to Empowerment' (2013) 9 *Journal of Global Ethics* 329.

kinds of liminal identity (for example, 'couple as prospective parents', 'surrogate as both mother and provider of a service', 'physician as innovator'), each of which exists in a state of in-between.

Until recent legislation, which has sought to curb the surrogacy sector heavily,[46] India was a particularly attractive destination for prospective parents. The surrogacy sector flourished under a pro-business political and economic culture, as well as a lack of legislation governing a million-dollar industry, leaving 3,000-plus surrogacy clinics largely to self-regulate, and surrogates to look after their own interests through surrogacy contracts.[47] These empty regulatory spaces have given rise to several high-profile cases, including the abandonment of children and children being left stateless as a result of conflicting national laws.[48] Engaging with surrogacy, especially contract-based pregnancies, as a processual endeavour allows us to recognise the various liminal identities of the actors involved, set in motion when an agreement for surrogacy is negotiated and eventually reached. Prospective parents, sometimes referred to as commissioning parents, having faced years of disappointment, enter a liminal phase characterised by hope and concern, teetering for months on the verge of potential parenthood. Their identities as parents are dependent on a successful pregnancy, on surrogates willing to give up the baby, and on regulation allowing for their formal recognition as parents. They are parents-in-waiting, in expectation of their lives to begin. Surrogacy is different from traditional methods of entering parenthood, however, as it requires the emotional and biological labour of another person.

The surrogate herself also enters a liminal phase, moving from her own identities as woman and mother into an uncertain phase of reproductive labour, which will not be rewarded by parenthood, but might be rewarded by other benefits: the pleasure arising from helping others, financial benefits which allow her further economic independence or to support her own family. Ethnographers have described the liminal identities of surrogates as necessary to the endeavour of contract-based pregnancy and its smooth governance. In discussing the Indian

[46] Bronwyn Parry and Rakhi Ghoshal, 'Regulation of Surrogacy in India: Whenceforth Now?' (2018) 3 *BMJ Global Health* 1.

[47] Agomoni Ganguli-Mitra, 'Exploitation through the Lens of Structural Injustice: Revisiting Global Commercial Surrogacy' in Monique Deveaux and Vida Panitch (eds), *Exploitation from Practice to Theory* (Rowman & Littlefield 2017) 139.

[48] Karen Smith Rotabi et al, 'Regulating Commercial Global Surrogacy: The Best Interests of the Child' (2017) 2 *Journal of Human Rights and Social Work* 64.

surrogacy sector, Pande describes the process triggering the surrogacy contract as a 'disciplinary project', where the establishment of a docile identity as 'mother-worker' produces a 'subject similar to a trained factory worker but one who is simultaneously a virtuous mother'.[49] Pande goes on to argue that, '[a]t each stage of the disciplinary process, the mother-worker duality is manipulated in ways that most benefit the mode of production'.[50] Surrogacy experiences can also, however, become sites of resistance, as Pande goes on to explore; in interacting with the surrogacy clinics and their structure, women negotiate their own identities and freedoms in this temporarily created space. The liminal identities of both prospective parents and surrogates are further mediated, and vulnerabilities potentially further exacerbated, by changing regulatory landscapes. Restrictions imposed on contract-based surrogacy have at times not only left parents-in-waiting in further limbo but also further marginalised surrogates who had embraced surrogacy as part of their own life plan. Thus, for example, as India has been seeking to pass increasingly restrictive legislation through subsequent assisted reproductive technology (ART) bills, concerns have been raised as to whether these are really implemented in the interest of the surrogates, as professed by the government.[51]

In thinking about surrogacy further, and at a time when several countries are implementing and considering legislative and regulatory reforms to surrogacy, a liminal lens reminds us that it is particularly important to consider whether the governance discourse further marginalises surrogates by (inadvertently) taking advantage of their liminal identities. In the context of voluntary childlessness, Anna Gotlib writes that '[t]o be liminal is to be in-between: to be seen and invisible; to speak, but not necessarily to be understood; to exist within a community but to not necessarily be of it'.[52] Applying this reading of liminality to the context of surrogacy, one can argue that on top of embraced identities are the ones imposed by ethical, regulatory and political discourse. Without rigorous ethical debate on the nature, justification and moral standing of surrogacy alongside legislative and regulatory development, surrogates can be treated by governance

---

[49] Amrita Pande, 'Commercial Surrogacy in India: Manufacturing a Perfect Mother-Worker' (2010) 35 *Journal of Women in Culture and Society* 969, 970.

[50] Ibid.

[51] Parry and Ghoshal (n 46).

[52] Anna Gotlib, '"But You Would Be the Best Mother": Unwomen, Counterstories, and the Motherhood Mandate' (2016) 13 *Journal of Bioethical Inquiry* 327, 342.

structures as either empowered and autonomous or, alternatively, exploited and commodified. Surrogacy clinics can then be seen as sites of employment or exploitation (or both), and prospective parents as supportive enablers or morally complicit in a web of exploitation and commodification. In regulation, the voice and interests of those who are contributing their bodies and labour should closely inform and steer any potential reform and development in this area. Without careful pathways of governance, reproductive labour and technologies, as well as those engaged with them, might continue to exist in states of per-manent chaos, where the interests and rights of those who are most closely affected are ignored or pushed aside. Surrogacy is paradigmatic to reproductive processes that take gestation outside the body of the intended mother and will no doubt prove to be a test-case for other emerging technologies that alter the physical location of gestation, sparking important repercussions for ethical and legal discourses, espe-cially around the moral and legal rights of those concerned.

## 5.4   Ectogenesis: A Liminal Lens

The processes of human reproduction and gestation, whether entirely *in vivo* or partially *in vitro* through the use of *in vitro* fertilisation (IVF), are undoubtedly liminal. Human embryos and foetuses are paradigmatic of liminal entities, constantly going through processes of evolution and change, yet biologically, legally and, for some, morally in a state of 'in-betweenness'. As Turner writes: '[l]iminal entities are neither here nor there; they are betwixt and between the positions assigned and arrayed by law, custom, convention, and ceremony'.[53] That liminality and the lim-inal processes that embryos are led through *in vitro*, for example,[54] are something to which we are now socially accustomed. New technologies continue to bring new liminal states to life before birth, especially with the recently introduced prospect of gestation *ex utero* (that is, ectogen-esis) via artificial womb technology (AWT). Technology has always modified the reproductive process,[55] yet ectogenesis via AWT has the potential to be one of the most disruptive technological disturbances to reproductive processes yet. To give some background, in 2017 a US research team announced that they had successfully maintained the

[53] Turner (n 7) 95.
[54] See McMillan (n 41).
[55] Ibid.

lives of extremely premature lambs within AWT for four weeks.[56] While not currently viable for use in humans, advances such as this have brought this possibility close to realisation. The use of AWT for partial ectogenesis (where only part of the gestational process takes place in an artificial womb) is on the more immediate horizon, mainly as a form of neonatal intensive care for premature babies.[57] This process would most likely involve placing a premature baby inside an artificial womb (as with the premature lambs) until it has been gestated 'full term' (around forty weeks).

The continuous advancement of science, including in the field of reproductive technologies, is irrefutably processual. This 'processuality' is visible from the micro level of the human experiences of actors in research (that is, donors or researchers) to the societal level where particular norms are disrupted and changed by those advancements.[58] We saw this with the birth of Louise Brown, the first baby to be born through IVF. This seismic event in the landscape of human reproduction triggered a series of further events, including heated public discussion (filled with Frankensteinian references),[59] and most notably the formation of the Warnock Committee and the production of the Warnock Report (as examined in Chapter 11 of this volume). It is arguable that the Warnock Committee may be cast as the 'representative of order' for the liminal phase that ARTs and research on human embryos were in at the time. Its deliberations on ethics and law[60] took us through a liminal moment and *out* the other side; this important process led to the Human Fertilisation and Embryology Act 1990, which allows for embryos *in vitro* to be created, used and stored for reproduction and research. The Committee's Report and the resulting 1990 Act were a seismic change in reproduction and research practice as we knew it.

The introduction of partial ectogenesis via AWT would present another profound moment of legal and social change with regard to how we view the 'natural' process(es) of gestation. Human ectogenesis, in any form, has the potential to change those processes as we know them, and lead us into what has been dubbed the 'third era of human

---

[56] Emily Partridge et al, 'An Extra-Uterine System to Physiologically Support the Extreme Premature Lamb' (2017) 8 *Nature Communications* 15112.

[57] Elizabeth Romanis, 'Challenging the "Born Alive" Threshold: Fetal Surgery, Artificial Wombs, and the English Approach to Legal Personhood' (2020) 28 *Medical Law Review* 93.

[58] See Laurie et al (n 42).

[59] See Michael Mulkay, 'Frankenstein and the Debate over Embryo Research' (1996) 21 *Science, Technology and Human Values* 157.

[60] Although IVF was not entirely unregulated before the 1990 Act; see Amel Alghrani, *Regulating Assisted Reproductive Technologies: New Horizons* (Cambridge University Press 2019) 24–5.

reproduction'.[61] Extant legal frameworks and precedent surrounding human reproduction (for example, the Abortion Act 1967) will be undoubtedly disrupted if/when this technology comes to fruition for human use. Yet how do we navigate that disruption?

One of the most notable disruptions to legal and social norms will be to the role of 'birth' as a legal 'line in the sand'. 'Birth' is a legally significant moment for many jurisdictions as it is the moment at which personhood is attained; having personhood lets us know which relationships, rights and interests are recognised and protected by law. In the UK, the unborn foetus attains legal personhood – along with the rights that come with the status of 'legal person' – only at birth.[62] Moreover, the foetus must be 'born alive'[63] in order to receive these rights and protection (for example, a stillborn cannot bring an action in tort).[64] Yet there is much uncertainty surrounding what 'born alive' means, which is likely to only deepen given the complex process of placing a premature foetus inside an artificial womb, which in many cases would require it to survive. Notably, ectogenesis is not the first advance to give rise to concerns surrounding the threshold of birth; over the past fifteen years or so, the threshold of viability has been pushed back significantly. At the moment, however, law ultimately relies on a 'natural' process – birth – to decide personhood. In the past, major disruptions to reproductive processes (for example, the advent of IVF) did not perturb legal rules surrounding 'birth' and personhood. The use of AWTs on humans, and thus ectogenesis, relies, however, on an entirely new process that will take place in an entirely new context: *ex utero*. Although the exact details of how partial ectogenesis would occur are yet to come to light, it is likely that a foetus would be either prematurely born or transferred from the mother's body to an artificial womb for a period of weeks or months, to be 'born' at the gestational age at which full-term babies are normally born. The disruption of the linear process that is 'normal' gestation will (and should) undoubtedly disrupt law's clear 'line in the sand' of 'birth', because that line becomes blurred by placing the foetus/baby within AWT.

---

[61] Stellan Welin, 'Reproductive Ectogenesis: The Third Era of Human Reproduction and Some Moral Consequences' (2004) 10 *Science and Engineering Ethics* 615.

[62] See *Paton* v. *BPAS* [1987] 1 All ER 1230; *Kelly* v. *Kelly* 1997 SC 285.

[63] For a detailed discussion on this, see Romanis (n 57); Amel Alghrani and Margaret Brazier, 'What Is It? Whose Is It? Re-positioning the Fetus in the Context of Research?' (2011) 70 *Cambridge Law Journal* 51; Elizabeth Romanis, 'Artificial Womb Technology and the Frontiers of Human Reproduction: Conceptual Differences and Potential Implications' (2018) 44 *Journal of Medical Ethics* 751.

[64] See the English case of *Burton* v. *Islington Health Authority* [1993] QB 204.

A liminal lens allows us to understand the (for now, fictional) ecto-geneic foetus, physically *suspended* in an artificial womb, as an entity that sits between legal convention, between the status of born and not born – person and non-person, perhaps even person and 'thing'. The possibil-ities that AWT brings will undoubtedly alter the legal, social and ethical thresholds that we rely on, especially the threshold of 'birth' that draws a clear line in the sand between person and not (yet) person in the UK. Indeed, the ectogenic foetus is between our known legal and social customary categories.[65] In order to bring the ectogenic foetus out of legal *and* physical liminality, when the time comes, we need to under-stand what is happening with the process itself.

We know from the literature on liminality that seeking understanding of this process raises a 'human experiential question'.[66] However, in order to give birth to the child, an intervention will be required. How and when that intervention takes place in ectogenesis are issues of moral and legal significance. Using liminal analysis, it becomes clear that someone needs to lead that ectogenic foetus out of its liminal state. That leading out, seen as a liminal moment, becomes significant because the timing will be crucial for personhood, inheritance and perhaps even the rights of the mother (for example, the right not to become a parent). Liminality does not give us a normative framework, but it does, as a lens, highlight important questions which will undoubtedly have normative implications. The important questions that a liminal lens raises for the regulation of the early stages of human life are, for example:

- At what point does a liminal entity, such as an embryo or foetus, become legally significant and a bearer of legal rights?
- If we remove 'birth' as the legally relevant threshold, which threshold(s) become legally relevant in its place?[67]
- Who makes those decisions? In other words, who gets to decide when these entities are *led out* of their liminal states into personhood?

What liminal moments of the past have shown us is that we need guidance through transition, and, in the case at hand, to this new reproductive era. From the literature, we know that crossing a threshold into a liminal sphere, whereby, for example, ectogenesis is possible yet un(der)regulated, that liminal pace will be characterised by

---

[65] See Thomassen (n 11).
[66] Laurie (n 10) 114.
[67] Ibid.

uncertainty and even be potentially chaotic. The ritual process, for van Gennep, was a way to manage that chaos and help those going through transformation to navigate that process.[68] This is where the 'Master of Ceremonies', or 'Representative of Order', steps in to steward those experiencing liminality through the liminal process. Turner has argued that, in this process, social structure is broken down and replaced by 'antistructure'; as Graeme describes, 'that is, there is a breaking down of pre-existing norms and the opening up of possibilities in the processes of transformation and change'.[69] It is thus clear that in transformational technological moments, such as the advent of AWT, a state of 'pure possibility' is opened not only with regard to how we regulate the technology itself; it also gives us a chance to reconsider some of the key pillars of the law of life before birth more generally.

While, on a societal level, deliberative policy groups such as the Warnock Committee may be cast as a Master of Ceremonies, on the individual level, up until now, the mother is undoubtedly the person in that role due to her physical entanglement with the foetus. But what happens when that physical bond is broken: should the mother still be the one who leads the ectogenic foetus out of liminality? There are good reasons why this should continue to be the case – for example, upholding the reproductive autonomy of women.[70] Yet this is not to say that we should 'copy and paste' current norms surrounding reproduction and personhood without proper forethought. A liminal lens warns us against mimesis; we should therefore be cautious of irreflexively miming legal norms of the past regarding personhood without robust policy discussions regarding the broader consequences of ectogenesis for women.

While we can look to law for greater clarity with regard to the future regulation of ectogenesis, we cannot look to it for firm answers. To mimic previous legal regimes irreflexively in the context of reproductive technologies, an area that has always evolved rapidly (and undoubtedly will continue to do so), is intellectually indefensible: it risks 'legal stasis',[71] a form of permanent liminality. If anything, the development of ectogenesis has the potential to be so disruptive that it highlights this risk. There is potential here for an 'opening up' of the way we regulate reproduction, averting us from the staleness of the law in this area. The legacy of

---

[68] Ibid., 116.

[69] Ibid., 117.

[70] See McMillan (n 41); see also Joona Räsänen, 'Ectogenesis, Abortion and a Right to the Death of the Fetus' (2017) 31 *Bioethics* 697.

[71] See McMillan (n 41).

liminality in this context is thus to empower social discussion by high-lighting the importance, and the intertwined nature, of legal and bio-logical thresholds. The lack of clarity surrounding long-used concepts in modern times (for example, 'birth') means that we cannot look to law for answers to the problems created by this disruptive technology. This is not to say that we cannot draw from law, but rather that law should not or will not be the *only* entity that leads technology out of ectogenesis (on a macro level) or the ectogeneic foetus (on a micro level) *out of* liminality. To accomplish these feats, the input of those who experience that limin-ality, namely the progenitors or intended parent(s) of the hypothetical ectogeneic foetus, will be crucial.

## 5.5   Conclusions

The legacy of Graeme's work on liminality, which extended this concept into the realms of HRR, helps us make sense of other uncertain, if not chaotic, areas of health governance, both in the present (surrogacy) and in the future (ectogenesis). It therefore seems pertinent when writing on Graeme's legacy through his work on liminality, within a volume on law and legacy within medical jurisprudence developed during a chaotic, uncertain time,[72] to return to one of the key points that Graeme has made in his writings throughout the Liminal Spaces project: '[i]f we seek to cast law as the Representative of Order, we must equally be alert to it assuming the guise of Trickster, or at least that it is perceived as such'.[73]

When writing about legacy, its role within law and regulation should be treated with caution. Law's legacy can indeed be a burden, as many chapters in this volume demonstrate. Yet, as described here, examining regulation through the lens of liminality also has positive potential. Liminality, as a lens, allows us to speak of and examine our present and, moreover, prepare ourselves for the future in liminal periods trig-gered by emerging technology and evolving social and political land-scapes. Key themes that arose from the Liminal Spaces project, such as processual regulation, can help us to consider how to think of 'new policy' in the field of health, ethics and law in a way that is suitably flexible and accounts for human experiences in scientific endeavour.

---

[72] This chapter was written primarily during the summer of 2020, in the midst of both the Covid-19 pandemic and the Brexit transition period.

[73] Here, Graeme uses the care.data debacle as an example. See Laurie (n 21) 71; see further Chapter 9 in this volume.

But the legacy of Graeme's work on this project lies within not only his exceptional scholarship but also his superb leadership, which fosters an encouraging environment whereby our research and academic identities can flourish on both individual and team levels. It is a true testament to his mentorship that each team member has been able to reflect on liminality in their own works and continues to draw on both the legacy of Graeme's scholarship and his leadership to forge their own paths in academia.

# 6

## On the Importance of Impact on Policy and Legacy

ERIC M. MESLIN

### 6.1  Introduction

You never forget your first publication. In late 1987, I experienced something that all authors enjoy only once – seeing their first article published in a respected, peer-reviewed journal in their field of study. Mine was published in the August/September issue of the *Hastings Center Report*.[1] It was not ground-breaking, but seeing my name in print for the first time was a source of pride, of feeling recognised for having something original to say. In those days, authors received an order form for reprints, which one would be free to distribute to friends and colleagues. 'Free' was a misnomer, of course, because reprints had to be purchased: the order was mailed with a cheque (before automatic debit) and, a couple of weeks later, a large brown envelope would arrive with the reprints. Dissemination followed thereafter, generally involving hand delivery or mailing (incurring additional costs) to a few friends, an influential professor, perhaps some family members. Dissemination was also much slower before PDFs, email, online subscriptions or pay-walls: mailing meant stamps, envelopes, post offices and more waiting. I still have my 'just in case' copy, carefully preserved in a plastic sheath in a three-ring binder along with every publication thereafter.

One reprint recipient was my maternal grandmother in Toronto who, like most grandmothers, told me how proud she was but added (paraphrasing): 'Your paper was very interesting. How much did they pay you to write it?' It was at that moment that I realised how oddly warped is the academic system of reward, incentive and punishment. Trying to explain

---

[1]  Eric Meslin, 'The Moral Costs of the Ontario Physicians' Strike' (1987) 17 *Hastings Center Report* 11.

the 'system' to Grandma Ida was a trip down a rabbit-hole of odd protocols: think of something that no one else has thought of, write it down, send it to a special academic journal likely to publish it for others to read, wait for a group of anonymous experts to review it and recommend it to an editor, who will decide whether the paper is 'accepted' for publication (and, if so, what changes are required). These steps are followed by a list of pre-publication tasks including reviewing galley proofs, declaring conflicts of interest, disclosing funding sources and (where appropriate) submitting approvals from any committees that previously authorised research on animals, humans or dangerous materials that may have been the basis for the paper submitted for publication. The process is repeated if the first journal rejects the paper, and so on. The process of applying for grants from funding organisations is similar, although often with additional requirements such as plans for how money will be spent, dissemination plans and, as discussed in Section 6.2.2, details of social or other benefits that might be expected to arise. An onerous list to explain; an even more onerous one to undertake.[2]

The idea that my paper might inform the actions or decisions of others was, frankly, not uppermost in my mind. I gave little thought to whether physicians or politicians would see the arguments as dispositive for resolving the concerns at issue or informing any future policy debate. It would have been presumptuous: I was neither a physician nor a politician, no data were presented, no evidence was synthesised. What impact could a single paper in a specialised journal have on issues of the day? At that time, being published was enough. I would never have allowed myself the immodest luxury of thinking that this type of work

---

[2] Previous studies have estimated that up to 40 per cent of researchers' time is spent applying for and seeking grant funding. See, for example, Editorial, 'Dr. No Funding. The Broken Science Funding System' (*Scientific American*, 25 April 2011) www.scientificamerican.com /article/dr-no-money/ (accessed 5 March 2021). Recognition of the disproportionate balance between seeking funding to conduct research and undertaking the research itself was slow to materialise, but proposals for greater efficiency have been made. See, for example, Johan Bollen et al, 'An Efficient System to Fund Science: From Proposal Review to Peer-to-Peer Distributions' (2017) 110 *Scientometrics* 521. Moreover, many funding organisations are proposing new streamlined and targeted funding models. See, for example, Diana Hicks, 'Grand Challenges in US Science Policy Attempt Policy Innovation' (2016) 11 *International Journal of Foresight and Innovation Policy* 22; Philippe Larrue, Dominique Guellec and Frédéric Sgard, 'New Trends in Public Research Funding' in *OECD Science, Technology and Innovation Outlook 2018* (OECD Publishing 2018); and Fiona Murray, 'Evaluating the Role of Science Philanthropy in American Research Universities' (2013) 13 *Innovation Policy and the Economy* 23.

was cutting any new conceptual or methodological cloth for the field of bioethics, let alone that it might influence the work of those coming after me, or leave a lasting impression.

Yet to say that thinking and practice have evolved about the role that academics play in civic discourse in the past few decades, and about the significance of publication and dissemination, would be an understatement. Not only are there more methods, platforms and processes for dissemination but the expectations for what the work itself is capable of are also expanding. The term often used to capture these diverse issues and changing expectations is *impact* – a somewhat formal term that this chapter will unpack.

But there is another term that we also use when referring to what academics contribute (or permit themselves to consider): *legacy*. Admittedly, this term is more often associated with the encomia prepared by pupils and students about retiring professors, given its biographical implications. Legacy, like impact, can be many things: a gift of property we leave for others, the story of our lives, knowledge imparted to students, or the setting of an initial standard for those that come after.[3]

It is the intersection of impact and legacy that drives the narrative of this chapter. First, the chapter will review different types of impact that academics have and can have both inside the academy – its many faces – through publishing in academic journals and presses, and outside the academy by translating knowledge to policy through participation in and leadership of committees and other policy organisations. Both environments also include an under-appreciated type of impact, namely on the legacy of one's work through the interactions with others. The chapter then describes the changing landscape in which knowledge production and dissemination occur, highlighting the growth of international, collaborative work, to place the changing faces of impact into a broader environmental context. Finally, these two strands of impact and legacy are brought together for some concluding reflections about their future importance.

---

[3] Legacy can also have a more tired and worn out meaning, which will be avoided here, as when the term applies to obsolete practices or technologies. See, for example, the Wikipedia entry for 'legacy system': '[i]n computing, a legacy system is an old method, technology, computer system, or application program, of, relating to, or being a previous or outdated computer system, yet still in use. Often referencing a system as "legacy" means that it paved the way for the standards that would follow it. This can also imply that the system is out of date or in need of replacement.' https://en.wikipedia.org/wiki/Legacy_system (accessed 5 March 2021).

## 6.2 The Many Faces of Impact

The term 'impact' is used within the academy for many purposes, including as a benchmark for assessing individual faculty 'performance'; as an expectation of funding agencies who seek to ensure that their money is well spent; and as an aspirational goal for civically minded scholars who wish to contribute to public discourse. What university would not wish to have a reliable metric for assessing the quality and productivity of their faculty? Which government agency or funder would not want to see its support for science translated into applied or practical use? Who does not want to see one's work have impact – in any form – beyond the narrow, specialised disciplines that much academic work is focused on influencing?

What has become obvious, however, is that while the general idea of impact as a worthy goal may enjoy a degree of consensus, less agreement exists as to what it should mean in more detailed terms, how to assess it meaningfully and, more practically, how to achieve it. This may be because the idea of impact must do a lot of work, both quantitative and axiological: it must serve as an objective and generalisable metric, and as a subjective representation of value and worth. On the one hand, impact can refer to the way knowledge influences action in a type of linear cause-and-effect relationship. We can imagine the ideal case of a definitive publication whose findings are so compelling and unavoidably valid that decision-makers have no choice but to adopt a policy based on them.[4] On the other hand, the subjective assessment of how valuable such studies are to policy is based on a theory of value about the role of science in forming policy that is still being debated.[5] It is a slippery concept ranging from the use of specific forms of evidence to inform policy decisions, to the more ephemeral and rhetorical ways in which expert individuals may influence or persuade others.

---

[4] This is more easily imagined than applied. Even a definitive study that smoking caused lung cancer took years to be translated into policy. See, for example, Ellen Hahn et al, 'Lung Cancer Incidence and the Strength of Municipal Smoke-Free Ordinances' (2018) 124 *Cancer* 374. This example is selected for another reason: the connection between smoking and cancer was one of the great achievements of public health epidemiology established in the 1950s by Oxford's Richard Doll and others. That Doll continued this work fifty years on (see Richard Doll et al, 'Mortality in Relation to Smoking: 50 Years' Observations on Male British Doctors' (2004) 328 *BMJ* 1519) is also evidence of his lasting legacy.

[5] Consider the long-standing debate, mentioned further later, about the role of basic or pure science as contrasted with applied research. See, for example, Alvin Weinberg, 'The Axiology of Science' (1970) 58 *American Scientist* 612; Donald Stokes, *Pasteur's Quadrant: Basic Science and Technological Innovation* (Brookings Institution Press 1997).

The person we honour in this collection of chapters has had impact across this spectrum, and in having done so is leaving a legacy of work and contributions for those who follow. By reflecting on this impact, we may better understand this elusive concept and gain insight into the relationship between impact and legacy. First, let us consider some of the most obvious ways in which we think about the impact of academics.

### 6.2.1 Publishing in Journals and Academic Presses

The academic life is often chosen because it affords the opportunity to pursue ideas of interest and relevance. A type of social contract is struck: in exchange for the privilege being paid to pursue such a life, there is an expectation of productivity. The most immediate expectation is conveyed by one's academic employer, charmingly referred to as 'publish or perish'.[6] But there is also a non-trivial, if abstract, expectation from society. While different disciplines judge publication impact differently, the expectation that academics actually write up and publish their research remains a mainstay of the agreement. At the time of this writing, Graeme has published more than 160 papers in the scholarly literature, beginning with his first in 1994.[7] Little did the world know what would follow, but three observations are apparent.

First, although his disciplinary home is the law, Graeme's publication record is multidisciplinary, stretching across the fields of law, medicine, science, health and ethics. It includes contributions on clinical negligence, genomics, governance matters, consent, electronic health records, biotechnology, patenting, pandemics and human rights, as well as exploratory papers on cultural relativism and subjectivity. In other words, the scholarship and productivity extend horizontally across broad disciplines and vertically within particular areas.

Second, the publications show a diversity of methodology and approaches, from philosophically minded pieces steeped in conceptual analysis, to policy proposals, legislative commentaries and an occasional quantitative paper. Even a cursory analysis of the full collection reveals

---

[6] According to Wikipedia, the earliest known use of the phrase was found in Clarence Case, 'Scholarship in Sociology' (1928) 12 *Sociology and Social Research* 323.

[7] Graeme Laurie, 'Damages, Duty and *Hamilton v. Fife Health Board*' (1994) 1 *Juridical Review* 110.

a set of different epistemic trajectories, most often grounding the work in legal and jurisprudential thinking, but not uncommonly taking on topics using applied ethics, human rights or social science frames. This diversity is consistent with the trajectories of like-minded scholars working at the intersection of law, medicine and ethics, just as it would be for those of us in the humanities and social sciences working at other 'intersections' in the disciplinary landscape, including applied ethics, science and technology studies, or global health, for example.

Third, whereas the first few years of Graeme's publication record are filled primarily with single-authored papers, the later years include more jointly authored works, as befits a senior scholar with an interest in and commitment to mentoring, but also one who has recognised that one of the most energising (and fruitful) ways of exploring complex topics at the intersection of law, medicine and science is to have co-authors from these fields. These collaborations are simply described as *multi*disciplinary, in that many approaches contribute to the final work. But a more careful reading suggests that they contribute to a rich conversation about *inter*-disciplinary and even *trans*-disciplinary research.[8] This conversation was started well before Graeme began writing, reminding us again of the value of the work of those who have come before.

Scholarly publications are the first face of impact and Graeme's 160-plus papers paint a special portrait – one that is multi-topical, multi-methodological and multi-participatory. If we are honest, these features contribute to what makes these publications so interesting. Yet, it is precisely because of these features that the impact of the publications is so difficult to assess. One obvious difficulty is separating the publication's impact from the person who wrote it. Chief among the difficulties is how to assign to an individual author any attributed impact from a multi-authored work, specifically in assigning publication credit when there are many 'co-creators' of the knowledge contained in the papers being assessed. In days gone by, a multidisciplinary, multi-authored publication record would be frustrating to evaluate for university promotion and tenure committees, who find it easier to assess the quality and impact of a paper as being

---

[8] Bernard Choi and Anita Pak, 'Multidisciplinarity, Interdisciplinarity and Transdisciplinarity in Health Research, Services, Education and Policy: 1. Definitions, Objectives, and Evidence of Effectiveness' (2006) 29 *Clinical and Investigative Medicine* 351. See further Chapter 1 in this volume.

indistinguishable from the author who wrote it.[9] Fortunately, thinking has evolved in higher education.[10]

The publishing world has also kept pace with these developments with respect to apportioning credit and responsibility for publications. The Open Researcher and Contributor ID (ORCID) system, introduced in 2012, is one such development[11] which allows for an individual to have a single designated identifier attached to each publication. Guidelines by the respected International Committee of Medical Journal Editors (ICMJE) provide further advice and standards.[12]

But attribution credit is merely the membership card for discussing impact. Who gets credit is a distinct question from what the credit is for. A much-promoted metric has been the impact factor, first developed in 1955 to compare the relative importance of a journal in which a paper has been published. One of many bibliometric methods in the citation analysis toolbox, the impact factor counts the number of times a paper, an author or their organisation has been cited in the scholarly literature.[13] It is also used to study patterns in scholarly communications, as evidenced by citations between authors or domains of knowledge.

---

[9] I still recall a conversation with a university reappointment committee in the early 1990s which, in reviewing my publication portfolio, expressed difficulty in assessing my contribution to a multi-authored paper, with one member asking somewhat wryly, 'what part did you write?'.

[10] Lesley Schimanski and Juan Alperin, 'The Evaluation of Scholarship in Academic Promotion and Tenure Processes: Past, Present, and Future' (2018) 7 *F1000Research* 1605.

[11] Editorial, 'Championing Authorship Attribution' (2017) 19 *Nature Cell Biology* 579.

[12] Alastair Matheson, 'The ICMJE Recommendations and Pharmaceutical Marketing – Strengths, Weaknesses, and the Unsolved Problem of Attribution in Publication Ethics' (2016) 17 *BMC Medical Ethics* 20.

[13] Citation analysis is also used for purposes other than assessing performance of an individual faculty member, including for assessing the impact of a discipline itself, and even of a country's impact in the world of science. For many years, organisations have attempted to capture the role and influence of countries. My organisation, the Council of Canadian Academies (CCA), has undertaken several studies of this kind including Expert Panel on the State of Science and Technology and Industrial Research and Development in Canada, 'Competing in a Global Innovation Economy: The Current State of R&D in Canada' (Council of Canadian Academies 2018); see in particular 34–5 table 3.1: The citation indicators for country performance developed by CCA include number of publications, specialisation index, growth index and growth rate, collaboration index, average relative citations (ARC), median relative citations, highly cited publications https://cca-reports.ca/wp-content/uploads/2018/09/Competing_in_a_Global_Innovation_Economy_FullReport_EN.pdf (accessed 5 March 2021).

The impact factor has been the subject of deep discussion and debate, particularly because of the incommensurability problem of comparing different standards for different disciplines. For instance, the most cited paper of all time, with more than 300,000 citations, is about the structure of a protein.[14] The paper is cited this often because it is expected (a type of deference to authority) whenever the history of this issue or its acknowledgement is used. In the social sciences, where books still retain a privileged position of influence, Elliot Green identified the twenty-five most cited books (as of 2016),[15] which hold a similar status of reverence; among them are Thomas Kuhn's *The Structure of Scientific Revolutions* with 81,311 citations (#1) and John Rawls's *Theory of Justice* with 58,594 (#8). These two are selected for illustration given their familiarity to and use by the community of scholars of which Graeme is a part: those at the intersection of law, science, ethics and so on. Similarly, for journal articles, one finds those by familiar authors with tens of thousands of citations including two of the most influential in behavioural economics: by Amos Tversky and Daniel Kahneman, 'Prospect Theory: An Analysis of Decision under Risk' with 39,558 (#5) and 'Judgment under Uncertainty: Heuristics and Biases' with 36,356 (#9).[16] How exactly should we compare the Lowry et al protein paper to these by Kahneman and Tversky? How to compare Kuhn to Rawls?

Allowing for Green's uncritical blurring of the social sciences and humanities in his assessment (Kuhn's work is in the philosophy of science, and arguably Rawls's work is in political and moral philosophy), we recognise that the challenge of comparing papers *within* traditional academic disciplinary categories like political science, philosophy or anthropology is as difficult as comparing *across* broader categories like biomedical science, the humanities, social sciences or the natural sciences. The attempt to compare reveals not only the limitations of assessing impact by citation numbers alone but also deep methodologic and epistemic value choices about the taxonomy of assigning knowledge to

---

[14] Oliver Lowry et al, 'Protein Measurement with the Folin Phenol Reagent' (1951) 193 *Journal of Biological Chemistry* 265.

[15] Elliot Green, 'What Are the Most-Cited Publications in the Social Sciences (according to Google Scholar)?' (*LSE Blog*, 2016) https://blogs.lse.ac.uk/impactofsocialsciences/2016/05/12/what-are-the-most-cited-publications-in-the-social-sciences-according-to-google-scholar/ (accessed 5 March 2021).

[16] See Green, ibid., for ranking. Citations for the papers are Daniel Kahneman and Amos Tversky, 'Prospect Theory: An Analysis of Decision under Risk' (1979) 47 *Econometrica* 263; and Amos Tversky and Daniel Kahneman, 'Judgment under Uncertainty: Heuristics and Biases' (1974) 27 *Science* 1124.

a particular category. The attempt to compare also misses the target of this chapter, namely that of impact and its many domains, including its influence on legacy. Chief among these domains are the political and civic environments where the fruits of knowledge produced in the academy are shared for the public benefit.

### 6.2.2 The Face of Impact Outside the Academy

The life of the academic has evolved over millennia, and yet modern academics share many of the same motivations as their predecessors. We wish to teach others what we know, we wish to have the opportunity to think and experiment (with ideas and actions), and we hope to add to the storehouse of knowledge. The privilege of working in the academy also comes with expectations to contribute to the political life of the academy itself: to volunteer one's time taking on certain administrative responsibilities, including supervising students, serving on various committees, accepting administrative leadership positions and undertaking academic community service.

But it is in the *external* engagement – the activity in civil society – where many an academic also seeks to have impact. Such opportunities come in many forms, but they flow from the general idea of being an expert in some capacity.[17] Without rehearsing all of his bona fides, Graeme Laurie's breadth of activity is increasingly typical of the highly engaged academic expert. He has taken editorial leadership roles as co-editor of the Cambridge Bioethics and Law Series of Cambridge University Press, and most recently as editor-in-chief of the *Asian Bioethics Review*, helping to shepherd the flow of new ideas through the traditional academic model. He has been an active expert engaged in the work of committees and study groups whose reports (part of the grey literature[18]) were widely disseminated. For example, he chaired

---

[17] Elsewhere, I have commented on the different forms that such expertise may take. See Eric M. Meslin, 'The Once and Future Role of Policy Advice for Health Regulation by Experts and Advisory Committees' in Graeme Laurie et al (eds), *The Cambridge Handbook of Health Research Regulation* (Cambridge University Press 2021).

[18] The term 'grey literature' is a broad category of publications, a definition of which was proposed at the Twelfth International Conference on Grey Literature in Prague in 2010:

> [g]rey literature stands for manifold document types produced on all levels of government, academics, business and industry in print and electronic formats that are protected by intellectual property rights, of sufficient quality to be collected and preserved by libraries and institutional

the Global Alliance for Genomics and Health's Privacy and Security Task Team, the Privacy Advisory Committee in Scotland, and the Council of Europe's Drafting Committee for revision of the Council of Europe Recommendation on Biomedical Collections. He has been a member of the Scottish Government Data Management Board, the Royal Society Working Party on Science as an Open Enterprise, the ESRC Understanding Society Data Access Committee, the Nuffield Council on Bioethics Working Party on Novel Neurotechnologies, the British Medical Association's Medical Ethics Committee and the Council of Canadian Academies Expert Panel on Access to Health and Social Data.

Graeme's experiences with these organisations have demonstrable impact. For instance, Graeme's research for the Scottish Health Informatics Programme (SHIP) was used in the Scottish Government's public consultation on cross-sectoral data linkage and in policy instruments, including its 2015 Action Plan, its 2015 Open Data Strategy and its 2015 Safe Havens Charter.[19] His leadership of an interdisciplinary team was used by the Nuffield Council on Bioethics Working Party on Biological and Health Data and the Expert Advisory Group on Data

---

repositories, but not controlled by commercial publishers; i.e. where publishing is not the primary activity of the producing body.

The Ruth Lilly Medical Library at Indiana University includes the following examples of such materials:

- reports (pre-prints, preliminary progress and advanced reports, technical reports, statistical reports, memoranda, state-of-the art reports, market research reports, and so on; these may be produced by research centers, or commercial, professional or non-profit organisations);
- government reports and documents (state, national and international);
- research initiatives (might appear as white papers, presentations, media, and so on);
- conference proceedings, papers, posters, presentations;
- theses and dissertations;
- technical specifications and standards; and
- clinical trials documentation and registration.

https://iupui.libguides.com/systreviews/greylit (accessed 20 March 2021).

[19] These examples are taken from Graeme's public bio-sketch, which provides the following references: 'Data Management, Collection and Use: Strategic Action Plan' (2015) www .gov.scot/Resource/0047/00471995.pdf (accessed 5 March 2021); 'Open Data Strategy' (2015) www.gov.scot/Resource/0047/00472007.pdf (accessed 5 March 2021); and 'Charter for Safe Havens in Scotland: Handling Unconsented Data from National Health Service Patient Records to Support Research and Statistics' (2015) www.gov.scot /charterforsafehavens (accessed 5 March 2021).

Access.[20] But he also leaves a legacy impact of another kind. His role as the inaugural chair of the UK Biobank's Ethics and Governance Council (EGC) is an example[21] both of the contribution of academic scholars to the growing policy debate on ethics and biobanks and of the legacy of leadership to those that follow. As one of the first national biobanks with a formal ethics and governance committee, the UK Biobank provided a roadmap for other initiatives of this kind, as well as for the type of leadership necessary to oversee these projects. Graeme was followed by the distinguished academic lawyer Roger Brownsword as EGC chair, who was followed by Baroness Helene Hayman, the equally distinguished legal scholar and parliamentarian. (I was honoured to serve as vice chair of the EGC when Baroness Hayman was chair.)

These are not unusual examples for people like Graeme. Serving on external expert committees remains a tangible route for civic-minded scholars to have an impact by participating in the publication and dissemination of materials that will be read and used by others. Indeed, the impact of committees (and the reports and recommendations arising from them) is an enduring topic in science and health policy. Here, too, assessing impact is as slippery as the concept itself, for epistemic and practical reasons.[22] Among the difficulties is accounting for the iterative process of relying on evidence to inform decisions: expert committees produce reports requested by or offered to particular sponsors; these committees rely on access to high-quality evidence (especially from high-impact journals) to inform their deliberations; the resulting reports and summaries may be incorporated into legislative or other policy instruments, which then give rise to further assessment. At most, an accounting of the impact of any one of the items in this epistemic chain can be only a rough proxy for the actual impact.

Just as it is difficult to attribute credit to a specific author of a multi-authored work, so too is it difficult to determine the impact of an expert committee's report on a particular policy.[23] An Illustration of this

---

[20] Graeme Laurie et al, 'A Review of Evidence Relating to Harm Resulting from Uses of Health and Biomedical Data' (2014) www.nuffieldbioethics.org/wp-content/uploads/A-Review-of-Evidence-Relating-to-Harms-Resulting-from-Uses-of-Health-and-Biomedical-Data-FINAL.pdf (accessed 5 March 2021).

[21] For a more detailed discussion of the UK Biobank topic, see Chapter 14 in this volume.

[22] See, for example, National Research Council, *Using Science as Evidence in Public Policy* (US National Academies 2012); and Sheila Jasanoff, 'Contested Boundaries in Policy-Relevant Science' (1987) 17 *Social Studies of Science* 195.

[23] One approach with which I am directly familiar was the assessment undertaken by the RAND Corporation for the US National Bioethics Advisory Commission to determine

challenge is seen in a recent large-scale study undertaken to determine how science was being used to inform policy decisions arising from Covid-19. Yin and colleagues reviewed more than 37,000 policy documents from 114 countries to determine whether and to what extent the science in the documents was being used to inform decision-makers.[24] Under 'science', the database on which they conducted their investigation included 'research, briefs, reviews, or reports written with the goal of influencing or changing policy' (in other words, the grey literature). Their conclusion illustrates what the analysis of this deep and diverse resource reveals about how science is having an impact, though with notable qualifications: 'Taken together, our results show that policy documents in the COVID-19 pandemic substantially access recent, peer-reviewed, and high impact science. At the same time, our reference-based measures are but a proxy for the use of science in policy, and policies may cite science for different reasons.'[25]

The Yin et al study also reminds us how much context matters, and that unless we understand the changing environment in which knowledge production occurs and adapt our approach to understanding broader notions of impact, we will have to continue to settle for incomplete proxies.

### 6.3   The Changing Environment of Knowledge Production and Dissemination

The capacity of individual scholars to have policy impact has always been limited, often by the conditions placed on their extramural activities by their employers (including the amount of time they can devote, issues of potential conflict of interest and so on). Less often discussed are the limitations in capacity and skill to engage with policy-makers on their terms, to understand broader ecosystem issues and to survive comfortably in the political world. Yet even this environment of scientific knowledge production and engagement has been changing. Many organisations – including learned societies, assessment organisations like my own, advisory committees, advocacy groups, think tanks and

---

the extent to which any of the 120 total recommendations in NBAC's reports were acted upon. See Elisa Eiseman, 'The National Bioethics Advisory Commission: Contributing to Public Policy' (RAND Corporation 2003) www.rand.org/pubs/monograph_reports/MR1546.html (accessed 5 March 2021).

[24]  Yian Yin et al, 'Coevolution of Policy and Science During the Pandemic' (2021) 371 *Science* 128.

[25]  Ibid., 30.

consultancies – are part of a changing knowledge production and trans-lation ecosystem.[26] Some of these features are identified next.

*Science is more collaborative than ever.* One outgrowth of the multi-authored paper phenomenon is the rise in interdisciplinary and international collab-oration. For instance, in a 2000 study, 14 per cent of published science and engineering journal articles included authors from two or more countries. By 2018, the number had risen to 23 per cent.[27] The United Kingdom, Australia, France, Canada, Germany and Spain all now have international collabor-ation rates over 50 per cent. Even in the United States, which collaborates less because of its larger pool of domestic researchers, rates of international collaboration doubled between 2000 and 2018, rising from 19 per cent to 39 per cent.[28] This rise in both disciplinary and multi-jurisdictional collab-oration further adds to the complexity of assessing short-, medium- and longer-term impact. Evidence has been accumulating that explains a growing trend in the number of countries engaged in research and knowledge production. In the fields of science and engineering, for instance, this growth is especially noteworthy as China has surpassed the USA as the producer of PhDs[29] and in scientific publications in many fields.[30]

*The sciences are becoming more specialised.* The academy has evolved since the days of the polymath, where an influential scholar might be expert in the natural and the physical sciences.[31] Many such multiply wise experts live and work among us, but the trend line is clearly arcing towards specialisation and further micro-specialisation within fields. Observers of these impact debates sometimes point to these

[26] Antonino Cartabollatta and Julie Tilson, 'The Ecosystem of Evidence Cannot Thrive without Efficiency of Knowledge Generation, Synthesis, and Translation' (2019) 110 *Journal of Clinical Epidemiology* 90.

[27] National Science Board, 'The State of U.S. Science & Engineering' (National Science Foundation 2020) https://ncses.nsf.gov/pubs/nsb20201 (accessed 5 March 2021).

[28] Ibid.

[29] National Science Board, 'Publications Output: U.S. Trends and International Comparisons' (National Science Foundation 2019) https://ncses.nsf.gov/pubs/nsb20206/ (accessed 5 March 2021).

[30] CCA's report (n 13) includes data on the top twenty countries ranked by number of scientific publications, including the change over two five-year periods: 2003–8 and 2009–14. China is second only to the United States for both periods but has dramatically increased over time from 13.4 per cent of the world's scientific publications (2003–8) to 20.1 per cent in 2009–14. The US share of publications has declined over those two periods, from 29.2 per cent to 24.3 per cent (p. 37) Only two other countries in the top ten have seen their share of publications rise: India and Spain.

[31] Peter Burke, *The Polymath: A Cultural History from Leonardo da Vinci to Susan Sontag* (Yale University Press 2020).

sub-specialities as examples of both helpful and unhelpful approaches to assessing quality, influence and impact. The differences between disciplines (such as law versus philosophy versus chemistry) are so dramatic that one wonders if they all should be considered equally measurable. But how are we to assess a paper with twelve authors, including lawyers, philosophers, physicians and social scientists, writing about a narrow area of ethics oversight for data science studies published in the high-impact journal *Science*?[32]

The challenges of measuring impact in its many forms for someone like Graeme (or any of us) working in the social sciences and humanities continue to be a subject of interest and commentary often summarised by the phrase 'not everything that can be measured matters, and not everything that matters can be measured'. For example, in its 2018 report *Competing in a Global Economy*, the Council of Canadian Academies spoke for many when it concluded:

> For the social sciences, arts, and humanities, metrics based on journal articles and other indexed publications provide an incomplete and uneven picture of research contributions . . . However, future assessments of R&D in Canada may benefit from more substantive integration of expert review, capable of factoring in different types of research outputs (e.g., non-indexed books) and impacts (e.g., contributions to communities or impacts on public policy). The Panel has no doubt that contributions from the humanities, arts, and social sciences are of equal importance to national prosperity. It is vital that such contributions are better measured and assessed.[33]

*More journals are publishing than ever before.* The evidence of this specialisation can be found in the explosion of journals. According to one source, by 2014 there were more than 28,100 English-language journals in the world, and another 6,450 non-English-language journals, which collectively publish about 2.5 million articles each year.[34] My anecdote at the outset of this chapter refers to the pre-eminent bioethics journal of the day, the *Hastings Center Report*, though the number of

---

[32] Edward Dove et al, 'Ethics Review for International Data-Intensive Research' (2016) 351 *Science* 1399.

[33] CCA's report (n 13) xvii.

[34] Mark Ware and Michael Wabe, 'The STM Report: An Overview of Scientific and Scholarly Journal Publishing; Celebrating the 350th Anniversary of Journal Publishing' (2015) International Association of Scientific, Technical and Medical Publishers https://digitalcommons.unl.edu/cgi/viewcontent.cgi?article=1008&context=scholcom (accessed 15 March 2021).

journals in this domain was small. There are now as many as twenty such journals, each with their own rankings.[35]

*There is more to know than ever.* In 2018, a special issue of *Popular Science* tried to catalogue the growth of information that humanity had created, beginning with Pliny's thirty-seven volumes of natural history (equalling approximately 3.06 MB), to the 5.5 million articles posted to Wikipedia (27,000 MB), to the Internet itself (in 2014, the estimate was 1,000,000,000,000,000,000 MB).[36] Among the implications of this type of big data problem is the increasing use of expert systems, including those using artificial intelligence better to access, curate and understand scientific information.[37]

*Access to information is easier than ever for more people.* While the amount of information available is staggering, the increase in the number of people who have access to information may be even more impressive, aided by an increase in educational attainment, school attendance and literacy, particularly among girls and women.[38] It is noteworthy that this chapter was completed during the period that will forever be known as the Covid-19 pandemic – not because the writing conditions were sometimes less than convenient but because the pandemic itself shed new light on many aspects of the issues raised above. Among the more impressive pivots in publishing, for instance, was the decision taken by journals and public media organisations to lower or eliminate paywalls on papers about Covid-19. This decision effectively opened the vault to a storehouse of useful knowledge that would otherwise have remained accessible only to those who could afford to pay. Such a decision was an accelerant to the already developing world of open data, open science and open access – each of which plays a key role in the impact lives of individual researchers and the teams, consortia, programmes, organisations and countries with which they are affiliated.

One such initiative that was underway well before Covid-19 is Plan S, a consortium of governmental research agencies that requires grantees to

---

[35] Michael Cook, 'Ranking Bioethics Journals' (*BioEdge*, 17 August 2019) www.bioedge.org /bioethics/ranking-bioethics-journals/13175 (accessed 15 March 2021).

[36] Sarah Chodosh, 'How Much Space Does All of Humanity's Knowledge Take Up?' (*Popular Science*, 14 March 2019) www.popsci.com/human-knowledge-infographic/ (accessed 15 March 2021).

[37] Andy Extance, 'How AI Technology Can Tame the Scientific Literature' (*Toolbox*, 10 September 2018) www.nature.com/articles/d41586-018-06617-5 (accessed 15 March 2021).

[38] Steven Pinker, *Enlightenment Now* (Penguin 2018) 236–8.

publish the results of their funded research in open-access journals.[39] The power of the Plan S idea is that funding agencies can use collective influence to ensure that research they fund in the public interest is widely accessible.[40] Plan S is part of a larger effort to democratise access to information generally, which many countries are now taking more seriously through 'cOAlition S'. The Open Data Barometer, which measures 'how governments are publishing and using open data for accountability, innovation and social impact', is one such instrument.[41] Using data available up to 2017, 30 countries out of 100 were assessed based on criteria including readiness, implementation and emerging impact; the top 5 countries were Canada (76), the UK (76), Australia (75), France (72) and South Korea (72).

*Publishing platforms are changing and expanding.* Specialty journals may be increasing in number, but this trend pales in comparison to the number of other media for sharing information. For example, in 2006, the search engine platform Technorati estimated that there were more than 35.3 million blogs, with their number doubling every six months.[42] By 2019, it was estimated that the number of blogs had risen to between 500 million and 600 million.[43] A Google search of the term 'COVID blogs' returned 910,000,000 results, which included several sub-results for 'Top Ten COVID19 blogs', each of which has tens of thousands of followers.

*Peer review and quality metrics are under stress.* The growth of journals and submissions has stressed the traditional peer review system, which has been the subject of critique and reform from its earliest days.[44] Then came Covid-19 and with it many positive benefits of open access, as well

---

[39] 'Plan S: Making Full and Immediate Open Access a Reality' www.coalition-s.org/ (accessed 15 March 2021).

[40] Koen Vermeir, 'Research Funding Agencies Are Redefining Science. Early Career Researchers Will Have to Adapt' (2020) 25 *Trends in the Sciences* 62.

[41] The Open Data Barometer https://opendatabarometer.org/?_year=2017&indicator=ODB (accessed 17 March 2021).

[42] David Sifry, 'State of the Blogosphere, April 2006 Part 1: On Blogosphere Growth' (*Sifry's Alerts*, 17 April 2006) https://web.archive.org/web/20130109014955/http:/www.sifry.com /alerts/archives/000432.html (accessed 17 March 2021).

[43] The number of blogs and bloggers should be considered with caution. For instance, Optinmonster.com estimated that 500 million blogs existed in 2019, 440 million of which belonged to Tumblr, and WordPress with about 60 million blogs https://optinmonster .com/blogging-statistics/ (accessed 17 March 2021). Growthbadger.com estimated the number of blogs in 2019 at 600 million https://growthbadger.com/blog-stats (accessed 17 March 2021).

[44] Alex Csiszar, 'Peer Review: Troubled from the Start' (2016) 532 *Nature* 306.

as legitimate concerns. A veritable firehose of publications – peer-reviewed publications across the academic spectrum, teaching and learning materials, grey literature, committee and task force reports, investigative news reporting and editorialising – became instantly available. The decision of many publishers to permit free access to Covid-19-related research and reporting in major journals and print newspapers was unprecedented. Perhaps this was pure benevolence, or a straightforward business strategy to attract customers and subscribers in the future, or a combination of both; time will tell.[45]

Along with greater access to quality information have come practices that increase the risk of misusing the very information being released. The reliance on pre-publication preprints[46] and announcements of research that has yet to be peer-reviewed – sometimes referred to as 'science by press release'[47] – places pressure on an already fragile peer-review system.[48] The trade-off of faster access means that the usual quality checks provided by peer review are unavailable. Speedier data sharing, even when in the public interest, is not without certain risks, not the least of which is that rushing to publish science undermines the science itself.[49] One of the implications of this phenomenon is the added risk of disseminating misinformation, recently described by the World Health Organization in relation to Covid-19 as an 'infodemic'.[50]

---

[45] Michael Luo, 'The Fate of the News in the Age of the Coronavirus' (*The New Yorker*, 29 March 2020) www.newyorker.com/news/annals-of-communications/the-fate-of-the-news-in-the-age-of-the-coronavirus (accessed 17 March 2021).

[46] A recent paper on this phenomenon captures the unique status of the issue. See Yulia Sevryugina and Andrew Dicks, 'Publication Practices During the COVID-19 Pandemic: Biomedical Preprints and Peer-Reviewed Literature' (*bioRXiv*, 21 January 2021) www.biorxiv.org/content/10.1101/2021.01.21.427563v1 (accessed 17 March 2021). The journal in which the paper appears is described as a 'preprint server for biology' and includes the following disclaimer: '[t]his article is a preprint and has not been certified by peer review'.

[47] Sanjay Gupta, 'Science by Press Release: When the Story Gets Ahead of the Science' (CNN, 27 June 2020) www.cnn.com/2020/06/27/health/science-by-press-release-gupta /index.html (accessed 17 March 2021).

[48] Jonathan Tennant and Tony Ross-Hellauer, 'The Limitations to Our Understanding of Peer Review' (2020) 5, 6 *Research Integrity and Peer Review* https://researchintegrityjour nal.biomedcentral.com/articles/10.1186/s41073-020-00092-1 (accessed 17 March 2021).

[49] Alex London and Jonathan Kimmelman, 'Against Pandemic Research Exceptionalism' (2020) 368 *Science* 476.

[50] WHO, 'Call for Action: Managing the Infodemic' (WHO, 11 December 2020) www.who .int/news/item/11–12–2020-call-for-action-managing-the-infodemic (accessed 17 March 2021).

Among the more worrisome platforms for disseminating misinformation are predatory journals and predatory publishers, estimated at more
than 8,000.[51] Their number and influence are seen as so consequential
that tracking organisations have been established and criteria for their
definition have been debated: 'Predatory journals and publishers are
entities that prioritize self-interest at the expense of scholarship and are
characterized by false or misleading information, deviation from best
editorial and publication practices, a lack of transparency, and/or the use
of aggressive and indiscriminate solicitation practices.'[52]

*Research funding priorities are changing.* As discussed earlier, support for
research has been part of the implied social contract for decades.[53] But
the contract has not remained static, changing as a result of social,
economic and even epistemic pressures. Some of the pressures are external, coming in the form of tighter budgets, leading to increased competition by applicants chasing fewer dollars. When conditions change, the
pressure-valve is released, permitting more research support to flow. This
pendulum of funding is neither predictable nor consistent, most notably
because funding bodies – whether public, private or philanthropic – have
had to grapple with many social, political, ethical and economic realities,
not the least of which is the ongoing debate about the role of funding and
how best to prioritise support for *basic* (sometimes called foundational or
curiosity-driven) research and applied research.[54]

---

[51] For initial estimates, see Cabells' Predatory Reports: Rick Anderson, 'Cabell's Predatory
Journal Blacklist: An Updated Review' (*The Scholarly Kitchen*, 1 May 2019) https://
scholarlykitchen.sspnet.org/2019/05/01/cabells-predatory-journal-blacklist-an-updated-
review/ (accessed 17 March 2021).

[52] Agnes Grudniewicz, 'Predatory Journals: No Definition, No Defence' (2019) 576
*Nature* 210.

[53] It is usual to cite Vannevar Bush's *Science: The Endless Frontier* (United States
Government Printing Office 1945) as the exemplar for the modern description of the
social contract between science and society, which arose from President Roosevelt's 1944
mandate letter to Bush. Given the historic impact of Covid-19, arising with the inauguration of Joe Biden as US President, it is equally appropriate to reference his mandate letter
to incoming science advisor Eric Lander as evidence of the renewed social contract.
https://buildbackbetter.gov/wp-content/uploads/2021/01/OSTP-Appointment.pdf
(accessed 17 March 2021).

[54] See, for example, Felix Bast, 'In Defence of Curiosity-Driven Basic Scientific Research'
(2020) 57 *Science* 21; Advisory Panel for the Review of Federal Support for Fundamental
Science, 'Canada's Fundamental Science Review' (2017) www.sciencereview.ca/eic/site/
059.nsf/vwapj/ScienceReview_April2017-rv.pdf/$file/ScienceReview_April2017-rv.pdf
(accessed 17 March 2021).

## 6.4   The Future Importance of Impact: From Policy to People

We may be living at the best possible time for knowledge to have impact on society. More has been produced, by more people, across more disciplines, on more subjects than at any other time in history. This larger knowledge base can be disseminated to more people in more ways than thought imaginable just a few decades ago. Against this observation is another: it is not only that we find ourselves in the presence of more information and opportunities for dissemination than ever before but that there is a powerful contribution ethic at work among those who wish to convert their knowledge into action, their ideas into impact.

More people can and wish to have impact. Funding organisations are taking seriously the idea that societal impact can be an expected criterion for assessing the merit of grant applications.[55] Importantly, impact and societal benefit, once obscure areas of interdisciplinary research,[56] are themselves the focus of scholarly study.[57] No doubt they will face the same comparative measurement challenges of all academic scholarship. The current and preferred expression of the idea of impact is for evidence to *inform* policy, an oft-repeated phrase by politicians who also pride themselves on recognising the limitations of the phrase evidence-*based* policy. Proponents of this mantra are well known and almost revered. Former US president Barack Obama announced in his 2008 inauguration: '[w]e will restore science to its rightful place and wield technology's wonders to raise healthcare's quality and reduce its costs'.[58] Shortly after

---

[55] For example, it has been almost twenty-five years since the US National Science Foundation (NSF) adopted 'societal impact' as a criterion for assessing grant applications; NSF now refers to these as 'broader impacts'. See 'NSF Proposal and Award Policies and Procedures Guide' (National Science Foundation 2018) www.nsf.gov/pubs/policydocs/pappg18_1/pappg_3.jsp#IIIA2b (accessed 17 March 2021). Other funders have similarly adopted criteria to value social or societal impact including the US National Institutes of Health and the Canadian Institutes of Health Research https://cihr-irsc.gc.ca/e/50604.html (accessed 17 March 2021).

[56] The most notable early example was the Ethical, Legal, and Social Implications Research program, supported by the Human Genome Project from its inception. See, for example, Eric Meslin, Elizabeth Thomson and Joy Boyer, 'The Ethical, Legal, and Social Implications Research Program at the National Human Genome Research Institute' 7 (1997) *Kennedy Institute of Ethics Journal* 291.

[57] Lutz Bornmann, 'Measuring the Societal Impact of Research: Research Is Less and Less Assessed on Scientific Impact Alone – We Should Aim to Quantify the Increasingly Important Contributions of Science to Society' (2012) 13 *EMBO Reports* 673.

[58] https://obamawhitehouse.archives.gov/blog/2009/01/21/president-barack-obamas-inaugural-address (accessed 19 March 2021).

taking office in 2015, Canadian Prime Minister Justin Trudeau said: '[w]e are a government that believes in science – and a government that believes that good scientific knowledge should inform decision-making'.[59] These statements came on the heels of the departing administrations of George W. Bush and Stephen Harper, respectively, whose attitudes towards science and scientists were regarded by many critics as unsupportive. That those statements had to be said at all is a reminder that the road from data to decisions, or from information to impact, is unevenly paved. This may account for the outpouring of support for newly inaugurated US President Joe Biden replenishing the deep well of knowledge at the Office of Science and Technology Policy (OSTP) with key appointments including Eric Lander as director and senior assistant to the President, and elevating Lander's position to Cabinet rank.

It is also here that we witness the reciprocity between impact and legacy. The Obama, Trudeau and Biden comments resonated because they each recalled a time when science seemed to matter more. They were drawing on a history of leadership and legacy that preceded them against which they were reacting, reminiscent of the oft-quoted sentiment used by scientists and politicians that their own work to advance knowledge and society is possible only by 'standing on the shoulders of giants'.[60]

This mutually reinforcing link – between the policy community that believes (or thinks it believes) it needs evidence to inform policy and the academic research community willing to provide it – also sets up mutually reinforcing expectations, some of which cannot help but be unfulfilled, as the demands of policy debates, sometimes best supported by a powerful anecdote,[61] may not always align with the norms of science.[62] New demands also inhibit the presumed reciprocity of science and society as one between experts alone and elected decision-makers. The emergence of diverse expertise, the wisdom of the crowd, advocacy organisations, new ways of disseminating (including the explosion of opinions sometimes masquerading as evidence and unburdened by

---

[59] https://pm.gc.ca/en/mandate-letters/2015/11/12/archived-minister-science-mandate-letter (accessed 19 March 2021).

[60] The history of the phrase is itself the source of academic debate but seems well captured in the explanation here: https://en.wikipedia.org/wiki/Standing_on_the_shoulders_of_giants (accessed 17 March 2021).

[61] John McDonough, 'Using and Misusing Anecdote in Policy' (2001) 20 *Health Affairs* www.healthaffairs.org/doi/10.1377/hlthaff.20.1.207 (accessed 17 March 2021).

[62] Robert Merton's four norms, which he took to be the ethos of science, are communism, universalism, disinterestedness and organised scepticism in *The Sociology of Science: Theoretical and Empirical Investigations* (University of Chicago Press 1973).

traditional expert peer review), new ways of knowing (including indigenous and local knowledge), the engagement of young academics without the protections afforded by tenure or endowed funding and the experiences of many publics all inform policy discussions.

And what of the future? Roger Pelke opens *The Honest Broker* with an illustration of the ways in which science (and scientists) can help (or have impact) on policy, describing four idealised roles:[63] the pure scientist, the science arbiter, the issue advocate and the honest broker of policy alternatives; he spends the rest of the book explaining how these roles work in practice before concluding: 'there are different visions of democracy and these different visions have profound implications for how we think about the roles of scientists and other experts ... Individual scientists should recognize that they have choices about how they engage with policy and politics and that their perspectives on these choices will likely be shaped by their preconceptions about democracy.'[64]

Some of us contributing to this volume, particularly those with more of our careers behind us than ahead of us, have occupied many of Pelke's roles, if by other names. Graeme Laurie has too. He has authored peer-reviewed papers with research funding, sat on or chaired committees whose publications have been requested by the organisations, and supported academic scholars and scholarship. He has mentored students and faculty, managed budgets and projects, and maintained a productive career of writing, teaching and advising. This volume is a testament to Graeme's contributions and diverse impact. As such, it is also an argument for expanding the idea of impact beyond the simplistic arithmetic of number of publications to include the contributions of collaborating, multidisciplinary, civically minded experts to policy.

At this point, we should pause to reflect on how impact can also be seen as something more profound than a mere policy metric. As noted throughout this chapter, in addition to different types of impact having their own metrics, impact can also be understood from the perspective of epistemic and personal *legacy*. The former can be seen from the vantage point of how work has informed new ways of knowing. The ELSI programme of the Human Genome Project was an early example of this type of epistemic legacy, especially in the way it normalised the idea of using collaborative, interdisciplinary research to tackle ethical,

[63] Roger Pelke, *The Honest Broker: Making Sense of Science in Policy and Politics* (Cambridge University Press 2007).
[64] Ibid., 152.

legal and social problems arising in genomics.[65] So too was Graeme's initial articulation of the idea of liminality in health law regulation,[66] a concept that has led to high-impact publications and funded research programmes. Each of these disrupted (positively) the ways of knowing that had been used before.

But it is the version of impact as personal legacy that warrants our deepest attention as it implicates the influence one has on other persons. This type of legacy is measured not by the number of papers published, or by $h$-index ratings, ARC scores, grant dollars awarded, or even the policies changed. Rather, personal legacy is also judged in how people are remembered, for the ideas they advanced, the risks they took, the experiments they tried. Each of these was lubricated by gifts of friendship, humour, collaboration and creativity that inspire others to pursue their own ideas, take their own risks, try their own experiments. Ultimately, this may be the way we should understand the future importance of impact: for the many ways in which it serves as the connecting legacy between people and policy. Graeme has done that exceptionally well.

---

[65] Jane Kaye et al, 'ELSI 2.0: A New International Collaboratory for Genomics and Society Research' (2012) 36 *Science* 673.

[66] Graeme Laurie, 'Liminality and the Limits of Law in Health Research Regulation: What Are We Missing in the Spaces in-Between?' (2017) 25 *Medical Law Review* 47.

# 7

## Breathing Life into Law

### What It Means to Take an Ethics+ Approach
### to Conceptualising Law in Research Governance

CALVIN WAI-LOON HO AND JUSTIN YUK CHEONG WONG

## 7.1 Introduction

When we study law and regulatory systems, we are not merely studying a set of rules and techniques to fixate social realities, or indeed the living beings that embody them, into friezes. There is little doubt that laws and regulations generally seek to secure regularity in social transactions and expectations, and thereby confer a degree of stability without which many aspects of social life will be arduous, if not impossible. From this vantage point, laws and regulations are conventionally seen as hierarchical, prescriptive, normatively conservative, rigid and often coercive. When applied to health-related research, laws and regulations are typically regarded as limiting and counterproductive; in contrast, scientific innovations are construed as disruptive forces that must be carefully managed, if not precluded altogether. This alterity and permutations of it are hard to miss when studying the regulatory governance of health-related research, whether in London, New York, Singapore or Hong Kong.[1]

On the legal and regulatory side of the alterity, Graeme Laurie reminds us that the regulatory governance (inclusive of laws, regulations and research administration) of health-related research should be purposive;

---

[1] These places are specified because of the familiarity of one of the authors with them, some of which having been his research field sites: see further Calvin Ho, *Juridification of Bioethics: Governance of Human Pluripotent Cell Research* (Imperial College Press 2016). It may be reasonable to say that this alterity is a common enough phenomenon and is reflected in the regulatory policies of many jurisdictions.

not in the negation of all risks or otherwise in rendering scientific endeavours predictable and thereby manageable, but in sustaining certain fundamental values and nurturing particular relationships. He warns against the adoption of a rule-based regulatory practice culture, which tends to promote a culture of mere compliance.[2] A complicated legal architecture that is built up around research approval promotes a tick-box mentality, which fosters unhealthy suspicion and favours procedure and caution at the expense of real engagement.[3] A manifestation of this mindset is when even ethical guidance starts to assume a mantle of obligation; to become non-negotiable and require additional measures of compliance. When compliance serves no purpose other than to standardise or regularise the relationship between researcher and research participant at a single moment (typically being the moment the consent form is signed), form prevails over function and the act that is regularised may well become meaningless to the individuals to which it relates. This tick-box approach to consent-taking fails to recognise the initial consent as merely the start of a research relationship, one that must – like any other relationship – be nurtured over time in order to cultivate trust.[4]

These concerns that Graeme brought to light offer us an insight into what a command-and-control (or rule-based) form of regulation could be like when (mis-)applied to health-related research. This mindset would perhaps broadly reflect an overt 'black-letter' attitude, which, in the common law tradition, is one that privileges certainty (and clarity) at the expense of flexibility, responsiveness and perhaps even contextual sensibility. For instance, the English common law rule that the dead body of a person does not have an owner and is not subject to property law is clear and broadly accepted by common law jurisdictions.[5] Where disposal of bodily remains of deceased individuals is concerned, this rule fits

---

[2] Graeme Laurie and Nayha Sethi, 'Towards Principles-Based Approaches to Governance of Health-Related Research Using Personal Data' (2013) 4 *European Journal of Risk Regulation* 42, 45.

[3] Graeme Laurie, 'Reflexive Governance in Biobanking: On the Value of Policy Led Approaches and the Need to Recognise the Limits of Law' (2011) 130 *Human Genetics* 347, 351.

[4] Graeme Laurie and Emily Postan, 'Rhetoric or Reality: What Is the Legal Status of the Consent Form in Health-Related Research?' (2013) 21 *Medical Law Review* 371, 411–12.

[5] Peter Skegg, 'Medical Uses of Corpses and the "No Property" Rule' (1992) 32 *Medicine, Science and the Law* 311. Over time, exceptions to this rule have emerged, notably in relation to certain bodily materials that have been collected and stored for reproductive purposes. See Shawn Harmon and Graeme Laurie, '*Yearworth v. North Bristol NHS Trust*: Property, Principles, Precedents and Paradigms' (2010) 69 *Cambridge Law Journal* 476.

well within a regulatory paradigm that thrives on certainty as well as protecting individual dignity and the interests of (surviving) significant others of the deceased. However, such an approach fits poorly within a paradigm that reflects the nature of health-related research, that is, one that deals in uncertainty, complexity and dynamism, and seeks to promote trust and the public interest as a means of satisfying the social value of research.[6] As Graeme explains, hard rules cannot cope with the myriad considerations which include uncertain risks, uncertain futures and uncertain outcomes.[7]

Governance of health-related research must be reflexive in order for a regulatory system to support organic policy development.[8] This system must be responsive to the demands of the social endeavour (be it research or some other social project) by taking into account a range of values and interests, particularly those of individuals or communities who are most affected (such as human participants where research is concerned). A reflexive approach to governance is premised on mutual learning and engagement rather than a 'them and us' culture of regulation. It is also a principles-based approach in that it offers space for discussion and negotiation while promoting partnership in governance and regulatory pathways forward.[9] The regulatory culture that it fosters is reflective and justificatory; it seeks to provide practical and effective support to researchers, research administrators and participants alike in navigating increasingly complex regulatory landscapes.[10]

This chapter focuses on the introspective approach that Graeme presents to us in thinking about the law and its relationship with the social beings and activities whose goals are broadly directed at advancing knowledge in the biosciences. Labelled the 'Ethics+' approach, it is important for at least three reasons: (1) from a legal standpoint, it

[6] Agomoni Ganguli-Mitra et al, 'Reconfiguring Social Value in Health Research through the Lens of Liminality' (2017) 31 *Bioethics* 87, 93. On the social value of research, see also Ezekiel Emanuel, David Wendler and Christine Grady, 'What Makes Clinical Research Ethical?' (2000) 283 *JAMA* 2701.

[7] Laurie and Sethi (n 2) 46. Laurie and Sethi further observe (at 47) that while rule-based governance tends to be a state-driven, vertically-oriented, top-down, command-and-control deployment of formal (hard law) instruments, principles-based or reflexive governance is often a far more horizontally-oriented enterprise, more likely driven by local actors and more reliant on soft law options such as guidance or professional codes.

[8] Laurie (n 3) 352.

[9] Laurie and Sethi (n 2) 57.

[10] Graeme Laurie, 'What Does It Mean to Take an Ethics+ Approach to Global Biobank Governance?' (2017) 9 *Asian Bioethics Review* 285, 296.

provides a critical perspective of the crucial role and limits of law in the regulation of research; (2) from a bioethical perspective, it provides insights into how regulatory governance constructs and constitutes the scientific cause and public trust; and (3) from a policy angle, it guides the formulation of an approach to the regulatory governance of challenges to come, such as the application of big data in health and research.

Overall, we reiterate the important legacy of Graeme's oeuvre, but without having to set 'law' so distinctively apart from 'ethics' as the 'Ethics+' approach appears to suggest. While we do not think that Graeme would himself adopt a dichotomous view of ethics and law, he might have considered the essentialisation of law as a particular form of practice in the governance of health-related research to be necessary to underscore the great need for reflexivity. In other words, Graeme's concern could be understood as one that relates to the pure instrumentalisation of law to meet limited and perhaps even blinkered motives, and without regard for its wider purposes and commitments. If our understanding is correct, then our view that there should be no fundamental difference between law as applied in a research context (or health law in brief) and health/medical jurisprudence (or, as it were, the 'spirit' of law) accords well with his after all.

## 7.2   The 'Ethics+' Approach

Writing mainly in the context of research involving human biological materials, Graeme presents to us what is known as the 'Ethics+' approach, the foundational elements of which have been stated as:[11]

(a) drawing us back to the strengths of bioethical reflection and the importance of sound ethical judgement;
(b) requiring and reinforcing the need to articulate and pursue the underlying values at stake;
(c) resembling governance processes rather than some pseudo-regulatory or quasi-legal framework in the sense that it must be designed to add value and not simply replicate regulations found elsewhere;
(d) involving a range of actors and stakeholders and, perhaps most importantly, requiring engagement of those actors in the deliberative

---

[11]   Ibid., 298.

and reflective processes so that mere compliance is never adequate; and

(e) requiring stewardship of these processes by trained actors who can support and facilitate the deliberative and reflective processes.

Legal (and regulatory) boundaries in the 'Ethics+' approach are not strictly immutable and non-negotiable, even if they have been erected to protect and promote core values and interests.[12] Elsewhere, Graeme explains that legal boundaries tend to reflect a particular state of science or ethical thinking at a particular time. With scientific or technological change, however, these boundaries may need to be reconsidered in a manner that advances the public interest. How these boundaries should be shifted or redrawn is facilitated by an agreed upon set of principles to be taken into account in ways that are cognisant of the likelihood of, and relative threats to, the principles and values that they promote.[13] While the 'Ethics+' approach is principles-based, we are warned against treating principles in a manner that is too rule-like. Rather, the discretionary element in such an approach needs to be recognised so that decision-makers are provided with sufficient guidance and support to temper discretion, while also promoting an appropriate culture of reflection and justification.[14] Principles-based regulation can be contrasted with rules-based regulation in that the former relies upon broad and looser principles to guide action, whereas the latter relies on stricter prescriptive (and often also proscriptive) rules for framing approaches to governance and decision-making.[15] Principles should therefore be seen as fundamental starting points to identify areas of disagreement, and to guide deliberation and action. Their purpose is to point actors or decision-makers in the direction of the relevant values and considerations to be taken into consideration,[16] and to forge overlapping consensus through deliberation and dialogue.[17]

---

[12] Shawn Harmon, Graeme Laurie and Gill Haddow, 'Governing Risk, Engaging Publics and Engendering Trust: New Horizons for Law and Social Science?' (2013) 40 *Science and Public Policy* 25, 28.

[13] Laurie and Sethi (n 2) 48–9.

[14] Ibid., 49.

[15] Ibid., 44.

[16] Ibid., 46. See also Graeme Laurie, 'The UK Biobank Ethics and Governance Council: How Valuable Is an "Ethics+" Approach to Governance?' in Kris Dierickx and Pascal Borry (eds), *New Challenges for Biobanks: Ethics, Law and Governance* (Intersentia 2009) 243.

[17] Laurie and Sethi (n 2) 48.

These insights that Graeme eloquently articulates are derived from within a particular socio-historical episode, and it will be instructive briefly to describe it. Fin-de-siècle regulatory developments in the United Kingdom relating to the handling, use and disposal of human bodies, organs and tissues for purposes that include biomedical research have been instructive to policy-makers, regulators, research institutions, academicians and other interested stakeholders well beyond its shores. Central to these developments are the enactment of the Human Tissue Act 2004 and the establishment of the Human Tissue Authority in 2005. As detailed in Chapter 9 in this volume, legislative intervention was considered necessary following the Alder Hey organs scandal, which involved the unauthorised removal, retention and disposal of human tissue at Alder Hey Children's Hospital in Liverpool between 1988 and 1995.[18] While these developments were not directed at biomedical research, studies that involved the collection and use of human biological materials nonetheless fell subsequently within the scope of regulatory oversight. An especially important research endeavour initiated around that time was the UK Biobank, established in 2006 as a large, long-term study on contributions of genetic predisposition and environmental exposure to the development of disease. As explained in more detail in Chapter 14 in this volume, UK Biobank operated within the standards set out in an Ethics and Governance Framework (EGF), which outlined safeguards that were considered necessary to ensure that biological materials and related data were used for scientifically and ethically appropriate purposes. For the purposes of this chapter, there are three points to note about the EGF: (1) it was developed by a group that included experts in law, research ethics, philosophy, science and social science, and consumer representation, and underwent public consult-ation too; (2) it was developed in anticipation that the research use of human biological materials and related data would raise ethical, legal and social concerns, and that it would evolve over time to adapt to scientific, ethical, legal and other developments; and (3) it was overseen by the Ethics and Governance Council (EGC), appointed by the funders of UK Biobank as an independent guardian of the UK Biobank and the EGF, until the EGC was replaced by the Ethics Advisory Committee (EAC) in 2018.

---

[18] 'The Royal Liverpool Children's Inquiry Report' (The Stationery Office 2001) www .gov.uk/government/publications/the-royal-liverpool-childrens-inquiry-report (accessed 22 January 2021).

Graeme served as the Chair of the UK Biobank's EGC from 2006 to 2010, and it would perhaps not be surprising at all to say that the EGF exemplified the 'Ethics+' approach. In a co-authored publication,[19] Graeme explains that, through the EGF, UK Biobank combined 'hard' governance (in the specification of rules) to protect the interests of participants as well as 'soft' governance (in the provision of guidelines), taking into account different values and interests and ensuring continuing participation by members of the public in the biobank and its governance process. He goes on to explain that the EGF illustrated the way in which government and governance function neither as two poles of a continuum nor as two completely intertwined entities but as a 'soft' wrapping of governance around a 'hard' core of government. This arrangement recognises that government alone would not provide a sufficient basis for the establishment of the biobank. It requires the active participation of publics and clinicians and, in a modern democracy, this cannot be obtained by central government edict. On the other hand, the legislative framework has provided a layer of protection for participants without which trust in the biobank would be unlikely to be gained.[20]

The storage and research use of 'leftover' or residual tissue from a therapeutic procedure or research protocol illustrate the range of interests that may be entailed. These include those of the UK Biobank and of potentially conflicting interest-based positions, notably scientific improvement, protection of participants and fair distribution of benefits, among others. In the past, tissue has been stored in repositories on the assumption that it is no longer wanted (or abandoned) by the person from whom it has been taken or has otherwise been collected for a clear purpose and end point (such as a pathological specimen maintained for medico-legal reasons). With technological advancement, small tissue repositories have grown in scale and complexity to take on infrastructural features such as biobanks that could support a variety of research over an extended period of time. For this reason, they are deliberately constructed to be purposively open-ended and enduring until these biological resources have been exhausted. Graeme highlights that this gives rise to an immediate tension between establishing policies and

---

[19] Graeme Laurie, Ann Bruce and Catherine Lyall, 'The Roles of Values and Interests in the Governance of the Life Sciences: Learning Lessons from the "Ethics+" Approach of the UK Biobank', in Catherine Lyall, Theo Papaioannou and James Smith (eds), *The Limits to Governance: The Challenge of Policy-Making for the New Life Sciences* (Ashgate 2009).

[20] Ibid., 51, 53 and 74.

procedures to *protect* adequately the interests of participants who have contributed to the establishment of the resource and establishing policies and procedures which *promote* the use of the resource as widely as possible. Mechanisms that can effectively balance up these two goals of protection and promotion are not readily available.[21] At one extreme, certain jurisdictions have limited the use of tissue to specific purposes for which they have been collected.[22] This approach could provide better assurance that the interests of tissue donors are safeguarded, but it does not otherwise promote the efficient use of the biological resources. Ironically, the need to seek recourse in a rules-based response – in choosing protection over promotion – points to the system as having already failed in being adequately responsive for balancing competing needs as a means of advancing the public interest.[23]

This is not to say that there is no place for 'hard' rules in research governance. Rather, the approach that Graeme advocates is one whereby principles and rules are not mutually exclusive in their operation and their deployment becomes a matter of good design rather than a preference for one over another.[24] This reflexive mode of governance is 'performed' in a manner that better reflects the dynamic nature of science and uses the law more effectively as a value- and institution-framing mechanism within a broader and more ground-up enterprise. Recognising the limits of law by embedding it in a more interdisciplinary-designed governance regime means that policy- and law-makers are better able to anticipate which challenges might arise and to build systems that are sufficiently adaptive and responsive.[25] The 'Ethics+' approach, as applied in the EGF, seeks to allow these different and often conflicting interests to be recognised, negotiated, respected and protected.

## 7.3 Relationality, Purpose and Trust

Being fundamentally participatory, the 'Ethics+' approach avoids some of the pitfalls associated with certain 'engagement' strategies adopted by

---

[21] Laurie (n 3) 348.

[22] See, for instance, Randy Mungwira et al, 'Is It Ethical to Prevent Secondary Use of Stored Biological Samples and Data Derived from Consenting Research Participants? The Case of Malawi' (2015) 16 *BMC Medical Ethics*.

[23] Laurie (n 3) 354.

[24] Laurie and Sethi (n 2) 47.

[25] Harmon, Laurie and Haddow (n 12) 31.

regulators and policy-makers,[26] such as those that give rise to the 'Collingridge dilemma' where 'attempts to intervene too early in a technology trajectory mean that insufficient information is available on which to act, yet to wait can mean that technologies become entrenched and influence and change become correspondingly more difficult to effect'.[27] The 'Ethics+' approach bypasses this problem through engagement with stakeholders on their own terms and experiences, and thereby co-produces pathways through the research process itself.[28] This is implicit in reflexive governance, which concerns both in-parallel partnership in governance in the face of future uncertainty and the facilitation of mutual learning from experience over time. As Graeme explains, reflexivity requires that actors have 'the capacities and the competencies to participate in and contribute to social learning; that they communicate and interact in relational and deliberative ways; that they engage in and learn from experimentation through collaborative forms of joint enquiry; and that their learning is informed by cognitive processes entailing the adjustment and redefinition of frames, representations and collective identities'.[29] However, this reflexivity is not purely a personal attribute or an acquired ability. It is one that is infused into the agents, processes and mechanisms of regulatory governance, and thereby also encodes the need for relational association by those who govern (at all levels, from policy to administrative) with the different stakeholders. For this reason, Graeme quite appropriately depicts 'Ethics+' as a processual phenomenon. Not only does this approach require reflection and deliberation on each step of a process; it also requires 'the identification of a telos for the process in question, and mechanisms for recalibration if novel events arise that might divert the actors from their course'.[30] In this sense, stewardship is not solely the responsibility of the 'governors' but must be a shared responsibility where all stakeholders commit to advancing the common purpose or what may be of social value to the collective.[31]

---

[26] Laurie, Bruce and Lyall (n 19) 59.

[27] Laurie (n 3) 348 citing David Collingridge, *Critical Decision-Making: A New Theory of Social Choice* (Macmillan 1982).

[28] Laurie (n 10) 297.

[29] Laurie (n 3) 351–2.

[30] Laurie (n 10) 297.

[31] Graeme explains that social value is pertinent since the process towards the realisation of social value will not be clear from the start of the research endeavor: see Laurie (n 10) 297. For an empirical analysis of regulatory stewardship in a research ethics review context, see

Drawing reference again to the UK Biobank, we have noted already that the EGC served as an independent guardian of the EGF and that its responsibilities included keeping the EGF up to date, monitoring and reporting publicly on the conformity of the UK Biobank with the EGF, and advising on the interests of research participants and the general public on matters within its remit.[32] Additionally, the EGC kept under review applications for access to the UK Biobank resource with regard to the interests of research participants and in accordance with the Intellectual Property and Access Policy, and provided approval for any transfer of the UK Biobank resource (or substantial parts of it) to a third party (should the UK Biobank cease to operate, for example). This governance arrangement, particularly in the relationship between the UK Biobank and the EGC, allowed 'real time interactions and ethical reflection about how the UK Biobank should respond to novel issues in the management of the resource that were never previously anticipated'.[33] Unlike clinical practice guidelines, which tend to be pre-scriptive and to limit discretionary judgement, the EGF set out principles that were to be considered and applied in the relational context within which the UK Biobank is nestled with its key stakeholders: participants, research users and society. These principles were to be seen as starting points for deliberation and action; they are less likely to be taken as sanctions-backed rules as no single course of action is mandated. Such an approach is better suited as a complement to rules in areas where there is genuine uncertainty, and where the exercise of judgement between two or more defensible options is needed.[34]

The relational turn in the 'Ethics+' approach to governance is espe-cially important because the EGF was treated as a 'living instrument' subject to ongoing revision as necessary over time,[35] and thereby also represented a clear articulation of the value basis upon which the model of governance was established and of how different ethical principles have been negotiated.[36] This is quintessential of reflexivity, which in turn created an obligation on the part of the EGC, in its governance capacity,

Edward Dove, *Regulatory Stewardship of Health Research: Navigating Participant Protection and Research Promotion* (Edward Elgar 2020).

[32]  See UK Biobank Ethics and Governance Council https://egcukbiobank.org.uk/ (accessed 22 January 2021).

[33]  Laurie (n 10) 289.

[34]  Laurie and Sethi (n 2) 47.

[35]  Laurie (n 10) 289.

[36]  Laurie, Bruce and Lyall (n 19) 66.

to make explicit the basis for much of its reasoning as well as what informed its advisory and monitoring role. A failure to do so could result in the fragmentation of the deliberative process along the lines of competing values and interests, thereby also stalling policy- and decision-making.[37] Graeme explains that, as a governance feature, this obligation is one that required the EGC to be open and participatory.[38] It is typified by ongoing engagement with values and interests, responsive and explicit advice and monitoring, and a commitment to explaining why particular policies or decisions have been adopted in a manner understandable to a majority of reasonable persons. It is also characterised by clear articulation of criteria for decision-making, transparency at every level, and an overall aim to reach decisions which are acceptable to (all) reasonable persons because the reasons (and values) behind them are at least understood, even if they are not agreed with.[39]

A result is the assurance of integrity of purpose, in the sense of setting realistic expectations based on cogent reasons for all stakeholders in the biobanking enterprise, and particularly the participants. Such integrity of purpose does not dictate a specific approach to any particular aspect of the operation of a biobank, whether by mandating informed consent or by requiring absolute anonymity of personal data. Rather, the principle focuses on the relationship between those with responsibility for the biobank and those who have contributed to it or might expect to benefit from it, which could include society at large. This broadly egalitarian and participatory approach is in turn constructive not only of a degree of reasonable consensus but also of trustworthiness. It further provides an assurance that the resource will be managed to bring about the core purposes for which the biobank was initiated as a social enterprise.[40]

Trust, then, arises from the common commitment to the principle of integrity of purpose, while the principle of reflexivity provides a means to realise it and to establish a relationship for moving forward.[41] Openness in the basis for decision-making makes explicit the pros and cons being balanced, the benefits and risks, and the different interests and value-preferences. The sharing of values, or the recognition of one's values in relation to those of others, is an important element in building

---

[37] Ibid., 72.
[38] Ibid., 66.
[39] Ibid., 73.
[40] Laurie (n 3) 349.
[41] Ibid., 354.

a relationship of trust.[42] The 'Ethics+' approach aims at neither identifying dominant values nor necessarily accommodating the majority of interests; rather, it seeks, through democratic participation, systematically to garner evidence and identify the range of values and interests at stake and to explore the basis of commonalities and differences, in order to develop policies and take decisions which are ultimately acceptable to a body of 'reasonable' stakeholders.[43] Choice then, as Graeme observes, can be an important governance tool and one that involves some degree of empowerment of participants as stakeholders. In the UK Biobank context, choice and trust are closely allied in the sense that choice in favour of UK Biobank is a measure of trust in the project. The options that it offers are, however, somewhat limited, such as the choice to participate (or not) and the choice to withdraw (or not). The processual character of 'Ethics+' will thereby also encapsulate mechanisms to measure and gauge participants' (and public) attitudes and to understand what is informing their choices. These mechanisms in turn confer on 'Ethics+' as a governance approach a degree of responsiveness to concerns or conflict, and a capacity to anticipate choices that are likely to be made.[44]

## 7.4   'Big Data' Research Governance

It is, we think, fitting to conclude with a brief account of how the 'Ethics+' approach continues to guide reflexive governance of emergent technologies and practices in the biosciences. As one of the chairpersons of a working group that recently promulgated an ethics framework for Big Data in Health and Research (hereafter, BDF),[45] Graeme instructively demonstrates that a similarly reflective, principles-based, processual and participatory approach could be applied in practical decision-making on ethical issues that arise from the use of big data in a variety of health and research contexts. Like the 'Ethics+' approach, the BDF is intended for a wide range of professional audiences that include policy-makers, ethics committees, data access committees and data controllers. Further similarities are apparent in the three main components of the BDF, these being: a list of values considered to be central to a number of big data

---

[42]   Laurie, Bruce and Lyall (n 19) 65.
[43]   Ibid., 51.
[44]   Ibid., 68.
[45]   Vicki Xafis et al, 'An Ethics Framework for Big Data in Health and Research' (2019) 11 *Asian Bioethics Review* 227.

contexts; a systematic deliberative decision-making process; and three rule-like 'considerations' that operate as a value- and decision-framing mechanism.[46]

It is less clear which actors should take on stewardship responsibility for these processes, but this will presumably be dependent on the specific context within which the BDF is applied. In keeping with its processual character, the BDF is not prescriptive of any decision or procedure; it seeks only to provide insight into the central role of underlying values in the decision-making process and in the justification of decisions that are made. Like the 'Ethics+' approach, the BDF gives emphasis to the relational dimension of governance, in respect of which the integrity of purpose is the cornerstone of trust and trustworthiness. From this vantage point, stewardship responsibility would entail facilitative acts that are undertaken within a collaborative space, even while the spatial domain is continuously evaluated and redefined in a purposive and participatory manner. With the growing use of big data digital tools in health care and related research, publication of the BDF is especially timely.

In health-related research, digital tools, including mobile sensing devices equipped with sensors to track mobility and fluctuations in a range of biomarkers of research participants, have been increasingly used to study mental health problems, for instance,[47] some of which involve children and young persons.[48] Major research funders (such as the National Institutes of Health in the United States) have provided support for the use of these digital tools, broadly categorised as mobile imaging, pervasive sensing, social media and location tracking (MISST) tools.[49] While there is still relatively limited guidance on ethical study design, digital tools applied in such research are nevertheless subject to

---

[46] Graeme Laurie and Tai Shyong (on behalf of the SHAPES Working Group), 'Delivering a Practical Framework for Ethical Decision-Making Involving Big Data in Health and Research' (2019) 11 *Asian Bioethics Review* 223.

[47] Florian Ferreri et al, 'How New Technologies Can Improve Prediction, Assessment, and Intervention in Obsessive-Compulsive Disorder (e-OCD): Review' (2019) 6 *JMIR Mental Health* e11643. See also Melanie Lovatt and John Holmes, 'Digital Phenotyping and Sociological Perspectives in a Brave New World' (2017) 112 *Addiction* 1286.

[48] Candice Odgers and Michaeline Jensen, 'Annual Research Review: Adolescent Mental Health in the Digital Age: Facts, Fears, and Future Directions' (2020) 61 *Journal of Child Psychology and Psychiatry* 336.

[49] Sarah Dunseath et al, 'NIH Support of Mobile, Imaging, Pervasive Sensing, Social Media and Location Tracking (MISST) Research: Laying the Foundation to Examine Research Ethics in the Digital Age' (2018) 1 *Digital Medicine* 20171.

research ethics review and must comply with regulatory requirements on personal data collection and use.

Recent contributions to the digital health and bioethics literature have identified ethical concerns that could arise from methodological limitations that make it difficult to draw definitive conclusions from the research,[50] along with additional ethical and regulatory considerations that should be taken up in research ethics review when digital tools and social media platforms are applied to locate, track and communicate with research participants.[51] Where digital tools such as mobile sensing devices are used on vulnerable populations, there is arguably an ethical imperative to collaborate with particular groups and communities who are part of the research at the design and implementation stage.[52] Online platforms are also being established to enable stakeholders in the digital health ecosystem collectively to shape dynamic and responsive ethical and responsible research practices.[53] The upshot of all of this is that digitalisation within a research context should be considered, measured, largely (on the part of the participants) voluntary and understood to be within a testing environment.

There will always be occasions for genuine and reasonable disagreement over the use of these digital tools, which, for some, will fail to strike an appropriate balance between protection of the (privacy) interests of participants and promotion of social value in research. Like the 'Ethics+' approach that precedes it, the BDF highlights the need for mechanisms to gauge participants' expectations as to their concerns and interests (such as privacy) and as to what counts as research that is of social value, which should be factored into decision-making processes. In addition, mechanisms are required to allow participants to voice their concerns about what might be happening to their data and to their privacy; to exercise certain

---

[50] Chris Hollis et al, 'Annual Research Review: Digital Health Interventions for Children and Young People with Mental Health Problems – A Systematic and Meta-Review' (2017) 58 *Journal of Child Psychology and Psychiatry* 474.

[51] Ananya Bhatia-Lin et al, 'Ethical and Regulatory Considerations for Using Social Media Platforms to Locate and Track Research Participants' (2019) 19 *American Journal of Bioethics* 47. See also Samuel Lustgarten and Jon Elhai, 'Technology Use in Mental Health Practice and Research: Legal and Ethical Risks' (2018) 25 *Clinical Psychology Science and Practice* e12234.

[52] Samantha Breslin, Martine Shareck and Daniel Fuller, 'Research Ethics for Mobile Sensing Device Use by Vulnerable Populations' (2019) 232 *Social Science & Medicine* 50.

[53] John Torous and Camille Nebeker, 'Navigating Ethics in the Digital Age: Introducing Connected and Open Research Ethics (CORE), a Tool for Researchers and Institutional Review Boards' (2017) 19 *Journal of Medical Internet Research* e38.

rights (such as the right to withdraw at any time and for any reasons without consequence); and to remain engaged in big data research as a social enterprise if they so wish. In this respect, Graeme continues to instruct us in the manner by which the BDF could be applied in deliberation of cross-sectoral sharing of data projects, comprising activities and arrangements that generate, use and link biomedical data beyond the health sector.[54]

The application of the BDF as a deliberative balancing approach is presented in six steps: (1) What exactly is at stake? (2) How do the substantive values in the BDF help the project? (3) What are likely actions that might be taken in response? (4) How should this deliberative balancing approach be given effect and how might the project engage dissenting or sceptical voices? (5) Which action has the strongest ethical weight and what are its likely influences? (6) How should the outcome be communicated? There will undoubtedly be more work to follow in terms of trained agents, processes and mechanisms, which will need to be worked into the research ethics review infrastructure. But reflexive governance already makes clear at an early stage that constructive engagement involving all stakeholders must be initiated: researchers should not be concerned only with form filling; research ethics committees and institutional review boards should not be concerned only with compliance; and data controllers and data privacy regulators should not be concerned only with prescribing rules. It is beyond the scope of this chapter to provide a detailed comparative examination of the 'Ethics+' approach and the BDF. Our goal here is simply to suggest that the former is not merely an analytical account of a historical episode; it is also one that continues to be immensely useful in steering and shaping regulatory governance of emerging concerns and developments.

## 7.5    Conclusion

The lived experience of law in medical practice and research is typified by intricate, sometimes complex and often mundane (and perhaps even ritualistic) procedural requirements. While some scholars have been content to limit the normativity of law to this account, Graeme Laurie reminds us that law is interconnected with ethics and that its distinctiveness may be better understood as a process, particularly in liminal spaces

---

[54] Graeme Laurie, 'Cross-Sectoral Big Data: The Application of an Ethics Framework for Big Data in Health and Research' (2019) 11 *Asian Bioethics Review* 372.

where the roles of ethics and law are blurred. This processual conception of law is in turn a component of governance regimes that Graeme depicts as 'Ethics+'. He argues that ethics is always a necessary component of a robust and defensible regime of health research that is rooted in the core values and principles at stake while concurrently enabling adaptation and accommodation. Law as an 'Ethics+' governance regime embraces uncertainty and the liminal nature of the health research journey. Moreover, it admits value-based objectives that can act as foci for all stakeholders. This ground-breaking insight represents a bright beacon that points the way to a rich and non-formalistic account of law, not simply as law in action or law on the books but law subsisting in-between. As we read Graeme, the purpose and the course of law should not be primarily directed by the exigencies of practice, or otherwise as a philosophical enterprise. In being essentially processual, law should be relational. In this chapter, we have shown how Graeme (along with his collaborators), drawing from his experiences and insights with the EGF and the EGC of UK Biobank, has built a body of legal knowledge on this relational approach to governance, as opposed to one that is more command-and-control or rule-based in character. For the purposes of this chapter, we have focused on one epistemic artefact that Graeme has presented to us: the 'Ethics+' approach. At a conceptual level, it explains how integrity of purpose relates to trust and trustworthiness, and why regulation (and governance more broadly) should ultimately remain relational and invested in the stakeholders. Practically, the 'Ethics+' approach serves as a guide to action, and one that is neither exclusively prescriptive (or proscriptive) nor permissive. We have also shown how the foundational elements of Graeme's 'Ethics+' account of law have moved beyond its constitutive contexts in the UK to the establishment of the BDF for the appropriate use of big data in health and research in the Far East. While the primary aim of the BDF is to provide practical guidance to a wide range of professional audiences, we have traced its conceptual origins in keeping with Graeme's vision of legal governance that is reflexive, responsive and, ultimately, relational.

We do not attempt (or think it possible) to reduce Graeme's immensely rich ideas and insights to a few commemorative legacies. Instead, we conclude with a brief account of how his work and insights have deeply shaped the work of one of us, and in three respects. First, the construct of 'Ethics+' has added to the vocabulary by which scholars have been able to render visible, as well as advocate, a less rule-based or command-and-control approach to the governance of health-related research. This epistemic development occurred in tandem with its public policy corollary on the research use of biological materials. As we discussed in Section 7.2, the regulatory framework that initially emerged in response to the Alder Hey events assumed a less prescriptive character when applied to the UK Biobank initiative. This development did not occur spontaneously but through deliberative and purposive engagement among regulators, administrators, researchers, research participants and other interested stakeholders. The key features of this regulatory development in the UK have been distilled and subsumed into the 'Ethics+' approach, which in turn helped to inform policy developments elsewhere (notably Singapore),[55] and in academic discussions on the complexification of biobank governance, particularly across the Asia and Pacific regions.[56]

Second, the 'Ethics+' approach explains why the law should itself be a learning system and how it could be so. Generally speaking, a command-and-control (rule-based) approach privileges certainty and efficiency. In contrast, a collaborative approach that is premised on fair-minded participation and reflexivity is more likely to be responsive and adaptive to change. Additionally, the latter approach better supports learning and promotes trustworthiness, as well as trust among stakeholders. In Section 7.3, we noted how Graeme has highlighted reflexivity on the part of the EGC as having created an obligation to make explicit the basis of its reasoning and the conditions that inform its advisory and monitoring roles. This openness and willingness to engage have also been a means by which consensus was (and was seen to be) built on reason, manifested in processual features that include sustaining engagement with varied values and interests, eliciting advice, monitoring and evaluating developments consistently, and explaining why particular policies or decisions have been adopted in a manner understandable to reasonable persons. As Graeme also explains, a regulatory approach that is capable of identifying a *telos* for a process in question and recalibrating itself without compromising the integrity of its purpose is better able to secure trustworthiness and promote trust. This more egalitarian and learning-oriented approach to regulation has been applied, through

---

[55] Bioethics Advisory Committee of Singapore, *Ethics Guidelines for Human Biomedical Research* (Bioethics Advisory Committee 2015) www.bioethics-singapore.gov.sg/files/publications/reports/ethics-guidelines-for-human-biomedical-research-report-only.pdf (accessed 22 January 2021).

[56] Calvin Ho and Karel Caals, 'Editorial: Special Issue on Biobanking' (2017) 9 *Asian Bioethics Review* 277.

conceptual cross-pollination, to the regulatory governance of medical devices based on artificial intelligence (AI).[57] As the concept of the liminal space becomes more prominent with increasing capacitation of machine learning in a growing number of medical devices, the 'Ethics+' approach – as exemplar – will obtain even greater purchase and currency.

Third, the deep insight that is implicit in the 'Ethics+' approach is its explication of the relational character of regulation or governance, often obfuscated by appeals to disinterest and objectivity (particularly evident in more technocratic approaches to regulation or governance). To secure integrity of purpose, Graeme reminds us that we must not forget the relationship between those with responsibility to regulate or govern, and those who have contributed to regulation or governance, or might expect to benefit from it. Whether a position is reasonable is thereby also determined within a specific relational context, rather than being devoid of it. In Section 7.4, we showed how this important feature is common to both the 'Ethics+' approach and the BDF. We have additionally explained why (in Section 7.4 and elsewhere[58]), in the light of emerging big data health-related research, this relational component will be crucial in building and sustaining trust and trustworthiness.

If the seemingly laconic 'Ethics+' approach suggests Graeme's lack of confidence in the law, such a proposition could not be further from the truth. Rather than draw on the analytic of alterity to critique the 'other', Graeme has instead turned the critical lens inward and demonstrated to us all what the law could and should be, particularly for those whose life and work are deeply enmeshed with it. Far from denigrating the relevance of law to health-related research, this deeply introspective approach reveals to us how the zest of law must itself be sustained. Graeme's work is demonstrative not only of analytical ingenuity but also of an illustrious and passionate life in the law.

---

[57] Calvin Ho et al, 'Governance of Automated Image Analysis and Artificial Intelligence Analytics in Healthcare' (2019) 74 *Clinical Radiology* 329.

[58] Calvin Ho, Joseph Ali and Karel Caals, 'Ensuring Trustworthy Use of Artificial Intelligence and Big Data Analytics in Health Insurance' (2020) 98 *Bulletin of the World Health Organization* 263.

# 8

# Biomedical Research Policy

## Back to the Future?

BARTHA MARIA KNOPPERS, RUTH CHADWICK AND
MICHAEL J. S. BEAUVAIS

## 8.1 Introduction

Almost thirty years ago, the physician and Yale law professor Jay Katz
opined that only when the Nuremberg Code (of 1947) is 'firmly put into
practice can one address the claims of science and the wishes of society to
benefit from science'.[1] He cautioned that when 'primacy [is afforded] to
consent . . . one [should] exercise the requisite caution in situations where
one may wish to make an exception to this principle but only for clear and
sufficient reasons'.[2] History bears testimony to these words of caution when
we look at international biomedical research norms established since the
Nuremberg Code. Indeed, since then, various flashpoints of scientific
breakthroughs or controversies – from Tuskegee (1932–72: syphilis experiment on African American men), to Louise Brown (1978: first in vitro
fertilisation (IVF) baby), to Alder Hey Children's Hospital (1988–95:
unauthorised organ removal), to Jesse Gelsinger (1999: gene therapy
death), to He Jiankui (2018: clustered regularly interspaced short palin-
dromic repeats (CRISPR) twin babies) – have served to remind us of the
limits of law and the consequent need for what Graeme Laurie has called
'reflexive governance', which seeks to foster mutual exchange and learning
among those implicated in biomedical research.[3]

---

[1] Jay Katz, 'The Nuremburg Code Consent Principle: Then and Now' in George Annas and
Michael Grodin (eds), *The Nazi Doctors and the Nuremberg Code: Human Rights in
Human Experimentation* (Oxford University Press 1995) 236.
[2] Ibid.
[3] Graeme Laurie, 'Reflexive Governance in Biobanking: On the Value of Policy Led
Approaches and the Need to Recognise the Limits of Law' (2011) 130 *Human Genetics* 347.

Beyond the limits of law, these flashpoints make clear the nexus among science, ethics, law and society more broadly.[4] None exist in isolation, as evidenced by the creation of norms (for example, in the fields of human rights[5] and health law[6]) as well as policy following these controversies. Indeed, specialised institutions of the United Nations (UN), such as the World Health Organization (WHO)[7] and the United Nations Educational, Scientific and Cultural Organization (UNESCO),[8] as well as regional organisations, such as the Council of Europe[9] and the European Union (EU),[10] and self-regulatory international professional societies, such as the World Medical Association (WMA),[11] the Council for International Organizations of Medical Sciences (CIOMS)[12] and the Human Genome Organization (HUGO),[13] have also provided guidance to scientists and physician-scientists engaged in research involving humans, their tissues and their data. In this chapter, these efforts to

---

[4] Bartha Maria Knoppers and Vural Özdemir, 'The Concept of Humanity and Biogenetics' in Britta van Beers, Luigi Corrias and Wouter Werner (eds), *Humanity across International Law and Biolaw* (Cambridge University Press 2014) 223.

[5] For example, Council of Europe, *Convention for the Protection of Human Rights and Dignity of the Human Being with Regard to the Application of Biology and Medicine: Convention on Human Rights and Biomedicine*, 4 April 1997, CETS No. 164 (Oviedo Convention).

[6] For example, the UK enacted the Human Tissue Act 2004 in direct response to the Alder Hey scandal. See David Price, 'The Human Tissue Act 2004' (2005) 68 *Modern Law Review* 798. See further Chapter 9 in this volume.

[7] See, for example, World Health Organization, 'Proposed International Guidelines on Ethical Issues in Medical Genetics and Genetic Services' (WHO, 1998) https://apps .who.int/iris/bitstream/handle/10665/63910/WHO_HGN_GL_ETH_98.1.pdf? sequence=1&isAllowed=y (accessed 17 February 2021).

[8] See, for example, United Nations Educational, Scientific and Cultural Organization, 'Universal Declaration on the Human Genome and Human Rights' (UNESCO, 1997) http://portal.unesco.org/en/ev.php-URL_ID=13177&URL_DO=DO_TOPIC& URL_SECTION=201.html (accessed 26 January 2021).

[9] See, for example, Council of Europe, *Additional Protocol to the Oviedo Convention concerning Genetic Testing for Health Purposes*, 27 November 2008, CETS No. 203.

[10] See, for example, European Parliament, Resolution on the Ethical and Legal Problems of Genetic Engineering, 17 April 1989, 1989 OJ C96/165.

[11] See, for example, World Medical Association (WMA), 'Declaration of Helsinki: Ethical Principles for Medical Research Involving Human Subjects' (2013) 310 *JAMA* 2191.

[12] See, for example, Council for International Organizations of Medical Sciences (CIOMS), *International Ethical Guidelines for Health-Related Research Involving Humans* (CIOMS 2016).

[13] See, for example, HUGO Ethical, Legal, and Social Issues Committee, 'Statement on DNA Sampling: Control and Access' (HUGO, February 1998) www.hugo-international.org /Resources/Documents/CELS_Statement-DNASampling_1998.pdf (accessed 26 January 2021).

control and to prevent future abuses or to frame emerging technologies in the field of human genetics and genomics will serve as examples and guideposts in our attempt to draw from the lessons of the past so as to map policy-making for the future.

It is our contention that one cannot properly speak of a legacy without reference to learning from the past. Building the future requires a foundation, one which is provided by a legacy informed by learning. We believe that the central arc that connects the past, present and future of biomedical research policy is the shift in focus from the atomised individual to situating the individual in a broad spectrum of relationships, from bacteria to human communities. Indeed, as biomedical and psychosocial research reveals new insights about the biological and the social human, biomedical research policy must keep pace. We further posit that policy developments do not happen on a clean canvas. With time and experience, policy and its underlying principles find themselves interacting with all that came before. Rare are those policy developments that are mere flashes in the pan. Instead, present and future policy can be properly understood only through knowing that which came before. Today's policy developments are tomorrow's legacy.

Our chapter builds on similar efforts undertaken by two of us in 1994,[14] 2005[15] and 2015.[16] In those decennial exercises, we examined how the advancement and globalisation of genomic research spurred novel directions in research policy. The first article used the international Human Genome Project as an example of the application of the classic 1978 Belmont principles of respect for persons, beneficence and justice, while adding the quality of the science as an ethical norm,[17] as illustrated by its inclusion in HUGO's 1996 Statement on the Principled Conduct of Genetic Research.[18] The second article, on emerging trends in ethics and human genetic research, revealed the limits of individualism in the

---

[14] Bartha Knoppers and Ruth Chadwick, 'The Human Genome Project: Under an International Ethical Microscope' (1994) 265 *Science* 2035.

[15] Bartha Knoppers and Ruth Chadwick, 'Human Genetic Research: Emerging Trends in Ethics' (2005) 6 *Nature Reviews Genetics* 75.

[16] Bartha Knoppers and Ruth Chadwick, 'The Ethics Weathervane' (2015) 16 *BMC Medical Ethics* 58.

[17] Knoppers and Chadwick (n 14).

[18] HUGO Ethical, Legal, and Social Issues Committee, 'Statement on the Principled Conduct of Genetics Research' (HUGO, December 1995) www.hugo-international.org /Resources/Documents/CELS_Statement-PrincipledConductofGeneticsResearch_1995. pdf (accessed 26 January 2021).

scientific endeavour. Indeed, the international HapMap, the 1,000 Genomes Project and the emergence of population biobanks in, for example, Estonia, Quebec, the UK and Japan served as exemplars for more societal endeavours. These population resources relied on the participation of citizens as ongoing donors of samples and data for future unspecified, approved research, thereby promoting the concepts of citizenry, reciprocity, mutuality, solidarity and universality.[19] The third article noted a new emphasis on the more procedural and technical aspects of ethical implementation in the era of international consortia and data-sharing, spawning the principles of governance, security, empowerment, transparency, the right not to know and globalisation.[20]

Throughout these exercises, we were able to abstract and postulate these trends without denying either their reliance on and coexistence with past principles or their influence beyond the genetic context. The legacy of earlier principles such as autonomy, beneficence and justice provides the foundation with which other, newer principles are in dialogue. Furthermore, genetics and biomedical research have become more inextricably linked to health generally as attested by the latest guidance from WHO/CIOMS, which specifically moved away (in its title) from biomedical research to embrace the broader term 'health-related research'.[21] This is also illustrated in the name of the Global Alliance for Genomics and Health (GA4GH), a non-profit organisation that emerged in 2013 to provide the framework, policies, tools and standards to build the bridge from genomic research to the clinic.[22]

What other specific legal tools and ethical principles can we discern from the past as guidance for the genomics and health trajectory (Section 8.2), in order prospectively to build the future upon this legacy of 'genomics policy' (Section 8.3)?

## 8.2 International 'Genomics' Policy: Lessons from the Past

The 1990–2020 genetic and genomic research and ethics trajectory detailed in Section 8.1 also found specific expression in different

---

[19] Knoppers and Chadwick (n 15).
[20] Knoppers and Chadwick (n 16).
[21] Council for International Organizations of Medical Sciences (CIOMS), 'International Ethical Guidelines for Health-Related Research Involving Humans' (CIOMS 2016) ix.
[22] Bartha Maria Knoppers, 'Framework for Responsible Sharing of Genomic and Health-Related Data' (2014) 8 *HUGO Journal* 3.

international legal instruments and guidance. The 1989 Resolution on the Ethical and Legal Problems of Genetic Engineering[23] of the European Parliament sought to address the broader welfare interests at stake in human genetics. It 'regard[ed] the restraints imposed on the freedom of science and research, arising in particular from the rights of third parties and the society they constitute, as the expression in legal terms of the responsibility assumed by society as a whole for the action of the scientist and for research'.[24] The European Parliament furthermore:

> ... call[ed] for the possible applications of research, diagnosis and therapy, particularly at the prenatal stage, to be the subject of legally binding definitions so that procedures involving live human embryos or foetuses or experiments on them are justified only if they are of direct and otherwise unattainable benefit in terms of the welfare of the child concerned and its mother and respect the physical and mental integrity of the woman in question.[25]

The interests of future children in the context of prenatal testing and screening were also raised in 1992 by the Council of Europe.[26] Across this thirty-plus-year span from 1989 to the present, we wish to highlight the development of three human rights delimiting biomedical research generally: (1) the rights of children and decisionally vulnerable adults in health-related research; (2) the right to science; and (3) the rights of future generations.

### 8.2.1   The Rights of Children and Decisionally Vulnerable Adults

Newly minted researchers, bioethicists and jurists could be forgiven for believing that children and decisionally vulnerable adults (that is, those having been deemed to lack capacity to make decisions themselves regarding their care) have always been included in biomedical research. Biomedical research policy and norms have gone from the express exclusion of these groups in research (for example, Article 1 of the Nuremberg Code mandates that participants themselves 'have legal capacity to give consent', thus foreclosing on any assent/authorisation from

---

[23]  European Parliament (n 10).

[24]  Ibid., para 8.

[25]  Ibid., para 32.

[26]  Council of Europe Committee of Ministers, 'Recommendation No. R (92) 3 on Genetic Testing and Screening for Health Care Purposes' (10 February 1992) https://rm.coe.int /16804e913a (accessed 26 January 2021).

the child or incompetent adult) to norms that ensure their inclusion in research in a way that ensures their protection.

### 8.2.1.1 Children

The hallmark 1989 UN Convention on the Rights of the Child[27] was ten years in the making and, to date, has been ratified by 196 countries.[28] (The USA remains the only country to have signed but not to have ratified.) It codifies and makes the consideration of the best interests of children primary in all decisions concerning their well-being (Article 3). Other rights include the right to the enjoyment of the highest attainable standard of health and the right to be heard and express their views in all matters concerning them with due weight given to their age and maturity.[29] The Convention does not explicitly address the involvement of children in biomedical research as consensus could not be achieved on this point. A child is defined as 'a human being below the age of 18'.[30]

Since the Convention, laws and ethics guidance has increasingly focused on the protection of children from harm, as well as their inclusion and involvement in research and in decisions affecting them. The ethical principle of distributive justice calls for making high-quality care available for all population groups. For example, the EU's Clinical Trials Regulation (2014) allows minors to participate in clinical trials that either create a direct benefit for the minor concerned that outweighs the risks that participation involves or create some benefit for the population represented by the participating minor and represent minimal risk to the minor.[31] Similarly, the EU's General Data Protection Regulation (GDPR), which came into effect in 2018 and covers 'scientific research' among other activities, recognises that children deserve special protection for data processing activities and so additional privacy and security safeguards for processing the personal data of children are required.[32] The data

---

[27] United Nations General Assembly, 'Convention on the Rights of the Child' (UN Treaty Series vol 1577, 20 November 1989, 3.

[28] Office of the United Nations High Commissioner for Human Rights, 'OHCHR Dashboard' https://indicators.ohchr.org (accessed 26 January 2021).

[29] United Nations General Assembly (n 27) arts 24 and 12, respectively.

[30] Ibid., art 1.

[31] Council Regulation 536/2014 of 16 April 2014 on clinical trials on medicinal products for human use, and repealing Directive 2001/20/EC, 2014 OJ L158/1, art 32.

[32] Council Regulation 679/2016 of 27 April 2016 on the protection of natural persons with regard to the processing of personal data and on the free movement of such data, and repealing Directive 95/46/EC (General Data Protection Regulation), 2016 OJ L119/1, recital 38, arts 6(1)(f) and 8.

subject's right to transparency of processing is furthermore adapted to the needs of children in the form of heightened plain language requirements regarding information given about processing activities.[33]

### 8.2.1.2 Decisionally Vulnerable Adults

Policy and norms with respect to biomedical research with decisionally vulnerable adults have followed a similarly cautious trajectory. The 2006 UN Convention on the Rights of Persons with Disabilities,[34] ratified by 182 countries, makes similar inroads on protection and inclusion.[35] It applies to all persons with disabilities (including cognitive) and emphasises respect for choices previously expressed as well as continued involvement in decision-making concerning health, with more state support of the elderly and the disabled. No direction is provided as concerns the participation of persons with disabilities in biomedical research.

With time, however, more attention has been given to the inclusion of incompetent adults within biomedical research. This is particularly true within the European normative space as evidenced by normative developments with regard to biobanking and the processing of health data. Consider the Council of Europe's 2016 Recommendation on research on biological materials of human origin,[36] for the revision of which Graeme served as the UK's representative on the Council of Europe Expert Group. Its earlier iteration[37] contained minimal provisions for individuals not able to consent. For example, Articles 15(2) and 15(3) specify the almost axiomatic proposition that the participant's legally authorised representative should have the ability to consent on behalf of the individual concerned and that where the individual concerned attains legal capacity, this now-capable adult should have the relevant rights to give, modify or withdraw consent.[38]

---

[33] Ibid., art 12(1).

[34] United Nations General Assembly, 'Convention on the Rights of Persons with Disabilities', United Nations Doc A/RES/61/106, 24 January 2007.

[35] Ibid.

[36] Council of Europe, Recommendation CM/Rec (2016) 6 of the Committee of Ministers to member States on research on biological materials of human origin, 11 May 2016, https://search.coe.int/cm/Pages/result_details.aspx?ObjectId=090000168064e8ff (accessed 26 January 2021).

[37] Council of Europe, Recommendation Rec (2006) 4 of the Committee of Ministers to member States on research on biological materials of human origin, 15 March 2006 https://search.coe.int/cm/Pages/result_details.aspx?ObjectId=09000016805d84f0 (accessed 26 January 2021).

[38] Ibid., art 15(2)–(3).

One innovation in the 2016 Recommendation is the obligation to involve decisionally vulnerable adults in the authorisation procedure in so far as possible, to respect any objection of the individual concerned and to take their previously expressed wishes into account.[39] (This is all to say nothing of the more robust provisions concerning the governance of collections in Chapter IV of the 2016 Recommendation, in which one feels Graeme's indelible mark.)

Similarly, the Council of Europe's 2019 Recommendation on the protection of health-related data advises that even for adult persons lacking legal capacity, if they are capable of understanding some level of the information given to data subjects, they should be informed about the data processing activities in addition to their legally authorised representative.[40]

### 8.2.2 The Right to Science

While the right to science is an 'old' right that traces its origins back to Article 27 of the 1948 Universal Declaration of Human Rights (UDHR),[41] its legal actionability was recognised only by the signing and ratification of 169 states of the 1966 International Covenant on Economic, Social and Cultural Rights (ICESCR).[42] Article 15 of the Covenant creates the obligation to 'respect the freedom indispensable for scientific research' and to recognise 'the right of everyone … to enjoy the benefits of scientific progress and its applications'.[43] A study of the reports submitted to the UN committee overseeing the implementation of the Covenant by its 123 state parties reveals an increasing interest in and support for the activation of this right via investment by countries in information technology (IT) and in data sharing as one of its possible realisations.[44] The final General Comment on this right from the UN

---

[39] Council of Europe (n 36), art 12(4).

[40] Council of Europe, Recommendation CM/Rec (2019) 2 of the Committee of Ministers to member States on the protection of health-related data, 27 March 2019, art 11.5 www .apda.ad/sites/default/files/2019–03/CM_Rec%282019%292E_EN.pdf (accessed 26 January 2021).

[41] United Nations General Assembly, Universal Declaration of Human Rights, United Nations Doc 217 A (III), 10 December 1948, art 27. See further Chapter 18 in this volume.

[42] United Nations General Assembly, International Covenant on Economic, Social and Cultural Rights, United Nations Treaty Series vol 993, 16 December 1966, 3.

[43] Ibid., art 15.

[44] Rumiana Yotova and Bartha Maria Knoppers, 'The Right to Benefit from Science and Its Implications for Genomic Data Sharing' (2020) 31 *European Journal of International Law* 665.

Committee on Economic, Social and Cultural Rights (CESCR) concluded that the right to science contains, at its core, the interrelated elements of availability, accessibility, quality and acceptability, which together secure both scientific advancement and the equitable sharing of its benefits.[45]

Open access to scientific knowledge, scientific freedom, citizen science and biomedical research funding are other recent avenues of expression of this right. UNESCO's 2009 Venice Statement on the Right to Enjoy the Benefits of Scientific Progress and Its Applications,[46] as well as the special report of the United Nations Human Rights Council in 2012,[47] and the work of the American Association for the Advancement of Science (AAAS) on polling its membership regarding the right to science, have explored these avenues.[48] Indeed, UNESCO's 2017 Recommendation on Science and Scientific Researchers specifically highlights this approach when it seeks to 'ensure the human right to share in scientific advancement and its benefits' by asking 'Member States [to] establish and facilitate mechanisms for collaborative open science and facilitate sharing of scientific knowledge while ensuring other rights are respected'.[49] At a minimum, 'the right has at least three main components: (1) the right of everyone to benefit from and contribute to scientific and technological progress (the "right to science" *sensu stricto*); (2) the right of scientists, for instance, to do research and push forward science and technology (the "rights of science"); and (3) countries' duty to provide an enabling environment'.[50] With such rich potential, it is unfortunate that the CESCR's final version of the General Comment on the right to science did not further elaborate on the implications of the right to science for

---

[45] United Nations Committee on Economic, Social and Cultural Rights (CESCR), General Comment No 25 (2020) on Science and Economic, Social and Cultural Rights (Article 15(1)(b), (2), (3) and (4) of the International Covenant on Economic, Social and Cultural Rights), UN Doc E/C12/GC/25, 30 April 2020.

[46] United Nations Educational, Scientific, and Cultural Organization (UNESCO), The Right to Enjoy the Benefits of Scientific Progress and Its Applications, United Nations Doc SHS/RSP/HRS-GED/2009/PI/H/1, 2009.

[47] United Nations General Assembly, Report of the Special Rapporteur in the Field of Cultural Rights, Farida Shaheed: The Right to Enjoy the Benefits of Scientific Progress and Its Applications, United Nations Doc A/HRC/20/26, 14 May 2012.

[48] American Association for the Advancement of Science (AAAS), 'Right to Science' www.aaas.org/programs/scientific-responsibility-human-rights-law/resources/article-15/about (accessed 26 January 2021).

[49] UNESCO, Recommendation on Science and Scientific Researchers in 'Records of the General Conference, 39th session, Paris, 30 October–14 November 2017, v. 1: Resolutions', United Nations Doc 39 C/RESOLUTIONS, 2018, 122.

[50] Andrea Boggio et al, 'The Human Right to Science and the Regulation of Human Germline Engineering' (2019) 2 *CRISPR Journal* 134, 136.

data sharing and scientific research beyond a high level of abstraction that does little to inspire.[51]

There are, however, limits to what the state can do to ensure the realisation of the right to science when there is a panoply of public and private actors engaged in the contemporary global scientific enterprise. Complementing this top-down approach of implementing the right to science by state parties to the Covenant are the bottom-up initiatives from the scientific and health-care communities. A notable example in this regard, and as previously described, is GA4GH, an international alliance of more than 3,000 members from 600 institutions across more than 90 countries, whose central mission is to promote data sharing so that all persons may share in the benefits of scientific achievement.[52] Founded on the right to science, GA4GH's Framework for Responsible Sharing of Genomic and Health-related Data gives substance to the right in the context of genomic and health-related research, with core provisions such as transparency, accountability and data security.[53]

GA4GH's varied initiatives, which espouse the ethos expressed in the Framework and span from the ethico-legal to the technical, ensure that the international community itself has resources at its disposal that foster open, responsible collaboration. For example, the Matchmaker Exchange, a federated platform for identifying novel genes in rare diseases, is built on GA4GH's technical and regulatory standards.[54] The platform brings together researchers from all over the world to share rare-disease data in a way that respects participant autonomy and medical needs, while furthering the global scientific endeavour. In a similar vein, GA4GH's Beacon application programming interface (API) allows for the discovery of genomic data within data repositories and the creation of federated networks across the globe, while at the same time protecting individual privacy.[55] A final GA4GH-initated effort that is closer to the nature of a clinical support tool is the BRCA Exchange. As a clinical-care online reference portal, it allows for collaborative variant curation in BRCA1 and BRCA2 genes, which is then coupled with expert

---

[51] CESCR (n 45).
[52] Global Alliance for Genomics and Health (GA4GH) https://ga4gh.org/about-us (accessed 26 January 2021).
[53] Knoppers (n 22).
[54] Anthony Philippakis et al, 'The Matchmaker Exchange: A Platform for Rare Disease Gene Discovery' (2015) 36 *Human Mutation* 915.
[55] Marc Fiume et al, 'Federated Discovery and Sharing of Genomic Data Using Beacons' (2019) 37 *Nature Biotechnology* 220.

interpretation to 'enable a more comprehensive understanding of the clinical significance of genetic variation in BRCA1 and BRCA2'.[56]

### 8.2.3 The Rights of Future Generations

Hitherto confined largely to debates concerning the environment, the idea of future generations themselves having interests and rights in the present may have the greatest implications for biomedical research policy. Although still in its nascent stages, this category of rights has received much attention in the context of heritable human genome editing (HHGE). The nature of HHGE means that future generations of biologically related individuals will be affected by the modification. Their rights may then be key to the development of policy to regulate the use of HHGE. Indeed, the relationship of the rights of future generations and HHGE demonstrates well the importance of leaving a flexible legacy that present and future generations may use to reach ethically acceptable decisions.

We first see the rights of future generations fleetingly mentioned in the Parliamentary Assembly of the Council of Europe's 1982 Recommendation on genetic engineering, which recommended the creation of a European policy for the legitimate application of 'techniques of genetic engineering' to both current and future generations of humans.[57] Then, in 1997, UNESCO adopted the Declaration on the Responsibility of the Present Generations Towards Future Generations and included the human genome,[58] Article 1 of which states that '[t]he present generations have the responsibility of ensuring that the needs and interests of present and future generations are fully safeguarded'.[59] Article 6 maintains that '[t]he human genome, in full respect of the dignity of the human person and human rights, must be protected and biodiversity safeguarded. Scientific and technological progress should not in any way impair or compromise the preservation of the human and other species.'[60] Consideration for future generations also appears in the 2005 Universal

---

[56] Melissa Cline et al, 'BRCA Challenge: BRCA Exchange as a Global Resource for Variants in BRCA1 and BRCA2' (2018) 14 *PLOS Genetics* e1007752.

[57] Parliamentary Assembly of the Council of Europe, 'Recommendation 934 (1982) on Genetic Engineering', Parliamentary Assembly, 26 January 1982, para 7(a) https://pace .coe.int/en/files/14968 (accessed 21 January 2021).

[58] UNESCO Declaration on the Responsibilities of the Present Generations Towards Future Generations, UNESCO General Conference, 29th session, 12 November 1997.

[59] Ibid., art 1.

[60] Ibid., art 6.

Declaration on Bioethics and Human Rights, where we read that '[t]he impact of life sciences on future generations, including on their genetic constitution, should be given due regard'.[61]

The development of a new generation of tools for gene editing, such as CRISPR, has been a catalyst for tailored HHGE policy and, in turn, for the development of the rights of future generations affected by germline editing. For example, the UK's Nuffield Council on Bioethics's 2018 report explicitly linked the rights of future generations to the debate on gene editing. The Council's conclusion regarding interventions in the human genome was

> . . . that interventions of this kind to influence the characteristics of future generations could be ethically acceptable, provided if, and only if, two principles are satisfied: first, that such interventions are intended to secure, and are consistent with, the welfare of a person who may be born as a consequence, and second, that any such interventions would uphold principles of social justice and solidarity – by this we mean that such interventions should not produce or exacerbate social division, or marginalise or disadvantage groups in society.[62]

To that end, intergenerational monitoring of any children following gene editing has been recommended as a way of 'tracking' the effects of such editing. This duty echoes a similar conclusion made in another report on gene editing from the National Academies of Sciences of the USA.[63]

The news of the birth of the 'CRISPR babies' came a few months following the publication of the Nuffield Council's report. Undoubtedly a controversy, potentially even a scandal, this watershed moment left a legacy that may actually be understood in positive terms. The event galvanised scientists, ethicists and jurists, bringing them together in a way that mirrors Graeme Laurie's vision for reflexive governance, which 'is about facilitating mechanisms of mutual learning in addressing genuine dilemmas as and when these arise'.[64] To this end, two international bodies have been constituted: an International Commission on the Clinical Use of Human Germline Genome Editing, sponsored by

---

[61] UNESCO Universal Declaration on Bioethics and Human Rights, 19 October 2005, art 16 http://portal.unesco.org/en/ev.php-URL_ID=31058&URL_DO=DO_TOPIC&URL_SECTION=201.html (accessed 26 January 2021).

[62] 'Genome Editing and Human Reproduction: Social and Ethical Issues' (Nuffield Council on Bioethics 2018) vii www.nuffieldbioethics.org/publications/genome-editing-and-human-reproduction (accessed 26 January 2021).

[63] National Academies of Sciences, Engineering, and Medicine et al, *Human Genome Editing: Science, Ethics, and Governance* (National Academies Press 2017).

[64] Laurie (n 3) 355.

national scientific and medical academies on the responsible pathway for the potential clinical use of HHGE,[65] and a WHO Expert Advisory Committee on Developing Standards for Governance and Oversight of Human Genome Editing on Ethics and Governance.[66] The work of these bodies demonstrates the importance of both scientific and ethical governance of biomedicine and, indeed, the seeming inseparability of science and ethics.

In a recent report, the International Commission on the Clinical Use of Human Germline Genome Editing expressly mentions the rights of future generations as a potential way to develop appropriate governance mechanisms for the potential use of HHGE.[67] As societal debate concerning HHGE continues, we will no doubt see further delineation of the contours and content of the rights of future generations and the ensuing responsibilities and duties in the context of gene editing, but also in the health arena, generally. Indeed, as we turn to mapping the future, we will see that policy responses to actual events such as gene editing and Covid-19 move the biomedical research map closer to one that encompasses humanity as a whole, both in the present and beyond.

To sum up Section 8.2, then, we consider that, together, these efforts amount to a strong endorsement of the right of children and the decisionally vulnerable to science and demonstrate a commitment to realising its potential in the interests of future generations. We maintain that this right may well come to fruition in the nascent international policy debate surrounding gene editing. Indeed, the issue of gene editing may serve further to shape both the rights of children and the right to science, but also to develop the hitherto neglected rights of future generations, which still remain largely confined to environmental issues.[68] Perhaps the most important lesson that can be drawn from past and current policy-making debates is the need for science to be in dialogue with society. Changing social attitudes and mores directly affect ethics and law and, in turn, the direction that science takes. If we were to forget all that came before, there would be not a single

---

[65] Victor Dzau, Marcia McNutt and Venki Ramakrishnan, 'Academies' Action Plan for Germline Editing' (2019) 567 *Nature* 175.

[66] Sara Reardon, 'World Health Organization Panel Weighs in on CRISPR-Babies Debate' (2019) 567 *Nature* 444.

[67] International Commission on the Clinical Use of Human Germline Genome Editing et al, *Heritable Human Genome Editing* (National Academies Press 2020) 158.

[68] Bartha Knoppers and Erika Kleiderman, 'Heritable Genome Editing: Who Speaks for "Future" Children?' (2019) 2 *CRISPR Journal* 285.

lesson learnt, nor could we reasonably say that there is a legacy upon which to build a future.

## 8.3 Mapping the Future: Legacies, Interpretation and Events

When we turn to mapping the future, we are operating under conditions of uncertainty. Indeed, it may be pertinent (if obvious) to say that the only thing of which we can be certain is uncertainty. We can, however, leverage the lessons learnt from past experiences to discern the parameters according to which we can seek to identify possible future trends. Graeme Laurie's contributions to our understanding of the proper role of ethics and governance in science provide us with a legacy that connects the past, present and future.

We can see the inevitability of uncertainty in the legal sphere even in relation to legacies which one might believe to be certain or watertight. In the context of the law of succession, legacies can and frequently do turn out in ways that are very different from those intended. As the popular Danish TV series *The Legacy* (*Arvingerne*) demonstrates, they can lead to years of family drama. More generally, there are at least two ways in which intentions can be frustrated. The first is through interpretation; the second is a result of events – as in the well-known story (which may or may not be authentic) that when UK Prime Minister (1957–63) Harold Macmillan was asked what was most likely to knock a government off course, the answer was 'events, dear boy, events'.

In relation to interpretation, we may take, as an example, the gift of a building in a will on condition that alcohol is not to be consumed on the premises, followed by an attempt to get around this by building a bar *under* the premises. In ethics, legacies are not quite like this, but a great deal of interpretation goes on. For example, there has been continual reinterpretation of the meaning of such terms as 'consent' and 'autonomy'. In fact, one of the purported reasons for the success of the original 'four principles' approach in biomedical ethics, espoused most famously by Beauchamp and Childress, is precisely that they are compatible with different moral theories and thus open to different interpretations; people from very different backgrounds and cultures can subscribe to them to some degree.[69]

---

[69] Raanan Gillon, 'Ethics Needs Principles – Four Can Encompass the Rest – and Respect for Autonomy Should Be "First Among Equals"' (2003) 29 *Journal of Medical Ethics* 307.

When we turn to events, it has arguably been the developments in science that have had most impact on the evolution of ethics – as described in Section 8.2 – both in the latter part of the twentieth century and at the beginning of the twenty-first. The most obvious of these has been the rapid advances in the field of genomics and related '-omics'. These have had effects, already noted, on the interpretation, selection and application of ethical principles.

Thinking forward, we suggest a number of ways in which either (1) interpretation or (2) events, or even a combination thereof, might continue to affect the further development of ethics, policy and regulation, emphasising the need for reflexivity that Graeme long called for in his own work.

### 8.3.1   Interpretation: Concepts

Beyond ethical principles, advances in science have challenged fundamental concepts upon which social life is based, as we can see in the field of reproductive medicine regarding the interpretation of concepts such as parenthood. Debate continues over the meaning and importance of having children 'of one's own' – for example, the importance of the genetic relation is one aspect of this, but there are also issues about whether having children of one's own should be taken to include access to womb transplants, for example.[70] Even more fundamental, however, is the concept of the person. Developments in different kinds of '-omics' have cast doubt on traditional accounts of the person as an autonomous individual with choices about how to respond to their environment. There is, of course, a wider debate to be had about the relationship between biological categories and social classifications, as we can see from rapidly developing debates about the rejection of binary classifications of sex and gender. In relation to the concept of 'person', however, the advent of what was initially called 'personalised (now "precision") medicine' required thought about the meaning of 'personal', along with questioning of traditional thought about 'respect for persons' in medicine, with more deeply associated questions about the concept of person itself.[71]

---

[70] Laura O'Donovan, Nicola Jane Williams and Stephen Wilkinson, 'Ethical and Policy Issues Raised by Uterus Transplants' (2019) 131 *British Medical Bulletin* 19.

[71] Ruth Chadwick, 'What's in a Name: Conceptions of Personalized Medicine and Their Ethical Implications' (2017) 4 *Lato Sensu* 5.

Both epigenomics and microbiomics have illustrated the, at best, partial understanding of the biological human, which inevitably has implications for our view of persons. Although biological facts do not determine how we understand or value persons, they are relevant. The implications of epigenomics include the suggestion that we need to have a much more environmentally situated view of the human person than has hitherto been the case. Also, more and more is being learned about the ways in which our microbiome affects our health and life. For example, researchers have recently established a link between gut microbiota and amyloid plaques in the brain, which are responsible for neurodegenerative disorders such as Alzheimer's disease.[72] Of course, it is possible to try to hold on to a view such as that what marks our personhood, as opposed to membership of the human species, is rationality, but as more evidence is gathered about the correlation between the microbiome and psychological well-being, the less it becomes feasible to ignore these communities of microbes in thinking about persons and ethics.

Likewise, one could describe traditional oppositions, such as that between therapy and enhancement, or between somatic and germline, as 'legacy divides'. Prior to using these in moral argument, there is a question about conceptual distinctions. The differences between somatic and germline cells have been challenged by stem cell science and by the possibility of turning somatic cells into reproductive ones. Gene editing has already challenged widespread consensus about the moral divide between somatic and germline and will no doubt continue to do so.

For regulators and policy-makers, the categorisation of the world carries with it normative implications. This is, after all, what gives ethico-legal distinctions their significance. Effective, robust policy, as a creature of ethics and law, requires some (but not total) cohesion with scientifically relevant categories. Where scientific advances blur the boundaries of certain concepts with either ethical or legal relevance, policy-makers must carefully interpret the implications of such advances. Attention to lessons learnt and their legacy helps prudence to become wisdom. This leads us to the consideration of events.

---

[72] See, for example, Moira Marizzoni et al, 'Short-Chain Fatty Acids and Lipopolysaccharide as Mediators between Gut Dysbiosis and Amyloid Pathology in Alzheimer's Disease' (2020) 78 *Journal of Alzheimer's Disease* 683.

### 8.3.2   Events: Challenges to Moral Consensus

The birth of the 'CRISPR babies' in 2018 is an example of an event that has led to challenge of a pre-existing, widespread – but not universal – distinction between somatic and germline modification. Children have now been born following germline genetic intervention, and debate has raged over whether the modification of the germline *itself* should be the main cause for concern rather than aspects of how it was carried out – for example, in the informed consent process.[73] An analogy has been drawn with the birth of the first 'test tube' baby, Louise Brown, in 1978, which at first gave rise to much controversy but eventually led to the acceptance of IVF and other assisted reproduction technologies. Will this be the direction of travel?[74] These examples relate, under the broad heading of 'events', to scientific developments. At the time of writing, however, there is an 'event' challenge for ethics of a completely different kind: the global pandemic of Covid-19.

Covid-19 made its appearance on the world stage almost at the very end of 2019, and, over the past two years, its effects on daily life and economic activity in almost every country of the globe (with a few notable exceptions) have been dramatic. It is essential to reflect in a systematic way on the implications for ethics – not only on immediate effects on people's behaviour but also on ethical thinking. One very striking aspect of this is the extent to which the principle of solidarity is appealed to in public discourse around this topic[75] (but there are others, which we tentatively try to elucidate further later in this section). Traditionally more popular in European than in North American contexts, solidarity emphasises the relational aspects of human life, rather than focusing primarily on individual autonomy. It has been appealed to in contexts of biobanking, for example, in relation to donating samples for the common good in terms of public health benefits.[76] One criticism that is

---

[73] Julian Savulescu and Peter Singer, 'An Ethical Pathway for Gene Editing' (2019) 33 *Bioethics* 221.

[74] See, for example, Mary Bergman, 'Perspectives on Gene Editing: Harvard Researchers, Others Share Their Views on Key Issues in the Field' (*The Harvard Gazette*, 9 January 2019) https://news.harvard.edu/gazette/story/2019/01/perspectives-on-gene-editing/ (accessed 26 January 2021).

[75] See, for example, European Group on Ethics in Science and New Technologies, Statement on European Solidarity and the Protection of Fundamental Rights in the COVID-19 Pandemic (2020) https://ec.europa.eu/info/sites/info/files/research_and_innovation/ege/ec_rtd_ege-statement-covid-19.pdf (accessed 26 January 2021).

[76] Barbara Prainsack and Alena Buyx, *Solidarity: Reflections on an Emerging Concept in Bioethics* (Nuffield Council on Bioethics 2011). See also Knoppers and Chadwick (n 15).

sometimes levelled at solidarity is that in so far as it emphasises groups of people standing 'shoulder to shoulder' with each other, it can be associated with the idea of sticking together against a common enemy, such as terrorist groups. It is a further step to portray the relevance of solidarity to the human species as a whole rather than to groups or subsets in particular circumstances, although this can be done in relation to the idea of the genome as the common heritage of humanity, for example.

In the Covid-19 context, the relevant group is indeed the human species, and the common enemy is a virus which threatens the welfare of humans wherever they live on the planet. It is perhaps noteworthy that although climate change is also a common threat which affects humans everywhere, the issue has been less successful in attracting the same support for solidarity. Economic interests, as well as appeals to justice in terms of the interests of currently less developed countries, have come into sharp conflict with the arguments of those who are most concerned about climate change. There is also, of course, the phenomenon of climate change denial, which may itself be influenced by economic interests. Denial is to a very considerable extent less feasible as a successful strategy in the case of Covid-19.

Beyond the phenomenon of solidarity moving centre stage, what other ethical impacts might there be? Two are ripe for consideration. One concerns intergenerational justice. This topic has already been of increasing importance in relation to matters such as the economic prospects of the young and changes in life expectancy in different social contexts. We have seen that both epigenomics and germline gene editing inevitably revive debates about obligations to future generations. Like germline gene editing, the intergenerational justice aspects of the effects of Covid-19 require monitoring. The second ethical impact concerns a cluster of issues around social inequalities (other than intergenerational) and how different actors in society are valued in the context of a globally interconnected world. Human futures themselves are up for debate. To date, that has largely been in the arena of the bioethical debate on human enhancement, posthumanism and transhumanism. The very real threats to human survival of both climate change and Covid-19 show that these debates are not 'only academic'.

To conclude Section 8.3, then, in mapping our ethical future, we need to have regard to the ways in which ethical legacies will continue to be challenged by interpretation, by events and by a combination of the two. Thinking about the possibilities of human solidarity, then, intergenerational justice and addressing social inequalities are clear candidates for further attention and reflexivity. Current events have breathed new life into these principles and concerns, and policy-makers would be unwise to ignore them. It would be relatively easy for international policy-makers to include these principles in future normative instruments. The more difficult task is ensuring that words become actions. Science exists within society and it must respond to society's demands and needs. The issues we face at present are the seeds of the policy of tomorrow. If legacy requires learning, then we also need the kind of sustained dialogue between the varied parties with interests in the development and/or use of new scientific outputs for which Graeme Laurie has advocated. It is only by working through difficult issues together and in tandem that our policy future can live up to its aspirations.

## 8.4  Conclusion

The intimate linkages between and among the past, present and future have underpinned this chapter. Developments in the 'past' can only properly be so called through the lens of time. The legacy of past events and subsequent developments shape our understanding of those events, give shape to our present moment and direct our future course. Since the Nuremberg Code, what continues to unite law, ethics and science is a concern for safeguarding the inherent dignity of all humans. As a community, we have at once progressed far beyond the Nuremberg Code and yet are always in its shadow, with the ever-present desire to uphold the dignity of each individual involved in biomedical research.

Recognising and giving effect to the inherent dignity of individuals in their capacity as research participants is a contextual question that depends on the interaction between the prevailing schools of thought and the science at issue. The past three decades, in particular, have borne witness to key breakthroughs and profound developments in how we think about the interaction of law, ethics and scientific research. Broadly speaking, we have seen ethico-legal principles shift from the classic Belmont principles of respect for persons, beneficence and justice, to reciprocity, citizenship and transparency, among others. The initial principles are never replaced; rather, there is a gradual accretion of experience and of wisdom that translates to new social and scientific contexts.

Against this background, we have highlighted the development of three types of human rights: the rights of children and of decisionally vulnerable adults, the right to benefit from scientific advancement, and the rights of future generations. As to the first group, norms and principles have shifted from largely leaving children and the decisionally vulnerable behind via their exclusion from biomedical research, to the genesis and maturation of international frameworks that place these groups of individuals within the biomedical research enterprise, recognising the imperative for them to share in the benefits of science while heeding the call for their increased protection and adaptation of traditional understandings of autonomy. As to the second human right – the right to science that furnishes every human with the possibility to benefit from scientific advancement – we have detailed its surprising rise from a dormant, rarely invoked right in the 1948 UDHR to one that informs discussions and policy-making at the highest levels in the political and scientific communities. The third and final right, that of future generations, has shown itself to be a nascent claim that is quickly developing. The growing recognition that we must secure a better future for individuals who are not yet born or even conceived has engendered a further shift to examining the relationship between scientific advancements, such as germline gene editing, and the effects that the use of such technologies will have on society in the future.

These developments over the past three decades demonstrate a shift from thinking about the 'here and now' to adopting a long-term vision that tries to anticipate and give a voice to those who do not yet have one. As part of this larger shift to thinking about the future, we have identified three issues that are at the forefront of policy: our understanding of personhood engendered by advances in epigenomics and microbiomics, germline gene editing, and pandemics such as Covid-19.

As to personhood, we have called attention to the growing body of knowledge that shows how the biological human must be seen within its environment, and that many aspects of our life, which we had previously thought could be explained by a relatively simple chain of causation, may be staunchly more complex in reality. The quickly developing ethico-legal debates regarding the use of germline gene editing tools in both research and clinical applications are likely to result in policy that no longer has an irreconcilable void between somatic and germline. Finally, much of the discourse surrounding the Covid-19 pandemic demonstrates that the principle of solidarity continues to grow in importance and is finding its articulation in concerns for intergenerational justice and for humankind more broadly. We are living in a rare moment where we are at once isolated, either in the imagined boundaries of the territorial jurisdiction of the state or in the four walls of our own homes, yet are also experiencing together something truly global. Very few people have seen their lives improve since the start of the current pandemic, and so there is a quasi-universal desire to improve the situation of humanity as a whole. In sum, each of these developments presents the potential to shake the foundations of our current understanding of the role of law, ethics and policy in biomedical research and to change our current course of action. We must learn, however, from the past and the present to produce a rich legacy upon which we can build the future.

A meta-trend that brings together the past lessons from and the future directions of policy-making examined in this chapter is the shift from a focus on only the individual to an additional focus on the relationships that individuals have to one another and on communities as a whole. The Nuremberg Code's central principle is respect for individual autonomy; it begins by stating that '[t]he voluntary consent of the human subject is absolutely essential'.[77] Yet genomics, epigenomics and microbiomics have taught us that the individual cannot be understood as an island unto themselves. Consequently, there is a need to respect both individual autonomy and relationality.[78] We have already seen the shift in focus from the individual to the collective in the context of biobanking initiatives, discussed earlier in the chapter. Graeme Laurie's work with the UK Biobank evidences the great benefits that may be reaped from the design of governance that shifts away from paradigm of the self-interested individual and towards an understanding of an individual who is motivated by solidarity. Challenging traditional forms of individual autonomy, biobanking was able to draw upon notions of citizenship and of trust to establish itself as a key research infrastructure in the biomedical research community. Recent developments such as the English High Court's decision in *ABC* v. *St George's NHS Trust & Others*[79] – where

---

[77] Nuremberg Military Tribunals, 'Permissible Medical Experiments' in *Trials of War Criminals before the Nuremberg Military Tribunals under Control Council Law No. 10, Nuremberg October 1946–April 1949* (US Government Printing Office 1949) 181.

[78] Ezekiel Emanuel and Charles Weijer, 'Protecting Communities in Research' in James Childress, Eric Meslin and Harold Shapiro (eds), *Belmont Revisited: Ethical Principles for Research with Human Subjects* (Georgetown University Press 2005) 99, 105.

[79] *ABC* v. *St George's NHS Trust & Others* [2020] EWHC 455 (QB). The case did not succeed against the defendants as it was found that although one of the defendant NHS trusts owed ABC a duty of care because of the close proximal relationship involved, that duty was to conduct a balancing exercise and the exercise had been undertaken appropriately (no such duty was owed on the part of the other defendants). The claim therefore failed. In further looking at the question of causation, the judge held that the claimant had not proved that she would have undergone a termination if notified of the risk during her pregnancy. Accordingly, the claim would have failed on causation even if it had succeeded on breach.

a physician was found to owe a novel duty of care to *consider* informing a patient's biological child (who was pregnant at the time) about the patient-parent's status as a carrier of Huntington's disease – further evidence a conception of autonomy (and of privacy) that is on the move.[80]

The Covid-19 pandemic has brought concerns of solidarity and of community to the fore. In the face of the trap of myopic, nationalistic responses to our current pandemic, Tedros Adhanom Ghebreyesus, Director-General of the WHO, has cautioned that 'global cooperation is our only choice against COVID-19'.[81] Furthermore, the European Group on Ethics in Science and New Technologies has described solidarity as a 'social vaccine' with 'enduring character' that erases the differences among groups, bringing them together in a common enterprise.[82] Notions of solidarity and of community-oriented justice are not new, either. Indeed, the USA's Belmont Report, whose famous tripartite principles of respect for persons, beneficence and justice have formed the bedrock of protection for research with human participants, has been criticised as needing a fourth principle: respect for communities.[83] The development of new frameworks for the ethical conduct of genomic research with indigenous communities shows that this principle is of growing importance.[84]

Implicit in each development we have detailed is the idea that the relationship between society and science that is encapsulated in policy-making is a reciprocal one. Each is progressing in response to what the other has done and in anticipation of what the other will do. Graeme Laurie's sustained efforts to bring ethical considerations to the fore of biomedical research and to ensure the development of agile,

---

[80] Edward Dove et al, 'Familial Genetic Risks: How Can We Better Navigate Patient Confidentiality and Appropriate Risk Disclosure to Relatives?' (2019) 45 *Journal of Medical Ethics* 504. See also Bartha Maria Knoppers and Kristina Kékési-Lafrance, 'The Genetic Family as Patient?' (2020) 20 *American Journal of Bioethics* 77.

[81] 'Global Cooperation Is Our Only Choice Against COVID-19, Says WHO Chief' (*UN News*, 6 August 2020) https://news.un.org/en/story/2020/08/1069702 (accessed 27 January 2021).

[82] European Group on Ethics in Science and New Technologies (n 76).

[83] Charles Weijer, 'Protecting Communities in Research: Philosophical and Pragmatic Challenges' (1999) 8 *Cambridge Quarterly of Healthcare Ethics* 501; Emanuel and Weijer (n 79).

[84] Gregg Pratt et al, *Genomic Partnerships: Guidelines for Genomic Research with Aboriginal and Torres Strait Islander Peoples of Queensland* (QIMR Berghofer Medical Research Institute 2019).

fit-for-purpose governance reflect this reciprocal relationship. Indeed, the silence of law at the forefront of biomedical science is an invitation for creative policy-making that is embedded within the scientific endeavour itself.

Governance and policy-making that are rooted in a desire to safeguard human dignity, and which operate from within the scientific enterprise, remind us that biomedical research is conducted for the sake of humanity and not for the sake of science.[85] Rigorous governance helps to ensure that science maintains its vocation of serving the interests of humanity as a whole and not the interests of a few. Yet with even the future of the very concept of a 'human' now up for debate due to biotechnological advances, and the panoply of normative effects that flow from such a determination, there is a greater need than ever for stewardship in policy-making.[86] As we stand now at the crossroads of the present and the future, with the lessons of the past also impressed upon us, it is incumbent upon us to concretise the growing calls for solidarity and justice within biomedical research.

---

[85] Eva Mozes-Kor, 'The Mengele Twins and Human Experimentation: A Personal Account' in George Annas and Michael Grodin (eds), *The Nazi Doctors and the Nuremberg Code: Human Rights in Human Experimentation* (Oxford University Press 1995) 58.

[86] Bartha Knoppers and Henry Greely, 'Biotechnologies Nibbling at the Legal "Human"' (2019) 366 *Science* 1455.

# The Burden of History

## How Past Scandals Have Shaped the Future Governance of Human Tissue and Health Data

NILS HOPPE AND JOSÉ MIOLA

## 9.1 Introduction: Legacy as a Driver for Regulation

Law, understood broadly as the normative frameworks which govern the actions of citizens and of the state, is in most cases a response. This response is based on the rationality of a legislature that is bounded by, among other things, prior experiences. The event to which it is a response is the identification of a regulatory need based on this experience. In contexts where citizens and state actors function seamlessly without the need to intervene with regulation, to regulate despite this would amount to an unwarranted intervention. It follows that actions are fundamentally unregulated until an actor's conduct gives rise to a need for regulation to intervene (consider, for example, doctrines such as *nulla poena sine lege*, or the *Lotus Principle* in international law). This means that it is appropriate to posit causation at each step from an event to the associated regulatory need and the subsequent regulation. It is a function of fundamental justice that, along that causal chain, assessments of need and the legislative response are proportionate and reasonable. Put another way, a regulation's energy, directed at the cause, ought not significantly exceed that which is required appropriately to address the regulatory need. This finely balanced system of regulatory kinetics is a core characteristic of the rule of law.

At the same time, laws are social constructs that enshrine a snapshot of societal perception of a given moment – out of date almost as soon as they enter into force, swiftly decaying as society changes its views. This is particularly the case in the context of science and medicine, where novel ideas and their application challenge our views of ethically volatile cases on an almost daily basis. In this chapter, we argue that the ethical volatility that surrounds the cause, which gives rise to the regulatory need, plays an important role in the strength of the regulatory response. In other words, the more scandalous a trigger event is, the more energy the subsequent regulation deploys. While stakeholders may accept this as proportionate in the immediate aftermath of the scandal itself, the resulting regulation very rarely applies only to that scandal; rather, it unfolds prospective power in all cases which cannot be adequately distinguished. The regulation is the scandal's legacy, impacting future actions that were not even contemplated when the regulatory need was identified. In these cases, the regulatory response is propelled by at least two discrete drivers: the actual regulatory need, which can be empirically ascertained and normatively addressed; and a societal perception of the undesirability of a practice, which is in some cases an epistemic issue which does not always overlap entirely with the normative challenge. This raises an important question: where the epistemic lack of clarity of a medical practice gives rise to a societal desire for a prohibition, but there is no corresponding empirically provable normative requirement, should we regulate? In other words: does the legitimacy of societal perception have an impact on the legitimacy of regulation?

It is a characteristic of the phenomenon we are describing that there are, by necessity, many examples of it in law. Two which we suggest are particularly worthy of closer inspection using the lens of the 'burden of legacy' are: (1) the genesis of the Human Tissue Act 2004 in the wake of the Alder Hey Scandal; and (2) the public response to the introduction of the *care.data* programme in England. Both examples illuminate the phenomenon from two different sides: overreaction and underreaction to a regulatory need. The ultimate shape that the Human Tissue Act 2004 was given was a response to a public outcry over the retention of children's organs without consent – to the lasting detriment of tissue-based research in the UK. The laudable and societally desirable objectives of *care.data* were permanently scuppered by the failure to anticipate an entirely foreseeable public outcry and to establish appropriate information governance – to the lasting detriment of data-driven medical research not just in England but, arguably, across the UK.

We will outline these two examples and put them in the context of the legacy they represent for the governance of biomedical research in the UK. We will then seek to make a connection between these two specific events and what we term the 'general direction of travel' of medical law as a whole.[1] We argue that medical law has shifted from being a doctor-centred enterprise to one that instead takes as its starting point the interests of patients and the level of care that they are entitled to expect. Therefore, while our two examples may seem unconnected at first glance, each conforms to the new model of medical law. We begin, however, with a discussion of the Alder Hey organ retention scandal.

## 9.2   Overreaction? The Legacy of Alder Hey in the Regulation of Human Tissue

Human tissue is a vital material for research in the UK and beyond. It is the basis for significant advances in understanding the causes and pathways of diseases, it enables *in vitro*-based research in cases where it used to be necessary to experiment with patients or with live animals, and it unlocks perspectives for new approaches to regenerative medicine. Biobanks and biorepositories are indispensable research infrastructures in modern biomedical research. These are not recent developments. Human tissues and cells have always held a level of significance in research which is hard to overstate: from anatomical experimentation in Egypt and Greece more than three thousand years ago, to the more recent cases of Henrietta Lacks[2] and John Moore,[3] the potential of research with tissues and cells is uncontentious, as is the potential for abuse.[4]

Access to these materials is clearly contingent on potential tissue donors' agreement, if at all possible, whether this be in the context of using excess blood drawn for diagnostic purposes in the UK or even in the context of collating genetic knowledge of indigenous groups in Panama.[5] It is this act of obtaining any meaningful kind of agreement

---

[1]  We realise that there is a heated debate, as noted in the Introduction, surrounding different terms such as 'medical law', 'health law', 'biomedical law', 'health-care law' and, of course, 'medical jurisprudence'. In our view, these are often used synonymously but do not, in fact, always overlap fully. We duck away from participation in this skirmish and invite the reader to make their own mind up from the context we provide.

[2]  See Rebecca Skloot, *The Immortal Life of Henrietta Lacks* (Crown 2011).

[3]  *Moore v. Regents of the University of California and others*, 793 P 2d 479 (Cal 1990). For a summary and discussion, see Nils Hoppe, *Bioequity: Property and the Human Body* (Ashgate 2009) 107.

[4]  Of which the Lacks and the Moore cases are prime examples.

[5]  Heather Widdows, 'Constructing Communal Models of Governance: Collectives of Individuals or Distinct Ethical Loci?' in Heather Widdows and Caroline Mullen (eds), *The Governance of Genetic Information: Who Decides?* (Cambridge University Press 2009) 82.

to the taking and subsequent use of tissues that has long been neglected in almost all countries. A strong argumentative focus was laid on the fact that many materials are leftover samples (that is, clinical waste), and a compelling ethical argument can surely be constructed in favour of using excess material for societally desirable research activities rather than having such material destroyed. Added to this was the simple reality of clinical logistics in modern medicine – in many cases, patients were admitted for and at that time consented only to the basics of the immediate diagnostics and care, and were then discharged without adequate contact information. It was simply no longer pragmatically possible to trace them to ask for additional permission, even if this was thought to be required. To enable important research under these conditions, regulatory frameworks over the world have in the past included the possibility to undertake research even when there is no consent (with some rudimentary safeguards aimed at protecting patients' informational self-determination).[6] In the context of human tissue regulation in the UK, these rules were fragmented across different instruments,[7] and certainly not easily identified either by patients or by researchers.

In addition to this regulatory backdrop, there was a by and large unregulated hunter-gatherer culture within the medical community: any material that was physically available was collected, stored (sometimes unsystematically, often using an eclectic array of home-made cataloguing systems) in old fridges in hospital corridors, and generally regarded as the property of the collecting physician. In the absence of a consolidating attempt at regulation,[8] the level of uncertainty and normative blurriness in the use of human tissues and cells for biomedical research had significant potential for abuse. In addition, the lack of clarity in relation to the provenance of cells clearly held risks for those tissues and cells that subsequently metamorphosed to a clinical application. In this adjoining (and sometimes overlapping) area, the European

---

[6] For a view on this, and an assessment of the justification of research without consent, see Luke Gelinas, Alan Wertheimer and Franklin Miller, 'When and Why Is Research without Consent Permissible?' (2016) 46 *Hastings Center Report* 1.

[7] Before the Human Tissue Act 2004 came onto the scene for England, Wales and Northern Ireland, relevant norms could be found in, among other instruments, the Human Tissue Act 1961, the Anatomy Act 1984, the Corneal Tissue Act 1986 and the Human Organ Transplants Act 1989.

[8] It is worth remembering that the Human Tissue Act 1961 was a deeply inadequate piece of legislation full of deficiencies and, indeed, inexplicable lacunae (David Price, 'The Human Tissue Act 2004' (2005) 68 *Modern Law Review* 798, 799). This is also noted in Chapter 10 of this volume.

Commission identified in 2002 a need for regulatory convergence within the European Union and presented a proposal for a directive that was meant to ensure that the quality and tracking of such material was the same across the EU. The aim was explicitly to foster confidence in tissue-based medicine, that is, in clinical application.[9] While the scope of the directive could be extended to some forms of research, these would be limited to where cells were used in a human for research purposes (but not for *in vitro* research).[10] The aim of the Commission was, in the end, to assist in establishing high standards for product development to protect consumers (patients) and further facilitate a common market in health products.

This reasonably clearly delineated EU initiative came just over a year after the publication of the Royal Liverpool Children's Enquiry Report (also known as the Redfern Report). The public perception of the Redfern Report, and the preceding public and very emotional debate on the practices at Alder Hey between 1988 and 1995, had produced a fertile policy ground for a comprehensive approach to regulating the use of human tissues and cells in the UK. Alder Hey Children's Hospital in Liverpool has been a leading paediatric hospital since just before the Great War. It was the first hospital to test penicillin, in 1914, and the first to establish a neonatal surgery unit.[11] Since the advent of the NHS in 1948, Alder Hey has been continuously pioneering in the care of children, establishing numerous initiatives which improved the health and quality of life of children in the UK.[12]

Between 1948 and 1988, there was a policy that entailed the wide-spread post-mortem collection and retention of samples from children treated at Alder Hey using established processes.[13] After 1988, the

---

[9] Proposal for a Directive of the European Parliament and of the Council on setting standards of quality and safety for the donation, procurement, testing, processing, storage, and distribution of human tissues and cells, COM(2002) 319 final, para 4.

[10] Ibid., paras 10 and 17. The proposal was subsequently adopted as Directive 23/2004/EC on setting standards of quality and safety for the donation, procurement, testing, processing, preservation, storage and distribution of human tissues and cells, 2004 OJ L102/48.

[11] Stephen Armstrong, 'Alder Hey's "Cognitive Hospital" Aims to Turn NHS Use of AI on Its Head' (2018) 362 *BMJ* k3791.

[12] For example, '[p]enicillin was tested on a child for the first time at Alder Hey . . . and we were the first to establish a neonatal surgical unit in the UK. Other "firsts" include curing the most commonly encountered congenital heart defect and pioneering various splints and orthopaedic appliances' (Alder Hey, *Our History*, https://alderhey.nhs.uk/about-us /our-history?q=%2Fabout-us%2Four-history (accessed 15 March 2021)).

[13] Hoppe (n 3) 35.

practice changed significantly following the appointment of a new paediatric pathologist, Dick van Velzen. In line with the widespread hunter-gatherer culture, van Velzen established a regime in which staff were instructed to collect all available specimens for, at this point, entirely unclear future uses.[14]

At the same time, the mother of an eleven-year-old girl who had died at Bristol Royal Infirmary was told that her daughter's heart had been retained without her permission. A public campaign was established to expose the practice at Bristol and to understand better why so many children were avoidably dying there. This led to an inquiry chaired by Professor Sir Ian Kennedy, which came to damning conclusions,[15] and during which numerous witnesses were called. One of these witnesses, heart specialist Robert Anderson, submitted in oral evidence in September 1999 that he did not consider that the consent-free retention practice at Bristol was particularly unique – after all, Alder Hey had a much larger collection.[16] This witness testimony caused some degree of upheaval and fuelled a strong suspicion that the practice of taking and keeping organs from deceased children was significantly more widespread across the UK. It became clear from the public discussion that followed on from Anderson's evidence that there had, at some point, been an uncoupling of biomedical research practice from legitimate public expectations. Indeed, Anderson himself conceded that pathologists had 'presumed too much when we made our collections'.[17] What followed was the Royal Liverpool Children's Inquiry and its subsequent 2001 Redfern Report into the practice at Alder Hey.

A census at Alder Hey revealed a collection which confounded even the most battle-hardened medical lawyers and ethicists and which proved not just that van Velzen had been randomly collecting samples but that there had been such a culture at Alder Hey going back to the 1960s. Some of the figures uncovered by the census make for uncomfortable reading: 2,128 hearts, 4,020 foetuses, 13 post-natal heads or parts of post-natal heads, 22 foetal heads, 188 eyes, the whole body of a child and the head of

---

[14] Ibid.
[15] Clare Dyer, 'Bristol Inquiry Condemns Hospital's "Club Culture"' (2001) 323 *BMJ* 181.
[16] This is described in some detail in Joseph Lawlor's non-academic work *Thief of Hearts* (Authorhouse 2011) 353; see also 'The Royal Liverpool Children's Inquiry Report' (House of Commons, 2001) 88, para 2.9 ('Redfern Report') https://assets.publishing.service.gov.uk /government/uploads/system/uploads/attachment_data/file/250934/0012_ii.pdf (accessed 27 January 2021).
[17] Professor Robert Anderson, quoted in http://news.bbc.co.uk/2/hi/health/background_ briefings/the_bristol_heart_babies/455738.stm (accessed 6 November 2020).

an 11-year-old in a container.[18] The tone of the Redfern Report makes the dismay of those involved in compiling it exceptionally clear. An example can be found in the paragraph outlining the census's findings in one of the many storage rooms in a basement:

> Ms Connell went through the various containers and books, and the summary of the collection makes sobering reading. She identified 13 post-natal heads/parts of head from children from a few days old to 11 years of age dating back to the 1960s and 22 heads from late premature/term fetus. There are containers with a whole body of a child in one jar with a separated head in another jar. Perhaps the most disturbing specimen is that of the head of a boy aged 11 years old. The most recent specimen was obtained in 1973.[19]

The ethical volatility and emotional weight of these findings can hardly be exaggerated and this was reflected in the public outcry that accompanied the process. The one identifiable common theme in the Alder Hey collection was that there was no policy to ask anyone for permission to procure, fix, store or use the samples and body parts. This was noticed at several points in time before the scandal erupted, with one consultant writing to the coroner on 16 February 1988, seeking clarification:

> [M]ost of these specimens from both Coroner's and Hospital autopsies over the last 35 years have been properly preserved and filed with the relevant data. In the light of the new Anatomy Regulations, I am not sure if the authority for possession of these specimens has been sought from the relatives of the deceased. I therefore wonder if it is possible to ask the relative for such a consent. If a consent is withheld then we have to dispose of the specimen properly after we have studied it microscopically.[20]

This position was correct in law then. While the Anatomy Regulations 1988 (SI 1988/44) did not formally cover the issue of consent (conventionally understood), they required those dealing with dead bodies to ascertain and record the wishes of the deceased and their family in relation to the disposal of the body (reg. 2(2)(e)) and stated that these wishes ought to be given effect (reg. 4(1)(e)). This was clearly not practised at the time. Even if the coroner had inexplicably determined that there were overriding reasons why it was appropriate to retain every organ from every child, the regulations also illustrate a compelling obligation from an ethics perspective: there seems to be no justification for

---

[18] Ibid.
[19] Redfern Report (n 16) 112 para 20.5.
[20] Ibid., 350 para 51.1.

not ascertaining the wishes of the relatives of the deceased children. The Redfern Report notes, in the same paragraph, that the consultant never received a response from the coroner, and the report is overall exceptionally critical of the role played by those who were meant to provide checks and balances on the post-mortem use of human bodies at Alder Hey. The reporting in national and international media that followed resulted in Alder Hey becoming synonymous with the cruel and cavalier exploitation of dead children in the name of medicine, science and personal hubris.

In the immediate aftermath of Alder Hey, and concurrently with the European Commission's initiative to establish a regulatory regime, there was a dramatic drop in the public's willingness to provide organs for transplantation, a drastic decrease of tissues and cells provided for research, and dwindling numbers of post-mortems.[21] Public trust in medicine and biomedical research had taken a severe hit and it was political consensus that the lessons learnt from Bristol and Alder Hey ought to result in a clarification of the law. A normative evolution can be traced from the timely publication of the Nuffield Council on Bioethics's recommendations for an ethical and legal framework for the use of human tissue,[22] via the organ retention scandals, to the transposition obligation derived from the implementation of the EU's Human Tissue Directive.[23] Taken together, the events along this pathway inevitably led to the changes that were implemented by the Human Tissue Act 2004. It is also, in all likelihood, the only time in the brief history of the UK's membership of the EU that a directive adopted in March was fully implemented by November of the same year (nearly a year and a half ahead of schedule). In contrast, the UK had, at the end of its membership, an average transposition delay of 7.2 months.[24] The UK's obligation to transpose the Human Tissue Directive therefore provided both an additional impetus to the regulatory drive that led to the Human Tissue Act 2004 and a welcome vessel for the UK government's policy initiative.

---

[21] David Price, 'From Cosmos and Damian to Van Velzen: The Human Tissue Saga Continues' (2003) 11 *Medical Law Review* 5.

[22] 'Human Tissue: Ethical and Legal Issues' (Nuffield Council on Bioethics, 3 April 1995) www.nuffieldbioethics.org/publications/human-tissue (accessed 10 July 2020).

[23] The nature of this pathway becomes particularly clear in the helpful debate during the Lords' second reading of the Human Tissue Bill, HL Deb 22 July 2004, vol 664, col 365.

[24] European Commission Single Market Scoreboard https://ec.europa.eu/internal_market/scoreboard/performance_by_member_state/uk/index_en.htm#transposition (accessed 27 January 2021).

Giving effect to the triumvirate of 'lessons learnt', 'public expectation' and 'supranational regulation' in one legislative approach meant that the resulting one-size-fits-all legislation had to have a solid footing in the wishes of patients and their families and would have to apply not just to research but to clinical use as well. This very quickly drew the criticism of medical professionals, who correctly pointed out the pragmatic limits of informed consent in real-life medicine.[25] In addition, the resulting framework of primary law, secondary legislation, guidelines, licensing and regulatory authority scrutiny may have made the law clearer for lawyers, but not for the intended users of the law. The approach also neglected to draw on decades of scholarship on the complex interplay among clinical care, biomedical research and the availability of the human body.

Simply reducing the issue to one of consent may be a quick fix to soothe the public post Alder Hey outrage and to put an immediate stop to the clearly inappropriate practices in UK hospitals. It was not, however, an approach that was likely to be prospectively proportionate, and neither – we argue – is it one that actually sought to make sure that the public's perception was footed on solid scientific evidence. It merely sought to quench the societal thirst for control that was caused by the lack of the involvement of parents in the decision-making previously. We do not argue that there ought to have been no control, but rather that the consent requirements ought to have been more finely nuanced to enable important research to be done. The Redfern Report notes that the formidable collection of children's hearts at Alder Hey contributed to the reduction of the mortality rate following cardiac surgery in children from 33 per cent to 3 per cent.[26] This was to some extent a result of the retention practices that were properly criticised, but it had no discernible influence on the public's perception, or on the granularity of the subsequent regulation.

Fifteen years on, the system has stabilised and more lessons have been learnt; inevitably, jurisprudence has developed the law and the Human Tissue Authority has become more confident and clearer in its guidance.

---

[25] M Bell, 'The UK Human Tissue Act and Consent: Surrendering a Fundamental Principle to Transplantation Needs?' (2006) 32 *Journal of Medical Ethics* 283. It should be noted, though, that the Act conspicuously avoids the term 'informed consent' and instead refers to 'appropriate consent', thereby creating its own, more malleable, consent regime. Indeed, an informed consent standard would be difficult to achieve in post-mortem scenarios, which make up a significant portion of cases.

[26] Redfern Report (n 16) para 1.

The previous hunter-gatherer culture at the interface between clinic and laboratory has diminished, and the procurement of tissue samples for research has taken on a significant bureaucratic burden – though some routine is now setting in. It would be naive to assume that this did not also result in a trammelling of the innovative power of medicine, and it seems obvious that there is some beneficial research that simply has not taken place following the change in the regime in relation to human tissues and cells.[27] The sustained energy of the scandal (caused by a grave misunderstanding of public expectations), wrapped in the coat of extrinsic, supranational obligations, resulted in a regulatory regime which can be argued to have caused as many new problems as it solved old ones: a legacy which still impacts the quantity and quality of biomedical research in the UK. We now turn to consider an example of legacy being used to *prevent* rather than *propel* change.

## 9.3  Underreaction? *Care.data*'s Legacy for Data-Driven Research

If anything, we can say the opposite for the disaster that was *care.data*. Here, we can see another example of the law being a social construct manifesting a snapshot of societal perception of the moment. However, perhaps significantly, the societal perception appears to have been well founded – although we would argue that it would have lost none of its legitimacy had it not been. Here, as we demonstrate in the following paragraphs, the scandal triggered such a strong critical response that the proposal was shelved. In relation to the substance of the issue, much of what we say above in relation to tissue applies to data. The NHS holds millions of pieces of data about patients, all of which is useful, particularly if aggregated. It can be used – at no physical risk to any patient – to ameliorate services for all.

In this respect, then, *care.data* had, on the surface, a laudable goal: to 'bring together health and social care information from different healthcare settings, such as GP practices, hospitals and care homes, in order to see what's working really well in the NHS – and what we could [improve]'.[28] The idea was to take this huge amount of information stored by the NHS and aggregate it with a view to using it to improve NHS services. Moreover, and contrary to what was assumed by many,

---

[27] Antonia Cronin et al, 'British Transplant Research Endangered by the Human Tissue Act' 37 *Journal of Medical Ethics* 512.

[28] NHS England, 'The *care.data* Programme' www.england.nhs.uk/ourwork/tsd/care-data/ (accessed 27 January 2021).

this was not to be done without the consent of patients. Rather, an opt-out system would be put in place, although consent would be assumed if a lack of consent was not communicated.[29] However, its timing could not have been worse, and the execution of the plan was just as bad. Thus,

> the method used to inform people about the possibility of opting out – sending letters that two-thirds of the public did not recall receiving – created the impression that the government was trying to sneak this through without anyone noticing. Moreover, this came in the wake of a scandal where 'millions' of NHS records were inappropriately sold to insurance firms.[30]

Indeed, things were so bad that the scheme was scrapped following a critical report that included an assessment of it.[31] Despite not being asked to look at care.data (and therefore in comments that can best be described as incidental findings), Dame Fiona Caldicott and her team within the National Data Guardian office still pointedly noted that '[i]n the light of the Review, the government should consider the future of the care.data programme'.[32] Here, the ethical volatility related not to the idea per se but to the safeguards surrounding the enterprise and, seemingly, the perception of a slippery slope rather than the actual existence of harm. Dame Caldicott did express concerns about the consent and opt-out models, but noted that care.data had already run into trouble due to a lack of support among stakeholders, notably the Royal College of General Practitioners (RCGP), the British Medical Association, and Healthwatch England.[33]

---

[29] It might well have been that the creators of care.data were thinking of the situation with organ donation here, where it is well established that far more people would be happy to be organ donors than had joined the organ donor register. We also recognise that presumed consent is not universally accepted as appropriate and, in many respects, we share the concerns.

[30] José Miola, 'Duties of Shared Membership in Research Ethics' in David Kirchhoffer and Bernadette Richards (eds), Beyond Autonomy: Limits and Alternatives to Informed Consent in Research Ethics and Law (Cambridge University Press 2019) 153. An account of the sale of the NHS records can be found in Laura Donnelly, 'Millions of NHS Records Sold to Insurance Firms' (Daily Telegraph, 17 June 2014) www.telegraph.co.uk/news/health/news/10906390/Millions-of-NHS-records-sold-to-insurance-firms.html (accessed 27 January 2021).

[31] National Data Guardian for Healthcare, 'Review of Data Security, Consent and Optouts' (National Data Guardian, 2016) ('Caldicott Report') https://assets.publishing.service.gov.uk/government/uploads/system/uploads/attachment_data/file/535024/data-security-review.PDF (accessed 27 January 2021).

[32] Ibid., 36 para 3.3.7.

[33] Ibid., 6 para 1.22.

Yet this was due to the lack of explanation of the safeguards to patients, and the resulting lack of trust, rather than the idea itself being unacceptable. As the RCGP noted:

> The RCGP believes that, if implemented correctly, *care.data* has the potential to deliver enormous benefits to patients by helping the NHS to improve the quality of care it delivers and to better prepare for outbreaks of infectious disease. However, we are concerned that many people remain uncertain about the safeguards that will apply. The public's trust in the way in which the NHS treats their personal data cannot be overvalued and it is paramount that we do everything possible to protect and uphold it.[34]

The issue – perhaps unsurprisingly given the sale of information – became one of trust, and the energy pushing against the viability of the scheme came from the reaction to those previous events. This was the case even though the idea itself was seen as a good one that had the potential to improve the effectiveness of the NHS. This was made plain by the RCGP, which argued that there should be '[c]onfirmation that any information disclosed by the Health and Social Care Information Centre (HSCIC) to third parties will not be sold for profit'.[35] This can also be seen in a survey conducted for Healthwatch at the time, which found that despite people being able to see the benefits of what *care.data* was trying to achieve, 69 per cent of respondents would not give permission for their information to be forwarded by their GPs.[36] As Healthwatch noted, one of the main reasons given was 'a lack of trust around misuse of data'.[37] Moreover,

> [s]everal people expressed concern that the data would be made available to private sector companies, such as pharmaceutical or insurance companies and many people seem unconvinced that the data will remain secure in the future, and fear that there may not be substantial mechanisms in place to safeguard the data from being released to other 'interested' companies. 'If the data was to only be used by the NHS I wouldn't have a problem, but to give it away to private firms is going down a dangerous path.'[38]

---

[34] 'RCGP Parliamentary Briefing – *Care.data*' (RCGP, 14 March 2014) www.rcgp.org.uk /-/media/Files/Policy/A-Z-policy/Care-data-RCGP-Parliamentary-Briefing.ashx?la=en (accessed 27 January 2021).

[35] Ibid.

[36] '*Care.data* Report' (Healthwatch Devon, March 2014) 2 www.healthwatch.co.uk/sites/health watch.co.uk/files/reports-library/20140301_Devon-%20Care%20data%20Report%20Final% 20March%202014.pdf (accessed 28 January 2021).

[37] Ibid., 6.

[38] Ibid.

These fears may or may not have been well founded, and it is not within the purview of this chapter to consider whether they were. What Healthwatch's findings do demonstrate, however, is that timing is critical. We mentioned in our introduction that laws are social constructs that enshrine a snapshot of societal perception of a given moment; they can go out of date almost as soon as they enter into force, swiftly decaying as society changes its views, or indeed as events overtake them. The story of *care.data* is that this snapshot is not just relevant to legal rules, and that legacy can prevent as well as erode; *care.data* never had the opportunity to prove the doubters right or wrong.

It is equally evident that such suspicions linger. The UK government's attempt to develop a 'track and trace' smartphone app in mid-2020 to help the fight against Covid-19 met the same fate, and for fundamentally the same reasons. The proposed NHSX app faced opposition from the start. In part, this was due to the fact that the UK government decided not simply to use the Google-Apple model that was being used by other countries; instead, it opted to design its own platform.[39] The key difference with the UK platform was that it centralised information, in contrast to the existing Google-Apple version. This led to specific concerns about privacy and large-scale collection of personal data. The Open Rights Group, for example, saw this as a fundamental issue and, just as with *care.data*, highlighted the fact that there were no safeguards to prevent the 're-use of contact tracing data for other purposes'.[40] Such reservations were not limited to pressure groups: indeed, the UK Parliament's Joint Committee on Human Rights came to the same conclusion, its Chair noting:

> Assurances from Ministers about privacy are not enough. The Government has given assurances about protection of privacy so they should have no objection to those assurances being enshrined in law.
>
> The contact tracing app involves unprecedented data gathering. There must be robust legal protection for individuals about what that data will be used for, who will have access to it and how it will be safeguarded from hacking. Parliament was able quickly to agree to give the Government sweeping powers. It is perfectly possible for [P]arliament to do the same for legislation to protect privacy.[41]

---

[39] 'NHS Rejects Apple-Google Coronavirus App Plan' (*BBC News*, 27 April 2020) www .bbc.co.uk/news/technology-52441428 (accessed 28 January 2021).

[40] 'NHSX Tracking App Privacy Assessment: Key Concerns' (Open Rights Group, 13 May 2020) www.openrightsgroup.org/blog/nhsx-tracking-app-privacy-assessment-key-concerns/ (accessed 28 January 2021).

[41] Joint Select Committee on Human Rights, 'Report on UK Tracing App Published' (7 May 2020) https://committees.parliament.uk/work/218/the-governments-response-

What we can see here, then, is the opposite of the story in relation to the law governing tissue donation. In the case of data and privacy, the government was prevented from changing rules by the legacy of previous (mis)behaviours and mistrust. Legacy, it would appear, operates both as a positive catalyst for change and as a conservative force that prevents it. These might be considered micro-interactions, but they do have one thing in common: in both cases, the interests of patients are protected at the expense of what might be seen as the greater good. This can be explained by looking at the wider picture and considering the general trajectory of medical law as a whole, where the impact of legacy is also evident.

## 9.4 The Totality of Medical Law

Individual issues are rarely devoid of context. Indeed, the opposite is often true, and they develop in a way that is responsive to the situation around them. In medical law as a whole, what can be seen is a very definite and particular direction of travel that cannot help but influence the rest. Put simply, through the span of Graeme Laurie's career, medical law has performed what can be seen as a 180-degree turn, away from doctors and towards patients.[42] When Graeme's work started, medical law was about doctors. The *Bolam* test was all pervasive.[43] It provided, or at least was interpreted to provide, that a doctor had acted reasonably as long as they could find other doctors who would confirm that they might have acted in the same way in similar circumstances. Significantly, the test for reasonableness was different for doctors than for any other profession.[44] The key question for judges in medical law cases seemed to be 'what are the duties of the doctor, and have they been discharged?'. In other words, medical law was judged for doctors and, essentially, by doctors. As Lord Scarman noted in the middle of the 1980s, the 'standard of care is set by the medical profession'.[45]

---

to-covid19-human-rights-implications/news/115237/report-on-the-contact-tracing-app-published/ (accessed 28 January 2021).

[42] We imagine medical law here as a clash between doctor and patient, where their interests are almost in opposition to one another, so to move away from one is to move towards the other. This view is somewhat reminiscent of the work of Ian Kennedy. See, for example, Ian Kennedy, *The Unmasking of Medicine* (Allen and Unwin 1981).

[43] *Bolam v. Friern Hospital Management Committee* [1957] 1 WLR 582.

[44] See, for example, Margaret Brazier and José Miola, 'Bye-Bye *Bolam*: A Medical Litigation Revolution?' (2000) 8 *Medical Law Review* 85.

[45] *Sidaway v. Board of Governors of Bethlem Royal Hospital* [1985] 1 All ER 643.

However, while Lord Scarman was referring to questions of diagnosis and treatment, it also became evident that *Bolam* was being used to judge medical conduct away from these parameters. Thus, for example, questions of best interests (including for sterilisation and whether to remove life-sustaining treatments from patients in a coma), whether to provide treatment without the knowledge of parents to children under the age of sixteen or how much information to give patients about risks, all came under *Bolam*'s increasingly large umbrella. Medical law as a subject distinct from criminal law and tort/delict was essentially founded on recognising two things from this: first, that the law was indeed being applied differently to doctors than to other professions; and, second, that it was possible to question the legitimacy of the determinative nature of the medical voice in the law. In relation to the latter, Professor Sir Ian Kennedy's famous quote beautifully encapsulates this questioning: 'Doctors make decisions about what is to be done. Some, but only some, of these decisions are matters of technical skill. I submit that the majority of decisions taken by doctors are not technical. They are, instead, moral and ethical. They are decisions about what ought to be done, in light of certain values.'[46] Equally, editions of *Mason and McCall Smith's Law and Medical Ethics*, the textbook that Graeme became involved in writing, have traditionally carried in the front matter a quote from the criminal law case of *R v. Instan*, stating that '[i]t would not be correct to say that every moral obligation involves a legal duty; but every legal duty is founded on a moral obligation'.[47]

It was this recognition that *Bolam* was being used to decide issues that went beyond the limits of medical expertise, combined with a series of medical scandals that affected public trust in the medical profession, that helped to create the conditions for change. These scandals ranged from the poorly performed paediatric arterial switch operations at Bristol Royal Infirmary, to the Alder Hey organ retention scandal discussed earlier, to the discovery of the heinous murders committed by the GP Harold Shipman. Change became inevitable given the strength of public feeling and revulsion that demanded a regulatory response, and what is clear is that the medical law that Graeme is leaving is very different from that at the beginning of his career as a consequence of this inevitability of change.

---

[46] Kennedy (n 42) 78.
[47] Graeme Laurie, Shawn Harmon and Edward Dove, *Mason and McCall Smith's Law and Medical Ethics* (11th edn, Oxford University Press 2019) ii.

As is well known, the story of medical law has been a metamorphosis that gained its energy in large part due to this recognition that the status quo – where medical decision-making outside of doctors' unique sphere of competence was privileged – was untenable. Significantly, and as a totem of this change, a long retreat from *Bolam* began, specifically rejected by the Mental Capacity Act 2005 as a method of deciding the best interests of incapable patients, and specifically ejected from the law relating to information disclosure in the landmark case of *Montgomery*.[48] In that case, Lady Hale expressed the view that the application of *Bolam* for any issues that did not relate to the exercise of technical medical skill would be 'quite inapposite'.[49] This has been accompanied by increased judicial willingness to challenge medical professionals, in the name of upholding the rights of patients. In essence, if courts used to begin by asking 'what are the duties of the doctor?', they now ask 'what are the rights of patients, and have they been upheld?'. Risk disclosure provides the clearest example of this phenomenon, as the courts have been open in their use of this approach, and equally open about changing the law when it was felt to be insufficiently protective of patient autonomy.[50]

This general 'direction of travel' by the body of medical law is important for two reasons. First, it can be seen to be consistent with the examples that we gave earlier. In relation to the Human Tissue Act, and indeed *care.data*, the energy for change, whether that energy was supportive of change or seeking to stifle it, was protective of what we might term a subcomplex understanding of 'patients' rights'. Any sense of collectivity is sacrificed in order to protect the right to self-determination of the *individual*. Second, and on a related note, it is also evident that this protection of individual autonomy is linked to a lack of trust in doctors and the medical profession as a whole. This will be at least in part due to the scandals outlined in this chapter, but why this has happened is less important for our purposes than the fact that it has done so. This is because the effect of this change in the corpus of medical law is that the law's protection of patient interests threatens to remove the morality from medical law, and instead see doctor–patient interactions as almost transactional. As Professor Sir Jonathan Montgomery has noted,

---

[48] See *Montgomery* v. *Lanarkshire Health Board* [2015] UKSC 11.
[49] Ibid., [115].
[50] See, for example, *Chester* v. *Afshar* [2004] 3 WLR 927.

the discipline of healthcare law is at risk of being transformed – moving *from* a discipline in which the moral values of medical ethics (and those of the non-medical health professions) are a central concern, *to* one in which they are being supplanted by an amoral commitment to choice and consumerism. In other words, that the morality is being taken out of medicine by legal activity.[51]

This quote is important for two reasons. First, it encapsulates the move from the 'old' to the 'new' medical law. It is important to note that the criticisms of the 'old' medical law by Professor Sir Ian Kennedy were both insightful analyses and perfectly reasonable critiques of the law as it was at the time that he wrote them. But, of course, so is Montgomery's now. Second, and consequently, we can also see another role for legacy: the creation of a pendulum. Montgomery's vision is as much a reaction to the state of the law as Kennedy's, and in time we can expect that the law will move back the other way as events conspire to show the limitations of prioritising the individual over the collective – and indeed whether there is even an optimum balance between the two. Perhaps Covid-19 provides an example of this. Within months of the pandemic, articles were published arguing for indemnity from negligence actions for medical professionals,[52] as well as an increased visibility of the moral nature of medical practice with such issues as allocation of scarce intensive care unit (ICU) beds and ventilators.[53]

The pendulum will move back and forth between these extremes of doctor-centric and patient-centric normativity. Every new scandal will inject fresh kinetic energy into the pendulum's swing and move it into new areas of regulatory experience: be it propelling or preventing the process of change, testing the moral and ethical spectrum that is available in society at that particular time. In other areas of law, it may be the objective to achieve a completely still pendulum when the sum of experience has permitted a normative equilibrium to take hold. Not so in medicine and science: the pendulum will continue to swing as long as values in society change with what is possible and desirable, catalysing frequent change along with social attitudes. We submit that this is the uniquely positive and attractive nature of medical law.

---

[51] Jonathan Montgomery, 'Law and the Demoralisation of Medicine' (2006) 26 *Legal Studies* 185.

[52] See, for example, the recent debate in Christine Tomkins et al, 'Should Doctors Tackling Covid-19 Be Immune from Negligence Liability Claims?' (2020) 370 *BMJ* m2487.

[53] See, for example, Ezekiel Emanuel et al, 'Fair Allocation of Resources in the Time of Covid-19' (2020) 382 *New England Journal of Medicine* 2049.

## 9.5 Conclusion: The Legacy of Regulating Human Tissue and Health Data

Legacies are meant to last, and to be a sustained marker for an experience had, or a value generated that was meaningful. In law, where the somatic effects of the anguish of a particularly painful societal experience are usually binding rules, aimed at preventing future anguish, it is a worthwhile exercise regularly to test rules to assess whether they can achieve this. They need to be proportionate, and we must not regulate conduct and restrict freedoms lightly. In other words, we need to understand the causes, drivers and effects of restrictive measures better to be sufficiently sure that they do what it says on the tin. This inevitably raises the question of what kind of impulse is appropriate to shape regulation which has a significant impact on a societally desirable activity, such as biomedical research. A violent public reaction to an emotionally charged and ethically volatile scandal is, on the face of it, unlikely to be an appropriate driver. The resulting legacy would be one of retribution rather than prevention.

At the same time, when the pendulum has swung towards being in favour of individual patients' choices and preferences, rather than medical professionals and health systems, we are automatically buying into a greater potential for non-expert expectations, seemingly unreasonable choices and expensive interactions. Taken together with the increasing political tendency to pander to the demands of the most vocal, rather than the most reasonable, this prepares the ground for the type of legislative legacies in medical law that, we submit, are neither helpful nor futureproof. This is starkly visible in our example of Alder Hey, which was a toxic combination of parental bereavement, public outcry, serendipity in cross-examination and supranational regulatory pressure. The resulting regulatory corset is a unique illustration of the vagaries of legislative legacy footed more on societal anguish than on a genuine desire to learn the lessons of the past. Our second example, *care.data*, takes the illustration of the power of public perception one step further; here is an initiative that seeks to do exactly that – learn the lessons of the past on the basis of the treasure trove of NHS data that is already available – but it does so in a way which squanders public trust in the shortest conceivable amount of time. The diffuse notion of 'the greater good' is thought to justify fast-tracking consent to the extent that it can barely be said to be an expression of autonomy. This is the same notion behind the 'hunter-gatherer syndrome' that we described when we outlined the background to Alder Hey: this is something we need to further the greater good, and it won't do for you to say no; so we won't ask you.

The missing link to understanding the fatal flaws in Alder Hey and *care.data* that are directly responsible for causing the legislative legacies we now see is this: individuals were seen as resources, rather than as agents. They were producers or providers of cells or of data. They were the means to another's end, rather than ends in themselves. The public's anaphylactic reaction to being treated as means to an end was then, and is now, foreseeable and understandable. What was needed was better communication and transparency, better science and better knowledge about how science is generated. This will inevitably lead to better law, and it will mean that the legislative legacy of lessons we need to learn as a society is a sustained and sustainable marker that is actually meaningful.

# 10

# Body Parts and Baleful Stars?

MARGARET BRAZIER AND ALEXANDRA MULLOCK

## 10.1 Introduction

Graeme Laurie has written extensively on almost every question of medical law and ethics. Many academics have become more and more specialist in particular, and sometimes narrow, fields of research. Were we to say simply that we devoted our scholarly effort to 'medical law', we might well be categorised as Jills of all trades? Graeme defies a culture of narrow specialism. He is one of the most distinguished scholars in medical law, with an international reputation, and there is scarcely an area of the terrain on which he has not written. We have yet to discover any evidence that Graeme has ever sacrificed depth for breadth. His personal intellectual legacy will be immense. The sheer range of Graeme's scholarship made it initially difficult to decide what to address in a chapter in his honour. We mulled over his publication profile and concluded that genetics and the law relating to the body were two areas in which he might be said to have 'majored'. We plumped for body parts.

Human bodies and human tissue are, and have been for centuries, crucial to the development of medicine. The anatomists in the 'anatomical Renaissance' required bodies to dissect.[1] Human organs and tissue are needed today for medical education and research and, of course, transplantation. Our focus in this chapter is principally on transplantation, on what we can learn from the unhappy legacy of the past about the prospects of success for new legislation in the United Kingdom

---

We are indebted to Marleen Eijkholt, Amber Dar and Javier Garcia Oliva for their assistance with this chapter.

[1] Jonathan Sawday, *The Body Emblazoned: Dissection and the Human Body in Renaissance Culture* (Routledge 1996).

introducing 'deemed consent', which is designed to increase the number of cadaver organs for transplant.

Baleful stars have too often blighted the development of medical science. We consider how a legacy of fear and distrust has again and again shaped laws and regulations relating to the uses of human corpses, from the donation by the Kings of Scotland and England of the bodies of executed criminals for dissection to the enactment of the Human Tissue Act 2004 and the Human Tissue (Scotland) Act 2006 in the wake of public outrage over non-consensual organ retention for research and teaching. Elsewhere in this Festschrift, Nils Hoppe and José Miola explore the genesis of the Human Tissue Act 2004, analysing regulatory response to scandal. The Act adopted explicit *consent* (opt-in) as the fundamental principle legitimising removal, retention and use of 'relevant material' from the living or the dead. In parliamentary debates, little attention was given to complexities relating to deceased donation and transplantation. How far should the wishes of the dead prevail? How might those wishes be discerned? What say, if any, should the family be accorded? And what about the interests of those on organ waiting lists?

The change from opt-in to opt-out ('deemed consent') in Wales, England and Scotland (the last of which adopts the term 'deemed authorisation') is intended to improve donation rates. However, as we discuss, whether laws prescribe opt-in or opt-out, grieving families will often determine whether donation is possible. Thus, relational factors together with creating a supportive, well-organised transplant system in hospitals at the point of death are just as important as debates about the pros and cons of opt-in or opt-out. *How* the new legislative frameworks for donation are implemented in practice will be as important as the words in the statute-books.

## 10.2    Baleful Stars

### 10.2.1    The 'Tail Wagging the Dog'

Graeme never had a high opinion of the Human Tissue Act 2004. In the seventh edition of *Mason and McCall Smith's Law and Medical Ethics*, he and the late Ken Mason commented that, in their view, the Act had been 'born under the wrong star' and was 'forced into service as the result of the widespread unauthorised retention of human body parts following post mortem examinations'.[2] The eleventh edition hits harder. Laurie

---

[2] JK Mason and Graeme Laurie, *Mason and McCall Smith's Law and Medical Ethics* (7th edn, Oxford University Press 2006) 493.

and his co-authors characterise the Act as in the 'nature of the tail wagging the dog'.[3] In the statute's emphasis on autopsies and subsequent retention and uses of body parts for non-therapeutic purposes, including education and research, transplantation was nigh on invisible, simply one of twelve scheduled purposes. The only provisions of the Act directly concerned with transplants were those sections continuing the ban on sales of organs for transplant. In parliamentary debates at Westminster, only cursory attention was given to the needs of transplant medicine and the case for an opt-out (deemed/presumed consent) system for procuring organs for transplantation. The 2004 Act was yet another example of the legacy of scandal and mistrust – concerning the use (and abuse) of human tissue in medicine – blighting the approach to organ donation.

The Human Tissue (Scotland) Act 2006 paid slightly more attention to transplantation, imposing on Scottish ministers (inter alia) a duty to promote and develop programmes of transplantation.[4] The 2006 Act also adopted the term 'authorisation' rather than 'consent'. We share *Mason and McCall Smith's* semantic preference for authorisation in the context of cadaver donation.[5] While the two statutes differ in detail, both Acts 'unequivocally adopt a central principle of opt-in … Organs could not be taken without explicit permission'.[6]

Sixteen years later, taking the lead from Wales,[7] a form of soft opt-out (described as deemed consent) for donation of organs for transplant is now in force in England[8] and, in early 2021, similar legislation came into force in Scotland.[9] The three statutes use different terminology but adopt the same basic principle. In the absence of evidence to the contrary, a deceased adult will be deemed to have consented to (or authorised) donation of material for transplant, subject to a list of excluded materials,[10] specified in regulations, for which express consent continues to be required. Such reform of the Human Tissue Acts was campaigned

---

[3] Graeme Laurie, Shawn Harmon and Edward Dove, *Mason and McCall Smith's Law and Medical Ethics* (11th edn, Oxford University Press 2019) 598.

[4] Section 1.

[5] Laurie, Harmon and Dove (n 4) 598.

[6] Margaret Brazier and Sheila McLean, 'Human Tissue: A Story from a Small State' in Voo Teck Chuan, Richard Huxtable and Nicola Peart (eds), *Healthcare Ethics, Law and Professionalism* (Routledge 2019) 104.

[7] The Human Transplantation (Wales) Act 2013.

[8] The Organ Donation (Deemed Consent) Act 2019.

[9] The Human Tissue (Authorisation) (Scotland) Act 2019.

[10] Referred to as 'excluded materials' in the Wales Act, 'excepted body parts' in the Scotland Act and 'not permitted materials' in the English statute.

for by the media and again opinion polls suggest that it also enjoys wide support from the public and the medical profession.[11] The law will not change in Northern Ireland.[12]

Has Mason and Laurie's 'wrong star' waned and ceased to blight transplant medicine? Has the dog asserted control over its tail? At first sight, the omens look promising. Opinion polls regularly indicate that the majority of people in all the four nations which currently comprise the UK support transplantation and, in theory, are happy to donate their own organs after death.[13] Yet theory has not translated into practice. There remains a huge gap between the number of organs needed and the number donated. In the UK in 2019/20, 6,138 patients were waiting for a transplant and 372 patients died while on the active waiting list, with a further 746 removed from the list due to deteriorating health.[14]

We urge caution. The history of legislation in the United Kingdom,[15] touching on the use of bodies and body parts from the dead, suggests that baleful stars have risen regularly, blighting attempts to implement laws permitting human remains to be used in the service of science and medicine. Preparing the first draft of this chapter, we were fairly optimistic that the new laws would trigger change in practice and attitudes. By 2022, we expected that there would be hard evidence indicating whether or not deemed consent embedded in improved procedures for communication with bereaved relatives and allied to a campaign of public education had resulted in an increase in the number of cadaver organs donated for transplant. In March 2020, the Coronavirus pandemic (Covid-19) suspended (albeit temporarily) most transplants and dominated media and public debate on health policies. Had a new baleful star risen?

---

[11] The BMA has 'long advocated a "soft" opt-out for organ donation across the UK'. See www.bma.org.uk/advice-and-support/ethics/end-of-life/organ-donation (accessed 29 January 2021).

[12] See Human Tissue Authority Code of Practice F Part 2, para 20.

[13] 'This Change in the Law on Organ Donation Will Save Hundreds of Lives' (*The Guardian*, 26 February 2019) www.theguardian.com/commentisfree/2019/feb/26/organ-donation-law-change-save-lives-max-johnson (accessed 29 January 2021).

[14] NHS, 'Organ Donation and Transplantation Activity Report 2019/20' https://nhsbtdbe .blob.core.windows.net/umbraco-assets-corp/19220/activity-report-2019-2020.pdf (accessed 29 January 2021).

[15] David Price, 'From Cosmos and Damien to Van Velzen: The Human Tissue Saga Continues' (2003) 11 *Medical Law Review* 1.

## 10.2.2 Baleful Stars: Organ Retention

Controversy sparked by revelations of unauthorised organ and tissue retention after post-mortem examinations, the tail that wagged the dog, is the baleful star decried by Graeme Laurie. Evidence emerged that organs and tissue removed from the body at post-mortem examination had, in thousands of cases, been retained and used for research and teaching without consent from the deceased or their families. The media focused on organs retained from children and the consequent distress suffered by parents who discovered that they had not buried their children whole. In some cases, the whole body of a foetus or stillborn child had been retained. In others, all a child's internal organs were retained and an 'empty shell' returned to the parents. In England, it should be noted that a significant number of instances related to adults. The family of an Orthodox Jewish man learned years after his death that his brain had been removed and stored for research, wholly contrary to the deceased's and his family's deeply held beliefs.[16]

The Bristol Interim Inquiry Report[17] and the more graphic Redfern Report[18] drew 'unprecedented media attention'[19] to organ retention *for purposes unconnected with transplantation* and caused 'outrage among affected families'.[20] The then secretary of state for health for England described the Redfern Report as the most shocking he had ever read.[21] It was in response to the controversy generated by the revelations relating to organ retention that the Human Tissue Acts of 2004 and 2006 were enacted, imposing requirements of explicit consent for any scheduled purpose.[22] The public and media outcry as well as several reports and inquiries revealed a huge chasm in attitudes to the bodies of the dead between, on the one hand, biomedical scientists, medical practitioners

---

[16] Department of Health, 'Isaacs Report: The Investigation of Events that Followed the Death of Cyril Mark Isaacs' (2003) http://image.guardian.co.uk/sys-files/Society/docu ments/2003/05/12/isaacs_report.pdf (accessed 29 January 2021).

[17] Ian Kennedy et al, 'Inquiry into the Management of Care of Children Receiving Complex Heart Surgery at the Bristol Royal Infirmary, Interim Report: Removal and Retention of Human Material' (Bristol Royal Infirmary Inquiry, 2000) 56.

[18] 'The Royal Liverpool Children's Inquiry Report' (House of Commons, 2001) ('Redfern Report') https://assets.publishing.service.gov.uk/government/uploads/system/uploads/attachment_data/file/250934/0012_ii.pdf (accessed 29 January 2021).

[19] See NHS Retained Organs Commission, 'Remembering the Past, Looking to the Future: The Final Report' (*Department of Health*, 2004) 7.

[20] Ibid.

[21] HC Deb 30 January 2001, vol 362, col 176.

[22] Brazier and McLean (n 7) 107–14.

and many bioethicists and, on the other, families affected by organ retention and much of the public. The bitter debates had uncanny echoes of earlier conflicts founded on mutual distrust and antipathy among sections of the public and biomedical science. In the Afterword to the second edition of *Death, Dissection and the Destitute*, Ruth Richardson describes the similarity between public unrest about dissection in past centuries and the organ retention controversy at the turn of the millennium.[23]

### 10.2.3   Baleful Stars: Distrust and Dissection

To treat the ills of the human body, doctors in the Renaissance needed to understand human physiology.[24] Dead bodies to dissect were valuable commodities. Finding a sufficient supply was a perennial problem. Richardson charts the uncomfortable history of supply of corpses in the United Kingdom. It is a bleak tale, in consequence of which dissection became tainted by links with criminality.[25] James IV of Scotland[26] and Henry VIII of England[27] granted surgeons a number of bodies of executed felons. The numbers of corpses kindly 'donated' by the Crown increased over time, but there were never enough bodies to meet demand. Legislation in 1752 allowed judges to impose dissection as an additional penalty to hanging for especially 'horrid' murders,[28] a sanction seen as worse than being hanged, drawn and quartered.[29] Those whose bodies were involuntarily donated to science were likely to be criminals, and dissection was worse than death itself. If such obloquy attached to the use of the bodies of the dead were not enough, the demand for more bodies led to more extreme measures. Body snatching and grave robbing were resorted to in order to fill the gaps between supply and demand.[30]

---

[23] Ruth Richardson, *Death, Dissection and the Destitute* (2nd edn, University of Chicago Press 2000) 409.

[24] Sawday (n 2).

[25] See Peter King, *Punishing the Criminal Corpse 1700–1840: Aggravated Form of the Death Penalty in England* (Palgrave Macmillan 2017).

[26] Richardson (n 24) 32.

[27] Ibid.

[28] 1751: 25 George 2 c37: The Murder Act: An Act 'for Better Preventing the Horrid Crime of Murder'. Available on the Statutes Project website: http://statutes.org.uk/site/the-statutes/eighteenth-century/1751-25-geo2-c37-murder-act/ (accessed 22 March 2021).

[29] See Elizabeth Hurren, *Dissecting the Criminal Corpse: Staging Post Execution Punishment in Early Modern England* (Palgrave MacMillan 2016).

[30] Richardson (n 24) 52.

Surgeons and other medical practitioners were well aware of the practice and sometimes actively involved in the enterprise.[31] In Edinburgh, Burke and Hare notoriously went further still – murdering their victims to sell their bodies to the surgeons.[32] A lively trade in corpses developed. Public protest often turned to violent disorder. And still there were not enough bodies.

Against this background of public unrest, Parliament sought to legislate to regulate anatomy schools and provide an adequate and ethical source of bodies. The first Bill had to be withdrawn, opposed by the Church and the College of Surgeons.[33] That Bill had provided that when any person died 'in prison, or in any hospital or workhouse', their body could be delivered up for dissection, unless within seventy-two hours after the death a relative claimed the body and there was reason to believe that the deceased would be duly buried by that relative. The 1829 Bill was at least honest about its policy to target prisoners and the destitute as the source of supply to ensure a sufficient pool of dead bodies for dissection. They were unlikely to have family willing to claim the body with the funds to ensure that the deceased was 'duly buried'.

The Anatomy Act 1832 was more cleverly worded, avoiding any direct reference to prisons or workhouses while still relying on unclaimed bodies to meet the anatomists' needs. Thomas Wakley,[34] who crusaded to reform the coronial courts and encourage post-mortem examinations, opposed the Bill. He (rightly) noted that it was likely to result in the bodies of the poor being dissected in greater numbers.[35] The wording of the 1832 Act encouraged workhouse masters and hospital managers to hand over unclaimed bodies of paupers. As Richardson established, the Anatomy Act 1832 added poverty to the list of factors that much of the public associated with medical uses of dead bodies. Such was the outrage generated by the 1832 Act that riots broke out. The Anatomy School in Cambridge came under attack in 1833. Its counterpart in Sheffield was destroyed in 1835.[36]

---

[31] Ibid., 57–9. For an account of the involvement in body snatching of John Hunter (sometimes described as the 'Father of Surgery'), see Wendy Moore, *The Knife Man* (Bantam Books 2005) 96–8.

[32] Richardson (n 24) 131.

[33] Ibid., 157–8.

[34] Ian Burney, *Bodies of Evidence: Medicine and the Politics of the English Inquest, 1830–1926* (John Hopkins University Press 2006).

[35] Richardson (n 24) 155–6.

[36] Ibid., 263.

A huge chasm separated much of the public and the educated elite. The latter applauded the development of scientific medicine condemning the opposition of the poor and uneducated to dissection as based on superstition, ignorance, prejudice and passion.[37] Nonetheless, with notable exceptions, such as Jeremy Bentham, the higher echelons of society took great care to ensure that their bodies did not fall into the hands of the anatomists.[38]

### 10.2.4   Waning Stars?

The first twentieth century Act of Parliament relating to use of body parts from the dead was blessed with a more benign horoscope. The Corneal Grafting Act 1952 established that it was lawful to remove corneas from cadavers on evidence either that the deceased had expressed a wish to 'bequeath' his corneas for therapeutic purposes or that there was no known objection on the part of the deceased, or his surviving relatives, to such a course of action. Parliamentary debate was brief. Emphasis was placed on evidence that corneal donation was common practice in other European countries,[39] and that the purpose of the Bill 'is to allow the eyes of the dead to be used for this beneficent purpose'.[40] The Act simply remedied a lacuna in the law, avoiding doubt about the lawfulness of any such procedure under the Anatomy Act or common law.

The Human Tissue Act 1961 initially excited little controversy.[41] The development of kidney transplantation and the potential for transplant of other organs created a demand for clarification of the law. This Bill was also described as 'mainly concerned with the removal of doubt'.[42] The Corneal Grafting Act 1952 was in part a cause of this doubt. If legislation was needed to authorise the removal of eyes, there thus arose 'a natural doubt about the possibility of removing other parts'.[43]

Introducing the Human Tissue Bill in the House of Lords, Lord Newton acknowledged 'a long tradition of bitter hostility to the dissection of bodies'.[44] Debates in Parliament on the Bill smugly compared

---

[37] Ibid., 156.
[38] Ibid., 80–1.
[39] HL Deb 27 May 1952, vol 76, col 1465.
[40] Ibid.
[41] See Lord Balneil's description of the Bill as 'not controversial' and not a Bill that 'has attracted any public attention': HC Deb 20 December 1960, vol 632, col 1244.
[42] Ibid., col 1231.
[43] Ibid.
[44] HL Deb 19 July 1961, vol 233, col 54.

'bitter and superstitious opposition'[45] to the Anatomy Bill with the more sophisticated and scientific milieu of the twentieth century. We can find no evidence of public controversy or, until 1970, much academic engagement with the Act. Had the baleful stars waned? Or were they simply hidden?

In 1970, Gerald Dworkin exposed practical weaknesses of the 1961 Act and highlighted the dangers of ad hoc legislation.[46] In the wake of revelations about organ retention, the Bristol Report condemned the complexity and obscurity of the 1961 Act.[47] Many medical practitioners whose practice was regulated by it were wholly unaware of its existence! The Act regulated the removal of body parts from the dead for therapeutic purposes and for the purposes of medical education and research. It was thus central to pathology. Any retention of body parts to promote research, medical education or public health was governed by the Act. In Parliamentary debates relating to it, however, the focus was on enabling *organ transplants* – promoting the miracle of transplant medicine. In the event, perception played a crucial role in creating the controversy around organ retention, and the 1961 Act failed in its vaunted objectives of enhancing the supply of organs for transplant.

### 10.2.5 Commodifying Organs: Human Organs Transplant Act 1989

The Human Organs Transplant Act 1989 responded to scandal relating to living organ 'donation', tarnishing the reputation of transplantation generally and reviving distaste at the notion of human organs as a commodity. In 1989, evidence of a commercial trade in organs for transplant attracted media attention. Three doctors were found guilty of serious professional misconduct by the General Medical Council. Four impoverished Turkish citizens had been paid to come to London in return for agreeing to the removal of a kidney to be transplanted into wealthy private patients. Evidence of 'kidney bartering' was not new in 1989. In 1985, a citizen of Pakistan received £2,000 to fly to London, where his kidney was transplanted into a private patient.[48]

---

[45] Dr Horace King MP, HC Deb 20 December 1961, vol 632, col 1243.
[46] Gerald Dworkin, 'The Law Relating to Organ Transplantation in England' (1970) 33 *Modern Law Review* 353; and see P Skegg 'Criminal Liability for the Unauthorised Use of Corpses in Medical Education and Research' (1992) 32 *Medicine Science and the Law* 51.
[47] Bristol Interim Report (n 18) 20.
[48] HL Deb 19 July 1989, vol 510, col 846.

The Act banning payments, including payment for cadaver donations as well as living donations, was rushed through Parliament. The government resisted attempts to start a coherent debate on laws regulating transplant medicine as a whole – stating that this was a 'short Bill', designed to deal 'with a specific problem in a specific way'.[49] The quality of debate was variable, to say the least, with some Members of Parliament (MPs) seeking to use the Bill to reopen the abortion debate.[50] Live donations where the donor and recipient were not closely genetically related became unlawful unless approved by the Unrelated Live Transplant Authority (ULTRA). Scrutiny to ensure that living donors comprehend what they are doing, and do so freely, might well be seen as desirable and is provided for today within the Human Tissue Acts. Exploitation and covert coercion are claimed as reasons to avoid commercialisation of organ donations. However, ULTRA's remit was confined to unrelated donors, overlooking the fact that the genetic family is the most obvious setting context for undue influence and emotional pressure to donate. The minister who introduced the Bill acknowledged that ULTRA's primary role was not to safeguard donor autonomy but to police possible organ sales: '[t]he main purpose of this Bill is to prohibit commercial dealings from taking place in Great Britain involving human organs intended for transplant'.[51] The Bill assumed that any trade in human organs was 'unacceptable' and that the government was determined to stamp out such 'abhorrent practices'. Discussion of the broader context of commercial dealings in human material is wholly absent.

### 10.2.6    Baleful Star: Legislating on the Hoof

The history of legislation touching on medical uses of human bodies and their parts was consistently marked by an unwillingness to engage in reflection about the significance of the body per se. The pendulum swung between unquestioning acceptance of scientific claims, and unthinking responses to moral panic and/or emotional life stories in the media, allied to a deplorable tendency to legislate ad hoc. People in need of a transplant linger on waiting lists. Are the new laws replacing requirement for express consent for cadaver donation with deemed consent, variously named presumed consent, or opt-out, the perfect compromise? If we

---

[49] HL Deb May 1989, vol 510, col 842.
[50] HC Deb vol 153, col 769.
[51] HL Deb vol 510, col 842.

have objections to donating organs, a few minutes on the Organ Donation Register ensures that our objection prevails. But, as Den Hartogh has examined,[52] the question of whether consent can be presumed/deemed, or whether that would be fictional consent, is deeply problematic.

## 10.3    Deemed Consent

When the government proposed legislation to introduce deemed consent in England, the seemingly modest proposal met with unexpected opposition. Dr Chris Rudge, a passionate advocate of transplantation and former medical director of UK Transplant and chair of the Organ Donation Committee, told journalists that he was 'horribly opposed' to the proposals: 'organ donation should be a present and [it is] not for the state to assume that they can take my organs without asking me'.[53] Hugh Whittall, the director of the Nuffield Council on Bioethics at the time, expressed misgivings. Noting the lack of evidence that similar legislation in Wales had as yet led to an increased supply of organs, Whittall commented: 'We fully endorse the aim of increasing the rate of donated organs, but we are concerned that making a legislative change based on poor evidence risks undermining public trust in the organ donation system, and could have serious consequences for rates of organ donation.'[54]

The doubts expressed by Rudge and Whittall emphasise how fragile is the trust, on which this field of medicine depends, that human material donated for the benefit of fellow humans will be used for the purposes of that 'beautiful gift',[55] to achieve a good end in the spirit of the original donation. Transplants of many internal organs, such as hearts, kidneys and sections of livers or lungs, have become routine. Yet, as David Price argued, all transplantation engages deeply personal and socially

---

[52] Govert Den Hartogh, 'Can Consent be Presumed?' (2011) 28 *Journal of Applied Philosophy* 295.

[53] 'Ex-transplant Chief Chris Rudge: My Doubts About New Donor Plans' (*The Times*, 8 October 2017) www.thetimes.co.uk/article/ex-transplant-chief-paul-rudge-you-wont-get-my-organs-p7tbjf03t (accessed 29 January 2021).

[54] 'Organ Donation Consent Law Change Could "Undermine" Public Trust, Ethics Experts Warn' (*The Independent*, 23 February 2018) www.independent.co.uk/news/health/organ-donation-opt-out-consent-law-public-trust-ethics-trust-nhs-healthcare-a8225756.html (accessed 29 January 2021).

[55] Michael Stephens, 'Opt-Out Organ Donation Systems: The Experience in Wales' (2018) 3 *Journal of Kidney Care* 38.

profound questions: 'By virtue of their nexus to "self", the retention and use of human material raises profound issue pertaining to the relationship between bodies and personal identity, and generates fundamental questions about who we are and what sort of society we want to live in.'[56]

Failure to heed Price and treating human material as simply a 'thing', akin to an artificial hip joint, risks undermining efforts to increase the number of organs for transplant and generating adverse publicity, which in turn might reduce the number of people prepared to donate organs. Taking organs on the basis of deemed consent could magnify the risk of treating the dead as a 'thing', a resource to be harvested. Echoing Richardson, different values may be attributed to the corpse by the team that carries out the transplant and the families of 'donors'. For the former, the deceased is the source of valuable human material: in Richardson's words, an anatomical object and a valuable commodity. For the latter, she is a loved mother. The bioethicist Alastair V Campbell, has noted:

> From a scientific perspective the human dead body – or 'cadaver' – is easily viewed in an impersonal way, as a source of knowledge of the causes of death or the effectiveness of therapy through autopsy, or as a source of benefit to others through the harvesting of organ and tissue. Such an objectified view of the body is however a universe of meaning removed from the perceptions of the bereaved family of the dead person. For them the body of the deceased represents all that they cared for and all that they have lost.[57]

We saw earlier that Dr Rudge conceptualised deemed consent as *taking* his organs, not allowing him to gift them. Reflection for a moment makes it clear that neither deemed consent nor the alternative formulation of *presumed consent* is in reality consent.[58] Silence cannot constitute consent.[59] Any presumption that 'if X has not communicated an express objection to donation, then X has consented' rests on shaky ground and so presumed consent is a fiction. While opinion polls indicate that most people would consent, the reliability of the data drawn from polls and surveys has been questioned.[60] Deemed consent is a slightly better

---

[56] David Price, *Human Tissue in Transplantation and Research* (Cambridge University Press 2010) 3.

[57] Alastair Campbell, *The Body in Bioethics* (Routledge 2009) 1.

[58] Price (n 57) 133.

[59] *Felthouse* v. *Bindley* (1862) 11 CB NS 869.

[60] Tobias Cantrell, 'The "Opt-Out" Approach to Deceased Organ Donations in England: A Misconceived Policy Which May Precipitate Moral Harm' (2019) 14 *Clinical Ethics* 63.

descriptor in the sense that, rather than presuming the unknowable state of mind of an individual, it applies an objective test. In light of the needs of organ recipients and prevailing opinion, a judgement is made that it is likely that X would have agreed and carries with it the connotation that X should agree. Opt-out best reflects the reality of the change. Donation becomes the norm, the decision expected of a citizen, subject to 'permission' to recuse oneself from such expectation.

'Hard opt-out' enables the taking of organs unless, and only unless, the deceased had formally objected. Views held by the family are irrelevant. Opt-out in the UK is 'soft': some might say so soft in England that it defeats the purpose of changing the law. In parliamentary debates, the MP who first introduced the Bill, Geoffrey Robinson, promised that soft-opt safeguards would be built into the legislation.[61] The Act per se is not obviously 'soft'. The Organ Donation (Deemed Consent) Act provides that bereaved families will still be consulted and can object, but only to provide 'information that would lead a reasonable person to conclude that the person concerned would not have consented'.[62] The Human Tissue Authority Code of Practice for England dilutes opt-out.[63] The Human Tissue Authority (HTA) makes it clear that consent, express or deemed, permits the taking of organs but does not mandate it.[64] Families still play a crucial role in the donation process. Their views must always be taken into account and have strong influence on the decision whether or not to proceed with the donation.

Dove and colleagues (including Graeme) have examined the family veto from a human rights perspective, following a Latvian case with a disturbing 'body-snatching' theme.[65] *Elberte* v. *Latvia*[66] involved a successful Article 3 European Convention on Human Rights (ECHR) (inhuman or degrading treatment) claim by a widow who alleged that she had been caused suffering 'that went beyond the suffering inflicted by grief following the death of a close family member' as a result of seeing her husband's body with his legs bound together and subsequently learning that tissue had been removed without his or her consent.

---

[61] Ibid., 64–5.
[62] Organ Donation (Deemed Consent) Act 2019, s 1(5).
[63] Human Tissue Authority, 'HTA Code of Practice F: Donation of Solid Organs and Tissue for Transplantation; Deceased Organ and Tissue Donation' (2020) www.hta.gov.uk/hta-codes-practice-and-standards-0 (accessed 29 January 2021).
[64] Ibid., 75.
[65] Edward Dove et al, '*Elberte v. Latvia*: Whose Tissue Is It Anyway – Relational Autonomy or the Autonomy of Relations?' (2015) 15 *Medical Law International* 77.
[66] *Elberte* v. *Latvia* (Application no 61243/08) [2015] ECHR1.

*Elberte* also opened the door to an Article 8 right (to respect for private life) for relatives to oppose the removal of a deceased relative's tissue irrespective of the wishes of the deceased. Unfortunately, the European Court of Human Rights (ECtHR) failed to pin down the precise nature of the relational interests at stake, but, by linking family consent to Article 8, the decision reflects the broader expansion of the right to respect for private life. It also highlights the difficulty in determining the scope of the family veto within a system that attends to relational interests but does not 'spell out the nature and scope of the rights, nor the corresponding duties of the parties in ascertaining and operationalising those views'.[67] Dove and colleagues suggest that when the law does not mandate family consent but makes it a policy position, family consent becomes a matter of local courtesy rather than a moral requirement.

The HTA Code of Practice requirement that account should be taken of the potential donor's faith and/or beliefs might also be seen as a matter of courtesy, but there is a practical aspect to the policy too, which seeks to avoid being tainted by 'body-snatcher' allegations.[68] Similarly, where consent could be deemed but there is no relative to consult, donation should not proceed because the risk to public confidence outweighs the possible benefit.[69] Unclaimed bodies are not to revive their role as the source of body parts. In paragraphs 13 and 14, the HTA guidance states as a general principle of its guidance that, in making decisions on donation, human considerations may mean that donation should not go ahead and that risk to public confidence must be borne in mind.

Supporters of opt-out consent may conclude that, in practice, little has changed, even in relation to those transplants where consent/authorisation can be deemed. Certain body parts are exempt from the change in the law, continuing to require express consent. All the lists are eclectic. Welsh legislation typifies the excluded materials as *novel*.[70] The pool of body parts utilised in transplant medicine is expanding. As is gradually happening with faces and limbs, once-rare transplants are now feasible and may become standard practice as expertise improves and the public becomes aware of the possibilities in relation to some of the exclusions. Will the excluded list be modified? The current excluded lists include brains, faces and also sexual and reproductive organs. Uterus and penis

[67] Dove et al (n 66) 78.
[68] https://content.hta.gov.uk/sites/default/files/2020-11/Code%20F%20part%202.pdf, paras 92–3.
[69] Human Tissue Authority (n 64) para 951.
[70] Human Transplantation (Wales) Act 2013, s 7(3).

transplants are possible now. What such body parts have in common are a significance and a sensitivity closely related to the donor's identity,[71] and so the donation of such parts is often a more difficult decision, both for the putative donor (if they engage with the list before death) and for the family facing a request to take organs and sensitive parts from a deceased or dying relative.

### 10.3.1  Gift, Sacrifice and Duty

Given the guidance from the HTA, the principal factor in the process of encouraging more families to consent, or not to object, remains the quality of the interaction with all staff (health-care and transplant team) involved with the family. Supporters of the new legislation consider that what has changed is the starting point for conversation about donation between the family and relevant staff.[72]

Understanding *why* families refuse consent is crucial in facilitating constructive discussion. Sque and Long-Sutehall have carried out extensive research with donor families drawing on concepts of donation as 'sacrifice'. They have emphasised the need to remember that the donor family is first a bereaved family, and ask us to think of donation as being as much a 'sacrifice' as a gift. Sque and Long-Sutehall's work draws from donor family experiences and explores how families who agree to donation derive comfort from continuing an internalised relationship with the deceased. Donation serves to highlight the positive personality of the deceased, whose generosity in life continues after death. The deceased donor may be described as an 'angel' or a 'hero', with the donation viewed as a further achievement of the deceased.[73] Some donor families may also derive comfort from the idea that part of the deceased lives on within the body of the recipient, which helps to give meaning to the life and death of the donor.

Sque and colleagues have subsequently studied how temporally interwoven experiences and global themes influence the family.[74]

---

[71]  Richard Huxtable and Julie Woodley, 'Gaining Face or Losing Face? Framing the Debate on Face Transplants' (2005) 19 *Bioethics* 505; Donna Dickenson and Guy Widdershoven, 'Ethical Issues in Limb Transplants' (2001) 15 *Bioethics* 110.

[72]  Stephens (n 56) 38–41.

[73]  Magi Sque and Tracy Long-Sutehall, 'Bereavement, Decision-Making and the Family in Organ Donation' in Anne-Maree Farrell, David Price and Muireann Quigley (eds), *Organ Shortage, Ethics and Pragmatism* (Cambridge University Press 2011).

[74]  Magi Sque et al, 'Bereaved Donor Families' Experiences of Organ and Tissue Donation and Perceived Influences on Their Decision Making' (2018) 45 *Journal of Critical Care* 82.

Unsurprisingly, the wish to respect the will of the deceased was a key 'past' factor, together with the families' preconceived attitude towards deceased donation. 'Present' factors affecting the decision were the sudden and shocking nature of events, and the way that information about the dying patient's condition and the possibility of donation were communicated and subsequently arranged. Families in shock over sudden or impending death will naturally struggle to make a decision if they are unsure what the deceased would want. While families were generally positive about the sensitive way in which information was communicated, once a decision was made, the paperwork and form filling – for example, 'the itemisation of body parts'[75] – had the potential to increase distress and, in one reported case, even led to a change of mind about allowing some 'parts' to be used. Fear about what would happen to the body of the deceased was an important factor for some families, who were concerned about mutilation, what the body would look like after organs were taken and/or the fact that their loved-one's body had already been through so much and should be left in peace. This wish to leave the body in peace is reflected in almost 20 per cent of reasons given for family refusal in the UK.[76] Finally, further themes reflected Sque and Long-Sutehall's earlier work (discussed above): families derived comfort from the fact that the death of their loved-one had helped others and thus continued the positive theme of their life. While most families did not see public recognition as important, some families thought that public recognition would help to promote donation and serve as a tribute to the deceased.

Understanding family experiences in order to develop systems that address the factors and themes that direct the family decision is essential. For some, the notion that donation is a 'gift' which characterises and affirms the generosity of the deceased seems appropriate. For other families, the donation is a difficult 'sacrifice' to be tolerated despite the distress. For families refusing to consent, the organs of the deceased are neither a gift to be given nor a sacrifice they are prepared to tolerate for the greater good. For some of these families, opposition may be immutable, but for others the refusal might have been averted and we return to this possibility in Section 10.4.

---

[75] Ibid., 87.

[76] NHS Organ Donation and Transplantation Activity Report 2019/20 (n 13): 9.1 per cent of refusals were because the deceased had 'suffered enough' and 9.9 per cent because the family did not want to see more surgery done on the deceased.

Worrying about 'gift' or 'sacrifice' and the impact on the bereaved family may, as the authors of *Mason and McCall Smith* comment, result in a disproportionate focus on the donor family. Given the competing interests at stake – family distress versus life/health for an organ recipient – should cadaver organs be regarded as a 'community asset'?[77] John Harris has argued that organs should be 'conscripted' into service to address the shortfall.[78] Graeme and his colleagues point out that conscription would mean that 'in some way the dead body falls into the custody of the state', exactly what Rudge vehemently objected to. Proposals for compulsion, ignoring the powerful distress occasioned to grieving families, often in the midst of shocking events, and the cultural beliefs of many communities in the UK, could provoke a backlash resulting in fewer, not more, organs.[79]

### 10.3.2 Deemed Consent: Spanish Lessons

Spain is known as the paradigm of success after switching to an opt-out stance in 1979. The first ten years after the change in the law, from 1979 to 1989, were disappointing. The Spanish success came only after the introduction of a well-resourced state system to support transplants. It is interesting that there is no national, state-run organ donor register, suggesting that recording consent or opposition is not a policy priority. The matter of formally registering to donate or registering one's opposition has been devolved to regional authorities.[80] State efforts have instead been directed at cultivating a positive social and medical climate in order to generate trust, which has led to Spain having the highest deceased donation rate in the world.

Fabre and colleagues argue that deemed consent is in fact 'dormant' in Spain[81] because what matters more than whether an opt-in or opt-out approach is in place is developing a climate of trust with effective systems co-ordinated by trained experts. Trust and effective systems have been shown to reduce the number of family vetoes. Enabling a grieving family

---

[77] Laurie, Harmon and Dove (n 4) 606.

[78] John Harris, 'Organ Procurement: Dead Interests, Living Needs' (2003) 29 *Journal of Medical Ethics* 130.

[79] Sheelagh McGuinness and Margaret Brazier, 'Respecting the Living Means Respecting the Dead Too' (2008) 28 *Oxford Journal of Legal Studies* 476.

[80] Article 30 Real Decreto 1723/2012 28 December. Art 9 states that therapeutic donation can take place unless there is explicit opposition by the deceased.

[81] John Fabre, Paul Murphy and Rafael Metasanz, 'Presumed Consent: A Distraction in the Quest for Increasing Rates of Organ Donation' (2010) *BMJ* c4973.

to perceive the donation of organs as not simply a service to the recipients but the final service that the donor can render others – and so a sacrifice that the family should make – is an art. It cannot be taught in the same way that, say, anatomy is taught. Imagination needs to be deployed and the possibility of 'failure' accepted with grace. The skills of the transplant teams at the bedside must also be deployed in the public arena. Media support to foster public awareness, as seen in Spain, will be an important factor in establishing public trust.

As the Spanish experience has illustrated, soft opt-out can be successful. Success depends on reassuring the grieving family such that they trust that donation is appropriate, which requires highly effective transplant infrastructure with staff who have been trained to undertake difficult conversations with grieving families. Fewer families seek to veto donation when they know that the deceased wished to donate. As Shaw has discussed, changing to opt-out means changing the 'default' for patients' families.[82] He suggests that families are more likely to veto donation by contending that their feelings should carry more weight when consent is merely presumed. Shaw's point accords with the research carried out by Sque and colleagues, which suggests that a crucial factor for the bereaved family is carrying out the wishes of the bereaved. If the family simply do not know the wishes of the deceased, a key objective within a deemed consent approach is to persuade the family that donation is the right decision.

Under an opt-in system, if the deceased had not opted in, a family refusal to donate might be seen as honouring the wishes of a loved-one who in life had not chosen to donate. Most recent data indicate that 25.4 per cent of family refusals were because the patient had previously expressed a wish not to donate, while for 14.1 per cent of refusals the family reported that they simply did not know what the deceased would have wanted.[83] Within an opt-out scheme, those choosing not to donate can now be certain – provided that they opt out – that their wishes will be respected. The family cannot veto an opt-out. But if the deceased had not opted out, their silence should be taken as deemed consent, which changes the nature of the family veto and opens the door to approaching the family with the message that silence means (deemed) consent whereas previously, at least superficially, silence meant dissent. This

---

[82] David Shaw, 'The Side Effects of Deemed Consent: Changing Defaults in Organ Donation' (2019) 45 *Journal of Medical Ethics* 435.

[83] NHS Organ Donation and Transplantation Activity Report 2019/20 (n 13) 137.

might help to avoid those cases where the family refuses because they are unsure what the deceased would have wanted.

Will deemed consent increase the number of organs for transplant in the UK? Will it reduce cases where families veto donation? The assertion that the change in the law will bridge the gap and save lives is central to the arguments that most people would therefore agree to donation and that any 'harm' occasioned by resiling from a requirement for express consent is offset by the greater good of saving or improving lives. We should note that the refusal rate has already fallen from 41 per cent in 2010 to 32.3 per cent in 2019–20.[84] It is still too high and especially so in some ethnic minority communities.[85] In Wales, although it may be too soon to reach any firm conclusion, early evidence suggests that, after a hesitant start, donation rates have improved under the opt-out system.[86] At first it seemed that the change had been in vain.[87] Then, happily, the system appeared to be yielding improvements, until the Covid-19 pandemic struck in March 2020. The timing of the introduction of deemed consent in the UK has, in that light, proved unfortunate. As Parsons and Moorlock make clear,[88] any campaign to inform the public that they now need to opt out (or have their consent to donation presumed) has been overshadowed by the pandemic – bidding to be a new baleful star. Parsons and Moorlock are sadly right to say that a valuable opportunity to inform the public of this important change has been lost in the midst of the crisis.

### 10.3.3   Deemed Consent: Why Only for Transplants?

Deemed consent will apply only to donation of cadaver organs for transplant. Retaining and using material for any other scheduled purpose – such as research or medical education, donating the whole body to a medical school, or for public display – will continue to require explicit consent/authorisation. These other purposes may be as valuable to medicine and ultimately to the community as transplantation. A multiple

---

[84] Ibid.

[85] Ibid. The refusal rate recorded in BAME families is 58.3 per cent.

[86] Seonad Madden et al, 'The Effect on Consent Rates for Deceased Organ Donation in Wales After the Introduction of an Opt-Out System' (2020) 75 *Anaesthesia* 1146 https://onlinelibrary.wiley.com/doi/full/10.1111/anae.15055 (accessed 29 January 2021).

[87] Jordan Parsons, 'Welsh 2013 Deemed Consent Legislation Falls Short of Expectations' (2018) 122 *Health Policy* 941.

[88] Jordan Parsons and Greg Moorlock, 'A Global Pandemic Is Not a Good Time to Introduce "Opt-Out" for Organ Donation' (2020) 20 *Medical Law International* 155.

donation of several organs for transplant can save, or improve the quality of, life for five or six recipients. Donation of organs and tissue for research may benefit thousands of people. Medical students need bodies to study anatomy. The foundation of scientific medicine from which we have all benefited today derives from the grisly activities of the anatomists learning the secrets of the human body in the dissecting rooms. Few corpses provide suitable material for transplant. The organs of those dying at an advanced age or as a result of certain conditions will not provide suitable organs for transplant. They may, however, have great value for research purposes. Rationally, if deemed consent is adjudged as justified by the goods of meeting the shortfall in organs, should it be for research? The authors of *Mason and McCall Smith* express initial regret that 'insofar as the therapeutic use of tissues is so far separated in the public mind from activities such as research and education[,] the oppor-tunity was not taken for the first time on a distinct conceptual plane'.[89] The difference in 'the public mind' seems to rest in the presence of a direct and immediate beneficiary.[90] Several families who were bitterly aggrieved when they discovered that their child's or other relative's organs had been retained without their knowledge or consent had ori-ginally offered those very organs for transplant.[91]

Other apparent irrationalities litter the law. Legislators have steered clear of any property model,[92] too swiftly aligning property with commodification.[93] 'Gift' is lauded without considering that, to be able to give, one must usually own what one gives. The Human Tissue Act 2004 treats taking consent for the use of tissue from the dead as a more serious matter than taking it from the living. In relation to using the tissue of the living for future research purposes, the prioritisation of industry interests means, as Quigley argues, that problematic exemptions make it inappropriate to designate the person from whom the tissue was sourced as 'the donor',[94] since no consent exists beyond the initial extraction. If we do not care too much about obtaining consent for the use of the tissue of the living, then why, Quigley asks, should we treat

---

[89] Laurie, Harmon and Dove (n 4) 599.

[90] Sque et al (2018) (n 74).

[91] NHS Retained Organs Commission (n 20) para 1.9.

[92] John Kenyon Mason and Graeme Laurie, 'Consent or Property? Dealing with the Body and Its Parts in the Shadow of Bristol and Alder Hey' (2001) 64 *Modern Law Review* 710 should be compulsory reading for any UK legislator considering human tissue.

[93] Muireann Quigley, *Self-Ownership, Property Rights, and the Human Body* (Cambridge University Press 2018).

[94] Human Tissue Act 2004, s 7(1)(b).

consent in relation to the dead as a more serious concern? Is the answer simply that, in the wake of the fall-out from the organ retention 'scandal', governments are wary of engaging in debate on uses of body parts other than for transplant?

## 10.4 Conclusions: Practice and Principles

The taking and uses of organs and tissue from the dead for transplant, research, education or other beneficent purposes are riddled with an array of contradictory arguments and uncertainty over the meaning, value and ownership of human tissue. Distrust, industry interests, a historical legacy of punitive dissection (and worse), matters of faith and culture, and reactive responses to scandals, leading to ad hoc legislation, have impeded past attempts to establish an effective system to improve the supply of sufficient organs and tissue for transplant. They have produced a treasure chest of questions to debate for philosophers, lawyers, social scientists, medical historians and many others.

Academically productive as these debates may be, they do nothing to help people on the transplant waiting list. Stories of people dying for want of a transplant and of mistakes when material is taken against the wishes or beliefs of the deceased and/or their family make equally good copy for the media. Soft opt-out as represented in the three UK Acts will not please everybody. It is a compromise in terms of principle.[95] The priority now should be to make it work in practice. Making the system work demands a number of actions.

When approaching families at the bedside to consider donation, the importance of the manner in which discussions are handled in the tragic moments when death and donation are first confronted by a family cannot be emphasised too strongly. The Spanish experience has demonstrated that sensitive communication, reassurance and well-supported formal arrangements are key to minimising family objections. The crucial role of any evidence of the wishes of the deceased highlights the requirement for effective public communication and engagement relating to organ donation.

Public education must make it clear that people who want to donate should not simply assume that, given the new law, they can rest happily in the knowledge that consent will be deemed. Signing the register to

---

[95] Margaret Brazier and John Harris, 'Does Ethical Controversy Cost Lives?' in Farrell, Price and Quigley (n 74) 15.

evidence your wishes as well as making sure your family know of your wishes offer further support to those engaged in the sad conversations about donation after your death. If a potential donor is aware that their immediate family are opposed to donation, they may wish to appoint a proxy to act on their behalf after their death. Even in such a case, transplant teams are not obliged to act on the proxy consent, but the case to present to the family is strengthened.

In the public arena, honesty and patience will be needed, and overly emotional rhetoric treated with care. The media played a key role in the change of the law in England, focusing on two children. Max was on the waiting list for a new heart. Keira was tragically killed in an accident. Her parents donated her heart, saving Max's life. So compelling was this story that the 2019 Act has been named 'Max and Keira's law'. While this story illustrated the good that organ donation can do, the 2019 Act and thus deemed consent apply only to adults. Far from all recipients of transplants will be as appealing as Max. In recent years, transplant surgeons have extended the range of older recipients and patients with other health conditions.

The change in the law was never going to result in speedy 'success' in terms of a swift closure of the gap between organs donated and organs needed. The number of patients needing and eligible for a transplant is growing rapidly. Improvements in the care of transplant recipients have resulted in many more patients surviving to need a second, third or fourth transplant. Success might prove to be that the gap does not grow. Patience would always have been needed. Success was never going to be achieved swiftly. Events alas have intervened to delay the day when 'deemed consent' can be evaluated.

The Covid-19 pandemic radically reduced the number of transplants possible for much of 2020 and, as this book went to press, there was ongoing disruption due to the impact of the pandemic on the NHS during 2021. No one who died of Covid-19 was suitable as a donor,[96] and generally only the most urgent transplants have taken place. The impact of the virus, the redeployment of staff and the sheer difficulty of conducting discussions about donation remotely during a period when relatives of dying patients have generally being prevented from being with the patients in hospital mean that we will have to wait some time

---

[96] Latest update (8 January 2021) NHS Blood and Transplant, Organ Donation website www.organdonation.nhs.uk/get-involved/news/coronavirus-the-latest-updates/ (accessed 22 March 2021).

until even any cautious judgement about the move to deemed consent can be made. The dominance of the pandemic in the media represents a lost opportunity to inform the public about the change to opt-out while the ink dries on the new statutes.[97] The lost opportunity may have long-term implications in terms of public understanding and trust unless, once transplants resume, a concerted effort is made to publicise the change. People who have objections to donation need to be aware that they must now opt out. Respect for the beliefs and values of those with whom we do not agree is required. Lack of respect, dismissing objections as superstition or ignorance, has been a recurring feature of discontent relating to uses of human tissue since the Renaissance, if not before.

A focus on practice, and on making law work, seems appropriate in a tribute to Graeme Laurie. He is a scholar who has never eschewed the messy business of putting principle into practice. He has built on the legacy of Ken Mason and made Edinburgh a star in the firmament of medical law scholarship and policy-making, a bright and benign star.

---

[97]  Parsons and Moorlock (n 89).

# 11

## The Legacy of the Warnock Report

EMILY JACKSON

## 11.1 Introduction

Graeme Laurie's legacies to the discipline of medical law are many and varied, but, in addition to his superb publications, Graeme has taken very seriously the 'public service' element of a senior academic's role. Committee work can be fascinating, but it can also be time-consuming and thankless. It is to Graeme's enormous credit that he has played such an active role in a very wide range of bodies, from the Nuffield Council on Bioethics to the UK Biobank's Ethics and Governance Council; and from the European Association of Health Law to the Royal Society Working Group on Science as an Open Enterprise and the British Medical Association's Medical Ethics Committee. I was a member of this last committee at the same time as Graeme, and I learnt a great deal from his calm, focused and knowledgeable contributions. Some members of the 'great and the good' collect committee roles as baubles, and like the sound of their own voices. Graeme is the exact opposite, and, as a result, he has made a real and tangible difference not only to the academic discipline of medical law but also to the ethical practice of medicine and scientific research in the UK.

My contribution to this Festschrift is about the legacy of a committee which completed its work nearly four decades ago. The Report of the Committee of Inquiry into Human Fertilisation and Embryology,[1] commonly known as the Warnock Report, has had the most profound impact

---

[1] Department of Health & Social Security, *Report of the Committee of Enquiry into Human Fertilisation and Embryology* (HMSO, 1984) hereafter 'Warnock' www.hfea.gov.uk/media/2608/warnock-report-of-the-committee-of-inquiry-into-human-fertilisation-and-embryology-1984.pdf (accessed 10 February 2021).

on the regulation of fertility treatment not only in the UK but worldwide. Fertility treatment in the UK continues to be regulated by an expert regulator, through a licensing and inspection regime, backed up by a series of criminal offences. This regulatory model, set up by the Human Fertilisation and Embryology Act 1990, has proved to be sufficiently flexible and liberal to be able to accommodate scientific and social change, while also being sufficiently strict and rigorous to maintain public confidence. At the same time, it should not be surprising that a statute based on recommendations made so long ago is 'inevitably showing its age'.[2]

In this chapter, I will reflect upon the legacy of the Warnock Report. I will argue that it has stood the test of time remarkably well, and that the licensing regime set up as a result of its recommendations has proved to be a flexible and robust way to regulate a fast-moving area of science and clinical practice. At the same time, the world was very different in 1982–4. Inevitably, some of the language in the Warnock Report sounds old-fashioned and judgemental today, particularly in relation to same-sex parenthood and surrogacy. And issues like trans parenthood were not considered at all – not only in 1984 but also in 2008 when the Act was amended substantially. At some point, it may be sensible to embark upon a law reform process that does not just tweak and update the current statute but goes back to first principles and starts again. Yet, while there may be some legacies of the Warnock Report which we could sensibly dispense with in the 2020s, those who work in the fertility sector, and the patients who have been treated within it, undoubtedly owe a debt of gratitude to Baroness Mary Warnock and her fellow committee members.

## 11.2  Warnock's Legacy on Process

Four years after the birth of Louise Brown, the first baby conceived through *in vitro* fertilisation (IVF), and as a result of 'growing public concern about new techniques for the treatment of infertility and new, related areas of research',[3] the government appointed Dame Mary Warnock, as she then was, to chair a Committee of Inquiry. The

---

[2] Sally Cheshire, 'Is the UK Fertility Sector Facing a Tipping Point?' (*Bionews*, 8 July 2019) www.bionews.org.uk/page_143760 (accessed 10 February 2021).
[3] Mary Warnock, 'Moral Thinking and Government Policy: The Warnock Committee on Human Embryology' (1985) 63 *Milbank Memorial Fund Quarterly: Health and Society* 504.

Committee's terms of reference were '[t]o consider recent and potential developments in medicine and science related to human fertilisation and embryology; to consider what policies and safeguards should be applied, including consideration of the social, ethical and legal implications of these developments; and to make recommendations'.[4] Although the Warnock Report addressed questions of morality, such as the moral status of the embryo and the legitimacy of surrogacy, its task was essentially a practical one: it had to come up with realistic proposals for legislation. Reflecting on the work of the Committee the following year, Mary Warnock commented that '[p]erhaps the most important point of agreement ... was that *some laws or other* need to be enacted, and soon, before the swift developments in embryology go much further' (emphasis in original).[5]

The Warnock Report did not just make recommendations about *when* it should be lawful to store and use gametes and embryos outside of a woman's body. Equally important were its recommendations about *how* this new area of scientific endeavour and medical practice should be regulated.

### 11.2.1  An Arm's-Length Regulatory Body

The Warnock Report recommended the setting up of an arm's-length body, independent of government and with a lay chairman and 'substantial lay representation'[6] (translated into law as a lay majority):

> The protection of the public, which we see as the primary objective of regulation, demands the existence of an authority independent of Government, health authorities, or research institutions. The authority should be specifically charged with the responsibility to regulate and monitor practice in relation to those sensitive areas which raise fundamental ethical questions. We therefore recommend the establishment of a new statutory licensing authority to regulate both research and those infertility services which we have recommended should be subject to control.[7]

The Warnock Report's view that professional self-regulation of fertility treatment was insufficient did not spring from nowhere. The idea that the professions, including the medical profession, required more external

---

[4] Warnock (n 1) para 1.2.
[5] Warnock (n 3) 521.
[6] Warnock (n 1) para 13.4.
[7] Ibid., para 13.3.

surveillance and control was a key theme of government policy in the 1980s.[8] In 1982, two prominent lawyers, Ian Kennedy and Geoffrey Robertson, had argued separately that discussion of IVF needed to be 'dragged into the open',[9] and should not take place behind 'a closed door marked "Medical Ethics – laymen and lawyers keep out"'.[10] In her column in *The Observer*, Katherine Whitehorn had been critical of Robert Edwards for saying that he did not understand what the fuss was about, arguing that 'if ever there was a case where it shouldn't be left to doctors and scientists alone, where society ought to have a say, as Ian Kennedy insisted in last year's Reith Lectures, this is it'.[11]

Mary Warnock herself had advocated public accountability for IVF through a 'system of surveillance' in an article published while the Committee was still hearing evidence.[12] As Duncan Wilson has explained, her enthusiasm for external oversight of scientists and doctors was not intended to be an impediment to medical and scientific progress; rather, it was intended to *protect* doctors and scientists.[13] Warnock argued that external oversight would allow scientists 'to get on with their work, without the fear of private prosecutions, or disruption by those who object to what they are doing'.[14] In short, the best way to deflect calls for new technologies to be banned was to demonstrate that they could instead be controlled and contained within limits set down in legislation, and enforced by an independent and publicly accountable regulator.

The Warnock Report's proposed new licensing authority was to have two functions: one advisory and one executive. In its advisory function, it would issue good practice guidance to clinicians and scientists, as well as advising government and ministers 'on specific issues as they arise'.[15] Its executive function would be to issue licences to clinicians and scientists

---

[8] See further Michael Power, *The Audit Society: The Rituals of Verification* (Oxford University Press 1997) and Duncan Wilson, *The Making of British Bioethics* (Manchester University Press 2014).

[9] Ian Kennedy, 'Ethical Guidelines on Fertilization' (*The Times*, 11 February 1982). See also Kennedy's Reith lectures, published as Ian Kennedy, *The Unmasking of Medicine* (George Allen and Unwin 1981).

[10] Geoffrey Robertson, 'The Law and Test Tube Babies' (*The Observer*, 7 February 1982).

[11] Katherine Whitehorn, 'Embryonic Problems' (*The Observer*, 3 October 1982).

[12] Mary Warnock, '*In vitro* Fertilization: The Ethical Issues (II)' (1983) 33 *Philosophical Quarterly* 238.

[13] Duncan Wilson, 'Creating the "Ethics Industry": Mary Warnock, in vitro Fertilization and the History of Bioethics in Britain' (2011) 6 *BioSocieties* 121.

[14] Warnock (n 3) 514.

[15] Warnock (n 1) para 13.5.

and, backed up by an inspectorate, it would ensure that all premises where fresh and frozen gametes and embryos were to be stored and used were licensed by the licensing authority.[16] Public confidence would be secured not only by the licensing authority's independence from government and from 'sectional interests', but also by ensuring that carrying out any licensable activity without a licence from the authority would be a criminal offence.

This regulatory model was ground-breaking and, for two reasons, it has proved remarkably resilient. First, by giving responsibility for drawing up detailed guidance to the regulator, rather than enshrining such guidance in primary legislation, it has enabled the Human Fertilisation and Embryology Authority's (HFEA) Code of Practice to respond to scientific, medical, social and legal developments that were unforeseeable in 1984. To take an example I will come back to later, attitudes to same-sex parents have changed dramatically in the intervening decades. In 1984, the Warnock Report expressed a clear preference for a particular family model: 'we believe that as a general rule it is better for children to be born into a two-parent family, with both father and mother'.[17] In contrast, the HFEA's 9th Code of Practice is clear that 'patients should not be discriminated against on grounds of gender, race, disability, sexual orientation, religious belief or age'.[18] Or, to take another example, the Warnock Report expressed a clear preference for donor anonymity: 'our general view is that anonymity protects all parties not only from legal complications but also from emotional difficulties. We recommend that[,] as a matter of good practice[,] any third party donating gametes for infertility treatment should be unknown to the couple before, during and after the treatment.'[19]

Donor anonymity continued to be the norm in the 1980s and 1990s, but attitudes were changing and, following Joanna Rose's judicial review action in 2002,[20] Regulations which came into force in 2005 made it unlawful to use anonymously donated gametes in treatment in licensed clinics.[21] When the law was changed, there was still some vocal

---

[16] Ibid., para 13.7.

[17] Ibid., para 2.11.

[18] Human Fertilisation and Embryology Authority (HFEA), 9th Code of Practice (2019) para 8.6 https://portal.hfea.gov.uk/media/1605/2019-12-03-code-of-practice-december -2019.pdf (accessed 10 February 2021).

[19] Warnock (n 1) para 3.2.

[20] *R (on the application of Rose)* v. *Secretary of State for Health* [2002] EWHC 1593 (Admin).

[21] The Human Fertilisation and Embryology Authority (Disclosure of Donor Information) Regulations 2004.

opposition to the abolition of donor anonymity – for example, from the British Medical Association and the British Fertility Society[22] – but this has since dwindled and, with a few notable exceptions,[23] there is now widespread agreement with the Nuffield Council on Bioethics's 2013 conclusion that 'other things being equal, it will usually be better for children to be told, by their parents and at an early age, that they are donor-conceived'.[24] Certainly, for many years the HFEA's Code of Practice has advised clinicians to 'encourage and prepare patients to be open with their children from an early age about how they were conceived'.[25]

Second, just as important as its capacity to respond to external developments was the toughness of the sanctions attached to this regulatory model. This new licensing regime would have teeth because a doctor or a scientist could go to prison if they carried out a licensable activity outside the terms of a licence from the HFEA. The general public and fertility patients could therefore be confident that only properly conducted fertility treatment and embryo research would take place in the UK.

The HFEA regulatory model – in which an 'arm's-length body' issues licences, backed up by criminal sanctions, and in which primary legislation is supplemented by regularly updated codes of practice – has since been used to regulate other areas of medical practice. The Human Tissue Authority (HTA), for example, regulates 'activities relating to the removal, storage, use and disposal of human tissue', and its 'overall goal' is 'to maintain public confidence by ensuring that the removal, storage and use of human tissue and organs are undertaken safely and ethically, and with proper consent, in accordance with the provisions of the Human Tissue Act 2004'.[26] Indeed, the similarities between the HTA

---

[22] Written evidence provided to the House of Commons Science and Technology Committee, 'Human Reproductive Technologies and the Law Fifth Report of Session 2004–05, Volume II Oral and written evidence' (2005) appendices 9 and 12 https://publications.parliament .uk/pa/cm200405/cmselect/cmsctech/7/7ii.pdf (accessed 10 February 2021).

[23] See, for example, Guido Pennings, 'Disclosure of Donor Conception, Age of Disclosures and the Well-Being of Donor Offspring' (2017) 32 *Human Reproduction* 969.

[24] 'Donor Conception: Ethical Aspects of Information Sharing' (Nuffield Council on Bioethics, 17 April 2013) para 5.46 www.nuffieldbioethics.org/publications/donor-conception (accessed 10 February 2021).

[25] HFEA (n 18) para 20.8.

[26] 'Annual Report and Accounts 2019–20' (Human Tissue Authority (HTA), 2020) www .hta.gov.uk/sites/default/files/CCS207_CCS0420471370-001_HC%20417%20Web% 20accessible%20%281%29.pdf (accessed 10 February 2021).

and the HFEA have meant that, on more than one occasion, the government has proposed merging their functions.[27] It could therefore be
argued that a further legacy of the Warnock Report is the HFEA as an
exemplar of the benefits to government of using an independent regulator to regulate an especially controversial area of medical practice.

### 11.2.2   The Importance of Line-Drawing

In 1984, IVF was still new and controversial. There had, according to the
Warnock Report, 'been some hundreds of such births throughout the
world' (now, there have been 8 million); and these births 'continue to
exercise considerable fascination'.[28] The Warnock Report was very clear
that, in relation to matters as controversial as embryo research and IVF,
lines had to be drawn. Although the Report acknowledged that there was
'a wide diversity in moral feelings' within society, what everyone could
agree upon is that lines must be drawn somewhere. As the Report
explains:

> There must be some barriers that are not to be crossed, some limits fixed,
> beyond which people must not be allowed to go. Nor is such a wish for
> containment a mere whim or fancy. The very existence of morality
> depends on it. A society which had no inhibiting limits, especially in the
> areas with which we have been concerned, questions of birth and death, of
> the setting up of families, and the valuing of human life, would be a society
> without moral scruples. And this nobody wants.[29]

So, while it was important to build in a degree of flexibility, through
allowing the licensing authority to issue good practice guidance, which
might change in the light of new developments, the legislation was to
have some lines that must not be crossed.

The paradigm example of such a line was the fourteen-day limit for
embryo research. Invoking the primitive streak as 'one reference point in
the development of the human individual', which 'marks the beginning
of individual development of the embryo', the Warnock Report recommended that 'no live human embryo derived from *in vitro* fertilisation,
whether frozen or unfrozen, may be kept alive, if not transferred to
a woman, beyond fourteen days after fertilisation, nor may it be used as

---

[27] Martin Johnson, 'HFEA Reprieved – For the Moment!' (2013) 26 *Reproductive
BioMedicine Online* 303.
[28] Warnock (n 1) para 5.5.
[29] Ibid., para 5.

a research subject'.[30] Just like in society as a whole, there was not unanimity within the Warnock Committee on the moral status of the embryo: three of its members opposed this recommendation,[31] and set out their objections to all embryo research in an appendix.

There were also those who had argued in the 1980s for a longer time limit,[32] but at that time this was purely theoretical because, until 2016, it was not possible to keep a developing embryo alive for more than about nine days.[33] The fourteen-day limit therefore had the appearance of being strict and rigorous while, in reality, it did not impose a significant constraint upon scientific practice until several decades after the Warnock Report was published. The time limit therefore fits with Duncan Wilson's contention that Warnock's preference for external control was intended to facilitate rather than curtail scientific and medical progress.

The Warnock Report did not use the term 'pre-embryo' to describe embryos before fourteen days, but Anne McLaren, the eminent developmental biologist and Warnock Committee member to whom the fourteen-day limit has been attributed,[34] did. McLaren argued that individual embryonic development did not begin until fifteen or sixteen days after fertilisation and, before then, the term conceptus or pre-embryo was more appropriate.[35] For a few years in the 1980s, the word pre-embryo, with its implication that there is something special and different about very early human embryos,[36] was in common usage. Interestingly, Colomer and Pastor have pointed out that once embryo research had become lawful and widely accepted, the term pre-embryo largely disappeared. By then, they argue, it had served its purpose.[37]

---

[30] Ibid., para 11.22.

[31] Madeline Carriline, John Marshall and Jean Walker.

[32] See, for example, Michael Lockwood, 'The Warnock Report: A Philosophical Appraisal', in Michael Lockwood (ed), *Moral Dilemmas in Modern Medicine* (Oxford University Press 1985) 155.

[33] Alessia Deglincerti et al, 'Self-Organization of the in vitro Attached Human Embryo' (2016) 533 *Nature* 251; and Marta Shahbazi et al, 'Self-Organization of the Human Embryo in the Absence of Maternal Tissues' (2016) 18 *Nature Cell Biology* 700.

[34] Duncan Wilson, 'What Can History Do for Bioethics?' (2013) 27 *Bioethics* 215; Mary Warnock, *Nature and Morality: Recollections of a Philosopher in Public Life* (Continuum 2003) 80.

[35] See, for example, Anne McLaren, 'Research on the Human Conceptus and Its Regulation in Britain Today' (1990) 83 *Journal of the Royal Society of Medicine* 209.

[36] Sheila Jasanoff, 'Making the Facts of Life' in Sheila Jasanoff (ed), *Reframing Rights: Bioconstitutionalism in the Genetic Age* (MIT Press 2011) 59, 65.

[37] Modesto Ferrer Colomer and Luis Miguel Pastor, 'The Preembryo's Short Lifetime: The History of a Word' (2012) 23 *Cuadernos de Bioética* 677.

## 11.3   Warnock's Legacy on Substance

Just as we cannot know what fertility treatment will involve in 2057, it was impossible in 1984 to predict what the provision of IVF services in the 2020s would look like. Here I draw attention to two developments that the Warnock Report did not anticipate and hence did not make provision for in its recommendations: first, the emergence of a lucrative market in fertility services; and, second, the increasing acceptance that fertility treatment should be available to would-be parents who do not conform with Warnock's preference for the 'two-parent family, with both father and mother'.[38]

### 11.3.1   Regulating a Market

In 1984, there were relatively few providers of fertility treatment, and there were 'lengthy hospital waiting lists for gynaecological treatment'.[39] The Warnock Report recommended wider availability of fertility treatment within the NHS, and the setting up of 'a working group at national level made up of central health departments, health authorities and those working in infertility, to draw up detailed guidance on the organisation of services'.[40] The Report suggested that one of this working group's first tasks should be 'to consider how best an IVF service can be organised within the NHS. Although private IVF clinics would continue to exist alongside those within the NHS, we believe it is important that there should be a sufficient level of NHS provision for childless couples not to feel that their only recourse is to the private sector.'[41] While the Warnock Report envisaged that private fertility services would continue to coexist with NHS provision, it did not foresee the development of a lucrative market in private fertility treatment. The Human Fertilisation and Embryology Act 1990 did not give the HFEA any control over the prices that clinics charge, for example. The HFEA's Code of Practice now requires clinics to give patients 'a personalised costed treatment plan' before offering treatment,[42] but the prices charged for investigations and treatment services are outside of the HFEA's control.

---

[38]  Warnock (n 1) para 2.11.
[39]  Ibid., para 2.17.
[40]  Ibid.
[41]  Ibid., para 5.11.
[42]  HFEA (n 18) para 4.9.

Contrary to the Warnock Report's recommendations, most fertility treatment in the UK is provided in the private sector.[43] In England, a 2013 National Institute for Health and Care Excellence (NICE) guideline recommended that the NHS should fund three full cycles of IVF (i.e. a fresh cycle followed by further cycles using the frozen embryos) for women under forty years old and one full cycle for women aged forty to forty-two, who must additionally not have received IVF treatment before and not have low ovarian reserve.[44] Implementation of this NICE guideline is not mandatory, however, and only 13 per cent of Clinical Commissioning Groups provide three full cycles of IVF to eligible women; 60 per cent offer one NHS-funded cycle (most of which fund only one fresh cycle), and 4 per cent fund no IVF treatment at all.[45]

The NICE guideline does not apply directly in Scotland, Wales and Northern Ireland. Access is more limited in Northern Ireland, where women under the age of forty are eligible for only one NHS cycle. In Wales, they are eligible for only two cycles, but, while this looks more restrictive than the NICE guideline, in practice the two cycles in Wales are actually provided more frequently than in England. In Scotland, since 2017, the Scottish Government has funded the three recommended cycles for women under the age of forty, or one for women aged forty to forty-two, following recommendations from the National Infertility Group.[46]

Throughout the UK, state funding is generally available only to those who have a clinical need for it, thus excluding people who need assistance because they do not have an opposite sex partner. The NHS will fund single and lesbian women's treatment, but this is usually on the grounds of infertility. This means that for many single and lesbian women, access to NHS-funded treatment is possible only after they have failed to conceive after a year of regular self-funded intrauterine insemination.[47]

---

[43] 'The State of the Fertility Sector 2017–18' (HFEA, 2019) www.hfea.gov.uk/media/2703/the-state-of-the-fertility-sector-2017–2018.pdf (accessed 10 February 2021).

[44] 'Fertility Problems: Assessment and Treatment Clinical Guideline [CG156]' (National Institute for Health and Care Excellence (NICE), 2013) www.nice.org.uk/guidance/cg156/resources/fertility-problems-assessment-and-treatment-pdf-35109634660549 (accessed 10 February 2021).

[45] See further https://fertilitynetworkuk.org/fertility-fairness-audit/.

[46] 'National Infertility Group Report' (Scottish Government, 2016) www.gov.scot/binaries/content/documents/govscot/publications/progress-report/2016/06/national-infertility-group-report/documents/00501403-pdf/00501403-pdf/govscot%3Adocument/00501403.pdf (accessed 10 February 2021).

[47] See further Atina Krajewska, 'Access of Single Women to Fertility Treatment: A Case of Incidental Discrimination' (2015) 23 *Medical Law Review* 620.

The Warnock Report did not consider the implications of a flourishing free market in fertility services, now estimated to be worth £320 million per year, and growing at 3 per cent each year.[48] When medical treatment is provided by for-profit companies, there is a risk of over-selling and over-treatment, which may additionally be invisible to patients in the UK, who are unfamiliar with having health-care services marketed to them in the same way as other consumer goods.

For example, fertility clinics increasingly offer a variety of 'add-on' treatments to patients. Add-ons are interventions that do not require a licence from the HFEA (because they do not involve the use and storage of gametes or embryos outside of the woman's body), so the HFEA's control over their marketing and use is limited. Although add-on treatments are presented to patients as interventions which may increase the chance of an IVF cycle working,[49] most of them lack any robust evidence base. Some (like acupuncture) are a waste of money, while others (like reproductive immunology) might also be positively harmful. But patients who are desperate for a child, who may be paying £5,000 for a single cycle of treatment, are often eager to 'try anything' to increase that cycle's chance of success. The potential for over-selling and sharp practices is therefore considerable. Even if clinic staff are honest with patients that there are no robust clinical trials supporting the use of a particular add-on treatment, they might also tell patients that they have had some success with it in their clinic. This is anecdote, rather than evidence, but it may be persuasive to patients who have financial as well as emotional reasons to try to maximise the chances that this IVF cycle will result in a baby.[50]

A new Human Fertilisation and Embryology Act might then give the HFEA more powers over the market in services, and over the provision of dubious treatments and poor-quality information to patients. It is not just the question of whether and when gametes and embryos can be used outside of a woman's body that raises ethical issues; rather, the over-selling of non-evidence-based treatments to patients is an important ethical issue in its own right. The Warnock Report did not foresee the fertility industry's 'pronounced predilection for over-diagnosis, over-use and over-treatment',[51] and the tools the HFEA has to control the market

---

[48]  HFEA (n 43).

[49]  Joyce Harper et al, 'Adjuncts in the IVF Laboratory: Where Is the Evidence for "Add-On" Interventions?' (2017) 32 *Human Reproduction* 485.

[50]  Jack Wilkinson et al, 'Reproductive Medicine: Still More ART Than Science?' (2019) 126 *British Journal of Obstetrics and Gynaecology* 138.

[51]  Ibid.

in non-evidence-based add-ons are undoubtedly more limited than they would have been if this had been a concern from the outset.

In 1976, the then CEO of Merck admitted to *Fortune* magazine that it was a pity that the market in new medicines was limited to sick people. Henry Gadsden said that his dream was to create drugs for healthy people, so that, 'like Wrigley's chewing gum', they could 'sell to everyone'.[52] Until relatively recently, the market for fertility treatments was similarly limited to people who want to have a baby now, and who are unable to do so without assistance. A newly successful egg freezing technique, known as vitrification, changes this because it facilitates what is known as 'social' egg freezing. Social egg freezing can be marketed to the very much larger pool of women who are not currently trying to conceive but who think that they might want to have a baby in the future. Clinics increasingly offer fertility MOTs, which involve ovarian reserve testing, in order to find out whether egg freezing is advisable – which it often is – and, if so, how many cycles of egg retrieval are likely to be necessary. Fertility MOTs cost a few hundred pounds, but the costs of egg freezing are substantial (one cycle of egg freezing costs in the region of £3,500–£4,000, with medication costs of around £1,000 on top).

As a result of this dramatically expanded and lucrative market for fertility preservation, it is important that clinics do not make exaggerated claims about the utility of social egg freezing, and that they do not overstate the chances of success. Most women who freeze their eggs are unlikely to return to use them in the future. And even if they do, while egg freezing may increase the chance that a future IVF cycle will work, it cannot offer any guarantees against future childlessness. The HFEA has limited powers over clinics' marketing materials, and while some clinics make sober claims for egg freezing – such as '[i]t should be clearly understood that there is no guarantee that the eggs will survive the freezing and the subsequent thawing processes, nor any guarantee that the eggs will necessarily fertilise'[53] – another large provider's website states that '[u]ltimately, egg freezing is a good option if you think you might want to start or grow your family in the future and would like to preserve your fertility, just in case'.[54]

[52] Ray Moynihan and Alan Cassels, *Selling Sickness: How the World's Biggest Pharmaceutical Companies Are Turning Us All into Patients* (Nation Books 2005) ix.

[53] 'Egg Freezing' www.bmihealthcare.co.uk/treatments/fertility/egg-freezing (accessed 7 August 2020).

[54] 'Egg Freezing and Storage' www.carefertility.com/treatments/fertility-preservation/egg-freezing-and-storage/ (accessed 7 August 2020).

In 2020, it was reported that some clinics are even advertising 'Prosecco parties', where women receive (marketing) information about egg freezing over drinks and canapés.[55] At the time of writing, it was possible to pay £49 via Eventbrite to sign up for this event at the Sheraton Grand Hotel in Park Lane, London:

> Join us on 30th January at the Mercante Italian Restaurant in Mayfair for an informal yet educational evening, to mingle with like-minded women over indulgent desserts and listen to leading Fertility Consultant[] Dr Irfana Koita talk about this empowering process.[56]

In 1984, the Warnock Report did warn against giving childless couples 'false or unrealistic hopes',[57] but its main object of concern was 'unease at the apparently uncontrolled advance of science',[58] rather than the apparently uncontrolled advance of advertising. As a result, the HFEA's powers are focused on the need to prevent scientists from 'going too far', and it has rather less teeth when it comes to the aggressive marketing of for-profit fertility services.

### 11.3.2 Diverse Families

Although the Warnock Report's preference for the heterosexual, two-parent family now looks dated and conservative, it is important to note that it did not recommend that there should be any statutory restrictions upon access to fertility treatment in the UK. Stating that 'we believe that hard and fast rules are not applicable',[59] the Report recommended that eligibility decisions should be for the individual consultant, who 'may, after discussion with professional health and social work colleagues, consider that there are valid reasons why infertility treatment would not be in the best interests of the patient, the child that may be born following treatment, or the patient's immediate family'.[60] The Warnock Report's recommendations on surrogacy were also restrictive, advocating

---

[55] Victoria Allen, 'Fertility Clinics Offer Women Prosecco and Wine and Cheese Events to Persuade Them to Spends Thousands Freezing Their Eggs for IVF' (*Daily Mail*, 6 January 2020) www.dailymail.co.uk/news/article-7855269/Fertility-clinics-offer-women-pro secco-promote-egg-freezing.html (accessed 10 February 2021).

[56] See www.eventbrite.co.uk/e/extended-choices-egg-freezing-party-tickets-77087596075? aff=erelexpmlt (accessed 10 February 2021).

[57] Warnock (n 1) para 5.12.

[58] Ibid., para 1.1.

[59] Ibid., para 2.13.

[60] Ibid., para 2.12.

that legislation should 'render criminally liable the actions of professionals and others who knowingly assist in the establishment of a surrogate pregnancy',[61] but stopping short of banning surrogacy altogether or criminalising surrogates and intended parents.

It is worth reminding ourselves that, in the early 1980s, Margaret Thatcher had advocated – without irony – a return to 'Victorian values', and traditional family values were 'a leitmotif of the [1983] election campaign'.[62] At the 1987 Conservative Party conference, Margaret Thatcher introduced the policy change that would become known as section 28, by saying that 'children who need to be taught to respect traditional moral values are being taught that they have the inalienable right to be gay'.[63] Section 28 of the Local Government Act 1988 inserted a new section 2A(b) into the Local Government Act 1986, which provided that 'a local authority shall not . . . promote the teaching in any maintained school of the acceptability of homosexuality as a pretended family relationship'.

Given this political context, it could be argued that by not ruling out single and LGBTQ women's access to fertility services, or recommending that surrogacy should be against the law, the Warnock Report was *relatively* progressive. It is also perhaps remarkable that a Conservative government in the late 1980s introduced legislation which did not restrict access to fertility services to heterosexual couples, and which, despite the original statute's requirement to consider the child's 'need for a father' before providing treatment,[64] in fact facilitated the creation, in certain circumstances, of legally fatherless children.[65]

Although it has always been possible for single women and same-sex female couples to receive treatment in licensed centres, refusing to treat a potential patient on the grounds of her marital status or sexual orientation would now be unlawful discrimination.[66] When the legislation was updated in 2008, the requirement that clinicians consider the future child's 'need for a father' was replaced by a duty to consider the child's need for 'supportive parenting',[67] and, more significantly in practice, it

---

[61] Ibid., para 8.18.
[62] Raphael Samuel, 'Mrs. Thatcher's Return to Victorian Values' (1992) 78 *Proceedings of the British Academy* 9.
[63] Philip Thomas, 'The Nuclear Family, Ideology and AIDS in the Thatcher Years' (1993) 1 *Feminist Legal Studies* 23.
[64] Section 13(5).
[65] Gillian Douglas, 'Family Law under the Thatcher Government' (1990) 17 *Journal of Law and Society* 411.
[66] HFEA (n 18) para 8.6.
[67] Section 13(5).

has been possible since 2009 for two women to be a child's only legal parents from birth.[68]

In relation to the Warnock Report's recommendations on surrogacy, fortunately the Surrogacy Arrangements Act 1985 did not criminalise anyone who assisted in the establishment of a surrogate pregnancy, but it did criminalise the operation of commercial surrogacy agencies,[69] and, following Warnock's recommendations, it specified that surrogacy agreements should be unenforceable.[70] But while the Warnock Report did not formally prohibit the use of fertility treatment and surrogacy to create non-traditional families, it could be argued that a further legacy of the Warnock Report is the assumption that children born as a result of the contribution of a third party should have two parents, and its affirmation of the common law assumption that 'the woman giving birth should, for all purposes, be regarded in law as the mother of that child'.[71] If the English and Scottish Law Commissions' 2019 proposals on surrogacy become law,[72] an exception to this will be created in order to enable, in certain circumstances, the intended mother to be treated as the child's mother from birth.

When an unknown donor's gametes are used in treatment, it is usually unproblematic to say that the child has a maximum of two legal parents because the donor will be not be identifiable until the child reaches the age of eighteen and will play no role in the child's upbringing. There are, however, an increasing number of cases in which a sperm or egg donor is known to the parents, who also intend the donor to be involved in the child's upbringing. The use of introduction websites, in which people seek out informal donors with the intention that the child will have a relationship with the donor during childhood, or that the donor will jointly bring up the child, poses a further challenge to the two-parent family model.

Similarly, following disputed surrogacy arrangements, there have been several cases in which the judge has decided that the child should live with, on the one hand, the surrogate and their partner, but have ongoing

---

[68] Human Fertilisation and Embryology Act 2008, ss 42 and 44.
[69] Surrogacy Arrangements Act 1985, s 2.
[70] Ibid., s 1B.
[71] Warnock (n 1) para 6.8.
[72] 'Building Families through Surrogacy: A New Law – A Joint Consultation Paper' (English and Scottish Law Commissions, 2019) https://s3-eu-west-2.amazonaws.com/lawcom-prod-storage-11jsxou24uy7q/uploads/2019/06/Surrogacy-consultation-paper.pdf (accessed 10 February 2021).

contact with the intended parents,[73] or, on the other hand, the intended parents, with ongoing contact with the surrogate and their partner.[74] In such cases, the child undoubtedly has more than two people in a 'parental' relationship with them; indeed, judges have sometimes been explicit that 'the reality is that Z does have two families and four parents'.[75]

In addition, trans parenthood poses a new set of challenges for the rules on the attribution of parenthood set out in the Human Fertilisation and Embryology Acts 1990 and 2008. Until relatively recently, the storage of gametes for future parenthood was not a routine aspect of preparation for gender reassignment. This has now changed, and the latest edition of the HFEA's Code of Practice contains guidance on the treatment of trans patients, including 'options for fertility preservation'.[76] But where a trans woman's stored sperm, or a trans man's stored eggs, are used in their partner's treatment, it seems likely that they could be recognised as the child's parent only through the 2008 Act's 'agreed parenthood conditions', rather than because they are the child's genetic parent.

If a female-to-male trans person's reproductive organs have not been removed, he might be able to give birth, and would then be treated in law as the child's mother. This was confirmed recently in *R (on the application of McConnell)* v. *Registrar General for England and Wales*,[77] in which a trans man who had given birth failed to persuade the court that his and his son YY's Article 8 ECHR rights required him to be recorded on YY's birth certificate as his father or his gender-neutral 'parent'.[78] Dismissing Mr McConnell's appeal against Sir Andrew McFarlane P's judgment that 'being a "mother" is the status afforded to a person who undergoes the physical and biological process of carrying a pregnancy and giving birth',[79] the Court of Appeal held that '[t]he view that Parliament has taken is that every child should have a mother and should be able to discover who their mother was, because that is in the child's best interests. Others may take a different view and in time may be able to persuade Parliament to take a different view.'[80] At first instance, this case also drew

---

[73] *Re M (A Child)* [2017] EWCA Civ 228.
[74] *Re H (A Child) (Surrogacy Breakdown)* [2017] EWCA Civ 1798.
[75] *Per* Russell J [107] in *Re Z (surrogacy agreements: child arrangements orders)* [2016] EWFC 34.
[76] HFEA (n 18) para 4.14.
[77] [2020] EWCA Civ 559.
[78] Ibid.
[79] [2019] EWHC 1823 (Fam) [279].
[80] [2020] EWCA Civ 559 [86].

attention to another important way in which the legislation is ill-equipped to deal with trans parenthood. Mr McConnell had undergone intrauterine insemination in a licensed clinic. The HFEA can issue licences for the provision of 'treatment services', which are defined in its section 2 as services 'for the purpose of assisting *women* to carry children' (my emphasis). As a result, Sir Andrew McFarlane P expressed 'some doubt that the treatment was lawfully provided under the HFEA regime'.[81] It must, he argued, 'be at least questionable whether the provision of treatment services to a man is within the range of activities that the HFEA is permitted to authorise by licence'.[82] Although 'not for determination in the present claim',[83] Sir Andrew McFarlane P 'anticipate[d] that these are matters that will now be considered closely by the Authority and by ministers'.[84]

## 11.4   Conclusion

It should not be surprising that, nearly forty years after the Warnock Committee was appointed, issues have arisen that were simply not within the Committee's contemplation. For example, when it expressed a preference for a child to have 'both father and mother', it would not have occurred to the Committee that a child's mother could be male. Nor is it surprising, and indeed it is to be celebrated, that attitudes towards the family have changed almost beyond all recognition from Margaret Thatcher's endorsement of Victorian values. Predictably, there have also been significant scientific developments, such as the development of gene editing technologies and vitrification. What is, perhaps, remarkable is that legislation which has its roots in a report published thirty-six years ago continues to be the basis of a modern, flexible and responsive regulatory system.

In part, this flexibility was 'designed into' the regulatory system proposed by the Warnock Report. Some aspects of the legislation were explicitly future-proofed, enabling changes to be made through regulations, rather than requiring new primary legislation. The statutory purposes for which research may be carried out on embryos, for example, were expanded in this way in 2001 in order to accommodate the possibility of stem cell research.[85] Through its regularly updated Code of

---

[81] [2019] EWHC 1823 (Fam) [127].
[82] Ibid., [155].
[83] Ibid., [159]
[84] Ibid.
[85] Human Fertilisation and Embryology Act 1990 Schedule 2(3A)(1).

Practice, the HFEA has been able to respond to new evidence and to scientific and social developments. Some changes have required new primary legislation, however, such as the replacement of the requirement to consider a child's 'need for a father' before providing a woman with treatment services. Following the *McConnell* case, it may be necessary to change the law in order to make it lawful to provide treatment services to men as well.

The HFEA has also had to respond to trends in regulation, from the pre-financial crash preference for 'light-touch' regulation, to moves towards greater openness and more public consultation.[86] Of course, the HFEA has its critics, and clinics complain about the volume of form-filling and paperwork; but the legacy of the regulatory framework which has its origins in the Warnock Report is that there continues to be considerable public confidence in the safety of fertility treatment in the UK, and in the robustness of the regulation of research on embryos.

It is unlikely to be a coincidence that the Warnock Committee's very considerable collective expertise, and the length of time it was allowed to deliberate, led to recommendations that have, on the whole, stood the test of time so well. If this or a future government decides that a fresh Human Fertilisation and Embryology Act is needed for the decades ahead, it would be well advised to adopt a similarly deliberative and expert-led approach to the development of new recommendations. This may look like an expensive approach to law reform, but any short-term financial costs are surely eclipsed by the longer-term benefits of constructing a regulatory system with such secure foundations that it continues to be a model for regulation worldwide nearly four decades later.

---

[86] See, for example, HFEA, 'Scientific Review of the Safety and Efficacy of Methods to Avoid Mitochondrial Disease through Assisted Conception' (HFEA, 2011) and HFEA, 'Mitochondria Replacement Consultation: Advice to Government' (2013) www .hfea.gov.uk/media/2618/mitochondria_replacement_consultation_-_advice_for_go vernment.pdf (accessed 10 February 2021).

# 'Only Time Will Tell'

## Escape from the Medically Assisted Suicide Spiral

MURRAY EARLE

## 12.1 Introduction

I first met Graeme Laurie when he started his lectureship at the University of Edinburgh. His comments on my PhD research then, and teaching now, have been a source of invaluable guidance. His own research is both well-known and influential, and will have been drawn on throughout this volume. In particular, for present purposes, Catriona McMillan and Agomoni Ganguli-Mitra have provided commentary on the Liminal Spaces project,[1] and this chapter explores a position of seemingly permanent liminality which has been occupied for two decades. It is reminiscent of the 'Empty Spaces' dimension of the project, in which legislation is required to push us over the legality threshold in order to render assisted suicide lawful.

I will not consider whether assisted suicide should be lawful; I am concerned with why it has *remained unlawful*, and what it may take to change that position. To do so, I will deconstruct two ostensibly straight-forward statements: 'the courts have said this is a matter for the legislature'; and 'the bill failed'. The chapter reflects on the judicial reasons for referring the issue to the legislature, and looks at a Bill in the Scottish Parliament with which Graeme was involved, both individually and through evidence from the Mason Institute, to demonstrate a congruence with some of the given reasons for those failures. Neither will I directly consider the doctrine of double effect under *R* v. *Adams*,[2] withdrawal of treatment in the patient's best interests under *Bland*,[3] or

---

[1] See Chapter 5 in this volume. See further www.liminalspaces.ed.ac.uk.
[2] *R* v. *Adams* [1957] Crim LR 365.
[3] *Airedale TNHS Trust* v. *Bland* [1993] AC 789.

where treatment is given that has no analgesic effect and will hasten death under *R v. Cox*.[4] While these decisions do come up in both court and parliament, they are not directly concerned with assisted suicide.

The scenario of interest is one in which a person is suffering from a terminal or incurable condition and has expressed a desire for an assisted death, in preference to allowing the disease to take its course or refusing life-saving treatment (which are within a patient's autonomous right under *Re B*,[5] or under an advance decision under the Mental Capacity Act 2005 and cases such as *Tracey*).[6] This scenario is explored in *Pretty*,[7] *Purdy*,[8] and *Nicklinson*,[9] which Graeme and colleagues consider to concern a narrow class of neuromuscular conditions not covered by existing provisions.[10] Such patients will not be physically able to take their own life, but are prohibited from being assisted in so doing by section 2(1) of the Suicide Act 1961. The constitutional question explored in the case law is whether the legislation is in conflict with Article 8 of the European Convention on Human Rights (ECHR). And yet, '[t]he law as it stands, therefore, leads to a professional, moral and/or legal impasse – as much of the recent judicial activity suggests'.[11]

'Only time will tell' are the closing words to Graeme's editorial for an edition of the *European Journal of Heath Law* dedicated to physician assisted suicide in Europe.[12] Written more than fifteen years ago and referring to a 'plethora of (failed) reforms',[13] those words remain both prescient and valid. The same is true of the issues raised by Graeme then: the autonomy argument is central to moving beyond the threshold of legality, but autonomy is wider than the individual involved; legislation needs not only to account for other actors involved, such as medical professionals, but also to include safeguards to protect those vulnerable to undue influence.

---

[4] *R v. Cox* (1992) 12 BMLR 38.
[5] *B v. An NHS Hospital Trust* [2002] EWHC 429 (Fam).
[6] *R (on the application of Tracey)* v. *Cambridge NHS Foundation Trust* [2014] Civ 822.
[7] *R (on the application of Pretty)* v. *Director of Public Prosecutions* [2001] UKHL 61 and *Pretty* v. *United Kingdom* (2002) 35 EHRR 1.
[8] *R (on the application of Purdy)* v. *Director of Public Prosecutions* [2009] UKHL 45.
[9] *R (Nicklinson and Another)* v. *Ministry of justice* [2014] UKSC 38.
[10] Graeme Laurie, Shawn Harmon and Edward Dove, *Mason and McCall Smith's Law and Medical Ethics* (11th edn, Oxford University Press 2019) para 19.60.
[11] Ibid.
[12] Graeme Laurie, 'Physician Assisted Suicide in Europe: Some Lessons and Trends' (2005) 12 *European Journal of Health Law* 5.
[13] Ibid., 8

The implicit question left hanging by Graeme is 'what can be done?'. There are two possible routes whereby the courts defer to the legislature – either with or without declaring section 2(1) incompatible with Article 8 – which in turn enacts change. There is also a route queried as 'a third way' by Emily Jackson,[14] in which the courts themselves can edge towards, though not quite get across, the legality threshold, where a partial defence is in effect available to those assisting suicide on compassionate grounds.[15] Unless and until any of these routes is followed, the UK runs the risk of a legacy of failure, which is out of kilter with the current medico-legal trend towards personal autonomy.

His own Festschrift chapter for Ken Mason,[16] from whom the 'medical jurisprudence baton' was passed to Graeme, is relevant to the current chapter in two respects: first, to underline that autonomy is relational; and second, to affirm that among the five key cases identified as most significant over the past thirty years are *R v. Cox* on conflicting autonomies in medically assisted death, and *Gillick*[17] on autonomy and consent. On the first issue, Graeme drew attention to what we will see later in this chapter came to be presented as among the key arguments against proposed assisted suicide bills.[18] Whereas 'Mason has himself pointed to the obvious answer to involving physicians in active euthanasia, namely, using specialists in the care of the terminally ill',[19] some politicians expressed a preference for improved palliative care, as opposed to permitting assisted death. Just as Mason was concerned with the need for a conscience clause in any new legislation, this is a matter Graeme brought to the attention of the Scottish Parliament Health and Sport Committee, during stage one of the Assisted Suicide (Scotland) Bill in 2015.[20] On the second issue, while at the time those five key cases

---

[14] Emily Jackson, *Medical Law: Text, Cases and Materials* (5th edn, Oxford University Press 2019) 958.

[15] This does not form an integral part of this chapter but, for completeness, Jackson cites Richard Huxtable, 'Splitting the Difference? Principled Compromise in Assisted Dying?' (2014) 28 *Bioethics* 472 and Heather Keating and Jo Bridgeman, 'Compassionate Killings: The Case for a Partial Defence' (2012) 75 *Modern Law Review* 697.

[16] Graeme Laurie, 'The Autonomy of Others: Reflections on the Rise and Rise of Patient Choice in Contemporary Medical Law' in Sheila McLean (ed), *First Do No Harm: Law Ethics and Healthcare* (Ashgate 2006) 131.

[17] *Gillick v. West Norfolk and Wisbech Area Health Authority* [1985] 3 All ER 402, HL.

[18] See Section 12.3.3 on autonomy and the palliative care alternative to legislating in favour of allowing assisted suicide.

[19] Laurie (n 16) 14.

[20] HC Deb 20 January 2015, col 35 though he also observed that it is a matter reserved to Westminster and is therefore not in the bill.

included *Gillick* on autonomy and consent, they would undoubtedly now include *Montgomery*,[21] as an indication of the extent to which society has placed an ever greater value on autonomy.

This chapter will first consider the case law on assisted suicide, in which judges have consistently found that the issue is one better dealt with by the legislature. That discussion highlights the relevant parts of the judgments that have broached this constitutional question. It also considers other jurisdictions such as Canada, Germany and Italy. Here, we see that while the legality threshold for assisted suicide remains a constitutional question in those jurisdictions, the underpinning constitutions are written ones that include a human rights dimension. This marks a difference from UK jurisdictions. What they have in common, however, is the courts requiring, on constitutional grounds, the legislature to progress any change. The chapter will therefore also consider the legislative changes which have been made in Canada, Germany and Italy, and the reasons for which UK legislatures have not done so. Does such a constitutional move amount to an escape from liminality?

## 12.2   The Case Law

Assisting a suicide adds an element of criminality to the conduct of the physician, or person assisting, where consent is no defence, as confirmed in both *Nicklinson*[22] and *Bland*.[23] Although in *Cox*, a genuine belief in the benefits of the treatment to the patient would serve as exculpatory,[24] the primary intention in assisted suicide is to help a person to end their life. The relevant criminal law is sections 2(1) and (2) of the Suicide Act 1961, under which suicide is legal, but complicity attracts a custodial sentence of up to fourteen years. That includes putting pressure on a person to attempt suicide. This Act applies to England and Wales only.[25]

The case law relevant to this chapter has considered whether section 2(1) is incompatible with the right to respect for private life under Article 8 ECHR. The cases are drawn from that narrow neuromuscular class, in

---

[21] *Montgomery* v. *Lanarkshire Health Board* [2015] UKSC 11. For a full discussion of autonomy and informed consent, in the context of personal data protection, see Chapter 17 in this volume.

[22] *Nicklinson* (n 9) paras 18, 22–6.

[23] *Airedale NHS Trust* v. *Bland* [1993] 1 All R 821 (HL), 890.

[24] *Cox* (n 4) 41.

[25] Suicide has never been an offence in Scotland, which means that assisting a suicide can in theory amount to the common law offence of murder or culpable homicide.

which the issue was assistance either in the act of suicide itself or in travel to a jurisdiction where medically assisted suicide is permitted. The courts also considered the constitutional question of why the issue is better left to the legislature.

### 12.2.1   Pretty

Diane Pretty[26] was diagnosed with motor neuron disease. It did not affect her mental competence, but its progressive and terminal nature meant that she would be unable to take her own life without her husband's assistance, which he was willing to give if he could be assured of non-prosecution. This would be prima facie in contravention of section 2(1) of the Suicide Act 1961. Under section 2(4), the Director of Public Prosecutions (DPP) may exercise a discretion for or against prosecution. This is not a general discretion but is to be applied in the circumstances of individual cases.[27].

While the European Court of Human Rights (ECtHR) found that Article 8 was engaged, it was not prepared to exclude that preventing an incapacitated person from choosing a dignified end to their life amounted to an interference with that right.[28] The Court also found that section 2 was designed to protect the vulnerable. Although Mrs Pretty had disputed that there was scope for allowing a margin of appreciation under Article 3 ECHR,[29] the ECtHR found that '[i]t is primarily for States to assess the risk and the likely incidence of abuse if the general prohibition on assisted suicides were relaxed or if exceptions were to be created'.[30] The Court held that the blanket ban on assisted suicide was not disproportionate; nor was the DPP's refusal to give an advance assurance of non-prosecution.[31]

Prior to the ECtHR case, Lord Steyn in the House of Lords had found: 'For her to succeed it is not enough to show that the European Convention allows member states to legalise assisted suicide. She must establish that at least that part of section 2(1) of the 1961 Act which

---

[26] *Pretty* (n 7).

[27] *R (on the application of Pretty)* v. *Director of Public Prosecutions* [2001] UKHL 61, per Lord Steyn paras 65–66; Lord Hope para 80. This was to play into the decision in *Purdy*, discussed in Section 12.2.2.

[28] *Pretty* v. *United Kingdom* (2002) 35 EHRR 1 para 67.

[29] Ibid., para 19.

[30] Ibid., para 74.

[31] *Pretty* (n 28) paras 76, 77.

makes aiding or abetting suicide a crime is in conflict with her Convention rights.'[32] He concluded that the logic of the ECHR 'does not justify the conclusion that the House must rule that a state is obliged to legalise assisted suicide. It does not require the state to repeal a provision such as section 2(1) of the 1961 Act.'[33] He did, however, find that 'such a fundamental change cannot be brought about by judicial creativity',[34] and that, on policy grounds, 'it must be a matter for demo-cratic debate and decision making by legislatures'.[35] Lord Hobhouse of Woodborough agreed with the 'inescapable conclusion' that the ques-tions raised and the formulation of new policies – in effect, amending or repealing section 2 of the Suicide Act 1961 – 'must under our system of parliamentary democracy be a matter for the Legislature[,] not the Judiciary'.[36]

## 12.2.2   Purdy

Debbie Purdy[37] suffered from primary progressive multiple sclerosis, a progressive and incurable neurological disorder. She argued that she and her husband were entitled to know the factors that the DPP would take into account in exercising his discretion to prosecute,[38] should her husband help her to travel to Switzerland for the purposes of assisted suicide at the Dignitas clinic. This was argued despite the DPP having published an explanation of his decision not to prosecute the family of Daniel James, paralysed playing rugby, for helping him to travel to Dignitas to end his life.

The House of Lords found that her Article 8 rights were engaged insofar as the DPP Guidance did not apply to the facts of her specific case. It was therefore more about section 2(4) than section 2(1) of the 1961 Act, which required guidelines of sufficient precision for an individual to act upon them.[39] Such a 'custom-built policy

---

[32] *Pretty* (n 27) per Lord Steyn para 41.

[33] Ibid., per Lord Steyn para 68.

[34] This level of 'judicial creativity' has been applied in other European countries, such as Germany and Italy. This is discussed in Section 12.2.4.

[35] *Pretty* (n 27) per Lord Steyn para 57.

[36] Ibid., para 120.

[37] *Purdy* (n 8).

[38] Nobody had or has been prosecuted, meaning no guidance could be gleaned from previous cases.

[39] *Purdy* (n 8) para 42. This chapter is concerned not with the specifics of the guidance but with the workings of Article 8 and the constitutional issue of courts' referrals to the legislature.

statement'[40] was published by the DPP in 2010. This issue resurfaced in the speech of Sir Keir Starmer MP on the Assisted Dying (No 2) Bill, speaking as the former DPP who had published the guidelines.[41]

### 12.2.3 Nicklinson

Like *Pretty* and *Purdy*, this case concerned an incurable neurological condition, but, unlike those cases, these three claimants were, as a matter of medical fact, unable to end their own lives when legal proceedings were initiated[42]. Following a stroke nine years prior, Tony Nicklinson was paralysed and could move only his head and eyes, and spell out words by blinking, which was interpreted by computer. He did not want to take the *Re B* route and refuse feeding and hydration, as death would be painful and protracted. He wanted to be injected with a lethal drug by someone else or by means of a machine that he could activate. He sought a declaration either that the former would be lawful if performed by a doctor or, failing that, that section 2(1) of the Suicide Act 1961 was incompatible with his rights under Article 8 ECHR. Both of these were refused by the High Court and the Court of Appeal (where Paul Lamb was added as a claimant),[43] and he appealed to the Supreme Court.

Following a car crash in 1990, Paul Lamb was able to move only his right hand and required twenty-four-hour care, with pain under permanent control of morphine. His claim was the same as that of Mrs Nicklinson,[44] and was similarly unsuccessful in the Court of Appeal. Like Nicklinson, Martin, the third claimant, could communicate only through slow hand movements and via an eye blink computer in this case following a brain-stem stroke. Aside from refusal of nutrition,[45] he felt his only option was to have somebody accompany him to Dignitas in Switzerland to end his life. He sought clarification of the 2010 DPP guidelines and of their modification to include carers. Although Martin's case in the High Court had failed, there was a degree of success insofar as Lords Dyson and Elias found that,

---

[40] Which Lord Brown of Eaton-Under-Heywood felt was necessary: *Purdy* (n 8) para 86.
[41] Discussed in Section 12.3.3.
[42] *Nicklinson* (n 9).
[43] Respectively, *R (on the application of Nicklinson)* v. *Ministry of Justice* [2012] EWHC 2381 (Admin), and *R (on the application of Nicklinson)* v. *A Primary Care Trust* [2013] EWCA Civ 961.
[44] In her own right and as administratrix of Mr Nicklinson's estate.
[45] Something he attempted following his High Court loss, but 'but abandoned it in distressing circumstances': *Nicklinson* (n 9) para 12.

in certain respects, the policy was insufficiently clear with respect to assistance by health-care professionals.

With the support of a considerable body of Strasbourg case law, based on similar facts as *Pretty* and *Purdy*, Lord Neuberger found that the state had a considerable margin of appreciation in this context.[46] Specifically, the blanket ban under section 2 of the 1961 Act falls within the UK's margin of appreciation.[47] It is also constitutionally open to UK courts to consider whether section 2(1) and Article 8 are compatible, since it is for domestic courts to determine whether there has been an infringement of ECHR rights in these circumstances.[48]

On whether section 2(1) is incompatible with Article 8, the appellants' argument was that the section was a disproportionate and unjustifiable interference with the rights of those who had made a voluntary and informed decision to end their lives, but who could not do so due to their physical circumstances.[49] A majority of justices found that it is constitutionally appropriate for the court to make such a determination, but only two of the seven found there to be an incompatibility.

Lord Neuberger argued that section 2 is a valid interference with Article 8 rights only if it satisfies the terms of Article 8(2), in this context 'the protection of the rights and freedoms of others'.[50] He found that the question turned on whether the terms of section 2(1) are no more than necessary to protect the weak and vulnerable, and whether they strike a fair balance between individual rights and community interest. On vulnerability, he concluded that the Act aims to protect those who may be in the same position as the appellants but who do not wish to end their lives, yet feel a pressure to do so by being a burden on others. Permitting assisted suicide would send such a message to those weak and vulnerable people. Because he had argued that it is institutionally appropriate for the legislature to consider the issue, he concluded by extension that it was inappropriate for the courts to modify section 2 of the 1961 Act, as the appellants had argued. He returned to Lord Sumption's arguments on the extent to which Parliament had already been involved in this issue.

Conversely, Lady Hale considered the law to be incompatible with ECHR rights because it fails to admit any exceptions. She contrasted the

---

[46] As did all seven justices.
[47] *Nicklinson* (n 9) paras 62–66.
[48] Ibid., paras 67–76.
[49] Ibid., para 55.
[50] Ibid., para 79.

present case with *Re B*,[51] in which Ms B was able validly to refuse life-saving treatment, even without the need to approach the court. Yet she did go to court because doctors refused to withdraw treatment, considering it tantamount to taking active steps to end her life. The difference between *Nicklinson* and *Re B* is that in *Nicklinson*, the appellants were able to breathe without artificial assistance, and could not avail themselves of the collapsed act/omission distinction. It is notable that since *Nicklinson*, the Court of Protection, with jurisdiction in England and Wales, has declared the withdrawal of clinically assisted nutrition and hydration to be lawful, and in the best interests of a patient in a minimally conscious state.[52]

Lady Hale went on to cite the ECtHR decision in *Pretty*, which had found that Article 8(1) was engaged by the prohibition in section 2(1); the way Dianne Pretty chooses to end her life is part of the act of living, and she has the right to ask that this should be respected. Since the decision in *Pretty*, she noted, the ECtHR has offered greater clarity on the scope of this right; it includes the right to decide the means and timing of death, which falls within the right to respect private life.[53] It does not depend on being physically capable of carrying out that wish; and yet it does not follow that such a person has the right to help from another person in carrying out that choice.[54] The question remained whether the blanket ban in section 2(1) is a proportionate interference with this right. As Lord Neuberger had done, Lady Hale found that, in order to be justified, such interference has to be:

(i)   for a legitimate aim important enough to justify interfering with a fundamental right,
(ii)  rationally connected to achieving that aim,
(iii) no more than reasonably necessary to achieve it and
(iv)  a fair balance between individual rights and community interests.[55]

Lady Hale found that a universal ban on assisting some – like the appellants – in ending their own lives was not reasonably necessary in order to protect the vulnerable from undue pressures. In a phrase which

---

[51]   *B v. An NHS Hospital Trust* (n 5).
[52]   *Re Briggs (No. 2)* [2016] EWCOP 53, [2017] 4 WLR 37.
[53]   *Nicklinson* (n 9) para 306 citing *Haas v. Switzerland* (2011) 53 EHRR 33 para 51 (repeated in *Koch v. Germany* (2013) 56 EHRR 6 para 52 and *Gross v. Switzerland* (2014) 58 EHRR 7 para 59).
[54]   *Nicklinson* (n 9) para 307.
[55]   Citing *R (Quila) v. Secretary of State for the Home Department* [2012] 1 AC 621 para 45.

resonates with the limited class of patients with which this chapter is concerned, she said that '[i]t would not be beyond the wit of a legal system to devise a process for identifying those people, those few people, who should be allowed help to end their own lives'; though she admitted that this had not been put forward in argument, she suggested that the requirements would be capacity, a free decision reached without undue influence, in full knowledge of available options and consequences, and the inability to carry out the decision without help.[56] Universally preventing those who might qualify under this rule from availing themselves of its provision amounts to a disproportionate interference with Article 8 rights.[57]

Before finding that section 2(1) is not compatible with ECHR rights, Lady Hale considered Parliament to be the 'preferable forum in which the issue should be decided' and 'the *only* forum in which a solution can be found which will render our law compatible with the Convention rights'.[58] As if pre-empting parliamentary action, she then set out ways to remedy the situation, including by Act of Parliament. This was picked up by Lord Pannick in the Committee stage of the House of Lords Assisted Dying Bill, agreeing with Lady Hale that a new law should require a judge to be 'satisfied in advance that someone has a voluntary, clear, settled and informed wish to die and for his or her suicide then to be organised in an open and professional way'.[59]

In *Nicklinson*, a majority of justices felt that these matters would be better assessed by Parliament. Lord Sumption gave a number of reasons.[60] First, where more than one rational choice is possible, this would normally be a matter for Parliament but would depend on the nature of the issue and whether it is 'essentially legislative in nature ... requiring a democratic mandate'.[61] He felt that the issue should be decided by Parliament because it involves a choice between mutually exclusive moral values. Second, this is a choice already made by Parliament, not only in the passage of the Suicide Act 1961, and its amendment under the Coroners and Justice Act 2009, but also by its activity on the range of bills that have been discussed (and will be considered later in this chapter). Lord Sumption's third point was that

[56] *Nicklinson* (n 9) para 314.
[57] Ibid., paras 317, 321.
[58] Ibid., para 300 (emphasis in original).
[59] HL Deb 7 November 2014, col 1853, speaking to proposed amendments in his name.
[60] *Nicklinson* (n 9) paras 230–4.
[61] Ibid., para 230.

parliamentary procedure was better at resolving controversial, complex, moral dilemmas, to take into account a range of views and interests.[62]

The case law considered above implicitly raises the question of whether the judiciary could be more creative, in the way Lady Hale suggested is possible, or even if its hand may be forced by repeated legislative inaction, as indicated by Lords Clark and Sumption in *Nicklinson* – that if Parliament does not do so, the courts might be prepared to deliver a declaration of incompatibility. Some of the case law and legislative acts from other jurisdictions are instructive in this regard, demonstrating a similar interplay between legislature and judiciary. That interplay illustrates how legacy-as-encumbrance can be overcome, or indeed has been overcome in other jurisdictions. The key theme that emerges is patient autonomy as a constitutionally protected value. That protection means, in turn, that criminal codes prohibiting assisted suicide are found to be unconstitutional by reason of incompatibility with human rights.

The rights invoked in these other jurisdictions are substantively similar to the Article 8 rights engaged in the UK cases, and the criminal codes are similar to the provisions in the Suicide Act 1961. An additional similarity is that specific guidance can be given to the legislature as to an appropriate direction of travel (as Lady Hale did in *Pretty*). It is therefore theoretically possible to overcome the burden of liminality in a comparatively similar way. Any UK legislature doing so would leave a legacy with an impact as considerable as that left by the legislatures in Canada and Italy, with Germany to follow.

### 12.2.4   Other Jurisdictions

#### 12.2.4.1   Canada

*Carter* v. *Canada*[63] involved a claim by Gloria Taylor on the constitutionality of the Canadian Criminal Code prohibiting assisted suicide. Ms Taylor had been diagnosed with amyotrophic lateral sclerosis (ALS), a fatal and progressive neurodegenerative disease. She did not want to die slowly, and in pain, or live bedridden and deprived of dignity. Without the resources to travel to Switzerland, she felt left with the

---

[62] Ibid., para 234.

[63] *Carter* v. *Canada* [2015] SCR 331 https://scc-csc.lexum.com/scc-csc/scc-csc/en/item/14637/index.do (accessed 21 September 2021).

'cruel choice' between early suicide while still physically able, and relinquishing control of her death.

The Supreme Court of Canada found that section 14 of the Criminal Code unjustifiably infringes section 7 of the Canadian Charter of Rights and Freedoms, which is incorporated into the Constitution Act, 1982. Section 14 is not dissimilar to section 2(1) of the Suicide Act 1961. It provides that '[n]o person is entitled to consent to have death inflicted on them, and such consent does not affect the criminal responsibility of any person who inflicts death on the person who gave consent'. Section 7 establishes that '[e]veryone has the right to life, liberty and security of the person and the right not to be deprived thereof except in accordance with the principles of fundamental justice'. This is analogous to Article 8 ECHR. The extent to which this analogy works exposes a circularity in UK Supreme Court case law, in that it is within that Court's competence to rule on an incompatibility but it ought not make such a ruling as Parliament is better suited to the role.[64]

The Supreme Court of Canada held that this incompatibility means that the criminal provisions are of no force where they prohibit physician-assisted death among competent adults who clearly consent and suffer from an irredeemable illness causing intolerable, enduring suffering. It is noteworthy that the medical condition does not need to be fatal, and the tolerability test is subjective. The decision was based on personal autonomy. Disallowing assisted dying 'interfered with the claimant's right [to liberty and security of the person] by depriving her of control over her bodily integrity, by depriving her of the choice of how to live, or cease to live'.[65] The judgment also made reference to the issue of vulnerability and undue pressure, finding that it calls into question the validity of consent if it involves a 'duty to live'.[66]

Referring to the decision in *Nicklinson* and the appropriateness of parliamentary action, the Canadian Supreme Court found that 'Parliament must be given the opportunity to craft an appropriate remedy.'[67] This led to Bill C-14, which, following Royal Assent in June 2016, became an Act to amend the Criminal Code and to make related amendments to other Acts (medical assistance in dying).[68] Despite stating that it did not wish to pre-empt legislative action, the

---

[64] See discussion of Lord Neuberger's judgment in *Nicklinson* (Section 12.2.3).

[65] *Carter* (n 63) para 64; Canadian Charter of Rights and Freedoms, in the Constitution Act, 1982, s 7.

[66] *Carter* (n 63) para 63.

[67] Ibid., para 125.

[68] https://parl.ca/DocumentViewer/en/43-2/bill/C-14/royal-assent (accessed 21 September 2021).

Canadian Supreme Court did observe that a physician's decision to participate is a matter of conscience.[69] Section 241.2(9) of the Criminal Code, under the heading 'Clarification', now reads in full: '[f]or greater certainty, nothing in this section compels an individual to provide or assist in providing medical assistance in dying'. The legislation applies only to medical practitioners or nurse practitioners and those aiding them, including pharmacists, when assisting a death upon a competent request. Health-care professionals providing information are also exempt from prosecution. Eligibility criteria under section 241 apply to Canadian residents and include being legally capable and above eighteen years of age, having made a voluntary and unpressured request, and having given their informed consent. Eligible persons must suffer from a 'grievous and irremediable medical condition', as defined, in an advanced state that causes subjectively unacceptable physical or psychological suffering, and where their natural death has become reasonably foreseeable.

Safeguards include that two independent medical or nurse practitioners take the view that the criteria are met, that the request was in writing and signed (proxy conditions apply) by two independent witnesses, and that a ten-day period is observed between the signing and the provision of assistance. Before that provision, the person must be given the opportunity to withdraw their request. It is a criminal offence to fail to comply with these safeguards. The minister for health is required as necessary to make regulations in respect of collection of data and formats of information to be provided. These issues came to the fore in the debates of UK bills, as will be discussed in Sections 12.3.2–12.3.4.

### 12.2.4.2   Germany

The German Federal Constitutional Court delivered judgment in February 2020 in a case that, like *Carter*, required legislative change,[70] and was based on the constitutionality of parts of the Criminal Code. The case was brought by Swiss- and German-based associations offering assisted suicide, people seeking to use such services, physicians and lawyers advising on such matters. Under paragraph 217 of the German Criminal Code 'anyone who, with the intention of assisting another person to commit suicide, provides, procures or arranges the opportunity for that person to do so and whose actions are intended as a recurring

---

[69] *Carter* (n 63) para 125.
[70] Judgment of 26 February 2020 www.bundesverfassungsgericht.de/SharedDocs/ Entscheidungen/DE/2020/02/rs20200226_2bvr234715.html (accessed 21 September 2021).

pursuit incurs a penalty of imprisonment for a term not exceeding three years or a fine'. Judge Andreas Voßkuhle found that the prohibition violated the general right of personality under Article 2(1) of the German Constitution (the Basic Law for the Federal Republic of Germany). That right includes a right to a self-determined death, and to seek, and use, the assistance of third parties. Assistance may include counselling and the provision of lethal medication, but not its adminis-tration, because actively causing someone's death on request is prohib-ited by section 216 of the Criminal Code (*Strafgesetzbuch*). A decision such as this would not help a person in the position of Debbie Purdy, who sought assistance when she is incapable of committing suicide, but it would be helpful insofar as she would be allowed assistance in getting to Switzerland.

The decision was seen as being in line with the ECHR, though the Court was no more specific than that. As was argued in *Nicklinson*, the restriction in national law was subject to a proportionality test on the same basis – that the provision 'has a legitimate purpose, is suitable and necessary for achieving that purpose, and strikes an appropriate balance between the purpose pursued and the resulting restrictions'.[71] The right does not allow assisted suicide to be linked to 'substantive criteria' such as diagnosis with an incurable illness.[72] This marks the German position as more liberal than any other jurisdiction considered in this chapter, raising some concerns that the preservation of life could become an obsolete principle for doctors because, no matter the rationale, it is permissible for people to take their lives, and to seek help in so doing.[73]

The judgment found that improvements in palliative care should not be seen as adequately addressing a disproportionate restriction on self-determination, yet the legislator may act to expand and strengthen palliative care so as to limit the call for assisted suicide due to illness. There was an oblique reference to conscientious objection, with the end of the judgment stating that 'there can never be an obligation, on anyone, to assist in another person's suicide'.[74] The Court also offered some

---

[71] See summary of the judgment in the German Federal Constitutional Court Press Release No. 12/2020 of 26 February 2020 www.bundesverfassungsgericht.de/SharedDocs/Pressemitteilungen/EN/2020/bvg20-012.html (accessed 9 February 2021).

[72] Ibid., section III.

[73] See, for example, the concern of Frank Ulrich Montgomery, President of the Standing Committee of European Doctors. See Rob Hyde, 'Germany Overturns Ban on Assisted Suicide' (2020) 395 *The Lancet* 774.

[74] Summary of the judgment of the German Federal Constitutional Court (n 71), section III.

guidance for the legislator when drawing up provisions that reflect this decision. For example, the legislature may act to prevent pressure on individuals to take their own life – perhaps due to the rising cost of long-term care – or for suicide to be viewed as a normal way to end life. The range of options open to the legislator included safeguards such as the provision of information, the observation of waiting periods, and the prohibition of dangerous forms of assistance. Referencing the judgment, section 217 of the Criminal Code was amended to include those promoting assisted suicide by commercial means (or a 'recurring pursuit') and to exclude from criminal liability those not acting commercially, the patient's relatives and those close to them.[75]

### 12.2.4.3   Italy

The *Cappato* case involved the trial of Marco Cappato, who assisted Fabiano Antoniani (known as Dj Fabo) along with his fiancée and her mother in travelling to Switzerland, where his assisted suicide took place. Dj Fabo had been blind and paralysed since a car accident in 2014. Cappato was arrested and charged on his return to Milan, under Article 580 of the Penal Code.[76] Drawing inspiration from *Carter* and *Nicklinson*, the (lower) Assizes Court in Milan found that, in some cases, assisting someone to commit suicide is not illegal. As in Germany and Canada, the decision was based on finding that Article 580 – which provides for five to twelve years' imprisonment for assisting a suicide or reinforcing a suicidal intent – is unconstitutional.[77] Article 580 needed to be read in accordance with the Italian constitutional precedent of 2017, which had recognised the right to refuse even life-saving treatment, including nutrition and hydration.[78] This was the ground on which the Milanese court referred the case to the Constitutional Court, as well as the fact that the Italian Parliament had not, by 24 September 2019, accepted the invitation to intervene.[79]

---

[75] Amended    s217    www.gesetze-im-internet.de/stgb/__217.html    (accessed    21 September 2021).

[76] Associazione Luca Coscioni, 'The Cappato Trial Step By Step' www .associazionelucacoscioni.it/the-cappato-trial-step-by-step/ (accessed 21 September 2021).

[77] Constitutional Court Decision No. 242 of 22 November 2019. See also Nicola Lupo, 'The Italian Constitutional Court and the Lawmaker: The "Cappato Case" (Order no. 207/ 2018)' (2019) *Anno Accademico 2018/2019, Dipartimento di Scienze Politiche Cattedra di Public Law* 33, which predates the Constitutional Court decision.

[78] Law No. 219 of 22 December 2017, on Informed Consent and Advanced Trials.

[79] For further constitutional reflections, see Pietro Faraguna, '"Constitutional Paternalism" and the Inability to Legislate: The Italian Constitutional Court's Decision on Assisted Suicide'

The Constitutional Court agreed with that precedent, but went further, finding that if medical treatment can be validly stopped, it followed that such a person is also not forbidden from ending their life with the assistance of a third party. That third party may not, under legislation applicable at the time, be a medical doctor who makes available or prepares the means of death. The Court cited a further precedent of 2018,[80] which required that the mentally competent 'suicide aspirant' be affected by an irreversible pathology that is the source of intolerable physical or psychological suffering, and that they are kept alive artificially. This limits the class of applicants to those who are already in a position to end their lives by a competent refusal of treatment.

That the Court came out in support of conscientious objection by health professionals suggests that its decision conferred a more general constitutional legitimacy on assisted suicide. The conditions for decriminalisation are redolent of many of the safeguards in proposed UK legislation, and yet are the result of a judicial ruling rather than a legislative process:[81]

- the ability to make free and conscious decisions,
- irreversible pathology or serious physical or psychological suffering, kept alive only through life-sustaining treatments,
- intolerable physical or psychological suffering,
- a pronouncement on the case by the territorially competent ethics committee,
- conditions and modality of the suicide approved by a public entity of the national health service,
- the aspirant having been adequately informed about the conditions, including the possibility of accessing palliative care or continuous sedation, and having rejected them,
- the aspirant having expressed their will clearly and unequivocally and
- the conditions having been verified by a judge in each particular case.

The trend, if it can be so described, emerging from this brief review of case law in other jurisdictions is for courts, on constitutional grounds, to

---

(*Verfassungsblog On Matters Constitutional*, 26 September 2019) https://verfassungsblog.de/constitutional-paternalism-and-the-inability-to-legislate/ (accessed 21 September 2021).

[80] Ordinance No. 207 of 2018.

[81] Dante Figueroa, 'Italy: Criminal Code Provision Outlawing Assisted Suicide Ruled Unconstitutional' (*Library of Congress: Law*, 7 January 2020) www.loc.gov/law/foreign-news/article/italy-criminal-code-provision-outlawing-assisted-suicide-ruled-unconstitutional/ (accessed 21 September 2021).

declare a constitutional incompatibility and pass the baton to the legislature, with or without being prescriptive on legislative scope. In contrast, requiring legislative action and setting its terms are constitutional steps that UK courts have been unwilling to take, save that Lady Hale indicated in *Nicklinson* that *if* the legislature did not act, she would be prepared to declare section 2(1) of the Suicide Act 1961 incompatible with Article 8 ECHR, as discussed in Section 12.2.3.

However, an important difference between the UK and other jurisdictions considered in this chapter is that a UK court ruling that an act or omission is, in effect, unconstitutional by virtue of its incompatibility with the Human Rights Act 1998 does not, in itself, compel the legislature to act on that ruling – either at the level of principle or in respect of specific conditions. Conversely, judicial rulings by Canadian, German and Italian courts have a more determinative power as far as a change of principle is concerned, as well as for outlining the shape of the conditions that require to be met to render the legislative provision constitutional.

## 12.3    Escape from Liminality: Crossing the Legality Threshold

### 12.3.1    Non-prosecution: A 'Third Way'

The DPP Guidance, in effect on non-prosecution in England and Wales, is covered in a number of textbooks on medical law. Hoppe and Miola argue that, in the case of family members, judges are trying to 'provide as much latitude as possible for people who help the terminally ill to die for compassionate reasons', and go on to argue that what is most telling is the 'total lack of prosecutions for assisting people to die at Dignitas'.[82] This was supported by a former DPP, Lord Macdonald, in a debate on the Assisted Dying Bill in the House of Lords, when he said that, as a DPP, he 'did not in a single circumstance authorise a prosecution against anyone who, through compassion, had helped a son, a daughter, a husband, a mother or a friend to die'.[83] Hoppe and Miola conclude their discussion on this point by arguing that, while a lack of prosecutions may be reassuring, such a 'half-way house' nudge towards legalisation 'certainly does not amount to much legal certainty'.[84] Indeed, it still does not get us

---

[82]  Nils Hoppe and José Miola, *Medical Law and Medical Ethics* (Cambridge University Press 2014) 270.

[83]  HL Deb 18 July 2014, cols 816–17.

[84]  Hoppe and Miola (n 82) 269, 270, referring to Keir Starmer, 'So far, we've got it right on assisted suicide . . . and it is thanks to you, the public' (*The Times*, 6 September 2011).

beyond the threshold at which, as judicially repeatedly stated, legislative action is required.[85]

In her textbook, Jackson proposes the addition of a 'third way', that is, 'treat[ing] euthanasia as a particular *type of killing*'.[86] Citing Huxtable,[87] and Keating and Bridgeman,[88] Jackson notes that a partial defence would operate at the level of compassion, which would serve the same purpose as that currently served by diminished responsibility and necessity, and which lowers the offence from murder to manslaughter. This is not far off the incremental approach advocated by Graeme and colleagues,[89] but it is different in that they stress the requirement for specific legislation,[90] as opposed to giving 'free reign' to individual doctors and their patients. It is perhaps this that led them to wonder whether legislation is needed, and to conclude that there are persuasive reasons for 'rejecting the legalisation of voluntary euthanasia'.[91]

At this point, my own view parts company with Graeme and colleagues, to a certain extent. We agree that progressive neuromuscular disease constitutes a special category,[92] and I accept that this would require either legislation aimed at a very narrow class of patient or a more formal judicial recognition of the 'third way'. Where we are not in agreement is in the need for legislative change. The courts are bound by precedent and, time and again, refer the matter to the legislature, in whose court the ball remains. It is not beyond the wit of legislative drafters to construct legislation that caters to the narrow class of patients considered earlier, and to address the majority of the oppositional concerns discussed in Sections 12.3.2–12.3.4. The case law is drawn from a quite specific and yet generalisable factual context of neuromuscular incapacity, in which patients do not have the option of suicide. That raises the question of whether any legislation can or should be confined to this narrow class of patients, in order to guard against the slippery slope.[93] Even tightly drafted legislation is fraught with difficulties as it tends to be based on 'intolerability' and a terminal diagnosis – the former

---

[85] As discussed in Section 12.2.
[86] Jackson (n 14) 958 (emphasis in original).
[87] Huxtable (n 15).
[88] Keating and Bridgeman (n 15).
[89] Laurie (n 10) para 19.115.
[90] Ibid., paras 19.90 & 19.114.
[91] Ibid., para 19.11.
[92] Ibid., para 19.78.
[93] Ibid., para 19.85 and discussion of legislators' concerns about the slippery slope.

very broad, and the latter fraught with definitional problems,[94] and in some cases excluding neuromuscular conditions.

These, among other factors, were extensively debated when proposals were considered by the UK legislatures, often repeatedly. As argued in this chapter, a move beyond the current liminality requires the legislature to approve assisted suicide; only then will the ping-pong between judiciary and legislature come to an end. This argument in turn raises the question of why parliamentarians have not yet enacted such a reform. Addressing that question requires a detailed consideration of arguments put forward both for and against the bills which failed.

### 12.3.2   Legislation and Members' Speeches

This section looks at specific arguments for and against three failed bills in UK legislatures. Divisions were not along party-political lines, as Members of Parliament (MPs) were given a free vote. That vote will have been guided in many cases by constituents who had been in contact with the MP, or by that MP's family or indeed their own advancing age.

First, the Assisted Dying Bill, HL Bill 6 in the House of Lords 2014–15, was a Private Member's Bill brought by Lord Falconer of Thoroton, a barrister (QC) and Labour peer. He proposed his Assisted Dying Bill in 2014, following the success of the Death With Dignity Act in Oregon. This Bill proposed that competent, terminally ill adults would be allowed assistance to end their lives. Assessments of prognosis and competence would be undertaken by two doctors, between the request and the delivery of the medication. The bill required self-administration of that medication but provided for a preloaded syringe with electronic driver. A conscience clause was included, and the Secretary of State could issue codes of practice on the operation of the Bill.[95] There was enough support at second reading for the Bill to progress to committee stage. The misgivings at second reading are indicated by the considerable list of amendments for that stage. Line by line examination of the Bill took place on 16 January 2015. Amendments discussed covered Clause 1 on assisted dying, including criteria such as age and capacity, and Clause 2 on the definition of terminal illness. The 2014–15 session of Parliament was

---

[94] See discussion of UK legislation (in Sections 12.3.2–12.3.4).

[95] See Lords Library briefing, 'In Focus: Assisted Dying Bill [HL], LIF 2014/006' (14 July 2014) https://services.parliament.uk/bills/2014-15/assisteddying.html (accessed 21 September 2021).

prorogued due to the 2015 General Election, and the Bill made no further progress thereafter.

Second, the Assisted Dying (No 2) Bill in the House of Commons was brought by Bob Marris MP in 2015, following the failure of the House of Lords Bill. It is substantially similar to the Lords Bill, though changes were made to address some of the concerns outlined above. For example, the voluntary informed wish of the person needed to be confirmed by a High Court judge, with further detail on how the application was to be made; terminal illness was defined as diagnosed by a registered medical practitioner as a progressive and terminal illness with an expected death within six months; further details were included on the workings of the 'cooling-off' period; the Chief Medical Officers were to monitor the operation of the Act; the 'democratic damage' issue was addressed by allowing regulations by the Secretary of State; and new offences were created for making false declarations or medical opinions.[96] The Bill was defeated by 118 votes to 330 at second reading on 11 September 2015.

Finally, the Assisted Suicide (Scotland) Bill 2015[97] aimed to legalise assisted suicide for competent people aged over sixteen with terminal or life-shortening illnesses. It required a preliminary declaration, followed by two requests fourteen days apart, both endorsed by two medical practitioners. It created the role of licensed facilitator to provide support. Death was to be accomplished by the individual's own action. The University of Edinburgh's Mason Institute submitted written evidence on the Bill, and Graeme gave oral evidence to the lead committee.[98] Congruence with the views of Members of the Scottish Parliament (MSPs) in the stage one debate is indicated below. The Stage One Report[99] of the Health and Sport Committee made no recommendation on the Bill, given that it is a matter of conscience. The same is true of political parties, as MSPs were given a free vote. The Report cited a wide range of concerns with the Bill, which were reiterated by MSPs arguing against the Bill at stage one.

---

[96] See Sarah Barber, Sally Lipscombe and Joanna Dawson, 'The Assisted Dying (No 2) Bill 2015' (*House of Commons Library Briefing Paper No 7292*, 4 September 2015) https://commonslibrary.parliament.uk/research-briefings/cbp-7292/ (accessed 21 September 2021).

[97] Scottish Parliament Stage One debate on the Assisted Suicide (Scotland) Bill 2015, SP OR 27 May 2015, cols 18–86.

[98] 20 January 2015. ASB395 written evidence to the Health and Sport Committee by the J Kenyon Mason Institute for Medicine, Life Sciences and Law, University of Edinburgh, directed at the time by Graeme.

[99] 6th Report 2015 (Session 4): Stage 1 Report on Assisted Suicide (Scotland) Bill.

A consideration of the arguments put forward on the basis of which the three bills outlined above failed, serves as a rationale for why UK jurisdictions have not moved in the direction of legal reform of assisted dying, which by implication is required in order to move beyond the current state of liminality and in the direction of novelty and evolved legacy. The legacy left by these points of opposition bears some similarity to the guidance of the Italian Court, to the relevant Canadian legislation and to some of the elements of UK case law considered earlier. The bases of failure were on the grounds of autonomy; relative lack of safeguards; the threat of a slippery slope (towards euthanasia); the availability of palliative care alternatives; and a lack of protection for the vulnerable. Each ground is considered in Sections 12.3.3 and 12.3.4.

### 12.3.3   Autonomy and the Palliative Care Alternative

Many comments, for and against the Assisted Dying Bill (HL Bill 6), included anecdotes about friends who had died.[100] Some arguing in support of the Bill did so not wishing to deny others what they might want for themselves: control at the end, even from a palliative care perspective.[101] This line of argument supports personal autonomy and choice, so widely promoted in society.[102] Some argued that there is a gap between allowing life support to be switched off – under either *Bland* if incompetent[103] or *Re B* for treatment refusals by those with capacity[104] – but no compassionate outcome is available to those with neuromuscular conditions. A change in the law is, moreover, supported by public opinion.[105]

On the other hand, some peers felt that the 'my rights, my life, my choice' attitude fails to recognise that we live in complex family and social

---

[100] For example, Lord Dubs, who had a friend die of motor neuron disease, in support of the Bill, HL Deb 18 July 2014, col 779.

[101] Lord Dubs, ibid., cols 779–80; Baroness Blackstone, ibid., col 804–5; Lord Stone of Blackheath, ibid., cols 814–15.

[102] Baroness Warwick of Undercliffe, ibid., col 800; Lord Birt, ibid., col 800; Baroness Blackstone, ibid., cols 804–5; Lord Alli, ibid., col 808; Viscount Craigavon, ibid., col 813–14; The Earl of Glasgow, ibid., col 795.

[103] Lord Lester of Herne Hill, ibid., col 780.

[104] Lord Joffe, ibid., col 789–90.

[105] Lord Dubs, ibid., col 779. This contention is supported by British Social Attitude Survey UK data, particularly in the case of terminal illnesses: see Kathleen Robson and Sarah Harvie-Clark, 'SPICe Briefing: Assisted Suicide (Scotland) Bill, SB 15/02' (8 January 2015) 18 https://archive2021.parliament.scot/ResearchBriefingsAndFactsheets/S4/SB_15-02_Assisted_Suicide_Scotland_Bill.pdf (accessed 21 September 2021).

relationships, including with social and health services.[106] This chimes with Lady Hale's comments in *Nicklinson*, considered in Section 12.2.3, on the 1961 law being incompatible with ECHR rights and, more particularly, with Lord Neuberger's nuance on that point, that interference with Article 8 rights must be considered in the context of interference with the rights and freedoms of others. That nuance was supported by Lady Hale, who had set out four conditions according to which interference with Article 8 rights would be justified.

Several peers argued that the Bill did little to assist the dying, when what is required is a bill to address the patchy availability of high-quality palliative care.[107] To support the choices of the dying, a bill should be centred on choices to refuse treatment.[108] Similarly, some referred to the sufficiency of the double effect rule and withdrawal of treatment.[109]

Like the debate on the Lords Bill, MPs debating the Assisted Dying (No 2) Bill in the House of Commons were concerned that its enactment could lead to negative effects on society's attitudes to ageing, death and dying, and people feeling that they are a burden (which could be addressed by improved palliative care) or have a 'duty to die'.[110] Some MPs referred to pressure from family members.[111] Although there was some general agreement that standards of palliative care were in need of improvement, many felt that this was a better alternative than assisted suicide.[112] At the same time, there was a perceived risk that passing the Bill would reduce resources available to hospice care.[113]

Other MPs who supported the Bill did so on the basis of the right to choose for those with a terminal illness, suffering pain and indignity. Many wanted to 'control their own exit'.[114] Even among those supporting the Bill there was concern over the limitations in the guidelines.[115] Sir Keir Starmer MP, who voted in support of the Bill at second reading, gave

---

[106] Lord Mawson, HL Deb 18 July 2014, col 799.
[107] Baroness O'Neill of Bengarve, ibid., cols 781–2, Baroness O'Cathain, ibid., col 801; Baroness Campbell of Surbiton, ibid., col 809.
[108] Baroness O'Neill of Bengarve, ibid., cols 781–2.
[109] Baroness Finlay of Llandaff, ibid., cols 791–2.
[110] Dr Philippa Whitford MP, HC Deb 11 September 2015, col 691; Caroline Spelman MP, HC Deb 11 September 2015, cols 663–5; Lyn Brown MP, HC Deb 11 September 2015, col 669.
[111] Dr Liam Fox MP, ibid., cols 679–80; Fiona Bruce MP, ibid., col 670.
[112] Dr Philippa Whitford MP, ibid., col 691; Caroline Spelman MP, ibid., cols 663–5.
[113] Caroline Spelman MP, ibid., cols 663–5.
[114] Jim Fitzpatrick MP, ibid., cols 665–7.
[115] Jim Fitzpatrick MP, ibid., col 666.

a detailed history of the guidelines that he had issued as DPP, when deciding whether to prosecute, for example, the father of Daniel James, the rugby player who became paralysed after an accident on the pitch. Based on his difficulty in drawing up the guidelines, he empathised with the House drawing up its own guidelines at Committee Stage. He referred to limitations in the current DPP guidelines: a person cannot have the assistance of medical professionals, and investigations can happen only after the event.[116]

These concerns over autonomy were discussed in the opening contribution to the stage one debate on the Assisted Suicide (Scotland) Bill 2015 by the Bill sponsor, Patrick Harvie MSP – for the most part arguing that they could be addressed at stage two once the general principles of the Bill were agreed.[117] Arguments made in support of the Bill recognised the shortcomings of the proposal, but it was felt that these could be 'ironed out' at stage two.[118] They included control of a person's own destiny.[119] This links to a point made by Graeme in his evidence to the committee, that the three most frequent reasons for choosing an assisted death were loss of autonomy, decreased ability to have an enjoyable life, and loss of dignity.[120]

Like the Lords and the Commons, several MSPs were against the Bill in principle,[121] including on the ground of autonomy,[122] which can support arguments on both sides.[123] The point on relational autonomy is something which came out in the evidence that Graeme gave to the Health and Sport Committee, where he also argued that 'protection of the autonomous nature of the decision is absolutely crucial'.[124] Members had difficulty with definitions, including defining what is *not* a crime rather than what is the crime,[125] as well as what is meant by 'life shortening'. On the basis of autonomy, Graeme questioned the scope of the Bill as focusing on life-shortening and terminal conditions but not on people who are 'in

---

[116] Sir Keir Starmer MP, ibid., cols 671–5.

[117] Patrick Harvie MSP, SP OR 27 May 2015, cols 29–30.

[118] Elaine Murray MSP, ibid., cols 49–51; Christine Grahame MSP, ibid., cols 59–62.

[119] SP OR HC 20 January 2015, col 20.

[120] SP OR HC 20 January 2015, col 20.

[121] Christian Allard MSP, SP OR 27 May 2015, cols 29–30; Rhoda Grant MSP, SP OR 27 May 2015, cols 36–7; Dave Thompson MSP, SP OR 27 May 2015, cols 40–1.

[122] Murdo Fraser MSP, ibid., cols 73–4; Alison McInnes, ibid., cols 51–3.

[123] Bob Doris MSP, speaking as Deputy Convener of the Health and Sport Committee, ibid., cols 23–7.

[124] SP OR HC 20 January 2015, cols 4–5, 10, 15.

[125] Christian Allard MSP, SP OR 27 May 2015, cols 29–30.

excruciating pain but whose life is not being shortened as a result'.[126] Indeed, the most regularly occurring objection to the Bill was that an improvement in palliative care services was preferable to allowing assisted suicide. This came with the explicit acknowledgement that palliative care services were in desperate need of improvement.[127]

### 12.3.4   Safeguards, the Slippery Slope and Protection of the Vulnerable

In the debate over the Assisted Dying Bill in the House of Lords, there were peers who considered that the time was right for a change in the law. They observed that the Supreme Court had held that Parliament should decide,[128] and that there is a risk that if it did not do so, a declaration of incompatibility (between Article 8 ECHR and the 1961 Act) may be made.[129] As noted in Section 12.2.1,[130] the ECtHR observed in *Pretty* that section 2 of the 1961 Act was designed to protect the vulnerable, and Lady Hale had found in *Nicklinson* that a universal ban on assisted suicide was not reasonably necessary in order to protect the vulnerable from undue pressures. She also indicated a preparedness to make such a declaration if the legislature did not act.[131]

The Lords Bill was tightly focused, with appropriate safeguards, supporters argued, and therefore there was no slippery slope that threatened the lives of the vulnerable,[132] or meant that terminally ill patients would feel pressure to end their lives.[133] Some argued that the Bill was not geared to

---

[126] SP OR HC 20 January 2015, col 10, evidence given by Graeme to the Health and Sport Committee of the Scottish Parliament. See also Laurie (n 98) 2–3.

[127] Paul Martin MSP, SP OR 27 May 2015, cols 76–7; Alison McInnes, SP OR 27 May 2015, cols 51–3; Nanette Milne MSP, SP OR 27 May 2015, cols 32–4; Shona Robison MSP, SP OR 27 May 2015, cols 27–9; Dr Richard Simpson MSP, SP OR 27 May 2015, cols 69–71; Dave Thompson MSP, SP OR 27 May 2015, cols 40–1.

[128] Lord Lester of Herne Hill, considering the decision in *Nicklinson*, HL Deb 18 July 2014, col 780; Baroness Jay of Paddington, HL Deb 18 July 2014, col 784.

[129] Baroness Jay of Paddington, ibid., col 784, quoting Lord Neuberger in *Nicklinson* at col 785; Lord Wigley, at col 787.

[130] See Section 12.2.3.

[131] Ibid.

[132] Lord Lester of Herne Hill, HL Deb 18 July 2014, col 780; Baroness Jay of Paddington, HL Deb 18 July 2014, col 784; Lord Purvis of Tweed, HL Deb 18 July 2014, col 785 citing the experience in Oregon (as did Baroness Meacher, HL Deb 18 July 2014, cols 811–12); Lord Alli, HL Deb 18 July 2014, col 808; The Earl of Sandwich, HL Deb 18 July 2014, cols 817–18.

[133] Lord Joffe, ibid., cols 789–90.

disability but to those with a terminal diagnosis,[134] reflecting on the view of
Baroness Campbell of Surbiton that while she, as a disabled peer, opposed
the Bill, there were those with disabilities who did not share her view.[135] On
the other hand, there were peers who argued that the Bill did *not* protect the
vulnerable, that there *was* a slippery slope (from terminal conditions to
'unbearable suffering' or disability),[136] and that safeguards were *in*sufficient.
Peers with health-care experience tended to oppose the Bill as running
contrary to their professional ethical obligations or as damaging to the
doctor- or nurse–patient relationship,[137] which had not been properly
thought through.[138] Others felt that with pressures on the health service,
doctors were unlikely to have the time and competence to deal with the
issues at a personal level.[139] It is difficult adequately to determine medical
capacity, and a doctor is in no position to judge external pressures such as
those placed by family, finances and the victim's condition.[140] There were
peers who questioned the importance of a six-month life expectancy, which
meant that an action would become lawful that before then would have
attracted a prison sentence.[141] On the other hand, some felt that the scope
was broad and almost anyone could be shoe-horned into it,[142] despite others
observing that a patient with motor neuron disease is unlikely to fit within it
as they would be unable to carry out the final act.[143] There were peers who
felt that the Suicide Act 1961 and the Coroners and Justice Act 2009 mean
that prosecutions are not automatic and are guided by the discretion of the
DPP.[144] This discretion would be dislodged by the Bill: 'If there were no
offence, none of these protections would remain.'[145]

---

[134] Lord Wigley, ibid., col 787.

[135] Lord Baker of Dorking, ibid., cols 810–11; Baroness Campbell of Surbiton, ibid., col 809.

[136] Lord Harries of Pentregarth, ibid., cols 805–6; Lord Cormack, ibid., cols 806–7; Baroness
Campbell of Surbiton, ibid., col 809; Lord Stirrup, ibid., cols 819–20. On the existence of
a slippery slope in the predecessor bill brought by Lord Joffe, see John Keown,
'Physician-Assisted Suicide: Lord Joffe's Slippery Bill' (2007) 15 *Medical Law Review* 126.

[137] Lord MacKenzie of Culkein as a former nurse, HL Deb 18 July 2014, col 794.

[138] Lord Empey, ibid., cols 803–4.

[139] Lord Mawson, ibid., col 798.

[140] Lord Tombs, ibid., cols 815–16, who argued that both assisted suicide and suicide are
illegal.

[141] Lord Mackay of Clashfern, ibid., col 778; Baroness Finlay of Llandaff, arguing that there
is no accurate test for a six-month prognosis, ibid., cols 791–2.

[142] Baroness Finlay of Llandaff, ibid., cols 791–2.

[143] Lord MacKenzie of Culkein, ibid., col 794.

[144] Lord Harries of Pentregarth, ibid., cols 805–6.

[145] Baroness O'Neill of Bengarve, ibid., col 782; Lord Harries of Pentregarth, ibid., cols
805–6.

Despite disagreement with the Bill, some peers still wanted it to move to committee stage further to discuss safeguards,[146] or due to the Supreme Court having asked Parliament to look at the issue.[147] There were peers who cited a danger to democracy because the Bill required executive oversight without reference to Parliament.[148] There was considerable concern over the potential for abuse, and people being forced to think that they are a burden and have a duty to die, and of helping to create a society with such an attitude to death, which was likely to increase with an ageing population.[149] This resonated with Lord Neuberger's comments in *Nicklinson* that the question of Article 8 ECHR compatibility turned on whether the terms of section 2(1) of the 1961 Act are no more than necessary to protect the weak and vulnerable.

Similarly, many MPs objected to the Assisted Dying (No 2) Bill in principle,[150] including those with medical experience, who felt that death was not a good treatment for anything,[151] or that the substance used is a poison rather than a medicine.[152] For many, that was linked to a dominant concern over damage to the doctor–patient relationship and the Hippocratic Oath,[153] particularly when there was no indication how doctors can satisfy themselves that a person's intention is settled, unencumbered by undue influence. Neither were MPs satisfied that reference to a High Court judge would be any better, as the judge will not have met the patient.[154] There was concern for the lack of detailed safeguards on the face of the Bill, which was left to codes of practice which *may* be issued by the Secretary of State. Despite changes to the Lords Bill, those concerns at the democratic level remained, with the Bill constituting a 'blank cheque' before safeguards may be considered.[155]

---

[146] Baroness Greengross, ibid., cols 786–7; Lord Harries of Pentregarth; Lord Cormack, ibid., cols 806–7.

[147] Baroness Finlay of Llandaff, ibid., cols 791–2.

[148] Lord Brennan, ibid., cols 802–3.

[149] Baroness Greengross, ibid., cols 786–7; Lord McColl of Dulwich, ibid., cols 797–8; Lord Brennan, ibid., cols 802–3; Baroness O'Cathain, ibid., col 801; Baroness Campbell of Surbiton, ibid, col 809; Lord Macdonald of River Glaven, a former Director of Public Prosecutions, ibid., cols 816–17; Lord Elton, ibid., cols 818–19.

[150] Dr Philippa Whitford MP, HC Deb 11 September 2015, col 691; Jim Shannon MP, HC Deb 11 September 2015, col 677 (speaking as a Christian).

[151] Dr Philippa Whitford MP, ibid., col 691 (speaking as a former breast cancer surgeon).

[152] Fiona Bruce MP, ibid., col 670; Nadine Dorries MP, ibid., col 676 (speaking as a nurse).

[153] Caroline Spelman MP, ibid., cols 663–5; Lyn Brown MP, ibid., col 669; Dr Liam Fox MP, ibid., col 679–80 (comments expressly based on his experience as a doctor).

[154] Fiona Bruce MP and Simon Hoare MP, ibid., col 670.

[155] Caroline Spelman MP, ibid., cols 663–5; Fiona Bruce MP, ibid., cols 670–1.

Concerns remained about a slippery slope to euthanasia, through future amendments to the scope of the Bill.[156]

Supporters of the Assisted Suicide (Scotland) Bill 2015 found that it did in fact distinguish assisted suicide and euthanasia, and that the safeguards proposed were sufficient.[157] On the other hand, several speeches drew attention to problematic definitions, including that of 'euthanasia', 'assisted suicide' and 'any drug or other substance or means'.[158] There were arguments, as presented to the Committee by Professor James Chalmers, that if 'assistance is the cause of death, the bill would not prevent somebody being charged with culpable homicide'.[159] In a reflection of the Commons debate, and discussion of non-prosecution in this chapter, MSPs noted that in England there have been few prosecutions of those who have assisted suicides.[160]

Some argued that the Bill was too widely drafted and therefore undermined the value of life, where any shortening of life justifies suicide.[161] There were comments to a similar effect from MSPs speaking as former health-care professionals:[162] the Bill would change the way society views suicide,[163] and have implications for the current suicide prevention strategy.[164] MSPs also felt that sixteen years of age was too young to act as a facilitator,[165] and generally found the safeguards proposed by the Bill to be insufficient to address public safety.[166] While Graeme considered

---

[156]  Lyn Brown MP, ibid., col 669, citing the experience in the Netherlands; Fiona Bruce MP, ibid., col 671; Jim Shannon MP, ibid., col 677; Dr Liam Fox MP, ibid., cols 679–80 (arguing that '[i]n practice it is impossible to distinguish between assisted dying and euthanasia. If we have one, because of the failures of process we will inevitably get the other').

[157]  Mary Fee MSP, SP OR 27 May 2015, cols 29–30.

[158]  Bob Doris MSP, ibid., cols 23–7; Alison McInnes, ibid., cols 51–3; Siobhan McMahon MSP, ibid., cols 62–4; Shona Robison MSP, ibid., cols 27–9; Mary Scanlon MSP, ibid., cols 57–9; Dr Richard Simpson MSP, ibid., cols 69–71.

[159]  Professor Chalmers' written evidence, which was discussed by the Health and Sport Committee on 17 February 2015, and referenced in the Health & Sport Committee 6th Report, 2015 (Session 4): Stage 1 Report on Assisted Suicide (Scotland) Bill. See also Rhoda Grant MSP, ibid., cols 36–7; Dr Richard Simpson MSP, ibid., cols 69–71, asserting that the safeguards were insufficient to address the issue of causation of death.

[160]  Christian Allard MSP, ibid., cols 29–30.

[161]  Nigel Don MSP, ibid., cols 66–8; Murdo Fraser MSP, ibid., cols 73–4; Alison McInnes, ibid., cols 51–3; Shona Robison MSP, ibid., cols 27–9.

[162]  Nanette Milne MSP, ibid., cols 32–4; Dr Richard Simpson MSP, ibid., cols 69–71.

[163]  Rhoda Grant MSP, ibid., cols 36–7; Stewart Stevenson MSP, ibid., cols 79–81.

[164]  John Mason MSP, ibid., cols 47–9.

[165]  Siobhan McMahon MSP, ibid., cols 62–4; this issue was also raised by the Mason institute, Laurie (n 98) 3.

[166]  Bob Doris MSP, ibid., cols 23–7; Shona Robison MSP, ibid., cols 27–9.

the three-step approach to be 'helpful', he questioned whether it might be too onerous for the individual.[167] Other MSPs felt the Bill had the potential to undermine the doctor–patient relationship.[168] The potential for undue influence or coercion remained under the Bill as drafted,[169] which Graeme felt should be an offence under any legislation.[170] The potential for a slippery slope also remained, as the Explanatory Memorandum considered widening the categories of those eligible.[171] The lack of a conscience clause was another concern,[172] also highlighted in Graeme's evidence.[173]

## 12.4   Conclusion

As we have seen, parliamentary arguments for and against parts of proposed legislation on assisted suicide are emotive and contentious. The fact that they have not led to reform indicates that the UK jurisdictions remain at the liminal threshold. Given the nature of representative democracy, there is an argument that it makes little difference whether there is public support for a proposal, whether there is or is not a slippery slope, whether safeguards are adequate for the protection of the vulnerable, whether definitions are sufficiently clear, or whether current or improved palliative care provision would serve to dissipate calls for assisted suicide. If the combined force of those opposing a bill coalesces around the concern that it represents the thin end of a wedge, with inadequate safeguards and unclear definitions, the bill will fail.

The workings of UK courts are clearly distinct from those in Canada, Germany and Italy, where courts have allowed assisted suicide and have done so on constitutional grounds. Despite demonstrating some form of interplay between judiciary and legislature, this route is less open to UK courts. We do not have a similar form of written constitution or criminal

---

[167]  SP OR HC 20 January 2015, col 5.

[168]  Stewart Stevenson MSP, SP OR 27 May 2015, cols 79–81.

[169]  Bob Doris MSP, ibid., cols 23–7; John Mason MSP, ibid., cols 47–9; Mary Scanlon MSP, ibid., cols 57–9; Dave Thompson MSP, ibid., cols 40–1. See Laurie's evidence, SP OR HC 20 January 2015, cols 4–5, 10, 25.

[170]  SP OR HC 20 January 2015, col 36.

[171]  Dave Thompson MSP, SP OR 27 May 2015, cols 40–1; Michael McMahon MSP, SP OR 27 May 2015, cols 44–5, quoted Prof. Theo Boer at Utrecht University: 'the very existence of a euthanasia law turns assisted suicide from a last resort into a normal procedure'.

[172]  Siobhan McMahon, ibid., cols 62–4.

[173]  SP OR HC 20 January 2015, cols 5, 26, and 35 on it being a matter reserved to Westminster.

code in the UK. There are constitutional elements in the judgments that indicate that Article 8 ECHR was engaged and that Article 8(1) supported the claimant's case, but this was offset by the public interest exception under Article 8(2). I would argue that our courts are constitutionally hamstrung when it comes to the judicial leadership demonstrated in other jurisdictions – or perhaps not, if they were to see the public interest in the form of autonomy not as an exception but as permitting assisted suicide. They might also recognise the similarities between the rights invoked abroad and the criminal provisions that infringed them.

I conclude by returning to my central question: how do we move across the threshold of the liminal space in the permissibility of assisted suicide? In the absence of a policy of non-prosecution, however tacit or formal, I must conclude in Graeme's own words: that while it is currently in the hands of the legislature (again) in the form of Baroness Meacher's Assisted Dying Bill 2019–21,[174] and will be in the hands of the courts when the next case comes before them, until then, 'only time will tell'.

---

[174] The Bill (HL Bill 69) is substantially similar to the Assisted Dying Bill in the House of Lords 2014–15 and the Assisted Dying (No 2) Bill in the House of Commons 2015. First reading took place on 28 January 2020. At time of writing a date for the second reading had been set as 22 October 2021. See https://bills.parliament.uk/bills/2875 (accessed 21 September 2021). It has also been announced that a Bill will be lodged in the Scottish Parliament by Liam McArthur MSP; see https://www.bbc.co.uk/news/uk-scotland-scot land-politics-57541231 (accessed 21 September 2021).

# 13

## Integrating the Biological and the Technological

### Time to Move Beyond Law's Binaries?[*]

MUIREANN QUIGLEY AND LAURA DOWNEY

## 13.1 Introduction

Donna Haraway famously asked, '[w]hy should our bodies end at the skin, or include at best other beings encapsulated by skin?'.[1] Similarly, Sebastian Abrahamsson and Paul Simpson have asked, '[w]here does one body end and another one begin? Is the limit of a body drawn at the skin, or does a body extend beyond its epidermis? If we both are and have a body then where does it/I end?'.[2] We pose these questions here not because we do (or can) answer them in what follows but to prompt us to confront our likely presuppositions about persons, bodies and things (specifically medical devices as 'things' for the purposes of this chapter). As Janelle Taylor notes, there is a 'tendency to presume, rather than ask, what a body is and where its significant boundaries are located'.[3] This presumptive tendency is notably evident if we probe the boundaries constructed within the law.[4] Significantly, the common law takes a bounded approach to both persons and objects. It considers

---

[*] This chapter is based on research generously supported by a Wellcome Investigator Award in Humanities and Social Sciences 2019–2024 (Grant No: 212507/Z/18/Z).

[1] Donna Haraway, 'A Manifesto for Cyborgs: Science, Technology and Socialist-Feminism in the Late Twentieth Century' in Linda Nicholson (ed), *Feminism/Postmodernism* (Routledge 1990) 191, 220.

[2] Sebastian Abrahamsson and Paul Simpson, 'The Limits of the Body: Boundaries, Capacities, Thresholds' (2011) 12 *Social and Cultural Geography* 331.

[3] Janelle Taylor, 'Surfacing the Body Interior' (2005) 34 *Annual Review of Anthropology* 741, 749.

[4] For a longer discussion of law's boundary-work in this respect, see Muireann Quigley and Semande Ayihongbe, 'Everyday Cyborgs: On Integrated Persons and Integrated Goods' (2018) 26 *Medical Law Review* 276.

that something is either a person (subject) or a thing (object), but not both.[5]

As we will see in this chapter, this conceptualisation of persons as bounded selves, and of objects as separate from persons, represents an encumbrance which goes to the very heart of law. The person–thing binary is so fundamental that it both structures the law conceptually and dictates its practical applications. We explore the consequences of this legacy in relation to 'everyday cyborgs' – that is, persons with attached and implanted medical devices – and argue that it creates a number of conceptual, normative and practical deficiencies. In so doing, the chapter is framed by a theme developed across much of Graeme Laurie's body of work regarding the inherent limits of the law. We recognise, as he does, that law in and of itself can sometimes be a blunt tool.[6] As such, our exploration takes inspiration from two significant and interrelated strands of Graeme's work: liminal analysis and processual governance. With his liminal analysis of law, part of Graeme's own legacy is a framework and set of insights with application well beyond the sphere of health research regulation (HRR) in which he originally developed it. After setting out some of the difficulties with the joining of persons and medical devices, we draw on Graeme's seminal insights to argue that recognising the inherent liminality of everyday cyborgs (and everyday cyborg technologies) allows us to look beyond law's binaries to more fully account for the 'spaces in-between'.[7] Following this, we ask whether a 'Laurie approach' to the regulation and governance of persons and medical devices, most recently in the form of processual governance, can help to overcome the difficulties which a bounded approach engenders. While the answer to this, for us, is broadly in the affirmative, we acknowledge that certain political and commercial realities may nevertheless curtail the implementation of the ideal processual approach in respect of medical devices.

---

[5] Donna Dickenson, *Property in the Body: Feminist Perspectives* (Cambridge University Press 2017) 5.

[6] Graeme Laurie and Shawn Harmon, 'Through the Thicket and Across the Divide: Successfully Navigating the Regulatory Landscape in Life Sciences Research' in Emilie Cloatre and Martyn Pickersgill (eds), *Knowledge, Technology and Law* (Routledge 2014) 121, 132; Graeme Laurie, 'Governing the Spaces in-Between: Law and Legitimacy in New Health Technologies' in Mark Flear et al (eds), *European Law and New Health Technologies* (Oxford University Press 2014) 191.

[7] Graeme Laurie, 'Liminality and the Limits of Law in Health Research Regulation: What Are We Missing in the Spaces in-Between?' (2016) 25 *Medical Law Review* 47.

## 13.2   Bodies, Boundaries and Legal Binaries

In the UK alone, hundreds of thousands of people, if not more, have attached or implanted medical devices of some form or another.[8] And every year these numbers rise. These include different types of device: (1) simpler technologies of the 'carpentry-kind'[9] such as artificial joint replacements or aesthetic prostheses; (2) wearable devices such as external insulin pumps and continuous glucose monitors; (3) implanted devices such as pacemakers and other cardiac devices; and (4) complex prostheses such as myoelectric prostheses, which are, to some extent, integrated with a person's nervous system.[10] Many of these medical devices have become more sophisticated in recent years. They are in essence mini-computers. As well as the hardware, they have integrated software. They can store data, they have algorithms which can analyse that data and they can transmit data either via hard links or wirelessly. The next generation of devices may also include those with artificial intelligence (AI) capabilities which use machine learning; for example, wearable devices which can collect and analyse data for stroke predication.[11] To varying degrees, devices might become integrated with persons physically (being internalised, partially internalised or remaining external yet attached); functionally (having a mechanical, physiological or other regulatory purpose); psychologically (becoming part of their lives and identities); or phenomenologically (becoming part

---

[8] From the National Joint Registry, the total number of operations in England, Wales, Northern Ireland and the Isle of Man relating to joint replacement carried out in 2019 was 147 www.njrcentre.org.uk/njrcentre/Healthcare-providers/Accessing-the-data /StatsOnline/NJR-StatsOnline (accessed 4 February 2021), 337. The numbers of new pacemakers and other cardiac devices implanted each year have risen steadily over the last ten years and, in England, the rate for cardiac resynchronisation therapy (CRT) implants has more than doubled in the last twenty years; see David Cunningham et al, 'National Audit of Cardiac Rhythm Management Devices: April 2015-March 2016' (2017) *National Institute of Cardiovascular Outcomes Research* (NICOR) 12–13 www .nicor.org.uk/wp-content/uploads/2019/02/crm-devices-national-audit-report-2015– 16_v2.pdf (accessed 4 February 2021).

[9] Haddow and colleagues talk about the distinction between 'technologies of the carpentry-kind' and other technologies in their discussion of smart devices: Gill Haddow, Shawn Harmon and Leah Gilman, 'Implantable Smart Technologies (IST): Defining the "Sting" in Data and Device' (2016) 24 *Health Care Analysis* 210, 212.

[10] Quigley and Ayihongbe (n 4) 279.

[11] Suzanne Hodsden 'Samsung Designs Wearable Stroke-Detecting Device' (*Med Device Online*, 27 January 2015) www.meddeviceonline.com/doc/samsung-designs-wearable-stroke-detecting-device-0001 (accessed 4 February 2021).

of how they experience the world).[12] The greater the physical integration with persons, the greater the support or replacement of bodily functioning, or the greater the dependency of persons on devices, the more the subject–object dichotomy breaks down. At the extreme end of this spectrum are devices which keep people alive, such as certain pacemakers and internal cardioverter defibrillators (ICDs). These have not just crossed the bodily boundary but, in virtue of keeping the person alive, have become constitutive of that person's subjecthood.[13]

This joining of persons with different types of medical device raises a number of issues for the law which have not yet been adequately examined, let alone resolved. Part of the reason for this is simply because, until relatively recently, the law has not had to deal with the joining of persons and things in this manner.[14] However, it creates a significant set of conceptual, normative and practical problems. As noted in the introduction, currently the law treats something as either a subject (a person) or an object (a thing), but not both. This has consequences for how the law operates and for its practical application. We see it in law's structure, which is broadly divided into law relating to persons and law relating to things – for example, assault and battery and medical negligence, on the one hand, and areas such as property law and sale of goods, on the other.[15] The subject–object dichotomy is also reflected in how the law deals with other divisions such as internal–external (for example, implanted versus wearable devices), biological–synthetic (for example, human origin versus artificial) and material–immaterial (for example, property rights in

---

[12] Muireann Quigley, *Self-Ownership, Property Rights, and the Human Body: A Legal and Philosophical Analysis* (Cambridge University Press 2018), 251; Quigley and Ayihongbe (n 4) 305.

[13] Ibid., 242, 252–3; Quigley and Ayihongbe (n 4) 306.

[14] There are, of course, examples of the joining of persons with things which are not so recent, all things considered. For example, the first recorded prosthesis was a wooden toe discovered on an Egyptian mummy; the first prosthetic legs were developed fairly early and consisted of wood and/or leather; and even metal hands were used to enable continued fighting as far back as the Middle Ages. For more on these, see Alan Thurston 'Paré and Prosthetics: The Early History of Artificial Limbs' (2007) 77 *ANZ Journal of Surgery* 114. However, these examples seem to be different in kind, scale and sophistication from the more recent, technologically advanced ones we are discussing.

[15] Quigley and Ayihongbe (n 4) 302–3. See also Catriona McMillan et al, 'Beyond Categorisation: Refining the Relationship Between Subjects and Objects in Health Research Regulation' (2021) 13 *Law Innovation and Technology*, DOI: 10.1080/ 17579961.2021.1898314.

tangible goods versus intellectual property rights in those goods or software). As one of us has previously argued:

> The bodily boundary seemingly marks out the person from the external world and, as such, it is often the mode by which the subject–object dichotomy is given effect in particular laws (e.g. damage to property versus assault and battery) ... [T]he subject–object boundary is taken to be an ontological one (i.e. an empirical reality). This is then imbued with a moral significance that we find reflected in law's structure and operative rules.[16]

However, 'everyday cyborgs',[17] or integrated persons[18] as we also call them, are person–thing hybrids. They are a subject–object nexus in which there is a merging of synthetic (and once external) objects with embodied biological persons.[19] As such, at a very fundamental level, there is a philosophical and conceptual mismatch between how the law operates and the reality of these integrated persons.

We can see the extent of this mismatch if we think about the varying degrees to, and dimensions along, which devices can become incorporated into or integrated with persons. At the extreme end of the spectrum – for instance, persons with pacemakers and ICDs – the subject–object distinction seems almost completely to break down. In such cases, without the object – the medical device – there would be no subject. The device is, in a very real sense, maintaining and constituting their subjecthood. This would seem to pose a problem for the standard way in which the law classifies and categorises.

As well as these types of conceptual and normative incompatibily, there is also a practical difficulty with the subject–object dichotomy within the common law. Specifically, within a bounded approach we might struggle to respond to new challenges. For example, it is not clear whether difficulties relating to everyday cyborgs and their technologies should be addressed within a subject- or object-orientated framework, or something else entirely. Nor is it clear what the consequences of choosing one or the other might be. If one is chosen rather than the other, this may end up being inappropriate either in analytical terms (for example, treating something as an object which ought more appropriately to be treated as part of the person) or in remedy terms (for instance,

---

[16] Quigley and Ayihongbe (n 4) 303. See also Quigley (n 12) 242–55.
[17] Gill Haddow et al, 'Cyborgs in the Everyday: Masculinity and Biosensing Prostate Cancer' (2015) 24 *Science as Culture* 484, 486.
[18] Quigley and Ayihongbe (n 4) 277.
[19] Ibid.

not attracting an appropriate corrective remedy or the right level of compensation for harms or wrongs done). To illustrate, consider the question of whether devices, on transgressing the bodily boundary and becoming integrated (be it physically, functionally or in other ways) with the body, should retain their property status (which they unquestionably have prior to implantation) or be treated as part of the person.[20] The answer to this question is not inconsequential. It has substantial and substantive implications regarding the size and type of, for example, remedies available for damage done and the appropriateness of legal routes to get to those remedies. Criminal law, for instance, generally treats harm to persons more seriously than damage to property,[21] something which is mirrored in tort law.[22]

Thus, the very literal transgression of the bodily boundary, represented by everyday cyborg technologies, poses a problem for *how* and *why* law constructs, incorporates and utilises different boundaries (including supposed ontological and moral ones). As Popat and colleagues note, '[t]he assemblage and the parts exist simultaneously on the ontological plane – their properties emerge from and are contingent upon their relationship with each other. The emergent properties and capacities of the whole are different from (not more or less than) the sum of the parts.'[23] Thinking in bounded and binary terms belies the complexity and 'ambiguous embodiment'[24] of everyday cyborgs and their technologies. Importantly, thinking in such terms forecloses new and potentially fruitful modes of enquiry.

In a recent paper, Catriona McMillan, writing with Graeme and other colleagues, argues that 'the relationship between the legal categories of "subject" and "object" is poorly understood, and that existing categorisations within HRR are inflexible and insufficient by obscuring the important transformations that take place between subjects and objects'.[25] We

---

[20] See more fully on this Quigley and Ayihongbe (n 4) 287–9. While an old Department of Health Notice in 1983 stated that devices become the property of the patient upon implantation, this is not supported by legal precedent.

[21] Ibid., 289–90.

[22] Ibid., 290.

[23] Sita Popat et al, 'Bodily Extensions and Performance' (2017) 13 *International Journal of Performance Arts and Digital Media* 101, 102.

[24] Gill Haddow, 'Animal, Mechanical, and Me: Organ Transplantation and the Ambiguity of Embodiment' in Natalie Boero and Katherine Mason (eds), *The Oxford Handbook of the Sociology of Body and Embodiment* (Oxford University Press 2019).

[25] McMillan et al (n 15) 3.

are urged by the authors in the title of their paper to go 'beyond categorisation'. In the rest of this chapter, we take up that challenge.

## 13.3  Regulatory Failures and Medical Devices as Bounded Objects

Graeme's work on liminal spaces aims at better understanding problems with 'the current regulatory spaces created in the health research environment'[26] and what is missed when we do not pay attention to the spaces in-between.[27] Part of his critique is that existing HRR is typified by a command-and-control response, with multiple overlapping regulatory regimes that are formed around legally constructed 'objects' as their targets.[28] This 'bounded object' approach includes 'tissue', 'data' and 'embryos', all of which are subject to bespoke regulatory instruments forming regulatory 'silos'.[29] Each silo deals with issues related to research governance, but limited learning between them leads to both inefficiency and increased regulatory burden as activities are subject to multiple overlapping regimes.[30] For example, research on human embryos is governed (minimally) by the Human Fertilisation and Embryology Act 1990 (as amended), the Human Tissue Act 2004 and the Human Tissue (Quality and Safety for Human Application) Regulations 2007, as well as a patchwork of multiple jurisdictional variations in law and regulation at international level.[31] Graeme argues that, by focusing on the *objects* involved in research, existing regulatory regimes do not pay sufficient regard to research *subjects*, neither capturing their experiences nor accommodating those experiences within the regulation.[32]

Both of the main difficulties which Graeme highlights – the siloed nature of regulation and its object-focus – can be seen in relation to medical devices. Law and regulation in this area not only focus on the

---

[26] Laurie (n 7) 71.

[27] Ibid., 63.

[28] Ibid., 49. This critique is developed further looking at issues of feedback loops and the (negative) inhibitory effects of command-and-control type regulation on health research practices in Samuel Taylor-Alexander et al, 'Beyond Regulatory Compression: Confronting the Liminal Spaces of Health Research Regulation' (2016) 8 *Law, Innovation and Technology* 149.

[29] Laurie (n 7) 50.

[30] Ibid.

[31] See Timothy Caulfield et al, 'The Stem Cell Research Environment: A Patchwork of Patchworks' (2009) 5 *Stem Cell Review* 82; cited by Laurie (n 7) 51.

[32] Laurie (n 7) 50.

devices as objects (rather than on the subjects as their recipients) but construct medical devices as different types of object, for example 'risk objects', 'marketised objects' and 'innovation objects'.[33] Although there is not space to unpack these constructions fully here (which in any case has been done elsewhere[34]), we note that much is linked to the framing of medical devices as 'products'.[35] This is something which is essentially rooted in EU law and, unless and until post-Brexit legislation alters this, it is also what drives domestic medical devices law.

What we find within the regulatory landscape at both UK and EU level (the former being still largely derived from the latter) is a narrow focus on the health and safety of products within the *market*.[36] While health and safety are clearly important in respect of medical devices regulation, as noted by Flear, the way the EU regulates health technologies 'narrow[s] the meaning and framing of technological risk to being principally about product safety at different stages of product development and ultimately marketing within the internal market'.[37] Flear argues that the rationale

[33] Quigley and Ayihongbe (n 4) 280.

[34] Ibid., 282–7.

[35] The basis for the jurisdiction of the EU over medical devices is rooted in the free movement of goods and harmonisation of the market. The Guide to the Implementation of Directives Based on the New Approach and the Global Approach ('Blue Guide') (2016), which provides guidance for the interpretation of EU legislation concerning products and goods, specifically encompasses the law relating to medical devices as stated in para 1.5. For further analysis of medical devices as 'products' and the emphasis on regulating their risk as about product safety, see Mark Flear, 'Regulating New Technologies: EU Internal Market Law, Risk, and Socio-technical Order' in Marise Cremona (ed), *New Technologies and EU Law* (Oxford University Press 2016) 74.

[36] UK legislation: Medical Device Regulations 2002 (SI 2002 No. 618) as most recently amended by the Medical Devices (Amendment etc) (EU Exit) Regulations 2019 (SI 2019 No. 791) and the Medical Devices (Amendment etc) (EU Exit) Regulations 2020. EU legislation: Council Directive 90/385/EEC of 20 June 1990 concerning active implanted medical devices, 1990 OJ L189/17 (AIMDD); Council Directive 93/42/EEC concerning medical devices, 1993 OJ L169/1 (MDD); Council Directive 98/79/EEC concerning in vitro diagnostic medical devices, 1998 OJ L331/1 (IVDD); Regulation 2017/45/EU on medical devices, 2017 OJ L117/1 (MDR); and Council Regulation 2017/746/EU on in-vitro diagnostics medical devices, 2017 OJ L117/176 (IVDR). Note that the MDR was due to be fully in force across the EU in May 2020 and would therefore have become part of UK law during the Brexit transition period in accordance with the Withdrawal Agreement. However, the timeline was extended until May 2021 due to the Covid-19 pandemic. The UK's 2019 regulations previously mirrored and implemented much of the MDR and the IVDR. However the 2020 regulations, passed late in 2020, removed these provisions and set in place a dual system of regulation for Great Britain and Northern Ireland, meaning that the MDR and the IVDR will come into force in Northern Ireland but not in England, Wales and Scotland.

[37] Flear (n 35) 77.

given for the new MDR 2017 and IVDR 2017 'further underscores the salience and centrality of product safety as the focus of technological risk regulation'.[38] He cites the Commission's proposal for a new medical devices regulation as expressly highlighting that 'substantial divergences in the interpretation and application of the rules have emerged, thus undermining the main objectives of the Directives, i.e. the safety of medical devices and their free movement within the internal market'.[39] In this way, the Commission links the need for a new regulation directly to the broader and prior aim of market freedom, which is further justified as facilitating competition and innovation in the medical device industry.[40] As such, within the EU's sociotechnical order, medical devices are the targets of regulation in virtue of the fact that they are 'products' as part of the market rather than, for example, being intimately connected to health as a good in and of itself.[41]

It is questionable whether the UK's post-Brexit approach will, in the long term, be much different. Certainly, the new Medicines and Medical Devices Act 2021 (MMD Act) does not, on the face of it, differ significantly in this respect. It is a skeleton Act creating extensive (arguably overly so[42]) delegated powers for the Secretary of State to make provisions via secondary legislation. Its stated purpose is to create a new legal basis for powers to amend the existing regulations on human medicines, veterinary medicines and medical devices. Pre-Brexit, any regulation-making powers in these areas derived from section 2(2) of the European Communities Act (ECA) 1972. However, the 1972 Act ceased to have effect in the UK at the end of the transition period.[43] Arguably, however, the delegated powers created by the MMD Act are not simply equivalent to those which were enabled by the 1972 Act. Section 2(2) ECA enabled the UK to implement EU legislation which had *already* been subject to

---

[38] Ibid., 113.

[39] European Commission, Proposal for a Regulation on Medical Devices, and amending Directive 2001/ 83/ EC, Regulation (EC) No 178/ 2002 and Regulation (EC) No 1223/ 2009, COM(2012) 542 final 2.

[40] Ibid.

[41] Flear (n 35) 115–17.

[42] See Muireann Quigley et al, 'Medicines and Medical Devices Bill 2019–2020 Briefing Paper' (2020) www.birmingham.ac.uk/research/artslaw/projects/everyday-cyborgs.aspx (accessed 4 February 2021). See also the 19th Report of the Delegated Powers and Regulatory Reform Committee (2020 HL 109).

[43] Medicines and Medical Devices Bill Memorandum from the Department of Health and Social Care to the Delegated Powers and Regulatory Reform Committee (14 February 2020) paras 8–9.

rigorous scrutiny within the EU law-making institutions. The powers conferred by the MMD Act, by contrast, allow for potentially radical changes to be made to extant regulation in these areas *without* being subject to the same parliamentary scrutiny that exists for primary legislation or that was in place within the EU regime.[44] The government's position is that these delegated powers are needed to ensure that the UK can continue to update the existing regulation in line with advances in technology, stressing that many updates will be very technical in nature and that it strikes the right balance between patient safety and encouraging such innovation.[45]

Indeed, elements of both the draft Bill as it passed through Parliament and the wording of the final Act continue to construct medical devices as innovation objects and commercial entities. For example, we can see the marketised framing in the so-called attractiveness clauses contained in earlier drafts of the Bill. Specifically, with respect to medical devices, the Bill contained a requirement that, in making regulations, the Secretary of State must have regard to the '*attractiveness* of the United Kingdom as a place in which to develop or supply medical devices'.[46] This was amended at the Lords Report Stage to remove 'attractiveness'.[47] Instead, the Act now requires that the Secretary of State have regard to the 'likelihood of the relevant part of the United Kingdom being seen as a *favourable place*' in which to develop and supply medical devices.[48] There seems to be little to distinguish this from 'attractiveness', and both imply the need for regulations to create or support particular market conditions.

Arguably, it is the construction and fixing of medical devices as bounded regulatory objects,[49] situated in a marketised context, which

---

[44] Ibid., para 4, where the government argues that most provisions will be subject to the affirmative procedure giving Parliament more scrutiny than it currently has over regulation in this area. This ignores the scrutiny that legislation in the EU undergoes in the European Parliament.

[45] Ibid., paras 3–4.

[46] Clause 12(2)(c) (our emphasis). This was mirrored in relation to medicines and veterinary medicines, in clauses 1(2)(c) and 8(2)(c) respectively in the Bill as introduced https://publications.parliament.uk/pa/bills/cbill/58-01/0090/cbill_2019-20210090_en_1.htm (accessed 24 March 2021).

[47] Introduced by Lord Bethell at the Lords Report Stage on the Bill, HL Deb (12 January 2021) vol 809 col 666.

[48] See the final wording in s15(3)(c) of the Medicines and Medical Devices Act 2021, replicated for human medicines and veterinary medicines in s2(3)(c) and s10(3)(c) respectively (our emphasis).

[49] Laurie (n 7) 48–9.

contributes to insufficient attention being paid to subjects (which Graeme emphasises in the HRR sphere). When the predominant regulatory framing is overtly and overly object-focused, the result is that the subject – patient, end-user, integrated person – is decentred.[50] In other words, '[t]hrough its object categorisation, the law can inadvertently spur an overly-technocratic view of the world which pays insufficient attention to human subjectivity and experience'.[51] This is something which is brought home in the recent Independent Medicines and Medical Devices Safety Review (Cumberlege Review),[52] where the decentring and marginalisation of patients and their experiences are laid out (sometimes in harrowing detail). The Review investigated a litany of institutional and regulatory failures in relation to three apparently disparate interventions: the hormone pregnancy test Primodos; the anti-epileptic drug sodium valproate; and surgical mesh for pelvic organ prolapse. Tying these together, however, are disquietingly similar narratives where patients' voices (in these cases, women's voices) went largely unheard. Among other things, the Review highlights 'the lack of information to make informed choices; lack of awareness of who to complain to and how to report adverse events; the struggle to be heard; not being believed; ... [and] a lack of interest in, and an inability to deliver, the monitoring of adverse outcomes and long-term follow-up across the healthcare system'.[53] The Review outlines problems with the fragmented and siloed nature of health-care and regulatory institutions, noting 'a system that does not work in a joined-up fashion'.[54] It also notes that the regulatory system for medical devices 'is relatively immature compared to medicines regulation'.[55] There is no licensing system for medical devices and, in general, the pre-market approvals process for these is much less stringent.[56]

Thus, the underdevelopment of the regulatory system in relation to devices, along with the regulatory framing of (and focus on) devices as objects and products within the market, is problematic. When health and safety is viewed through a marketised lens and devices are constructed

---

[50] Ibid., 51.
[51] McMillan et al (n 15) 6.
[52] Report of the Independent Medicines and Medical Devices Safety Review, 'First Do No Harm' (*Aps Group*, 2020), www.immdsreview.org.uk/downloads/IMMDSReview_Web .pdf (accessed 4 February 2021).
[53] Ibid., para 1.12.
[54] Ibid., para 1.19.
[55] Ibid., para 5. 108.
[56] Ibid., para 5. 109.

predominantly as products within that frame, then a regulatory boundary is erected which distances those objects from the subjects into whom they are (to be) implanted. In this manner, the law is neither sufficiently 'attentive to the conjoined futures for which such devices are destined'[57] nor to the experiences of persons in reaching or navigating that future. In the HRR context, Graeme argues that a more coherent understanding of the processes and experiences of becoming a research subject, the position and experiences of researchers, the research project in general and the objects that are the target of regulation can be achieved through recourse to the anthropological concept of liminality.[58] Drawing on this work, in Section 13.4 we make the case for the inherent liminality of everyday cyborgs and their technologies, exploring how a liminal lens could help us better to appreciate the ambiguous embodiment of persons with attached and implanted medical devices.

## 13.4   Liminality, Blurred Boundaries and Ambiguous Embodiment

Key in Graeme's work on liminality and liminal spaces in law is the idea of the 'in-between': in-between regulatory spaces and in-between legal statuses. The sticking point for the law is that it is not particularly adept at accounting for the in-between. It also cannot take account particularly well of transitions between different spaces or statuses, or the transformations that take place as persons or objects pass from one space or status to another. One example given by Graeme is that of mature minors who are in a transitionary phase, somewhere in-between childhood and adulthood.[59] Their autonomy (like them) is in a developing, liminal state, something with which the courts in *Gillick* v. *West Norfolk & Wisbech Area Health Authority*[60] and subsequent cases[61] have attempted to grapple.[62]

Thus, liminality can refer to a phase of transition or transformation, where persons are in a state of becoming, or are in-between states or (legal) statuses, and in which the norms and conventions that normally

---

[57]  Quigley and Ayihongbe (n 4) 282.
[58]  Laurie (n 7) 53.
[59]  Laurie (n 7) 56.
[60]  [1986] AC 112 (HL).
[61]  *Re R (a minor) (wardship: medical treatment)* [1992] Fam 11 and *Re W (a minor) (medical treatment)* [1992] 4 All ER 627.
[62]  Laurie (n 7) 56.

structure behaviour may be in flux.[63] Transitions and transformations can occur over protracted periods of time or may be short moments of becoming. They can be localised or occur on a wider scale. Perhaps most importantly for Graeme, a liminal analysis enables us to take account of persons' experiences and acknowledges critical 'temporal and spatial dimensions'.[64]

Moving beyond liminality as traditionally applied to persons (as it is in the anthropological literature), Samuel Taylor-Alexander, along with Graeme and others, posited that it 'can also account for the changing relations that people have with the world and the things around them'.[65] The paradox, as they put it, is that while liminality has failed hitherto to account for things, regulation all too often fails to account for experiences of subjects 'in relation to things'.[66] Yet, as the Cumberlege Review highlights, the consequences can be dire when those experiences are neglected or ignored. If Taylor-Alexander and colleagues are correct that 'liminality can be applied as well to things',[67] then medical devices seem apt for its application.

### 13.4.1 Medical Devices, 'Ubjects' and 'Active Subject-Objects'

Let us begin with medical devices themselves. Where these are destined for conjoined futures with persons, they are objects in transition. They are in transition (in a very literal sense) since they are on a journey from manufacturer to patient. A pacemaker, for example, may change hands from manufacturer, to supplier, to NHS trust, and finally to patient, whereupon implantation takes it across the bodily boundary. But this transition from object in the external world to being inside the human body raises questions of transformation. How are we to view medical devices – both ontologically and legally speaking – which have crossed the bodily boundary and become internalised? As noted in Section 13.2, there are varying degrees to which such devices become incorporated into or integrated with persons. Consequently, there are varying degrees to which the subject–object boundary is challenged. In the case of devices which keep persons alive, where the devices essentially become constitutive of a person's subjecthood, the supposed ontological boundary

---

[63] Ibid.
[64] Ibid., 56 and 60. See also Taylor-Alexander et al (n 28) 155.
[65] Taylor-Alexander et al (n 28) 158.
[66] Ibid., 159.
[67] Ibid.

between person and thing falls away. Such medical devices can be viewed as having undergone a transformation; albeit the crucial question is, transformation to what? While it seems inappropriate to continue to view them purely or merely as objects, it is not clear that we ought to view them as wholly part of the subject.

When medical devices become part of persons' (lives) in this way, simply asking whether we ought to consider them as objects or part of the subject belies the complexities involved. When talking about contested (bio)materials such as cells, tissues, organs, bodies, bone, metal parts, implants and so on, Klaus Høyer argues that 'subject or object' places the terms in immediate opposition and impacts (negatively) on the framing of any subsequent debate. To avoid this framing, he introduces the term 'ubject' with the aim of providing an analytical vocabulary that is free of the suppositions usually present. For him, this captures any '[m]aterial[] which is ambiguously related to bodies and to persons [and] is neither fully subject nor fully object'.[68] He has also previously called them human boundary objects, a term which likewise serves to reflect the potentially ambiguous nature of a range of materials which become associated with persons. Yet 'ubject' is not entirely synonymous with the materials themselves. Instead, ubject is intended to capture a 'temporal relation'.[69] In this respect, it represents the *movement* of the materials in question between subject and object. It is the space in-between, neither one nor the other, and can represent a fluctuating status over time and in different contexts. Høyer's terminology and analytical frame remind us of the ambiguities which exist and of how they sit in tension with the boundary-work inherent in the approach of the law.[70] There are clearly important parallels with Graeme's approach to liminality, with its focus on uncertainty, transition and how to deal with the in-between.

Given the connection of medical devices to the persons to whom they are attached or into whom they are implanted, the assemblage of integrated persons and devices seems like a particularly concrete instantiation of what Taylor-Alexander and colleagues conceptualise as 'active subject-objects'.[71] They apply this term specifically to research participants' separated biomaterials and personal data. For them, 'active

---

[68] Klaus Høyer, *Exchanging Human Bodily Material: Rethinking Bodies and Market* (Springer 2013) 5.

[69] Ibid., 7, 167.

[70] Quigley and Ayihongbe (n 4) 302–4; Taylor-Alexander et al (n 28) 170–2.

[71] Taylor-Alexander et al (n 28) 163. See also Catriona McMillan, *The Human Embryo In-Vitro: Breaking the Legal Stalemate* (Cambridge University Press 2021), ch. 5.

subject-object' is a means of describing and articulating the enduring metaphysical links and interests that subjects have with these (physically) separated biomaterials and associated data. These are not mere objects and should not be viewed as having transitioned to 'mere passive objects ... devoid of significance'.[72] Instead, there is a need properly to recognise the enduring ties to, and impact upon, the subject.[73] It is these enduring ties and interests (and often fluctuating status) of such materials which are challenging in regulatory terms. Biomaterials and personal data are examples of things which were unambiguously part of the subject but which then take on (sometimes liminal) life in the external world: not always or appropriately wholly subject; not always or appropriately wholly object.

Attached and implanted devices are examples of the reverse of this process. These can be seen uncontroversially as beginning life as mere objects. Yet, as alluded to in Section 13.2, when they become physically incorporated into or integrated with the person, it may not be appropriate (ontologically, morally or legally speaking) to continue to treat them as mere objects. But neither might it suffice to view them entirely as 'part' of the subject. Both medical device and subject have a conjoined future. Thus, we suggest that integrated persons themselves can be seen as active subject-objects in a very literal sense.

### 13.4.2  Ambiguity and Navigating the In-Between

This transformation of the object – the medical device – or 'ubject', with its ontological and phenomenological ambiguity, mirrors the process of becoming and being an everyday cyborg. Gill Haddow argues that embodiment itself is ambiguous.[74] By this, she means that the extent to which individuals may experience their subjectivity – their sense of self – as both being and having a body is 'a dynamic and fluid process that becomes more or less important to everyday living depending on the circumstances that bring it to the fore'.[75] This description speaks to potential liminality in being and becoming cyborg. It also encompasses the potential ambivalence which persons can experience regarding this. Haddow's work highlights some of the factors influencing this altered, ambiguous and ambivalent experience. Such experiences speak to the

---

[72] Taylor-Alexander et al (n 28) 163.
[73] Ibid., 159–63.
[74] Haddow (n 24).
[75] Ibid., 12.

liminality which may occur (on multiple levels) when persons become conjoined with attached or implanted medical devices. Haddow has found that material matters in terms of feelings about (potential) implants. In a study of participants' reactions to replacement organs, a general preference was expressed for implants as close to one's own person as possible, ranking living donation and (hypothetical) bio-printed organs over mechanical alternatives and xenotransplantation.[76] Reactions to mechanical replacements reflected the participants' concep-tualisations of themselves as human; with some saying that they would 'feel less human' or 'I don't want to be a cyborg'; in contrast, others expressed a generally positive outlook with regards to the technology and placed trust in it.[77]

Often, in becoming an integrated person, the individual is contending with status and identity changes as a result of becoming ill or of no longer being an able-bodied person (and the new physical experience and psychological impact of this). Such changes have a social element with changes in perceptions of identity, including both how the individual views themselves and how others (or how they imagine others) view them. For example, Haddow and colleagues found that men recovering from prostate cancer perceived this particular cancer, and their own diagnosis, as stigmatised, viewing themselves as 'leakers and bleeders', something which formed a threat to their own masculinity.[78]

The location of an implanted device can also affect the recipient's perception of it. For instance, identity-constituting locations in the body (such as the brain or proximity to sexual organs) impact on the perceived risk of implanted devices.[79] This threat to identity (and health) seemed to motivate a willingness to become cyborg (in these cases, to be implanted with a biosensor) as a means of exerting positive control over one's health (and by implication identity) into the future.[80]

Yet, paradoxically, greater physiological integration of a device may represent a lessening of the integrated person's autonomy and control. This is because the device essentially functions in the background and

---

[76] Ibid., 6.

[77] Ibid., 9.

[78] See Gill Haddow et al, 'Cyborgs in the Everyday: Masculinity and Biosensing Prostate Cancer' (2015) 24 *Science as Culture* 484, 492.

[79] Shawn Harmon, Gill Haddow and Leah Gilman 'New Risks Inadequately Managed: The Case of Smart Implants and Medical Device Regulation' (2015) 7 *Law, Innovation and Technology* 231, 239.

[80] Haddow et al (n 78).

these functions are often unknowable to the person.[81] This is the case particularly in relation to devices such as ICDs, which act autonomously in the body delivering shocks in the case of adverse events. The implant is not controlled by the patient, but they are nevertheless aware (starkly and painfully so) of something having gone wrong when they receive a shock, something which can lead to increased anxiety despite the device working to keep them alive.[82] This lack of control may create the uncertainty, ambivalence and ambiguity characteristic of liminality. Moreover, an ongoing lack of control over device functioning may render integrated persons unable to transition out of liminality to a point of stability. This is not to say that integrated persons necessarily desire greater control over the functioning of such devices (although they might, as we will see presently). Indeed, their own lack of knowledge or inexperience on technical matters may be a factor in their trust in clinicians or the technology itself to do as it is designed.

The level of control which integrated persons might want over their devices will vary from person to person and may be dependent on their satisfaction with existing devices. This can be seen in growing biohacking movements. For example, dissatisfaction with the functioning of existing diabetes technologies has led to community-developed DIY artificial pancreas systems. Persons with diabetes developed open-source software which, when installed on a smartphone or small computer, allows their continuous glucose monitors and insulin pumps to 'speak' to each other. This enables real-time glucose monitoring and corresponding adjustments to the insulin delivered by the pumps.[83] However, the degree of knowledge and expertise which integrated persons have may influence their willingness to alter their embodiment and relationship with their devices. Not all patients will be able (for a variety of reasons) to make the transition to reliance on more technologically advanced devices/systems to manage their illnesses.

---

[81] Haddow, Harmon and Gilman (n 9) 210.

[82] Ibid., 222.

[83] Dana Lewis and her husband are key figures in the #WeAreNotWaiting movement and have gone on to become founders and collaborators on online platform OpenAps.org, which hosts the open-source software, and the community improving and adding to the code, which is required in hacking devices to create the 'closed loop' insulin delivery system, or artificial pancreas. See https://diyps.org/about/dana-lewis/ (accessed 4 February 2021). See also Joseph Roberts, Victoria Moore and Muireann Quigley, 'Patients Are Doing It for Themselves: DIY Artificial Pancreas Challenge for Doctors' (*Everyday Cyborgs Blog*, 9 March 2020) https://blog.bham.ac.uk/everydaycyborgs/2020/03/09/patients-are-doing-it-for-themselves/ (accessed 21 December 2020).

Our point is that the circumstances in which a person becomes integrated with a medical device, in addition to the characteristics of different types of device and perceptions of risk associated with these, can lead to varying and disparate impacts on a person's sense of self and experiences of (altered) embodiment. Hence, the process of becoming an integrated person or everyday cyborg can be regarded as paradigmatic of liminality. Integrated persons as beings in transition – from one state to another – can be said to occupy a liminal space (or, perhaps more accurately, multiple liminal spaces). What is more, we can view this liminality as paralleling the different modes of integration of devices with persons, which we set out in Section 13.2. As such, we suggest that the everyday cyborg may experience transformation – passing through the in-between – physically (as the devices alter their body and corporeality); functionally (due to mechanical, physiological and/or bio-regulatory alterations); psychologically (as they adjust to their new embodiment and any impact on their identity); and phenomenologically (due to potential changes in how the world is experienced).

The question remains, however, how should such transitions, transformations and the in-between be dealt with legally speaking? This is an important question. How these potentially ambiguous transformations are navigated and experienced may have a significant impact on how and whether integrated persons can complete their transition and reach an endpoint with regards to liminality. This endpoint occurs when a person can navigate out of the in-between state (which can be typified by uncertainty and anxiety).[84] This might occur, for example, with the person adjusting well to life as an everyday cyborg and accepting their attached or implanted medical device as part of a course of care, or something which facilitates a restoration of health. Yet this may not occur for all. There is a risk that some may get stuck in a phase of 'permanent liminality';[85] where individuals and/or their objects/ubjects (and their relationships with each other) may permanently 'go through the uncertainties of the in-between'.[86] As we will see in Section 13.5, this may occur, for example, where something goes wrong with integrated devices and implants resulting in physical (or other) harms to the everyday cyborg. We will also see that the response to such crises and how they are navigated can have proximate, enduring and adversely life-changing

---

[84] Laurie (n 7) 69.
[85] Ibid., 58.
[86] Taylor-Alexander et al (n 28) 160.

impacts for individuals. In short, the implications of mismanaged liminality can be calamitous.

### 13.5 Integrated Persons, Medical Devices and Processual Regulation?

Regulation of medical devices in the EU and the UK, as noted in Section 13.3, constructs and fixes medical devices as different kinds of regulatory object: risk objects, marketised objects and innovation objects. The Cumberlege Review brought systemic failures, including the siloed nature of regulatory institutions and failures in the regulatory framework itself, into sharp relief. In addition, it highlighted the general failure to listen to patients' (women's) voices and experiences. While regulatory failure, and thus the need for reform, is emphasised, the fundamental structuring around the bounded regulatory object of the medical device is not recognised. Yet our analysis suggests that the object-focus present in current regulation is problematic. It does not properly reflect the uncertainties, ambiguities or inherent liminality of either medical devices or everyday cyborgs.

Graeme is clear that while liminality provides a useful lens for analysing specific problems and issues, it cannot tell us what we should do in response.[87] His recommendation for HRR is that 'more attention should be paid to *process* and *transformation*'.[88] He distinguishes a *processual* approach to regulation and governance from mere processes[89] or procedural approaches,[90] instead drawing our attention to 'the dynamics and the (inter)actions of the actors engaged in processes'.[91] We can see this as a continuation and evolution of his work on reflexive governance. This earlier work set out a number of desirable features of good governance. These include: flexibility; learning from experience over time; integrity of purpose; proportionality and reflexivity in establishing governance mechanisms; and an emphasis on partnerships and the co-production of regulation (especially with research participants).[92] The more recent

---

[87] Laurie (n 7) 69.
[88] Ibid (emphasis in original).
[89] Graeme Laurie, 'What Does It Mean to Take an Ethics+ Approach to Global Biobank Governance?' (2017) 9 *Asian Bioethics Review* 285, 287.
[90] Ibid., 297.
[91] Ibid., 287.
[92] Graeme Laurie, 'Reflexive Governance in Biobanking: On the Value of Policy Lead Approaches and the Need to Recognise the Limits of Law' (2011) 130 *Human Genetics* 347, 349, 352; Laurie and Harmon (n 6) 131; and Laurie (n 89) 290, 296.

focus on the processual adds to this, emphasising in particular the experiences of subjects of research and their ongoing relationships with their biomaterials and data.[93]

With McMillan and colleagues, Graeme suggests that a processual approach to regulation is one which:

1. [a]cknowledges and articulates the often-enduring connection between subjects and objects;
2. [r]eflects the reality that fluidity can occur between the categories of subject and object in health research;
3. [r]ecognises the potential implications of these relationships for a subject/research participant's identity; and
4. [e]mbraces the view that health research needs to be seen holistically, as an endeavour that continues beyond the categorisation (subject, object, research, consent, etcetera) that HRR currently acknowledges.[94]

In practical terms, they argue that this requires a number of things including: more meaningful engagement of research participants in research processes; allowing subjects greater input on the direction of research; feedback to research participants on research findings and the uses of their materials and data; and greater recognition of subjects' ongoing connections to their excised materials and data in the form of opportunities for the co-production of regulation.[95]

In short, a processual approach 'requires a temporal-spatial examination of regulatory spaces and practices as these are experienced by all actors, including the relationship of actors with the objects of regulation'.[96] As we have already seen in this chapter, and will elaborate further in this section, the relationship of integrated persons with their medical devices – to wit, the objects of regulation – is not adequately considered or taken account of within the existing regulatory framework. Given this, we suggest that a Laurie-type processual approach could help us to navigate some of the ambiguities and difficulties which can arise when medical devices are attached to or integrated with persons. In particular, such an approach could aid with preventing and addressing crisis points regarding medical devices, where everyday cyborgs are unable to navigate 'the uncertainties of the in-between'.[97]

---

[93] Laurie (n 89) 290, 296; Taylor-Alexander et al (n 28) 175–6; and McMillan et al (n 15) 33.
[94] McMillan et al (n 15) 26.
[95] Ibid.
[96] Taylor-Alexander et al (n 28) 175.
[97] Ibid., 160.

Throughout the Cumberlege Review, the neglected narratives of those experiencing crises in health care are set out. In each case something has gone wrong, but no process was available properly to investigate or rectify this. For some, this meant being stuck in a phase of 'permanent liminality',[98] that is, stuck in a state of permanent crisis, ambiguity or uncertainty, and thus unable to complete their journey through a phase of transition or transformation.[99] We can see this in some of the descriptions set out in the Review:

> Many of those affected by the interventions under review have expressed their frustration at the lack of a clear pathway for them to make a complaint or raise concerns about aspects of their care.[100]
>
> Patients struggle to navigate the complaints system and it may take some time to find the correct organisation to complain to. All the while patients are still living with the complications that led to the original complaint, and may have had further upsetting experiences including surgeons dismissing their pain and other complications – patients described being 'broken' by this journey.[101]
>
> We have frequently heard in both our patient engagement events, and in direct communication from those affected that this Review has been the first time they felt able to tell their story to someone who would listen.[102]

With no adequate systems in place, some patients were left to experience decades of crisis, ambiguity and uncertainty relating to the interventions (including medical devices) which they had received. In being ignored and not listened to, they were unable to move beyond the transitional, liminal space in which they found themselves. There was no person or entity to which they could turn for guidance or counsel.

Had the infrastructure and practices for the kind of processual approach suggested by Graeme and colleagues been available, it is possible that the stories might have been different. When institutional and regulatory failures like those investigated by the Cumberlege Review occur, it is unlikely that those most affected will be able to transition out of crisis, and its attendant liminality, without adequate and appropriate systems being in place. In this respect, Graeme notes that 'the importance of rites of passage emerges as a means to manage transitions through liminal periods and spaces'.[103] Specifically, he says that a 'central

---

[98]  Laurie (n 7) 58.
[99]  Ibid.
[100]  Independent Medicines and Medical Devices Safety Review (n 52) para 2.40.
[101]  Ibid., para 2.41.
[102]  Ibid., para 2.42.
[103]  Laurie (n 7) 54.

feature of such processes is the role of an independent actor to guide those persons experiencing liminality through the liminal phase and out the other side'.[104] In this vein, we suggest that an independent patient safety commissioner (PSC) as recommended in the Cumberlege Review, and which has since been mandated in the form of the Commissioner for Patient Safety by the MMD Act, could potentially fulfil this role and facilitate a more processual approach with regards to the regulation of medical devices.[105] The PSC would, in Graeme's schema, fulfil the role of 'guide', helping to lead integrated persons – and perhaps parts of the wider health-care and regulatory systems – through periods of crisis and uncertainty and out the other side.[106] Ideally, it might even help prevent them in the first place.

In her letter to the Secretary of State at the beginning of the Review's report, Baroness Cumberlege outlines her vision for the PSC. They would be

> ... a person of standing who sits outside the healthcare system, account-able to Parliament through the Health and Social Care Select Committee. The Commissioner would be the patients' port of call, listener and advo-cate, who holds the system to account, monitors trends, encourages and requires the system to act. This person would be the golden thread, tying the disjointed system together in the interests of those who matter most.[107]

As thus described, a PSC could enable the kind of meaningful engage-ment required by a processual approach. Having a mechanism via which patients and patient groups can give feedback and make their concerns heard would give greater space to their voices and experiences. The very act of creating such a mechanism and means of being heard has benefits.

---

[104] Ibid.

[105] We note the recent paper by Victoria Moore, 'Regulating Patient Safety during Hospital Discharges: Casting the Patient Safety Commissioner as the Representative of Order' (forth-coming) *Medical Law International*, https://doi.org/10.1177%2F09685332211023531. In it, Moore also draws on Graeme's liminal spaces analysis and provides a detailed discussion of the potential for a PSC to fulfil the specific role of Representative of Order in liminal processes in hospital discharges. At 22-4, Moore argues, among other things, that a PSC could help guide and co-ordinate the multiple actors involved in the regulatory space of hospital discharges, and ensure that reports on patient safety in this context are not lost but are responded to and acted upon. In our analysis, we address how a PSC may help to meet some of the general elements of a processual approach outlined by Graeme and colleagues as but one measure of many that may be needed in such a processual approach.

[106] Laurie (n 7) 62.

[107] Independent Medicines and Medical Devices Safety Review (n 52) ii.

In and of itself, the creation of a PSC may help to guard against persons being stuck in a state of permanent liminality, unable to gain a resolution, when crisis points arise. In being a conduit for communications from the public in relation to concerns about medicines and medical devices, a PSC could serve a vital function in preventing patients from feeling as though they have been 'broken' by the system (health-care and regulatory). A PSC could be in a position to adopt more flexible, reflexive approaches which promote learning over time.[108] With principles such as these built in from the beginning, a PSC could, as envisaged by the Cumberlege Review, help to promote and improve patient safety. This would involve not only developing principles of better patient safety[109] but also setting out steps to be taken to improve it. This could safeguard against future crises, as well as have the potential more quickly to resolve any current ones. Perhaps most significantly for a processual approach, the creation of the role of PSC could become a means of co-producing regulation with regards to medical devices.

The MMD Act offered a timely opportunity to implement the Cumberlege Review's recommendations in respect of a PSC. During the Lords Committee Stage, Baroness Cumberlege herself tabled an amendment which would have mandated the establishment of this role,[110] but, at report stage, the government tabled its own version which is now in the Act.[111] While this is undoubtedly positive and a step in the right direction, the devil is in the detail. There is still much we do not know about the form that the PSC role (or Commissioner for Patient Safety as it is in the final wording of the Act) will take or how they will operate in practice. Crucial to their success will be ensuring that the role is properly resourced, in both monetary and staffing terms. As is apparent from the types of device listed at the beginning of Section 13.2, 'medical devices' covers broad ranges of categories. As such, it is likely that the scope of issues arising for any PSC would be correspondingly

---

[108] Laurie (n 89) and Laurie and Harmon (n 6).

[109] Independent Medicines and Medical Devices Safety Review (n 52) para 1.31.

[110] See the amendment tabled after clause 38 inserting a new clause 'Independent Patient Safety Commissioner' in HL Medicines and Medical Devices Bill 116-I Corrected Marshalled list for Grand Committee 30 https://publications.parliament.uk/pa/bills/lbill/58-01/116/5801116-I(Corrected).pdf (accessed 21 December 2020).

[111] See the amendment tabled before clause 1 inserting a new clause 'The Commissioner for Patient Safety' and before Schedule 1 inserting a new Schedule 'Further Provision about the Commissioner for Patient Safety' in HL Medicines and Medical Devices Bill 154 Running List of All Amendments on Report 1 https://publications.parliament.uk/pa/bills/lbill/58-01/154/5801154-RL.pdf (accessed 21 December 2020).

broad. Given that a PSC would also have responsibility for medicines and other aspects of patient safety, then, even with a team of people, questions of both proper resourcing and relevant expertise would arise. Both of these would need to be addressed in order to facilitate the kind of governance approach envisaged by Graeme.

The MMD Act could also have been an opportunity to tighten consultation duties in relation to the creation of any new medicines and medical devices regulations (something which the Review also recommended).[112] While the final Act does contain a duty to carry out a public consultation before any regulations are made under the main parts of the Act,[113] it does not specify *who* should be consulted or how extensive such consultations should be. If there is to be meaningful engagement with patients in relation to medicines and medical devices, then this gap needed to be addressed. An amendment to the Bill was tabled which would have partially addressed this gap.[114] However, it did not make it into the final Act.

Despite some of the positive changes facilitated by both the Cumberlege Review and the MMD Act, questions remain about how a more processual type of regulation in relation to persons and medical devices could be realised. Even if the amendments to the MMD Bill had been successful in tightening up duties of consultation, this is no guarantee that the government would act faithfully on any findings from such consultations. Similarly, without concurrent powers of enforcement, there are no guarantees that a PSC will be able to make changes which they deem necessary. Moreover, we should not forget about the powerful role of industry in shaping the current regulatory landscape with respect to medical devices. There are no legal duties for manufacturers to consult or include patients or would-be integrated persons in their processes. The current regulatory framework relies upon commercially set up 'approved bodies' (previously known as 'notified bodies') to assess and grant market authorisations for devices, and thus relies to a large degree on industry self-regulation.[115] What is more, as noted in the Cumberlege Review

---

[112] The PSC is envisaged to be under a duty to consult with patients and patient groups as part of wider powers and functions relating to research and review; see Independent Medicines and Medical Devices Safety Review (n 52) appx 2 para 32.

[113] S 45.

[114] See the amendments tabled to clause 41 in HL Medicines and Medical Devices Bill 116-I Corrected Marshalled list for Grand Committee 35 https://publications.parliament.uk/pa/bills/lbill/58-01/116/5801116-I(Corrected).pdf (accessed 21 December 2020).

[115] Part V Medical Device Regulations 2002 currently set out the conditions and designation of notified bodies in the UK. Independent Medicines and Medical Devices Safety Review

report, '[a]t present the MHRA [Medicines and Health products Regulatory Agency] has no involvement in the pre-market phase of medical device development'.[116] This, coupled with the fact, noted in the Report, that there is a high degree of regulatory capture by industry at the MHRA,[117] means that there is little to compel industry to take appropriate account of patient voices and experiences or to involve them in co-producing its (self-)regulatory processes (except where this might appeal to their own market interests).

For these reasons, it might be the case that a more reflexive, processual approach cannot stand on its own, and that there is a need to recognise that aspects of the underlying legal framework are in need of reform if such approaches are to work in practice. Graeme has previously argued, albeit specifically in relation to biobanks, that the point of reflexive (and we might add processual) governance is to be a means of improving the learning of systems, and that recourse to law and enforcement would itself be a sign that the systems in place had failed.[118] However, given the marketised nature of the medical devices sector and regulatory framework, without a compelling legal duty to engage in processual regulation (and to treat it seriously) there is a danger that neither existing regulatory actors nor industry will engage. While there may be some scope within the current system to move further towards the ideal of a processual approach, political and commercial realities potentially mean that a firmer line is required. And this is something which may necessitate a restructuring and rethinking of the extant regulatory framework as it relates to medical devices.

Outlining the exact contours of such restructuring and reform, along with any attendant pitfalls and negative consequences, is a task for another day (and years in order to think it through); as such, we do not make any detailed suggestions here beyond what has already been said. What we have hopefully done, however, is to contribute to the analytical work which must necessarily precede change. Put simply, we must first recognise and analyse the challenges and difficulties inherent in law's fixed boundaries and binaries before we can think about dismantling and

---

(n 52) para 2.60 also recommends the overhaul of the Medicines and Healthcare Products Regulatory Agency (MHRA) to ensure that patients' interests are prioritised over business interests, a recommendation sparked by concerns of a revolving door between industry and staffing of the MHRA.

[116] Independent Medicines and Medical Devices Safety Review (n 52) para 1.45.

[117] Ibid., paras 2.59–2.60.

[118] Laurie (n 92) 354.

moving past them. But engaging in the analytical process in order to do this is an important and necessary step towards more reflexive, responsive (and potentially more radical) regulation of the type envisaged by Graeme.

## 13.6  Concluding Thoughts

Previously, Graeme observed that law can be a blunt tool,[119] offering neither reassurances nor guarantees that the broader range of persons' interests is recognised or promoted. With regards to integrated persons, in this chapter we have found this to be the case in both doctrine and implementation. At the level of doctrine, we have seen that there is a fundamental mismatch between the structure of the law and its everyday operation, on the one hand, and the complexities of the assemblage of persons and medical devices, on the other. As particularly tangible, concrete and literal instantiations of 'active subject-objects', integrated persons trouble boundaries and binaries (be they ontological, moral or legal) in profound ways. In being overtly and overly object-focused, the current regulatory framework in relation to medical devices fails to recognise and appropriately deal with this. Consequently, as the details in the Cumberlege Review exemplify, not only does the regulatory system not acknowledge or take account of broader complexities relating, for instance, to the everyday cyborg's altered embodiment and identity but it has failed even to protect persons' narrowly construed interests with respect to safety.

We saw that many of the difficulties, in line with Graeme's findings in the HRR sphere, rest on the siloed and object-focused nature of both health-care and regulatory systems and institutions. Along with McMillan and colleagues, Graeme contends that '[i]n today's world, where lines between common legal categories are increasingly blurred (especially "person" and "thing"), and a plethora of technological development is taking place (much faster than law and regulation can keep up with), processual regulation as an adaptive framework can help us to tackle these relatively new challenges in law and society'.[120] With regards to persons and medical devices, we hope that the arguments in this chapter show that we generally agree. We agree wholeheartedly that the lines between legal categories are becoming (or, at the very least, ought to

---

[119]  Laurie and Harmon (n 6) 132; Laurie (n 6) 191.
[120]  McMillan et al (n 15) 27.

be becoming) increasingly blurred. In the case of persons and medical devices, this is partially because the ontological lines between persons as subjects and medical devices as objects are blurring as technology advances.[121] We also agree that liminality can be a useful 'lens that helps us more closely to interrogate the spaces *between* conventional legal spaces'.[122] By applying Graeme's analysis to the assemblage of persons and medical devices, the inherent liminality of both everyday cyborgs and their technologies was revealed. When a person receives an attached or implanted medical device, both object and person can go through transitions and transformations. We saw that, in this respect, the everyday cyborg may occupy multiple liminal spaces, passing through the in-between physically, functionally, psychologically and phenomenologically.

We also saw that a liminal analysis can help us to better understand crisis points, where harms occur and integrated persons become stuck in the in-between, unable to transition to a point of stability. This risk of permanent liminality is well-illustrated by the findings from the Cumberlege Review, which highlight abject failures to take seriously either patient voices or experiences. As a result, decades of opportunities to prevent further harms and crises were missed. We explored whether a more processual type of regulation, of the kind favoured by Graeme, might help to avoid these failures in the future. It is here that a hint of caution creeps in. It is clear that adequate systems (health-care and regulatory) were not in place to deal with the various failures (lack of information, no complaints systems, not being believed regarding harms, and so on) and we suggested that a more processual approach could have helped to mitigate some of this. A flexible, reflexive system which is open to learning is more likely to be able to resolve crises as they arise and prevent future ones from occurring. In this respect, we explored whether a 'guide' in the form of a PSC could facilitate this. In principle, a PSC could do a lot to enable a more processual approach, but this all depends on implementation and, potentially, enforcement.

It also does not change the fact that if the underlying legal and regulatory framework and principles are in need of reform, we are going to encounter ongoing difficulties in relation to the joining of persons and medical devices. To move forward, we may need to recognise, as McMillan argues we should, that sometimes law itself can be

---

[121] Quigley (n 12) 251–5.
[122] McMillan et al (n 15) 27.

liminal, that 'static, unchanging regulation ... is a form of permanent liminality'.[123] The fixing of medical devices as different kinds of regulatory object in part occurs because the law – or, at least, the normative framework within which it is made and operationalised – has become fixed. This fixing is an encumbrance which keeps boundaries and binaries in place. As we have shown throughout this chapter, this legal legacy can have significant consequences. It can result in both persons and devices existing within a 'regulatory purgatory'[124] which is inadequate to address the challenges wrought by sociotechnological change. What is clear is that both Graeme's liminal analysis of law and his framework for processual regulation offer us a different and potentially fruitful vision of persons, bodies and devices with which to examine the relevant regulatory and governance architecture. As such, part of Graeme's legacy has been to give us a much-needed analytical apparatus with which to begin to look beyond boundaries, beyond binaries and 'beyond bodies'.[125]

---

[123] McMillan (n 71) ch. 5, section 3.4.

[124] Ibid.

[125] The exhortation to go beyond the strictures of usual legal, regulatory and academic constraints and enquiry is a thread which runs through a lot of Graeme's work. 'Beyond bodies' is a nod to one of the research themes of Edinburgh's Centre for Biomedicine, Self and Society, which Graeme was part of setting up.

# 14

# UK Biobank and the Legal Regulation of Genetic Research

## Preserving the Legacy and Empowering Future Regulation

JEAN V. MCHALE

## 14.1 Introduction

In 2003, UK Biobank, the huge genetic database created with funding from Wellcome, the Medical Research Council and the Department of Health, established an Interim Ethics and Governance Group (IEAG) to develop its ethical framework, which was subsequently taken forward by the UK Biobank's Ethics and Governance Council (EGC). This approach of creating an ethical framework for a distinct research initiative, interpreted by a specially appointed body with the ability to hold the researchers and funders to account, could itself be seen as innovative but also (as we see in Chapters 9 and 10 of this volume) as a legacy of the era in which trust in medicine had been shaken by organ retention scandals and there were notable concerns over the potential implications for use of genetic material and data in the light of the sequencing of the human genome. Graeme Laurie played a critically important part in developing and implementing that framework as both a member of the IEAG and also subsequently a chair of the EGC itself. The UK Biobank developments were hugely influential both nationally and internationally in contributing to the debate as to how such genetic databases should be operated.[1] Yet, in 2018, the EGC was, without noticeable fanfare, disbanded as a separate organisation at arm's length from UK Biobank. It has since been replaced by a new UK Biobank Ethics Advisory Committee (EAC), with its chair becoming a member of the board of UK Biobank.

---

[1] See generally Mark Stranger and Jane Kaye, *Principles and Practice in Biobank Governance* (Routledge 2009).

What is, and will be, the long-term legacy of UK Biobank's EGC? This chapter will begin by exploring how the legacy of the scandals, controversies and legal uncertainties over regulation of the use of tissue and data in an era of increasing potential for use of genetic information formed the backdrop to the creation of the UK Biobank's EGC. The second part of the chapter will explore the EGC's establishment and operation, its innovative actions and also some of the regulatory challenges it faced. Finally, the chapter will explore what is now and what will be in the future the legacy left by the EGC. It asks how that legacy can be preserved and used to empower future regulation both domestically and globally.

## 14.2   The Legacy of Scientific Innovation, Scandal and Uncertainties

The backdrop to the regulation of genetic databases can be seen as rooted in the events of the preceding decade. The 1990s were notable for the rise of genetics and genomics. The sequencing of the human genome was a scientific milestone which led to governments and the scientific community globally seeing the need to map the future.[2] The use of genetic information provided new opportunities for research. The advantages of collection (and use) of genetic material and information for research purposes in a genetic database became recognised. From the late 1990s onwards, a number of notable genetic databases were established, such as the Avon Longitudinal Study of Children and Parents (ALSPAC), more commonly known as the Children of the 1990s study.[3] In Iceland, the major deCODE Iceland Health Sector Database was created.[4] Given these developments, it was not surprising that in the UK there was a willingness to take forward biobanks at national level; so, for example, in 1999, the House of Lords Select Committee adopted the approach taken by George Poste, the then Chief Scientific Officer of GlaxoSmithKline,

---

[2] John Venter et al, 'The Sequence of the Human Genome' (2001) 291 *Science* 1306.

[3] ALSPAC www.bristol.ac.uk/alspac/ (accessed 20 February 2021).

[4] Hróbjartur Jónatansson, 'Iceland's Health Sector Database: A Significant Head Start in the Search for the Biological Grail or an Irreversible Error?' (2000) 26 *American Journal of Law and Medicine* 31; Jeffrey Gulcher and Kári Stephansson, 'The Icelandic Healthcare Database and Informed Consent' (2000) 342 *New England Journal of Medicine* 1827; and Graeme Laurie, *Genetic Privacy* (Cambridge University Press 2002) 287–93.

for the creation of an NHS population biobank.[5] The UK government itself committed to UK Biobank in the NHS Plan in 2000.[6] The NHS saw the development of UK Biobank as effectively a case study for a national genetic database.[7] However, right from the outset, concerns were raised. In 1999, in evidence to the House of Lords Science and Technology Committee, the Department of Health indicated that there were various issues raised by a large-scale biobank:

- [I]s the use of personal health information in [a] large[-]scale database justified by the potential research and treatment benefits?
- [S]hould data be anonymised?
- [S]hould explicit consent from an individual be required before entering information on a database, even if the data are anonymised?
- [W]hat safeguards or legal controls should be required to protect confidentiality, consent and use?[8]

As we shall see below, what is striking is that more than twenty years on, these are issues which still remain the subject of considerable discussion and debate.

While this was an era of considerable excitement about the potential of genetic research, there was, at the same time, a diminishing level of trust in medical research – fuelled by scandal. At the time when UK Biobank was envisaged, the use and the retention of human material were a matter of acute controversy due to the major inquiry reports regarding the unauthorised retention of human material at Bristol Royal Infirmary[9] and the Royal Liverpool Children's Hospital (commonly known as Alder Hey Hospital).[10]

---

[5] See further Robin Fears and George Poste, 'Building Population Genetics Resources Using the UK NHS' (1999) *Science* 284; and the extensive discussion on the background to UK Biobank in Genewatch UK, 'Bioscience for Life Appendix A: The History of UK Biobank, Electronic Medical Records in the NHS, and the Proposal for Data-Sharing without Consent' (2009) www.genewatch.org/uploads/f03c6d66a9b354535738483c1c3d49e4/UK_Biobank_fin_2.pdf (accessed 20 February 2021).

[6] NHS, 'The NHS Plan' (CM 4818-I, 1 July 2000) https://dera.ioe.ac.uk/4423/1/04055783 .pdf (accessed 20 February 2021).

[7] See Genewatch (n 5).

[8] Memorandum by the Department of Health, 'Genetic Databases' (*Select Committee on Science and Technology* 2nd Report, Session 1999–2000) discussed in Genewatch (n 5) www.publications.parliament.uk/pa/ld199900/ldselect/ldsctech/11/1101.htm (accessed 20 February 2021).

[9] See further Jean McHale, 'The Human Tissue Act 2004: Innovative Legislation – Fundamentally Flawed or Missed Opportunity?' (2005) 26 *Liverpool Law Review* 169.

[10] For a full report into the extent of the unauthorised holdings of human material, see House of Commons, The Royal Liverpool Children's Inquiry Report (30 January 2001) https://assets.publishing.service.gov.uk/government/uploads/system/uploads/attach

These Reports formed the basis for the eventual reform of the law premised on consent for use of human material for treatment and research in the form of the Human Tissue Act 2004 in England, Northern Ireland and Wales.[11] This was a consent-based law with provision for criminal penalties for infringement of its provisions and the creation of an oversight body in the form of the Human Tissue Authority.[12] But although the Act was rooted in the principle of 'appropriate consent', what this precisely meant was not defined in the legislation. Those operating biobanks were also faced with the piecemeal nature of the legal regulation of health research.[13] Although there are some specific statutory provisions in relation to certain areas,[14] the application of law in this area must otherwise be ascertained by analogy to general principles of criminal and civil law. It was not until 2011 that a national oversight body for research in the form of the Health Research Authority was established, initially as a special health authority,[15] and subsequently placed on a statutory footing under the Care Act 2014.[16]

A further notable issue left unresolved by the Human Tissue Act 2004 was the acutely controversial question of property in human material. While there are no property rights in the human cadaver itself,[17] in contrast, excised human material may constitute property.[18] There

---

ment_data/file/250934/0012_ii.pdf (accessed 20 February 2021). There were also a number of further specific inquiries concerning organ retention: Department of Health, *Isaacs Report: The Investigation of the Events that Followed the Death of Cyril Mark Isaacs* (TSO 2003); Scottish Executive, 'Final Report of the Independent Review on the Retention of Organs at Post Mortem' (*Scottish Executive* 2002) www .sehd.scot.nhs.uk/scotorgrev/Final%20Report/ropm-01.htm (accessed 20 February 2021). It should also be noted that such controversies were not confined to the UK: see, for example, David Jones, *Speaking for the Dead: Cadavers in Biology and Medicine* (Ashgate 2000) regarding the New Zealand position.

[11] Stephen Pinnock, 'Human Tissue Bill Could Jeopardise Research, Scientists Warn' (2004) 328 *British Medical Journal* 1034; Kathleen Liddell and Alison Hall, 'Beyond Bristol and Alder Hey: The Future Regulation of Human Tissue' (2005) 13 *Medical Law Review* 170.

[12] Human Tissue Act 2004, s 13 and sch 2.

[13] See also *Yearworth and others v. North Bristol NHS Trust* [2009] EWCA Civ 37.

[14] For example, under the Medicines for Human Use (Clinical Trials Regulations) 2004 and the Mental Capacity Act 2005.

[15] Health Research Authority (Establishment and Constitution) Order 2011 (SI 2011/2323); Health Research Authority Regulations 2011 (SI 2011/2341).

[16] Care Act 2014, ss 109–117.

[17] See Paul Matthews, 'Whose Body; People as Property' (1983) 36 *Current Legal Problems* 195; Peter Skegg, 'Human Corpses, Medical Specimens and the Law of Property' (1976) *Anglo-American Law Review* 412.

[18] *R v. Kelly* [1999] QB 621; Andrew Grubb, 'Theft of Body Parts; Property and Dead Bodies' (1998) 6 *Medical Law Review* 247; *Yearworth v. North Bristol NHS Trust* (2009) EWCA Civ 37; Muireann Quigley, 'Property: The Future of Human Tissue' (2009) 17 *Medical*

have been concerns over time as to the consequences of individuals whose human material had been used for scientific exploitation subsequently bringing actions in the tort of conversion.[19] Were an individual to bring a property law action arguing that their genetic material stored in a biobank had been used for purposes which went beyond the scope of an original consent for use, this could result not only in considerable financial loss but also in large-scale reputational damage to any biobank involved in such litigation and, by extension, to its funders. Furthermore, there were questions regarding the extent to which the development of such biobanks could be seen as compatible with fundamental principles of human rights.[20] Such uncertainties provided a complex backdrop for any ethics and governance body to operate within.

## 14.3   UK Biobank: Ethics and Governance

UK Biobank was established in 2005.[21] It was funded by two main national bodies involved in funding research, the Medical Research Council and Wellcome, and also by the Department of Health. The intention was to create a large-scale database which would form the basis for extensive epidemiological research. It enrolled 500,000 participants ranging in age from 40 to 69 years, with the aim of tracking them for a period eventually extended to 30 years.[22] There was controversy regarding its establishment; some questioned whether it was

Law Review 457. See also the discussion in Rohan Hardcastle, *Law and the Human Body: Property Rights, Ownership and Control* (Hart 2007) and Muireann Quigley, *Self-Ownership, Property Rights, and the Human Body: A Legal and Philosophical Analysis* (Cambridge University Press 2018).

[19] *Moore v. University of California* (1990) 793 P 2d 479; see generally Bernard Dickens, 'Living Tissue and Organ Donors and Property Law: More on Moore' (1992) *Journal of Contemporary Health Law and Policy* 73.

[20] For an early discussion of the interface between human rights and biobanks in a report of a Working Group (which Graeme convened), see Graeme Laurie et al, 'Genetic Databases; Access to the Benefits and the Implications on Humans and Patients' Rights – A WHO Report' (2003) 11 *European Journal of Health Law* 87.

[21] For a fascinating examination of the background to the establishment of UK Biobank drawn from sources including interviews with those involved in the process, see Mairi Langan, 'A Contemporary History of the Origins and Development of UK Biobank 1998–2005' (PhD thesis, University of Glasgow 2007) http://theses.gla.ac.uk/104/ (accessed 20 February 2021).

[22] Pallab Ghosh, 'Will Biobank Pay Off?' (*BBC News,* 24 September 2003) http://news .bbc.co.uk/1/hi/health/3134622.stm (accessed 21 February 2021). Roger Highfield, '£62 Million Biobank May Not Be Worth It, Says Professor' (*Daily Telegraph,* 15 September

scientifically valid and some viewed it as politically motivated; in contrast, others saw it having the potential to produce a hugely valuable resource.[23]

UK Biobank was established as a charitable company. It is run by the board of the Biobank company, which includes representatives from funders and academic institutions that host the Biobank. The project has a Steering Committee whose members 'provide expert knowledge on how UK Biobank might best achieve its aims to enhance the resource through detailed, accurate data collection'.[24] It is also supported by an International Scientific Advisory Board, providing advice on 'UK Biobank's scientific direction, strategy, operations and the furtherance of its scientific mission'.[25]

From the outset, it was intended that the Biobank's resources would be available to a range of users, from both academic and commercial organisations.[26] The safeguards were, first, that information used was to be anonymised and, second, that researchers would be required to obtain approval for the research from a specifically designated Multi-Centred Research Ethics Committee. Biobank raised considerable ethical questions, including those concerning consent, use of information generated through research and feedback of findings. The funders were very aware of this and were concerned to ensure that the project was subject to ethical oversight. They initially established the IEAG – as noted in Section 14.1 and which was chaired by Dr William Lowrance, a consultant in health research ethics and policy – to develop an ethical framework for the Biobank.[27] Graeme was one of the members of this

2004) www.telegraph.co.uk/news/uknews/3310025/62m-Biobank-may-not-be-worth-it-says-professor.html (accessed 20 February 2021).

[23] See further Virginia Barbour, 'UK Biobank: A Project in Search of a Protocol' (2003) 361 *The Lancet* 1734; House of Commons Science and Technology Committee Report, The Work of the Medical Research Council, Third Report of Session 2002–03, HC 132; and Helen Wallace, 'The Need for Independent Scientific Peer Review of Biobank UK' (2002) 359 *The Lancet* 2282.

[24] www.ukbiobank.ac.uk/learn-more-about-uk-biobank/governance/steering-committee (accessed 20 February 2021).

[25] www.ukbiobank.ac.uk/learn-more-about-uk-biobank/governance/international-scien tific-advisory-board (accessed 20 February 2021).

[26] Naomi E Allen, Cathie Sudlow, Tim Peakman, Rory Collins and on behalf of UK Biobank, 'UK Biobank Data: Come and Get It!' (2014) 6(224) *Science Translational Medicine* 224ed4.

[27] Dr William Lowrance had previously developed a report for the Nuffield Trust, *Learning from Experience: Privacy and the Secondary Use of Data in Health Research* (Nuffield Trust 2002) www.nuffieldtrust.org.uk/research/learning-from-experience-privacy-and-the-secondary-use-of-data-in-health-research (accessed 20 February 2021).

group, as was the author of this chapter.[28] The resulting Ethics and Governance Framework (the 'Framework') sets out the principles within which the Biobank would operate.[29] A review of the Framework in 2015 suggested that it 'may be seen as a living constitution for the UK Biobank project and as such is central to the functioning and legitimacy of the EGC and the UK Biobank project'.[30] It sets out the relationship with participants, with research users and with society. The relationship with participants is seen in terms of initial recruitment, consent and confidentiality. That with research users addresses stewardship of data and samples as well as research access to data and samples. Finally, that with society is concerned with issues including the management and accountability of the Biobank, its external governance and benefit sharing.

The EGC was deliberately established as a body acting at arm's length from the funders. Members, including its chair, were appointed under the Nolan principles. It was to be the guardian of the Framework, providing monitoring and advice on the extent to which the UK Biobank Project conformed to it.[31] It also had a more general role to advise on the role of the interests of research participants and the general public regarding UK Biobank. The first chair of the Committee was Professor Alastair Campbell, a bioethicist. He was followed by Graeme from 1 September 2006.[32] Graeme himself was succeeded by Professor Roger Brownsword, a law professor at Kings College London, from 20 January 2011.[33] The final chair (from December 2015) was Baroness

---

[28] The Interim Advisory Group membership was Dr William Lowrance (Chair), Professor Alastair Campbell, Professor Erica Haimes, Dr Graeme Laurie, Professor Chris Mathew, Professor Jean McHale, Mrs Helen Millar, Baroness O'Neill of Bengarve and Mrs Madeleine Wan.

[29] See further 'UK Biobank Ethics and Governance Framework: Summary of Comments on Version 1.0' (Wellcome Trust, 2004) https://wellcome.org/sites/default/files/wtd003285 .pdf (accessed 20 February 2021).

[30] https://egcukbiobank.org.uk/meetingsandreportsc575.html?page=6 (accessed 20 February 2021).

[31] Adrienne Hunt, Martin Richards and Graeme Laurie, 'UK Biobank EGC: An Exercise in Added Value' in Jane Kaye and Mark Stranger (eds), *Principles and Practice in Biobank Governance* (Ashgate 2009) 229.

[32] UK Biobank EGC, 'Ninth Meeting' (25 September 2006) https://egcukbiobank.org.uk/sites/ default/files/meetings/EGC9%20agenda%20and%20report.pdf (accessed 20 February 2021).

[33] UK Biobank EGC, 'Twenty-Fifth Meeting' (6 December 2010) https://egcukbiobank .org.uk/sites/default/files/meetings/EGC25%20agenda%20and%20report.pdf (accessed 20 February 2021).

Helene Hayman, who had previously been a chair of the Human Tissue Authority and of Cancer Research UK.[34]

What was the EGC's role in practice? We have seen how it developed ethics policy and advice, but to what extent did its role extend beyond this? The very name 'EGC' is important. It was not simply a 'committee' or some form of advisory meeting. The Council discussed the nature of its role at its meeting of 1 November 2007:

> The Council discussed the use of the words 'guardian' and 'watchdog' as a means of conveying the EGC's role. The word 'watchdog' was felt to be misleading as it may suggest the Council has powers above and beyond its advisory and monitoring role. The word 'guardian', as appears in the EGC's remit, was favoured as this draws on the role of the EGC as the overseer of the project and suggests a flexible role which can respond to the changing environment in which UK Biobank and the EGC operate.[35]

Nonetheless, its function was to persuade; it had no power to enforce. Instead, the only 'sanctions' available to members of the ECG were those of either resignation or (and related to this) going public in the press and media generally as to their concerns. The creation of ad hoc bioethics committees with no clear powers can be seen as problematic if relationships with funders prove problematic. The resignation/publicity approach can simply be seen as a 'nuclear option' which could destroy entirely public confidence in the Biobank.[36] This in turn could mean that participants withdraw en masse, with the consequent collapse of the project. Without some sanctions, an ECG could be said to be a 'toothless tiger'. The issue of independence is critical here. The EGC was in existence due to the determination of the funders. Its power was ultimately drawn from those who themselves were not wholly detached from the Biobank project. On the other hand, it could be argued that an effective ethics and governance process would be possible through trust and co-operation on both sides. Here, I explore this in relation to aspects of its role in relation to consent and feedback, as well as its Access and IP Policy. The discussion draws upon the papers produced by the EGC and

---

[34] https://wellcome.ac.uk/news/new-appointments-uk-biobank-ethics-and-governance-council (accessed 20 February 2021).

[35] UK Biobank EGC, 'Thirteenth Meeting' (1 November 2007) https://egcukbiobank.org.uk /sites/default/files/meetings/EGC13%20agenda%20and%20report.pdf (accessed 20 February 2021).

[36] Jean McHale, 'Accountability, Governance and Biobanks: The Ethics Committee as Guardian or as Toothless Tiger' (2011) 19 *Health Care Analysis* 231.

the minutes of the meetings of the EGC made publicly available on its website.[37]

## 14.4   UK Biobank and Consent

A major practical question for any database involving long-term storage of personal data and samples is the question of consent. In a standard research project, the consent process concerns one-off consent to participation in a specific project, the information consequently generated to be used for a purpose defined in advance. In contrast, a situation where information and material are held in a database, and where information and/or future access to the participants whose material is in the database is sought by a range of researchers, is far more challenging. One approach is that of 'broad consent'.[38] Here, rather than consenting to a particular use, individuals give consent to their materials/data being stored in the biobank itself. There is then the assumption that subsequent uses of that material/data will be justifiable without the need to return to the participant each time for their approval. Moreover, participants may view themselves as having 'donated' their material and data to the biobank. The language of gift was used in the early days in relation to UK Biobank. When launching the project in September 2003, Professor John Newton, the UK Biobank Chief Executive, noted that '[t]he participants are saying [] yes we would like to support this project in the nature of a gift to biomedical science'.[39] Participation in such long-term genetic research was viewed in terms of social solidarity and a duty to help others.[40] Broad consent can also be seen as a pragmatic solution when dealing with the prospect of re-contacting many individuals for specific consent in relation to a wide range of research projects who may in turn see such re-contact as an inconvenience.

An alternative is that of 'specific consent'. Specific consent for each subsequent use can be seen as being aligned with respect for fundamental human rights, by respecting an individual's right to privacy through

---

[37] UK Biobank Ethics and Governance Council, https://egcukbiobank.org.uk/ (accessed 20 February 2021).

[38] See further Margaret Otlowski, 'Developing an Appropriate Consent Model for Biobanks: In Defence of "Broad" Consent' in Kaye and Stranger (n 31).

[39] Tim Radford, 'Gene Study Will Provide 30 Years of Human Data', *The Guardian* (24 September 2003) www.theguardian.com/uk/2003/sep/24/research.genetics (accessed 5 March 2021).

[40] Ruth Chadwick and Kåre Berg, 'Solidarity and Equity: New Ethical Frameworks for Genetic Databases' (2001) 2 *Nature Reviews Genetics* 318.

promoting their decision-making autonomy. It also recognises that, in
relation to a genetic database, a person's views as to what forms of
scientific research are legitimate may change over time. It has been
suggested that privacy concerns in relation to use of tissue and data can
be addressed through anonymisation.[41] However, while anonymisation
may mean that some privacy concerns consequent upon a person's
identity are removed, it does not address the element of privacy concerned with autonomous *control* over personal data. An individual may
be perfectly happy for their material to be used for one specific project,
such as for NHS research, but may not be happy for their personal data
and related genetic data to be used in a project which involves commercial exploitation by a pharmaceutical company.[42] In the original consultation exercises regarding UK Biobank, there was considerable support
for ongoing consent:

> Ongoing consent was considered essential due to uncertainty both about
> the precise uses of the resource and the frequency of recontact / level of
> inconvenience encountered by participants. While some members of the
> public were willing to place their faith in the project to protect their best
> interests, others (including several stakeholders) believed it would be
> important to seek re-consent for future uses of the resource (e.g. that
> individuals should be given the opportunity to opt out of individual
> studies or to consent to batches of studies).[43]

However, the Framework produced by the IEAG and subsequently
adopted by UK Biobank followed the model of broad consent. It can be
argued that this choice was not unduly problematic as UK Biobank did
give participants a right to withdraw from participation. But a real right
to withdraw depends on participants themselves being very aware of the
detail of the research which has been undertaken by UK Biobank and by
those allowed to use the research resource.[44]

The Framework provided:

> Consent will be sought 'to participate in UK Biobank'. Participation will
> be cast as an opportunity to contribute information that in the long term

---

[41] See *R v. Source Informatics Limited* [2000] 1 All ER 786; see, for example, discussion in
Deryck Beyleveld and Elise Histed, 'Betrayal of Confidence in the Court of Appeal' (2000)
4 *Medical Law International* 277.

[42] Human Genetics Commission, 'Inside Information: Balancing Interests in the Use of
Personal Genetic Data' (HGC 2002).

[43] 'Summary of the UK Biobank Consultation on the Ethics & Governance Framework'
(Opinion Leader Research, August 2003).

[44] See Laurie (n 4) 312 regarding the impact of a right to withdraw.

may help enhance other people's health. Because it will be impossible to anticipate all future research uses, strong governance and safeguards will be in place to protect participants interests and the public interest.[45]

Note here the emphasis placed upon strong governance safeguards; the role of the EGC as an independent body could be seen as critical. The need for clarity in consent from the outset, and the participants needing to be aware of the range of potential uses and indeed the limits of their 'rights', was something which emerged in the discussions over the development of consent forms for participants.[46] Originally, when consenting, participants were given the right to withdraw from the project and were told that their data would be destroyed. However, it was reported in 2007 that, in fact, it was 'not possible for UK Biobank to destroy all of a participant's data due to the project's back-up and audit system'.[47] The EGC was asked for its advice on this issue and discussion with Professor Collins from UK Biobank confirmed that 'UK Biobank can still guarantee the main principle behind this option i.e. that there will be no further use of the data by researchers.'[48] Ultimately, it was decided that the information provided would be amended to ensure that participants were informed as to important developments with the project, including changes in process.

Questions as to the scope and nature of consent, and the need to ensure that participants remain engaged and informed, were a recurring theme in the work of the EGC. So, for example, in the 2016–17 report of the EGC, it was noted that 'we are aware from UK Biobank participant events that one of the most common questions is what's my data being used for'.[49] Moreover, what material was recognised as being included within a person's data was by no means straightforward. For instance, there was debate regarding whether tumour tissue from persons who were part of

---

[45] UK Biobank, Ethics and Governance Framework, v. 2003, ibid., section I.A.1. cited in Jean McHale, 'Regulating Genetic Databases: Some Legal and Ethical Issues' (2004) 12 *Medical Law Review* 70, 86.

[46] See, for example, in relation to adding the word 'commercial' to documents providing information regarding consent, UK Biobank EGC, 'Eighth Meeting' (12 June 2006) https://egcukbiobank.org.uk/sites/default/files/meetings/EGC8%20agenda%20and%20report.pdf (accessed 20 February 2021).

[47] UK Biobank EGC, 'Twelfth Meeting' (12 June 2007) https://egcukbiobank.org.uk/sites/default/files/meetings/EGC12%20agenda%20and%20report.pdf (accessed 20 February 2021).

[48] UK Biobank EGC, 'Annual Review 2007' (2007) https://egcukbiobank.org.uk/sites/default/files/meetings/EGC%20annual%20review%202007.pdf (accessed 20 February 2021).

[49] UK Biobank EGC, 'Review 2016–17' (2017) 10 https://egcukbiobank.org.uk/sites/default/files/UKBEGC_Review2016_2017.pdf (accessed 20 February 2021).

UK Biobank could be accessed and used as part of a participant's health record.[50] What is apparent is the need for accountability of a biobank if issues arise, as here in relation to the reality of consent and its withdrawal. The need for continuing oversight of the consent process, particularly as the project continues and new issues arise, can be seen as critical; and a flexible ethics and governance process, with a body such as the EGC, can be seen as one which can facilitate it. Such issues are likely to be ongoing: for example, the consequences of reusing material once participants lack capacity.

## 14.5    Feedback of Findings

While individuals may have agreed to sign over the use of their samples and data, did this also mean that should any clinically relevant findings personal to them arise from the project, these should be passed to them? On the one hand, it could be seen as clinically advantageous if information emerged in relation to an individual's health which could lead them to seek treatment. If research findings uncovered issues which were potentially detrimental or indeed clearly harmful to the health of the research participant, UK Biobank itself might be seen to have a duty of care to participants to disclose information revealed during the research in relation to their health and indeed this could be seen as part of their 'right to know'.[51]

Feedback was initially addressed by the IEAG and then also subsequently considered by the EGC. Generally, in relation to research, the expectation would be that the researcher would not be acting in a clinical capacity and would have no obligation to respond and feed back clinically relevant information to a participant. But should that approach be taken in relation to UK Biobank? Initially, the Ethics and Governance Framework took the approach that feedback would not be provided. As the EGC meeting in November 2004 noted, '[t]he Council were firm in their view that the recruitment process for UK Biobank should not be described as a "health check". This would obscure UK Biobank's fundamental character as a long-term research resource and could be

---

[50]  Ibid., 14.

[51]  See, for example, the Convention for the Protection of Human Rights and Dignity of the Human Being with Regard to the Application of Biology and Medicine: Convention on Human Rights and Biomedicine (otherwise known as the Oviedo Convention), ETS No 164, 4 April 1997, which entered into force 1 December 1999.

construed as an inducement to participate. However this issue arose once it was in operation.'[52] However, the minutes went on to say:

> A uniform approach of not providing feedback could work in many cases, but there were bound to be difficulties as UK Biobank was aiming to include individuals with prevalent disease. Some members felt that it would be insufficient (legally and ethically) for UK Biobank simply to assert that it did not owe a duty of care by virtue of its being a research project. The Council will advise UK Biobank on the development of a policy on what, if any, of this information could be fed back to participants.[53]

it had been argued that a duty of care was indeed owed by UK Biobank to participants and that such information should be fed back.[54] Johnston and Kaye suggested that this could be seen in terms of a moral obligation owed by UK Biobank.[55] Provision of unwanted information can, of course, be considered intrusive and it has been suggested that individuals may have a right not to know.[56] In contrast, Johnston and Kaye suggested that it was likely that there will be only rare circumstances in which individuals would not want to be informed. Furthermore, they suggested that failure to feed back in a situation in which an individual's life was at risk could damage public trust in researchers and institutions such as UK Biobank.[57] At the same time, Johnston and Kaye commented that '[i]t seems unacceptable that individuals who have agreed to participate in the UK Biobank for altruistic reasons involving an active commitment for many years for the public good should be denied information that could save their lives on the basis that to do so would be too time-consuming and costly'.[58]

---

[52] UK Biobank EGC, 'Induction Meeting' (29 November 2004) https://egcukbiobank.org.uk/sites/default/files/meetings/EGC1%20agenda%20and%20report.pdf (accessed 20 February 2021).

[53] Ibid.

[54] Carolyn Johnston and Jane Kaye 'Does UK Biobank Have a Legal Obligation to Feedback Findings to Participants?' (2004) 12 *Medical Law Review* 239.

[55] Ibid., 242.

[56] See further Ruth Chadwick, Mairi Levitt and Darren Shickle, 'The Right to Know, the Right Not to Know and the Emerging Debate', Graeme Laurie, 'Privacy and the Right Not to Know: A Plea for Conceptual Clarity' and Kadri Simm, 'Biobanks and Feedback' in Ruth Chadwick, Mairi Levitt and Darren Shickle (eds), *The Right to Know and the Right Not to Know: Genetic Privacy and Responsibility* (2nd edn, Cambridge University Press 2014).

[57] Johnston and Kaye (n 54), 244.

[58] Ibid.

The whole question of feedback kept re-emerging over the following decade. In 2005, the UK Biobank's Science Committee proposed that some information derived from the enrolment process should be fed back to participants and this was discussed by the EGC.[59] The EGC took the approach that some limited feedback of measurements undertaken by research nurses in the initial enrolment should go ahead but that care should be taken not to provide an interpretation as this was not a clinical setting.[60]

Subsequently, however, concerns were raised as to what the impact would be if the health professional undertaking participant recruitment believed that information should be disclosed.[61] Following this, by 2007,[62] the minutes of the EGC's Eleventh Meeting summarised the provisions for the feedback of interim findings through the UK Biobank Standard Operating Procedures. This meant that while it was not the role of UK Biobank to provide interpretation of findings during recruitment, none-theless, in some circumstances, it may be appropriate to draw attention to measurements such as high blood pressure or conditions with potentially life-threatening consequences such as suspected melanoma. Participants were to be directed to relevant information (such as leaflets) and also to contact their general practitioner (GP) as soon as possible.[63]

More recently, the UK Biobank Imaging Study demonstrates a contextualised approach to the feedback of clinical findings. This is a project which undertook a range of brain, cardiac and body magnetic resonance imaging (MRI), dual-energy X-ray absorptiometry and carotid Doppler ultrasound on some 100,000 individuals.[64] The intention was to create a vast multimodal imaging data set. In relation to the study, it was determined that, as incidental findings were anticipated, information would be returned to participants and participants' GPs. This was to apply where radiographers ascertained that there were findings which could 'indicate the possibility of a condition which, if

[59] UK Biobank EGC, 'Third Meeting' (4 April 2005) https://egcukbiobank.org.uk/sites/default/files/meetings/EGC3%20agenda%20and%20report.pdf (accessed 20 February 2021).

[60] UK Biobank EGC, 'Report: Public Meeting of the UK Biobank EGC 28th November 2005' (2 February 2006) https://egcukbiobank.org.uk/sites/default/files/meetings/Public%20meeting%20report.pdf (accessed 20 February 2021).

[61] UK Biobank EGC, 'Seventh Meeting' (13 March 2006) https://egcukbiobank.org.uk/sites/default/files/meetings/EGC7%20agenda%20and%20report.pdf (accessed 20 February 2021).

[62] UK Biobank EGC, 'Eleventh Meeting' (12 March 2007) https://egcukbiobank.org.uk/sites/default/files/meetings/EGC11%20agenda%20and%20report.pdf (accessed 20 February 2021).

[63] Ibid.

[64] www.ukbiobank.ac.uk/explore-your-participation/contribute-further/imaging-study (accessed 31 March 2021).

confirmed, would carry a real prospect of seriously threatening life span or of having a substantial impact on major body functions or quality of life' and this was subsequently confirmed by a radiologist.[65] In its Annual Review of 2016–17, the EGC noted that this study had revealed some 2 per cent of potentially serious incidental findings.[66] The issue of feedback represents the EGC (and UK Biobank itself) in 'responsive' mode, recognising that what may have been standard practice in relation to scientific research in traditional time-limited defined studies may not always be appropriate in this type of longer-term, multi-levelled study.

## 14.6    Access and Intellectual Property

An important issue for the operation of UK Biobank relates to the question of access to the Biobank resource itself, and also to any intellectual property consequently developed. Here, due to space constraints, the main focus of discussion is on access to the UK Biobank resource. This was the subject of robust engagement and extensive input by the EGC to try to inform the approach that UK Biobank undertook. Essentially, the question here concerned the basis on which the material should be able to be utilised by researchers. The EGC developed a living document advising on the public interest and the public good with important questions of public policy underpinning the discussion.[67] These included 'who should have access to the UK Biobank resource?' and 'should access be confined to the UK or should the resource be made more broadly accessible?'.[68]

The need for research published by the resource to be made available in open access journals was highlighted. The EGC saw that it could have a

[65] See further Lorna Gibson, Jonathan Sellors and Cathie Sudlow, 'Management of Incidental Findings on Multimodal Imaging in UK Biobank' in Sabine Weckbach (eds), *Incidental Radiological Findings* (Springer 2017).

[66] UK Biobank EGC *Annual Review 2016–7*: https://egcukbiobank.org.uk/sites/default/files/ UKBEGC_Review2016_2017.pdf (accessed 31 March 2021).

[67] UK Biobank EGC, 'Preface and Report: "Access to the UK Biobank Resource: Concepts of the Public Interest and the Public Good"' (3 July 2008) https://egcukbiobank.org.uk/sites/default/ files/Access%20to%20the%20UK%20Biobank%20Concepts%20of%20the%20Public% 20Interest%20and%20the%20Public%20Good.pdf (accessed 23 February 2021).

[68] 'UK Biobank Access and Intellectual Property Procedures' (29 October 2008) https:// egcukbiobank.org.uk/sites/default/files/meetings/Questions%20to%20consider%20dur ing%20the%20development%20of%20access%20and%20intellectual%20property% 20procedures.pdf (accessed 23 February 2021).

monitoring role to ensure that relevant processes regarding access and intellectual property (IP) were in place.[69] It emphasised the need for engagement with participants in developing its Access and IP Policy (AIP Policy). This was taken forward by UK Biobank in providing information in a newsletter which was being produced and which would be the first 're-contact' with all UK Biobank participants.[70] As the AIP Policy evolved, the EGC continued to have input. It stressed the importance of a principled approach to these issues.[71] Graeme's term of office as chair was coming to an end at that point and the EGC recommended that he should continue to have a role assisting the development of these procedures after he stepped down as chair.[72] The EGC recommended that the 'ethics input should be integral to the access review process' and this was taken forward by UK Biobank with the intention that the Access Sub-Committee, established to consider applications to the Biobank Resource, would be chaired by a person having ethics/legal expertise.[73] In addition, a contract was given to the Ethox Centre at the University of Oxford to provide ethics advice to support the Sub-Committee's work.[74] The AIP Policy was produced in 2011 and is still applicable.[75]

The need to safeguard the public interest in this process continued to be raised as the AIP Policy was developed.[76] At times, it appears that these discussions were perhaps not always as smooth as they might have been. By

---

[69] UK Biobank EGC, 'Twenty-First Meeting' (7 December 2009) https://egcukbiobank.org.uk/sites/default/files/meetings/EGC21%20agenda%20and%20report.pdf (accessed 23 February 2021).

[70] UK Biobank EGC, 'Twenty-Fourth Meeting' (27 September 2010) https://egcukbiobank.org.uk/sites/default/files/meetings/EGC24%20agenda%20and%20report.pdf (accessed 23 February 2021).

[71] UK Biobank EGC, 'Twenty-Fifth Meeting' (6 December 2010) https://egcukbiobank.org.uk/sites/default/files/meetings/EGC25%20agenda%20and%20report.pdf (accessed 23 February 2021).

[72] Ibid.

[73] UK Biobank EGC, 'Twenty-Sixth Meeting' (14 March 2011) https://egcukbiobank.org.uk/sites/default/files/meetings/EGC26%20agenda%20and%20report.pdf (accessed 23 February 2021). The original chair of the committee was a lawyer, Tara Camm.

[74] UK Biobank EGC, 'Twenty-Seventh Meeting' (6 June 2011) https://egcukbiobank.org.uk/sites/default/files/meetings/EGC27%20agenda%20and%20report.pdf (accessed 23 February 2021).

[75] 'Access Procedures: Application and Review Procedures for Access to the UK Biobank Resource' (November 2011) www.ukbiobank.ac.uk/media/omtl1ie4/access-procedures-2011–1.pdf (accessed 23 February 2021).

[76] UK Biobank EGC, 'Twenty-Eighth Meeting' (26 September 2011) https://egcukbiobank.org.uk/sites/default/files/meetings/EGC28%20agenda%20and%20report.pdf (accessed 23 February 2021).

the time of the twenty-ninth meeting, the EGC considered the terms of a draft public statement on access and proposed changes: '[t]he statement aims to (1) re-state the nature of the EGC's monitoring and advisory role in relation to the access phase and (2) indicate the issues that the EGC regards as important to keep under review as UK Biobank gains experience of the access process in operation'.[77] It was suggested that the EGC could input into the review of access process by UK Biobank and that the EGC itself may be able to review full applications with the aim of assessing 'whether there are any significant ethics or public good issues and to see how these were managed through UK Biobank's adjudication system'.[78] This point is significant. As we have seen, the EGC did not have 'teeth' as such, but the prospect of publicity may have been seen as a mechanism for accountability. The EGC also emphasised the need to ensure that the public interest was incorporated into (among other things) guidance for researchers applying for access to UK Biobank.[79]

The EGC was initially involved with reviewing lay summaries of applications to the resource but stated that, having reviewed them, this would not be sufficient. This concern was raised with UK Biobank.[80] Ultimately, it was decided that the EGC would continue to review these summaries, but it could access full applications on request on a case-by-case basis. By 2013, the discussions on access and review of proposals were still ongoing and it was suggested that the EGC role should be that of an auditor of applications. There were discussions as to how this could also be compatible with safeguarding the interests of participants.[81] Later, in 2013, the chair of the Access Sub-Committee attended an EGC meeting, which facilitated understanding of that Committee's role and led to discussions as to how the EGC audit function could be undertaken.[82] UK Biobank proposed a trial so that the EGC could audit the entire application

---

[77] UK Biobank EGC, 'Twenty-Ninth Meeting' (12 December 2011) https://egcukbiobank .org.uk/sites/default/files/meetings/EGC29%20agenda%20and%20report.pdf (accessed 23 February 2021).

[78] Ibid.

[79] UK Biobank EGC, 'Thirtieth Meeting' (5 March 2012) https://egcukbiobank.org.uk/sites/ default/files/meetings/EGC30%20agenda%20and%20report.pdf (accessed 23 February 2021).

[80] UK Biobank EGC, 'Thirty-First Meeting' (21 May 2012) https://egcukbiobank.org.uk/sites/ default/files/meetings/EGC31%20agenda%20and%20report.pdf (accessed 23 February 2021).

[81] UK Biobank EGC, 'Thirty-fifth Meeting' (20 May 2013) https://egcukbiobank.org.uk /sites/default/files/EGC35%20agenda%20and%20report.pdf (accessed 23 February 2021).

[82] UK Biobank EGC, 'Thirty-sixth Meeting' (10 September 2013) https://egcukbiobank.org.uk /sites/default/files/EGC36%20agenda%20and%20report.pdf (accessed 23 February 2021).

database.[83] Subsequently, a 'three strand governance model for access oversight involving: (i) alerting, (ii) reporting and (iii) auditing; with a light touch audit being undertaken by a qualified third party' was proposed, and this would be followed by a Memorandum of Understanding.[84] Under this process, it would be for UK Biobank to alert the EGC to certain kinds of application.[85] Thus, ultimately, the EGC was seen as an integral part of the access structure. However, the EGC does not appear to have undertaken further direct engagement in evolving the AIP Policy over time, which, given the importance of this issue, is concerning.

The EGC played a notable role in highlighting fundamentally important issues and testing approaches in the context of consent, feedback and access. At the same time, its advice has not always proved conclusive. The current chair of the Access Sub-Committee is neither a lawyer nor an ethicist.[86] And, as we shall see in Section 14.7, the abolition of the EGC has meant that the prospect of comprehensive arm's-length oversight of governance access appears to have been lost.

## 14.7   Reconfiguring the EGC

During its existence, the funders (the Medical Research Council and Wellcome) established reviews of the EGC's work in 2010 and 2015. The focus here is particularly on the 2015 review, which can be seen as the catalyst to the developments that led ultimately to the EGC's abolition. In 2015, an Expert Review Panel ('the Panel') – chaired by Professor Eric Meslin, a bioethicist at Indiana University at the time – was established.[87] The Panel gave a strong endorsement to the work of the EGC:

[83] UK Biobank EGC, 'Thirty-seventh Meeting' (9 December 2013) https://egcukbiobank.org.uk /sites/default/files/EGC37%20agenda%20and%20report.pdf (accessed 23 February 2021).

[84] UK Biobank EGC, 'Thirty-Ninth Meeting' (2 June 2014) https://egcukbiobank.org.uk /sites/default/files/Final%20EGC39%20minutes.pdf (accessed 23 February 2021).

[85] UK Biobank EGC, 'Fortieth Meeting' (9 September 2014) https://egcukbiobank.org.uk /sites/default/files/Final%20EGC40%20minutes.pdf (accessed 23 February 2021). See also 'Annex A The EGC's Oversight in Relation to UK Biobank's Administration of the Access Process (Final 13/11/14)' in minutes of UK Biobank EGC, 'Forty-First Meeting' (8 December 2014) https://egcukbiobank.org.uk/sites/default/files/Final%20EGC41% 20minutes.pdf (accessed 23 February 2021).

[86] The current chair is Professor Martin Bowbrow, an emeritus professor of medical genetics at the University of Cambridge.

[87] The other panel members were Professor Martin Bobrow, Cambridge University (who was also chair of the UK Biobank Expert Advisory Group on Data Access); Dr Jennifer Harris, Norwegian Institute of Public Health; Professor Debbie Lawlor, University of

The continued presence of an ethics and governance body is integral to the ongoing success of the UK Biobank project and provides necessary reassurance to both participants and the general public. The Panel further concurs with the 2010 Expert Panel that the EGC's existence helped satisfy the informal 'social contract' between UK Biobank, participants and the public. There is both an important symbolic and practical requirement for large-scale studies of this kind to have a governance structure in place to provide an assurance to the funders, the research community and the public that the UK Biobank aspires to the highest ethical standards.[88]

Nonetheless, the Panel made a series of recommendations which would have the effect of altering the EGC's composition and work. It was clear from the EGC's response to the findings that aspects of these were unexpected, such as the reduction of meetings to two per annum in addition to an annual general meeting. Here, the EGC minutes noted that '[t]here was a background concern that the new model was[,] in effect, asking the EGC to switch on and switch off over time, with fluctuating involvement as issues arise, rather than running regularly throughout the year'.[89]

The Panel proposed that the size of the Council should be reduced to between five and eight persons. There were concerns that a new structure could in fact lead to more work for members between meetings (for example, there would be fewer members to participate in the work of sub-groups). There would be a chair appointed according to Nolan principles; however, the Panel said that the Council should not be required to include a 'lay member' and that a participant perspective could come from an annual general meeting (AGM).[90] The EGC responded by indicating that the Panel may have misunderstood the composition of the EGC, as it had never had a lay member and, moreover, 'would not equate lay membership with participant representation'.[91] The Panel had recommended that the Secretary to the EGC would have their time commitment reduced by 40 per cent and this prompted considerable concern from the EGC including 'placing serious question marks about

Bristol, an epidemiologist; and Professor Jonathan Montgomery, UCL, a health lawyer and chair of the Nuffield Council on Bioethics.

[88] Medical Research Council and Wellcome Trust, 'Review of the UK Biobank EGC: Report of the Expert Review Panel' (June 2015) https://egcukbiobank.org.uk/sites/default/files/EGC%20Review%20FINAL%20June15.pdf (accessed 23 February 2021).

[89] UK Biobank EGC, 'Forty-Fourth Meeting' (8 September 2015) https://egcukbiobank.org.uk/sites/default/files/Final%20EGC44%20minutes.pdf (accessed 23 February 2021).

[90] Ibid.

[91] Ibid.

its ability to discharge its inward-facing responsibilities'.[92] Following the Panel's report, this led to ongoing discussions, including as to the extent to which the EGC should undertake an auditing role, which appeared ongoing up until the disbanding of the EGC.[93]

One question which remains, however, is whether the EGC had by that point simply run its course. Was the idea of an oversight body dated? There is certainly a practical issue as to whether an individual biobank governance body can effectively, on its own, address all issues which arise. On this question, the Panel recommended:

> The Funders should explore the idea of supporting development of a national EGC that would interface with all UK biobanks and cohort studies. Such a council would need sufficient expertise in bioethics plus other practical experience in issues such as data access so that the UK can maximize the scientific return from their collective biobank and longitudinal studies endeavours. The Panel did not consider it its place to discuss details, such as, whether this body could be formed from a pre-existing council or whether a fresh council would need to be established.[94]

The EGC was very supportive of this proposal and would be keen to establish close links with such a body and indeed with other biobanks.[95] To date, however, the idea has not been taken forward. But a question of national level oversight is not a matter that should simply be left to individual funding bodies. It is something which should be undertaken by the government giving the task to an independent review group.

The reconfiguring of the EGC and what happened next is the point at which we perhaps need to reflect on its legacy.

### 14.8   UK Biobank Ethics and Governance: The Legacy

The Panel's recommendations clearly signalled the direction of travel for UK Biobank's EGC. The Council was to morph into a smaller body with less direct oversight, fewer resources and less public engagement. Following the review, Professor Brownsword's term of office was coming to an end and Baroness Helene Hayman took over as EGC chair from 1 January 2016. The Council then met in May 2016[96] and

---

[92]  Ibid.

[93]  UK Biobank EGC (n 89).

[94]  Review of the UK Biobank EGC (n 88).

[95]  Ibid., 13.

[96]  UK Biobank EGC, 'Forty-Sixth Meeting' (27 April 2016) https://egcukbiobank.org.uk /sites/default/files/Final%20EGC46%20minutes.pdf (accessed 23 February 2021).

October 2016.[97] During this period, UK Biobank was in the process of amending the Framework. The last two meetings of the EGC were reported on the website as having taken place in March 2017 and October 2017 – although, in relation to the latter, no papers exist on the EGC website. The report of the penultimate meeting, in March 2017, noted that there had been a planning review meeting between UK Biobank and the EGC.[98] The website records no minutes or information concerning any meetings in 2018. Subsequently, in 2018, the EGC was disbanded and replaced with a new Ethics Advisory Committee (EAC).[99]

> The remit of [the EAC] shall be to provide advice to the Board on ethical issues that arise during the maintenance, development and use of the UK Biobank resource, including:
>
> - identifying, defining and examining relevant ethical issues;
> - providing advice, guidance and recommendations on relevant ethical issues; and
> - reviewing and advising on policies which have an ethical dimension that is relevant to UK Biobank.[100]

Such an abrupt change is somewhat perplexing. First, while the Panel did indicate that the EGC's role was to be reduced and its membership limited, it nonetheless endorsed the importance and the utility of the EGC and a new EGC chair had only recently been appointed. Second, the very essence of the EGC was its independence. As we have seen in this chapter, it was deliberately established at arm's length from UK Biobank, with an independent chair. Such perceived detachment is inevitably lost once its status is altered in this way, with the new EAC chair as a member of the main Biobank board, running a committee which feeds into it. The UK Biobank website was revised in January 2021 and states that the EAC has five members, including the chair.[101] There is an attempt to assert

---

[97] UK Biobank EGC, 'Forty-Seventh Meeting' (3 October 2016) https://egcukbiobank .org.uk/sites/default/files/Final%20EGC47%20minutes.pdf (accessed 23 February 2021).

[98] UK Biobank EGC, 'Forty-Eighth Meeting' (15 March 2017) https://egcukbiobank.org.uk /sites/default/files/EGC48%20agenda%20and%20report.pdf (accessed 23 February 2021).

[99] www.ukbiobank.ac.uk/learn-more-about-uk-biobank/governance/ethics-advisory-committee (accessed 31 March 2021).

[100] Ibid.

[101] At the time of writing these are, in addition to the chair, Professor Anneke Lucassen, a professor of clinical genetics at the University of Southampton: a lay member, Mr Nick Ross, a broadcaster; Professor Susan Halford, a professor of sociology at the University of Bristol; Dr Neil Manson, a senior lecturer in philosophy at Lancaster University; and

some independence in that '[a]ll of the members shall be independent of the day-to-day management of UK Biobank'.[102]

However, this is critically an *ethics advisory* committee – it is no longer concerned with both the ethics *and the governance* of UK Biobank, and it is a committee and not a council. This reduces the ultimate scope of accountability of UK Biobank. The terms of reference state that '[m]embers of the EAC shall be selected and appointed by the Board after consultation with the funders'.[103] There is no mention of a Nolan appointment process. The members are to have 'relevant expertise in epidemiology and biobanking, bioethics and public policy, and community engagement and communications'.[104] The terms of reference also state:

> 2.1 The general remit of the ESC is to advise and make recommendations to the Board and the Access Sub-Committee (ASC) on ethics issues which relate to the development, maintenance, and use of the UK Biobank resource, particularly as such issues may impact on the participants.
> 2.2 This remit will include:
> > 2.2.1 identifying, defining and examining relevant ethical issues;
> > 2.2.2 providing advice, guidance and recommendations on relevant ethical issues;
> > 2.2.3 reviewing and advising on policies which have a relevant ethical dimension; and
> > 2.2.4 advice in relation to communication and participant engagement.[105]

Exactly how the EAC has been operating in practice since its establishment in 2018 remains unclear. The website does not contain a list of the meetings with relevant papers. This demonstrates a notable contrast in transparency as to its operation as compared with the EGC, with its clear, independent website containing details of meetings and public availability of accompanying papers. A further notable aspect of the EGC's work was that of its public meetings. Such meetings are an important means of

Dr Susan Wallace, a lecturer in population and public health sciences at the University of Leicester. Professor Lucassen and Dr Wallace previously served terms as members of the EGC.
[102] Terms of reference, para 1.1.
[103] Ibid., para 1.2.
[104] Ibid.
[105] Ibid.

obtaining engagement and feedback.[106] However, as we saw, the Panel recommended that the EGC should step back from public engagement, with the exception of holding an annual general meeting. It remains to be seen whether the EAC will undertake such a role in the future. The new EAC does, however, have a '[r]esearch-led arm' with the appointment of a researcher in the area of ethics/social science who will 'undertake detailed empirical and conceptual research'.[107] This is intriguing. While, on the one hand this can be seen as a useful, up-to-date resource, it raises questions, on the other hand, as to how the diversity of views will be addressed by the work of the EAC itself.

As a body, the EGC was in a unique position. It was established by, and financially dependent on, the funders and, while able to work at arm's length, it was not constituted in the way in which statutory regulatory bodies ordinarily operate. In short, the EGC lacked full autonomy. Nonetheless, as we have seen, the EGC was able to make strong recommendations and raise issues of fundamental importance, such as access to the resource and development of the AIP Policy. As noted, one way in which the EGC's role was conceptualised was as that of a 'guardian'. Reflecting on the EGC in 2011, Graeme described its role as that of a 'critical friend'.[108] Furthermore, he suggested that, as an example of 'reflexive governance', it was able to be responsive as unforeseen challenges arose, as we saw in relation to the inability to maintain a commitment to destroy the data of those participants when permission was withdrawn.[109] Graeme saw reflexive governance as a mechanism that could address biobank challenges without a specific law being needed.[110]

In 2014, during a UK Biobank conference, Roger Brownsword expanded on the theme of the 'critical friend', arguing that '[i]n the final analysis, it is for UK Biobank to adopt principles and practices

---

[106] See, for example, UK Biobank EGC, 'Report: Public Meeting of the UK Biobank Ethics and Governance Council 28th November 2005 Royal College of Physicians, London' (2 February 2006) https://egcukbiobank.org.uk/sites/default/files/meetings/Public%20meeting%20report.pdf (accessed 23 February 2021).

[107] UK Biobank, Ethics Advisory Committee https://prod.ukbiobank.ac.uk/learn-more-about-uk-biobank/governance/ethics-advisory-committee (accessed 23 February 2021).

[108] UK Biobank EGC, 'Past, Present, Future: The Ethics and Governance of Big Biobanks Conference 3rd–5th November 2014' 5 https://egcukbiobank.org.uk/sites/default/files/UKBEGC_ConferenceReport.pdf (accessed 23 February 2021).

[109] Ibid.

[110] See Graeme Laurie 'Reflexive Governance in Biobanking: On the Value of Policy Led Approaches and the Need to Recognise the Limits of Law' (2011) 130 *Human Genetics* 347.

that it is prepared to defend as ethically sound; the role of the EGC is to help UK Biobank to understand the issues, not to impose an EGC view (if it has one)'.[111] He added that '[t]he EGC should encourage UK Biobank to "internalise" its ethical responsibilities', and that '[t]he EGC and UK Biobank share a common aspiration but the EGC has its own priorities (especially to protect participants) within the governance network'.[112]

Graeme and his Liminal Spaces colleagues have suggested that the EGC can be seen as regulatory stewardship in action.[113] Such a stewardship role is in addition to any existing legal regulatory functions. It can be seen as a mechanism involving co-operation between regulators and other actors. It can operate without a legal basis for such a role. Furthermore, such a body may be involved in 'negotiating uncertainty about the relevance of particular legal regimes or rules within regulatory frameworks'.[114] The EGC can be seen as a notable example of such regulatory stewardship. Ultimately, the EGC could raise issues, but it could not compel. Its powers were of persuasion and also dependent on ears that, at least for a considerable amount of time, were receptive. But, ultimately, it was dependent upon the funders' conception of its role.

Was the EGC itself outdated? It is suggested that it was not. The questions faced by the EGC – the nature and scope of consent, the problems of long-term storage of data and samples, who exactly should have access to the resource and the question of subsequent commercial exploitation of such material – live on as enduring questions. Indeed, the EGC was influential at an international level and has shared its experiences with those operating biobanks in other jurisdictions.[115] To follow Graeme's argument that this can be seen in terms of reflexive governance, there was so much that UK Biobank could have learned from such an experienced body in the years to come.

If genetic databases are effectively a matter of public concern, and certainly if they utilise information from the NHS, they should be seen as such. In that light, perhaps one legacy and lesson drawn from the last

---

[111] See n 108.

[112] Ibid.

[113] Graeme Laurie et al, 'Charting Regulatory Stewardship in Health Research: Making the Invisible Visible' (2018) 27 *Cambridge Quarterly of Healthcare Ethics* 333; and 'Regulatory Stewardship: A Concept Note' (2021) www.law.ed.ac.uk/sites/default/files/2021-03/Regulatory%20stewardship%20concept%20note.pdf (accessed 31 March 2021).

[114] Ibid., 343–4.

[115] See, for example, UK Biobank EGC 2014 (n 108).

sixteen years is that this should be a matter for comprehensive national oversight. The Panel reviewing the EGC mooted the establishment of a broader national body. Such a body may be well placed to learn from the legacy of the EGC. There needs to be clarity and consistency in the ethical parameters employed in such databases across the jurisdiction, and these need to be clear and appropriately proportionate.[116] However, this on its own, it is suggested, is not enough. It should be accompanied by a comprehensive and detailed review of the whole legal regulation of health research itself, to give greater clarity to researchers going forward. What is critical is that we ensure that the work of the EGC, of Graeme and of his colleagues does not become simply a matter of reference by medical historians or a brief footnote in health law textbooks in the future. Engagement with this legacy is critical to inform the future regulation of biobank research in the UK and beyond.

---

[116] See further discussion in Graeme Laurie, Shawn Harmon and Edward Dove, *Mason and McCall Smith's Law and Medical Ethics* (11th edn, Oxford University Press 2019) 701–2.

# 15

# Overcoming Regulatory Impasse in Stem Cell Research and Advanced Therapy Medicines in Argentina through Shared Norms and Values

FABIANA ARZUAGA

## 15.1  Introduction

The medical and scientific advances that have occurred in the field of regenerative medicine throughout the last twenty years, especially as a result of the incorporation of new biotechnologies, have generated new areas for research at both academic and industrial levels. They have also posed new challenges for the regulation of therapeutic products. Treatments that use cells as therapeutic agents, such as cell therapy, gene therapy and tissue engineering – in recent times commonly termed 'advanced therapies medicinal products' (ATMPs) – are carried out by administering cell preparations containing (somatic or stem) cells after they have undergone a series of physical or chemical procedures (manipulation) to activate their restorative or therapeutic function. These preparations are live substances with great proliferative and differentiation potential that, unlike a traditional drug, continue their metabolic action within the recipient organism.

It has been clear that since the advent of so-called regenerative medicine research, there is much that is unknown in this field, including the full catalogue of risks that affect the safety of human beings who receive these therapies; and this, of course, is a critical topic to consider. For this reason, there is a consensus among the medical, scientific and regulatory communities that these types of intervention must not be included in current medical practice and administered for therapeutic purposes to humans unless and until safety and efficacy are verified using accepted and peer-reviewed clinical research. In Argentina, science and

332

technology regulatory authorities have considered regenerative medicine and cell therapies as a 'strategic area' within the health sector. Since 2006–7, it is possible to see the construction of this technology as a 'State priority in terms of research and development',[1] based on a growing trend of institutional creation, funding programmes, regional network generation, and actions towards the governance of this technology.[2]

This chapter aims to document and analyse the initial steps taken to shape those frameworks: the landscape that was envisioned, developed and evolved; and the challenges that have arisen and how they have been managed in order to create governance structures based in social values. Such values are the core of a system aimed to protect the human rights of the recipients of advanced therapies, to promote equal conditions for researchers and industry to develop future products, and to facilitate access to new treatments. There were, of course, many actors and factors involved in this complex process, but a key and foundational actor who facilitated the creation of a vision and its materialisation was Graeme Laurie, along with his team at the University of Edinburgh. The ideas, synergy and interactions deployed in an open and receptive scenario were essential elements of identifying critical points in regulating for uncertainty and practising the methodology of foresight in law. This contribution is inspired by the spirit of our collaborative work, which was born as an academic project and helped, through its strength and coherence, to create a future that was shared by many people in my country.

## 15.2 Building Capacities through International Collaboration

Since the early 2000s, (somatic/stem) cells therapies have acquired priority in health research agendas worldwide. While the United States, the European Union, Israel and Japan started to develop important research and development (R&D) programmes, and specific regulatory frameworks governing them, many middle-income countries such as India, China, Brazil, Malaysia and Argentina, among others, started to implement national strategies for the rapidly developing field of regenerative medicine, through capacity-building programmes and the effort to create specific regulations.[3]

---

[1] Verónica Palma et al, 'Stem Cell Research in Latin America: Update, Challenges and Opportunities in a Priority Research Area' (2015) 10 *Regenerative Medicine* 785.
[2] Fabiana Arzuaga, 'Stem Cell Research and Therapies in Argentina: The Legal and Regulatory Approach' (2013) 22 *Stem Cells and Development* 40.
[3] Achim Rosemann et al, 'Global Regulatory Developments for Clinical Stem Cell Research: Diversification and Challenges to Collaborations' (2016) 11 *Regenerative Medicine* 647.

In the case of Argentina, it has actively pursued regenerative medicine and stem cell solutions to health problems, but in the early 2000s there were no regulations, nor any studies related to ethics and the law in this field. In 2007, as a result of Graeme's sabbatical visit to the School of Law at the University of Buenos Aires, numerous academic links were created with local colleagues, which resulted in the formalisation of a Collaborative Agreement between the recently created Argentine Advisory Commission on Regenerative Medicine and Cellular Therapies (the 'Advisory Commission') at the Secretary of Science and Technology and the University of Edinburgh's AHRC SCRIPT Centre.[4] This collaboration was continued by the new Ministry of Science, Technology and Productive Innovation (MOST) and a new Minister for Science, Technology and Productive Innovation with a background in the life sciences, and it combined with other efforts to create an opportunity addressed in greater detail in the rest of this chapter.[5] The collaboration was a key factor in facilitating knowledge construction and decision-making during the creation of the governance framework for ATMPs in Argentina and, in that way, its impact extended to 2019, well after the initial project was completed.

### 15.3   Objectives, Tensions and Governance

The bespoke, empirical, Argentina-based yet collaborative research programme was enriched by the sharing of experience and lessons learned in the UK, which is seen as a vanguard country in regulating new technologies in health. This helped Argentinean counterparts to recognise and manage some issues that were emerging around the process for creating a governance framework. Key tensions included:

a) finding criteria to define the nature of cell therapies as a treatment, a procedure or a *sui generis* device;
b) understanding the evolving regulatory scenario at the international level, recognising trends and taking a position regarding the adoption of a model which would be the most appropriate for Argentina;
c) identifying and understanding the social values that should underlie the regulation and cope with a myriad of interests influencing the process; and

---

[4] AHRC Research Centre for Studies in Intellectual Property and Technology Law.
[5] Dr Lino Barañao was Minister of Science, Technology and Productive Innovation during three periods (2007–11, 2011–15 and 2015–17).

d) identifying critical points in regulating for uncertainty and practising the methodology of foresight in law to create a shared vision and be able to recognise when futures might materialise.

Each of these tensions is described in this chapter, but I do want to emphasise at this point that the support in identifying both problems and the resources to find answers and solutions to them was without a doubt one of the most relevant aspects of Graeme's legacy.

### 15.3.1   Product, Procedure or Sui Generis Development?

Since their advent, cell therapy technologies (using somatic or stem cells) have raised hopes for novel treatments for a wide range of diseases that currently have no cure, and expectations for new patentable and marketable developments. At the same time, and as background to the project's context, the construction of societal expectations regarding the potential therapeutic applications of this technology was increasing year by year, mainly disseminated by mass media and social networks. In this scenario, and for the past decade, the Advisory Commission issued a plethora of press releases, alone or jointly with a great number of stakeholders such as scientists, bioethicists, scientific societies and patient organisations, warning against the risks of experimental treatments with cells. All of these communications helped to create awareness and promote dialogue about the necessity of developing a specific framework to regulate these emerging technologies and practices, setting standards in relation to quality, safety and effectiveness.[6]

However, controversies arose regarding how to design appropriate regulation for cell-based treatments, and how they would adequately address the many safety issues at play. The 'risk-based approach' was a concept that had the consensus of all the Advisory Commission members, but for a long time it was difficult to align competing positions with

---

[6] See, for example, 'Declaración Acerca de la Guarda de Células Madre de Sangre de Cordón Umbilical' (2009) ('Statement regarding cord blood stem cells banking') www.celulas madre.mincyt.gob.ar/Documentos/DECLARACION_CELULAS_MADRE_CORDON _UMBILICAL.pdf (accessed 19 February 2021); 'Claves Para el Debate Sobre Células Madre' (2009) ('Key issues in the debate on stem cells') www.celulasmadre.mincyt.gob .ar/Documentos/CLAVES_PARA_EL_DEBATE_SOBRE_CELULAS_MADRE.pdf (accessed 19 February 2021); and 'No Existe en la Actualidad Ninguna Evidencia que Justifique el Uso de las Células Madre Como Tratamiento Establecido en Ninguna Enfermedad Neurológica' (2014) ('There is currently no evidence to justify the use of stem cells as an established treatment in any neurological disease') www.argentina.gob.ar/ sites/default/files/sobre_las_enfermedades_neurologicas.pdf (accessed 19 February 2021).

regard to the legal 'umbrella' under which cell therapies should be regulated: under transplant legislation as a procedure or under drugs law as a medicinal product. It is important to point out that in 2017, and after several years of discussion, the concept of 'cell-as-medicine' was the position held by the Advisory Commission, and it was the recommendation made to the Ministers of Science and Health. This understanding and consensus was reached by the Commission's members as a result of some activities developed in Edinburgh in 2011 supported by the Genomics Forum,[7] a visit of officers of the Spanish Medicines Agency (AEMPS) in 2013, and further in-house training in the headquarters of the AEMPS in Spain in 2014 and 2018.[8]

In 2017, the Interministerial Commission in Advanced Therapies ('Interministerial Commission'), which included professionals from both the Ministry of Health (MOH) and MOST, as well as the National Administration in Food, Drugs and Medical Technology (ANMAT) and the Unique Central Institute for Ablation and Implantation (INCUCAI),[9] was formed. It had the mission to 'propose a regulatory framework for Advanced Therapies harmonized with international standards' (the US Food and Drug Administration (FDA) and the European Medicines Agency (EMA)), that is to say that advanced therapies would be considered as a biologic medicine and would be regulated and approved for commercialisation by the medicines authority (ANMAT).

During 2017 and 2018, the Interministerial Commission drafted a specific regulation on ATMPs (ANMAT 179/18), which was issued in September 2018.[10] This regulation includes more specific definitions of the products that fall within the ATMP's subcategories of cellular therapy, gene therapy and tissue-engineered products. In addition, it

---

[7] On 7–8 November 2011, Fabiana Arzuaga and Shawn Harmon, with support from the Genomics Forum, organised an interactive two-day workshop with experts and scholars interested in the field, which aimed to explore the evolving regulatory state of affairs for regenerative medicine and cellular therapies in Argentina; report on the findings of the Governing Emerging Technologies: Social Values and Stem Cell Regulation in Argentina project; draw on the experience of the UK and Europe with a view to formulating recommendations for proceeding in Argentina; and offer participants an opportunity to reflect on the robustness of UK and EU regulatory mechanisms. For further discussion, see Shawn Harmon, 'Regenerative Medicine Governance: The EU Experience and Argentine Possibilities' (2011) 8 SCRIPTed 323.

[8] Ibid.

[9] Ministry of Health and the Ministry of Science, Technology and Innovation, Joint Res.-E1 /2017.

[10] Disposition 179/18 ANMAT.

provides clearer guidance on the role and legal competencies of INCUCAI and ANMAT.[11] The former will be responsible for regulating the donation, obtention and verification of cellular tissue. In turn, ANMAT will oversee the production, registration, approval and surveillance of ATMPs. The manufacturing site will have to follow manuals of Good Manufacturing Practices and clinical trials will have to comply with Good Clinical Practice guides that apply to all clinical research. It is expected that INCUCAI will soon issue specific regulations for the stages of ATMP development that fall within its competence. The two agencies are expected to work in a more co-ordinated way in the future.

### 15.3.2   Regulatory Harmonisation or Self-Regulatory Diversification?

Another problem that we faced was centred on defining the structure of the regulatory framework, and which entity would have the authority to regulate and enforce it. It was a central issue because Argentina is a federal country where the exercise of the right of health is retained by the provinces. However, the main legislation related to health (Medicines Law, Transplants Law) takes the form of national laws, issued by the Argentinean Parliament.

At international level, during the last decade, regulatory developments in most jurisdictions were debated between two central dynamics – attempts for harmonisation versus a process of regulatory diversification – and these trends influenced local discussions and decision-making processes. The first trend, towards harmonisation, was led by regulatory authorities in the United States and the European Union (EU) and is exemplified by legislative instruments such as the Regulation for Human, Cellular and Tissue Products (HCT/Ps) in the USA and the Advanced Therapy and Medicinal Products (ATMP) legislation in the EU[12] (both in 2007); and by the Guidelines for Stem Cell Research and Clinical Translation by the International Society for Stem Cell Research (2008).[13] These harmonisation processes have evolved from a pharmaceutical model of drug development and the ideal of evidence-based medicine (EBM) towards a multiphase clinical trial model. This tendency aims to facilitate particular forms of global cell therapy

---

[11]  INCUCAI is the Argentine Transplant Authority.

[12]  Regulation 1394/2007/EU on advanced therapy medicinal products and amending Directive 2001/83/EC and Regulation (EC) No 726/2004, 2007 OJ L324/121.

[13]  www.isscr.org/docs/default-source/all-isscr-guidelines/clin-trans-guidelines/isscrglclini caltrans.pdf?sfvrsn=fd1fa5c8_6 (accessed 18 March 2021).

governance, framing the task for national regulators and including capacity-building processes that may be required to adapt local capacities
and processes to global standards. The related laws and regulations
combine to form a reasonably comprehensive normative system applicable to research, market access approval, and pharmacovigilance for
ATMPs, and they are largely harmonised with international standards
in force in the USA and Europe.

On the other hand, there has been an increase in the emergence of
multi-standardisation (or diversification) politics that propose alternative methods and forms of evidence for clinical innovation in the cell
therapies field, to reduce the costs of clinical testing and to increase
access to non-systematically proven innovative interventions at an
earlier stage. Many of these regulatory impulses have come from Asia,
in countries such as Japan, India, China and South Korea. As Bortz and
colleagues write, 'the ways in which governments and regulatory
authorities respond to these tensions and conflicting regulatory choices
are not only a matter of "control", but they create different types of
(state-desired) futures for technological development, which affect
issues such as, priority selection, allocation of public expenditure,
capacity building, the construction of expectations, accessibility and
risk management'.[14]

In the case of Argentina, it moved towards the centralised model to
harmonise with the EMA and the US FDA, both regulatory bodies that
have served as models to create the ANMAT. The newly amended
Argentine Civil Commercial Code 2015 establishes the ethical-legal
requirements for clinical trials. Specifically, Article 58 states that investigations in human beings through interventions, such as treatments,
preventative methods and diagnostic or predictive tests, whose efficacy
or safety are not scientifically proven, can be carried out only if specific
requirements are met, such as adherence to consent and privacy, ethics
approval and so on. ATMPs are medicines for human use that are based
on genes, tissues or cells.[15] They can be classified into three main types:
gene therapy medicines, somatic-cell therapy medicines and tissue-
engineered medicines. In addition, some ATMPs may contain one or
more medical devices as an integral part of the medicine; these are

---

[14] Gabriela Bortz, Achim Rosemann and Federico Vasen, 'Shaping Stem Cell Therapies in
Argentina: Regulation, Risk Management and Innovation Policies' (2019) 21 *Sociologias*
116, 131.
[15] Medicines Law 16.463 and ANMAT Disposition 179/2018.

referred to as combined ATMPs. An example of this is cells embedded in a biodegradable matrix or scaffold.[16]

All ATMPs are authorised centrally via the ANMAT. As with all medicines, the ANMAT continues to monitor their safety and efficacy after they are approved and marketed. Cells that are to be used as a starting material for an ATMP are regulated by the Transplant Authority (INCUCAI).[17]

### 15.3.3   Social Values for the Bioscience Governance Setting

It is generally recognised that law (and regulation) must have some moral basis if it is to be persuasive and legitimate, particularly where the subject's conduct has some potential to harm. Ultimately, moral values are important to the realisation of both good science and good governance, particularly where human health and well-being are implicated, and there is ample justification for their formulation in 'biolaw', which, by necessity, concerns matters having a strong a moral element.[18] However, values are often more assumed than explicit, and are often extremely opaque or hidden, and therefore invisible. A research project funded by Innogen and the University of Edinburgh (GET: Social Values) was undertaken to make visible and explicit some of the values that Argentine stakeholders felt should influence the biomedical research setting and the legal and regulatory solutions created to solve actor problems in this arena.

Fieldwork was run during 2008/9 and was led by me and Dr Shawn Harmon, who at the time was based at the University of Edinburgh.[19] Respondents were asked to identify important and/or valued sources or

---

[16] Gene therapy medicines are medicines that contain genes that lead to a therapeutic, prophylactic or diagnostic effect. They work by inserting 'recombinant' genes into the body, usually to treat a variety of diseases, including genetic disorders, cancer or long-term diseases. A recombinant gene is a stretch of DNA that is created in the laboratory, bringing together DNA from different sources. Somatic-cell therapy medicines are medicines that contain cells or tissues that have been manipulated to change their biological characteristics or cells or tissues not intended to be used for the same essential functions in the body. They can be used to cure, diagnose or prevent diseases. Tissue-engineered medicines are medicines that contain cells or tissues that have been modified so they can be used to repair, regenerate or replace human tissue.

[17] Transplant Law No. 27.447 and its Regulatory Decree articles 1 and 2, Resolution 28/2020 (Starting material for MTA).

[18] See further Chapter 16 in this volume.

[19] Semi-structured interviews were carried out face-to-face with stakeholders from the medical, scientific, academic, policy, legislative and regulatory communities in Argentina. Purposive selection was used to choose participants. This was a cross-sectional one-off study.

shapers/informers of moral values. Collectively, they felt that core moral values should be derived from conversations around different relevant topics. Such a 'conversation' was viewed as essential insofar as it would encourage a range of stakeholders to consider the consequences of actions, and therefore a range of options, before acting. The idea of discussion and debate was felt to be important to uncovering, exploring and refining values. Respondents specifically noted the social and dynamic nature of morality for which there could be no universal rule, and they felt that values must come from society and from informed people who are prepared to debate and openly articulate moral values and defend the research boundaries they inform. In short, respondents told us that social sources need to be consulted to generate good evidence and understanding.[20] Respondents also articulated a broad range of values that they considered to be important not only to the bioscience and regulatory setting but also to Argentine society more generally. The values which they felt were broadly important (for Argentina and beyond) were dignity, human well-being, solidarity, justice, democracy, knowledge, autonomy, safety, scientific freedom and transparency/trust.[21]

Evidence was also gathered through interviews with key stakeholders, meetings and international workshops. The workshops were directed at the scientific and patient communities as well as regulators and legislators, including representatives from MOST in Argentina and leading experts from the EU and the UK. They covered topics relevant to the needs of local colleagues, and international speakers were asked to be as open and critical of their own experiences as possible to enable their Argentinian colleagues to identify key lessons and possible opportunities to 'leapfrog' and go down certain routes, but not others. This research revealed that there was a will among key stakeholders to fill a gap in the governance arrangements for stem cell research with top-down regulation. It also helped to identify suitable instruments.[22]

---

[20] For more information about the findings, see www.law.ed.ac.uk/research/impact-and-engage ment/moral-and-legal-aspects-of-stem-cell-research-in-argentina (accessed 19 February 2021).

[21] Shawn Harmon, 'Guiding Values: Argentine Stem Cell Research and Regenerative Medicine' (2010) 4 *SCRIPT Opinions*, AHRC Research Centre for Studies in Intellectual Property and Technology Law, https://core.ac.uk/download/pdf/43703613.pdf (accessed 28 February 2021).

[22] Shawn Harmon, 'Argentina Unbound: Governing Emerging Technologies: Social Values in Stem Cell Regulation in Argentina' (2008) presented at European Association of Health Law, 'The Future of Health Law in Europe' (Conference 10–11 April 2008) www.research .ed.ac.uk/portal/en/publications/argentina-unbound-governing-emerging-technologies (10c2153f-f774-49f0-bdb7-bc239894fe65).html (accessed 19 February 2021).

Early dissemination of these findings through workshops and policy briefings (some of which were published on the MOST website) helped to shape conversations in the Advisory Commission that fed directly into a document it authored and which resulted in a draft Life Sciences Law (setting standards for regenerative medicine research and patient care) that MOST presented in a seminar at the Argentinian Senate in 2013.[23] Thereafter, the Advisory Commission worked with legislators on a related modification to the Civil Code that came into force in 2015, and on the final model law.

Importantly, and interestingly, though many stakeholders in the 2011–17 period reported a preference for command-and-control models of regulation (i.e. state-led, top-down approaches characterised by rules enforced by regulators), and many elements of the prevailing regime do now reflect this, the framework itself emerged through a bottom-up, iterative process which sought to connect abstract concepts and models of governance with actual experience and with the national social and legal normative culture. Ultimately, social values were the key elements in the construction of the governance framework for ATMPs, which evidences the power of legacy.

### 15.3.4    Foresighting in Law: Shared Vision and Materialisation of Futures

We, as a society, have not always been prepared, and are not adequately equipped, to confront concerns and possibilities around technologies in an early, explicit or effective manner. Indeed, some of the most important and ubiquitous technological innovations of the modern era were 'rolled out' with very little consideration on the part of developers and contemporary commentators of the profound social and legal impacts they might have. For example, few recognised the extensive social and commercial influencing potential of the Internet until it had already been taken up. Technology-driven uncertainty has emerged as a result of the advent of cell therapies, querying how we might better regulate in the emerging sociotechnological setting, which is characterised by promise and consternation, fluidity and pace, fragmentation and complexity. We have explored the possibilities for foresighting in the legal setting,

---

[23] Agencia CyTA www.agenciacyta.org.ar/2013/08/advierten-sobre-tratamientos-no-aprobados-con-celulas-madre/ (accessed 19 February 2021).

arguing that 'legal foresighting' is imminently justifiable and needs to be expanded and enhanced.[24]

Very briefly, our project understands 'legal foresighting' to mean the identification and exploration of possible and desirable future legal or quasi-legal developments aimed at achieving valued social and techno-logical ends. It is a fundamentally active and outcome-oriented reform process; while it offers us the opportunity to subject technological trajec-tories and social trends as well as legal conditions, inertias and develop-ments to early, rational, contemplative reflection, it is its shaping capacity that makes it particularly valuable. Legal foresighting should help us create pathways into the unknown, and part of that creation may mean (or demand) a fundamental re-visioning of the legal setting itself, its instruments, institutions and regulatory or governance mechanisms. We must be prepared to ask whether existing systems (and their assumptions and values) are capable of responding to the demands being made of them and of delivering the future that we want.[25]

While the Advisory Commission, together with a key circle of actors, shaped the process, a wide variety of stakeholders from academia, regu-latory bodies, medical societies, researchers, patients and social media co-operated to advance the field. Their efforts were very much an example, imperfectly realised, of legal foresighting.[26] A proof of this concept was the alignment of strategies and postures with local patient organisations. Far from advocating for deregulation or the creation of regulatory alter-natives to access experimental treatments, many organisations raised awareness of the diseases and the risks associated with experimental therapies, denounced the construction of 'unreasonable expectations' from the media, and advised patients who sought these alternative treatments.[27]

As an example of this exercise, we could cite the launching of the Argentine Network of Patients for Advanced Therapies (APTA Network) in 2013 under the auspices of the Advisory Commission and MOST and integrated with forty-five patient organisations. This network

---

[24] See also Chapter 18 in this volume.
[25] Graeme Laurie, Shawn Harmon and Fabiana Arzuaga, 'Foresighting Futures: Law, New Technologies, and the Challenges of Regulating for Uncertainty' (2012) 4 *Law, Innovation and Technology* 1.
[26] Ibid.
[27] Sonja Erikainen, Anna Couturier and Sarah Chan, 'Marketing Experimental Stem Cell Therapies in the UK: Biomedical Lifestyle Products and the Promise of Regenerative Medicine in the Digital Era' (2020) 29 *Science as Culture* 219.

provides a space for dialogue among scientists, regulators and patient organisations. Its creation also involved the advice and support of the Genetics Policy Institute, which helped with defining objectives to help Argentine patient groups to organise as a national network and to create critical mass. The Network's aims were to co-ordinate efforts, raise awareness about cellular therapies, promote legislation, position this issue on the public agenda, and inform patients and their families about advances in stem cell research and the risks of experimental treatments.[28]

The APTA Network has established links with research groups, funding agencies, regulatory bodies, international patient advocacy groups and other relevant actors, and it aims at strengthening the voice of patients in the field of advanced therapies. Allied with scientists from Argentina and abroad, and mobilising scientists, authorities and resources, patient organisations have begun to generate local records of pathologies, setting up medical histories, building international databases and establishing further ties with international patient groups. They advocate the development of new studies validated through clinical trials: trials that are approved by the competent regulatory authorities, with informed consent procedures, free to patients, and with detailed follow-up of patients and possible future complications.[29]

## 15.4   Conclusion

Argentine science and technology and health authorities have considered regenerative medicine and cell therapies as a 'strategic area' within the health sector and, to that end, they deployed institutional, regulatory and financing actions to build endogenous capacities in the area, informed by international standards. The design and adoption of a governance framework for these technologies has been a more-than-a-decade-long undertaking, which has relied on the strengths and commitment of key government institutions, ongoing engagement with a wide range of local stakeholders and the invaluable support of an

---

[28] Federation of Patients Associations for Rare Diseases of Argentina (FADEPOF) https://fadepof.org.ar (accessed 19 February 2021).

[29] La Asociación de Pacientes y Padres de Niños con Enfermedad de Stargardt (Stargardt APNES), 'Siete jóvenes argentinos viajaron a China para un ensayo clínico contra una discapacidad visual', www.stargardt.com.ar/novedades_detalle.php?link=Siete_jovenes_argentinos_viajaron_a_China_para_un_ensayo_clinico_contra_una_discapacidad_visual (accessed 19 February 2021).

international collaboration with Graeme Laurie and his team at the University of Edinburgh. This collaboration fuelled the knowledge and decision-making of the Advisory Commission at MOST and helped it to become a key driving force in the governance of advanced therapies in Argentina. This process received the input of serious and scientific research projects that evidenced the social values that Argentinian stakeholders desired, as well as a central normative guidance and oversight which, through the Advisory Commission, was converted into recommendations – in force today – on how to regulate. This process also facilitated the mobilisation of a close network of Argentine and UK researchers and regulators, which enabled swift policy movement.

To achieve the current normative framework, it was necessary to amend existing legal instruments and to issue new laws and regulations. The new framework exemplifies a more joined-up regime that is harmonised with other important regulatory agencies, like EMA and the FDA, and has the support of all stakeholders. The resulting framework is robust and responds to the vision of a desirable technological future, focused on promotion of R&D, the prevention of unproven treatments and the construction of a governance framework for advanced therapies. However, there are still challenges to overcome, such as the development of clinical testing, production and marketing. This opens a new discussion on what goes beyond R&D, and how to align novel elements to build the utility of this technology – as a strategic technology – to facilitate access and deliver concrete social benefits.

The legacy that, thanks to Graeme, we were able to leave for Argentina is of great value not only because we have achieved the goal of regulating new technologies in health but also because of the lessons learned through the process. It demonstrated to us that the power of a vision accompanied by hard work, and centred in values and principles, can certainly result in a great contribution to the country and to future generations.

# Institutions, Interpretive Communities and Legacy in Decision-Making

## A Case Study of Patents, Morality and Biotechnological Inventions

AISLING MCMAHON

## 16.1 Introduction

Institutional theories highlight the development of shared understandings or ways of doing things within various organisations or institutions, including branches of law or decision-making fora.[1] Over time, such shared understandings can become engrained and develop into interpretative patterns of thinking and practice.[2] Similarly, certain concepts within law can become imbued within a relatively fixed body of past practice (for example, via judicial precedent, legislative interpretation and so on), becoming *institutional* in nature, and this in turn can make

---

[1] Parts of this chapter draw on my earlier doctoral research completed under the supervision of Graeme Laurie and Gerard Porter – I am very grateful to both for their insights, and for our discussions on the morality provisions in patent law. The main sources of institutional theories drawn on in this chapter include sociological literature; see, for example, Paul DiMaggio and Walter Powell, 'The Iron Cage Revisited: Institutional Isomorphism and Collective Rationality in Organizational Fields' (1983) 48 *American Sociological Review* 147. In the political context, see Edwin Amenta and Kelly Ramsey, 'Institutional Theory' in Kevin Leicht and Craig Jenkins (eds), *The Handbook of Politics: State and Civil Society in Global Perspective* (Springer 2010) 15; and Peter Hall and Rosemary Taylor, 'Political Science and the Three Institutionalisms' (1996) 44 *Political Studies* 936; and in the legal context, see Neil MacCormick, 'Norms, Institutions and Institutional Facts' (1998) 17 *Law and Philosophy* 301.

[2] Aisling McMahon, 'Regulatory Authorities and Decision-Making in Health Research: The Institutional Dimension' in Graeme Laurie et al (eds), *The Cambridge Handbook of Health Research Regulation* (Cambridge University Press 2021): 'Institutional theories examine the way in which policies and decisions are structurally determined by institutions. "Institutions" traditionally included state institutions such as the legislature and executive, but can also refer to embedded systems of rules, branches of law, etc. evident within particular organisational contexts.'

legal change difficult to achieve. Indeed, in some cases, even when legal change is suggested on paper (for example, within a legislative text), practice within a field may still be drawn back to historical conceptions or institutional understandings of legal concepts within that decision-making framework. In this vein, legacy within a decision-making context is a significant influence on end outcomes of decision-making.

In this chapter, I examine two aspects of institutional 'legacy': (1) the legacy within particular decision-making frameworks, including normative predispositions that may develop within approaches to decision-making or influence decision-making actors in that framework; and (2) legacy in terms of shared institutional understandings and historical legacies around a particular concept or provision within that decision-making framework. Such legacies can become engrained, making legal change difficult to achieve without institutional intervention. In this way, shared institutional understandings can act as an encumbrance to law's responsiveness to societal or technological change. The chapter uses the morality provisions in the Biotechnology Directive 98/44/EC ('the Directive') – which provide that inventions are excluded from patentability where their commercial exploitation is against *ordre public* or morality – and examines as a case study how these provisions have been interpreted by the European Patent Office (EPO) since the adoption of the Directive.[3] In doing so, the chapter makes three related arguments specific to this context. First, I argue that traditional predispositions or experiences within the EPO framework, together with shared understandings within the EPO of the role, or lack thereof, of ethics within the patent system, have become engrained, making adaptation difficult to achieve in this context.

Second, I argue that despite the increased focus on ethical considerations around patents for biotechnological inventions in the text of the Directive, the EPO, as patent examination and granting body for 'European' patents, has continued to show a reluctance to engage deeply with the morality provisions or other ethical provisions within the Directive in practice. In this vein, it must be noted that the European Patent Organisation (EPOrg), which is the overarching organisation within which the EPO is based, is not an EU entity. Instead, it is an inter-governmental organisation of thirty-eight states comprising all twenty-seven EU Member States and eleven non-EU states.[4] All

---

[3] Council Directive 98/44/EC on the legal protection of biotechnological inventions (1998) OJ L213/13.

[4] For a full list of states, see www.epo.org/about-us/foundation/member-states.html (accessed 4 February 2020). This categorisation of non-EU states includes the United Kingdom.

thirty-eight states are Contracting States to the European Patent Convention 1973 (EPC) (the primary 'European' legislation governing patent law in Europe). While the EPO is the patent grant and examination body for patents applied for using the 'European' patent route in all EU countries, this route allows applicants to apply for a patent in more than one European country at the same time and is consequently a popular avenue for those seeking European patent protection.[5]

Although the EPO is not directly bound by EU law, the EPOrg adopted the Directive as supplementary interpretation for the EPC following the Directive's adoption, suggesting a commitment that the EPO would apply principles set out in the Directive for patent grant and examination for biotechnological inventions. Notably in this vein, the general morality provision in the Directive is virtually identical to the general morality provision already contained in the EPC (Art 53(a)). However, the Directive incorporated specific exclusions against patentability based on the morality provisions that were not previously contained within the EPOrg context. After the Directive's adoption, the EPOrg also adopted these provisions via Implementing Regulations to the EPC, discussed in Section 16.2. Indeed, this commitment was arguably necessary for the EPO to remain as the patent examination/grant body for EU countries under the 'European' patent route. Thus, broader questions of institutional congruence and fit vis-à-vis the EPOrg and the EU are relevant in this context, but these questions are outside the scope of this chapter.[6] Instead, the key focus here is how the EPO's shared understandings, and the legacy of morality provisions within the EPOrg framework, arguably continue to dominate the EPO's interpretation and approach to moral/ethical issues posed by patent grant and, specifically, its approach to the interpretation of the morality provisions

---

[5] If the application is granted, the applicant acquires a bundle of national patents for the states applied for, whose post-grant life is considered individually under the jurisdiction of each national European state.

[6] Such institutional issues vis-à-vis the EU and EPOrg in this context are considered in Aisling McMahon, *The Morality Provisions in the European Patent System: An Institutional Examination* (PhD thesis, University of Edinburgh 2016); Aisling McMahon, 'An Institutional Examination of the Implications of the Unitary Patent Package for the Morality Provisions: A Fragmented Future Too Far?' (2017) 48 *IIC International Review of Intellectual Property and Competition Law* 42; and Antonina Bakardjieva-Engelbrekt, 'Institutional and Jurisdictional Aspects of Stem Cell Patenting in Europe (EC and EPO): Tensions and Prospects' in Aurora Plomer and Paul Torremans (eds), *Embryonic Stem Cell Patents in Europe: European Law and Ethics* (Oxford University Press 2009) 227.

in its consideration of the patentability of biotechnological inventions. This continued influence of such legacies and shared institutional understandings is despite the EPO's adoption of the Directive as supplementary interpretation and the broader commitment to engaging with ethical considerations for biotechnological patents that appears evident within the Directive's text.

Third, the chapter's overarching argument is that the continued marginalisation of the morality provisions and other ethical considerations within EPO decision-making is in large part due to institutional reasons; specifically, to the fact that the interpretative communities within the EPO have remained static despite the EU's adoption of the Directive. Accordingly, engrained conceptions or institutional understandings of the limited role of the morality provisions and ethics within patent law continue to dominate within EPO decision-making. In effect, the role of legacy within the institutional setting is starkly evident in this context and offers broader lessons on the role of institutions in achieving legal change within patent law, and the role of institutional legacies more generally in other decision-making contexts.[7]

As a caveat, whether patent law *should* have a broader role in relation to ethical issues at grant stage is debated and the purpose of this chapter is not necessarily to address this normative question.[8] Rather, the focus here is on legacy and the argument made is a more nuanced one; namely, that as currently institutionally configured, the legacy within the EPO is not one which easily accommodates broader consideration of ethical issues within patent law at grant stage. Moreover, the chapter argues that if broader consideration of ethical issues posed by patent grant is sought in Europe, then the role of institutions and legacy within European patent law requires scrutiny.

Such arguments and issues resonate with questions examined in Graeme Laurie's work on patents and biotechnology, which highlights the insular nature of patent law.[9] Graeme observed that, 'despite far more interaction today than has ever occurred in the past, it is still possible to

---

[7] See McMahon (n 2).

[8] For a recent discussion on such issues, which argues in favour of a broader development and consideration of such provisions in European patent law, see Karen Walsh and Naomi Hawkins, 'Expanding the Role of Morality and Public Policy in European Patent Law' in Paul Torremans (ed), *Intellectual Property and Human Rights* (4th edn, Wolters Kluwer 2020).

[9] Graeme Laurie, 'Should There Be an Obligation of Disclosure of Origin of Genetic Resources in Patent Applications? Learning Lessons from Developing Countries' (2005) 2 *SCRIPTed* 265, 266.

detect strong enduring reluctance to see, or accept, the patent system as part of a greater whole'.[10] He also previously argued that the advent of biotechnology led to objectors seizing upon the opportunity to use the morality provisions in an attempt to challenge such provisions, but with limited success as the 'first problem was to persuade the patent examiners in the European Patent Office that considerations of morality were within their sphere of responsibility and competence'.[11] This fundamental issue is still evident within the EPO context and this chapter argues that it stems largely from an institutional legacy within the EPO, which has viewed itself as outside or disconnected from other systems – and as a system whose role is not to delve into questions of morality or ethics.

To advance these arguments, the chapter is structured as follows. Section 16.2 provides an overview of the morality provisions and the focus on moral and ethical considerations in the drafting and adoption of the Biotechnology Directive. It argues that, despite the incorporation of ethical considerations within the Directive's text, and such provisions being key to its eventual adoption, in practice such ethical considerations, including the morality provisions, have remained largely marginalised within EPO decision-making. Section 16.3 examines the role of institutional legacies as an explanation for why there is a marginalisation of the morality provisions and other ethical considerations within the EPO context. First, it examines the historical development and background of the morality provisions and the traditional exceptionalisation of such provisions within the EPO framework. Second, it examines the institutional legacy within the EPO decision-making framework attributable to the type of personnel within the EPO, which the chapter argues produces a distinct interpretative community wherein the background of personnel within the EPO reinforces an institutional predisposition favouring a minimal role for broader ethical considerations within patent examination and decision-making. Section 16.4 concludes, arguing that if greater engagement with ethical issues is sought within European patent law at grant stage, then institutional or legislative change, or both, is needed. Crucially, institutional factors and legacies must be given greater consideration within patent law and within legal decision-making more generally, as without such legacies being accounted for, they stand as

---

[10] Ibid., 267.
[11] Graeme Laurie, 'Patenting and the Human Body' in Andrew Grubb (ed), *Principles of Medical Law* (2nd edn, Oxford University Press 2004) 1079.

significant potential encumbrances to legal change and to law's responsiveness.


## 16.2   Biotechnology, Patents and the Morality Provisions within the EPO

A patent is an exclusionary right allowing the patent holder to exclude others from using the patented invention for the duration of the patent (generally twenty years). Historically, patent law was relatively insulated from ethical considerations,[12] and the grant of a patent was viewed primarily in technical or economic terms, focusing on its role in incentivising innovation.[13] Patent law developed a tendency to be 'relatively insular',[14] with patents perceived as technical in nature, sealed off from broader ethical considerations. In effect, patent law was 'continually presented as a neutral inert system, which is above or beyond ethics, politics or cultural concern'.[15]

However, the advent of biotechnology fundamentally challenged such conceptions of patents as being technical inert devices because ethical questions quickly arose around the appropriateness of granting patents over certain biotechnological 'inventions'.[16] These included questions around the appropriateness of granting patents over life-forms (for example, patents over transgenic animals);[17] questions around the

---

[12] Arguably, an exception to this is in the access to medicines context; however, such debates around patents' effects on broader rights and interests in such contexts are generally framed primarily in terms of *access* as opposed to '*ethics*' per se.

[13] Aisling McMahon, 'Biotechnology, Health and Patents as Private Governance Tools: The Good, the Bad and the Potential for Ugly?' (2020) 3 *Intellectual Property Quarterly* 161.

[14] Laurie (n 9) 266.

[15] Lionel Bently and Bradley Sherman, 'The Ethics of Patenting: Towards a Transgenic Patent System' (1995) 3 *Medical Law Review* 275.

[16] Biotechnological inventions are defined in the EPC as 'inventions which concern a product consisting of or containing biological material or a process by means of which biological material is produced, processed or used' (Rule 26(2)–(3) Implementing Regulations EPC). See also Articles 3(1) and 2(1) of the Biotechnology Directive. For a general discussion of biotechnologies, see 'Emerging Biotechnologies: Technology, Choice and the Public Good' (Nuffield Council on Bioethics 2012) xviii www .nuffieldbioethics.org/publications/emerging-biotechnologies (accessed 4 February 2021). For an overview of uses of biotechnologies in the patent system, see Oliver Mills, *Biotechnological Inventions: Moral Restraints and Patent law* (revised edn, Ashgate Publishing 2010) 7.

[17] *Harvard/Oncomouse* [1990] OJ EPO 476; [1992] OJ EPO 589. See more generally Deryck Beyleveld and Roger Brownsword, *Mice, Morality and Patents* (Common Law Institute of Intellectual Property 1993).

patentability of elements of the human body (for example, patents on isolated human genes);[18] and questions around the ethical issues raised by patents over contentious technologies, such as human embryonic stem cell–related inventions.[19] It also became evident that, depending on how patents were used over health-related biotechnologies, patents could have significant implications for access to and delivery of health care.[20]

As an aside, some individuals and groups sometimes seek to use patent grant challenges as a means to object to broader ethical concerns around the development of biotechnologies more generally.[21] However, depending on the aim of such objections, this can be problematic given that patents are a negative right – they merely allow the rights-holder to stop others from using a technology; thus, refusing a patent over a technology on the basis of the morality provisions potentially gives more freedom to use that technology to third parties rather than less.[22] Accordingly, the use of the patent grant stage to address ethical objections to a technology itself has been highlighted by some as futile.[23] Nonetheless, the lack of a patent could form a disincentive for commercial development of a particular area, and hence be used as part of a broader regulatory toolbox in such contexts; however, such arguments are beyond the scope of this current chapter.[24]

In Europe, the advent of biotechnologies led to significant questions around how biotechnological inventions should be accommodated within patent law and the ensuing uncertainty led to legislative action and the EU's eventual adoption of the Biotechnology Directive 98/44/EC.

[18] *Howard Florey/Relaxin* [1995] EPOR 541.
[19] EPO decisions involving human embryonic stem cells include: Case T1079/03 *Edinburgh University* (Unreported) [2003] OD EP 94913174.2; Case T522/ 04 *California Institute of Technology (CIT)* (Unreported) [2003] ED EP 93921175.1; Wisconsin Alumni Research Foundation (WARF) (G002/06), Decision of the Enlarged Board of Appeal of 25 November 2008; *TECHNION/Culturing stem cells* [2014] EPOR 23; *ASTERIAS/ Embryonic stem cells* [2015] EPOR 9.
[20] Aisling McMahon, 'Gene Patents and the Marginalisation of Ethics in Patent Law' (2019) 41 *European Intellectual Property Review* 608.
[21] See Mills (n 16).
[22] Shawn Harmon and Graeme Laurie, 'Dignity, Plurality and Patentability: The Unfinished Story of *Brüstle* v. *Greenpeace*' (2013) 38 *European Law Review* 92.
[23] See Mills (n 16); Graeme Laurie, 'Biotechnology: Facing the Problems of Patent Law' in Hector MacQueen (ed), *Innovation, Incentive and Reward: Intellectual Property Law and Policy* (Edinburgh University Press Hume Institute: Hume Papers on Public Policy vol 5(3), 1997) 46.
[24] See generally Aisling McMahon, 'Regulating Emerging Biotechnology: Patents and Licensing for "Ethical" Use' (Working Paper, 2021).

However, the Directive had a tumultuous drafting history, taking more than ten years from inception to its final adoption in 1998.[25] A key stumbling block to its adoption were the ethical issues posed by patents over biotechnological inventions.[26] The first draft of the Directive was rejected by the European Parliament in March 1995.[27] It was subsequently amended by the Commission, which placed greater emphasis on the ethical issues. A revised proposal was submitted in December 1995 and adopted in May 1998.[28] Arguably, central to the Directive's final adoption was the inclusion of ethical considerations for patenting biotechnological inventions within the revised text.

The subsequent adoption of the Directive as supplementary interpretation for the EPOrg's EPC[29] signified a commitment to applying principles contained within the Directive in EPO decisions on patent examination and grant; as noted, this created a curious institutional set-up, but this move was also arguably institutionally necessary to retain the EPO's role as patent grant body under the EPC system for EU countries.

Three main avenues to account for ethical issues posed by patent applications for biotechnological inventions are evident within the Directive, namely: the morality provisions under Article 6; references to the influence of human dignity considerations in the patentability of biotechnologies under recitals 16 and 38;[30] and recital 43, which underpins the role of human rights considerations in decisions on patenting biotechnologies.[31] Nonetheless, despite the references to morality, human dignity and human rights within the Directive, there is limited evidence of broader engagement with such concepts in EPO decisions.

---

[25] The first draft was introduced by the Commission on 17 October 1988; see Gerard Porter, 'The Drafting History of the European Biotechnology Directive' in Plomer and Torremans (n 6) 7.

[26] Ibid., 10.

[27] Ibid., 13.

[28] Ibid., 14.

[29] Regulation 26(1) of the Implementing Regulations to the EPC.

[30] Recital 16 Directive states: '[w]hereas patent law must be applied so as to respect the fundamental principles safeguarding the dignity and integrity of the person'. Recital 38 states: 'whereas processes, the use of which offend against human dignity ... are obviously also excluded from patentability'.

[31] Recital 43 contains a caveat indicating human rights underpin the Directive's interpretation. It states: '[w]hereas pursuant to Article F(2) of the Treaty on European Union, the Union is to respect fundamental rights, as guaranteed by the European Convention for the Protection of Human Rights and Fundamental Freedoms signed in Rome on 4 November 1950 and as they result from the constitutional traditions common to the Member States, as general principles of Community law'.

Instead, a reluctance by the EPO to engage in broader deliberation on such concepts appears evident both before and after the Directive's adoption. Moreover, in the (relatively small number) of decisions where human rights are discussed by the EPO in this context, the analysis tends to be often scant and lacking in depth.[32] Instead, a marginalisation of such issues is arguably evident within EPO decision-making.

The reluctance of the EPO to engage with ethical considerations in patent examination is demonstrated by examining its cases on the morality provisions. The morality provision contained in Article 6 of the Directive includes a general and specific morality exclusion. The general morality provision in Article 6(1) excludes patents on inventions where their commercial exploitation is against *ordre public* or morality. This provision replicated the existing Article 53(a) EPC 1973, which applied to all inventions, not only biotechnologies. Article 6(2) was an addition to the morality provisions inserted by the Directive, comprising a list of four specific inventions or processes excluded from patentability based on the general morality provisions, namely:

> (a) processes for cloning human beings; (b) processes for modifying the germ line genetic identity of human beings; (c) uses of human embryos for industrial or commercial purposes; (d) processes for modifying the genetic identity of animals which are likely to cause them suffering without any substantial medical benefit to man or animal, and also animals resulting from such processes.

The general morality provision in Article 6(1) provides the main avenue through which moral or ethical objections have been made to the patentability of emerging biotechnologies; however, such challenges have had limited success in practice within the EPO. Instead, the EPO has generally shown a marked reluctance to engage in the analysis of 'morality' or *ordre public* considerations, or to deny patents over biotechnologies based on the morality provisions – both before and after the

---

[32] For example, Case T0149/11 of 24 January 2013: Method and device for processing a slaughtered animal or part thereof in a slaughterhouse. This is one of the few cases where the EPO engages directly with human rights in the context of the morality provisions but does so with limited depth of analysis. See McMahon (2016) (n 6) 140. See also Aurora Plomer, 'Human Dignity and Patents' in Christophe Geiger (ed), *Research Handbook of Human Rights and IP Rights* (Edward Elgar 2015) 493. For an important, broader critique of the role of human rights within patent law as currently designed focusing on access to medicines, see Sivaramjani Thambisetty, 'Improving Access to Patented Medicines: Are Human Rights Getting in the Way?' (2019) 4 *Intellectual Property Quarterly* 284.

adoption of the Directive – and express statements to this effect are evident within the EPO's decisions. For example, prior to the Directive's adoption, in its 1995 decision in *Greenpeace v. Plant Genetic Systems*, the EPO stated that the morality provisions should be 'narrowly construed' in practice because the drafting history of the EPC suggested that patentability would be as wide as possible.[33] Similarly, after the adoption of the Directive, in its 2001 decision in *Leland Stanford*,[34] the EPO's Opposition Division held that the role of the EPO was not to act as a 'moral censor' for emerging biotechnologies. It stated that, in its view, the role of the general morality provision was a limited one, to be used to deny patent on 'extreme subject matter' such as letter bombs where technologies were 'regarded by the public as so abhorrent that the grant of a patent would be inconceivable'.[35] In *Euthanasia Composition/ Michigan State University*,[36] the EPO's Technical Board stated that it is generally accepted that '. . . Article 53(a) is to be construed narrowly and that such a restrictive interpretation is, while having regard to the particular circumstances of each individual case, not only correct but also justified'.[37] Furthermore, where the morality provisions are invoked in practice, the EPO has adopted high thresholds which must be met before patentability can be excluded on this basis. In the same case, the Technical Board stated that the exploitation of an invention infringes the morality provision only if 'it is regarded as reprehensible by society in general or at least by the trade concerned'.[38] Alongside these statements within EPO decisions, the EPO Guidelines for Examination state that the morality provisions are likely to be invoked only in 'rare and exceptional cases'.[39] The Guidelines also state that a 'fair test to apply is to consider whether it is probable that the public in general would regard the invention as so abhorrent that the grant of patent rights would be inconceivable'.[40]

---

[33] Decision of the Board of Appeal of the European Patent Office, *Greenpeace Ltd* v. *Plant Genetic Systems*, decision of 21 February 1995, T 356/93, 1. See also Case T 0866/01 Decision of the Technical Board of Appeal 3.3.02 of 11 May 2005.
[34] EPO Opposition Division, *Leland Stanford*, 16 August 2001 (2002) EPOR 2, para 44.
[35] Ibid., para 51.
[36] Case T 0866/01 Decision of the Technical Board of Appeal 3.3.02 of 11 May 2005.
[37] Ibid., para 5.4.
[38] Ibid., para 6.12.
[39] EPO, 'Guidelines for Examination' www.epo.org/law-practice/legal-texts/html/guidelines/e/g_ii_4_1.htm (accessed 4 February 2021).
[40] Ibid. See further Amanda Warren-Jones, 'Identifying European Moral Consensus: Why Are the Patent Courts Reticent to Accept Empirical Evidence in Resolving

Such statements in both past EPO decisions and the EPO Examination Guidelines indicate a light-touch approach taken by the EPO to the examination of the general morality provisions. In practice, such provisions are generally used only in rare and exceptional circumstances to deny patents on biotechnologies, and the EPO has shown limited appetite to date for engaging in deeper analysis of the ethical issues posed by patents on biotechnologies under these provisions. Moreover, while it is conceded that, in contrast to the general morality provision, the specific exclusions under Article 6(2) of the Biotechnology Directive have been used to deny patents on inventions (primarily for human embryonic stem cell inventions or related technologies under Article 6(2)(c)),[41] this does not necessarily mean that the EPO has developed a broader ethical engagement in such contexts. Instead, a purely definitional test applies to the specific exclusions under Article 6(2), and the EPO's task is merely to assess whether inventions fall within the definition of the exclusions set out by legislators under Article 6(2) of the Directive, as replicated in the EPC's Implementing Regulations after the Directive's adoption. If applications fall within such definitions, they are automatically excluded from patentability. However, if they do not fall within such definitions, then the specific exclusions do not apply. In that event, ethical issues related to patentability would need to be considered under the general morality provision, in relation to which it has been demonstrated that the EPO adopts a light-touch approach – hence such challenges are highly unlikely to be successful given EPO practice.

The definitional nature of Article 6(2) arguably means that the potential for institutional legacies within the EPO to influence its application is limited as, in theory, EPO discretion on what falls to be excluded by these provisions is removed by reducing the EPO's role to one of definitional application of the legislative provisions. Nonetheless, the key shortcoming here is that biotechnologies have advanced significantly since the Directive's adoption in 1998 and this means that, in practice, the EPO's interpretation of Article 6(2)'s application to biotechnological advances

---

Biotechnological Cases?' (2006) 28 *European Intellectual Property Review* 26; and Amanda Warren-Jones, 'Finding a "Common Morality Codex" for Biotech: A Question of Substance' (2008) 39 *International Review of Intellectual Property and Competition Law* 638. For a more recent critique of the EPO's approach to such provisions, see Justine Pila, 'Adapting the Ordre Public and Morality Exclusion of European Patent Law to Accommodate Emerging Technologies' (2020) 38 *Nature Biotechnology* 555.

[41] Wisconsin Alumni Research Foundation (WARF) (G002/06), Decision of the Enlarged Board of Appeal 25 November 2008.

is still needed. In effect, as technologies develop, definitions under Article 6(2) become stretched and require reinterpretation in practice to discern whether they apply to new contexts. For example, Article 6(2) excludes patents on uses of 'human embryos for industrial or commercial purposes'; as technologies developed, EPO decision-makers had to consider whether this would also exclude patents on human embryonic stem-cell technologies, which it answered in the affirmative.[42]

Thus, the EPO's discretion starts to re-emerge as important in such contexts due to the difficulty for law in keeping apace of science and the fact that the specific exclusions are reflective of legislative thinking around biotechnologies from 1998, which is now nearly 25 years ago. Accordingly, as technologies develop, it is more likely that they will fall outside the Article 6(2) exclusions, instead to be considered within Article 6(1) and then, if the arguments in this chapter are borne out, the EPO's legacy favouring a light-touch application will continue to dominate. Similar issues can be observed in terms of the role of dignity within the Directive. Despite the Directive adopting this as a principle to be considered in the patenting of biotechnologies, in practice it has been interpreted in a highly restrictive manner by the EPO, far removed from the broader conception of this principle within bioethics or medical law.[43] Similarly, human rights, although alluded to within the Directive, have also taken a limited role within EPO decision-making in practice.[44] However, given the limits of space, these points are not considered in detail here.

The broader question that arises from the foregoing analysis is why, if the Directive adopted provisions providing for moral and ethical considerations to be accounted for in the patenting of biotechnologies, and as the Directive was adopted by the EPOrg as supplementary interpretation

---

[42] G 0002/06 (Use of embryos/WARF) of 25 November 2008. Subsequently, the Court of Justice of the European Union had to consider whether technologies involving parthenotes (human eggs stimulated to mimic early-stage embryo development) would be patentable, and stated that such technologies were not excluded under Article 6(2)(c) as they were not currently capable of developing into a human being: Case C-364/13 *International Stem Cell Corporation* v. *Comptroller General for Patents*, EU:C:2014:2451.
[43] T Arvind and Aisling McMahon, 'Commodification, Control, and the Contractualisation of the Human Body' in Elodie Bertrand, Marie-Xavière Catto and Alicia Mornington (eds), *The Limits of the Market: Commodification of Nature and Body* (Mare & Martin 2020) 43. See also discussion in Graeme Laurie, 'Patents, Patients and Consent: Exploring the Interface between Regulation and Innovation Regimes' in Han Somsen (ed), *The Regulatory Challenge of Biotechnology* (Edward Elgar 2007) 214.
[44] McMahon (2016) (n 6) 226–7.

for the EPC, have such considerations remained relatively marginalised by the EPO's decision-making? Several aspects contribute to this, and a full account is beyond the scope of this chapter; however, one key aspect is the role of institutions[45] and, as part of this, the role of legacy within the EPO context, which I now turn to consider.

## 16.3 Institutions and Interpretative Community within Patent Law: The Role of Legacy

Legacy is a multifarious concept, encompassing 'something that is a part of your history or that remains from an earlier time'.[46] This section uses the lens of institutional theory to focus on legacy arising from two distinct avenues within legal decision-making. First, I look at the legacy of legislative provisions in terms of how past practice or previous decisions on such provisions, as well as the legislative history behind them within that decision-making framework, can influence or bind their future applications. Second, I examine institutional legacy relating to the body of past knowledge and experiences of decision-makers within a given framework, which provides an important interpretative community for applying a particular provision in practice.[47] Legacy in both of these senses can have a significant influence on a decision-making body's interpretation of such provisions, or analogous provisions, making legal adaptation difficult to achieve without tailored institutional intervention.

This section considers these two aspects of legacy within the European patent system for biotechnological inventions, arguing that they are significant factors in the restrictive application of the morality provisions and other ethical considerations by the EPO for biotechnological inventions.

### 16.3.1 Legacy within Law: Precedent and Legislative Histories

Historical institutionalism is a useful avenue to explore how past decisions within an institutional context can bind a decision-making body or influence it to follow similar patterns in future analogous matters even where there is no direct binding precedent. Historical institutionalism is

---

[45] For a broader discussion, see ibid.

[46] Cambridge Dictionary, https://dictionary.cambridge.org/ (accessed 10 February 2021).

[47] The term 'interpretative community' derives from Stanley Fish, *Doing What Comes Naturally: Change, Rhetoric and the Practice of Theory in Literary and Legal Studies* (Duke University Press 1989).

a diverse field,[48] which, in broad terms attempts to explain 'how the past influences the present and the future, the way incremental institutional change affects the choice set at a moment of time and the nature of path dependence'.[49] Within historical institutionalism, institutions are generally understood to be formal rules or organisations,[50] although they may also be informal rules and norms. Such institutions are assessed under historical institutionalism to see how they influence behaviour or the adoption of policy.[51]

A crucial element of historical institutionalism is the idea of path dependency which, in general terms, is how historical actions influence present acts.[52] Path dependency implies that 'what happened at an earlier point in time will affect the possible outcomes of a sequence of events occurring at a later point in time';[53] defined in this way, it can be viewed as a form of legacy of decisions. A prime example of this is precedent within common law systems, with path dependency encapsulated by *stare decisis*, which 'creates a seamless web connecting the past to the present and future'[54] and whereby 'reliance upon binding precedents leads courts to begin every case with an examination of the past'.[55] However, this in turn also means that past decisions of a body on a particular concept or provision may become difficult to adapt or change. Where discretion arises in favour of decision-makers, historical institutionalism suggests that decision-makers will tend to seek to ensure that they follow past precedent within a legal context (where this is binding); even where no precedent is evident, the decision-maker may be influenced by how analogous provisions or concepts have been

---

[48] Amenta and Ramsey (n 1) 16.

[49] Douglas North, *Institutions, Institutional Change and Economic Performance* (Cambridge University Press 1990) 3; as cited in Antonina Bakardjieva-Engelbrekt, 'Copyright from an Institutional Perspective: Actors, Interests, Stakes and the Logic of Participation' (2007) 4 *Review of Economic Research on Copyright Issues* 65, 70.

[50] Wolfgang Streeck and Kathleen Thelen (eds), *Beyond Continuity: Institutional Change in Advanced Political Economies* (Oxford University Press 2005).

[51] Sven Steinmo, 'What Is Historical Institutionalism?' in Donatella Della Porta and Michael Keating (eds), *Approaches in the Social Sciences* (Cambridge University Press 2008) 159.

[52] Oona Hathaway, 'Path Dependence in the Law: The Course and Pattern of Legal Change in a Common Law System' (2001) 86 *Iowa Law Review* 101.

[53] William Sewell, 'Three Temporalities: Toward an Eventful Sociology' in Terrence McDonald (ed), *The Historic Turn in the Human Sciences* (University of Michigan Press 1996) 245, 262–3.

[54] Hathaway (n 52) 601–65.

[55] Ibid.

interpreted in that decision-making framework. Thus, past decisions can be both prescriptive and predictive in their influences on decision-making outcomes.[56]

Reflecting on the morality provisions applicable in European patent law, historical institutionalism implies that the past practice of the EPO will be influential in how these provisions are applied. This includes how the EPO applied such provisions prior to the Directive's adoption by the EU in 1998, which curiously did not trigger any guidance within the EPO on the need for a change in interpretative practice around the general morality provisions for biotechnological inventions. As discussed in Section 16.2, the EPO historically showed strong reticence to deny patents based on the morality provisions, adopting high thresholds and discussing such provisions as exceptional in nature. Moreover, the general morality provision contained within Article 53(a) EPC since 1973 was virtually identical in wording to the provision adopted as Article 6 of the Directive. Thus, without the EPOrg expressly indicating an institutional change of practice in how this general provision should be applied for biotechnologies, it is unsurprising that the EPO retained a light-touch approach to the morality provisions. Hence, despite the emphasis on ethical considerations within the Directive and the EPO's acknowledgement that the morality provisions can provide an avenue to consider human rights and other ethical concerns in its later decisions,[57] in practice these provisions continue rarely to be used to deny patents on biotechnologies and, instead, arguably the EPO's light-touch approach to ethical issues continues.

Furthermore, the legacy of the current morality provisions encompasses the drafting history of the morality provisions within the EPOrg context, which is a crucial influence for their current application, particularly because of the identical wording of the general morality provision in the EPC and in the Directive. The morality provisions within the EPC developed from Article 2(a) of the Strasbourg Convention 1963,[58] which was adopted for all technologies within the EPC in 1973 under

---

[56] McMahon (2016) (n 6).

[57] Case T0149/11 of 24 January 2013: Method and device for processing a slaughtered animal or part thereof in a slaughterhouse; where the EPO Board stated at para 2.5 that 'ordre public' must be seen as defined 'by norms that safeguard fundamental values and rights such as the inviolability of human dignity and the right of life and physical integrity'.

[58] It provided: '[t]he Contracting States shall not be bound to provide for the grant of patents in respect of: (a) Inventions the publication or exploitation of which would be contrary "ordre public" or morality, provided that the exploitation shall not be deemed to be so contrary merely because it is prohibited by law or regulation'.

Article 53(a) EPC. Notably, according to Armitage and Davies, the morality provision was not introduced by the EPOrg as an essential feature of the substantive law; rather, 'the morality check has to be seen as merely an optional, conventional feature on the margins of the system'.[59] It was adopted in the EPC without controversy as an 'unremarkable but necessary marginal safeguard'.[60] Indeed, Armitage and Davies state that 'it seems plain to us, however, that to move from the traditional light regime [in terms of the application of the morality provision] to a regime of interventionist moral judgment would be a severe change in direction for the patent system'.[61] Thus, the legislative background of the general morality provision within the Strasbourg Convention and the EPC demonstrates that, historically, it was perceived as a marginal provision within European patent law. Given this historical legacy, it is unsurprising that EPO decision-makers charged with applying this morality provision continue to marginalise it in practice.

This legacy is likely to continue to foster a light-touch application of the provisions and limited intervention by the EPO in relation to ethical issues with European patent law, unless institutional change is adopted within the EPO. EPO guidance alone is unlikely to be sufficient to change the EPO's approach, as such engrained institutional legacies require sustained and bottom-up change for an institution to adapt. Accordingly, despite additional ethical principles being incorporated within the EU's Biotechnology Directive and this being adopted by the EPOrg as supplementary guidance, it is unsurprising and, indeed, to be expected that the legacy of how such provisions were historically interpreted by the EPO continues to influence the EPO. Arguably, this is a key factor in entrenching a light-touch interpretation of the provisions and a predisposition in favour of patent grant as opposed to the refusal of patent applications in this context.

### 16.3.2   Legacy of Interpretative Communities and Encumbered Practices

Looking beyond the legacy of a legal provision itself, the role of legacy in terms of the experiences that decision-makers from a particular body

---

[59] Edward Armitage and Ivor Davies, *Patent and Morality in Perspective* (Intellectual Property Institute 1994) 20. This analysis was based on their reflections on the drafting of the Strasbourg Convention.
[60] Ibid., 24.
[61] Ibid., 43.

bring to decision-making is also significant. The decision-making body, as Stanley Fish described,[62] provides the 'interpretative community'[63] for decision-making. The composition of and experiences within that interpretative community are vital to the end outcomes of decision-making given that they can create shared understanding or normative biases. As Peter Drahos argued, 'it is the patent community working with a shared set of assumptions, understandings, conventions and values that settles issues and problems of interpretation within the patent system'.[64] Drahos claimed that, in doing so, 'the patent community probably exercises more influence on the direction and content of patent policy than legislatures, which in any case rely on committees of specialists to advise them on matters of patent policy'.[65] Support for such arguments is provided by drawing on sociological institutionalism and, particularly, Powell and DiMaggio's work,[66] which demonstrates the significance of legacy in terms of the decision-makers' experiences and backgrounds as predictive influences on decision-making.

In this vein, the concept of 'isomorphism' discussed by Powell and DiMaggio is relevant. They describe isomorphism as 'a constraining process which forces one unit in a population to resemble other units that face the same set of environmental constraints'.[67] One type of isomorphism is normative isomorphism associated with professionalisation within a field,[68] as professionalisation creates 'a pool of almost interchangeable individuals who occupy similar positions across a range of organisations and possess a similarity of orientation and disposition that may override variations in tradition and control that may otherwise shape organizations'.[69] In effect, within professionalised

---

[62] Fish (n 47).

[63] There have been criticisms of Fish's usage of this term, including R Gill, 'The Moral Implications of Interpretive Communities' (1983) 33 *Christianity & Literature* 49; Robert Scholes, 'Who Cares about the Text?' (1984) 17 *A Forum on Fiction* 171; and Walter Davis, 'The Fisher King: Wille zur Macht in Baltimore' (1984) 10 *Critical Inquiry* 668.

[64] Peter Drahos, 'Biotechnology Patents, Markets and Morality' (1999) 21 *European Intellectual Property Review* 441, 441–2.

[65] Ibid., 442.

[66] Paul DiMaggio and Walter Powell, 'The Iron Cage Revisited: Institutional Isomorphism and Collective Rationality in Organizational Fields' (1983) 48 *American Sociological Review* 147.

[67] Ibid., 149.

[68] Ibid., 150.

[69] Charles Perrow, 'Is Business Really Changing?' (1974) *Organizational Dynamics* 31; as cited in DiMaggio and Powell (n 66) 152.

fields, such as within patent law, a filtering process develops whereby 'manager and key staff are drawn from the same universities and filtered on a common set of attributes, [thus] they will tend to view problems in a similar fashion, see the same policies, procedures and structures as normatively sanctioned and legitimated, and approach decision in much the same way'.[70] Accordingly, a legacy of similar experiences and credentials of personnel can develop within specialised areas. If the main decision-making personnel are drawn from similar backgrounds with limited variance of experiences, similar ways of doing things can become entrenched, making adaptation that deviates from traditional roles or experiences of the organisation's personnel difficult to achieve. The interpretative community in effect develops its own legacy of experience and expertise and, without intervention, this can act as a strong encumbrance to change.

This form of isomorphism is highly likely within the EPO given that, within the three main avenues for the interpretation of the morality provisions at patent grant and adjudication stage – the Examining Division, the Opposition Division and the Boards of Appeal – personnel are composed primarily of technical scientific experts who are qualified patent attorneys, which is a niche and highly specialised field. Moreover, the legal experts involved within these fora are also drawn primarily from patent practice and likely from within the legal commercial field. Both technically and legally qualified members are working within areas which would generally involve limited broader engagement with ethical issues or human rights and, arguably, this further entrenches a focus on the economic and scientific aspects of patents with limited engagement with the broader ethical issues posed by patents. For example, the EPO's Examining Division is important for the morality provisions because it is the primary decision-making body for assessing patent grant within the EPO and makes the day-to-day decisions on patent grant or refusal. It plays a hugely significant role in shaping the contours of the morality provisions in practice because it is only when its decisions on patent grant are appealed or challenged that other EPO bodies can shape these provisions. The Examining Division is composed of three technically qualified examiners; it can add a legally qualified examiner if it considers that the 'nature of the decision' requires this. However, even when added, the legal examiner often deals with technical procedural points.[71]

[70] DiMaggio and Powell (n 66) 153.
[71] Plomer (n 32).

Furthermore, there is little evidence of EPO Examining Division members being selected based on an awareness of the ethical issues posed by emerging technologies. The eligibility requirements for technical members of the Examining Division are: citizenship of any EPC Contracting State; a university degree in physics, chemistry, engineering or natural sciences relevant to the technical field in which they wish to work; and knowledge of one official language of the EPO and the ability to understand the other two.[72] Candidates are expected to have a 'genuine interest in technology, an eye for detail and an analytical mind'.[73] However, there is no reference to the need for an awareness of the potential ethical issues raised by patents on emerging technologies. Examiners undertake a two-year training course which could incorporate guidance on such ethical issues. Yet no explicit mention of a significant ethics component being required as part of the training programme is made on the EPO website. Such factors suggest that the Examining Division is institutionally predisposed – and, moreover, institutionally *configured* – to apply a light-touch, narrow application of the morality provisions, or indeed other ethical considerations within patent law. This limited (or lack of) experience in dealing with ethical issues in patent adjudication reinforces an institutional legacy which is insulated from broader ethical issues.[74]

Similar arguments can be made in respect of the other EPO decision-making stages such as the Opposition Division and Boards of Appeal, which – with the exception of the Legal Boards of Appeal – are composed primarily of technical, not legal, decision makers;[75] and, in all cases, limited or no emphasis is placed on having broader ethical awareness or experience for such legal or technical decision-making personnel.

The focus on selecting members of EPO decision-making bodies based on patent law and technical expertise is entirely sensible given that they will be adjudicating upon patent issues. Nonetheless, institutional theories highlight the pervasive diffusion of common thinking or normative positions among personnel in an organisational field like this, which suggests that even if drawn from different technical areas or professions,

---

[72] See www.epo.org/about-us/jobs/examiners/profile.html (accessed 4 February 2021).
[73] Ibid.
[74] For a detailed discussion see McMahon (2016) (n 6).
[75] The Opposition Division is composed of three technically qualified experts, two of whom cannot have taken part in the proceedings which granted the application (Article 19(2) EPC), while the Technical Boards of Appeal are generally composed of two technical experts and one legal expert.

personnel within a field such as patent law will resemble each other in terms of their training and normative values. Hence, this will likely further perpetuate normative positions. Taken alongside the recurring lack of reference to the need for an awareness of, or experience in, ethical issues surrounding emerging technologies, it reinforces an engrained institutional legacy within the EPO, which is arguably predisposed to marginalise ethical considerations in the application of the morality provisions in practice and more generally in other contexts.

In short, the composition of the interpretative community within the EPO decision-making system likely perpetuates the EPO's insulation from the ethical issues posed by the patentability of biotechnologies.[76] Given this institutional legacy, it is unsurprising that the morality provisions are not interpreted more broadly by the EPO. If such broader consideration of ethical issues is desired, a bottom-up reform of the institutional system within the EPO would be needed.

## 16.4   Conclusion

Drawing on institutional theories, this chapter has argued that legacy around how legislative provisions have developed and have historically been applied by decision-makers is a highly significant influence on decision-making. Alongside this, the chapter has argued that the institutional legacy of a decision-making body is significantly influenced by the past experiences, expertise and shared understandings of personnel within that decision-making body, which forms the interpretative community for applying these provisions in practice. Moreover, if decision-makers are drawn primarily from similar backgrounds or from within the same field, this is more likely to reinforce predispositions and existing legacies in that context, which can act as an encumbrance to adaptation or legal change.

Notably, the potential for encumbrance created by these types of legacies is not necessarily negative in nature. There are often important reasons why a decision-making body will produce and be shaped by specific legacies, which may relate to the legal competences of that body or to ensuring that the body does not act ultra vires its own powers. However, as has been seen, at times, legacy within decision-making contexts can act to perpetuate past ways of doing things where discretion applies in favour of the decision-making body. This can be problematic as

---

[76] McMahon (2016) (n 6).

it limits the scope for adaptation within legal decision-making and potentially limits law's responsiveness.[77] Legacy as encumbrance can be particularly problematic within the medico-legal space given that science and medicine are advancing at pace, and related social norms are also constantly evolving. This in turn may lead to a heightened need for decision-makers to interpret existing laws for evolving situations within the medico-legal context and require the exercise of discretion to facilitate legal adaptation or responsiveness.

Based on the foregoing analysis, two main avenues can arguably be used to overcome the potential for negative effects of legacy as encumbrance in this context. First, we could limit discretion for decision-makers, which in turn would limit the role that legacy could play in such contexts; it forces decision-makers to merely apply definitional tests, thereby limiting their interpretative roles. However, given that science and medicine, and the social norms pertaining to these fields, are in many respects constantly evolving, limiting discretion within the medico-legal and patent space both can be difficult to achieve in practice and can render laws quickly obsolete. Moreover, legislative drafting is generally a slow process, and relying on new legislation each time situations change would severely limit law's responsiveness in such contexts.

Second, the potential for legacy to act as encumbrance could be limited by ensuring that the interpretative community is carefully considered when any legal change is adopted, including consideration of whether the site for change is appropriate depending on the outcome desired; and whether the decision-making actors within that framework are drawn from appropriately varied backgrounds to deliver such change, or whether a modification of the institutional structure within that interpretative community is needed to deliver the change desired. The analysis has also provided strong justification for ensuring that decision-makers are drawn from interdisciplinary backgrounds, rather than from the same or similar specialised bodies of expertise or fields, as this will limit the pervasive influence that professionalisation can have in leading to normative isomorphism. This in turn will likely encourage greater varied considerations within decision-making frameworks.

In short, institutional influences and the legacies they create are highly significant factors in the end outcomes of decision-making. Such factors

---

[77] For a discussion on legal responsiveness in the medical context, see T Arvind and Aisling McMahon, 'Responsiveness and the Role of Rights in Medical Law: Lessons from Montgomery' (2020) 28 *Medical Law Review* 445.

must be considered when legal change is sought. Beyond developing the text of a legal provision, we must also consider *who* will interpret that provision, the *institutional legacy* which that interpretative community will bring to this role, and *historical legacies* surrounding particular provisions which may influence their future interpretations. Put simply, institutional legacies are (often) instrumental factors in decision-making which have important positive and negative effects and warrant much greater consideration within medical jurisprudence, particularly if law is to be responsive to social change and to scientific and medical advances.

# Towards a New Privacy

## Informed Consent as an Encumbrance to Group Interests

MARK J. TAYLOR AND DAVID M. R. TOWNEND

## 17.1 Introduction

In an information society, data can dictate the conditions of opportunity. This is true of personal data, which relate to identifiable individuals. It is also true of data that inform policy applicable to many. Increasingly, data relating to individuals as members of groups are of significance to those individuals and groups and to society. As a result, taking an individualist approach to data management in the data age is becoming difficult; the paradigm underpinning informational privacy has become an encumbrance to many of the things that we want to see in society – we have become so scared of being exploited (and with Cambridge Analytica, it appears that our fears had some grounding) that individuals and regulators have retreated to a bunker of isolated individualism. This is as true in the context of health-related research as it is in other aspects of society.

A difficulty in adequate governance of group data in the context of health research emerges, at least in significant part, because of the underpinning concept of privacy that is used in the interpretation of the key legislation. The interpretation of privacy is tilted towards an almost absolute individualist, self-determination conceptualisation, which is impacting on protections of groups and opportunities for solidarity. It is manifest in the operation of privacy in the regulation of research through Research Ethics Committees (RECs) and Institutional Review Boards (IRBs), and in the priority associated with 'informed consent' as a safeguard. So, in the midst of Covid-19, when solidarity is at the heart of the defence of our private lives, privacy becomes a barrier to track-and-trace and to medical research.

Informed consent is a central tool in the operation of this individual privacy. Informed consent, on the one hand, becomes a matter of the individual choosing to participate as an individual, without procedural reference to responsibilities or recognitions of others who might have interests in or be impacted by the decision. On the other hand, it has become burdened with our hopes for adequate protection, but it fails to deliver because of its unnegotiated, click-wrap protection; the safeguard, it seems, is not for the citizen but for the corporation or research sponsor.

In this chapter, we argue that an individualist conception of privacy, tied to the idea of individual autonomy and safeguarded by individual informed consent, is a secure foundation only for future failure. This is because the debate we need as a society is distorted. An individualist conception of privacy, if taken as axiomatic and the foundation for negotiation, assumes too much normatively. Individuality (individual privacy) is posed against the public interest – in binary opposition.[1] The Human Cell Atlas;[2] transfer of data to the USA; track-and-trace – all become situations where it is claimed that privacy inhibits social advance. Informed consent becomes a necessity for the protection of self-determination and yet makes desirable social ends impossible. And in commercial settings, informed consent operates simply to impose the draconian terms of multinational service providers upon individuals who cannot penetrate the corporate privacy shield to see the abuse of data that is sanctioned by the click of consent that pretends to safeguard the very interest that it destroys.[3]

We draw inspiration for our argument from two concepts that are developed within Graeme Laurie's work. First, his preferred model for governance is rooted in the concept of 'regulatory stewardship'. Personal data are to be respected as the individuals to whom the data relate are to be respected; stewardship manifests the interplay of legal and ethical responsibilities that ensure and facilitate that respect. This is well

---

[1] This seems to be especially clear in the difference between medical research ethics (with its focus on individual privacy rights) and public health ethics (with its focus on the common good).

[2] Human Cell Atlas www.humancellatlas.org (accessed 19 February 2021).

[3] Carole Cadwalladr and Emma Graham-Harrison 'Revealed: 50 Million Facebook Profiles Harvested for Cambridge Analytica in Major Data Breach' (*The Guardian*, 17 March 2018) www.theguardian.com/news/2018/mar/17/cambridge-analytica-facebook-influence-us-election (accessed 11 February 2021); Margaret Hu, 'Cambridge Analytica's Black Box' (2020) *Big Data & Society* 1.

known and accepted as a practical concept in the area.[4] Second, we draw from a concept upon which the practical 'stewardship' theory rests. In his early book *Genetic Privacy: A Challenge to Medico-legal Norms*,[5] Graeme developed a concept of privacy that challenges the dominant paradigm that privacy is about individual control. He demonstrates that this underpinning concept is not the only one available. Indeed, he has argued for a different approach that, in this chapter, we argue deserves a much more prominent place in the privacy governance discourse. This is the idea of 'privacy as separateness'. Maximally shorn of normative commitment, this conception invites and allows debate regarding which states of separateness *ought* to be protected and respected.

There is a need to revisit what it means to protect privacy in the context of health research, and this involves reconsidering the role of 'informed consent' as a privacy safeguard. It requires a shift from individualistic privacy and a fresh negotiation of relevant interests to a focus on the reordering of respecting individuals in community. It is first necessary to see 'privacy' as a paradigm – and, as such, a contestable concept. Graeme's work is invaluable here: recognising what is lost through any attempt to reduce privacy to autonomy helps to contextualise both autonomy and informed consent within a broader debate of the privacy norms that ought to be upheld. Informed consent is an important safeguard. It need not, however, be an overriding concern from a privacy perspective. Rather than an individualistic or atomistic conception of privacy, a more useful concept of privacy can locate individual self-determination in a moral community. It will include a respect for autonomy but under conditions of reciprocal respect. This is consistent with the European Court of Human Rights's (ECtHR) positive privacy idea, which extends privacy to duties to nurture each other to enable us to define our personalities and fund authenticity.[6] It does not leave an individual alone to bear the load that the current architecture of privacy places upon them: there is a common responsibility to recognise and protect the privacy norms – for example, the norms of data exclusivity – that are critical to culture and to community.

---

[4] Graeme Laurie et al, 'Charting Regulatory Stewardship in Health Research: Making the Invisible Visible' (2018) 27 *Cambridge Quarterly Healthcare Ethics* 333.

[5] Graeme Laurie, *Genetic Privacy: A Challenge to Medico-legal Norms* (Cambridge University Press 2002).

[6] Graeme points this out in Laurie (n 5) ch. 5, citing *Guerra and Others* v. *Italy* (1998) 26 EHRR 357. At para 60, the Court states that it 'reiterates that severe environmental pollution may affect individuals' well-being and prevent them from enjoying their homes in such a way as to affect their private and family life adversely'.

It has never been more important that the orthodoxy regarding information privacy be held up to challenge. Data relate to individuals, but rarely only to single atomised individuals. Especially in health research, personal data relate to more than one individual, linked by familial or kinship ties, or cultural and social connections that make them useful to more than the object data subject. Indeed, understanding the nature of the relationship of personal data to a particular individual often depends on understanding the significance of such data to others. Graeme's conceptualisation goes some way to releasing the concept of privacy from the paradigmatic straitjacket in which it is currently constrained. It enables us to reach for an idea of privacy better suited to our shared future.

The theme of this volume is the different dimensions of legacy in medical jurisprudence, and we consider the legacy of privacy as one of encumbrance. However, we move between encumbrance as a positive and encumbrance as a negative.[7] The starting point of the chapter is to consider the protection of privacy through the safeguard of informed consent and the positive protection of participants in research. However, we suggest that this safeguard becomes a negative encumbrance as informed consent becomes restrictive, limiting privacy issues such that group interests are lost and solidarity undermined.[8] We then show how Graeme's conceptualisation of privacy opens the way to an alternative paradigm: privacy as an opportunity for, and a product of, discourse and negotiation. We consider how the operation of this concept would impact on individual and group interests, and how such a conceptualisation might facilitate the ECtHR's view of privacy as including a duty in society to assist the individual in the fulfilment and enjoyment of their private life. In this way, we conclude this chapter with the possibility that the legacy that could be constructed for privacy in its next iteration is one of facilitation more than encumbrance.

---

[7] Barriers and encumbrances as positives is a theme that Laurie and Townend explore in their work (with Sorbie and Gueddana) in the Wellcome-funded project *DataTerms*. Far from being negative encumbrances, barriers such as ensuring the reach-through protection of data subjects in secondary processing of data, or effective curation of metadata in research datasets, are positive benefits. See Annie Sorbie, Wifak Gueddana, Graeme Laurie and David Townend 'Examining the Power of the Social Imaginary through Competing Narratives of Data Ownership in Health Research' (2021) 8 *Journal of Law and the Biosciences* lsaa068, doi: 10.1093/jlb/lsaa068.

[8] For discussion of solidarity, its potential to 'overcome the unproductive dichotomy between personal and common benefit' and the reflection it represents of 'commitments to accept costs to help others with whom we recognise similarity in a relevant respect', see Barbara Prainsack and Alena Buyx, *Solidarity in Biomedicine and Beyond* (Cambridge University Press 2017) 13, 43.

## 17.2 Privacy and the Parallel Rise of Institutional (Ethics) Review and Informed Consent: From a Legacy of Positive Encumbrance to Negative Encumbrance

Humans are curious animals. We want to know where we came from, what we are doing here, and where we might go after this world; we need a story that satisfies our imaginations. And within these questions, scientific enquiry, including medical research, is part of that realm of human curiosity. At the same time, it has always required a degree of external governance.[9] Whereas the limitations were, until the late nineteenth century, largely cultural constraints,[10] they are established today in the institutions of professional standards, clinical ethics, RECs and IRBs. And at the heart of this protection is the substantive gold standard of 'informed consent'. Consent is not always required before research involving a human being takes place, but where it is not so required under regulation, invariably its absence is abnormal and requires substantive justification. This justification itself involves processes and additional levels of governance.[11]

It is fair to say that the science community has brought external scrutiny upon itself. Interventions to prevent or address excess come from scientific abuse of the dignity of individuals. The list of abusive research practices is long, with a number of notorious cases: Albert Neisser's work on syphilis and gonorrhoea; the experiments in the Nazi death camps; the syphilis scandal of Tuskegee and a dehumanising of the individuals who were 'subjects' of the research (contrasting with a notion of participation in research). Science needs to be held to account for its choices. However, the Swedish sterilisation scandal[12] and Oppenheimer's 'Manhattan Project' show that dehumanisation through science is not only through the choices of scientists; politicians and society are also complicit in some of the choices. The regulation of science must itself be held up to scrutiny and debate if it is not to slip towards dehumanisation. At the heart of the abuses were physical assaults on the individual participants. The nature of the research interventions was physical mistreatment – infection with syphilis or gonorrhoea, denial of treatment to

---

[9] Roy Porter, *Blood and Guts: A Short History of Medicine* (Allen Lane 2002).

[10] Liminal Spaces project www.liminalspaces.ed.ac.uk (accessed 19 February 2021).

[11] See, for example, the UK Health Research Authority's Confidentiality Advisory Group www.hra.nhs.uk/about-us/committees-and-services/confidentiality-advisory-group/ (accessed 11 February 2021).

[12] Declan Butler, 'Eugenics Scandal Reveals Silence of Swedish Scientists' (1997) 9 *Nature* 389.

individuals, exposure to extreme cold, sterilisation, murder. It was not only physical assault that was endured; all dimensions of individual privacy were violated: physical, informational, decisional and proprietary.[13]

Society responded through two major institutions: the Nuremberg Code and the Declaration of Helsinki, in the 1940s and 1960s, respectively; and the Belmont Report and the emergence of principlism in the late 1970s. The response to physically demeaning research activity was the principle that individuals had a right to individual self-determination. In research, individuals had the right to be informed about the consequences of their participation, and to make an individual choice as to whether or not to participate. We would not seek to suggest that this response was improper. Indeed, this point, in relation to informed consent, raises an interesting question about 'encumbrance'. An encumbrance, colloquially and in law, is a restriction, a block on something, a limitation. But the notion of a barrier to an activity, especially in the area of law, is not necessarily one-sided or wholly negative. The legal encumbrance of, for example, a hypothec[14] enables protection and mutual co-operation and benefit. Informed consent has enabled the effective recognition of the dignity of, for example, a research participant – or, more generally, the participation of legally competent individuals in modern society.[15]

Self-determination is a positive element of human dignity that must be protected. A competent person's dignity is respected through offering choice and respecting the decision. A failure to offer choice and respect decisions can be profoundly wrong. However, our argument is that we must not allow the fact that informed consent serves well in some circumstance to blind us to its limitations in others. Informed consent may serve well to protect specific privacy interests – particularly those disrespected by past indignities – but it may be neither necessary nor sufficient to protect the privacy interests engaged by data-intensive health research. Two such situations come to mind: first, circumstances

---

[13] Anita Allen, 'Genetic Privacy: Emerging Concepts and Values' in Mark Rothstein (ed), *Genetic Secrets: Protecting Privacy and Confidentiality in the Genetic Era* (Yale University Press 1997) 31, 33.

[14] Somewhat equivalent to a mortgage or legal charge in different jurisdictions.

[15] Where there is a presumed equality of bargaining power, the individual is deemed to be capable of sufficiently informing themselves; in the fiduciary situation, the imbalance of power is redressed by a requirement to inform and operate in the paramount interests of the beneficiary.

where profound information and power asymmetry corrupt the conditions for meaningful consent; second, where the implications of participation in research are not only for the research participant themselves but for groups of individuals. These situations challenge the sufficiency and necessity of informed consent as a privacy protective safeguard for individuals as well as the families and communities that their data may represent. In relation to this second aspect, the issue of group protection or the protection of others is not only about the responsibilities of the researcher or regulator. Individuals not only have rights regarding the operation of informed consent, they also have responsibilities in a moral community and our individual claims to the protection of self-determination are mutually restrained. Our shared responsibility to the conditions necessary to protect others from unjustified harm is not always effectively discharged by abandoning individuals to protect their own interests: individuals also owe a duty of care to others in their group and community, and this is not discharged necessarily through the operation of individualist informed consent.

The problem of where informed consent has slipped its initial moorings in the protection of the individual in physical intervention situations concerns a shift of emphasis from protection to individual determination. Edward Dove noted in his observation of NHS RECs in the UK, which consider a broad range of research ethics applications, that there was a general tendency towards a liberal mindset that recognised that individuals should be empowered to make decisions for themselves: '[t]he prevalent view I observed is that provided risks are outweighed by potential benefits (or there is a "fair balance" between risk or burden and potential benefits), and participants are provided with all material information during the consent process, then the choice to participate should be theirs to make, not the REC's'.[16]

There is a risk that the idea of self-determination, rather than individual protection, slips into a belief in the almost perfect autonomy and individualism of the person. This is expressed in the theory of 'ethical egoism' of Ayn Rand, and it is implied in modern, populist appeals. What is missing from such appeals and theory, however, is the contextualisation of the individual within society; individuals have a degree of dependency upon each other. It is difficult to argue such dependency in the face of the reality that individuals have the economic power to buy their own

---

[16] Edward Dove, *Regulatory Stewardship of Health Research: Navigating Participant Protection and Research Promotion* (Edward Elgar 2020) 111.

independence (at least apparently), but the argument has been made, even in the strongest texts of liberalism. John Locke's property theory – that one has the inalienable right to private property by the mixing of personal effort with raw materials – lasts only as far as there is sufficient raw material left for others. Adam Smith rests his classic theory of market capitalism on his work *The Theory of Moral Sentiments*, which argues for an empathetic understanding of the needs of individuals as a necessary moral platform for the operation of the market. John Stuart Mill, perhaps the greatest advocate of personal freedom, accepts that personal freedom ends where the individual poses a harm to another person. Immanuel Kant's Categorical Imperative, demanding moral action from agents through their duty to others, again limits personal freedom with the requirement that individuals should not instrumentalise others. Each theorist of liberalism requires the individual to exercise their personal freedom with responsibility for others. In classical liberalism, self-determination is exercised or defended not in isolation but in society.

We have stepped away from the positive protection of the individual against researcher malpractice, and towards the idea that an individual can begin to choose to isolate him or herself from the society within which he or she lives. This moves informed consent from a *beneficial* encumbrance to an *exclusionary* encumbrance. An example of this can be seen in the Human Cell Atlas project,[17] the aim of which is to use already gathered information about human cells, from various repositories, to map human cells. Until 2018 and the implementation of the EU General Data Protection Regulation (GDPR) (2016/679),[18] these personal data – gathered with broad consent to allow the use of the data for future research – were available to the researchers; de-identification was used, and individuals' data could be processed for the secondary purpose of mapping. However, the data remained personal data, as the ability existed to re-identify the individuals by mosaicking the data with other datasets. This required the data to remain under the purview of personal data protection law.

The effect of the GDPR is to tighten the operation of informed consent with respect to the processing of data subjects' personal data. Whereas the legislative language used between the Regulation and the Directive that it replaces is very similar, the rhetorical conceptualisation of

---

[17] Human Cell Atlas www.humancellatlas.org (accessed 19 February 2021).
[18] Regulation 2016/679/EU on the protection of natural persons with regard to the processing of personal data and on the free movement of such data, and repealing Directive 95/46/EC, 2016 OJ L119/1.

informed consent within the Regulation is that it is narrowed, and perishable.[19] Therefore, even in the face of Recital 33 of the Regulation's preamble (and its inclusion of a possibility for 'broad consent' for processing data for scientific research purposes), researchers have become more cautious: perhaps in part driven by a fear of the heavy fines that can be imposed under the Regulation; perhaps in part by the changed language surrounding the GDPR to assert greater individual autonomy and control in relation to personal data. The outcome is that the caution requires that new, narrow consents are gained for the specific secondary processing of already gathered data. And the same problem is seen across 'big data' science. The presumption is that the individual data subject's sensitivities and privacy will be violated unless they not only are informed about the new research but also have the opportunity to choose to participate in the new research. The new approach is potentially devastating for such data processing because of the obvious issues of tracing data subjects and paying for the exercise. This, one might argue (given the limited potential harms posed by such a secondary use of an individual's data), is a disproportionate response and a distortion of the legacy of (positive) encumbrance that the initial intervention in science sought to impose.

As Samuel Warren and Louis Brandeis wrote in the opening of their seminal 1890 *Harvard Law Review* article on 'The Right to Privacy', '[t]hat the individual shall have full protection in person and in property is a principle as old as the common law; *but it has been found necessary from time to time to define anew the exact nature and extent of such protection*'.[20] If the main concern that prompted the use of informed consent as a safeguard for the protection of research participants was physical integrity, the Declaration of Helsinki soon came to include informational privacy.[21] There are clearly questions about the privacy of

---

[19] The language used in relation to the GDPR is almost suggestive of the data not merely 'relating to' the data subject but *belonging* to it (although ownership in personal data is hotly contested). The rhetoric is about the data subject having control of their data; the rights and duties reflect the data subject's new power of processing determination. This is, one might suggest, outside an analysis and discussion of the potential harm of the processing to the data subject, the potential to mitigate any harm by other measures, and the potential benefit from the research or processing.

[20] Samuel Warren and Louis Brandeis 'The Right to Privacy' (1890) 4 *Harvard Law Review* 193 (emphasis added).

[21] World Medical Association, Declaration of Helsinki www.wma.net/policies-post/wma-declaration-of-helsinki-ethical-principles-for-medical-research-involving-human-sub jects/ (accessed 19 February 2021).

individuals' personal data and their processing for research purposes. However, the question that has not been fully discussed is, does research using already gathered personal data in more social science contexts pose the same 'privacy' questions as research threatening the physical integrity of an individual? If it is not the same privacy at stake, perhaps the processes we adopt to reconcile, and trade off, relevant interests are flawed. If we uncritically turn to look at a new object through a lens ground for another, then we should not be surprised to find our view unfocused.

The nature of the protection needed now extends beyond 'individual control' and autonomy (and reciprocal responsibility) to include the responsibilities of others – particularly in relation to 'for profit' activity – in order to avoid uses of data that contribute to social inequity. If individuals have responsibilities to others that ought to be recognised, then so ought the responsibilities owed by those who collect information from them. The voluntary surrender of personal data, for the sake of others, should not carry with it risks that the data will come to be used in ways incompatible with the protection and interests of those providing them.[22]

## 17.3   The Crippling Priority of Autonomy

There is a legacy of 'informed consent' in the research context that enshrines a particular view of the individual in society – and that translates into a privacy of individualism, where self-determination (through informed consent) is paramount. There may be nothing wrong with this if it protects the individual without undue harm to others, but it does not. The approach is limited in its ability to protect collective interests,[23] including the idea of 'group privacy'.[24] Similarly, the limits of 'informed

[22] Barbara Prainsack notes that any assumption that individuals who refuse to grant access to personal or health data are being 'selfish or ignorant' is problematic as 'it involves a slippage from the social responsibility and accountability we should expect from corporate actors to what we should expect from individual citizens'. See Barbara Prainsack, 'Data Mining in Systems Medicine and the Project of Solidarity: The Interface of Genomics and Society Revisited' in Dana Mahr and Martina von Arx (eds), *De-sequencing, Health Technology and Society* (Springer 2020), 102. We agree that such slippage would be problematic: corporate responsibility should not be so easily evaded. We suggest that individuals have responsibilities to others, but they should not be leveraged to promote further corporate control over data.

[23] Henry Greely, 'Informed Consent and Other Ethical Issues in Human Population Genetics' (2001) 35 *Annual Review of Genetics* 785.

[24] Jennifer Suh et al, 'Distinguishing Group Privacy from Personal Privacy: The Effect of Group Inference Technologies on Privacy Perceptions and Behaviours' (2018) 2 *Proceedings of the ACM on Human-Computer* 1, 18.

consent' as a means to protect individual interests have been well characterised.[25] In short, individuals operating under conditions of bounded rationality may not be best placed to protect their own interests or those of others.

The problem is a systemic one. Not only is 'informed consent' insufficient to protect valued individual or collective interests but the primacy of individualism has a corrosive effect on the operation of other safeguards. It has never been the case that informed consent is the only lawful basis for health research – nor do we propose that it has ever been the only safeguard. Alternative safeguards, and justifications for health research, such as reside in public interest arguments, have always been possible. Our argument is that the priority of autonomy, manifest in an overriding concern with informed consent, is apparent even when consent is not required. The very framing of alternatives to consent as alternatives can prejudice the range of interests legitimately brought into consideration within any balancing exercise and positions public interest considerations as opposed to a narrow individualist conception of privacy.

This kind of framing is illustrated by the circumstances surrounding the establishment of Ireland's private, for-profit, genomic repository: known first as Genomics Medicine Ireland and then Genuity Science.[26] Genuity gained access to genomic data through arrangements and contracts with Irish hospitals, universities, charities and general practitioners. One hospital, Beaumont Hospital, has partnered as part of a brain tumour study. Genuity led an application for access to the tumour samples held by Beaumont without patient consent: a lawful possibility in Ireland if the application is approved by the Health Research Consent Declaration Committee (HRCDC).[27] The HRCDC must consider the application through the lens of Ireland's Health Research Regulations 2018.[28] The Regulations make explicit consent the default for processing personal data, but the HRCDC may make a Declaration permitting research without consent. The HRCDC may make such a Declaration

---

[25] Onora O'Neill, 'Some Limits of Informed Consent' (2003) 29 *Journal of Medical Ethics* 4; Neil Manson and Onora O'Neill, *Rethinking Informed Consent in Bioethics* (Cambridge University Press 2007); Gail Henderson, 'Is Informed Consent Broken?' (2011) 342 *American Journal of the Medical Sciences* 267.

[26] Genuity Science https://genuitysci.com (accessed 19 February 2021).

[27] Health Research Consent Declaration Committee (HRCDC) https://hrcdc.ie (accessed 19 February 2021).

[28] Data Protection Act 2018 (Section 36(2)) (Health Research) Regulations 2018, SI No 314 of 2018 (Ireland).

only where satisfied that the public interest in the research outweighs the public interest in requiring the explicit consent of the data subject, and other requirements are met.

When the HRCDC considered the application, it refused the Declaration.[29] Committee members did not think that the relevant statutory thresholds had been met. They were of the 'strong opinion'[30] that explicit consent should be sought and did not consider that the case had been made 'for the impossibility of'[31] seeking consent. They also took the view that 'the involvement of a "for-profit" organisation processing personal data introduced a higher risk that data subjects may have a deeper concern for their privacy rights'.[32] Furthermore, when considering the public interest, the Committee questioned whether use and commercialisation would result in 'direct benefit back to the patients whose data has been used to underpin the research, considering the high cost of any drugs that may be developed'.[33] On the one hand, the view that the public interest in the research might be outweighed by the public interest in requiring explicit consent only when consent was 'impossible' supports our claim regarding the priority afforded consent and demonstrates the value attached to it by the Committee – itself reflecting the priority accorded consent by the Regulations. However, that said, we may be heartened by the relatively broad view of privacy interests recognised to be relevant: extending beyond individual control, the Committee saw that questions of access to the benefits of the research, and the involvement of a 'for-profit' organisation, should form part of the public interest evaluation *and* may reflect a deep concern for privacy rights.

Genuity Science appealed the decision. The Appeal Panel overturned the Committee's position and, with conditions attached, supported the application for a Declaration enabling access without consent.[34] While the Appeal Panel supported the view that 'where it is relatively easy to obtain the consent of the data subjects, it is difficult to envisage circumstances in which the public interest in obtaining such consent would be

---

[29] Health Research Consent Declaration Committee, 'Minutes of the Meeting – 13th June 2019' https://hrcdc.ie/wp-content/uploads/2019/07/HRCDC-Meeting-Minutes-13 .06.2019-APPROVED-.pdf (accessed 19 February 2021).

[30] Ibid., 8.

[31] Ibid.

[32] Ibid.

[33] Ibid., 9.

[34] HRCDC Appeal Panel, 19–006-AF3 Appeal Panel Decision (24 September 2019) https:// hrcdc.ie/wp-content/uploads/2019/11/Appeal-Panel-DECISION-03.09.2019.pdf (accessed 19 February 2021).

significantly outweighed',[35] it did not agree that the relevant test was that of impossibility or impracticability. It imagined circumstances where difficulty might be sufficient.[36] The Panel also doubted the Committee's finding that the involvement of a for-profit organisation might introduce a higher risk of a deeper concern for privacy. The Panel was satisfied that privacy rights were adequately protected on the basis of submissions relating to individual patient confidentiality.[37] The Panel was also satisfied that the public interest in the research was demonstrated by the likelihood of new therapies, diagnostics and targeted drugs for patients with brain tumours.[38] It did not engage with the Committee's argument that those who contributed may not themselves benefit due to high costs or any suggestion that this may be a privacy concern.

Superficially, this might seem an odd case to cite as part of an argument that the legacy of the rise of informed consent has been to establish unwelcome encumbrance. It is, after all, an example of research being permitted without patient consent. However, as already noted, our claim is not that informed consent is always accorded priority – exceptions to a requirement of consent have always been possible. Our claim, rather, is that its rise to paramountcy as a safeguard has framed the debate in unhelpful ways: it has supported an atomised view of society and a particular narrative with regards to what relevant privacy interests are at stake and what is to be 'weighed in the balance' against public interests distinguished from privacy concerns. It has helped to frame a relatively narrow range of individual concerns *against* a public interest in access that competes with individual control. It constructs an artificial contest between privacy conceived as concealment of identity or individual control of identifiable information – or a right to be 'let alone' – pitched against the broader needs of society. Although the Appeal Panel was willing to recognise the need for consent to be displaced more readily than the Committee, it was ultimately a narrow range of interests, on behalf of patients, that appeared to count in the balance. As long as patient information was 'confidential', and improvements to health care could be anticipated, then establishing the extent of control that could practically be extended to individuals in the circumstances all but exhausted the relevant concerns. The relevant interest was framed as the public interest *in obtaining consent*. The problem is reducing it to a trade-off between the interest in 'informed

---

[35] Ibid., 2.
[36] Ibid.
[37] Ibid.
[38] Ibid., 3.

consent' and the interest in health research. There is no overriding consideration attached to the public interest in ensuring that reasonable expectations regarding use of data or a broader range of individual or collective interests are protected.

Our claim here is that there is a problem with broader social concerns being set up in opposition to individual autonomy: a focus on individual autonomy can skew the debate *even if it is being overridden*. This failure to recognise collective interests in personal and non-personal data, and the public interest in (non-personal) data protection, have profound implications for an information age. It is increasingly important to recognise that groups are affected by the use of data qua groups and as individual members of groups irrespective of whether they are individually identifiable. The fact that individuals may be identified only as members of a group offers no protection from the kinds of group harm that may associate with the 'insights' gathered through analysis of non-personal data. Group privacy is of increasing interest in an information age characterised by machine learning of big data sets.[39] Patterns and profiles generated through such analysis establish the conditions of opportunity for people seeking to contract with, or work for, organisations that segment and stratify potential customers and employees. Group harms may be 'dignitary' or tangible in character, the latter being realised through discrimination and stigma: poorer chances to thrive in an information society. Governance mechanisms generally, including those associated with ethics review, need to be able to bring such broader societal concerns into view. The questions about how we want to live together in an increasingly digital society are urgent and inadequately dealt with through an informed consent process.

We need today, more than ever before, to recognise privacy as a *collective* concern. Effective stewardship is dependent on an appreciation of the full range of interests that are to be protected. A coherent governance response requires the different parts of the regulatory system to work together. That does not preclude conflict or tension: a system may be designed with checks and balances and these must sometimes pull against each other in order for balance to be achieved and maintained. It does mean that *some* part of the system must be capable of adequately representing collective interests. If it does not, then governance will not

---

[39] Brent Mittelstadt, 'From Individual to Group Privacy in Biomedical Big Data' in *Big Data, Health Law, and Bioethics* (Cambridge University Press 2018); Linnet Taylor, Luciano Floridi and Bart van der Sloot (eds), *Group Privacy: New Challenges of Data Technologies* (Springer 2017).

be properly weighted. Any apparent balance will be achieved using dishonest scales. A failure to enable and empower governance to address broader social concerns consistently and other than through the vehicle of individual consent risks systemic failure.

## 17.4   Graeme's Guiding Light: Reclaiming a Potential for a Legacy of Positive Encumbrance for Privacy

In his *Genetic Privacy* monograph, Graeme introduces a strong concept of privacy as more than personal information but rather a 'sphere of separateness'. He suggests that it is preferable to conceive of privacy as a state or condition as this approach 'avoids the criticism associated with the use of value-laden language and allows us to see privacy for what it is, as distinct from what we think it ought to be'.[40] From this perspective, privacy 'becomes a sphere of separateness that deserves recognition as being inviolable, and not merely an issue of control of information'.[41] For Graeme, the relevant state of separateness 'encompasses both physical or psychological separation (spatial privacy), and the separateness of personal information (information privacy)'.[42] As he goes on later to state, '[i]f privacy is conceived not simply as a desire to control personal information, but rather as a general sphere of separateness from others and so also encompasses notions of spatial separateness, then it is no answer to say that an action that is concerned solely with information is an acceptable solution to privacy invasions'.[43] Relevant separation includes the state or condition of being unobserved and this extends to observation that records no data about us: it is possible for privacy to be invaded by unwarranted observation alone.[44] It thus resists any assumption that either anonymity or control of data will exhaust relevant privacy interests. How, though, does 'privacy as separateness' help us to address the blind spots generated through conflation of privacy and autonomy and the pitching of 'informed consent' against public interest? A concept of privacy as separateness creates a space for negotiation: it opens the possibility of privacy as an active enabler of participation in society – and, moving beyond axiomatic deference to autonomy, it also opens the door to stewardship.

[40]  Laurie (n 5) 55.
[41]  Ibid., 63.
[42]  Ibid., 64.
[43]  Ibid., 250–1.
[44]  Ibid., 65.

### 17.4.1    From Privacy as Separateness to Privacy as Nurturing

Our central thesis is that Graeme's concept of privacy helps us to recognise the normative assumptions implicit within current governance models that regard informed consent as the primary privacy protective safeguard. Understanding privacy as a state of separateness enables us to look anew at what warrants protection and clears the way for a recognition of our responsibilities to maintain the necessary conditions of effective stewardship. This does not require us to abandon all previous normative commitments. For example, it is not at odds with the approach of the ECtHR. In describing the extent of the legal right to privacy that has been defined by the ECtHR, Graeme shows how the Court has accepted a much broader view of privacy than simply atomistic privacy.[45] This reaches into the practical meaning of privacy being given normative weight through stewardship. It invites an active citizenship as privacy becomes an open space where everyone becomes a participant steward not only of their own privacy but of understanding and realising the privacy perspectives of others.

Within such a framing, the 'right to be let alone'[46] may be a right to a space to explore and define 'who I am' – but it may also entail reciprocal duties to respect and protect that space for others. This goes to the heart of the question, 'what is it to respect another's privacy?' Privacy has been framed as a freedom from interference (a negative privacy), but positive privacy offers an opportunity for privacy norms to be established consistent with a duty to nurture one another (while respecting the individual's rights to decline assistance).[47] Within this framing, the rights to education, to health care, to participate in the cultural and scientific life of one's community – to the nurturing of the private self – may be privacy rights that we have a duty to extend to our neighbours.[48] There is, within this framing, the possibility to construct constantly newly negotiated privacies.

We do not here have the space fully to construct an alternative privacy paradigm to that which holds sway. Nor do we need to do so in order to

---

[45] Ibid., 249.

[46] Warren and Brandeis (n 20).

[47] And this brings privacy rights into line with the duty to participate found in Article 29 of the Universal Declaration of Human Rights.

[48] United Nations General Assembly, 'International Covenant on Economic, Social and Cultural Rights' (UNGA Resolution A/RES/2200A(XXI) adopted 16 December 1966, in force on 3 January 1976) www.un.org/en/development/desa/population/migration/generalassembly/docs/globalcompact/A_RES_2200A(XXI)_economic.pdf (accessed 19 February 2021).

demonstrate its limitations. Our point is only that privacy as separateness creates the normative space for a fresh look at how to discharge our collective responsibilities in a modern information society: it creates the space for other commitments, such as those immanent to the idea of distributed stewardship, to be seeded and from which privacy as nurturing may follow.

### 17.4.2 Distributed Stewardship in the Context of Health-Care Data

If we project ourselves forward, through what we imagine necessary to establish freshly negotiated reasonable expectations of privacy in the context of a modern health-care system, then we can begin to imagine also how such an exercise might manifest the collective responsibilities inherent in stewardship to be distributed across all actors.[49] Let us imagine that, following the negotiation, there remains a mutual regard for the separateness necessary for self-determination. Privacy remains, at least in part, about the right to self-definition – the right to find one's own authenticity. In the context of health care, we might each expect to have the opportunity to avail ourselves of medical care within an environment of privacy and confidentiality. The construction of this environment – consistent with a mutual regard for self-determination – does not require all information to be kept separate in all circumstances. It may be a matter of privacy to expect that there will be a discussion of the parameters of data sharing with those whom we burden with the responsibility of our care. For example, in the context of a 'right not to know', it may be legitimate for those caring for me to expect me not to leave them questioning about fundamental objections I might have to the normal expectations about health care (that is, that I might be told of clinically significant outcomes or findings of processes in which I engage or that might reasonably be expected to be in my interests), thus avoiding leaving the physician decision-makers in a place where they have to guess what a reasonable subject might think about the return of information. This goes to privacy as part of the social contract – not 'a' social contract but an imperative reality of the relationship among individuals in society.

---

[49] 'Normatively, and crucially, we propose that regulatory stewardship is a responsibility for all actors engaged in health research regulation. The failure to see regulation as an inherently collective responsibility will stand in the way of the optimization of effective regulation' (Laurie et al (n 4) 344).

## 17.5   So What? Going Beyond Positive Encumbrance to Find a Legacy of Facilitation?

We have established that a distinctive merit of Graeme's conception of privacy as separateness is that, maximally shorn of normative assumption, it opens space for negotiation regarding what *ought* to be permitted with regards to data use and disclosure. Different ideas about what should constitute protected privacy interests can be discussed with minimal presumption of legitimacy. One of the consequences of this is that any legitimacy must be demonstrated, rather than presumed. Those who claim a normative position regarding data use and disclosure – claiming that some uses of data *ought* not be permitted, or that individuals or groups *ought* to have control over who accesses what data in what circumstances – are challenged to justify their position. Graeme's conception of privacy does not permit us the luxury of lazy normative assumption.

This does risk upsetting, however, the convenient overlapping consensus regarding what constitutes privacy rights, established over the past fifty years or so through international instruments, and decries unquestioning adoption of privacy tropes – such as 'the right to be let alone' – established in the academic literature. Yet it also enables provocation to reset privacy claims in a way that might work better for those of us living in a modern information-driven society. We are enabled to negotiate a new position that attaches due weight to a respect for autonomy – and the safeguard that informed consent represents – but that contextualises it among other valuable interests and responsibilities of a data steward: it locates the seed within the soil. What follows is our collective responsibility. One thing it does make clear, however, is the folly of abandoning an individual to make decisions under conditions of bounded rationality with any expectation that they will be able to act to protect their best interests and the best interests of the community affected by data that relates to them.

Recognition of the pervasive asymmetries in information and imbalances of power and bargaining position that exist in the health research context, particularly with regards to *further* processing of personal data, challenges us to move beyond consent as the mechanism to protect even individual interests in privacy. When we open space to recognise the interests that individuals may have in data that relate to them, not only as individuals but also as individual members of a group, and as members of groups qua groups, then we establish the need to find new ways of doing things. At the very least, it allows us to bring into focus the collective interests that individuals have in data. There is a spectrum of possibility when it comes to the possible change that might follow. It ranges from relatively trivial tinkering with the current approach to fundamental reform.

Practical questions that might be opened include which data are included in the discussion, and where might these open negotiations take place? The atomised, individual conceptualisation of personal data produces immediate questions of scope and inclusion. Where the normative value of personal data is predetermined by the limitation of individual privacy, it is easier to exclude the data of particular individuals or groups of individuals on the basis of their perceived importance in society; individuals are excluded when the cultural and normative setting is not part of the discussion.[50] The conception of privacy as separateness further allows us to ask the question whether non-personal data also ought to be controlled. The distinction between personal data and other data – for example, commercial data – in the individualistic privacy framing of value again excludes particular individuals from access to meaning and value in data that relate to them or to groups to which they belong. In the open space of separateness, presumptions of relationships among individuals (and their groupings) in relation to data lose their presumed order and have to be negotiated afresh; the exclusion of property in personal data from the data subject or the indigenous group, while accepting property in the same information in the hands of a commercial institution through intellectual property, becomes challengeable.

The spaces where these dialogues should happen can emerge through the spaces where individuals negotiate the transactions around their data. An imperative to stewardship expected of anyone holding data makes closing of spaces a contestable position. The imbalance of power among individuals must be a focus for institutional redress. One space where such redress could start is that of the REC/IRB. How, for example, might society avoid another Cambridge Analytica situation? Strengthening RECs and opening commercial practice to ethics scrutiny (and not limiting such scrutiny to research settings) could be one possibility. Currently, the rigour of ethics review is reduced where data do not relate to identifiable individuals. Given the significance of group data, this may

---

[50] See, for example, Caroline Criado Perez, *Invisible Women: Data Bias in a World Designed for Men* (Chatto and Windus 2019).

not be normatively defensible – particularly given the commercial interests in model profiles. The increasing reliance upon commercial organisations to contribute to research as partners carries risks (as with, for example, the UK's Information Commissioner's Office's censoring in 2017 of DeepMind's involvement with the Royal Free London NHS Foundation Trust[51]). The decision of the HRCDC Appeal Panel, discussed in Section 17.3, to reject the contention that involvement of a for-profit might challenge privacy concerns is an example of this. This, of itself, does not address the continuing difficulties of individualism and informed consent.

Although the challenges with 'informed consent' as a safeguard are well documented, we are not suggesting that it has no value or should be abandoned entirely. What we could do to improve it is to extend our understanding of what an informed consent process looks like. For example, the idea of an ideally informed consent might extend to include ongoing (updated) information about impact upon groups and collective interests. This could be done by extending the information that is provided to an individual about the purposes of processing: ensuring that purposes post-aggregation or anonymisation, and the anticipated consequences of that processing for groups, are declared. It could also be done by recognising the possibility in some circumstances of a group consent. There is evidence of this in relation to indigenous groups, such as that reflected in the UN Special Rapporteur's draft Recommendation on the Protection and Use of Health-Related Data.[52] Important considerations apply to questions concerning data sovereignty in relation to indigenous groups. That said, there may be much to be learnt, about how collective interests in data can be navigated, and group consents achieved in practice, from these communities that may be of broader application. Of course, this will not always be appropriate or practical. Most obviously, it is challenged when individuals do not recognise themselves as being members of relevant groups. There are other issues with

---

[51] Information Commissioner's Office, 'Royal Free – Google DeepMind Trial Failed to Comply with Data Protection Law' https://ico.org.uk/about-the-ico/news-and-events/news-and-blogs/2017/07/royal-free-google-deepmind-trial-failed-to-comply-with-data-protection-law/ (accessed 28 February 2021).

[52] United Nations Human Rights – Office of the High Commissioner, 'The Protection and Use of Health-Related Data: Report' www.ohchr.org/EN/Issues/Privacy/SR/Pages/HealthRelatedData.aspx (accessed 19 February 2021). See also 'Draft Recommendation on the Protection and Use of Health-Related Data' www.ohchr.org/Documents/Issues/Privacy/SR_Privacy/DraftRecommendationProtectionUseHealthRelatedData.pdf (accessed 19 February 2021).

representation and the practice and process of decision-making within a group that may be difficult and, in some cases, render this an inappropriate response. An extended understanding of consent is not the only way that collective interests can be recognised.

This reform need not be entirely radical. If we were to recognise an extended range of privacy interests and to acknowledge the responsibilities that individuals owe to consider the impact of processing on others, then there are other ways we might extend the reach of existing data protection law beyond enhancing information provision. A similarly incremental approach may be offered by an interpretation of the requirement for 'fair' processing. This requirement could be extended to recognise an individual's privacy interests *as a member of a group* alongside those they have as an identifiable individual. The concept of fair processing could be developed beyond a relatively thin conception of transparency and faithfulness to promises to include substantive considerations of fairness.[53]

This approach might take us some considerable distance, but it does not address the scope of privacy and data protection law: personal data means data relating to an identified or identifiable individual. We may tinker with an interpretation of that definition,[54] but we are stretching elastic that is anchored, at one end, to an individual identifiable person. We are unable to recognise the significance of governance extending to protect vulnerabilities that are not capable of protection through individual control: societal safeguards at a macro level. However, we might read Graeme and feel an invitation to find the suggested extension of data protection law to include group data within the definition of personal data: personal data could be defined to include 'data relating to a group of identified or identifiable individuals' and, as the consequences of such an inclusion were worked out, one would see that the world did not end; an inclusive rather than exclusionary privacy would protect a wider range of interests, and enable the negotiation of privacies that could release individuals' duties to contribute to flourishing in society.

## 17.6   Conclusion

Privacy does not have to be construed as the individualist charge of 'get off my land'. Privacy as separateness and stewardship becomes 'this land

---

[53] Mark Taylor and Jeannie Paterson, 'Protecting Privacy in India: The Roles of Consent and Fairness in Data Protection' (2020) 16 *Indian Journal of Law and Technology* 71.

[54] Mark Taylor, '"Personal Information" and Group Data under the Privacy Act 1988 (Cth)' (2020) 94 *Australian Law Journal* 730.

is our land' as the better construction – the negotiation of the space and the understanding of all the interests. The concepts work together to create the space for negotiation and to make explicit the normative commitments that may constrain it: they may ground a new idea of privacy. While the content of this new privacy needs to be established through the negotiation, we lean on the collective responsibility inherent in Graeme's notion of stewardship and tentatively label it a new privacy in solidarity. It is a privacy that might suggest a shift in access to personal data in the commercial and quasi-commercial environment, but respected by, for example, access to medicines and non-exploitation of interaction. Currently, we seem content that individual privacy protection can produce a market approach whereby the altruism of consented participation is met with a hard competitive commercialism for the developer. One might expect a more rounded, solidaristic, spatial privacy to require that *altruism in* from the participant is met with a starting presumption of *altruism out* from the developer – stepping from an isolating individualism to an empathetic empowered individualism in society. Privacy can move from an encumbrance to an opportunity of empowerment that is both part of democracy and part of the broader ECtHR agenda.

At the moment, however, the relationship between informed consent and a narrow range of privacy interests blinkers effective governance. Informed consent makes normative assumptions with regards to the necessity, sufficiency and desirability of individuals making decisions for themselves that have impacts upon not only them but also associated others. In many situations, we assume that autonomy and self-determination are sufficiently protected by an individual making their own decisions about what is in their best interests; we operate with the principle 'caveat emptor' ringing in our ears – 'let the buyer beware' – and it is a matter for the wit and guile of the individual (as consumer) to negotiate their world, making the best choices as they see fit and suffering the consequences of their bad bargains. This, it is argued, respects autonomy and decisional privacy; it avoids paternalism. However, this is not the only societal construction that we use. 'Caveat emptor' presumes an equality of bargaining power. Very often, individuals are not on an equal footing; one participant has enormous advantages.

In an environment of considerable power and information asymmetry, and also one in which the use of one person's personal information can have significance for their family, group and society at large, we are obliged to consider whether current safeguards are fit for purpose. Are they capable of protecting an individual's own interests, of recognising their responsibilities to others and of promoting incremental evolution towards civil society and moral community?

Many times, we want to preserve the knowledge imbalance as that is what we are seeking to exploit: we go to a doctor or a lawyer, or to a mechanic or skilled artisan, precisely to benefit from another's knowledge where ours is insufficient. We do not want to 'level the playing field'; we want to ensure that the tilt works for everyone. In common law jurisdictions, an imbalance in power is sometimes addressed by the concept of fiduciary duty: the individual with the knowledge advantage must act to protect the vulnerability of the other party.[55] Arguably, this is a long-standing challenge to the idea that privacy concerns self-determination, and that the individual is best placed to protect their own interests. Although not yet litigated, it would be very interesting to see if the researcher/participant situation would be considered one requiring a fiduciary duty in equity. If so, this would require a reversal of the position taken by RECs about the importance of informed consent: the researcher, and the REC, would have to act in such a way as to ensure that the potential participant was fully informed about the potential dangers of participation, and so as to ensure the welfare of their participants where full information was not possible. Would this extend into a duty not to ask individuals to participate in 'too risky' research? It was not that the participants of Neisser's study, or the Nazi 'experiments', or Tuskegee, were not asked if they would be willing to participate; it is that they should never have been put in that position in the first place: some research is, essentially, demeaning to human dignity and should not take place. But this does not sit easily with the individualist conceptualisation of privacy. Can this be reconciled with modern privacy?

In this chapter, we have sought to illustrate how a legacy of Graeme Laurie's work is that it points the way to a paradigm-shifting intellectual and regulatory agenda, specifically one that acknowledges that individual interests (in privacy) contain group responsibilities and benefits – and that individuals owe and need 'solidaristic responsibility' to function in a (liberal) society. Refreshing anew the states of separateness necessary to maintain the conditions conducive to a negotiated privacy may also reveal our shared responsibilities with regard to distributed stewardship.

---

[55] Taking English Equity as an example, cases such as *Keech* v. *Sandford* [1726] EWHC Ch J76, 25 ER 223, (1726) 2 Eq Cas Abr 741 and *Boardman* v. *Phipps* [1967] 2 AC 46, [1966] 3 All ER 721, [1966] UKHL 2 show that the courts are prepared to make seemingly extreme interpretations of the duty to protect the perceived 'weaker' party.

Graeme's conception of 'privacy as separateness', when placed together with the idea of stewardship, may allow us to rebalance respect in a way that allows us to encompass collective interests as fundamental to self-determination.

What we have sought to do here is to recognise the value of renegotiating the interests and expectations protected by the regulation of health research and the significance of Graeme's preferred conception of privacy for enabling such negotiation. We have pointed to a possible renegotiation of privacy that steps beyond the blinkers of individualism to realise a broader interpretation of human rights and human dignity – to rethink the duties of researchers and other actors, as well as the human right to participate in and enjoy the cultural and scientific benefits of society, and the human duty to participate in one's society. We do not argue to impose this (somewhat) radical change. We have argued for *a* radical change but left open-ended the possibilities. In other words, we have argued for a space to discuss it.

# A Tale of Two Legacies

## Drawing on Humanist Interpretations to Animate the Right to the Benefits of Science

SHAWN H. E. HARMON

## 18.1 Introduction

Having never before contributed to a Festschrift, and now being rather removed from the (impressive, collegial and much-missed) team assembled by Graeme Laurie in Edinburgh, I was unsure about the extent to which a chapter in a work such as this should (i) tackle a social/legal matter within the subject's field of interest with some appropriate reference to his (in this case) work; or (ii) critically engage with or critique his body of scholarship; or (iii) reverently and biographically muse about the person himself. In the present case, I shall lean towards (i) with a nod towards (iii), and in the effort I shall try to avoid interpreting his work inaccurately or appearing too obsequious. Having said that, my remit is to explore 'legacy' in some respect, and I think that necessitates a positive engagement; an approach made easier here as I admit to having no sense of any negative aspect or consequence of my academic mentor's contributions.

In this chapter, I engage with 'legacy' in two respects. First, I argue that Article 15 of the International Covenant on Economic, Social and Cultural Rights (ICESCR),[1] known as the 'right to science', has no legacy. By this, I mean that this provision and the collection of rights and obligations to which it gives voice have generated no significant real-world impact (and

---

[1] United Nations General Assembly, 'International Covenant on Economic, Social and Cultural Rights' (UNGA Resolution A/RES/2200A(XXI) adopted 16 December 1966, in force on 3 January 1976) www.un.org/en/development/desa/population/migration/generalassembly/docs/globalcompact/A_RES_2200A(XXI)_economic.pdf (accessed 18 February 2021).

indeed very little direct academic discussion).[2] Second, I recall some of the published pieces from Graeme's impressive and vibrant body of scholarship, highlighting a legacy that I think is discernible. For introductory purposes, it can be described as giving the experience and wisdom of 'people' a role in decision-making within this multidisciplinary field that is 'health' (that is, a motivation to move medical jurisprudence both through, and in ways that are responsive to the needs of, people and communities). I then suggest that the manifestation of that legacy – the calling upon of that legacy – is what we need to generate legacy (any kind of legacy) for Article 15 ICESCR, which remains largely, though not entirely, untheorised, under-appreciated and unrealised. It remains all potential. We should draw from Graeme's legacy to help animate that sadly fallow 'right to science' so that it might one day have a legacy of its own.

As a preliminary point, I should state that my critical perspective is conditioned by my 'humanist' approach. By humanist, I mean an approach to social, legal and economic development in the world, and to relations across communities and peoples and borders, that is solidaristic and that places the well-being of people and communities above other considerations, including the parochial interests of powerful actors. This humanist approach was modelled, encouraged and facilitated by Graeme, who was my mentor,[3] and it colours how I think the law should be used, and what I consider Graeme's legacy to be. As a humanist lawyer, I believe that it is incumbent on us as justice-conscious policy actors and legal advocates to resist the machinations of those who would keep the right to science (and other rights) somnambulant, and to expend efforts to give that right a positive and robust – a word of which Graeme is particularly fond – interpretation *and application* so that it might help us generate a more equitable society as we move deeper into the

---

[2] Although there are a few exceptions, and they are referenced later in the chapter.

[3] I believe that our shared view of the role of law as a servant of the people, though not necessarily the most important servant, has facilitated both our friendship and our collaborations. A shared humanist approach is also, I think, one of the reasons that caused Graeme's long-time collaboration with his mentor, Ken Mason, to be so satisfying and fruitful. Ken, who mentored and inspired Graeme, was also a compassionate person and a humanist scholar: Shawn Harmon, 'Rigorous and Incisive, but a Humanist First!' (*In Honour of Ken Mason*, 4 April 2017) http://masoninstitutekenmemories.blogspot.com /2017/04/rigorous-and-incisive-but-humanist-first.html (accessed 18 February 2021). As a celebration of Ken's contributions, Graeme named the institute that we founded in Edinburgh The J Kenyon Mason Institute in Medicine, Life Sciences and Law. I feel that this Festschrift is both necessary and insufficient to celebrate the contributions that Graeme himself has made.

Anthropocene, which is characterised by dislocation, dynamism, uncertainty and precarity (of human survival).

## 18.2 An Unrealised Legacy: The Right to the Benefits of Science

We begin with an assessment of the law rather than the man (that is, an exploration of the 'right to science'). Article 15 ICESCR states:

15(1) The States Parties to the present Covenant recognize the right of everyone: (a) to take part in cultural life; (b) to enjoy the benefits of scientific progress and its applications; (c) to benefit from the protection of the moral and material interests resulting from any scientific, literary or artistic production of which he is the author.

(2) The steps to be taken by the States Parties to the present Covenant to achieve the full realization of this right shall include those necessary for the conservation, the development, and the diffusion of science and culture.

(3) The States Parties to the present Covenant undertake to respect the freedom indispensable for scientific research and creative activity.

(4) The States Parties to the present Covenant recognize the benefits to be derived from the encouragement and development of international contacts and co-operation in the scientific and cultural fields.

In order to understand what these provisions mean and require, it is important to consider not only their ordinary meaning but also their purpose and context;[4] such is in keeping with the 'dynamic' approach to interpretation that has been commended in relation to international human rights.[5]

As a preliminary matter, then, it is important to recall that the Universal Declaration of Human Rights (UDHR),[6] from which the ICESCR sprang, states in its Preamble:

> WHEREAS recognition of the inherent dignity and of the equal and inalienable rights of all members of the human family is the foundation of freedom, justice and peace in the world,

---

[4] Vienna Convention on the Law of Treaties (UN Treaty Series 1155 adopted 23 May 1969, in force 27 January 1980) 331, Articles 31–2.

[5] David Harris et al, *Harris, O'Boyle and Warbrick: Law of the European Convention on Human Rights* (2nd edn, Oxford University Press 2009) 5–8.

[6] UNGA Resolution A/RES/217(III) 10 December 1948.

WHEREAS the peoples of the United Nations have in the Charter reaffirmed their faith in fundamental human rights, in the dignity and worth of the human person and in the equal rights of men and women, and have determined to promote social progress and better standards of life in larger freedom,

WHEREAS Member States have pledged themselves to achieve, in co-operation with the United Nations, the promotion of universal respect for and observance of human rights and fundamental freedoms,

WHEREAS a common understanding of these rights and freedoms is of the greatest importance for the full realization of this pledge,

NOW, THEREFORE THE GENERAL ASSEMBLY proclaims ... that every individual and every organ of society, keeping this Declaration constantly in mind, shall strive ... to secure their universal and effective recognition and observance .....

Article 28 UDHR stipulates that everyone is entitled to a social and international order in which the UDHR's rights and freedoms can be fully realised, and Article 29(1) UDHR goes on to remind us that everyone has duties to the community so that others may develop their personality and enjoy the rights and freedoms articulated.

In essence, the rights articulated are considered to be universal, vested in each person by virtue of their common humanity, and independent of recognition or implementation within legal orders. They are also expected to impose obligations on a range of actors to ensure that they are realised:[7] first and foremost governments, but also non-state actors.[8] The centrality of dignity and the disposition of the human rights framework expressed in the UDHR were reiterated in the ICESCR, which is an international legal instrument that is binding on the 171 State Parties that have ratified it to date;[9] it therefore represents a collection of enforceable legal norms, directives and standards within and with respect to those State Parties. In keeping with the UDHR, the ICESCR was founded on the dual convictions, stated in the Preamble, that:

- freedom from fear and want can only be achieved if conditions are created whereby everyone can enjoy a range of economic, social, and cultural rights; and

---

[7] James Nickel, *Making Sense of Human Rights: Philosophical Reflections on the Universal Declaration of Human Rights* (UCLA Press 1987).

[8] Yvonne Donders, 'The Right to Enjoy the Benefits of Scientific Progress: In Search of State Obligations in Relation to Health' (2011) 14 *Medicine, Health Care & Philosophy* 371.

[9] UN High Commissioner for Human Rights, 'Status of Ratification Interactive Dashboard' https://indicators.ohchr.org/ (accessed 18 February 2021).

- individuals have duties to others and to the community to strive for the promotion and observance of rights.

Bearing the above in mind, we turn to the right to science more specifically, and any understanding of that right must begin with a sensitivity to 'science' and the 'scientific undertaking'. The term science, as acknowledged at the 2009 UNESCO meeting on the right to science,[10] must be taken to apply to all fields of science or intellectual inquiry (not just the natural or technical sciences). This broad sense of science must further be understood as being aimed at the pursuit of knowledge and the improvement of the human condition. While the latter aim might be viewed as a secondary one, it is important because without it, significant portions of scientific research would be unethical as a misuse of public funds or an unnecessary endangerment of human lives; it is the anticipated benefit that moves people to bear risks, and that justifies research ethics committees in permitting such risks to be borne.[11] Thus, what is engaged is the pursuit of knowledge balanced with the need to benefit (all of) humanity. This imperative is confirmed by Articles 2(1), 11(2) and 23 ICESCR,[12] and the fact that Article 15 is an enabler of many other rights.

With respect to the scientific undertaking, it is not inconsequential that, at the time that the ICESCR was adopted, science was viewed as a public good (with governments playing a key role in its development), and the benefits of science were considered to be not the property of the few but the heritage of humanity.[13] Shortly after the adoption of Article 15, it was opined that science is a *public enterprise* advancing fundamental knowledge about the world, with shared values (such as disinterestedness, universalism, communism and organised scepticism) for governing activities that are considered to be scientific, and with standardised methods for certifying knowledge.[14] The wide dissemination of findings

---

[10] UNESCO, 'The Right to Enjoy the Benefits of Scientific Progress and Its Applications' (Experts' Meeting, 16–17 July 2009) https://unesdoc.unesco.org/ark:/48223/pf0000185558 (accessed 18 February 2021).

[11] Sheelagh McGuinness, 'Research Ethics Committees: The Role of Ethics in a Regulatory Authority' (2008) 34 *Journal of Medical Ethics* 695.

[12] Which instruct states to render technical assistance to others, and to make full use of technical and scientific knowledge to improve methods of production, conservation and food distribution.

[13] Johannes Morsink, *The Universal Declaration of Human Rights: Origins, Drafting and Intent* (University of Pennsylvania Press 1999).

[14] Robert Merton, *The Sociology of Science: Theoretical and Empirical Investigations* (University of Chicago Press 1973).

through publication remained the norm, with patenting and other economic considerations often eschewed.[15]

Ultimately, then, the right takes as axiomatic that the material benefits of science should be enjoyed by everyone in everyday life, regardless of location or whether they contributed to the specific scientific advancement or application at issue. Of course, the inclusion of a practice in a legal instrument is not to impose a time-bound or static understanding of that practice. Key concepts must move with the times, where the purpose, words and context permit, if the law is to remain relevant.[16] Having said that, it is safe to say that the primary aims of science – being to advance knowledge and improve the human condition – remain largely unchanged.[17] A practical ambition for Article 15 was, and therefore must remain, the closing of existing gaps in the enjoyment of the benefits of everyday scientific advancements (such as electricity, telephones, and agricultural and medical innovations, which were known to be unevenly enjoyed as a result of income levels, infrastructure and institutions) and the avoidance of further gaps that profoundly compromise human well-being.[18] In pursuit of this human rights aim, State Parties have obligations to:[19]

- facilitate the participation of individuals in science through the provision of education and programmes and institutions that encourage ethical science and technological innovation;

---

[15] Amy Carroll, 'Not Always the Best Medicine: Biotechnology and the Global Impact of U.S. Patent Law: A Review of Recent Decisions of the United States Court of Appeals for the Federal Court' (1995) 44 *American University Law Review* 2433.

[16] Michael Van Alstine, 'Dynamic Treaty Interpretation' (1998) 146 *University of Pennsylvania Law Review* 687.

[17] Angela Potochnik, *Idealization and the Aims of Science* (University of Chicago Press 2017).

[18] Maria Green, 'Drafting History of Article 15(1)(c) of the International Covenant on Economic, Social and Cultural Rights' (ECOSOC Document E/C.12/2000/15, 9 October 2000) www.un.org/en/ga/search/view_doc.asp?symbol=E/C.12/2000/15 (accessed 18 February 2021); UN Development Program, *Human Development Report 2001: Making New Technologies Work for Human Development* (Oxford University Press 2001); William Schabas, 'Study of the Right to Enjoy the Benefits of Scientific and Technological Progress and Its Applications' in Yvonne Donders and Vladimir Volodin (eds), *Human Rights in Education, Science and Culture* (Ashgate 2007) 273; Hans Haugen, 'Human Rights and Technology – A Conflictual Relationship? Assessing Private Research and the Right to Adequate Food' (2008) 7 *Journal of Human Rights* 224.

[19] Amrei Müller, 'Remarks on the Venice Statement on the Right to Enjoy the Benefits of Scientific Progress and Its Applications (Article 15(1)(b) ICESCR)' (2010) 10 *Human Rights Law Review* 765.

- ensure that the salutary outcomes of science and innovation are deployed for the benefit of society without discrimination; and
- avoid and mitigate the anticipatable harms that might arise from the pursuit and application of science and technology.

And while non-state actors might not have these same obligations, or at least not to the same extent, they nonetheless have duties (even if they are commercial enterprises) to refrain from undermining or interfering with states in the proper pursuit of their obligations.[20] This should impose limitations on the ability of private actors advancing their commercial interests to challenge state actions pursuing the public interest (but it has not).

The above aims have obviously not been achieved,[21] and the above obligations have not been taken up in a serious way. While the reasons are undeniably complex, with both macro and micro elements, much of the 'blame' can be laid at the feet of the architects and benefactors of neo-liberalism (for example, the International Monetary Fund, the World Trade Organization (WTO), the World Bank, a range of international corporations and their host states, which include Japan, the EU, the UK, the USA, and others). Through decades of free-market advocacy and support, trade liberalisation, privatisation of public services, and austerity measures levelled against the populations least able to accommodate them, these actors have eroded both the international human rights framework and the collective vision of what that framework might achieve.[22] In addition, they have sidelined and rendered largely invisible a range of international human rights, including the rights to solidarity (Article 1 UDHR), to non-discrimination on grounds of economic position (Article 2 UDHR), to just and favourable work conditions (Article 7 ICESCR), to adequate standards of living (Article 11 ICESCR), to free higher education (Article 13 ICESCR) and to science (Article 15 ICESCR). While references within the ICESCR to its 'progressive

---

[20] Ibid.; Schabas (n 18).

[21] To confirm this, we need only consider the uneven health of peoples and the profound inequalities in their access to medicines: see further Margaret Chan, 'Ten Years in Public Health 2007–2017' (WHO 2017) https://apps.who.int/iris/bitstream/handle/10665/255355/9789241512442-eng.pdf;jsessionid=B9303B69E84B9DBB52324C10A6CB12D3?sequence=1 (accessed 18 February 2021).

[22] See Gillian MacNaughton and Diane Frey, 'Teaching the Transformative Agenda of the Universal Declaration of Human Rights' (2015) 103 *Radical Teacher* 17, who lament that even international poverty eradication policy is driven by neo-liberal logic; under the Sustainable Development Goals, economic growth is the key platform for poverty reduction.

realisation' (Articles 2, 13, 14 and 22), together with an absence of bespoke enforcing bodies, have probably contributed to this sidelining, it is undeniably a consequence of invested actors constructing these rights as 'aspirational', as unenforceable, as too expensive and as concerned with 'others' towards whom they consider that they have no direct duties.[23]

With respect to science, they have aggressively advanced a market-oriented worldview, which spread significantly in the 1980s alongside a commercialisation agenda that was extended to research. The drivers and symptoms of this agenda, and associated shift in understandings of science, include the following:

- a reconceptualisation of the role of the state (driven in no small part by the US political culture's suspicion of government) so as to reduce its regulatory and redistributive function, and privatisation campaigns that further limited the state's ability to deliver public services and realise human rights for its subjects;[24]
- the introduction and pursuit of a profit motive in scientific undertakings, which began to determine research priorities, methodologies and values;[25]
- adoption of the Bayh-Dole Act in the USA, which prompted the US and other governments to encourage the commodification of all things (with an emphasis on exploitation and consumption), and further to develop publicly funded research through for-profit commercial enterprises;[26]
- the linking of science and intellectual property (IP) protection with trade under the WTO, and through laws crafted in closed negotiations

---

[23] Ellen Wiles, 'Aspirational Principles or Enforceable Rights? The Future for Socio-economic Rights in National Law' (2006) 22 *American University International Law Review* 35.

[24] Audrey Chapman, 'A Human Rights Perspective on Intellectual Property, Scientific Progress, and Access to the Benefits of Science' in WIPO/OHCHR, *A Panel Discussion to Commemorate the 50th Anniversary of the Universal Declaration of Human Rights* (WIPO 1999) 127.

[25] Audrey Chapman, 'Towards an Understanding of the Right to Enjoy the Benefits of Scientific Progress and Its Applications' (2009) 8 *Journal of Human Rights* 1.

[26] Albert Borgmann, 'Communities of Celebration: Technology and Public Life' in Frederick Ferre (ed), *Research in Philosophy and Technology* (JAI Press 1990) 335; Ian Barbour, *Ethics in an Age of Technology* (Harper Collins 1993); and National Research Council Committee on Issues in the Transborder Flow of Scientific Data, *Bits of Power: Issues in Global Access to Scientific Data* (NRC 1997).

dominated by industry intent on expanding its control over key high-science fields increasingly critical to human health and health care;[27]

- an erosion of the distinction between basic and applied science, with the result that IP protection moved far upstream and selective publication of research outcomes began to shroud product ineffectiveness or harms;[28]
- the regularisation of conflicts of interest in the research process resulting from corporate sponsorship, direct financial interests of researchers in their work, and university IP and commercialisation policies.[29]

This neo-liberal agenda has almost entirely colonised our minds, with the result that neo-liberalism and its programmes – even those that conflict with international human rights – have become invisible to us;[30] its character as only one of multiple ideologies or social structuring concepts has been lost, and many have lost, in consequence, the capacity to imagine an alternative world.

Despite the anti-egalitarian neo-liberal project, interest in enlivening the rights contained in Article 15 ICESCR has grown, perhaps in recognition of the failure of that project to deliver well-being equitably (or at all, one might argue, given the state of the global ecosystem and its peoples[31]). In 2009, UNESCO issued its Venice Statement on the Right to Enjoy the Benefits of Scientific Progress and Its Applications ('Venice Statement'),[32] which describes the 'right to science' as containing the following elements:

---

[27] David Downes, 'The 1999 WTO Review of Life Patenting under TRIPS' (*CIEL Discussion Paper*, 1999) www.ciel.org/wp-content/uploads/2015/03/WTOReviewofLPunderTRIPS .pdf (accessed 18 February 2021).

[28] Marcia Angell, *The Truth about Drug Companies* (Random House 2004). In this regard, note the adoption of the TRIPS Agreement by the WTO in 1994, and its imposition on all WTO members. It expanded the subject matter of IP rights to knowledge in foundational scientific fields, and to the tools and processes of science. The regenerative medicine field, for example, is cluttered with some 16,000 gene patents granted by the US Patent & Trademark Office: see further Aurora Plomer, 'The Human Rights Paradox: Intellectual Property Rights and Rights of Access to Science' (2013) 35 *Human Rights Quarterly* 143.

[29] Sheldon Krimsky, *Science in the Private Interest* (Rowman & Littlefield 2003).

[30] MacNaughton and Frey (n 22).

[31] Paul Crutzen, 'The "Anthropocene"' in Eckart Ehlers and Thomas Krafft (eds), *Earth System Science in the Anthropocene* (Springer 2006) 13; Madeleine Fagan, 'On the Dangers of an Anthropocene Epoch: Geological Time, Political Time and Post-Human Politics' (2019) 70 *Political Geography* 55; and Leslie Sklair, 'The Corporate Capture of Sustainable Development and Its Transformation into a "Good Anthropocene" Historical Bloc' (2019) 19 *Civitas* 296.

[32] UNESCO, 'Venice Statement on the Right to Enjoy the Benefits of Scientific Progress and Its Applications' (2009) www.aaas.org/sites/default/files/VeniceStatement_July2009.pdf (accessed 18 February 2021).

- academic or investigative freedom;
- opportunities for all to contribute to the scientific enterprise;
- participation of individuals and communities in decision-making;
- access by everyone, without discrimination, to benefits and applications; and
- conservation, development and diffusion of science and technology.

Given that many low- and low-middle-income states will not have the capacity to meet the more onerous obligations imposed by the right, it must (still) be viewed as imposing stepped obligations based on income level. But it was agreed in the development of the Venice Statement that actions must include financial and funding measures, education and monitoring measures, and standard-setting and access measures,[33] which ought to have a legislative element. In addition to states, the scientific community and the private sector were also identified as having obligations, including:

- Scientific Community: developing a greater awareness of the right and its application to the conduct of science, and participating in further development and elucidation of the right;[34]
- Civil Society: preparing reports relating to violations of the right;[35]
- Private Sector: acting in ways that advance rather than frustrate the right, including giving greater attention to the basic needs of disadvantaged and marginalised groups.[36]

While there is little substantive guidance in the Venice Statement on what concrete steps the private sector should take, it makes reference to the Human Rights Guidelines for Pharmaceutical Companies in relation to Access to Medicines (2008).[37] Those Guidelines observe that while pharma companies are subject to standards and to monitoring and accountability, they are rarely held accountable in relation to their human rights responsibilities to enhance access to medicines. Such companies are advised to, inter alia, adopt human rights policy statements (Article 1); integrate human rights into their commercial strategies

---

[33] Ibid., Arts 13–16.
[34] Ibid., Art 25.
[35] Ibid., Art 26.
[36] Ibid., Art 27.
[37] Contained as an Annex in Special Rapporteur Hunt, 'Report of the Special Rapporteur on the Right of Everyone to the Enjoyment of the Highest Attainable Standard of Physical and Mental Health' (UN Doc A/63/263, 11 August 2008) https://undocs.org/A/63/263 (accessed 18 February 2021).

(Articles 2 and 5); increase their transparency in relation to information they have bearing on access to medicines (Articles 6–8); adopt targets and management systems in relation to access to medicines, addressing the same in their annual reports (Articles 9–14); adopt anti-corruption policies and weed out counterfeiting (Articles 15–16); ensure that their own manufacturing process are appropriate and their clinical trials ethical (Articles 20–2); commit to researching neglected diseases (Articles 23–5); and commit to facilitating the flexibilities in the Trade-Related Aspects of Intellectual Property Rights (TRIPS) Agreement, including issuing non-exclusive voluntary licences, making available test data and not seeking patents on trivial modifications of existing medicines (Articles 26–32).

In 2017, the American Association for the Advancement of Science (AAAS) reported on its international survey on government actions necessary to give meaning to the 'right to science'. Key findings from the responses were that government needs to increase funding for scientific infrastructure and research; provide adequate science education to the general public; promote a positive view of science and scientists among the public; ensure open access to scientific information; and promote and protect academic freedom.[38] Also in 2017, UNESCO adopted its Recommendation on Science and Scientific Researchers (UNESCO Recommendation),[39] which is aimed at articulating the needs of researchers and the conditions for good research.

There are now emerging calls for heightened attention to the right to science, and there are recommendations that states should report more fully on their implementation of the right in their periodic reports to the CESCR, with the CESCR asking more specific and pointed questions in its exchanges with states about same.[40] There are also calls for increased international co-operation and partnering in different scientific fields, with an emphasis on the needs of marginalised peoples.[41] All told, though, the current state of affairs in relation to the right to science is one characterised by preliminary suggestions and demands rather than

---

[38] J Wyndham et al, 'Giving Meaning to the Right to Science: A Global and Multidisciplinary Approach' (AAAS 2017) www.aaas.org/sites/default/files/s3fs-public/reports/Right_to_Science_Report.pdf (accessed 18 February 2021).

[39] UNESCO, 'Recommendation on Science and Scientific Researchers' (39th Session of the General Conference of UNESCO, 13 November 2017) http://portal.unesco.org/en/ev.php-URL_ID=49455&URL_DO=DO_TOPIC&URL_SECTION=201.html (accessed 18 February 2021).

[40] Müller (n 19).

[41] Chapman (n 25).

concrete action.[42] It is with this unfortunate lack of legacy in mind that we turn to Graeme's rich legacy. Though neither the UDHR nor the ICESCR features significantly in Graeme's work, that work can be understood, in its broadest sense, as an effort to vindicate the human rights framework enshrined in these instruments, at least within the health and innovation setting.

### 18.3   A Notable Legacy: A 'Humanist' Approach to Health Innovation and Law

Obviously, Graeme's work has multiple strands and targets, though he has been and remains concerned with what can and ought to guide actors in the health-care setting, and how law might be deployed to assist in this regard; while also creating action spaces that are encouraging, sensible and comprehensible, all within environments where the law might be quite limited in what it can accomplish. While this is a broad church, one can see a consistent concern with the subject (or scientific artefact) of data – whether genetic data, health data more broadly, or administrative data used in health-related research – and governance in the new forms of research that are emerging. Different strands of Graeme's work can also be viewed as unified by a number of interrelated objectives, which, stated very broadly, are to improve the behaviour of life science innovators, the performance of health system regulators, and the outcomes of life science and health research and medical interventions. And, finally, it can be said to have at its centre the empowerment of people and communities, particularly those who have traditionally been silenced or pushed to the peripheries of decision-making.

For present purposes, my aim is to distil a narrower 'legacy' from Graeme's scholarship, and I do this through a brief tour of some of his published works. I begin with some work that we did together between 2008 and 2012.[43] This project, which concerned the collaborative

---

[42]  With all due respect to, and acknowledgement of, the work of Chapman and Donders, cited herein, and the work of Knoppers. See, for example, Bartha Knoppers et al, 'A Human Rights Approach to an International Code of Conduct for Genomic and Clinical Data Sharing' (2014) 133 *Human Genetics* 895, which explicitly considers the implications of the right to science developing standards for international data sharing in the genetic research setting. More recently, see Rumiana Yotova and Bartha Knoppers, 'The Right to Benefit from Science and Its Implications for Genomic Data Sharing' (2020) 31 *European Journal of International Law* 665, which further explores Article 15 ICESCR in this setting.

[43]  This work was undertaken within two projects, the ProReg Biotech Project, led by Graeme and funded through the ARHC SCRIPT Centre, and the GET Social Values Project, led by me and funded by the ESRC.

formulation, from the ground up, of regulation for regenerative medicine research and practice in Argentina, was informed by a shared conviction that the law, when it is relied on, must encourage positive social and health outcomes for individuals and communities. We took the opportunity offered by this work to remind those tasked with developing the law that they should be much more attuned than in the past to this objective and to the values that are necessary to achieve it. While the outcomes of that work – which was carried on by protagonists in Argentina long after the projects came to a close – were mostly legal (producing changes to the Civil Code and a new statute),[44] we also theorised how actors might better regulate in the emerging sociotechnological setting, which was and continues to be characterised by promise and consternation, dynamism and complexity, and fragmentation and uncertainty. In doing so, we developed the concept of 'legal foresighting'.

The aims of legal foresighting are to identify and explore possible and desirable future legal or quasi-legal developments aimed at achieving valued social and technological ends.[45] It is a fundamentally outcome-oriented reformative process; while it offers the opportunity to subject technological trajectories, social trends, and legal conditions, inertias and developments to early, rational, contemplative reflection, it also helps *create* pathways into the unknown, and part of that creation may mean (or demand) a fundamental revisioning of the legal setting itself as well as its instruments, institutions and regulatory or governance mechanisms. It is, at base, about collaboratively articulating the values that move us and the future we want, and then designing laws across mutually influencing (but rarely joined-up) systems to help deliver that future. We argued that the *nature* of the role that law can play in shaping health-related innovation is often misunderstood, with the result that law is often misdirected. We went on to offer a preliminary three-dimensional matrix or framework for undertaking such foresighting,[46] which was designed to ensure that actors undertake a wide-ranging and fulsome exploration of the field to be regulated and thereby empower themselves to appreciate how the law can be most effectively used and what the law might need to remain fit for purpose as we move into the unknown.

---

[44] For more on this, see Chapter 15 in this volume.
[45] Graeme Laurie, Shawn Harmon and Fabiana Arzuaga, 'Foresighting Futures: Law, New Technologies, and the Challenges of Regulating for Uncertainty' (2012) 4 *Law, Innovation & Technology* 1.
[46] Ibid.

Our work on legal foresighting is, however, just one example of Graeme's contribution to regulatory development and evolution, which, in my experience, he always perceived as a social exercise to be influenced by people – broader categories of people than were traditionally able to gain access to the regulation-making and regulatory process. It is therefore important, if we wish to appreciate the legacy that I am seeking to highlight, to take notice of some additional pieces of Graeme's work. These pieces begin, as did our work, with a keen interest in reminding actors to appreciate the 'public' nature of science and health-related research, and so the need to be cognisant of the public's (or publics') interests. In 2010, in the course of examining the foundation of publicly funded biobanks,[47] which are meant to serve as resources of genetic data and material to a wide range of future research, Graeme and colleagues commended the positive nature of 'public interest'. They argued that, contrary to many contemporary deployments of public interest arguments, the public interest could and should be understood as an 'encourager' and an 'enabler' rather than as a 'red light' barrier. In other words, rather than functioning to highlight and help avoid socially harmful outcomes, the public interest could also – and more helpfully – underscore the desirable, providing it was sufficiently explored and unpacked. The central thesis was as follows: '[S]cientifically sound, ethically robust research using biobanks is manifestly in the public interest. We would, in fact, go further and suggest that there is a positive moral obligation to promote use of these research resources in ways that, in turn, promote the public interest. That can only happen through access.'[48] In advancing this thesis, and as a means of discerning the content of public interest in this context, it was argued that *participants* in biobanks should have a say in the use of the resources, offering advice to resource custodians on the level at which to set privacy protections, and where further or specific negotiations over access might be warranted. In other words, publics (here, participants) should engage with research resource decision-makers in defining and redefining that public interest as it relates to biobank use and privacy protection relating thereto. The argument continues:

> [B]roadly speaking, the public interest should include acts or conduct which further society's better interests as well as providing adequate

---

[47] Graeme Laurie et al, 'Managing Access to Biobanks: How Can We Reconcile Privacy and Public Interests in Genetic Research?' (2010) 10 *Medical Law International* 315.

[48] Ibid., 322.

protection of the general public from harm. It is therefore arguable that the public interest in the context of biobanks should include genetic research for the benefit of society as a part of public health and welfare, the promotion of wider collective interests where appropriate, and this may also include personal security and the fight against crime. More specifically, and because the value of the principle of solidarity in the context of biobanks is particularly strong, broad engagement with publics and participants should inform the process of deciding what it means to manage a biobank 'in the public interest'.[49]

In difficult cases, decision-makers (that is, resource custodians) must consider effectiveness, necessity and balance in an effort to achieve fairness for all parties concerned. The article also considered benefit sharing as a means of achieving reciprocity.

Graeme would go on to articulate a 'good governance' framework for biobanks.[50] He argued that quality governance frameworks should contain the following:

- designed-in interoperability with respect to scientific and governance approaches;
- designed-out approaches restrictive of sharing, co-operation, flexibility and mutuality;
- *policies and procedures to protect adequately the interests of participants;*
- *policies and procedures that actively promote use of the resource in keeping with its purposes;*
- carefully articulated and managed access policies and stewardship arrangements; and
- governance policies and mechanisms that are kept fit for purpose over time.

At least two of the above features speak to Graeme's persistent concern for understanding and vindicating the interests of those actors who have habitually been left out of governance and policy-making: participants and publics. The principles underlying this framework, and which might be called upon to resolve conflicts between objectives, are, he suggested, 'integrity of purpose', 'proportionality of action' and 'reflexivity of approach'.[51] In defining these principles and advocating for his model, Graeme was, as ever,

---

[49] Ibid., 324.
[50] Graeme Laurie, 'Reflexive Governance in Biobanking: On the Value of Policy Led Approaches and the Need to Recognise the Limits of Law' (2011) 130 *Human Genetics* 347.
[51] Ibid., 349–50.

careful to point out that the law has its limits and cannot be relied on to solve all governance challenges, or to achieve all public interest-informed ends.[52] While the law might shape structures and place certain limits on conduct, research resources like biobanks are best governed by bespoke structures that permit reflexivity, anticipation and mutual learning (that is, learning on the part of all interested parties). In this respect, Graeme wrote extensively about the utility of a 'critical friend' to the biobank,[53] one of which he chaired (the UK Biobank's Ethics and Governance Council (EGC)).[54]

What the above hints at, and what was later given more direct attention,[55] is that it is important for innovators to understand the 'social licence' under which health-related research pursues its outcomes. Here 'social licence' refers to the expectations of society in relation to an activity in a particular field that goes beyond the requirements of formal regulation applicable to that field. The social licence related to – or the social acceptance of and participation in – health-related research is deeply influenced by whether, and the extent to which, it is viewed as a socially valuable enterprise conducted in the service of the public good.[56] Given that individual co-operation with specific research studies is usually moderated through (i) expectations about how research is conducted and regulated, (ii) trust in the institutions and individuals who recruit and interact with participants and (iii) beliefs in the 'wholesomeness' and public value of the research endeavour,[57] the conditions for social licence in this field include:

[52] Shawn Harmon, Graeme Laurie and Gill Haddow, 'Governing Risk, Engaging Publics and Engendering Trust: New Horizons for Law and Social Science?' (2013) 40 *Science and Public Policy* 25.

[53] Graeme Laurie, 'Role of the UK Biobank Ethics and Governance Council' (2009) 374 *The Lancet* 1676; Graeme Laurie, Ann Bruce and Catherine Lyall, 'The Roles of Values and Interests in the Governance of the Life Sciences: Learning Lessons from the "Ethics+" Approach of UK Biobank' in Catherine Lyall, Theo Papaioannou and James Smith (eds), *The Limits to Governance: The Challenge of Policy-Making for the New Life Sciences* (Routledge 2009) 51; Martin Richards, Adrienne Hunt and Graeme Laurie, 'UK Biobank Ethics and Governance Council: An Exercise in Added Value' in Jane Kaye and Mark Stranger (eds), *Principles and Practice in Biobank Governance* (Ashgate 2009) 229; and Graeme Laurie, 'What Does It Mean to Take an Ethics+ Approach to Global Biobank Governance?' (2017) 9 *Asian Bioethics Review* 285.

[54] The EGC has since been replaced by the UK Biobank Ethics Advisory Committee: see www.ukbiobank.ac.uk/ethics/ (accessed 18 February 2021). See further Chapter 14 in this volume.

[55] Pam Carter, Graeme Laurie and Mary Dixon-Woods, 'The Social Licence for Research: Why care. data Ran into Trouble' (2015) 41 *Journal of Medical Ethics* 404.

[56] Ibid., 405.

[57] Ibid., 406.

- reciprocity, which must begin with sound two-way communication;
- non-exploitation, which must exclude the spectre of disempowerment; and
- service of the public good, which need not exclude an economic agenda so long as there is confidence that research governance and information governance systems can hold those with decisional and custodial responsibility to account.

Here we see a confluence of several concepts that Graeme has consistently advanced: that of furthering the public good, engaging and collaborating across actor groups interested in the research undertaking, and joint development of governance mechanisms with some element at arm's length to the research undertaking.

Further elaborations of the good governance framework came in Graeme's work with the Scottish Health Informatics Programme (SHIP)[58] and Administrative Data Research Scotland (ADR Scotland),[59] both collaborative projects concerned with understanding 'big data' as a regulated space, and with marshalling and redeploying government- and health-care system–held administrative data.[60] In both cases, Graeme and colleagues developed decisional tools to facilitate ethical access to health data so that research in the public interest could be advanced. More recently, in the context of his Liminal Spaces project,[61] Graeme and colleagues argue that 'stewardship' is increasingly being called for in the research data context, but that its use is not consistent and its demands are not well understood.[62] They contend that, to understand and realise effective and ethically sound 'stewardship', actors need to:[63]

---

[58] SHIP www.scot-ship.ac.uk/ (accessed 18 February 2021).

[59] ADR Scotland www.adruk.org/about-us/our-partnership/adr-scotland/ (accessed 18 February 2021).

[60] See Graeme Laurie and Nayha Sethi, 'Towards Principles-Based Approaches to Governance of Health-Related Research Using Personal Data' (2013) 4 *European Journal of Risk Regulation* 43; and Graeme Laurie and Leslie Stevens, 'Developing a Public Interest Mandate for the Governance and Use of Administrative Data in the United Kingdom' (2016) 43 *Journal of Law and Society* 360.

[61] See 'Confronting the Liminal Spaces of Health Research Regulation' (Wellcome Trust) at https://europepmc.org/grantfinder/grantdetails?query=pi%3A%22Laurie%2BG%22%2Bgid%3A%22103360%22%2Bga%3A%22Wellcome%20Trust%22 (accessed 18 February 2021).

[62] Graeme Laurie et al, 'Charting Regulatory Stewardship in Health Research: Making the Invisible Visible' (2018) 27 *Cambridge Quarterly of Healthcare Ethics* 333.

[63] Ibid., 334.

- identify and communicate the meaning of the principles behind, and the responsibilities that arise from 'stewardship';
- recognise, defend and implement 'regulatory stewardship' as the collective responsibility of all stakeholders involved across all areas of health-related research (that is, stewardship is not a responsibility of regulators or researchers alone); and
- articulate and embed appropriate regulatory responsibilities not only in law and regulation but also in any training and awareness-raising for stakeholders.

It is in the second and third points that we find Graeme's consistent messaging that (i) multiple actors have contributions to make to the governance endeavour, and rightly have burdens to bear; and (ii) some behavioural standards will be imposed through formal legal instruments, but much (appropriately) exists beyond state-regulated practices.[64] And, again, the objective is a 'valued end-point in the form of a recognised public good and its association with a responsibility to support other actors toward the realisation of such a public good'.[65] Graeme and colleagues propose in that paper 'that regulatory stewardship is a responsibility for all actors engaged in health research regulation. The failure to see regulation as an inherently collective responsibility will stand in the way of the optimization of effective regulation. It requires both individuals and institutions, and researchers and regulators alike, to commit to the common goal of progress in human health and well-being.'[66]

That is, I think, an appropriate statement on which to conclude our tour of Graeme's scholarship. Through its various strands, the public good (and the well-being of persons and communities) is positioned at the centre of the undertaking, not the periphery where the patient and the community are often exiled. The responsibilities to create and manage resources, to undertake research, to deliver outcomes effectively and equitably, and to govern the entire enterprise are diffuse and borne by multiple actors. Thinking in terms of 'legacy', then, we can discern a programmatic effort to shape relationships among those diverse actors interested in health-related research and its outcomes, so that *just and useful* social ends are achieved (public goods) and *justified* trust is generated (partnerships).

---

[64] See also Graeme Laurie, 'Liminality and the Limits of Law in Health Research Regulation: What Are We Missing in the Spaces in-Between?' (2017) 25 *Medical Law Review* 47.
[65] Laurie et al (n 62) 342.
[66] Ibid., 344.

## 18.4  Drawing on Legacy to Achieve Legacy

Despite the hurdles represented by the above social/political conditions, the right to science could hardly be more important in our current science-reliant, technology-saturated, global society, a society which is characterised by massive disparities among nations and among peoples with respect to all kinds of determinants of health and well-being. With respect to science, the following has been noted:

> Rapid scientific and technological developments result in drastic changes in the daily life of both individuals and the societies they live in. Access to the benefits of scientific progress not only allows improving one's socio-economic situation, but also gives the opportunity to take a meaningful part in the life of communities whether they are local, national or international. Restriction of access to scientific progress may lead to stagnation, regression and exclusion.[67]

However, it is well known that there exist widespread concerns around (i) the misuse of techno-scientific advances; (ii) the growing gaps in science capacities and access to technologies; and (iii) the widely divergent interests between public bodies and private actors, and what each takes into account when determining and pursuing their objectives.[68] More recently, in its 2020 General Comment No. 25,[69] the UN CESCR has acknowledged that the intense and rapid development of science and technology has visited uneven and unequal benefits and burdens on different states and peoples, prompting a growing discussion on the relationship between science and other rights. General Comment No. 25 goes on to state:

> Accessibility means that scientific progress and its applications should be accessible for all persons, without discrimination. It has three dimensions: first, States parties should ensure that everyone has equal access to the applications of science, particularly when they are instrumental for the enjoyment of other economic, social and cultural rights. Second, information concerning the risks and benefits of science and technology should be accessible without discrimination. Third, everyone should have the open opportunity to participate in scientific progress, without

---

[67] UNESCO (n 10) 4.
[68] Committee on Economic, Social and Cultural Rights (CESCR), 'Report of the General Discussion on the Right to Enjoy the Benefits of Scientific Progress' (9 October 2018) www.ohchr.org/EN/NewsEvents/Pages/DisplayNews.aspx?NewsID=23714&LangID=E (accessed 18 February 2021).
[69] CESCR, General Comment No. 25 (2020) on Science and Economic, Social and Cultural Rights (Doc E/C.12/GC/25, 30 April 2020) https://undocs.org/E/C.12/GC/25 (accessed 18 February 2021).

discrimination. Thus, States parties should remove discriminatory barriers that impede persons from participating in scientific progress, for
instance, by facilitating the access of marginalized populations to scientific
education.[70]

This is a useful starting point, but it hardly suggests what states and other
actors need to do to truly operationalise the right to science both locally
and regionally. Questions remain. How do we rise above current
approaches to rights claims in this area that favour corporate interests
and scientific competitiveness? How can we develop and give content to
a right to science that is both sufficiently robust and sufficiently authoritative that all pertinent parties are bound to comply? How do we reshape
budgets and policies across borders to create a positive and harmonious
use of science for the public good? How do we understand the right and
the obligations it imposes in very different developmental settings?[71] In
other words, how do we forge some positive legacy for this long-
suppressed right?

The answer, I suggest, is in Graeme's legacy, which, in essence, is about
redefining the social contract among actors in the health setting
(researchers, regulators, patients, publics, health-care system operators
and health-care professionals). Whether concerned with legal foresighting, biobank oversight and support, or health and administrative database stewardship, Graeme has advocated (and practised) engagement
and participation in the development of regulatory instruments and in
the performance of regulatory processes. A starting point might be to
explore the concept of stewardship and assign its necessary responsibilities. As Graeme and colleagues have noted, the important concept of
stewardship demands that all actors have a role to play – we are *all*
stewards, though some have clear and/or pre-existing legal duties, and
some have more of a moral mandate. But we all have (or ought to have)
a role in determining both the scope and application of the right to
science, and the trajectories of science more generally.

Of course, the nature of our different stewardship roles is not entirely
clear, and the roles currently adopted (by the private sector, for example)
are not at all salutary. As such, the stewardship roles and responsibilities
of the full range of interested actors must first be clearly identified, and

---

[70] Ibid., para 17.

[71] In this regard, General Comment No. 25, ibid, para 48, establishes that all states should
contribute, to the maximum of their available resources, to this common task of developing science. Recommending that poor states focus exclusively on applied science actually
increases the gap and the unfair distribution of knowledge and power among states.

their fulfilment enabled, and this must be done – Graeme might advise us – through collaborative processes involving actors recruited from all levels of society. Drawing on our foresighting work, I contend that that process should first explore the future that we wish to create in the face of (and perhaps limited by) the unfolding conditions of the Anthropocene. It needs to arrive at shared socio-moral values, shared social objectives, and wide-ranging but shared views on the scientific pursuits and technologies that are considered to be most promising, at least in the short and the medium term.[72] From this common ground might emerge a more concrete understanding of the capabilities and essential responsibilities of the different actors from the perspectives of 'stewardship' and of stewards pursuing the 'public good'.

Once the broad (stewardship) roles of different actors are satisfactorily articulated, then all parties can get on with the more substantive goal of refining the law that shapes both scientific and commercial practices so that the right to science can be effectively advanced. In doing this, a much clearer understanding of the meaning, significance and consequences of Article 15 ICESCR should emerge. To truly explore what Article 15 ICESCR could mean, and what could be achieved if we enable a robust understanding of it, diverse actors, working collaboratively in bespoke institutions and forums, need to unpack and discuss the possibilities under the widely accepted obligations to respect, protect and fulfil this right. Core concerns might include the following:

- ensure ongoing public engagement and outreach around the nature and achievements of science, the appropriate aims and trajectories of science, and developments in the methodologies and tools supporting science;
- set equitable and human rights–sensitive science priorities through more open discussions and decisions around science investment and partnering;
- develop policies, institutions and laws that enable improved science/outcome assessment and actor monitoring, with the public good at its centre, together with accountability mechanisms; and
- revise fields of practice defined by law so that they can achieve better outcomes in keeping with the spirit of the right (that is, IP regimes, data use regimes and so on).

The first objective is aimed at advancing Article 15(1)(a) ICESCR, which relates to participation in cultural life. One aspect of this is ensuring

---

[72] Laurie, Harmon and Arzuaga (n 45).

sufficient public funding for robust science, technology, engineering and mathematics (STEM) education, commencing at the elementary level and continuing throughout the course of education. Another is developing sufficient training around ethics and human rights, and continuing education for science practitioners and participants. A third aspect is educating publics about how various sciences affect our lives and can help us manage the rapidly evolving conditions of the Anthropocene. At base, people – including, critically, science practitioners – must better understand how science is entangled with and part of the human rights regime, and how it affects other human rights; they cannot leave the 'ethics' or the 'rights' elements of the scientific undertaking to others, nor can they dismiss as irrelevant to their work the ways that science and its outputs can be used. Importantly, these campaigns and education standards will be most effective if they are shared and complementary across borders.

The second and third objectives are aimed at advancing Article 15(1)(b) ICESCR, which relates to the benefits and application of science. They have capacity elements (education, skills development, certification), funding elements, policy elements (ensuring, at base, that policies are grounded in sound science, counteracting disinformation and pseudo-science) and legal elements.[73] With respect to legal elements, law reform is necessary to:

- ensure that all policy decisions are based on sound scientific advice,[74] and take a 'health in all policies' and 'habitat in all policies' approach;[75]
- eliminate rules, standards and practices that unjustifiably or discriminatorily limit access to knowledge, information, services or facilities related to science;
- eliminate unjustifiable limits to the freedom to pursue scientific research (in the public good);
- enable equal enjoyment of this right, including the articulation of enforceable remedies for violations of the right; and
- develop enforceable strategies relating to the conservation of science (or, rather, its insights and practical tools and applications).

---

[73] For a list of core state obligations, see General Comment No. 25 (n 69) para 52.

[74] In this regard, consider the profound damage that has been caused to the environment and to the health of people as a result of thirty-plus years of policies grounded on pseudo-science (or fantasy) by the climate change deniers that have occupied positions of power. For more, see General Comment No. 25 (n 69), paras 53–5.

[75] For more on a HIAP approach, see Shawn Harmon, 'In Search of Global Health Justice: A Need to Reinvigorate Institutions and Make International Law' (2015) 23 *Health Care Analysis* 352; and Shawn Harmon et al, 'Imagining Global Health with Justice: Ebola, Impoverished People and Health Systems' (2015) 15 *Medical Law International* 3.

Ultimately, policies and laws must be discussed and adopted which address multiple concerns and shortfalls, handling them in a way that is sensitive to human rights.

The last objective is aimed at Article 15(1)(c) ICESCR, which relates to the protection of moral and material interests in science. In our work on legal foresighting, we encouraged actors not to dismiss the possibility that whole fields or sectors (and the legal frameworks that regulate them) may need to be reimagined and profoundly realigned if we are to achieve the positive futures – informed by human rights – that we envision through our collaborative policy-making exercises.[76] In this regard, it behoves us seriously to consider how commercial, IP and trade regimes – all of which have proven particularly problematic,[77] and which are no more than social constructs which are subject to reimagination – have undermined trust in science. For example:

> [M]any commercial agendas operate in the various research milieux and threaten to undermine the trustworthiness of scientific knowledge. In the biomedical field, for example, more than 60% of the clinical research conducted in the United States between 2003 and 2008 was funded by private corporations. This funding can introduce bias into scientific output, as has been shown by many studies analysing the impact of conflicts of interest on research results. For example, the research funded by the pharmaceutical or agri-food industries produces results that are favourable to those industries much more frequently than the results from research funded by other sources. Moreover, the influence of funders is often exerted in a relatively subtle and discreet way since, in some cases, it is research methods that are affected and not the research results directly. These commercial agendas also influence the editorial choices of scientific journals. Again, in the case of biomedicine, the scientific journals in this field sometimes receive considerable funding from industry (in advertising purchases, for example), which can alter the thrust of both the editorial line and the published research. Furthermore, journal editors are not always obliged to disclose these types of financial partnership.[78]

Ultimately, a variety of regimes must be (at least) refined to ensure that the pursuit of material benefits (by scientists and innovators) does not preclude others' rights to benefit in real and material ways. This may

---

[76] Laurie, Harmon and Arzuaga (n 45).

[77] Aurora Plomer, *Patents, Human Rights and Access to Science* (Edward Elgar 2015).

[78] Cécile Petitgand, Catherine Régis and Jean-Louis Denis, *Is Science a Human Right? Implementing the Principle of Participatory, Equitable, and Universally Accessible Science* (Canadian Commission for UNESCO 2019) 13–14.

mean ensuring that more scientific tools and outcomes remain in the public domain.

As should be clear from the discussion in Section 18.3, the suggestions advanced here are preliminary only. The nature and the content of the obligations that arise under Article 15 ICESCR need to be explored through sustained participatory activities that include diverse communities of interest. They need to be undertaken locally (at the regional and state level) and internationally, and efforts must be taken to ensure that harmonised understandings are arrived at and complementary programmes are designed. Further, and importantly, a humanist scholar like Graeme would perhaps remind us always to bear in mind that 'science' is not the end. We must not reify or sanctify science. We must instead appreciate that the end is in fact reliable knowledge, widely disseminated, that will enrich the human experience, and the constant, diligent and equitable improvement of the human condition. As such, we should be extremely cautious about how we approach economic, social and cultural rights; they are not equally compelling and should not be viewed as equally imperative.

Unfortunately, while the Venice Statement makes reference to the participation of individuals and communities in decision-making around science,[79] and while the UN Special Rapporteur has indicated that this right imposes obligations to ensure that individuals, communities and peoples can participate in science-related decision-making,[80] the UNESCO Recommendation is silent on the role of publics with respect to the critical activities of:

- developing the aims, objectives and scope of scientific programmes and projects;
- decision-making in relation to scientific boundaries and access to scientific resources; and
- determining how, to whom and under what conditions the outcomes of science should be distributed, and how benefits should be shared.

This lacuna must be viewed as a significant gap in UNESCO's consideration of how the still embryonic (and legacy-lacking) right to science should be understood and pursued. Having said that, General Comment No. 25 does explicitly stipulate the necessity of 'a culture of active citizen

---

[79] Venice Statement (n 32) Art 13.

[80] UN Special Rapporteur Shaheed, 'The Right to Enjoy the Benefits of Scientific Progress and Its Applications' (UN Doc A/HRC/20/26, 14 May 2012) https://undocs.org/en/A/HRC/20/26 (accessed 23 August 2021).

engagement with science, particularly through a vigorous and informed democratic debate on the production and use of scientific knowledge, and a dialogue between the scientific community and society'.[81] And the Canadian Commission for UNESCO has stated that '[r]esearchers ... must question not only the scientific relevance, but also the social implications of their investigations, by engaging in dialogue with their peers and the general population. This ultimately raises the question of research equity: what questions do researchers ask in the first place? And are the answers for researchers or society as a whole?'.[82] An axiom of Graeme's work is that rights should not be discussed and cannot be operationalised in the absence of collectively articulated notions of the public good, an appreciation of social licence, and the interests of individuals and communities. In short, because the outcomes are borne by society (good or bad), the answers are for society as a whole to determine.

## 18.5 Conclusion

The gap between 'have' and 'have not' nations in science, as well as their ability to apply scientific advances, is growing,[83] as is the gap between 'have' and 'have not' communities and peoples.[84] The recent dislocations caused by the Covid-19 pandemic, and the further ones we can expect as vaccines are rolled out in quantities that will leave large sections of the population unimmunised or under-immunised, demonstrate that (health) justice has not yet been achieved, and that there is much to do to animate a legal provision about the enjoyment of the benefits of science and its applications.

In this chapter, I have argued that Graeme's work can be understood as an exploration meant to redefine the social contract among actors in the health setting. It is less about advancing substantive claims about what science should be aiming at or should achieve, and more about developing and refining the tools that we could profitably use to help shape science in positive ways that are determined collaboratively. Grounded in

---

[81] General Comment No. 25 (n 69) para 54.
[82] Canadian Commission for UNESCO (n 78) 12.
[83] InterAcademy Council, 'Inventing a Better Future' (2003) www.interacademies.org/sites/default/files/publication/full_s%26t_report_final.pdf (accessed 18 February 2021).
[84] UN Department of Economic and Social Affairs, 'World Social Report 2020: Inequality in a Rapidly Changing World' (UN 2020) www.un.org/development/desa/dspd/wp-content/uploads/sites/22/2020/02/World-Social-Report2020-FullReport.pdf (accessed 18 February 2021).

the public good, it seeks to broaden the range of people who contribute to decision-making in the science and health settings. Article 15 ICESCR desperately needs key actors to take up this cause, and to put into action some of what Graeme's legacy demonstrates is a positive and useful undertaking.

The widely participatory discussions I envision must be designed to cut across different fields of practice, encouraging actors to appreciate that their diverse activities are in fact connected (and that the law should also engage with that connectedness). The scale of the collective reimagining required should not be underestimated.[85] But, again, Graeme's work offers us some of the tools that will be helpful. Legal foresighting, for example, cast as a proactive and participatory method of policy/law development, could assist in this regard, as could the touchstones of public good and stewardship. However, only with the inclusion of historically excluded actors throughout this process will the equity and well-being aims of the human rights project be given a chance to do their work.

---

[85] The broad swathe of the considerations necessary to give life to the right to science are outlined in Chapman (n 25).

~

# Afterword

## The Great Coronavirus Pandemic: A Pivotal Moment for Health Law and Ethics

### LAWRENCE O. GOSTIN

This Festschrift for Graeme Laurie could not have come at a more catastrophic, yet opportune, moment in modern history. The world is experiencing a once-in-a-lifetime pandemic that has devastated human health, social well-being and economic prosperity. The Great Coronavirus Pandemic started in Wuhan, China in December 2019 and has since swept the world. It has strained health systems to the brink, revealed unconscionable health inequalities and upended international institutions.

Leadership and good governance have emerged as perhaps the best predictor of how successfully nations have responded, both during the worst peaks of the pandemic and in the rollout of multiple successful vaccines (including participation in global equitable access schemes such as COVAX).[1] Public trust in government has been indispensable for curtailing the spread of the virus, severe acute respiratory syndrome coronavirus 2 (SARS-CoV-2). Health law and the rule of law itself have never been more important.[2] Societies everywhere on earth have been faced with deeply consequential choices on how to respond to Covid-19 in ways that are effective, but also ethical and equitable.

---

[1] Lawrence Gostin, 'The Great Coronavirus Pandemic of 2020 – 7 Critical Lessons' (*JAMA Health Forum*, 13 August 2020) https://jamanetwork.com/channels/health-forum/fullarti cle/2769600 (accessed 25 February 2021). See also World Health Organization, 'COVAX: Working for Global Equitable Access to COVID-19 Vaccines' (2021) www.who.int/initia tives/act-accelerator/covax (accessed 25 February 2021).

[2] Lawrence Gostin et al, 'The Lancet Commission on Global Health and the Law: The Legal Determinants of Health: Harnessing the Power of Law for Global Health and Sustainable Development' (2019) 393 *The Lancet* P1857.

Graeme's legacy is quintessentially about responding to the most complex health challenges in ways that abide by the rule of law and are also deeply moral and humane. As founding director of the J Kenyon Mason Institute for Medicine, Life Sciences and the Law based at the University of Edinburgh's School of Law, Graeme has been a pioneer in the field of health law and ethics. There is plenty of evidence of this throughout his twenty-five years of scholarship, beginning with his PhD at the University of Glasgow under the supervision of the legendary health law scholar Sheila McLean, and continuing through his brilliant articles and books, many of which were co-authored with his long-time academic collaborator (and another legend in the field) Ken Mason.

Graeme's commitment to interdisciplinary research at the interface of health, law and ethics – most recently reflected in his Liminal Spaces project – has been deeply prescient. It has been abundantly clear that multiple disciplinary perspectives are essential to solving complex problems of human and animal health. Sound public health law is grounded in science, including medicine, biostatistics and epidemiology. But it also requires anthropology, sociology and health education to shape how policy influences risk behaviours in communities. Think about the importance of burial ceremonies on the spread of Ebola Virus Disease in West Africa (2014–16). Or the deep public distrust of government, and the ensuing violence, during the Ebola epidemic in the Democratic Republic of Congo (2019–20). What makes the public trust (for example, Taiwan, South Korea, New Zealand, Germany) or distrust (for example, Brazil, Iran, the United States in the recent past) a government? That understanding can help to facilitate, or impede, health behaviours such as social distancing, personal hygiene and masking.

The legal determinants of health are a core contributor to what makes a population safe and secure. By establishing the rules and frameworks that shape social and economic interactions, laws exert a powerful force on all the social and commercial determinants of health. Well-designed laws can help to build strong health systems, ensure safe and nutritious foods, evaluate and approve safe and effective drugs and vaccines, create healthier and safer workplaces, improve the built and natural environments, and respond to infectious disease threats – all encompassed in Graeme's legacy. Graeme also taught us that laws which are poorly designed, implemented or enforced can harm marginalised populations and entrench stigma and discrimination, as occurred with the AIDS pandemic.[3]

---

[3]  To this end, see Graeme's discussion of laws on disclosure of notifiable diseases in previous editions of *Mason and McCall Smith's Law and Medical Ethics*; in his monograph

The Covid-19 pandemic has underscored the importance of nearly all these determinants of health. Weak health systems cannot contain outbreaks or effectively care for and treat patients. As the world searched for, and continues to develop, safe and effective therapeutics and vaccines, strong regulatory systems became essential. Workplaces (for example, meatpacking plants), congregate settings (such as nursing homes, prisons, cruise ships) and large indoor gatherings (for example, church services) have become amplifiers of the pandemic. So too have businesses like bars, pubs and restaurants. Even chronic non-communicable diseases have played a major role in determining who is at risk for hospitalisation or death.

Health laws have been used in unprecedented ways, twisted nearly beyond recognition in a declared health emergency. How could even the impeccable scholars at the Mason Institute have imagined that a pandemic would prompt a complete lockdown of mega-cities like Beijing, Delhi, London or New York? Or that health and education agencies would close virtually all businesses and schools around the world? Could we have envisioned location applications on smartphones tracking entire metropolises, often without regard to privacy? When China shuttered Wuhan and greater Hubei province, practically imprisoning 60 million people, I thought a similar approach could simply not happen in a liberal Western democracy. But it did, and virtually everywhere.

What legal safeguards can empower effective, evidence-based action while still respecting human rights and personal freedoms? Beyond human rights is the rule of law itself. Populist leaders (such as those currently in power in Brazil, China, Mexico, Hungary, Russia and, until 2021, the United States) used Covid-19 as a subterfuge for extending their own power, or at least trying to. Democratic freedoms and abiding faithfully to the rule of law are crucial determinants of health and stability, particularly in a health crisis. We need the wisdom of health law and ethics leaders to guide us.

Health law scholars are perfectly placed to advocate for change to advance health outcomes and the rights to health and to justice. As activists, we can confront populist leaders who undermine public health agencies and ignore scientific evidence. We fight for legal and social

Graeme Laurie, *Genetic Privacy: A Challenge to Medico-legal Norms* (Cambridge University Press 2002) 17–18; and in his book review Graeme Laurie, 'Book Review: AIDS: A Guide to the Law (Second Edition)' (1996) 2 *Medical Law International* 183.

change, such as for universal health coverage and pandemic preparedness. As international law specialists, we can analyse and urge reforms of
international agreements like the International Health Regulations or the
Pandemic Influenza Preparedness Framework. We can support international institutions like the World Health Organization. And so much
more.

Of course, the idea of 'legacy' can both advance and impede our work.
We can build on the best ideas and learn from the methods, analyses and
conclusions of the health law giants whom we emulate, including
Graeme. But 'legacy' can also create a rigid, antiquated or narrow way
of thinking about complex problems. When I began in my health law
career, much of the conversation was about the doctor–patient relationship, but it soon moved to broader health systems, public health and now
global health. Health law has the capacity to grow and to expand its lens,
most importantly as a lens of health justice.

Even before the Great Coronavirus Pandemic, unconscionable health
inequities became the prevailing global narrative. But Covid-19 virtually screamed inequity. The well-off could work remotely with a secure
income and stocked cupboards. Not the poor. At the same time, essential workers, including health workers, became infected at disproportionate rates. And so did racial minorities, the elderly and other
vulnerable or marginalised communities. The world developed highly
safe and effective vaccines with lightening speed. But most of the benefit
thus far has been to high-income countries, with the poor left behind –
yet again.

It is a truism that pandemics affect us all. We are truly 'all in this
together'. But it is just as true that even infectious diseases reveal, and
amplify, striking health/social/racial inequalities in society. It is unsurprising that the Black Lives Matter protests of the Spring of 2020 coin-
cided with Covid-19 not just in the United States but also globally.
Populations everywhere are fed up with unconscionable and enduring
health, social and economic injustices.

The field of 'medical jurisprudence', to use the University of
Edinburgh parlance, has come a long way. It is not just about medicine
and what happens in the clinic; it also explores health systems, including
public health services. It is not just about health systems but also
upstream social and commercial determinants of health. And it is not
just all-of-government but also all-of-society.

Fundamentally, the field is about identifying and investigating elements of
good governance like transparency, stewardship and accountability, as

applied in health. And it is about evidence-based, and fair, health laws and policies, along with the rule of law. The foundational scholarship of Graeme Laurie, the Mason Institute and all the founders of the field of health law and ethics have given the world so much. And yet, there is so much more thinking and giving to do.

# INDEX

For EU product safety concerns, contact us at Calle de José Abascal, 56–1º, 28003 Madrid, Spain or eugpsr@cambridge.org.

www.ingramcontent.com/pod-product-compliance
Ingram Content Group UK Ltd.
Pitfield, Milton Keynes, MK11 3LW, UK
UKHW020433240426
470322UK00017B/496